CHINA

Adapting the Past
Confronting the Future

Edited by

THOMAS BUOYE, KIRK DENTON
BRUCE DICKSON, BARRY NAUGHTON
MARTIN K. WHYTE

CENTER FOR CHINESE STUDIES
THE UNIVERSITY OF MICHIGAN
ANN ARBOR

PUBLISHED BY CENTER FOR CHINESE STUDIES
THE UNIVERSITY OF MICHIGAN, ANN ARBOR, MICHIGAN, 48104-1608

Printed and made in the United States of America

The paper used in this publication conforms with the American National Standard for Information Sciences—Permanence of Paper for Publications and Documents in Libraries and Archives ANSI/NISO/Z39.48—1992.

Library of Congress Cataloging-in-Publication Data

China : adapting the past, confronting the future / edited by Thomas Buoye … [et al.].
   p. cm
  ISBN 0-89264-156-8 (acid-free)
    1.   China. I Title: Adapting the past, confronting the future. II. Buoye, Thomas M.

DS706 .C4896 2002
951—dc21

2002073525

CONTENTS

Part 3: SOCIETY
Edited by Martin King Whyte

Part 6: FUTURE TRENDS
Edited by Bruce Dickson

INTRODUCTION   547
Bruce Dickson

READINGS

EDITORS' NOTE

This volume uses *pinyin* romanization throughout the introductory essays and the headnotes that precede each of the readings. Readings from sources using the Wade-Giles system have not been altered, and British spellings have been retained in excerpts from British publications. In their original form a number of the readings contained footnotes and other references, which do not appear in this volume.

A volume of this scope and complexity could not have been produced without the unstinting support and forbearance of an excellent publications staff at the Center for Chinese Studies at the University of Michigan. The editors wish to thank Professor Noriko Kamachi, director of publications, for her support, guidance, and helpful suggestions that have enhanced and enriched the creation of this volume. Similarly, Terre Fisher has devoted untold effort and countless hours to coordinating permissions work, editing and proofreading, and otherwise shepherding the book through the production process. Joseph Mooney is to be commended for his careful work on the readings; Ben Powers, Yachen Chi, and Victoria Chien all did yeoman's duty securing permissions. We also wish to thank University of Tulsa graduate students Justin McCrackin and Eric McDaniel, and Toy Kelley, History Department secretary, at the University of Tulsa.

We owe special thanks to the artist, Mr. Chen Shun Chu of Taiwan, for graciously agreeing to share his work for the volume cover. Finally, this book would not be possible without the wealth of excellent scholarship from a broad range of authors and scholars. The editors appreciate their generosity in sharing their work with us.

PREFACE

China: Adapting the Past, Confronting the Future, is the latest textbook on contemporary China from the Center for Chinese Studies at the University of
Michigan. The first classroom text appeared in 1986, a decade after Mao
Zedong's death. By that time the relaxation of Communist Party control over
economic, social, cultural, and political institutions was already beginning to
transform the face of modern Chinese society. Outwardly China still bore the
stamp of Maoist autarky in the mid 1980s: Most people dressed in blue or green
cotton suits, shopped for a limited variety of goods in state-run stores, and rode
black bicycles to and from work. With no private restaurants and few
entertainment or commercial venues, Beijing streets were dark and empty by
nightfall. Wide-ranging policy changes, similar to the dismantling of the
commune system in the countryside, were underway, but their effects had yet to
be felt. Today Beijing residents can shop in luxury department stores, the
evenings glow with neon signs and outdoor advertisements, closed access
expressways burst with automobile traffic, and dining out can range from simple
dumplings or Western fast food to the most exotic foreign and Chinese cuisines.
Despite the progress of the last quarter century, however, more than one hundred
million citizens remain below the officially determined poverty level. For the
most part Chinese citizens appear to be cautiously optimistic about the future,
though there have been troubling signs of income inequality, political
corruption, and social unrest along with the growth and prosperity.

Paradoxically, the Chinese Communist Party (CCP), which has presided
over the transition to a market-based consumer economy, remains firmly in power
despite its abandonment of nearly every principle of communist ideology. In
fact, many sons and daughters of high-level CCP leaders have been among the
principal beneficiaries of the economic boom. In a development that would have
been unthinkable under Mao, the CCP has recently invited successful businessmen to join its ranks. Despite its blurring of ideological boundaries and pragmatism
in the economic arena, the CCP has shown no willingness to tolerate dissent or
to relinquish its monopoly on formal political power. The brutal suppression of
the Beijing Spring of 1989 tragically illustrates the Party's single-minded determination to hold power. Similarly, despite the renewed economic prosperity in the
1990s and the successful transfer of power after the death of Deng Xiaoping, the

harsh crackdown and vehement denunciation of the Falun Gong religious movement in 1999 seems to indicate that the current regime will not brook any threat, real or perceived, to its authority.

Still, after a quarter century Chinese efforts at reforming their economy continue to confound and surprise outside observers. Over the past twenty-five years some experts have issued urgent warnings that China may be headed for political disintegration or economic collapse. The most recent dire predictions are based on China's entry into the World Trade Organization. Will Chinese agriculture and state-run industry wither when fully exposed to international competition, leading to widespread unemployment and social unrest as some analysts predict, or will full exposure to the international market enrich and strengthen the Chinese economic miracle? Similarly, U.S.-Chinese relations have remained tense over issues like human rights, trade policy, nuclear proliferation, and the status of Taiwan. Still Sino-American relations have weathered many storms, most notably the Tiananmen crackdown and the NATO bombing of the Chinese embassy in Belgrade. The downing of a U.S. spy plane in 2001 and the Bush administration's apparent shift in policy toward Taiwan threatened to endanger relations once again until the tragedy of 9/11 focused attention on a common threat. Whether it has been economic reform or relations with its most important trading partner, Chinese leaders have shown a remarkable ability to navigate exceptionally tumultuous seas. It remains to be seen whether the next generation of leaders will be as adept or as lucky as their predecessors.

The primary focus of this volume is the changes that have occurred since Mao's death. Clearly there has been a dramatic break with the Maoist past but there is an equally clear continuity with modern China's quest for wealth and power that began in the late Qing. Although Deng and his successor have broken dramatically with the policies of the Mao era, the consequences of their policies, both intended and unintended, have resonated with both China's recent and distant past. In the struggle to forge a modern society the Chinese people realize that their past can be both a source of inspiration and an obstacle to change. As the title indicates, the editors believe that the current changes must be examined in light of the richness of Chinese history and culture. *China: Adapting the Past, Confronting the Future* and the companion study guide can serve as the anchor to a multidisciplinary course on contemporary China that will enable students to understand the complexity and diversity of contemporary China and appreciate the important issues that will shape China's future.

China: Adapting the Past, Confronting the Future is divided thematically into five major sections: history and geography, politics; society; economy, and culture. A sixth section speculates on future trends. Each section includes an original essay that provides a broad historical and interpretive framework for the selected readings that follow. The readings draw on a wide range of primary sources: leading academic research, Chinese literature, and Western media reports. To enhance the learning experience, each section also includes a list of suggested readings and the companion study guide presents learning objectives, an overview of each chapter, key concepts, review questions, and suggestions for complementary China-related internet resources, documentary films, and Chinese cinema. Together the textbook and study guide lead instructors and students to a broader array of supplementary resources and serve as the foundation for a multidisciplinary, multimedia course on contemporary China in the best tradition of area studies.

Finally, the editors would like to note the untimely passing of Michel Oksenberg (1939–2001), a distinguished scholar of Chinese politics and a major contributor to the development of Chinese studies at the University of Michigan. Through his scholarship and government service over the last quarter century, Michel Oksenberg had an enormous influence in the field of Chinese studies and was an architect of the U.S.-China rapprochement. Over the course of his distinguished career he served as Director of the Center for Chinese Studies at the University of Michigan, Senior Staff Member of the National Security Council in Washington, D.C., with a special responsibility for China and Indochina, and President of the East-West Center. For those of us who were privileged to know him personally, Mike was an inspiring mentor, a generous colleague, a caring friend, and a true mensch. He enriched our lives and he will be sorely missed. This volume is dedicated to his memory.

Part 1

GEOGRAPHY AND HISTORY

Edited by Thomas Buoye

INTRODUCTION
Thomas Buoye

The Land and Its People

China ranks third in the world in total area and is just slightly larger than the United States. As J. R. McNeill's essay on environmental history reveals, China has an abundance of ecological, ethnic, and linguistic diversity (reading 1). From north to south, the country encompasses a broad range of climates and ecological systems from subarctic to tropical, with rich and varied flora, fauna, and natural resources. So bountifully endowed, China has demonstrated a remarkable degree of ecological resilience that has enabled it to sustain the world's largest population throughout most of recorded history.

Home to more than 1.3 billion people, China displays a high degree of ethnic diversity that is succinctly described by Dru Gladney (reading 2). The Chinese government recognizes fifty-six official nationalities. More than 90 percent of the population are "Han Chinese," but even among this vast majority, there are eight major linguistic groups. The remaining fifty-five "official" nationalities include those numbering in the millions, such as Mongols, Tibetans, Zhuang, and Yi, as well as many smaller groups that may include only few thousand people. In regions suitable for sedentary agriculture, Chinese civilization has overwhelmed and absorbed many smaller ethnic groups, but historically those based in the arid steppes and the high mountains on the peripheries of Han Chinese civilization were more successful at preserving their individual identities. To this day the largest concentrations of minority nationalities remain in the country's western half. Relations between the Han Chinese and other nationalities were not merely, however, a case of the majority dominating the minority. As we shall see below, two of the last three Chinese dynasties, the Yuan (Mongol) and the Qing (Manchu), were non-Han dynasties.

3

The Ancient Period

Chinese civilization spans more than 3,500 years, and no brief overview can adequately do justice to its richness and complexity. Modern historians usually begin their narratives of Chinese history with the Shang dynasty (1766–1122 B.C.). Bronze technology, settled agriculture, walled cities, and the earliest form of Chinese writing distinguished Shang society from earlier Neolithic cultures. Bronze vessels cast to commemorate important events and "oracle bones," tortoise shells and ox scapula used in divination ceremonies, provide the earliest evidence of Chinese writing as well as insights into the political institutions, social customs, and religious practices of the Shang people. The Shang people produced agricultural surpluses sufficient to support walled cities that were ruled by the Shang royal clan.

The Shang civilization dominated the north China plain, but competing kingdoms were present on the fringes of its territory. In 1122 B.C. the kingdom of Zhou, situated on the western border of Shang, overthrew the Shang king and established a new dynasty (1122–256 B.C.). Establishing an important political precedent, the ruler of the Zhou justified his conquest on the grounds that the last Shang ruler was an immoral tyrant and therefore Heaven had revoked his mandate to rule. The concept of the "mandate of Heaven" became a mainstay of Chinese political philosophy. The Zhou dynasty survived in name well into the third century B.C., but the weakness of the Zhou ruling house was apparent as early as 771 B.C. What had been a relatively stable, if decentralized, polity of city-states knitted together by kinship ties and vassalage began to break down after this time, eventually spiraling down into internecine warfare that would continue for centuries.

In his day, Confucius (551–479 B.C.) was just one of many Chinese thinkers seeking a solution to the problems of the crumbling Zhou political order. Confucius studied the past for an answer to the crisis of his day and concluded that the early Zhou rulers and the sage kings of antiquity had perfected rituals that adhered to the basic patterns of nature and human nature. Confucius saw his own role as a transmitter of an ancient culture of morality. Referring to the *Analects*—dialogues between Confucius and his students—Jonathan Will illustrates some of the enduring elements of Confucian teaching (reading 3). Confucius believed that a ruler should lead by moral example. He also believed the wise ruler promoted men of talent regardless of their social standing. Women were not permitted to serve in government. Confucius used the term *junzi*, which literally meant son of the ruler, to refer to the learned and moral individuals who should serve in government. According to Confucius, competence, not heredity, should determine who would serve. The appropriation of this term was revolutionary in that it implied that anyone who received the proper education and who attained the proper degree of moral growth was both eligible and obligated to serve society. Confucius advocated benevolence in governance and respect for hierarchy and order. While only one of many philosophies current in its day, Confucian thought would eventually emerge as the sanctioned orthodoxy in later dynasties.

The First Emperor

The final breakdown of the Zhou political system occurred during a period aptly known as the Warring States era (403–221 B.C.). After more than a century and a half of constant warfare the hundreds of states that began the Warring States era were reduced to seven major powers. In 221 B.C. China's first ruler to assume the title of emperor, Qin Shihuangdi, led his state to victory, founded the Qin dynasty (221–206 B.C.), and unified China under a centralized bureaucratic state. A ruthless adherence to legalism, a political theory that relied on a strictly enforced all-embracing code of laws to maintain political power, was the hallmark of Qin Shihuangdi's reign. During his reign, weights and measures, currency, and written Chinese were standardized. Despite his accomplishments, Qin Shihuangdi is not universally regarded as an admirable figure in Chinese history. Later Confucian scholars, while recognizing his achievements as a unifier, cited his reliance on law and force to rule as evidence that only a benevolent emperor who set a high moral tone could establish a long-lasting dynasty. Nevertheless, Qin Shihuangdi's centralized bureaucratic state with the emperor at its apex became the model for all future Chinese dynasties.

The Qin was succeeded by the Han dynasty, which ruled from 202 B.C. until 6 A.D., when the throne was usurped. The dynasty was restored in 25 A.D. and lasted until 220 A.D. The Han had a great influence on subsequent dynasties. Confucian thought was adopted as the official orthodoxy, and the political institutions of the Han, which were not very different from those of the Qin dynasty, set the standard for future dynastic governments. The Han political system has been described as one of Confucian ideological principles supported by a Legalist bureaucratic structure. The Han dynasty also witnessed a new flowering of Chinese culture in art, philosophy, music, and literature. The use of "Han nationality" to identify the majority ethnic group in China today indicates deep and ongoing pride in the Han cultural heritage. The boundaries of the dynasty expanded, and Chinese merchants plying the Silk Road, which crossed Central Asia, engaged in indirect trade with the Roman Empire.

Period of Disunity

When the Han dynasty finally collapsed in 220 A.D., China was divided for over three centuries. A series of dynasties founded by nomadic invaders from the grasslands on China's northwestern frontiers ruled China in the north, while Han Chinese who considered themselves the guardians of authentic Chinese culture ruled the south. Despite the fact that non-Han dynasties dominated the north, they adopted many of the Han political institutions. During this time Buddhism, a religion that originated in India, spread in both the north and south. In 589 A.D. the Sui dynasty (589–619) reunified most of the old Han territories. The Sui rulers restored order and consolidated control over all of China, but like the Qin, which reunified China after the Warring States period, the Sui proved transitory. The excesses of the Sui rulers provoked an uprising led by the founder of what would become the Tang dynasty (619–908), and the Sui dynasty ended after only three decades of rule. The Tang dynasty has often been compared with the Han in terms of longevity and cultural splendor. With imperial greatness restored, Tang China dominated the culture of East Asia. Literature and the arts, especially poetry, flourished. The Tang legal code became the standard for East Asia, and emissaries throughout the region, most notably Japan, came to China to study its political institutions. Buddhism, which along with Daoism enjoyed extensive imperial patronage, flourished throughout China among both the elite and the masses.

Late Imperial China

The Song dynasty (960–1279) succeeded the Tang and marked an important turning point in Chinese history. Although it faced repeated threats on its northern frontiers that culminated in the Mongol conquest in 1279, unprecedented economic development, population growth, and urbanization were also hallmarks of the Song. Politically, the Song civil service examination system became the primary means of official recruitment. The use of the civil service exam coincided with a rise of an educated elite, commonly called the "literati," who derived political power and influence from their mastery of the literary skills necessary to compete in the exams. In effect, this opened an avenue to political power to any man who could obtain the requisite education to master the core curriculum of the new examination system. Women were not permitted to sit for the exams. While this marked a new move toward a merit-based system of political recruitment, only the wealthy had a realistic chance of obtaining the education needed to succeed. The Song dynasty also witnessed a revival and enrichment of Confucian thought. Joining traditional philosophy with metaphysical concepts borrowed from a variety of sources, Western scholars have termed this new synthesis Neo-Confucian thought.

Economically, the production of iron, steel, and metal goods reached levels that all of Europe would not exceed until the eighteenth century. Population growth peaked at well over 100 million. Kaifeng, the capital until 1127, when Jurchen invaders from the northeast forced the Song to retreat south, and Hangzhou, the capital of the Southern Song in the Yangzi valley, both had populations over one million. For the first time in Chinese history, more Chinese lived south of the Yangzi River than north. The settlement of southern China would not have been possible without advances in hydraulic technologies and the introduction of new strains of rice that shortened growing seasons and effectively doubled output. Printing with moveable type was common in this period, which preceded Gutenberg in the West by centuries, and technological advances in agriculture and handicrafts were widely disseminated in printed manuals.

Despite its successes, military threats from its northern neighbors remained a constant. Eventually, Mongol invaders demolished the Song dynasty and established their own—the Yuan dynasty (1279–1368). In an effort to win the support of his Chinese subjects, Kubilai Khan, the first Mongol emperor, adopted the trappings of a Chinese emperor. Unfortunately, Kubilai's successors lacked his political skills, and the Yuan was toppled in less than a century by the Ming dynasty (1368–1644). Established by Zhu Yuanzhang, a Han commoner who led a popular uprising, the Ming dynasty drove the Mongols from China. Under Ming rule China surpassed the levels of economic commercialization and population growth achieved during the Song. During the early Ming (1405–1433), seven Chinese maritime expeditions sailed the Indian Ocean as far west as Africa and the Arabian Peninsula. Interestingly, Chinese political institutions did not change much despite the marked social and economic developments that unfolded during the Ming, although the relationship between the emperor and his officials did. The Ming founder had undertaken reforms that increased the power of the emperor and placed greater barriers between the ruler and government officials. In contrast to the rulers of previous dynasties, the Ming emperor held court from a raised dais while officials knelt before him. The concentration of power and prestige in the hands of the emperor meant that efficient and effective government was virtually impossible unless the emperor was a talented and competent individual. This was painfully apparent in the later years of the dynasty, when court eunuchs manipulated weak emperors with disastrous results for China.

The Last Imperial Dynasty

In 1644 Manchu invaders established the Qing dynasty (1644–1911). Prior to entering China, Manchu leaders had spent four decades welding the fractious Manchu tribal groups together into a powerful nation. As their dominance of the northeast grew, the Manchus gained political control over Han Chinese who had settled beyond the Great Wall and established alliances with their Mongolian neighbors. The absorption of Chinese advisors facilitated the adoption of standard Chinese political institutions and provided administrative strength to the new regime. The combination of Chinese administrative techniques and the Manchu banner system of military organization produced a potent force that was ready to assume power when peasant uprisings toppled the woefully corrupt Ming court in 1644. Ultimately, the Manchu-led Qing witnessed both the peak and the nadir of late imperial Chinese political, economic, and cultural development.

The early Qing emperors faced tremendous challenges in their efforts to consolidate control over the vast empire. Fighting between rebel peasant armies and Ming government troops had left large areas of China devastated, and it took the Manchu rulers several decades to consolidate control. During that time the Qing armies successively quelled persistent peasant uprisings, reestablished control over Taiwan, and eradicated the last remnants of Ming loyalist forces in southern China. When fighting finally ended in 1683, a period of recovery ensued that created the foundation for over a century of political stability and economic prosperity.

Politically, the Manchu conquerors implemented several important institutional innovations designed to safeguard the power of the alien minority, but the daily administration of the empire remained largely in the hands of about 20,000 Han Chinese bureaucrats recruited through the civil service examination system. Sharing a common class and ideological background, these bureaucrats faced the challenging task of administering an ever-growing population and an increasingly complex economy. Over time this task became extremely burdensome: By 1800 the population had surpassed 300 million, but despite the economic and demographic expansion of the eighteenth century, the size of the imperial bureaucracy remained fixed. Practical as well as political constraints limited the size of government. Historically, Confucianism had always advocated a small government, and when the Kangxi Emperor (1661–1722) froze the land tax in 1712, he placed a major fiscal constraint on any future expansion of the bureaucracy.

The eighteenth century brought an increased specialization and commercialization of agriculture, rising prices for grain, an extension of the area under cultivation, and an intensification of agriculture on existing farmland. Large-scale migrations and unprecedented levels of population growth also took place in this period. These developments created powerful economic incentives to define and enforce property rights in land more strictly. In the short term, efforts to alter property rights often led to lawsuits and, in the worst instances, violent disputes. Population growth stimulated migration to marginal areas, particularly highland regions, that were often home to non-Han minorities. As these migrations continued, social conflict between new settlers and long-term residents was not uncommon. An expanding market system transformed China's millions of small farming households, increasing their wealth in the best of times but also making them susceptible to its vagaries.

The volume and geographic scope of interregional and international trade also expanded over the course of the eighteenth century and transformed the landscapes of several important urban trading centers. Corporate guilds based on common origin or trade organized handicraft production and commerce. These guilds also served as vehicles for social, religious, and political activities. Clearly, there were social consequences associated with the prosperity of the eighteenth century. Commercialization created risks as well as opportunities, and a burgeoning population indicated prosperity but also heightened competition for resources.

Dynastic Decline?

Since the days of Confucius, Chinese scholars have valued the study of the past. One of the first tasks of every new dynasty was the compilation of an official history of the previous one. The purpose of writing these histories was to learn from the mistakes of the fallen dynasty, and the annals of past dynasties indicated that there were unmistakable signs of decline—for example, popular uprisings or foreign encroachment. History taught that all dynasties would eventually end, and this gave rise to a cyclical view of history. To the extent that this approach to history has fostered an image of a "changeless" China trapped within repeating cycles of dynastic decline, it has warped perceptions of China's past. Despite its obvious limitations the dynastic decline concept has even been invoked to explain twentieth-century China. To compare the rule of an emperor who commanded 20,000 bureaucrats to the head of a modern state who exercises power through the 60 million member Chinese Communist Party (CCP), and who has access to modern communications and coercive power is, at best, a gross misuse of historical analogy.

At first glance the events of the late eighteenth and early nineteenth century seem to resemble familiar patterns of dynastic decline. But in fact, modern historians have pointed to the unprecedented population growth, economic development, and social change of the eighteenth century as indications that China may have been on the threshold of a dramatic break with the past. In retrospect, events of the late eighteenth century, particularly the outbreak of popular rebellion and the first signs of conflict with the British, were harbingers of the double-barreled dilemma China would face during the last century of Qing rule. Under the rubrics of "imperialism," shorthand for the foreign military and economic exploitation of China, and "feudalism," shorthand for the stifling weight of traditional political and social institutions, John Fairbank (1907–1991) discusses China's military, economic, and cultural confrontation with the West and the decline of traditional political and social institutions (reading 4). Imperialism and feudalism are highly charged terms and, as Fairbank notes, the debate over their relative importance in understanding modern Chinese history continues. Nevertheless, most historians agree that the history of modern China cannot be understood without addressing both concepts.

Beneath the surface of this final flourishing of imperial China, the broad economic changes of the eighteenth century engendered tensions that erupted violently as the century came to a close. The White Lotus Rebellion (1795–1804) was the most serious of the various rebellions that marked the close of the eighteenth century. The inspiration and organizational foundation of this uprising was the centuries-old Buddhist White Lotus sect. White Lotus healing practices attracted believers among the poor and disaffected who, under normal circumstances, were law-abiding. Knowing full well that religion had inspired dynasty-toppling rebellions in the past, the Qing, like Chinese governments past and present, closely monitored popular religions and actively suppressed groups it deemed to be subversive. Ironically, government suppression often provoked rather than prevented rebellion. Such was the case in 1795, when White Lotus leaders preached the impending arrival of the Maitreya Buddha and the dawning of a new age. Rebellion quickly spread throughout north central China and lasted for almost a decade, in part due to the ineffectiveness of government forces employed to suppress it. In some regions the government had to call upon local literati-led militias to contain the insurrection. Although the Qing ultimately restored order, the White Lotus Rebellion revealed the deficiencies of both its military and civilian administration.

Coincidentally, 1795 was also the year that the Qianlong Emperor (1736–1795) issued the first edict forbidding the importation of opium. Before British traders began importing the drug to China in sizeable quantities in the late eighteenth century, it was not widely used. Opium was produced in India, which the British East India Company had controlled as a British colony since 1757.

The Chinese government closely monitored and controlled trade with the West. In 1759 China limited maritime commerce to the southern port of Canton (Guangzhou). Meanwhile, British merchants, with the support of the British government, were anxious to expand the scope of trade and to establish it on a more advantageous basis. In 1793 and again in 1816, British emissaries were sent to China to expand trade and establish diplomatic relations with China. The Qing court, however, rebuffed both missions.

By the end of the eighteenth century, opium smuggling had become an important component in the British trade with China at Canton. Prior to the introduction of opium, foreign trade had usually favored China, and because there was little demand for British commodities, British traders had to pay for Chinese imports with silver. Although the British East India Company, the official British monopoly empowered to conduct trade in the Far East, never directly engaged in opium trade, silver that Western opium smugglers earned was deposited with the British monopoly, and paid for the British importation of tea. Without opium Britain ran a trade deficit with China.

As opium imports steadily increased over the first four decades of the nineteenth century, tensions between Britain and China mounted. It did not take long for hostilities to begin once China decided to crack down on this illicit drug trade.

The Opium War

The story of the Opium War (1839–1842) is one that every Chinese school child learns. Of course the events surrounding the Opium War were complex. Western opium smuggling could not have succeeded without the cooperation of corrupt government officials and an indigenous Chinese underworld. But for many Chinese, the Opium War symbolizes the greed and unscrupulousness of the West and the need for China to maintain a modern military force. In fact, the British were determined to open Chinese markets to British manufactured goods and would likely have clashed with China, with or without the opium issue. Still, the fact that Chinese efforts to eradicate the opium trade precipitated the war has contributed to the emotionally charged atmosphere that surrounds any discussion of this shameful episode in Sino-Western relations.

China's defeat in the Opium War was only the beginning of a series of humiliations at the hands of the Western powers that punctuated the waning decades of the Qing dynasty. The embarrassing terms of the Treaty of Nanjing, which ended the Opium War, forced China to open five ports to trade, and to cede the island of Hong Kong to Britain. It also allowed foreign merchants and missionaries to own property and to reside in the open ports. It was not long before renewed Western aggression further expanded the treaty port system. After China's defeat at the hands of the British and French in the Arrow War (1856–1860), every major port on the Chinese coast as well as some inland ports along the Yangzi River were open to trade and foreign residence. Foreign enterprises dominated trade and shipping with the West. Within the treaty ports foreigners lived in special concessions areas which for the most part were outside Chinese administrative and judicial control. Shanghai was the largest and most notorious foreign concession area. While these islands of foreign culture were mortifying signs of Chinese weakness, they were also centers for the transmission of Western ideas and culture, and they often served as sanctuaries for Chinese radicals and revolutionaries.

Internal Rebellion

The foreign threat was undeniably significant, but it paled in comparison to the dangers of internal rebellion. No Chinese ruler could long ignore the will of the common people. Peasant uprisings, in fact, had toppled many of China's greatest dynasties, including the two previous dynasties the Yuan (1279–1368) and the Ming (1368–1644). During the mid-nineteenth century the Qing dynasty simultaneously faced several major popular uprisings. The deadliest and most threatening was the Taiping Rebellion (1851–1864). The leader of the Taipings, Hong Xiuquan, was a modest scholar from Guangdong Province. Hong had failed the civil service exam several times. Overwrought by his third failure, he suffered a physical and mental breakdown. During his period of convalescence, which followers later claimed lasted forty days and forty nights, Hong had visions of a venerable old man who presented him with a sword and told him to drive the demons from China. Later, Hong interpreted these visions in terms of a limited Chinese translation of the Bible. Hong believed that he was the younger brother of Jesus Christ and that God had charged him with driving the Manchus out of China. Not only did Hong and his followers plan to end the Qing dynasty, they were determined to end the dynastic cycle and establish a new political order in China.

As Hong's following grew, it became the object of government suppression, not unlike religious movements in China both past and present. Finally, the movement erupted in full rebellion and in 1851 threatened to topple the Qing dynasty. Within a few short years the Taiping movement, its ranks swollen with millions of new followers, controlled large portions of central China. The Taipings ruled their kingdom from the former Ming capital of Nanjing, which they renamed "New Jerusalem." The Taiping Rebellion was undoubtedly the bloodiest civil war in the history of the world. Estimates of casualties range from 20 to 30 million. The Taipings, like the White Lotus Rebels in 1795, once again exposed the weakness and corruption of regular Qing military forces.

Ultimately, the rebellion was suppressed only when the Qing court granted provincial officials, all of whom were ethnically Chinese, broad powers to raise taxes and organize military forces. Zeng Guofan, the leader of the government forces arrayed against the Taipings, used his network of relatives, friends, and colleagues among the local literati to unite local militias into an army that was bound together by personal and provincial ties. Zeng painted a stark picture of Taiping depredations and cruelty and forcefully unleashed his eloquence against their heterodox belief and abandonment of "several thousand years of Chinese ethical principles" (reading 5). In a broad appeal to the rural masses, Zeng also attacked the Taiping destruction of Buddhist and Daoist temples. Still, Zeng's rhetoric was primarily designed to inspire the elite leadership of rural society. Zeng urged the Chinese elite to fight against the Taipings not merely to save the dynasty, but also to protect the mostly deeply cherished beliefs of Chinese antiquity. It was a powerful plea that, when backed up with promises of official titles and rewards for those who joined the cause, ensured the support of the elite. In the end, Zeng crushed the rebellion and saved the dynasty, but the primitive communism and iconoclasm of the Taiping Rebellion inspired future revolutionaries as diverse as Sun Yat-sen and Mao Zedong.

Efforts at Reform

The Taiping Rebellion was finally defeated in 1864, ushering in an era of "self-strengthening." Chinese officials who had distinguished themselves defending the dynasty against the mid-century rebellions emerged to lead the self-strengthening efforts of the late nineteenth century. Chief among them was Li

Hongzhang (1823–1901). Li led a modernized army based in north China, established one of China's first modern naval fleets, supported the first steamship company in China, sent Chinese students abroad to study, and established a variety of industrial enterprises, including arsenals, cotton mills, and gold mines. Li's activities were emblematic of self-strengthening. Chinese leaders believed they needed to learn the technology that formed the basis of Western military superiority, whose efficacy was amply demonstrated during the suppression of internal rebellions. While China turned to the West for practical needs, self-strengtheners maintained that Chinese ethics and social, cultural, and political institutions were superior to those of the West. For self-strengtheners, these institutions required restoration, not reform.

The failure of Chinese reform efforts became painfully clear in 1895, when the recently modernized military forces of Japan soundly defeated Chinese forces in the Sino-Japanese War (1894–1895). Although China had suffered numerous military setbacks at the hands of the Western powers, defeat by the Japanese sent shock waves through Chinese political and intellectual circles. Historically, the relationship between China and Japan was akin to that between elder and younger brothers. But now it was painfully apparent that Japan had launched its own, more successful reform and modernization program. To make matters worse, the Japanese initially demanded exclusive control over Chinese territory in Manchuria as part of the peace settlement. They withdrew the demand only after France, Germany, and Russia intervened, citing the principles of maintaining Chinese sovereignty and territorial integrity. Within two years, however, all the major foreign powers, with the exception of the United States, demanded and received exclusive concessions or leaseholds over Chinese territory, triggering a "scramble for concessions" by the foreign powers. This new round of imperialist incursions was far more intrusive than those of the past. Within the leaseholds foreign companies controlled rights to mine, build railroads, and construct factories. They also stationed troops to protect their investments. For better and for worse, foreign imperialism had a much more direct impact on the Chinese people in the concession areas than it had had under the treaty port system established after the Opium War.

During the 1870s and 1880s China appeared to be making progress toward the goal of modernizing its military. At the same time, conservative officials who came together around the powerful Empress Dowager Cixi (1825–1908) blunted more radical efforts at political reforms. A powerful female leader, Cixi has been subjected to a great deal of criticism and ridicule. While one might argue that she made questionable decisions, particularly her support of the Boxer

Uprising (1900), in fact she was a shrewd politician who enjoyed the support of a significant segment of China's ruling elite. She was undoubtedly one of the most competent leaders of China in modern times. But, within the hierarchy of the traditional Chinese polity, neither Cixi, who was simply regent for a child emperor, nor anyone else who lacked the authority of a powerful formal office, could ever govern China as effectively as a strong and competent emperor. Defeat in the war with Japan concretely demonstrated the inadequacies and mismanagement of the self-strengtheners and led to renewed debates over modernization strategies after 1895. Proponents of far-reaching institutional reforms, led by Kang Youwei, briefly gained the ear of the sympathetic Guangxu Emperor (1875–1908), who began ruling in his own right after the "retirement" of the Empress Dowager Cixi in 1889. For one hundred days in 1898 China was awash in imperial edicts ordering a wide range of political and social reforms, but the effort abruptly collapsed when conservative forces persuaded the empress dowager to end her retirement and place the emperor under house arrest. The reemergence of the empress dowager set the stage for the Boxer Uprising and the subsequent occupation of Beijing by an eight-nation foreign army.

The Boxer Uprising

The Boxer Uprising was a complex event encompassing all the problems that plagued the Qing dynasty in its waning years: rural unrest, foreign imperialism, and a lack of decisive leadership in the Qing court. By the end of the nineteenth century Western missionaries had penetrated deep into local society. Most of these missionaries were well intentioned: in addition to proselytizing, they also built schools, orphanages, and hospitals to serve the local communities. But their presence in the Chinese countryside was often disruptive and commonly viewed as a challenge to the influence of local elites. Less scrupulous missionaries meddled in local affairs to protect Christian converts. Local government officials were cautious about offending foreign missionaries who could appeal to their government representatives in China to intercede with the Beijing government. But local government officials risked alienating their constituencies if they appeared too compliant to Western demands. Not surprisingly, anti-Christian propaganda was widespread, and anti-Christian violence was a persistent source of social unrest that brought the Qing court into direct conflict with the Western powers.

The Boxer Uprising broke out in the northeastern province of Shandong in 1900. Prior to the uprising several major incidents of anti-foreign violence had occurred in Shandong, and resentment toward foreigners and Chinese Christians ran high. Coincidentally, large parts of northern China also experienced a severe drought in 1899, idling many farmers and raising the specter of famine. In these troubled times, young men banded together in local market towns and practiced martial arts, which explains why foreigners referred to them as "Boxers." Many of them believed a centuries-old notion that individuals could obtain supernatural powers after a deity or spirit "possessed" them. Similarly, many folk religions taught that sincere believers could become invulnerable to weapons, a fallacy tragically demonstrated when hapless Boxers attacked Western soldiers equipped with state-of-the-art firearms.

Initially, Boxers were hostile to the Qing court as well as to foreigners and Chinese Christians. But when factions in the Qing court became interested in supporting the Boxers as a potential force to expel the foreigners, despite the warnings of local officials who had exposed the fraud of invulnerability rituals, the Boxers responded and dropped their anti-Qing slogans. As Paul Cohen notes, by the spring of 1900 Boxers had moved north and laid siege to the foreign legations and a major Christian church in Beijing, provoking an international intervention (reading 6). The siege of Beijing was finally lifted in June when an eight-nation army made up of 20,000 foreign troops occupied Beijing and dictated a settlement to the prostrate Qing court. This disgraceful situation triggered a new round of intensive reform efforts, but it was too late. In October 1911 a troop mutiny in the city of Wuhan set off a chain of events that let to the abdication of the Qing emperor and the formation of the first Chinese republic in 1912.

Republican China

The fall of the Qing dynasty and the founding of the People's Republic of China bracket the era known as the Republican period (1912–1949). This periodization is convenient, but it masks the true complexity of political and social crosscurrents of that time. The overthrow of the Qing dynasty represented a watershed in Chinese history, but the 1911 Revolution did little to strengthen China's hand against foreign imperialism or change Chinese society. On the contrary, foreign powers took advantage of Chinese weakness in the fall of 1911 to advance their ambitions in China. The persistence of imperial traditions was readily apparent when after only four years of republican rule the first president, Yuan Shikai (1859–1916), attempted to establish a new dynasty with himself as emperor. Yuan died shortly after his ill-fated efforts came to naught. The years from 1916 to 1927 are known as the Warlord period. A nominally "central" government that the foreign powers recognized continued to exist in Beijing, but control of China was really divided among an ever-changing group of military leaders who struggled to expand their individual control over ever-greater areas. Weak and divided, China was unable to resist further imperialist inroads, especially from Japan. Chinese reformers and revolutionaries, many of whom naively assumed that the overthrow of the Qing would pave the way for China's modern development, expressed anger and frustration.

The Rise of Chinese Nationalism

In 1919 Chinese delegates walked out of the Paris Peace Conference to protest the failure of the Western powers to support the Chinese demand for the return of a German leasehold in Shandong that Japan had occupied in 1915. This event sparked the accumulated anger and frustration of Chinese intellectuals and students, who erupted in protest on May 4, 1919. Student-led protestors demonstrated in the streets of Beijing and other major cities, voicing their disgust at this latest affront to Chinese nationalism. The immediate impact of the "May Fourth" protests was limited but, as Vera Schwarcz demonstrates, the long-term consequences were far-reaching, because at this juncture Chinese intellectuals identified traditional culture itself as the major impediment to China's political and social transformation and the source of China's weakness (reading 7). The Chinese students who protested in 1919 were part of a new generation of Chinese intellectuals who had come of age after the fall of the Qing. An older generation of progressive intellectuals, many of whom were professors at China's leading universities, had taught this younger generation that they were China's salvation. Chen Duxiu (1879–1942), who in 1915 created the journal *New Youth,* which became essential reading for the May Fourth generation, was the dean of arts and sciences at Beijing University in 1917, and a founding member of the Chinese Communist Party in 1921. He urged Chinese youth to be independent, progressive, aggressive, cosmopolitan, scientific, and utilitarian. Chen juxtaposed these traits to the subservience and conservatism that traditional Chinese culture had inculcated in China's youth.

As a result of the May Fourth Movement, young Chinese intellectuals turned to political activism with unprecedented enthusiasm. In the 1920s the city of Canton (Guangzhou) in Guangdong Province was the base of Sun Yat-sen (1866–1925), whose revolutionary activities dated back to the late nineteenth century. Sun led the Nationalist Party or Guomindang (GMD, also Kuomintang or KMT in older romanizations), which became the recipient of military, financial, and political aid from the Soviet Union. The centerpiece of Soviet aid was the establishment of the Whampoa Military Academy. Sun's speech, marking the opening of the Whampoa Academy, embodied the patriotic and nationalist rhetoric prevalent at the time, and it indicates that training a politically enlightened revolutionary army was considered critical to GMD success (reading 8). Soviet aid was contingent upon Sun's allowing members of the recently formed Chinese Communist Party to join the Nationalists. The top priority of the GMD-CCP alliance was to establish a modern army capable of defeating the warlords, but the movement was also committed to reforming society and raising the political consciousness of the Chinese masses. The GMD-CCP alliance established a women's federation, organized labor unions, and trained young intellectuals to set up peasant associations in rural areas. Through newspapers and other forms of propaganda the alliance sought to build a mass base of support for political change.

After the death of Sun Yat-sen in 1925, the tenuous alliance between the GMD and the CCP became severely strained. Chiang Kai-shek, Sun's military advisor, assumed the leadership of the GMD and launched the long-awaited Northern Expedition (1926–1928), an ambitious military campaign directed against China's warlords. Starting in Guangdong Province, the campaign's ultimate destination was Beijing. During the initial stages of the Northern Expedition the GMD and CCP cooperated to good effect. The CCP, through its dominance of mass organizations, particularly peasant associations and labor unions, provided political support for the military. In the industrial center of Shanghai, Communist-run labor unions took control of the city before Chiang's army arrived. Tragically, it was also in Shanghai that Chiang Kai-shek launched a preemptive strike against his erstwhile allies. On April 12, 1927, forces loyal to Chiang attacked the labor unions of Shanghai, precipitating an open break with the CCP. Many Communists were executed or jailed in the bloody crackdown that ensued. The GMD issued an official statement condemning the CCP and accusing it of usurping power. Chiang's assault on the CCP was crippling. It undermined the Communist-controlled labor unions and forced the CCP to go underground in urban areas.

By the end of 1927 Chiang Kai-shek had either defeated the remaining warlords or made agreements with them, and he established a new national government in Nanjing. From 1927 to 1937, the "Nanjing Decade," the GMD government exercised nominal control over China. In fact, major warlords who had joined the government, such as the powerful Manchurian warlord Zhang Xueliang, retained a large degree of autonomy. Progress was made under the

GMD government in the recovery of rights from the foreign powers, in economic development, and in the modernization of education. But Chiang Kai-shek faced two great challenges—the resilience of the rural-based Communist movement and the encroachment of Japanese imperialists. Chiang insisted that the Communist threat was more dangerous and, while acquiescing to the Japanese seizure of Manchuria in 1931, the Nanjing government initiated several large-scale military efforts to eradicate the Communists.

The Rise of Mao Zedong

After the break between the GMD and CCP, the Communists established base areas in remote rural areas. The most famous of these was the Jiangxi Soviet, where Mao Zedong (1893–1976) emerged as a key leader. Even before the GMD purge forced Communists to seek refuge in the countryside, Mao had enthusiastically advocated support for the peasantry in his report on the peasant movement in his home province of Hunan (reading 9). Mao spoke in apocalyptic terms, stating that "several hundred million peasants will rise like a mighty storm." He justified rural violence against "local tyrants, lawless landlords, and evil gentry" and urged the CCP to take a leading role in guiding the revolution in the countryside. This report foreshadowed the strategy of peasant revolution that would eventually propel Mao to victory, but in 1927 few observers could have imagined that Mao's achievements would match his lofty rhetoric. Nonetheless, by the early 1930s the CCP was successfully expanding its rural base area and carrying out an aggressive program of land redistribution, while simultaneously fending off GMD encirclement campaigns.

By 1934 the GMD encirclement campaigns had nearly succeeded in destroying the Jiangxi Soviet, but survivors of the campaigns walked nearly 6,000 miles out of Jiangxi on the legendary "Long March" and established a new base area in Yan'an in China's northwest in 1935. Over the course of the Long March Mao steadily consolidated his control over the Communist movement, but he recognized how weakened the Communists were, so he shrewdly appealed to Chiang Kai-shek to end the civil war and unite to fight the Japanese. The CCP's public appeal to nationalism was an effective propaganda tool and gained renewed support from patriotic Chinese who were frustrated at the GMD government's failure to stem the tide of Japanese encroachment. In December 1936 Zhang Xueliang, the former warlord of Manchuria and second in command to Chiang Kai-shek in the GMD regime, kidnapped Chiang during a visit to the Zhang's headquarters in Xian. Chiang had traveled to Xian to order

Zhang personally to resume the attack on the CCP. Instead, Zhang forced Chiang to agree to resist Japan in a "united front" with the Communists.

The Japanese Invasion

The so-called Xian Incident changed the political landscape in China. After Xian no Chinese leader could survive if he appeared to be soft on Japanese aggression, and skirmishes between Chinese and Japanese troops in north China increased. When the Japanese military launched an all-out invasion in July 1937, the GMD government initially fought hard. With only the Soviet Union supplying aid, China could not resist the superior Japanese forces, however. By the end of 1937, every major coastal city and most of the key cities in central China were under Japanese control. The GMD government retreated to the city of Chongqing in the southwest, where it remained until the Japanese surrender in 1945. From their base area in remote Yan'an in the northwest, the Communists fought a guerilla war against the Japanese throughout north China, spreading their political influence and garnering popular support. When Japan attacked American and British bases in the Pacific in 1941, China was no longer alone in its struggle. The U.S. government almost immediately began supplying military, financial, and humanitarian aid to Chiang Kai-shek's government. In wartime summit meetings Chiang Kai-shek met with Franklin Roosevelt and Winston Churchill, boosting his political prestige at home and abroad. From 1941 to 1945 Chiang's government stockpiled American aid while avoiding direct confrontation with Japanese forces. For many Chinese and some foreign observers, GMD efforts against the Japanese paled in comparison to CCP resistance. In fact, American observers in Yan'an praised the Communist-led guerilla war in the north. Still, aid to Yan'an remained limited.

Civil War

After the Japanese surrender in 1945, GMD and CCP forces rushed to accept the surrender of Japanese forces. Chiang's government, with the support of the U.S. Air Force, took control of every urban center in China. But the Communists were militarily strong in the countryside and not without supporters and sympathizers in the cities. The United States attempted to broker a coalition government between the GMD and CCP—to no avail—for neither side was interested in sharing power. By 1947 China was mired in civil war. After some initial setbacks CCP forces inflicted a series of stunning military defeats on the

GMD which, riddled with corruption and crippled by hyperinflation, rapidly lost popular support. The American scholar, A. Doak Barnett (1921–1999), who traveled throughout China from 1947 to 1949, described the widespread disintegration of public support for the GMD among people of all walks of life (reading 10). Nevertheless, the swift and total collapse of the GMD stunned most contemporary observers. Facing failure on all fronts, Chiang Kai-shek "retired" on January 21, 1949, but not without taking most of the navy, air force, and national treasury with him when he fled to the island province of Taiwan. In December 1949, after the loss of the last remaining strongholds in southern China, the remainder of the GMD government joined Chiang Kai-shek in Taiwan, which, as the Republic of China, remains beyond the control of Beijing to this day.

People's Republic of China

With the establishment of the People's Republic of China in 1949 the CCP succeeded where other twentieth-century revolutionary movements had failed. Regardless of their political orientation, most war-weary Chinese welcomed an end to the many years of conflict. For Mao Zedong the Communist success was a vindication of his strategy of rural-based revolution. After more than a decade of foreign invasion and civil war, the immediate goal of the new government was restoration of the economy and social order. During its first few years the new government moved slowly and cautiously in its effort to transform Chinese society. Many early initiatives, particularly in the area of public health and its attacks on prostitution and drug addiction, were quite popular. Similarly, the Marriage Law of 1950 outlawed arranged marriages and upheld the rights of women to divorce and to own property. With the important exceptions of land reform and women's rights, the new government initially refrained from radical reforms. Land reform, which had begun in north China as early as 1946, was extended to the entire country after 1949. Internationally, the United States imposed a trade embargo and continued to recognized the GMD regime in Taiwan as the legitimate government of China, while Mao made his first trip outside China to the Soviet Union where he negotiated the Sino-Soviet Treaty of Friendship, Alliance, and Mutual Aid. Whatever hopes there might have been for a Sino-American rapprochement were quickly dashed when American and Chinese forces clashed in the Korean War in 1950–1953. Normal diplomatic relations were not restored between China and the United States until 1979.

Sino-American Relations in Retrospect

Misperceptions and ambiguities clouded relations between the United States and China from the start. During the late nineteenth century, the United States played a relatively minor, but benign role in Chinese foreign relations compared with the European powers. American missionaries were active in China, and their appeals for support, which often depicted the Chinese as impoverished and pitiable, aroused sympathy and colored popular American perceptions. Participation in the suppression of the Boxer Uprising was the first major American military involvement in China. As foreign powers scrambled to extract exclusive concessions at the close of the nineteenth century, the United States called for an Open Door Policy that would respect the sovereignty, territorial integrity, and administrative independence of China. The policy was not based on altruism, however, but was designed to limit exclusive foreign spheres of influence and allow equal access to Chinese markets. Other unattractive aspects of American-Chinese relations included the 1882 American Exclusion Act (reading 11). Racism against Chinese immigrants to the United States was sufficient to gain passage of a law forbidding Chinese immigration to America. Nineteenth-century Chinese perceptions of foreigners were often similarly inaccurate (reading 12).

During the twentieth century the United States found itself increasingly at odds with Japanese efforts to extend their influence in China. The U.S. government continued to promote the principles of the Open Door Policy, but diplomacy proved ineffective as militarists gained the upper hand in Tokyo. When Japan invaded Manchuria in 1931 and established the "independent" state of Manchukuo, the United States responded with a policy of nonrecognition. As Japanese aggression escalated, America responded with diplomatic and economic sanctions, but it was only after the bombing of Pearl Harbor that America provided the Chinese direct military support. During World War II the United States supported the GMD government and actively promoted Chiang Kai-shek as a future leader of post-World War II East Asia. Continued U.S. support for the GMD government based in Taiwan led to a deterioration of Sino-American relations, which was not fully repaired until President Jimmy Carter reestablished diplomatic relations with the People's Republic in 1979. Over the past two decades foreign trade, tourism, and educational exchanges between China and the United States have grown steadily, but tensions over trade imbalances, human rights, and Taiwan continue to trouble Sino-American relations.

GEOGRAPHY AND HISTORY
Readings

1

China's Environmental History in World Perspective

J. R. McNEILL

For thousands of years the people of China have skillfully exploited the abundant and varied natural resources of their land to sustain one of history's greatest civilizations. As J. R. McNeill explains below, success was partly due to the country's "portfolio of ecological diversity" and partly due to the human alterations of the Chinese landscape. Throughout Chinese history the state took an active role in the construction and maintenance of large-scale waterworks, flood control, and reforestation. In the rice-growing south, keeping the paddies, terraces, polders, dikes, and canals in working order took enormous amounts of human labor. Some historians have argued that the "dynastic cycle"—the rise and fall or successive ruling houses—was related to the management of the environment. As J. R. McNeill notes, however, over the long term the pattern reveals "a slow drawdown of biological resources and the elimination of ecological buffers." McNeill also dispels the common misconception that Chinese beliefs, such as Daoism, which emphasize harmony between human beings and nature, restrained the human tendency to alter the environment.

The Chinese have river systems as useful as any in terms of transport, and have tirelessly tried to improve upon nature's gift for more than three thousand years. China has a Nile in the north, a Ganges in the south, and a man-made Mississippi linking them. The Yellow River, like the Nile before the Aswan Dam, carries irrigation water and fertile silt through an arid land. It floods seasonally. It is navigable to about 600–800 kilometers inland—as far from the sea as the first cataract of the Nile. The Yangzi flows through the rice basket of China, providing irrigation water and cheap transport, as the Ganges does in India. The Yangzi is navigable 2,700 kilometers upstream, as far as Chongqing (compared to only 1,600 kilometers on the Ganges-Jumna). But because of the difficulties of sailing though the gorges, large traffic on the Yangzi goes only as far as Wuhan, about 1,100 kilometers from the sea, about as far as the upstream limit for large ships on the Ganges (Allahabad). Between the Yangzi and Yellow rivers the Chinese state has built and for 1,400 years (usually) maintained as artificial Mississippi, the Grand Canal, a transport artery linking the north and south of the country. Taken together these waterways form a gigantic fishhook, a huge fertile crescent united by cheap and safe transport. Countless capillaries—smaller rivers and feeder canals—connected the main arteries to a broad hinterland. The system even extended to the West/Pearl River in the far south via the Ling Qu canal (first built c. 230 B.C.) No land-based transport network could rival this one for cheapness until the railway age. No inland waterway system in world history approaches this one as a device for integrating large and productive spaces. . . .

With its waterways the Chinese state from Song times forward kept under its control (most of the time) a huge diversity of ecological zones with a broad array of useful natural resources. The Song, who developed the south, ruled over a belt of about twenty degrees of latitude, extending as far south as Hainan, well into the tropics. The Ming and Qing, with Manchuria and eventually (after 1760) Xinjiang, controlled a span of thirty degrees of latitude and ecologies ranging from the tropical to the subarctic. Consequently the Chinese state had available great stocks and wide varieties of timber, grains, fish, fibers, salt, metals, building stone, and occasionally livestock and grazing land. This portfolio of ecological diversity translated into insurance and resilience for the state. It provided the wherewithal for war—except for horses, a constant concern resolved only by the Qing conquest on Mongolia. It assured that should crops fail and revenues dwindle in one part of the empire, the shortfall could be made good elsewhere. Forest fires, epizootics, or crop pests could devastate several localities without threatening the stability of the state. The role of ecological diversity as insurance helps explain the resilience of the Chinese state. No other state ever quite matched it—until the era of European overseas empire.

Thus China was, from about A.D. 650 to 1800, almost always the most ecologically resilient and resourceful state on earth. Indeed, during this millennium China was probably the most ecologically diverse polity in the history of the world before Britain assembled its far-flung overseas empire. State and society gradually corroded China's diversity, simplifying ecosystem in the interest of maximizing the human crop. Over the centuries China lost many of its ecological buffers, its forests, wetlands, wildlands. But it remained for more than eleven centuries the state with the greatest ecological complementarity.

Similarly, Chinese society was probably the most epidemiologically experienced. By virtue of its long urban tradition China had domesticated almost all the crowd diseases, such as measles and smallpox. By virtue of its animal husbandry, particular the keeping of pigs and fowl, the Chinese had vast experience with those diseases humankind shares with animals—influenza for instance. By virtue of its great expanses of surface water, China had plenty of waterborne infections, mosquito breeding grounds, and parasites. By virtue of its hot south, many Chinese immune systems were familiar with malaria, dengue, and other tropical fevers. These ecological circumstances amounted to a double-edged sword. Malaria and other tropical killers limited Chinese settlement and control over the far south. Illness and death haunted all of China, and the toll on children and other immunological naifs probably ranked among the highest anywhere in the world. But those who survived childhood, especially in southern China, where the variety of lethal infections was greatest, probably had the most alert and active (human) immune systems on earth. Consequently, the Chinese had less in the way of disease to fear from strangers than virtually anyone else, and strangers had much to fear from them. The Chinese were safe from the microbial imperialism of other peoples, and able to inflict its costs upon their less epidemiologically experienced neighbors. This probably helped China to expand at the expense of forest dwellers in the south, southwest, and northeast of modern China, and at the expense of Tibetans and the steppe peoples. Had the fifteenth-century Ming overseas voyages continued, had junks rather than caravelles linked the whole planet, China's brand of ecological imperialism presumably would have transformed landscapes and societies as thoroughly as Europe's did.

The inland waterway system created in China a far more unified market, polity, and society than existed over comparably large and rich spaces elsewhere in the world. Consumer or government demand in one part of the empire influenced production patterns, land use, resource exploitation, in very distant provinces—wherever the capillaries of the waterway system reached. This was true not merely for expensive military and luxury goods, but for bulk goods— grains, timber, salt. So China's environmental history, like its economic history, is more integrated, less the mere sum of its local parts than is the case elsewhere. This integration, this cohesion, meant that state policy and the character of the prevailing economic system conditioned China's environmental history to an unusual degree. . . .

The Chinese agricultural landscape, and eventually almost every hectare of inner China, was thoroughly anthropogenic. People chose (sometimes unwittingly) which animals and plants lived. People governed (as best they could) the paths of the waters. Even the soil was a human construct. All agricultural landscapes are of course man-made (or in many cases woman-made). Rice paddies are more so than most. But even north China, the land of wheat and millet, was sculpted by human labor to an unusual degree.

But China's terraces, paddies, polders, dikes, dams, and canals needed massive and constant labor and investment. Should the supply of either of these fail, rapid and costly deterioration (from the human point of view) would inevitably follow. A sudden loss of population, whether deriving from epidemic or war, could easily lead to heightened erosion, flooding, waterlogging of fields, silting up of river beds and canals—damage that might take decades of favorable conditions (abundant labor and a strong state) to repair. Should the state crumble or merely withdraw its funding from waterworks, neglect and decay followed, with the same high ecological costs. Equivalent demographic or political events in northern Europe or southern Africa—or any land without terracing and significant waterworks—would lead only to contractions in arable and resurgence of spontaneous vegetation. A single year of favorable conditions (adequate labor and a good burning season) could restore such lands to full production. Thus it is fair to say that the Chinese landscape was unusually dependent on demographic and political stability, and unusually vulnerable to disruption by neglect. . . .

The rapid and thorough ecological change provoked in China by neglect could be repaired in time. A new, strong, and solvent dynasty could restore waterworks, drain lowlands, and (least likely) reforest hills, thereby restoring high productivity until the next disruption. This situation gives the strong appearance of cycles, suggesting a long-term ecological equilibrium in which the hyperanthropogenic landscape deteriorated and recovered in an irregular rhythm defined by imperial finance, epidemics, and war.

Such a cycle may well have existed over centuries, and if so it distinguished China from most other societies. But over millennia a deeper pattern asserted itself, more linear than cyclical: the slow drawdown of biological resources and elimination of ecological buffers. The progressive replacement of forests and wetlands by fields and people—progress most would say—put China in periodic crisis, necessitating either spatial expansions or technological revolutions permitting great leaps upward in agricultural productivity. In this, China's environmental experience is typical of the world at large. . . .

Probably the two greatest environmental changes in the last three thousand years of Chinese history have been destruction of forests and the reorganization of surface waters. In both these matters the Chinese rank among the most enthusiastic and proficient of peoples, but their conduct, ambition, and motives are perfectly consistent with other societies'. Conversion of forests to arable and pasture is one of the hallmarks of civilization. Peoples round the world have used fire and ax to create landscapes capable of supporting (at least temporarily) the maximum human load. Sixteenth-century Amerindians probably burned more North American forests every year than the continent's current inhabitants do (although even after ten thousand years they had more forest standing than today's North Americans have after four hundred years). Polynesians cut down and burned off lowland forests in virtually every island they settled. Europeans cleared 80 percent of their forests, Indians—with help from the British—somewhat more of theirs. . . . China's replacement of trees by people easily fits the general pattern of the last ten thousand years. Its fuel wood and timber shortages resemble the experience of countless societies, ancient and modern, temperate and tropical.

China's record of water manipulation may involve more impressive technologies than found elsewhere (until 1750 at least). And certainly the scale of operations in China exceeded that elsewhere until the nineteenth century. But numerous other peoples have rerouted their waters with much the same aims and results as the Chinese. Dryland irrigation, channeling, and diking existed in Mesopotamia and Egypt before they did in China. In Central Asia the Syr Darya has been managed (off and on) since 2300 B.C. Finely articulated mountain irrigation systems existed in pre-Columbian Mexico and Peru, throughout the ancient Mediterranean and later Muslim worlds, and Ethiopia, not to mention Japan and China's southeast Asian neighbors. In most cases, states took a prominent role in building and operating these waterworks. In all cases, heightened production came at the cost of vulnerability to catastrophe in the form of disruption of the waterworks, which inevitably led to food crises. In all cases, rearranging surface waters incurred ecological costs, although these varied in nature and severity. Mesopotamia perhaps paid most heavily—at least until the recent debacles in Soviet Central Asia. Again, there is nothing eccentric about the Chinese record as regards water manipulation. Only scale distinguishes it from others.

Much the same holds true for the other components of Chinese environmental history. The slow extension of arable into marginal environments, semiarid grasslands, or ever steeper hillsides is a familiar tale with countless parallels.

The doubling and redoubling of silt loads in the rivers, the progradation of deltas into the sea, the alteration of microclimates following vegetation change, even the modern crises of chemical pollution, in all these China's history is different only in detail, in timing perhaps, or in scale.

. . . China has pursued ecologically unsustainable patterns for three thousand years, avoiding total breakdown by periodically adapting to crisis with new technologies or new spatial expansions. This pattern too is a common one, although since no other societies can show three thousand years of cultural continuity it is not easy to see. But taken at the aggregate, global level it is clearer: two crucial ecological transitions have relaxed constraints on human population growth. Hunting and foraging societies may have invented agriculture out of necessity, in response to food crisis brought on by population pressure. Even if invented for other reasons, the new technologies of food production allowed for far greater populations. But agriculture frequently entailed the slow (and sometimes fast) drawdown of fundamental resources, such as fertile soil, fresh water, and combustible fuel. In the eighteenth century, worldwide population growth brought matters of food and fuel to a head and in England produced the second great transmutation of the human condition, the intensive use of fossil fuel and machine power known as the industrial revolution. Through heightened agricultural productivity, better transport, and associated improvements, it not merely forestalled Malthusian crises, but allowed a further expansion of population and in places, of wealth.

The industrial revolution now threatens a new crisis in the shape of mounting pollution loads and perhaps depletion of scarce resources too. Pollution loads are now occasionally great enough to damage human health directly, most widely perhaps in Russia and Eastern Europe, and to alter basic biogeochemical cycles on which all life depends. (I refer to the depletion of stratospheric ozone and the buildup of atmospheric carbon dioxide and other greenhouse gases.) Pollution (chiefly with organochlorides) has even begun to affect the biological capacity to reproduce among many species—ours included—by disrupting endocrine systems (these produce hormones that regulate metabolism and sexual development, among other things). A third transmutation awaits us. The past, Chinese and global, suggests—but cannot guarantee—that after much suffering we will find another clever but unsustainable solution. . . .

2

The Uniting of China

DRU C. GLADNEY

The ethnic and linguistic diversity of China has often been poorly understood in the West. Historically, the arc of land extending from the Pamir Mountains in the west through Central Asia and the area south of Siberia and north of the Great Wall to the Pacific Ocean was the homeland of many ethnic groups that challenged and sometimes overwhelmed the Han Chinese empire. This area encompasses about half the territory of the Peoples' Republic of China and remains a sensitive area of great strategic concern for the present leadership in Beijing. Some of the major nationalities, such as the Tibetan, Mongolian, and Manchu, are well known, but Chinese ethnic and linguistic diversity is far richer than most outside observers realize. Even among the approximately 90 percent of the Chinese people who belong to the Han nationality, there are "eight mutually unintelligible linguistic groupings." Dru Gladney's essay introduces the fifty-six "official nationalities" of present-day China and discusses the politics of ethnic identity.

China is a multicultural and ethnically diverse nation-state with tremendous cultural, geographic, and linguistic diversity among its dispersed population. Yet, China usually is not thought of as multiethnic country, but rather as one nation with one majority population, the Han, and a few inconsequential minorities on its border areas. Discussions of China generally take cultural uniformity for granted and China is often portrayed as an "homogeneous" monoethnic state. This study takes exception to this conceptualization of China and its population; not only is there tremendous ethnic diversity among China's "official" minority nationalities, but there are equally important cultural differences among China's majority population, identified as the "Han" people. This cultural and ethnic diversity will be of increasing importance and vibrancy in the post-Cold War era, with a rising politics of difference that we must take seriously if we are to understand China in the 1990s. . . .

The People's Republic of China is comprised of 56 "official" nationalities. These include a total population of 91 million "official" minorities, living in every

31

province, region, and county, speaking a wide variety of languages that belong to four of the world's largest language families, including Sino-Tibetan (Mandarin, Tibetan, Kam-Tai, Miao-Yao), Turkic-Altaic (Kazakh, Uygur, Mongolian, Manchu-Tungus, Korean), Austro-Asiatic (Hmong, Vietnamese), and Indo-European (Tadjik, Russian; see Table 1.1) These groups have always been important for China's domestic and international relations. The significance of these official nationalities has increased dramatically in the 1990s, now that China is confronted with several new nations that have significant similar populations on both sides of the border. Ethnic separatism is a major concern to leaders in Beijing.

In addition to the official minority nationalities, the state-recognized majority nationality, known as the Han, which in 1990 occupied 91 percent of the total population, is comprised of a wide variety of culturally and ethnically diverse populations, including eight mutually unintelligible linguistic groupings (Mandarin, Wu, Yue, Xiang, Hakka, Gan, Southern and Northern Min). There is also marked linguistic and cultural diversity among these Chinese language subgroups. Among the Yue language family, for example, the Cantonese and Taishan speakers are barely intelligible to each other, and among southern Min speakers, Quanzhou, Changzhou, and Xiamen dialects are equally difficult to communicate across. The North China dialect, known as Mandarin, was imposed as the national language in the first part of the twentieth century and it has become the *lingua franca* (medium of communication between peoples of different languages) most often used by these peoples to communicate with each other, but it still must be learned in school. Yet, as any Mandarin-speaking Beijinger will tell you, buying vegetables or radios in Canton and Shanghai is becoming increasing difficult due to the growing expressions of pride in the local languages of these areas, with nonnative speakers always paying a higher price. Despite strong restrictions and discouragement from the state government, the appearance and resurgence of local languages, such as Cantonese, in film, radio, and television is just one indication of this increasing interest in cultural difference.

Yet, despite growing awareness of the enormous cultural and ethnic diversity within China, most introductions of the study of China have devoted themselves primarily to the larger issues of state and society, especially economics, politics, religion, family, and the arts, with little attention to the impact of cultural diversity on any of these issues. When cultural differences have been noted, generally they have been explained as "regional" and not important for our understanding of national identity in China. When ethnic identity is addressed, usually it has been devoted to the study of the official minorities who are generally marginalized to the geographic and sociopolitical

Table 1.1
CHINA'S OFFICIALLY RECOGNIZED NATIONALITIES, 1982 AND 1990 CENSUS

Number(s) of Group	1990 Population	1982 Population	Percent Increase	Language Family	Location
Achang	27,708	20,441	36%	Tibeto-Burman	South: Yunnan
Bai	1,594,827	1,132,010	41%	Tibeto-Burman	South: Yunnan
Bao'an (Bonan)	12,212	9,027	35%	Mongolian	North: Gansu
Benglong	15,462	12,295	26%	Mon-Khmer	South: Yunnan
Bulang (Blang)	82,280	58,476	46%	Mon-Khmer	South: Yunnan
Buyi	2,545,059	2,122,389	20%	Kam-Tai	South: Guizhou
Dai (Thai)	1,025,128	840,590	22%	Tai	South: Yunnan
Daur	121,357	94,014	29%	Mongolian	Manchuria, Xinjiang
Dong (Kam)	2,514,014	1,426,335	76%	Kam-Tai	South: Guizhou
Dongxiang (Santa)	373,872	276,347	34%	Mongolian	North: Gansu
Dulong (Drung)	5,816	4,682	24%	Tibeto-Burman	South: Yunnan
Elunchun (Oroqen)	6,965	4,132	68%	Tungus	North: Manchuria
Evenki (Ewenk)	26,315	19,343	36%	Tungus	North: Manchuria
Gaoshan	2,929	1,549	87%	Austronesian	Taiwan, Fujian
Gelao	437,997	53,802	714%	Maio-Yao	South: Guizhou
Hani	1,253,952	1,059,404	18%	Tibeto-Burman	South: Yunnan
Hezhe	4,245	1,476	19%	Tungus	North: Manchuria
Hui	8,602,978	7,227,022	19%	Diverse	Nationwide
Jing (Vietnamese)	18,915	11,995	58%	Mon-Khmer	South: Guangxi
Jingbo	119,209	93,008	28%	Tibeto-Burman	South: Yunnan
Jinuo	18,021	11,974	51%	Tibeto-Burman	South: Yunnan
Kazakh	1,111,718	908,414	22%	Turkic	North: Xinjiang
Kyrgyz	141,549	113,999	24%	Turkic	North: Xinjiang
Korean (Chaoxian)	1,920,597	1,766,439	9%	Altaic	North: Manchuria
Lahu	411,476	304,174	35%	Tibeto-Burman	South: Yunnan
Li	1,110,900	818,355	36%	Tai	South: Hainan
Lisu	574,856	480,960	20%	Tibeto-Burman	South: Yunnan
Luoba (Lhopa)	2,312	2,065	12%	Tibeto-Burman	Tibet
Manchu (Man)	9,821,180	4,304,160	128%	Tungus-Manchu	North: Manchuria
Maonan	71,968	38,135	89%	Tai	South: Guangxi
Menba	7,475	6,248	20%	Tibeto-Burman	Tibet
Miao (Hmong)	7,398,035	5,036,377	89%	Miao-Yao	South
Mongolian (Meng)	4,806,849	3,416,881	41%	Mongolian	North
Mulao (Mulam)	159,328	90,426	76%	Tai	South: Guangxi
Naxi (Moso)	278,009	245,154	13%	Tibeto-Burman	South: Yunnan

Table 1.1 Continued

Number(s) of Group	1990 Population	1982 Population	Percent Increase	Language Family	Location
Nu	27,123	23,166	17%	Tibeto-Burman	South: Yunnan
Pumi (Primi)	29,657	24,237	22%	Tibeto-Burman	South: Yunnan
Qiang	198,252	102,768	93%	Tibeto-Burman	South: Sichuan
Russian (Eluosi)	13,504	2,935	360%	Indo-European	Manchuria, Xinjiang
Salar	87,697	69,102	27%	Turkic	North: Gansu
She	630,378	368,832	71%	Miao-Yao	South: Fujian
Shui (Sui)	345,993	286,487	20%	Tai	South: Guizhou
Tadjik	33,538	26,503	27%	Indo-European	North: Xinjiang
Tatar	4,873	4,127	18%	Turkic	North: Xinjiang
Tibetan (Zang)	4,593,330	3,874,035	19%	Tibeto-Burman	Tibet, Qinghai, Sichuan
Tu (Monguor)	191,624	159,426	20%	Mongolian	North: Qinghai
Tujia	5,704,223	2,834,732	101%	Miao-Yao	South: Hunan
Uygur (Weiwuer)	7,214,431	5,962,814	21%	Turkic	North: Xinjiang
Uzbek	14,502	12,453	16%	Turkic	North: Xinjiang
Wa	351,974	298,591	19%	Mon-Khmer	South: Yunnan
Xibo	172,847	83,629	107%	Tungus	Manchuria, Xinjiang
Yao (Mien)	2,134,013	1,403,664	52%	Miao-Yao	South
Yi (Lolo)	6,572,173	5,457,251	20%	Tibeto- Burman	South
Yugur	12,297	10,596	16%	Turkic	North: Gansu
Zhuang	15,489,630	13,388,118	16%	Kam-Tai	South: Guangxi
Other nationalities still unidentified	749,341	881,838			
Chinese citizens of foreign origin	3,421	4,842			
Total Minorities	91,200,314	67,295,217	35%		
Han Majority	1,042,482,187	940,880,121	10%		
Total Population	1,224,882,815	1,075,470,555	12%		

borderlands of Chinese society. Although the official minorities are certainly important in terms of their overall estimated population of 91 million, and groups such as the Tibetans, Mongols, and Uygurs have gained international attention, their occupying only 8 percent of China's total population makes them inconsequential to most studies of China's overall economy, politics, and society. Discussions of ethnicity in China have generally been restricted to these official minorities, and since they are such a small proportion of China's population, little attention has been paid to ethnicity outside the official groups. . . .

The Politics of Ethnic Identification

Shortly after the founding of the People's Republic, state planners in Beijing sent teams of researchers, social scientists, and Communist Party cadres to the border regions of China to identify and recognize groups seeking to be registered as official nationalities (*minzu*), a generic term with a complex and relatively recent history in China that has been translated in English as "nation," "nationality," "ethnicity," or "people." Although more than 400 separate groups applied for nationality recognition, only 41 nationalities were initially listed in the first census in 1953. The 1964 census included 53 nationalities, and the 1982 and 1990 census identified 56 separate nationalities. What happened to the nearly 350 other groups who applied to be recognized? Some of them are still trying. There are at least 15 groups who are officially being considered for nationality recognition, including the Sherpas, Kucong, and Chinese Jews. Significantly, the 1990 census revealed that there are still 749,341 individuals still "unidentified" and awaiting recognition. This means that these people are regarded as ethnically different, but do not fit into any of the official nationality categories recognized by the state.

The majority of the groups that did not get recognized were either considered to belong to the Han majority or were grouped with other minorities with whom they shared some similarities. While there has not been much written about the exact nature of how some groups were recognized or others excluded, Fei Xiaotong, China's preeminent social anthropologist, revealed that the nationality categories employed by the Soviet Union in its identification programs were also influential in China. Known as the "four commons," outlined by Joseph Stalin, these categories included "a common language, a common territory, a common economic life, and a common psychological makeup," what Stalin later generalized as a common "culture." It is clear that language was a major factor in the identification of China's 56 nationalities. . . .

Other groups, however, have been more successful. The Jinuo, who live on the border of north Burma and southern Yunnan, were the most recent group to be officially recognized. They were granted official minority nationality status in 1979. In 1978, even though they no longer practiced Islam, approximately 30,000 Fujianese who were able to prove descent from foreign Muslims were recognized as members of the primarily Islamic Hui nationality.

In this case, their genealogical proof of descent from foreign Muslim officials and traders who settled on the south coast between the ninth and fourteenth centuries was sufficient for recognition. This led the way for many groups to begin to press for nationality recognition based on the historical records of foreign ancestry alone, even though they may lack any cultural markers of ethnicity, such as language, locality, economy, or religion [see Map 1.1].

Why would anyone want to be recognized as an official minority nationality in China, and why would the government want to recognize them in the first place? The answer may lie in the history of the Chinese Communist Party (CCP) and the influence of the "Long March" of 1934–1935, which was the Party's 6,000-mile escape from the threat of annihilation by Chiang Kai-shek's Kuomintang forces. During the Long March, the Chinese communist leaders became acutely aware of the vibrant ethnic identity of the many diverse peoples they encountered on their arduous trek from the southwest to the northwest. The march led them through the most concentrated minority areas of China, where they encountered peoples not always sympathetic to the communist cause. Edgar Snow graphically described the desperate plight of the Long Marchers, harried on one side by the Japanese and the Kuomintang, and on the other side by the "fierce" barbarian tribesmen (Snow, 1938). The Party was faced with the choice of extermination or making promises of special treatment to the minorities, specifically including the Miao, Yi (Lolo), Tibetan, Mongols, and Hui, should the CCP ever win national power. Once the Long Marchers reached the relatively safe haven of the mountain caves of Yan'an, they had to devise a plan to appease the numerous Mongols in the north, Hui Muslims to the west, and their powerful warlord Ma Hongkui of Ningxia. One solution was to promise recognition of the Hui as a separate nationality and establish the first minority autonomous region in Tongxin, in southern Ningxia. These pledges of recognition and autonomy, in exchange for support for the Communists, were just a few of the many promises made to minorities prior to the establishment of the People's Republic in 1949.

From the beginning, the Chinese Communist Party followed the Soviet policy of offering the possibility of true secession for its minority republics, a policy that ultimately resulted in the dissolution of the USSR in 1991. China, however, did not maintain its commitment to a secessionist policy after founding of the People's Republic. Before coming to power, Chairman Mao Zedong had followed and frequently referred to Article 14 of the 1931 CCP constitution, which clearly stated that the Party "recognizes the right of self-determination of the national minorities in China, their right to complete separation from China, and to the formation of an independent state for each minority." This policy was supported right up to the establishment of the PRC. In 1948, Liu Shaoqi stated that the CCP "advocates the voluntary association and voluntary separation of all nations." Once the PRC was founded, however, all real possibilities of secession were revoked as no longer necessary.

Aside from the strategic enlistment of a "united ethnic front" in support of China's precarious new nation, there was another issue at stake in the formulation of the minority identification policy: the nature of the Chinese nation itself. Since early in the century, Chinese reformers, whether Kuomintang or Communist, were concerned that the Chinese people lacked a sense of nationhood, unlike the British, Germans, Japanese, and even the Tibetans and Manchu. In Dr. Sun Yat-sen's poignant words:

> The Chinese people have shown the greatest loyalty to family and clan with the result that in China there have been family-ism and clan-ism but no real national-ism. Foreign observers say that the Chinese are like a sheet of loose sand. . . . The unity of the Chinese people has stopped short at the clan and has not extended to the nation.

The identification of certain groups within China as "minorities" and the recognition of the Han as a unified "majority" played a fundamental role in foreign a unified Chinese nation. For the Kuomintang, this reformation of national identity as one people, with one history, helped to galvanize a sense of identity in relation not only to China's internal ethnic peoples, but also toward the foreign nations encroaching on China's soil.

This idea of Han unity became fundamentally useful to the Communists, who incorporated it into a Marxist ideology of progress, with the Han people in the forefront of development and civilization. In the Communists' portrayal, the Han were placed in the "vanguard" of the people's revolution. The minorities were induced to follow the Han example. The more backward, or primitive, the minorities were, the more advanced and civilized the so-called Han seemed and the greater the need for a unified national identity.

The Politics of Han Nationalism

Recently, there has been an outpouring of scholarly interest in Chinese nationalism and China's "quest" for a national identity. However, most studies have continued to conflate the issue of the creation of the Han majority with larger

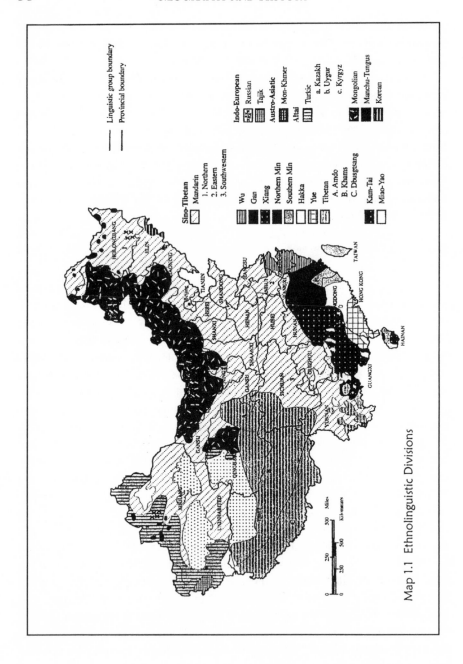

Map 1.1 Ethnolinguistic Divisions

questions of Chinese identity. Few have questioned how the Han became the 91 percent majority of China, merely accepting the Han as representative of the Chinese in general.

The notion of "*Han ren*" (Han person) has clearly existed for many centuries as those descendants of the Han dynasty (206 B.C.–220 A.D.) that had its beginnings in the Wei River valley. However, the nation of "*Han minzu*" (Han nationality) is as entirely modern phenomenon, which arose with the shift from Chinese empire to modern nation-state. While the concept of a Han person certainly existed, it probably referred to those subjects of the Han empire, just as "Roman" referred to those subjects of the Roman Empire (roughly concurrent with the Han). This tells us little about their "ethnicity," however, and we would be hard-pressed to determine who was Roman today. The Han are still thought to be around, however. The notion of a unified Han nationality, now said to occupy 91 percent of China's population, gained its greatest popularity under Sun Yat-sen. The leader of the republican movement that toppled the last empire of China in 1911, Sun was most certainly influenced by strong currents of Japanese nationalism during his long-term stay there. The Chinese term *minzu* is taken directly from the Japanese term *minzoku* and does not enter the Chinese language until the start of the twentieth century. Sun argued that the ruler-subject relation that had persisted throughout China's dynastic history would need to be fundamentally transformed if a true nationalist movement were to sweep China and engender support among all its peoples. More practically, Sun needed a way to mobilize all Chinese against the imperial rule of the Qing, a dynasty founded by a northeastern people who became known as the Manchu. By invoking the argument that a vast majority of the people in China were Han, Sun effectively found a symbolic national countermeasure against the Manchu and other foreigners to which the vast majority of the diverse peoples in China would surely rally.

Sun Yat-sen advocated the idea that there were "Five Peoples of China" (*wuzu gonghe*): the *Han, Man* (Manchu), *Meng* (Mongolian), *Zang* (Tibetan), and *Hui* (a term that included all Muslims in China, now divided into the Uygur, Kazakh, Hui, etc.). This recognition of the Five Peoples of China served as the main platform for his republican revolution that overthrew the Qing empire and established the first Republic. The notion of the peoples of China became key to the success of a people's revolution. The critical link between Sun's Five-Peoples policy and his desire to unify all of China is made clear from his discussion of nationalism, the first of his Three People's Principles (*Sanmin zhuyi*), which he argued was a prerequisite for Chinese modernization.

It is also not all surprising that Sun should turn to the use of the all-embracing idea of the Han as the national group, which included all the diverse peoples belonging to Sino-linguistic speech communities. Sun was Cantonese, raised as an overseas Chinese in Hawaii. As one who spoke heavily accented Mandarin, and with few connections in Northern China, he would have easily aroused traditional northern suspicions of southern radical movements extending back to the Song dynasty (960–1279 A.D.). The traditional antipathy between the Cantonese and northern peoples would have posed an enormous barrier to his promotion of a nationalist movement. Sun found a way to rise above deeply embedded north-south ethnocentrisms. The employment of the term *Han minzu* was a brilliant attempt to mobilize other non-Cantonese, especially northern Mandarin speakers and the powerful Zhejiang and Shanghainese merchants, into one overarching national group against the Manchu and other foreigners then threatening China. The Han were seem to stand in opposition to the "internal foreigners" within their borders—the Manchu, Tibetan, Mongol, and Hui—as the "external foreigners" on their frontiers, namely the Western imperialists. By identifying these "internal foreigners" in their midst, the Nationalists cultivated a new, broadly defined identity of the Han. In Benedict Anderson's terms, Sun was engaged in helping to construct a new "imagined community" of the Chinese nation, by "stretching the short tight skin of the nation over the gigantic body of the empire."

The Communists stretched this skin even further, following the Soviet model, by identifying not five, but fifty-six nationality groups, including the Han majority. Both for the Nationalists and the Communists it was not only the political necessity of enlisting the support of the ethnics on their borders that led them to recognize minority nationalities, but it was the desire to unify the nation against the outsiders, by de-emphasizing internal difference. Now that China no longer faces an external threat, internal differences must be considered if we are going to understand the full complexity of local politics and identity in contemporary China. . . .

3

CONFUCIUS

JOHN E. WILLS, JR.

Very few individuals in history have had as great or long-lasting an influence as Confucius (Kongzi) has had on China and East Asia. Several themes permeate his thought and his political programs. First was a strong ethical sense. Confucius believed that a moral order governed the cosmos and that human affairs could prosper only when they were in harmony with the moral nature of the universe. Second was an emphasis on social responsibility. The purpose of education was to prepare an individual for government service. Third was the rational approach to human problems. Confucius was concerned with the immediate problem of governing. Fourth, Confucius believed that societies as well as individuals were perfectible. John Will's essay uses the Analects, *dialogues between Confucius and his disciples, to illustrate the major tenets of Confucian thought.*

Confucius was a scholar who idealized the government and culture of an age five hundred years before his own, and who sought to convince the rulers of his time that all would be well in their states if they would concentrate on winning the trust of their people and setting a good example for them, would keep warfare and corporal punishment to a bare minimum, and would place scholars like him in charge of the governing of their states. In a time of rapid social, economic, and political change and of increasing warfare among the states of the Chinese world, it is not surprising that he failed. In his old age his only hope to influence the future lay in his scholarship, his students, and the presentation in his own life and in his teachings of an image of human goodness and steadfastness in adversity that can move even those who do not share his dreams. Out of his bitter failure he had made a moral triumph, and his life and his teachings are at the heart of Chinese optimism about what man can be and can accomplish in this world. In his recorded sayings we seem to get a picture of a real person, afraid, frustrated, moved by music, growing old, convinced that each of us can be truly humane at any moment if only we will really try. I think it is the oldest piece of literature in the world in which such a human portrait emerges. . . .

By Confucius's time, power in many of the states had shifted from the rulers' families to great ministerial families. The latter maintained themselves for several generations and frequently encroached on the prerogatives and powers of the ruling families, but themselves had no standing in the old Zhou feudal order. In some cases it is clear that these families rose to power in the state-building process and maintained themselves through control of new state organs, especially military commands. The dominance of people who rose as ministers and remained ministers in form . . . is an important source of the idealization of the ministerial role that emerged in these centuries and was associated with the memory of the duke of Zhou. In some states several families struggled for dominance while neighboring states sought to fish in the troubled waters. Diplomacy was intricate and formal, with much attention to the formalities of meetings and oaths and to the persuasive use of classical texts, but also cynical and brutal. Some *shi*, men of aristocratic but modest background, were beginning to make names for themselves as administrators, diplomats, military adventures. The rise of the *shi* is one of the most important trends of Confucius's times and the two centuries after.

This, then, was the world into which Confucius was born in 551 B.C.E., a world that he deplored and sought to reform but that gave him and his disciples opportunities they would not have had in the early Zhou order they idealized. Confucius was a native of the state of Lu, which was by no means powerless but was somewhat in the shadow of Qi to the north, Chu to the southwest, and Jin to the northwest. Lu had a strong sense of special connection to the early Zhou order; its ruling family were descendants of the duke of Zhou. "Confucius" is a latinization of "Kong Fuzi," "Master Kong," which has been used by Western students of China since the seventeenth century Jesuit missionaries. His personal name was Kong Qiu; "Kong Zi," a shorter form of "Master Kong," is the form of reference most readily recognized by Chinese today.

No coherent biography of Confucius has survived from his own times, and those written in later centuries obviously incorporate many legendary elements. His collected sayings, the famous *Lun yu* (*Analects*), are by far the best source of knowledge of him, but they are fragments of his teachings and his conversations with his disciples, sometimes loosely organized around a theme, sometimes completely random in sequence, never dated or in chronological order. A few important passages can be found in the *Zuo zhuan* and in the book of the philosopher Mencius. Thus a modern reader can get a convincing sense of some Confucius's deepest convictions and emotions, but can know only fragments of a chronology of his movements and political involvements.

In one of his most famous passage of self-revelation, Confucius said: "At fifteen I set my heart on learning; at thirty I had a place to stand; at forty I came to be free from doubts; at fifty I understood the decree of Heaven; at sixty I could hear [that decree] and submit; at seventy I followed my heart's desire without overstepping the bounds" (II, 4)*. . . .

In the passage of the *Analects* in which they are developed, explicit references to the great men and institutions of earlier ages are not common, but none of his teachings is fully comprehensible apart from Confucius's fascination with antiquity. Confucius once insisted that he was "a transmitter but not a creator" (VII, I); I would prefer to take seriously his vocation as a transmitter of an ancient culture but also to insist that he was a highly creative transmitter. He created the role of the scholar-minister, studying and passing on an ancient heritage and holding it up as a mirror to his ruler's conduct. He changed, universalized, moralized the meanings of some words found in the early Zhou texts. Above all, he created a world view of profound optimism about the goodness of human nature and the possibility of benign government, which he and later Confucians could not have sustained if they had not been so thoroughly convinced that human moral and political perfection actually had existed in the early Zhou and in the days of Yao, Shun, and Yu.

Confucius's search for a ruler who would listen to him and employ him was very near to the core of his values. He would have been shocked by present-day dismissals of "just politics" and "just like a politician." For him there was no higher calling than government, and the man who was not involved in government was radically incomplete. In the words of Zi Lu, "Not to enter public life is to ignore one's duty. Even the proper regulation of old and young cannot be put aside. How, then, can the duty between ruler and subject be set aside? This is to cause confusion in the most important of human relationships simply because one desires to keep one's unsullied character. The gentleman takes office in order to do his duty" (XVIII, 7). The Confucian aspired to be recognized by a ruler and chosen as minister. The ruler should "Set an example for your officials to follow; show leniency to minor offenders; and promote men of talent" (XIII, 2). The common people, as we have seen, had to be looked after and allowed to prosper, but they played a fundamentally passive role, grass before the wind of the teaching of their superiors. The basic grammar of politics here defined was generally accepted from Confucius's time down to our own

---

* All quotations from the *Analects* are followed by a reference to chapter and section, following the numbering and in general following the interpretation in D. C. Lau's translation.

century: a common people politically passive except in times of gravest crisis, officials watching over them who were morally independent but politically completely dependent on appointment by a ruler. It also was generally accepted that government produced nothing, that its revenues represented a dead loss to the people, and thus that taxes should be kept as light as possible. This, the selection of good officials, and the setting of good moral examples should suffice to keep order. "The Master said, 'Guide them by edicts, keep them in line with punishments, and the common people will stay out of trouble but will have no sense of shame. Guide them by virtue, keep them in line with ceremonies, and they will, besides having a sense of shame, reform themselves'" (II, 3).

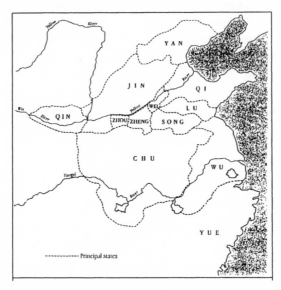

Map 1.2. China in Confucius's time

The disciple Zi Gong asked about government. Confucius said, "Give them enough food, give them enough arms, and the common people will have trust in you." Zi Gong then asked, "If one had to give up one of these three, which should one give up first?" "Give up arms." Which next? "Give up food. Death has always been with us since the beginning of time, but when there is no trust, the common people will have nothing to stand on" (XII, 7).

Rulers listening to such advice may have recognized that it embodied basic wisdom from which they could learn much, but at the same time they knew that it was no substitute for advice on what to *do right* now about bandits descending on peasant villages or the army of a neighboring state poised to invade. A bias toward fundamental analysis of problems and the proposal of long-run solutions was characteristic of many Confucian statesmen down to our time. It could be a source of great strength of systematic administration in times of flux and crisis. We might agree that good men, rulers and ministers, were the most basic and long-term solution to political problems and still sympathize with the ruler who needed advice of more immediate applicability.

If I am right that Confucius became disillusioned about the possibility of a quick return to the early Zhou system, the long-run solution he came to focus on had at its center the idea that every ruler, every minister or would be minister, should aspire to be gentleman, a *junzi*. There are many sayings about the gentleman in the *Analects*. Quite a few of them are brief and contrast the attitudes and behavior of the gentleman with those of the "small man." Some if this is apt guidance for anyone's moral striving:

The gentleman is troubled by his own lack of ability, not by the failure of others to appreciate him. (XV, 21)

What the gentleman seeks, he seeks within himself; what the small seeks, he seeks in others. (XV, 21)

The gentleman is easy of mind, while the small man is always full of anxiety. (VII, 37)

Others are more specific to the situation of the minister or would be minister, and these help to fill out an understanding of ministerial ethics. The minister should not associate with others to amass power or limit the ruler's freedom of decision: "The gentleman enters into associations but not cliques; the small enters into cliques bit not associations" (II, 14). "The gentleman is not a vessel" (II, 11). In the latter passage, of just four characters, "vessel" (*qi*) means especially a sacrificial vessel, something with a specialized and ornamental use. The gentleman is not a specialist but a moral generalist, and he must be given real responsibility, not just made an ornament of a court. *Qi* also means "tool" or "instrument," and the gentleman must be treated as morally autonomous individual, not just a tool of the ruler who employs him.

. . . The expression *junzi* itself packs a complex history and set of associations. The characters literally mean "son of the prince," and that and the frequent contrast with the "little man" make it clear that this term has a background of class feeling, of contrast between the values and actions appropriate to rulers and those for the ruled, much like the history of "gentleman" in English and many other important moral terms. In early Zhou texts *junzi* usually simply means "the ruler." It was Confucius's great achievement to insist that not only those who had a hereditary right to office could aspire to be gentlemen, but anyone who sought education, moral growth, and involvement in governing; his gentleman is a highly appropriate ideal for the rising class of the *shi*, the lowest aristocracy with no hereditary right to office. Certainly there was a great deal of class feeling left in the term, and he probably intended it to apply more to impoverished *shi* like himself than to farmers and artisans, but it was basically an ideal of moral striving open to anyone.

Men from modest backgrounds could aspire to the life of the gentleman only if they could obtain the necessary education. One of Confucius's greatest achievements was his emphasis on education. The *Analects* paints a picture of a teacher who would accept any student, no matter how meager the gift or payment that student was able to make (VII, 7). This teacher was thoroughly aware of the varying abilities and temperaments of his disciples and of the different ways in which they needed to be taught: some needed to be held back, others to be urged on (XI, 22). The future of his great cause depended entirely on its transmission to the next generation; this made him reverent, loving, demanding:

> I never enlighten anyone who has not been driven to distraction by trying to understand a difficulty or who has not got into a frenzy trying to put his ideas into words. When I have pointed out one corner of a square to anyone and he does not come back with other three. I will not point it out to him a second time. (VII, 8)
>
> It is fitting that we should hold the young in awe. How do we know that the generations to come will not be the equal of the present? Only when a man reaches the age of forty or fifty without distinguishing himself in any way can one say, I suppose, that he does not deserve to be held in awe. (IX, 23)

Another famous passage literally says "In teaching no classifications" (XV, 39); traditionally it has been taken to mean that in education there should be no class distinctions, but it also has been read as making the very different but important point that in teaching there should be no separation into hard and fast categories or specializations.

In China Confucius has always been known as the First Teacher. His example is at the root of the extraordinary respect for education and teachers still to be found in all Chinese communities today. The First Teacher set an example for his students by being himself constantly engaged in learning, in the study of ancient texts and the application in his own life of the moral lessons to be found in them, and in learning through discussion. The human mind might have the roots of goodness in it, but they were better developed by these forms of learning than by absorption in the solitary mind. The process was demanding, but it also brought the joys of growing understanding and of encounters with the great men and great writings of the past.

> I once spent all day thinking without taking food and all night thinking without going to bed, but I found that I gained nothing from it. It would have been better to spend the time in learning. (XV, 31)

> Is it not a pleasure, having learned something, to try it out at due intervals? Is it not a joy to have friends come from afar? Is it not the way of a gentleman not to take offence when others fail to appreciate your abilities? (I, 1)

> Even when walking in the company of two other men, I am bound to be able to learn from them. The good points of the one I copy; the bad points of the other I correct in myself. (VII, 22)

The term that best sums up the focus of Confucius and his disciples is "the Way" (*dao*). "The Master said, 'He has not lived in vain who dies the day he is told about the Way'" (IV, 8). For Confucius and his followers this meant, among other things, the Way of the Former Kings, the institutions and moral examples inherited from Yao, Shun, Yu, and the Zhou founders. But, as seen in the stories about the sage kings, this Way was neither an accidental human invention nor an arbitrary command of god or gods, but the result of the discovery by the sages of the basic patterns of nature and human nature and the elaboration of a way of life based on them that made it possible for people to be fully human, to live in harmony with nature and their fellow human beings. Chinese thinkers also came to call these basic patterns the Way—the way of nature, the way the world works. There was no radical distinction between the two; the Way of the Former Kings was firmly rooted in the Way of Nature.

This is especially clear in Confucius's treatment of the very important complex of values and customs referred to by the awkward phrase "filial piety," which involved the obedience of young people to their parents, kind and generous care of aged parents, prolonged and heartfelt mourning after their deaths, and reverence for earlier ancestors in the male line. Filial piety sometimes is thought of as a repressive and unnatural system, and it certainly produced come bizarre phenomena in later centuries, but in the view of it that Confucius helped to shape, it was a life-enhancing expression of natural emotions. When one of Confucius's disciples suggested that the traditional three years of mourning for a parent (actually twenty-seven months) was too long, Confucius said that if he really would feel at ease going back to ordinary life after just one year he should do so. But after the disciple left Confucius said, "How unfeeling Yu is!" A child ceases to be nursed by his parents only when he is three years old. Three years' mourning is observed throughout the Empire. Was Yu not given three years' love by his parents?" (XVII, 21). In several other passages he emphasized that it was the genuineness of reverence for aged parents and of grief over their deaths that counted most, not the food given them while they lived or the details of the funeral ceremonies (II, 7; II, 8; II, 4).

This attitude toward funeral ceremonies is an excellent example of Confucius's attitude toward ceremony in general. He may have lost his early faith in the political changes that could be brought about by restoring the early Zhou ceremonial order, but he always took seriously the usefulness of traditional ceremonial patterns for regulating relations among members of the ruling class and diplomacy among states. Expertise in these matters was the most important asset that made Confucius and his disciples employable. "If it is really possible to govern countries by ceremony and yielding, there is no more to be said. But if it is not really possible, of what is ceremony?" (IV, 13).

Confucius contributed to the emergence in his time of a unified under-standing of ceremony (*li*) that has been accepted by most Chinese down to our own time. It included two friends bowing and exchanging courtesies when they met; a son making sure his father's coffin was appropriate to his rank and them mourning for him for twenty-seven months; two rulers and their ministers subtly adjusting indications of relative status before a diplomatic encounter; ministers taking their places before their ruler according to their ranks; rulers performing sacrifices to Heaven, Earth, spirits if local places and natural forces, and their own royal ancestors. In this unified understanding, all these forms of ceremony were manifestations of the interactions of the Way of Nature and the Way of the Former Kings, and kept them meshed in one patterned harmony of feelings, acts, and the natural cycles of the seasons and the transitions of human life and death. Confucius advanced this unified view by taking family ceremonies and proprie-ties and ceremonies of political hierarchy very seriously as foundations of political order, and by turning resolutely away from the preoccupation of many of his contemporaries with the use of ceremonies to manipulate the forces of the spirit world and ward off supernatural disasters. Moreover, ceremony played a large part in the development of the human capacities of the gentleman; their orderly beauty gave him great joy, and at the same time the necessity of per-forming ceremonies correctly was a form of conquest of oneself (XII, 1). The same combination of form, discipline, and emotion is to be found in music, which Confucius also loved. . . .

The view of Confucius developed above relies almost entirely on the *Analects*. Followers of Confucius's teachings in later centuries also drew on many other sources. In some biographies he was represented as a child prodigy, a man of great height and strange appearance, an expert on all kinds of abstruse ancient lore, a semidivine figure of great historical destiny, a high official in Lu who brought good order to that state in a very short time; all quite a distance from the magnificent portrait of moral fervor and human frustration in the *Analects*.

Less at variance with the attitudes found in the *Analects* were the teachings ascribed to him and his favorite disciples in a number of short texts that were more connected in exposition and more abstractly philosophical than the *Analects*; traditional Chinese scholars accepted these texts as records of Confucius, but modern researchers believe them to be of later date and not reliable records of the Master's words. In the *Xiao jing* (Classic of Filial Piety), Confucius is shown explaining this key virtue: "To establish yourself and follow the Way, exalting your name to latter generations, and thus casting glory upon your father and mother, is the beginning of filial piety." The *Da xue* (Great Learning) made dogmatically clear the Confucian emphasis on the priority of study and moral effort:

> Only when affairs are investigated is knowledge extended; only when knowledge is extended are thoughts sincere; only when thoughts are sincere are minds rectified; only when minds are rectified are our persons cultivated; only when our persons are cultivated are our families regulated; only when families are regulated are states well governed; and only when states are well governed is there peace in the world.

The *Zhong yong* (Doctrine of the Mean) showed benevolence as the sum of all the virtues, the fullest realization of what it is to be a human being, but also went beyond this to an ideal of sincerity (*cheng*), or perfect harmony of word and actuality, in which this moral sincerity opened the way to a harmony with the cosmos:

> Only those who are absolutely sincere can fully develop their nature. If they can fully develop their nature they can fully develop the nature of others. If they can fully develop the nature of others, then they can fully develop the nature of things. If they can fully develop the nature of things, they can assist in the transforming and nourishing process of Heaven and Earth. If they can assist in the transforming and nourishing process of Heaven and Earth, they can thus form a trinity with Heaven and Earth.

Despite the great power and beauty of these texts and their teachings, nothing in them quite matches the depth of insight into the human condition that comes from reading and rereading the *Analects* in all their disorder and diversity. In the *Analects*, even an exploration of the most abstract and mysterious of Confucius's teachings, that on benevolence, leads right back to the beloved disciple Yan Hui whose early death he mourned so bitterly. Confucius seems to have found it altogether appropriate that his disciples should know of his joys and sorrows, his angers at abuses of power and his own terrible frustration about his failure to obtain office. He let his disciples see him as a man, not as some kind of near-divine being standing above human desires and frustrations. And the disciples who put together the *Analects* thought it fitting that should preserve these very human expressions of emotion by their Master.

If Confucius had succeeded in his search for political office he might be remembered as one of a number of wise statesmen of the Chunqiu periods, or as the author of an interesting experiment in restoring the early Zhou order in Lu. It was because of his failures and frustrations that he concentrated more on teaching and scholarship, developed the ideals of the gentleman and benevolence. He valued worldly success, but also knew how to make something even greater than success out of frustration and grief, and he gave us a teaching and a human example that can sustain us in success and in failure. In the words of the great disciple Zeng Zi, "A gentleman must be strong and resolute, for his burden is heavy and the road is long. He takes benevolence as his burden. Is that not heavy? Only with death does the road come to an end. Is that not long?" (VIII, 7)

For Confucius time flowed ceaselessly, like a river: "While standing by a river, the Master said, 'What passes away is, perhaps, like this. Day and night it never lets up'" (IX, 17). People missed chances, mourned, died. But that made the joys of being human nobler, keener. At a particularly bitter and discouraging moment in his travels, the governor of She asked the disciple Zi Lu about Confucius, and Zi Lu told his master he had not known how to answer. The Master said, "Why didn't you simply say something like this: He is the sort of man who forgets to eat when he tries to solve a problem that has been driving him to distraction, who is so full of joy that he forgets his worries and who does not notice that old age is coming on?" (VII, 19). As we read him and come to our own understanding of his teaching—and we must, for no summary does it justice, and it is above all the sense of a man we must confront—we may come to feel about his Way as did the gifted Yan Hui, whose early death almost broke Confucius's heart: "The more I look up at it the higher it appears. The more I bore into it the harder it becomes. I see it before me. Suddenly it is behind me.

The Master is good at leading one on step by step. He broadens us with culture and brings us back to essentials by means of the ceremonies. I cannot give up even if I wanted to, but, having done all I can, it [his Way] seems to rise sheer above me and I have no way of going after it, however, much I may want to" (IX, II).

4

History and China's Revolution

JOHN KING FAIRBANK

From his position at Harvard University, the historian John King Fairbank (1907–1991) was a founding father of the field of Chinese studies in America. His scholarly writings were voluminous, and he trained a generation of American China scholars. In the following selection Fairbank discusses the "broad cultural gaps" that divided the major protagonists of modern Chinese history. These gaps included intercultural ones between the expansionist Western powers and China, but also internal ones between the conservative Chinese ruling class and burgeoning revolutionary movements. The dean of American historians of China, Fairbank furnishes a broad overview of the historical forces at work during the twilight of late imperial China and provides a balanced explanation of the controversies surrounding interpretations of modern Chinese history.

The history of modern China—what is now thought to have happened there—is full of controversy. Major events are known but their significance is disputed. Meanwhile many minor events remain unknown or disregarded.

The first cause of controversy is widespread historical ignorance due to the lack of a generally accepted body of research and writing in this under-developed field. I say 'historical ignorance' because the task of history is to understand the circumstances, motives, and actions of *all* parties concerned, and an unbalanced knowledge, of one side only, may leave us still quite ignorant of the other side in a conflict, and therefore less able to comprehend it. . . .

A second cause of controversy is the broad cultural gap that separated the major historical protagonists—not only the cultural differences in language, thought, and values between the foreign invaders of China and the resistant Chinese ruling class in the nineteenth century, but also the similar differences between that ruling class and the great mass of the Chinese people, once they became revolutionary in the twentieth century. In short, China's modern history records two great dramas—first, the cultural confrontation between the expanding

Western civilization of international trade and warfare, and the persistent Chinese civilization of agriculture and bureaucracy; and second, arising out of the first, the fundamental transformation of China in the greatest of all revolutions.

These vast movements of conflict and change—between China and the outside world, between China old and new—have produced distinct points of view in the historical record and among historians. Most obvious to Western historians is the Victorian view of the world with which the British, French, and American expansionists set up the unequal treaty system in the mid-nineteenth century. They believed in the nation state, the rule of law, the benefits of individual rights, Christianity, and scientific technology, and the use of warfare in the service of progress.

Similar identifiable is the old Chinese ruling-class view of the world which believed in the classical Confucian teachings and the universal supremacy of the Son of Heaven, who maintained his rule by the edifying example of his virtuous conduct at the top of a harmonious social order of hierarchy and status. In this *ancien régime* the classical learning tolerated only changed-within-tradition, the extended family system dominated the individual, a doctrine of duty eclipsed any doctrine of rights, civil administrators controlled the military and used the merchants, and the principles of moral conduct took precedence over human passions, material profit, and the letter of the law. Truly, two civilizations stood embattled.

As the more ancient and less rapidly changing civilization gradually gave way before the more modern and dynamic, a pioneer generation of Chinese scholars and administrators pursued goals of reform, gradually working out a new view of the world and of China's place in it. This new view, in an era of collapse, inevitably lacked the unity of its predecessor. Confusion of ideas grew as central authority declined, and only in the mid-twentieth century could a new historical orthodoxy become established through the application of Marxism-Leninism to China in the thought of Mao Tse-tung (Mao Zedong). . . .

Although the foci of historical concern shift about from generation to generation, in the case of modern China certain unresolved problems of interpretation seem likely to pre-empt attention for some time to come. One major problem of interpretation is the degree and nature of foreign influence. Foreign activity in China increased markedly during the nineteenth century, becoming steadily more influential and pervasive and eventually contributing to a metamorphosis of Chinese life from top to bottom. Yet the process of foreign impact and Chinese response began gradually, almost imperceptibly. The perception of this process has developed through a succession of phases with increasing intensity and sophistication.

In the first phase it was recognized by observers both foreign and Chinese that the old agrarian-bureaucratic empire of China was no match for the expanding British and other empires of international trade and gunboats. The tempo of foreign aggression on China steadily accelerated. The Opium War of 1840–1842 was followed within fifteen years by the Anglo-French invasion of 1857–1860, within another decade or so by Russia's occupation of Ili in 1871 and Japan's take-over of Liu-ch'iu in 1874, and within still another decade by the Sino-French war of 1883–1885. Nine years later came the smashing Japanese victory over China in 1894–1895, followed by the Scramble for Concessions of 1898 and the Boxer War of 1900. These dramatic disasters were accompanied by a less tangible but more far-reaching collapse of China's traditional self-image, her Sino-centric view of the world.

In retrospect, China's nineteenth-century experience therefore became a stark tragedy, an unforeseen and certainly enormous decline and fall almost without equal in history. This tragedy was the more bitter because it was so gradual, inexorable, and complete. The old order fought a rearguard action, giving ground slowly but always against greater odds, each disaster followed by a greater, until one by one China's asserted superiority over foreigners, the central power of the emperor at Peking (Beijing), the reigning Confucian orthodoxy, and the ruling elite of scholar-officials were each in turn undermined and destroyed.

A second perception gained ground among Chinese revolutionaries of the early twentieth century, who found themselves in a different world, as nation-alists in an expanded international world of nationalisms. Under imperialist pressure the *ancien régime* of the Ch'ing (Qing) dynasty in China had taken on during the late nineteenth century an increasing burden of foreign special privilege. This had been indexed in the steady expansion of the unequal treaty system: the increase in the number of treaty ports from five in 1842 to about fifty in 1911; the extension of extraterritorial consular jurisdiction over treaty-power nations, their property, trade, and industry; the expansion of foreign shipping in Chinese waters from gunboats on the coast to steamship lines on main rivers; the employment of foreign administrators not only in the maritime customs but also in some native customs, post office, and salt revenue administrations; the spread of missionary work into every province and into the fields of education and medicine; an a multitude of other features like foreign garrisons in Peking after 1900 and pre-emption of customs revenues after 1911 to pay off foreign loans and indemnities. All this represented the special influence in Chinese life of people from outside the country. For modern nationalists, what could be more provocative of patriot indignation? More and more, from the period of World War I, this foreign invasion was called 'imperialism', and imperialism was seen as a humiliation that must be wiped out.

Another perception accompanied this view: that imperialism in China had been facilitated by Chinese weakness, not merely in military terms but in moral terms—in a lack of patriotic devotion, manifested in working for foreigners and profiting with them from the vicious traffic in opium or in coolies as well as from the evils of industrial exploitation of labor in port cities. Moral degeneracy was equally evident in warlord particularism, landlord selfishness, family-first nepotism. Most of all China's weakness had inhered in the old ruling-class strata—the alien Manchu court, the out-of-date officials trained in ancient classics, the literati whose prerogatives let them monopolize higher learning and culture, the landlords who exploited impoverished tenants. All this complex of institutions and practices could be summed up under 'feudalism'.

In this way China's nineteenth-century disaster was perceived in the twentieth century under twin headings of feudalism and imperialism. These terms and the explication of them by Marx, Engels, Lenin, Stalin, and Mao have been used in the People's Republic to describe China's modern history. In a vast land still overwhelmingly agrarian, still mindful of the Japanese aggression of the 1930s and 1940s, the native ruling class and foreign invasion stand out as the two major evils inherited from the past and still to be combated today.

The concept of imperialism has been expanded during its use in China. The role of imperialism as seen in retrospect has grown steadily since the 1920s in the thinking of both the Kuomintang and the Chinese Communist Party. It is built into the thought of Mao Tse-tung. Imperialism was at work from the Opium War onward, long before the rise of the Leninist type of finance-capitalist imperialism in the 1890s. Maoist imperialism not only goes further back in time to include the wars and gunboat diplomacy of the era of commercial expansion in the early Victorian age; it also expands the scope of imperialism to include nearly all forms of foreign contact in the nineteenth century, including Christian missions as cultural imperialism. Since the often-aggressive expansion of Western activities is plain in the record, historians generally feel justified in the broad conclusion that the Chinese people were invaded, exploited. and victimized by imperialism. This can hardly be disputed as a generalization. The aggressive expansion of Europe and its latter-day offshoots is a major fact of modern world history. . . .

Since China's historical consciousness has changed in the process of revolution, it is imperative to understand the Chinese self-image under the old order as well as the conditions of life then. Such an investigation, once undertaken, begins to fill out the picture of imperialism. From a unilateral force which overwhelms China from the outside, it becomes a result of interaction, and as this interaction between China and the outside world is studied further, imperialism as a generality breaks down into a variety of factors and circumstances.

It appears first that Chinese society was enormous in mass and extremely various in its local conditions. Because of its size, it was less easily influenced from abroad, and the reactions to foreign contact were diverse and separated rather than uniform and concentrated. In general, China was remarkably self-sufficient: first of all in foreign trade, which remained a comparatively unimportant part of the economy. In the second place, the Ch'ing empire, by its conquest of Ili in the 1750s and its successful dealings with the Russians at Kiakhta and the British at Canton, had established a seemingly strong defensive position militarily. Finally, the ideology of imperial Confucianism under the Ch'ing was almost impervious to the acceptance of foreign political concepts. All these factors made for a remarkable self-sufficiency. But still another historical tradition also made China unresponsive to foreign aggression—this was the tradition of barbarian invasion and the absorption or neutralization of the barbarians in the vastness of China's society and culture. For this reason, imperial Confucianism had become a supranationalistic system which could not easily appreciate the sentiments of nationalists from outside countries.

In this way the picture emerges of a Chinese state and society which, in the early 1800s, was self-sufficiently absorbed in its own domestic life and not capable of quick reaction to a Western invasion. The subsequent Chinese interaction with the invaders did not meet the foreign system on its own terms. The Ch'ing dynasty, for example, was not primarily concerned with foreign trade and investment as functions important to the state. The Ch'ing regime was mainly concerned with preserving the agrarian social order over which it presided, and from which it derived its main sustenance. Foreign relations were a marginal concern. It was at first assumed that Westerners could, in fact, be taken marginally into the Chinese polity and social order and be permitted to function on its periphery, as other foreigners had done in the past.

As a result of these conditions of size, self-sufficiency, unresponsiveness, and lack of concern among the ruling class, the Ch'ing empire was ill-prepared for Western contact. Put in more positive terms, when this contact materialized in modern times, one clue to China's collapse lay in the very success which

China's civilization had achieved in pre-modern times. To understand the collapse one must appreciate the earlier success, for it had been so great that China's leaders were unprepared for disaster. As the reformer Liang Ch'i-ch'ao put it as late as 1896, 'Here is a big mansion which has lasted a thousand years. . . . It is still a magnificently big thing, but when wind and rain suddenly come up, its fall is foredoomed. Yet the people in the house are still happily playing or soundly sleeping . . . quite indifferent.'

5

A Proclamation Against the Bandits of Guangdong and Guangxi, 1854

Historians estimate that over 20 million people died in the Taiping Rebellion (1851–1864), making it the bloodiest rebellion in world history. Taiping ideology combined utopian ideals from native religions and Buddhism with Christian beliefs derived from a partial translation of the Bible. Virulently anti-Manchu, the Taipings employed racist and nationalistic rhetoric to win popular support. Zeng Guofan (1811–1872), a distinguished government official, led the suppression of the Taipings. As the following selection illustrates, Zeng appealed to pride in Chinese culture and Confucian principles to win support of the educated elite. According to Zeng, the Taiping threat was not just a matter of the survival of one dynasty but "the most extraordinary crisis of all time for the Confucian teachings." He also highlighted the devastation the revolt was causing and appealed to elite self-interest. Although ultimately crushed, the Taiping challenge to traditional authority and their primitive communist ideals were sources of inspiration for later revolutionary leaders.

Zeng Guofan (1811–1872) was from a middle-peasant landowning family in Xiangxiang, Hunan. In 1838 he obtained his *jinshi* degree and was appointed a Hanlin Academy scholar. He was noted for his clear and practical suggestions for addressing affairs of state. In 1852 when his mother died, in accord with the traditional mourning practice, he resigned his post as the vice minister of the Board of Rites and went back to Hunan where he received the imperial order to form militia units to fight the Taiping.

The Qing efforts to repulse the Taiping were uphill struggles in the early years and Zeng's efficiency as the commander was hampered by the chronic lack of funds. His situation improved, however, when he was given official sanction to take control of the tax revenues in the provinces where his armies were operating.

Zeng Guofan's proclamation of 1854 was a powerful evocation of the scholar-literati's view of the rebels. . . . The document was notably anti-Christian and its references to the "kingly way" and the ethos of the Confucian *junzi* draw a clear line between the forces of orthodox "light" and heterodox "darkness."

It has been five years since the rebels Hung Hsiu-chüan [Hong Xiuquan] and Yang Hsiu-ch'ing [Yang Xiuqing] started their rebellion. They have inflicted bitter sorrow upon millions of people and devastated more than 5,000 *li* of *chou* [regions] and *hsien* [counties]. Wherever they pass, boats of all sizes, and people rich and poor alike, have all been plundered and stripped bare; not one inch of grass has been left standing. The clothing has been stripped from the bodies of those captured by these bandits, and their money has been seized. Anyone with five taels or more of silver who does not contribute it to the bandits is forthwith decapitated. Men are given one *ho* [1/10 pint] of rice per day, and forced to march in the forefront in battle, to construct city walls, and dredge moats. Women are also given one *ho* of rice per day, and forced to stand guard on the parapets at night, and to haul rice and carry coal. The feet of women who refuse to unbind them are cut off and shown to other women as a warning. The corpses of boatmen who secretly conspired to fell [*sic?*] were hung upside down to show other boatmen as a warning. The Yüeh [Guangdong and Guangxi] bandits indulge themselves in luxury and high position, while the people in our own Yangtze provinces living under their coercion are treated worse than animals. This cruelty and brutality appalls anyone with blood in his veins.

Every since the times of Yao, Shun, and the Three Dynasties, sages, generation after generation, have upheld the Confucian teachings, stressing proper human relationships, between ruler and minister, father and son, superiors and subordinates, the high and the low, all in their proper place, just as hats and shoes are not interchangeable. The Yüeh bandits have stolen a few scraps from the foreign barbarians and worship the Christian religion. From their bogus ruler and bogus chief ministers down to their soldiers and menial underlings, all are called brothers. They say that only heaven can be called father; aside from him, all fathers among the people are called brothers, and all mothers are called sisters. Peasants are not allowed to till the land for themselves and pay taxes, for they say that the fields all belong to the T'ien Wang [Heavenly King]. Merchants are not allowed to trade for profit, for they say that all goods belong to the T'ien Wang. Scholars may not read the Confucian classics, for they have their so-called teachings of Jesus and the New Testament. In a single day several thousand years of Chinese ethical principles and proper human relationships, classical books, social institutions and statutes have all been completely swept away. This is not just a crisis for our Ch'ing (Qing) dynasty, but the most extraordinary crisis of all time for the Confucian teachings, which is why our Confucius and Mencius are weeping bitterly in the nether world. How can any educated person sit idly by without thinking of doing something?

Since ancient times, those with meritorious accomplishments during their lifetimes have become spirits after death; the Kingly Way governs the living and the Way of the Spirits governs among the dead. Even rebellious ministers and wicked sons of the most vicious and vile sort show respect and awe toward the spirits. When Li Tzu-ch'eng reached Ch'ü-fu [Confucius' birthplace in Shandong province], he did not molest the Temple of the Sage. When Chang Hsien-chung reached Tzu-t'ung, he sacrificed to Wen Ch'ang [the patron spirit of literature]. But the Yüeh bandits burned the school at Shen-chou, destroyed the wooden tablet of Confucius, and wildly scattered the tablets of the Ten Paragons in the two corridors all over the ground. Afterwards, wherever they have passed, in every district, the first thing they have done is to burn down the temples, defiling the shrines and maiming the statues even of loyal ministers and righteous heroes such as the awesome Kuan Yü and Yüeh Fei. Even Buddhist and Taoist temples, shrines of guardian deities and altars to local gods have all been burned, and every statue destroyed. The ghosts and spirits in the world of darkness are enraged at this, and want to avenge their resentment.

I, the Governor-General, having received His Imperial Majesty's command leading 20,000 men advancing together on land and water, vow that I shall sleep on nettles and ship gall [to strengthen my determination] to exterminate these vicious traitors, to rescue our captured boats, and to deliver the persecuted people, not only in order to relieve the Emperor of his strenuous and conscientious labors from dawn to dusk, but also to comfort Confucius and Mencius for their silent sufferings over the proper human relationships; [not] only to avenge the millions who have died unjust deaths, but also to avenge the insults to all the spirits.

Therefore, let this proclamation be disseminated far and near so that all may know the following: Any red-blooded hero who assembles a company of righteous troops to assist in our extermination campaign will be taken in as my personal friends, and the troops given rations. Any Confucian gentleman who cherishes the Way, is pained at Christianity running rampant over the land, and who, in a towering rages, wants to defend our Way, will be made a member of the Governor-General's personal staff and treated as a guest teacher. Any benevolent person, stirred by moral indignation, who contributes silver or assists with provisions, will be given a treasury receipt and a commission from the board of Civil Appointments for a donation of 1,000 chin (jin) [1 chin = $1^1/_3$ lb.] or less, and a special memorial will be composed requesting a liberal reward for a donation of over 1000 chin. If anyone voluntarily returns after a long stay among the bandits, and kills one of their leaders or leads a city to surrender, he will be taken into the army of the Governor-General to the Emperor, [and] will be given an official title. Anyone who has lived under the bandits' coercion for some years, whose hair has grown several inches long, but who discards his weapon when the fighting is about to commence and returns to the fold barehanded, will receive an amnesty from the death sentence, and will be given travel expenses to return home.

In the past, at the end of the Han, T'ang (Tang), Yuan, and Ming, bands of rebels were innumerable, all because of foolish rulers and misgovernment, so that none of these rebellions could be stamped out. But today the Son of Heaven is deeply concerned and examines his character in order to reform himself, worships Heaven, and is sympathetic to the people. He has not increased the land tax, nor has he conscripted soldiers from households. With the profound benevolence of the sages, he is suppressing the cruel and worthless bandits. It does not require any great wisdom to see that sooner or later they will all be destroyed.

Those of you who have been coerced into joining the rebels, or who willingly follow the traitors, and oppose the Imperial Crusade [are warned that] when the

Imperial forces sweep down it will no longer be possible to discriminate between the good and evil—every person will be crushed.

I, the Governor-General, am scant in virtue and of meager ability. I rely solely on two words, trust and loyalty, as the foundation for running the army. Above are the sun and the moon, below the ghosts and spirits; in this world, the vast waters of the Yangtze [Yangzi], and in the other world, the souls of loyal ministers and stalwart heroes who gave their lives in battle against previous rebellions. Let all peer into my heart and listen to my words.

Upon arrival, this proclamation immediately has the force of law. Do not disregard it!

6

The Boxer Uprising

PAUL A. COHEN

The Boxer Uprising, like no other single event, encapsulated all the social and political dilemmas of the Qing dynasty at the close of the nineteenth century. Foreign economic encroachment, disruption of local society by Christian missionaries, weak leadership in the Qing court, popular resentment of the foreign imperialism, and the military dominance of the foreign powers, all played a role in the catastrophe that was the Boxer Uprising. Severe drought in Shandong Province created an atmosphere of crisis and social unrest at the close of the nineteenth century which was further fueled by increasing foreign penetration, particularly German investments in railroads and mining, and the proliferation of foreign missionaries. Because it was not uncommon for missionaries, who had the military might of their home governments behind them, to shield Chinese converts from criminal prosecution or law suits, many Chinese resented their presence and that of their Chinese converts. In 1900 the Boxers, practitioners of Chinese martial arts and invulnerability rituals, marched on Beijing. They laid siege to the foreign legations and precipitated a disastrous confrontation between the Qing court and an eight-nation foreign army sent to relieve the foreigners.

Internationalization of the Boxer Experience: The Outbreak of War

As long as the Boxers confined their activities to northwestern Shandong, they had remained an essentially local phenomenon. The dramatic expansion of the movement in Zhili during the first months of 1900, however, elicited a growing response from an increasingly nervous foreign community. And the escalating foreign response, in turn, forced the Chinese court, which had vacillated for months in its policy, eventually to adopt a clearer and more explicit (although not necessarily consistently implemented) stand with respect both to the Boxers and the foreign powers. A triangular field of forces thus came into play, consisting of the Boxers, the foreign governments, and the Chinese authorities, each of which affected, through its changing behavior, the responses of the other two.

For a long time there was little awareness of the Boxer phenomenon among foreigners in general. Protestant missionaries in western Shandong and southern Zhili first reported skirmishes between Boxers and local Christians in April–May 1899. But, as W. H. Rees of the London Missionary Society observed from Jizhou in southern Zhili, "such incidents are not uncommon in our mission centre." Certainly, as of spring 1899, there was still no sense—it would have been far more remarkable if there had been—of a major uprising in the offing.

By the fall this situation had changed dramatically. Notice of the Boxers began to appear in foreign newspapers in early October. Later in the same month, missionaries in the Beijing area reported on the spreading unrest in Shandong. Rees, in mid-December, described "the rebellion" as "spreading like a prairie fire." The murder of the British missionary Brooks at the end of December raised foreign alarm to a new level. Sir Claude MacDonald, the British minister, in his dispatch of January 5 to the Foreign Office, took note of the growing turmoil "secret societies" were creating in northern Shandong and made specific reference to "an organization know as the 'Boxers,'" which had attained "special notoriety" and whose "ravages [had] recently spread over a large portion of Southern Chihli [Zhili]." The growing danger to native Christians and foreign missionaries, MacDonald added, had been the subject of "repeated representations" by the foreign ministers, especially those of Germany, the United States, and Great Britain, to the Chinese government.

The Chinese court, although evincing concern over the murder of Brooks and moving quickly to bring about a settlement of the case, issued a decree on January 11 which announced that people drilling for self-defense and for the protection of their villages were not to be considered bandits; the decree went on to instruct local authorities to pay attention only to whether people fomented disorder and conflict, not to whether they happened to be members of this or that society or sect. The foreign representatives in the capital reacted with apprehension to this decree, which they interpreted, not unreasonably, as an effort on the throne's part to provide the Boxers with a degree of protection and perhaps even encouragement. On January 27, Britain, the United States, France, Germany, and Italy sent identical notes to the Zongli Yamen—the Chinese government office in charge of foreign affairs—requesting publication of an imperial edict ordering the immediate suppression of the Boxers in Shandong and Zhili.

During the next few months the tug of war persisted. The diplomatic corps in Beijing made periodic representations to the Chinese government, protesting the inadequacy of the measures thus far taken to put down the rising, while the court, for its part, far from adopting a firmer policy of suppression, as late as mid-April reiterated the view that it was quite all right for good people to organize for the defense of their communities and in early May even flirted with the idea of formally organizing these local self-defense groups into "militia." Increasingly frustrated by the lack of Chinese official action, despite rapidly escalating Boxer-related violence in the countryside, several of the powers in April raised the level of pressure a notch by parading warships before the Dagu forts guarding the approaches to Tianjin, in a flagrant display of old-style gunboat diplomacy.

If the Chinese government was being pushed, from one side, by the foreign powers, it was being pushed even harder, from the other side, by the Boxers. Inevitably, as disturbances in Zhili mounted in both frequency and severity, government forces came into direct conflict with Boxers, and the more this happened the harder it became for pro-Boxer officials to maintain the simple fiction that the Boxers were community protectors, whose main raison d'être was to guard against disruptive heterodox elements. The problem was illustrated—and also greatly aggravated—by a series of engagements between Boxers and Qing troops that took place in May in Laishui county, midway between Beijing and Baoding. The initial explosion took place in Gaoluo village in Laishui, where there had been a long history of animosity between Catholic and non-Catholic inhabitants. Boxers began to arrive in the area in the spring, and a boxing ground was established in the temple of the northern section of the village in April. Not long after this, on the evening of May 12, the Boxers, with the aid of confederates from nearly villages, burned down the church and, after killing all the Catholics (more than thirty families), disposed of their bodies in a wellpit (graphically described years later by the Gaoluo Boxer chief's grandson as a "flesh mound grave") and set fire to the victims' homes (located in the southern part of the village).

Faced with this provocation, a small force of government soldiers led by Col. Yang Futong closed the boxing ground in Gaoluo on May 15 and, the following day, after being ambushed by several hundred Boxers, killed sixty of them in a one-sided government victory. A couple of days later Yang's men took twenty Boxers captive, whereupon a large force of outraged Boxers from the entire area came together to rescue the prisoners and avenge the deaths of their comrades. On May 22, in Shiting, a market town ten miles north of the Laishui county seat, the Boxers took the government soldiers by surprise and killed Yang Futong.

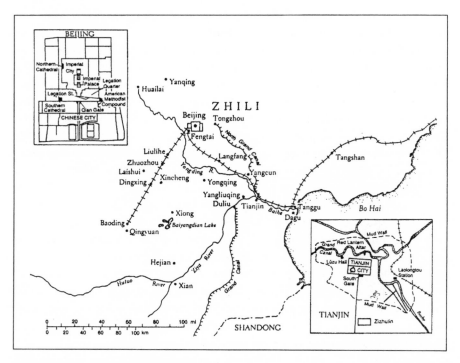

Map 1.3. The Beijing-Tianjin region

The death of Yang, the first Qing commander to be killed by the Boxers, had a catalytic effect on the movement, which now shifted into higher gear in central Zhili. During the last ten days of May a force of more than ten thousand Boxers took Zhuozhou, just northeast of Laishui on the rail line to the capital. Beginning on May 27, the Boxers also launched a succession of attacks along the Beijing-Baoding railway, ripping up tracks, destroying stations and bridges, and severing telegraph lines. On May 28 they burned down the Fengtai station on the Beijing-Tianjin railway, about ten miles from the capital. A few days later, in early June, Boxer involvement in the Baoding area also escalated.

The court's initial reaction to this upsurge of activity was to seek to avoid further confrontation with the Boxers, partly because Qing military forces in Zhili were stretched perilously thin. But, by the late May, as the situation worsened, the well-armed troops of Nie Shicheng (himself strongly anti-Boxer) were deployed against the Boxers along the Beijing-Tianjin railway, and in early June Governor-General Yulu for the first time urged the Zongli Yamen to request that orders be given to Nie and other Qing commanders to take decisive action to suppress the Boxer movement without further delay.

If the government had moved against the Boxers with firmness a few weeks earlier, it might still have been possible to bring the rising under control and avoid serious international repercussion. As of mid-May, Boxer violence had been directed almost exclusively against native Christians and their churches and homes, only one foreign life (that of Brooks) had been lost, and no attacks had yet been launched against the railways and telegraphs. By the end of May, the situation had changed so radically that, even if the court had been strongly inclined to suppress the Boxer movement (which it was not), it is doubtful it could have succeeded.

In addition to the development already noted, on May 28, after the destruction of the Fengtai station, the foreign ministers in the capital, fearing the loss of the rail link to the coast, called up several hundred legation guards, the first large contingent of these arriving by rail from Dagu on May 31. On the same day, four French and Belgian railway engineers, attempting to escape to Tianjin from Baoding after the cutting of the Beijing-Baoding line, were killed by Boxers, and on June 1 two British missionaries met their deaths in Yongqing, directly south of Beijing. Manifestly, the Boxer movement, in the last days of May and the first days of June, had rounded an important bend, venturing into territory it had previously only threatened to enter.

Accompanying this shift in direction, antiforeign feeling among the population at large now became rampant, aroused by the calling up of the legation guards, the news that two dozen foreign ships of war had assembled opposite the Dagu forts (in early June), the initiation of direct attacks on foreigners and on the rail and telegraph lines, the conspicuous increase in the numbers of Boxers crowing the thoroughfares to Beijing and Tianjin, and, undergirding everything, the continuation of severe drought. Significantly, when primitively armed Boxers sustained heavy casualties in a series of fierce engagements with Nie Shicheng's men along the Beijing-Tianjin railway in the first days of June (480 Boxers were killed near Langfang on June 6 alone), the Boxers, instead of being cowed into submission, became even more aggressive, emboldened by the widening support of an increasingly angry and frightened populace.

Although it would be foolhardy to point to any one factor that was of greater moment than all the others in shaping the crisis that now emerged, driving China and the foreign powers inexorably toward war, a number of historians have pointed to the decisive importance of the summoning of the legation guards in late May. . . . on May 29, in the aftermath of the killing of Yang Futong and the assaults on the rail line, the court, for the first time since the beginning of 1900, issued instructions to "annihilate" Boxers who refused to disperse. These orders were, however, reversed almost immediately, after the foreign ministers made known their plans to summon the guards, thereby strengthening the hand of the pro-Boxer faction at court; on June 3 explicit orders were given *not* to annihilate Boxers. . . .

In early June governors-general in the Yangzi Valley provinces, fearful of imminent foreign intervention, urged the court to take forceful action immediately to suppress the Boxers. But, although the court dispatched a number of emissaries . . . to attempt to persuade the Boxers to disperse and return to peaceful pursuits, this effort came to nought, and when Nie Shicheng, also acting on imperial orders, took much stronger action against the Boxers . . . he was severely reprimanded. This pattern of inconsistency and indecisiveness continued until June 10. On the morning of this date, acting in response to an urgent telegram from the British minister, stating that the situation had become "extremely grave" and that unless arrangements were made for the immediate dispatch of a relief expedition to Beijing, it would be too late, Adm. Edward Seymour left Tianjin by train with the first contingent of an international force that by June 13 had reached almost 2,000 men. Unlike the calling up of the legation guards, which had been discussed with and partially approved in advance by the Zongli Yamen, the sending of the Seymour expedition was completely without Chinese authorization. The court's response was immediate. Later on the same day (June 10), Prince Duan, a leading Boxer supporter, was appointed to the Zongli Yamen, along with three other pro-Boxer officials; Prince Duan replaced Prince Qing, a staunch opponent of the Boxers, as head of the yamen. The hand of pro-Boxer forces at court was significantly strengthened by this move, and within days preparations were being made for war.

The Seymour expedition proceeded very slowly. Frequent repairs of the railway had to be made en route, and this made it easier for bands of Boxers to engage in harassing actions. By June 18, the expedition was still bogged down at Langfang, midway between Tianjin and the capital. On this day Qing forces, led by Nie Shicheng and Dong Fuxiang, joined a large contingent of Boxers in attacking the expedition, and the Chinese side won a major victory. Unable to advance further, Seymour led the relief force back to Tianjin, which was reached on June 26, after suffering heavy casualties.

While the drama of the abortive Seymour expedition was being played out, the situation in Beijing was rapidly worsening. On the evening of June 10 Boxers destroyed the British summer legation in the Western Hills outside the capital. The following day, the secretary of the Japanese legation, Sugiyama Akira, was killed near the railway station by the soldiers of Dong Fuxiang (who, unlike Nie Shicheng, was sympathetic to the Boxer cause). On the afternoon of June 13 a large force of Boxers swarmed into the city and began setting fire to churches and foreign homes; the Southern Cathedral (Nantang), in which several hundred Chinese Catholics had taken refuge, was burned to the ground, resulting in a large number of deaths. The next day, in the evening, Boxers engaged in sporadic attacks on the guards of the foreign legations.

The situation was not much different in Tianjin, where the Boxer presence had grown steadily since early March. By late May–early June, the streets of the walled Chinese city (two miles northwest of the foreign settlements) had come under effective Boxer control. Officials, in encountering Boxers, were forced to get out of their sedan chairs and demonstrate their subservience. Churches and Christian homes—and eventually any establishments with foreign associations—were plundered and burned. A prison was broken into and the inmates set free. Yulu, whose residence was in Tianjin, was coerced into opening the government's arsenals to the Boxers. Faced with a situation that was getting increasingly out if hand and that presented an immediate danger to the foreign civilian population in the concession areas, foreign ships off the coast issued an ultimatum to the occupants of the Dagu forts on June 16 and seized them the following day.

Although the court did not find out about the ultimatum until June 19 (telegraphic communication between Tianjin and Beijing having been severed), the Empress Dowager Cixi, in the course of a series of important conferences begun on June 16, was already moving toward a decision to go to war. The news of the foreign ultimatum settled the matter. The diplomatic corps was informed that it had twenty-four hours in which to effect the evacuation of foreigners from the capital. The foreign ministers, concerned about the safety of a large number of foreigners, including women and children, making their way to the coast, were hesitant to comply with the Chinese government's orders. Their hesitation proved justified when, on the following day, the German minister Baron Clements von Ketteler was shot dead by a Chinese soldier while on his way to a meeting at the Zongli Yamen. Within hours of the killing of von Ketteler, Protestant missionaries, many from elsewhere in North China who had taken refuge, along with hundreds of native Christians, in the Methodist Episcopal (American) compound in the capital, were brought (with their converts) under armed escort to the legation quarter. More than 3,000 Catholics including foreign priests and nuns (and 43 Italian and French marines), had meanwhile secured themselves in the sturdily built Northern Cathedral, two miles northwest of the legation. On the afternoon of June 20, Chinese troops, joined by Boxers, opened fire on both the legations and the cathedral, commencing sieges that were to be carried on, with varying degrees of determination, until August 14. On June 21, the court issued a "declaration of war," and the Boxers, after being officially renamed "righteous people," were enlisted in militia under the overall command in the capital of Prince Zhuang, Gangyi, and Prince Duan. The climactic phase of the Boxer episode had begun.

The geographical spread of the Boxer movement widened dramatically after the throne's declaration of war, extending into Shanxi and Henan in North China, and beyond North China into Inner Mongolia and Manchuria. The number of deaths resulting from the movement also escalated, well over two hundred foreigners and untold thousands of Chinese Christian being killed before the bloodbath finally ended. The level of violence and disorder, on the other hand, varied greatly according to the degree to which provincial and local authorities were sympathetic to the Boxer cause. Thus high officials in the lower Yangzi provinces, determined to keep the war from spreading to the south, were able to work out an arrangement with the foreign consuls of Shanghai, according to which the Chinese authorities were to put down any antiforeign disturbances within their jurisdictions in return for which the powers would keep their armies from entering the area. In Shandong also, although the Boxers (and Big Swords) experienced a revival following the clarification of the court's stance, the staunchly anti-Boxer governor, Yuan Shikai, took effective measures to prevent loss of foreign life. Although more than 300 Chinese Christians were killed in the province, by far the largest number if casualties were Boxers who ignored Yuan's orders to proceed to the Tianjin-Beijing area to assist in the fighting against the foreigners.

Forming a sharp contrast to the Yangzi provinces and Shandong was Shanxi, where the uncompromisingly antiforeign Yuxian had been appointed governor in March. On July 9, forty-four foreigners (including children), after being summoned to the provincial capital (Taiyuan) for their protection, were executed under the governor's personal supervision, and by summer's end an indeterminate number of additional foreigners and some 2,000 Chinese Christians had also been put to death, many of the killings inspired directly or indirectly by the authorities.

Bordering on Shanxi to the north, Inner Mongolia was another area with a high death toll for both foreigners and Chinese. Boxers, mainly from Shanxi and Zhili, had streamed into the region in early summer, with support from the local officialdom. They were soon joined by Manchu-led government forces, and when one of the large churches they laid siege to was overpowered, some 3,000 Chinese Christians (mostly Catholics) were killed. Although it is impossible, because of the way in which the figures were presented at the time, to establish an internal breakdown between the number of foreign lives lost in Inner Mongolia and the number lost in Shanxi, the grand total for both areas appears to have been just shy of 180, of whom 159 were Protestant.

Manchuria, northeast of Zhili, was another important arena of Boxer activity. Circumstances here were different from those in North China. There was much popular hostility in the southern part of the region to the South Manchurian Railway, which had been constructed by the Russians. Boxers began to appear in Manchuria in the spring and by late June, together with Manchu troops, had commenced destruction of the railway, in part to hinder Russian military intervention. There were also numerous attacks on Protestant and Catholic missions, resulting in the killing of more than 1,500 Chinese Christians (but few foreigners). A draconian order was reestablished in Manchuria with the Russian occupation of the entire area in the summer and early autumn.

Although all told, the greatest number of foreign deaths in the summer of 1900 (over three quarters of the total) occurred in Shanxi and Inner Mongolia, a particularly serious incident took place in the Zhili provincial capital of Baoding, where on June 30 and July 1 fifteen Protestant missionaries (including children) were killed. The largest number of Chinese Christian deaths also occurred in Zhili, where the Christian population was relatively numerous, the roots of the Boxer movement were deep, and the incidence of armed conflict was widespread. The greatest concentration of Christian casualties in the province was doubtless in and around the cities of Beijing and Tianjin, areas that were under effective Boxer control through most of the summer.

The only other province to experience significant Boxer-related violence was Henan, which like Zhili and Shanxi had suffered from severe drought for many months. The damage resulting from Boxer activities in Henan was, however, largely confined to church burnings; no missionaries and relatively few Chinese Christians were killed.

Although the most serious anti-Christian violence of 1900, as above summarized, took place after the court's declaration of war and may clearly be viewed as part of the "Boxer War" in the widest sense, in the narrower sense of armed conflict between foreign and Chinese combatants the war may be divided into several partly overlapping phases. The first two of these—the Seymour expedition of June 10–26 and the assault against the Dagu forts on June 17—have already been noted. A third phase, which because of its idiosyncratic nature is beyond the scope of this narrative to more than take note of, was the Sino-Russian conflict in the three Manchurian provinces, which began on a sporadic basis in June in the south, heated up considerably in mid-July in the Amur region, and concluded with the Russian army's entry into Mukden on October 1.

Overlapping in time with the third phase of the Boxer War was a fourth, the Battle of Tianjin, which began with Chinese shelling of the foreign settlements in the city (Zizhulin) on June 17. The period from June 17 to June 26, when the first of several foreign relief contingents arrived from the coast, was the time of greatest danger for the nine hundred foreign civilians in Tianjin (Herbert Hoover, who was there, referred to it as the period of "the black fear"). The siege, which resulted in heavy casualties on both sides, lasted until July 13, when the arrival of a final wave of reinforcements (bringing the combined strength of the foreign force to between five thousand and six thousand troops) permitted the storming of the walled Chinese city and its seizure after a day of heavy fighting. The foreign victory, which was followed by several days of unrestrained killing, looting, and raping, dealt a severe blow to Boxer prospects in the Tianjin area.

The warfare in Tianjin, which pitted some of China's best-equipped troops (including the army of Nie Shicheng, who was killed on July 9) as well as Boxers against a foreign force consisting mainly of Russians and Japanese, was of a more or less conventional sort. Nothing could have been less conventional, on the other hand, than the fifth phase of the Boxer War: the assaults on the diplomatic quarter and the Northern Cathedral in the capital. Although there had been intermittent attacks earlier, both sieges began in earnest on June 20 and lasted until the arrival of the international relief force from Tianjin on August 14. The two sieges were unconventional in different ways. The assault on the Northern Cathedral was principally in the hands of some ten thousand Boxers under the overall command of Prince Duan. In almost two months of unremitting attacks, using mines, rifles, and some cannon but mainly depending on fire, the Boxers were unable to take the structure, an outcome they attributed to the superior magical powers of the foreigners within. . . .

The assault on the legations was more conventional in outward appearance. The several thousand civilians within were defended by some one hundred foreign soldiers and over a hundred volunteers. Although there was some Boxer participation, primary responsibility on the Chinese side was borne by regular government forces, under the command of Dong Fuxing and Ronglu. The latter, although wary of antagonizing the Empress Dowager, was not sympathetic to the Boxers, clearly understood the folly of China's having taken on all the powers at once, and made sure the siege was never pressed home. After a month of fighting that was sometimes quite heavy, a brief truce commenced in mid-July, as the court, in the wake of the news from Tianjin, tried to reach a negotiated solution to the crisis. The return of the staunchly antiforeign Li Bingheng to Beijing in late July, however, strengthened the hand of the pro-Boxer faction and stiffened Cixi's determination to continue the war. In late July and early August five officials known for their anti-Boxer views and past friendliness toward foreigners were executed by imperial order, and in early August full-scale bombardment of the legations was resumed.

In both of the Beijing sieges Chinese casualties were high. Many foreigners also suffered, mainly in the assault on the legations, in which at least 66 died and well over 150 were wounded. In the sixth phase of the war, the march overland from Tianjin to Beijing of the eight-power relief expedition, Chinese casualties were heavy (many of them civilians in villages and towns razed by the advancing troops), foreign casualties relatively light (if one discounts the hundreds who were unable to continue because of the paralyzing heat). Owing to interminable squabbling and to the competing commitments of several of the participants in other parts of the world, the expedition did not finally get started until August 4. The force numbered some twenty thousand, half of them Japanese. Once under way, it piled up one victory after another against hastily assembled and poorly led imperial troops. In the wake of the defeat of the Chinese army on August 6 at Yangcun, twenty miles out of Tianjin, Yulu shot himself. Li Bingheng, who left Beijing for the front in early August, took poison on August 11, after his own forces had twice gone down to defeat and were in flight everywhere. On August 14 foreign troops entered the capital. Most Boxers had by this time abandoned their weapons and identifying red (or yellow) clothing and slipping back into the population. The Empress Dowager, Emperor, and other high court officials, disguised as ordinary people, fled westward under armed escort early on the morning of August 15.

The final phase of the Boxer War consisted in mopping up and punitive expeditions by foreign soldiers, mainly in Zhili. These took place in two stages. In the first stage, military operations involving soldiers from various foreign countries were conducted in September against Duliu, an important center of Boxer activity southwest of Tianjin, and against Boxer strongholds south and north of the capital. The second stage, lasting from October into the following spring, was carried out under the command of German Field Marshal Alfred von Waldersee (who did not arrive in China until late September), and, although the soldiers of several of the powers took part, Germany took the clear lead. The city of Baoding, the site of one of the most serious Boxer actions, was devastated in October, its officials condemned to death by a makeshift military tribunal, and its citizenry forced to pay the costs of foreign occupation. From mid-December to the following April several dozen additional punitive expeditions were launched under von Waldersee's direction. Although most were aimed at objectives in Zhili, German and French forces crossed the border into eastern Shanxi on a number of occasions and also threatened to move into Shandong.

Although the ostensible purpose of the punitive expeditions was to clear the countryside of Boxer remnants, it was never very clear how Boxers were to be distinguished from non-Boxers. "It is safe to say," Major General Adna Chaffee, commander of the American relief force, said to a journalist, "that where one real Boxer has been killed since the capture of Peking, fifteen harmless coolies or labourers on the farms, including not a few women and children, have been slain." One motive for the key role Germany arrogated to itself in the expeditions was clearly the wish to avenge the killing of von Ketteler in June and in the process expand German influence in the Far East. Kaiser Wilhelm, in a speech at Bermerhaven on the occasion of the departure in late July of the first contingent of German troops for the Far East, had asserted: "Just as the Huns, a thousand years ago, under the leadership of Attila, gained a reputation by virtue if which they still live in historical tradition, so may the name of Germany become known in such a manner in China that no Chinese will ever again even dare to look askance at a German." A more immediate German purpose, of course, was to pressure the Chinese government into acceding to foreign demands at the negotiating table. The process of negotiating a settlement of the Boxer War had gotten under way almost immediately after the foreign occupation of Beijing. It took a year to run its course, the final results being incorporated in a protocol signed in the capital by eleven foreign ministers and two Chinese plenipotentiaries on September 7, 1901.

The Boxer Protocol stipulated that Yuxian was to be executed, several other high court officials (including Prince Zhuang) were to die by their own hand, and that Prince Duan was to be exiled for life to Xinjiang in the far northwest. Official missions were to be sent to Germany and Japan to convey regrets for the deaths of von Ketteler and Sugiyama, and a monument erected in Beijing on the spot where the German minister had been killed. In order to ensure the future security of the powers, the forts at Dagu and other key military installations were to be destroyed; also a two-year prohibition was placed on Chinese importation of arms, an enlarged legation guard was to be permanently stationed in Beijing, and foreign troops were to be positioned at specified points between Beijing and the coast. The indemnity imposed in the Chinese was huge: 450 million taels (U.S. $333 million), to be paid in thirty-nine annual installments along with 4 percent interest on unpaid principal.

Thus was written the final chapter of the Boxer episode. The detailed provisions of the diplomatic settlement were less important than the impact it had on the Chinese government and population. The severity of the indemnity greatly intensified the already considerable grip of the foreign powers over China's governmental finances and forced the Qing, in a desperate effort to generate new revenues, to begin laying the foundations for a modern state. The draconian character of the settlement, together with the generally poor showing of the Chinese military in the summer of 1900 and the court's humiliating flight to Xi'an in August, placed the weakness of the Qing dynasty on full view and energized the forces of both reform and revolution in Chinese society. The court also, however reluctantly, embarked after 1900 on a program of reform that went for beyond anything previously tried and completely reshaped the environment within which Chinese politics were carried on. This environment, as it turned out, proved to be one in which the dynasty itself was unable to survive.

7

The Chinese Enlightenment

VERA SCHWARCZ

The May Fourth Movement has often been compared to the European Enlightenment of the eighteenth century. Previously, many modern Chinese reformers had supported technological change and modernization while defending the superiority of Chinese culture and ethical values. The May Fourth Movement began in 1919 as a protest over China's treatment at the Paris Peace Conference and quickly developed into the first broad public condemnation of traditional Chinese culture and Confucian values as an obstacle to China's modern development. For the first time in modern Chinese history national salvation was directly linked to cultural and political awakening. Although the participants in the May Fourth Movement represented a broad range of political viewpoints, they shared a common belief that intellectuals had an obligation to play an active role in Chinese politics and nation building. Inspired by slogans of "Science" and "Democracy," the driving force behind the May Fourth Movement were Chinese college students. The following essay by Vera Schwarcz discusses the intellectual challenges that modernity posed for twentieth-century Chinese intellectuals.

Enlightenment and The Quest for Modernity

In twentieth-century China, as in Europe a hundred and fifty years earlier, the discovery of critical reason has been heralded as a sign of transition from tradition to modernity. In both contexts, this transition turned out to be neither as clear-cut nor as easily consummated as first envisaged by advocates of enlightenment. The lingering hold of outworn values, Christian as well as Confucian, on supposedly modern men and women, continues to shock those who had hoped to replace superstition and prejudice with objective doubt. For Chinese intellectuals, this shock had added reverberations. Having witnessed, participated in, and survived several political revolutions, they have more reason than European philosophers to fear the reemergence of old habits of mind.

Efforts to launch China onto the path of genuine modernity have, from the beginning, been marked by the intellectuals' awareness of the protean nature of traditional culture. These critics of native habits of mind needed an alternative place to stand from which they might continue to call into question the values that so many of their contemporaries considered to be natural and immutable. So, they turned to the West (or, more frequently, to Japanese interpretation of Western texts and ideas). The more Chinese radicals relied on the perspective of cultural relativism, the more they risked being accused of imposing a Western concept of modernity upon a unique Chinese civilization. Those who took that risk did so because events in Chinese history itself confirmed, and continue to reconfirm, the tenacity of feudalism at the heart of a supposedly modernized, even revolutionary society.

The question of how to become a modern nation antedates the problem of enlightenment in Chinese history. From the mid-nineteenth century onward, Confucian officials have tried to find the best way to increase the power and prestige of the state so as to enable it to withstand foreign aggression. The formula worked out in the 1880s by the reform-minded scholar Zhang Zhidong still appeals to patriotic revolutionaries determined to ensure China's survival in a world of rapacious nation-states. Zhang's suggestion was simple enough: "Chinese learning as the goal, Western learning as the means" (*zhongxue wei ti, xixue wei yong*). This *ti-yong* formula became more complicated in practice, however. Political reformers discovered that embedded in Western "means"— that is to say, in technological expertise—were distinctive goals that were inimical to the fundamental values of Chinese, or more precisely Confucian, civilization. The inseparability of means and ends in both Western and Chinese learning posed an awkward and lasting dilemma for cultural conservatives. It also provided the key opportunity for cultural radicals who sought to revive and to strengthen China by reevaluating native traditions with the tools of critical reason learned from abroad.

The first generation to take issue with Zhang Zhidong's *ti-yong* formula emerged during the first decade of the twentieth century. Having traveled to Japan and Europe, these still-Confucian scholars began to voice publicly their doubts about the superiority of Chinese learning, especially those elements of it that were codified in and rewarded by the imperial examination system. Their criticism of the native cultural legacy became sidetracked . . . by the passions of China's first nationalist revolution—the anti-dynastic revolution of 1911. Bent upon reforming Confucian education, most of these intellectuals ended up fighting against the "foreign" Manchu rulers whom they envisaged as the chief obstacle to national salvation and renewal. Thus, it fell upon subsequent generations to follow through with the implications of an early twentieth-century insight: that . . . national salvation, depends first and foremost on a commitment to . . . the salvation of mankind, or more precisely, to a critical-minded humanism.

This insight about the primacy of culture may be traced to the failure of political revolution in 1911. Once the optimism of anti-dynastic mobilization wore off, the tenacity of outworn cultural values became all the more apparent. A group of erstwhile revolutionaries now embarked upon the quest for a new worldview. This quest was more thorough than any of the quests previously undertaken by the Confucian reformers. Founders of *Youth* magazine (later renamed *New Youth*), these intellectuals tried to make sense of the reemergence of old habits of mind, in particular of the emperor-worship mentality, even after there was no longer an actual Son of Heaven on the throne in Beijing. Their conclusion was that China needed a radical transvaluation of values. The object of their New Culture movement was to dig up the common tendencies toward self-submission and expose them. Such tendencies, in their view, had prevented their compatriot from taking advantage of the possibility of national and individual autonomy opened up by the revolution of 1911. Rallying around the slogans "Science" and "Democracy," this first generation of enlightenment intellectuals looked to their descendants to actualize the hope of emancipation from the ethic of subservience. They wanted this "new youth" to prove that a truly modern nation-state could not come into existence in China unless it first sanctioned the human rights of critically minded citizens.

Thus, the stage was set for the historic action of a new generation—called here the May Fourth generation. Comprised of students who had congregated in and around National Beijing University (Beida) in 1919, this group of younger intellectuals took it upon themselves to carry through the vague hopes of their iconoclastic mentors. Their age and their educational experiences before entering Beijing University made them more distant from the Confucian tradition and therefore less angry at it. In contrast to their teachers, who had been obsessed with the tenacity of feudal habits of mind ever since the failure of the revolution of 1911, these students were more rational in their cultural criticism. Also, they were less pessimistic about political action and thus were able to respond more promptly to the political crisis occasioned by the end of World War I.

This generation's rallying point was the event of May 4, 1919. What began as a demonstration to protest China's treatment at the Paris Peace Conference developed during the following year into a national movement for cultural and political awakening. This broader movement included literary and family reforms as well as an increasing commitment by the educated elite to gain a mass hearing for their radical views. Spreading their ideas through street lectures, this younger group of intellectuals was able to put their mentors' ideas to the test of practical social action. They emerged from this first encounter with the unawakened masses full of confidence both in themselves and in critical reason—the tool with which they aimed to rouse their less enlightened contemporaries. Luo Jialun, one of the leaders of the student demonstration and also a founder of the New Tide Society, wrote one year after the event of 1919 that the glory of May Fourth lay in shaking China out of its prolonged backwardness:

> Before, we Chinese students had claimed to be able to smash heaven with our words and aimed to overturn the earth with our pens. . . . Only this time [during the May Fourth movement] did we begin to struggle with the forces of darkness with our bare fists. . . . China before the May Fourth movement was a nation gasping for breath. After the May Fourth movement, it is a more vital, lively nation. The glory of the May Fourth movement lies precisely in getting China to move.

This rather dramatic claim to having gotten China to move was and remains the core of the myth of May Fourth. It suggests the appealing possibility of an irrevocable and total break with the past. Beneath this myth . . . lies the more prosaic but more enduring significance of May Fourth. Far from having set China on the irreversible, glorious path of enlightenment, the event of 1919 marked the first of a series of incomplete efforts to uproot feudalism while pursuing the cause of a nationalist revolution. Intellectuals were at the forefront of this effort then, as they are now. Relatively immune to "the forces of darkness" by virtue of their modern scientific education, this minority has been able to infuse new vigor in a "nation gasping for breath." They were, as we shall see, in a particularly good position to shake off the burden of the *ti-yong* formula. This meant that they were no longer compelled to subordinate Western scientific rationality to the claims of China's spiritual civilization. Their capacity for and interest in cultural relativism set them apart from most of their compatriots—the less educated masses as well as the Confucian guardians of "national essence." Thus, when they claimed to have "moved" China, or at least to have gotten it moving, they were reaffirming the need for something more than a national salvation effort based on "Chinese ends" and "Western means."

8

Sun Yat-sen Opens the Whampoa Academy, 1924

Sun Yat-sen (1866–1925) left China as a youth and was educated by missionaries in Hawaii. When he was denied a license to practice medicine in the British colony of Hong Kong, Sun became involved in anti-Qing movements. From 1895 until the fall of the Qing dynasty in 1911, Sun used his connections to Chinese secret societies and his ties to overseas Chinese communities to organize armed uprisings against the Qing. Sun was a tireless revolutionary who reached the pinnacle of his power and influence late in life as leader of the Guomindang (Nationalist Party). In the 1920s Sun established a government in Guangzhou (Canton) and gained the support of Soviet Union. A key element in Soviet aid was assistance in the establishment of Whampoa Military Academy. The mission of the Whampoa Academy was to train a revolutionary army that would wrest control of China from warlord control. Many of the greatest political and military leaders of both the Guomindang and Communist Party were instructors or students at Whampoa. By emphasizing the importance of revolutionary spirit and political enlightenment, Sun distinguished the Guomindang revolutionary army from the crass militarism of the warlord regimes that controlled much of China.

Honored guests, faculty, and students, today marks the opening of our academy. Why do we need this school? Why must we definitely open such a school? You all know that the Chinese Revolution has gone on for thirteen years; although these years have been counted as years of the Republic there has been, in reality, no Republic. After thirteen years of revolution, the Republic is just an empty name and, even today, the revolution is a complete failure.

How have revolutions elsewhere in the world that began after out revolution fared? Six years ago, during the European War, in a neighboring country, a country larger than China, a country that shares a border of more than ten thousand *li* with China and that touches both Asia and European, a revolution broke out some six years after our revolution. What country was this? It was Russia.

Despite the fact that the Russian Revolution took place six years after that of China, they have thoroughly succeeded in obtaining revolutionary results. . . .

We can obtain a great lesson from tracing the causes for the difference between the results of the Russian and Chinese revolutions. And it is because we understand this lesson that we have come together to begin this school today. What is the lesson? When the revolution broke out in Russia, revolutionary party members served as the vanguard in the struggle against the Russian Czar. After the success of the revolution, they immediately organized a revolutionary army that continuously struggled for the revolution, it achieved success in a short period of time despite the numerous obstacles it encountered.

Because of the struggle of revolutionary martyrs in China, when the revolution broke out in Wuchang, the various provinces responded, overthrew the Manchu dynasty, and established the Republic. Our revolution, then, was partially successful. But later there was no revolutionary army to continue the goals of the revolutionary party and, therefore, although there was a partial success, warlords and bureaucrats continue today to usurp the power of the Chinese Republic. As for the basis of our Republic, there is none. Simply speaking, the reason is that our revolution is supported by the struggle of a revolutionary party but not by the struggle of the revolutionary army. Because we lack the struggle of a revolutionary army, bureaucrats and warlords are able to control our republic and our revolution is incapable of completely succeeding.

What is our hope in starting this school today? Our hope is that from today on we will be able to remake our revolutionary enterprise and use the students of this school as the foundation of a revolutionary army. You students will be the basic cadres of the revolutionary army of the future. With such excellent cadres as soldiers of the revolutionary army, our revolutionary enterprise will definitely succeed. Without a good revolutionary army, the Chinese revolution is doomed to failure. Therefore, in opening this military academy here today, our sole hope is to create a revolutionary army to save China from extinction!

What is a revolutionary army? What sort of resolve should those of you who have come to this school to study possess to become revolutionary soldiers? What qualifications should you have to call yourselves revolutionary soldiers? To become revolutionary soldiers, you should take the martyrs of the revolution as your models, you should learn from revolutionary party members, and you should study the revolutionary struggle of the party. Only when the struggle of the party and army are the identical is there a revolutionary army. None of the armies that have taken part in China's revolutionary struggles in the last thirteen years have shared the same goals as the revolutionary party. I venture to say that in these years there has been no revolutionary army. Quite a few armies in Guang-dong have worked with us in the struggle of our revolutionary party, but none of them can be called a revolutionary army. But if these armies have worked with our revolutionary party, why do I dare not call them revolutionary armies? The reason I cannot call these armies revolutionary armies is that the elements who make them up are too complicated, have had no revolutionary training, and have no revolutionary foundation. What is a revolutionary foundation? A revolution-ary foundation is something that inspires the same behavior as that of martyrs of the revolution. . . .

You gentlemen who have come to study here from the far corners of China, were no doubt aware even before you arrived that it is our goal to build a kind of revolutionary army. To join our revolutionary enterprise, you must surely possess a sort of powerful resolve. Where should the starting point of the revolutionary enterprise be? It should be in your own heart. You should eradicate from your hearts all bad thoughts and habits; you should eliminate all animalistic or evil traits of character that are not in keeping with humanity and righteousness. Therefore, if you want to make a political revolution you should start by making a revolution in your hearts. If you can revolutionize your hearts, there is hope that you will succeed in the political revolution. If you cannot make a revolution in your hearts, even though you study military science in this fully equipped military academy, you cannot become a revolutionary soldier here in the future or accomplish the revolutionary enterprise. Therefore, if you gentlemen want to make a revolution you must have a revolutionary will and if you have this revolutionary will, then in the future you can become the commanders and generals of the revolutionary army. If we want to succeed in our revolution, we must resolve today that for our whole lives we will not have the idea of "becoming officials and making money." We seek only to save the people and the nation and to enact the Three People's Principles and the Five Power Constitution. Only by wholeheartedly pursuing revolution can we reach the goals of the revolution. Otherwise, even if you gentlemen start your own armies, win many battles, obtain much land, and control tens of thousands of people, you still can not be called revolutionary soldiers. . . .

Whether an army can make revolution depends upon whether its generals and soldiers have a revolutionary resolve; it does not depend on how good its weapons are. . . . In the future, when you graduate and organize a revolutionary army you should be willing to give up your lives to overcome obstacles facing the Republic and have the spirit of one person fighting to overcome one hundred. What is the source of such a spirit? What sort of person should you use as a model to be a revolutionary soldier? Simply put, you should use the martyrs of the revolution as your model and study their behavior. Like them you should sacrifice yourselves for humanity and single-mindedly sacrifice all of your rights to save the country. Only then can you become a revolutionary soldier with no fear of death. . . . Death is something we welcome. To die before the bullets and shells of the enemy is something we especially welcome. With such great courage and resolve, one can defeat one hundred. The enemy believes that to live is to be happy; we believe that to die is to be happy and that when we die we reach our goals. There is such an enormous difference regarding life and death between the enemy and us that they are no match for us and we are invincible.

9

Report on an Investigation of the Peasant Movement in Hunan

MAO ZEDONG

Mao Zedong was a founding member of the CCP, but his unorthodox views regarding the role of the peasantry in a communist revolution kept him from assuming a major leadership role until after the Long March (1934–1935). During the 1920s Mao worked at the Guomindang-organized Peasant Training Institute where he prepared young Chinese intellectuals to return to their home regions to organize peasant associations. After personally investigating the situation in his home province of Hunan, Mao wrote this emotionally charged report that contained scant reference to the Marxist ideology of the CCP. Blaming rural elites for driving the peasantry to extreme measures, Mao unabashedly advocated violence against the "patriarchal-feudal class of local tyrants, evil gentry, and lawless landlords." It is no wonder that many of his more sophisticated Marxist colleagues within the CCP found his views dangerously unorthodox. But, after the Guomindang suppression forced the CCP to rely on rural base areas, Mao eventually emerged as the Communists' paramount leader.

The Importance of the Peasant Problem

During my recent visit to Hunan I made a first-hand investigation of conditions in the five counties of Hsiangtan (Xiangdan), Hsianghsiang (Xiangxiang), Hengshan, Liling and Changsha. In the thirty-two days from January 4 to February 5, I called together fact-finding conferences in villages and county towns, which were attended by experienced peasants and by comrades working in the peasant movement, and I listened attentively to their reports and collected a great deal of material. Many of the hows and whys of the peasant movement were the exact opposite of what the gentry in Hankow (Hankou) and Changsha are saying. I saw and heard of many strange things of which I had hitherto been unaware. I believe the same is true of many other places, too. All talk directed against the peasant movement must be speedily set right. All the wrong measures taken by the

83

revolutionary authorities concerning the peasant movement must be speedily changed. Only thus can the future of the revolution be benefited. For the present upsurge of the peasant movement is a colossal event. In a very short time, in China's central, southern and northern provinces, several hundred million peasants will rise like a mighty storm, like a hurricane, a force so swift and violent that no power, however great, will be able to hold it back. They will smash all the trammels that bind them and rush forward along the road to liberation. They will sweep all the imperialists, warlords, corrupt officials, local tyrants, and evil gentry into their graves. Every revolutionary party and every revolutionary comrade will be put to the test, to be accepted or rejected as they decide. There are three alternatives. To march at their head and lead them? To trail behind them, gesticulating and criticizing? Or to stand in their way and oppose them? Every Chinese is free to choose, but events will force you to make the choice quickly.

Get Organized!

The development of the peasant movement in Hunan may be divided roughly into two periods with respect to the counties in the province s central and southern parts where the movement has already made much headway. The first, from January to September of last year, was one of organization. In this period, January to June was a time of underground activity, and July to September, when the revolutionary army was driving out Chao Heng-ti (Zhao Hengdi), one of open activity. During this period, the membership of the peasant associations did not exceed 300,000–400,000, the masses directly under their leadership numbered little more than a million, there was as yet hardly any struggle in the rural areas, and consequently there was very little criticism of the associations in other circles. Since its members served as guides, scouts and carriers of the Northern Expeditionary Army, even some of the officers had a good word to say for the peasant associations. The second period, from last October to January of this year, was one of revolutionary action. The membership of the associations jumped to two million and the masses directly under their leadership increased to ten million. Since the peasants generally enter only one name for the whole family on joining a peasant association, a membership of two million means a mass following of about ten million. Almost half the peasants in Hunan are now organized. In counties like Hsiangtan, Hsianghsiang, Liuyang, Changsha, Liling, Ninghsiang (Ningxiang), Pingkiang (Pingjiang), Hsiangyin (Xiangyin), Hengshan, Hengyang, Leiyang, Chenhsien (Zhenxian) and Anhua, nearly all the peasants have combined in the peasant associations or have come under their leadership. It was on the strength of their extensive organization that the peasants went into action and within four months brought about a great revolution in the countryside, a revolution without parallel in history.

Down with the Local Tyrants and Evil Gentry!
All Power to the Peasant Associations!

The main targets of attack by the peasants are the local tyrants, the evil gentry and the lawless landlords, but in passing they also hit out against patriarchal ideas and institutions, against the corrupt officials in the cities and against bad practices and customs in the rural areas. In force and momentum the attack is tempestuous; those who bow before it survive and those who resist perish. As a result, the privileges which the feudal landlords enjoyed for thousands of years are being shattered to pieces. Every bit of the dignity and prestige built up by the landlords is being swept into the dust. With the collapse of the power of the landlords, the peasant associations have now become the sole organs of authority and the popular slogan "All power to the peasant associations" has become a reality. Even trifles such as a quarrel between husband and wife are brought to the peasant association. Nothing can be settled unless someone from the peasant association is present. The association actually dictates all rural affairs, and, quite literally, "whatever it says, goes." Those who are outside the associations can only speak well of them and cannot say anything against them. The local tyrants, evil gentry and lawless landlords have been deprived of all right to speak, and none of them dares even mutter dissent. In the face of the peasant associations' power and pressure, the top local tyrants and evil gentry have fled to Shanghai, those of the second rank to Hankow, those of the third to Changsha and those of the fourth to the county towns, while the fifth rank and the still lesser fry surrender to the peasant associations in the villages.

"Here's ten yuan. Please let me join the peasant association," one of the smaller of the evil gentry will say.
"Ugh! Who wants your filthy money?" the peasants reply.

Many middle and small landlords and rich peasants and even some middle peasants, who were all formerly opposed to the peasant associations, are now vainly seeking admission. Visiting various places, I often came across such people who pleaded with me, "Mr. Committeeman from the provincial capital, please be my sponsor!"

In the Ching (Qing) dynasty, the household census compiled by the local authorities consisted of a regular register and "the other" register, the former for honest people and the latter for burglars, bandits and similar undesirables. In some places the peasants now use this method to scare those who formerly opposed the associations. They say, "Put their names down in the other register!"

Afraid of being entered in the other register, such people try various devices to gain admission into the peasant associations, on which their minds are so set that they do not feel safe until their names are entered. But more often than not they are turned down flat, and so they are always on tenterhooks; with the doors of the association barred to them, they are like tramps without a home or, in rural parlance, "mere trash." In short, what was looked down upon four months ago as a "gang of peasants" has now become a most honorable institution. Those who formerly prostrated themselves before the power of the gentry now bow before the power of the peasants. No matter what their identity, all admit that the world since last October is a different one.

"It's Terrible!" or "It's Fine!"

The peasants revolt disturbed the gentry s sweet dreams. When the news from the countryside reached the cities, it caused immediate uproar among the gentry. Soon after my arrival in Changsha, I met all sorts of people and picked up a good deal of gossip. From the middle social strata upwards to the Kuomintang right-wingers, there was not a single person who did not sum up the whole business in the phrase, "It's terrible!" Under the impact of the views of the "It's terrible!" school then flooding the city, even quite revolutionary minded people became down-hearted as they pictured the events in the countryside in their mind's eye; and they were unable to deny the word "terrible." Even quite progressive people said, "Though terrible, it is inevitable in a revolution." In short, nobody could altogether deny the word "terrible." But, as already mentioned, the fact is that the great peasant masses have risen to fulfill their historic mission and that the forces of rural democracy have risen to overthrow the forces of rural feudalism. The patriarchal-feudal class of local tyrants, evil gentry and lawless landlords has formed the basis of autocratic government for thousands of years and is the cornerstone of imperialism, warlordism and corrupt officialdom. To overthrow these feudal forces is the real objective of the national revolution. In a few months the peasants have accomplished what

Dr. Sun Yat-sen wanted, but failed, to accomplish in the forty years he devoted to the national revolution. This is a marvelous feat never before achieved, not just in forty, but in thousands of years. It's fine. It is not "terrible" at all. It is anything but "terrible." "It's terrible!" is obviously a theory for combating the rise of the peasants in the interests of the landlords; it is obviously a theory of the landlord class for preserving the old order of feudalism and obstructing the establishment of the new order of democracy, it is obviously a counterrevolutionary theory. No revolutionary comrade should echo this nonsense. If your revolutionary viewpoint is firmly established and if you have been to the villages and looked around, you will undoubtedly feel thrilled as never before. Countless thousands of the enslaved—the peasants—are striking down the enemies who fattened on their flesh. What the peasants are doing is absolutely right; what they are doing is fine! "It's fine!" is the theory of the peasants and of all other revolutionaries. Every revolutionary comrade should know that the national revolution requires a great change in the countryside. The Revolution of 1911 did not bring about this change, hence its failure. This change is now taking place, and it is an important factor for the completion of the revolution. Every revolutionary comrade must support it, or he will be taking the stand of counter-revolution.

The Question of "Going too Far"

Then there is another section of people who say, "Yes, peasant associations are necessary, but they are going rather too far." This is the opinion of the middle-of-the-roaders. But what is the actual situation? True, the peasants are in a sense "unruly" in the countryside. Supreme in authority, the peasant association allows the landlord no say and sweeps away his prestige. This amounts to striking the landlord down to the dust and keeping him there. The peasants threaten, "We will put you in the other register!" They fine the local tyrants and evil gentry, they demand contributions from them, and they smash their sedan-chairs. People swarm into the houses of local tyrants and evil gentry who are against the peasant association, slaughter their pigs and consume their grain. They even loll for a minute or two on the ivory-inlaid beds belonging to the young ladies in the households of the local tyrants and evil gentry. At the slightest provocation they make arrests, crown the arrested with tall paper-hats, and parade them through the villages, saying, "You dirty landlords, now you know who we are!" Doing whatever they like and turning everything upside down, they have created a kind of terror in the countryside. This is what some people call "going too far," or "exceeding the proper limits in righting a wrong," or "really too much." Such talk may seem plausible, but in fact it is wrong. First, the local tyrants, evil gentry and lawless landlords have themselves driven the peasants to this. For ages they have used their power to tyrannize over the peasants and trample them underfoot; that is why the peasants have reacted so strongly. The most violent revolts and the most serious disorders have invariably occurred in places where the local tyrants, evil gentry and lawless landlords perpetrated the worst outrages. The peasants are clear-sighted. Who is bad and who is not, who is the worst and who is not quite so vicious, who deserves severe punishment and who deserves to be let off lightly—the peasants keep clear accounts, and very seldom has the punishment exceeded the crime. Secondly, a revolution is not a dinner party, or writing an essay, or painting a picture, or doing embroidery; it cannot be so refined, so leisurely and gentle, so temperate, kind, courteous, restrained and magnanimous. A revolution is an insurrection, an act of violence by which one class overthrows another. A rural revolution is a revolution by which the peasantry overthrows the power of the feudal landlord class. Without using the greatest force, the peasants cannot possibly overthrow the deep-rooted authority of the landlords which has lasted for thousands of years. The rural areas need a mighty revolutionary upsurge, for it alone can rouse the people in their millions to become a powerful force. All the actions mentioned here which have been labeled as "going too far" flow from the power of the peasants, which has been called forth by the mighty revolutionary upsurge in the countryside. It was highly necessary for such things to be done in the second period of the peasant movement, the period of revolutionary action. In this period it was necessary to establish the absolute authority of the peasants. It was necessary to forbid malicious criticism of the peasant associations. It was necessary to overthrow the whole authority of the gentry, to strike them to the ground and keep them there. There is revolutionary significance in all the actions which were labeled as "going too far" in this period. To put it bluntly, it is necessary to create terror for a while in every rural area, or otherwise it would be impossible to suppress the activities of the counter-revolutionaries in the countryside or overthrow the authority of the gentry. Proper limits have to be exceeded in order to right a wrong, or else the wrong cannot be righted. Those who talk about the peasants "going too far" seem at first sight to be different from those who say "It's terrible!" as mentioned earlier, but in essence they proceed from the same standpoint and likewise voice a landlord theory that upholds the interests of the privileged classes. Since this theory impedes the rise of the peasant movement and so disrupts the revolution, we must firmly oppose it. . . .

10

Collapse of Public Morale

A. DOAK BARNETT

After the Xian Incident in December 1936, the Communists and Nationalists (Guomindang) were ostensibly united in resistance Japanese aggression. Both sides harbored deep animosities and suspicions, but neither side was willing to break the alliance while China suffered under Japanese occupation. When Japan surrendered on August 15, 1945, however, the struggle for control quickly reemerged, and by 1947, China was engulfed in full-scale civil war. While costly military blunders hurt the Nationalists on the battlefield, maladministration, hyperinflation, and lack of trust in government were also responsible for the rapid collapse of the central government. A. Doak Barnett (1921–1999), a founding father of Chinese studies in America, was in China reporting on the civil war from 1947 to 1949. In this essay Barnett describes the erosion of popular support that hastened the demise of the Nationalist government.

As the battle for central China nears a climax in the Hsuchow (Xuzhou)-Pengpu (Pengbu) area, hysterical rumors and speculation pour out of the national capital. Contradictions and official denials make the news almost incomprehensible to the average reader, and Chinese distant from the centers of military and political activity must rely on guesswork to piece together a picture of what is happening to their government and their country in this national crisis.

One persistent rumor, persistently denied, claims that the Central Government is preparing to evacuate Nanking (Nanjing). Canton, Taiwan, Chungking (Chongqing), and Hengyang are mentioned as possible places of refuge for various branches of the government.

This rumor, and the obvious military threat to Nanking, has stimulated widespread discussion of what will happen if and when—and most people now believe it is a question of when rather than if—Nanking falls to the Communists. Will the Central Government attempt to move south as an intact unit? Will it attempt to reorganize and continue resistance to the Communists from new geographical bases? If the answer to these questions is affirmative, what are its chances of success?

At present it appears that if the Nationalists decide to shift their capital and continue fighting, the decision will be made at the last minute, and the move will be a disorganized scramble for safety. I was in Canton last week and saw no evidence that careful preparations had been made, or were under way, to receive a large influx of government personnel. Reports of such preparations in other possible evacuation centers are conspicuously lacking in press dispatches. In Nanking, furthermore government spokesmen continue to deny that any move is under consideration. These facts do not necessarily indicate that the government will not attempt to move. They do suggest, however, that if a move is made, it may be disorderly and uncoordinated.

The possibility of continuing military action against the Communists from a new Nationalist capital will depend in part upon the success with which public support can be mobilized and a spirit of resistance revived. In short, the general morale of people south of the Yangtze (Yangzi) River will become a vital element in the political situation in China, if Nanking falls.

Recently, I completed a trip by train and car through the provinces of Kiangsu (Jiangsu), Chekiang (Zhejiang), Kiangsi (Jiangxi), Hunan, and Kwangtung (Guangdong). Political demoralization in these areas is almost universal, and morale is incredibly low. Almost no spirit of resistance against the Communists remains, and faith in the Central Government seems to have vanished. I talked with people of many sorts-businessmen, educators, rickshaw coolies, civil servants, technicians, merchants. All were psychologically prepared for a basic shift of political control and a change of regime.

This low morale stems from numerous factors: the difficulty of ordinary living, a longing for peace and stability, and a growing mistrust of the Central Government, as well as the ominous reports from fighting fronts. Remarks such as "This can't go on" or "Any change will be for the better" are accompanied by solemn head shaking and dour expressions. The people with whom I talked face the future, and the prospect of a Communist-dominated government, with emotions that mix resignation, relief, and apprehension in varying degrees.

The "mood of the people" is an intangible thing that cannot be described in neat formulas or measurable terms. In China, the difficulty of defining the political mood is magnified by the scarcity of media of public expression. Whatever its validity elsewhere, the concept of "public opinion" is not generally applicable in China because the majority of the population is politically inarticulate. Furthermore, millions of people without access to reliable information have no clear-cut opinions about national political events. They react emotionally to such stimuli as grapevine rumors, incomplete news, distorted reports—and the local price of rice. They feel, rather than understand, political trends. The people I met between Shanghai and Canton feel that the time is ripe for a major political change in China. Even those who fear change seem to accept its inevitability with helpless resignation.

The literate, politically conscious minority in Nationalist China tries to obtain accurate information on current events, but can seldom find it in newspapers or elsewhere. The government's indirect censorship of news, whatever its motives, has discredited both the press and the government itself. "When Central News announces that a city has been 'saved,'" a railway engineer said to me, "we suspect that it has been lost or is about to fall." Cynicism, based on bitter past experience, is widespread. Lack of information is equally widespread. "What is going on in north China?" a group of Changsha professors and doctors asked when I was there. They were eager to hear a firsthand report from someone who might have access to reliable information. They knew nothing of the Communists' capture of Mukden, which had taken place nine days previously.

Many Chinese do not believe anything their government says now. When Generalissimo Chiang admits that it will take eight years to defeat the Communists, people remember irresponsible statements of a short while ago promising victory in six months. An increasing number of people feel that the Central Government has deceived and cheated them. The collapse of the recent economic reform program, more than anything else perhaps, has created public distrust of new government policies. Many people now regard the reforms as a clever fraud, a device whereby one kind of paper money was substituted for another as a means of gathering in the gold, silver, and foreign currency savings of the public. The number of people who are willing to make excuses for government mistakes and failures is decreasing.

Among government officials themselves, old patterns of thinking and acting persist, and as the general situation deteriorates, the public is less tolerant of them. Self-delusion, rationalization, and wishful thinking among officials and others closely allied to the Nationalist regime have often prevented them from attacking problems honestly and solving them efficiently. In the present gloomy political atmosphere, their wishful thinking is fast disappearing, but self-delusion and rationalization continue in the face of disaster. One of the most characteristic manifestations of these tendencies is the search for scapegoats and the refusal to accept blame for political failures or even to recognize failures.

"There are two main causes for the present economic chaos in China," a young government worker said to me in Nanchang, capital of Kiangsi Province. "One is President Truman's refusal to recognize the new Chinese currency. The other is manipulation of the black market in large cities by Russian agents and traitors hired by them." This young man refused to believe that the Central Government's economic reform measures might have been poorly conceived and implemented. He supported his "facts" with unquestionable "proof." In a speech two days previously, the most prominent Kuomintang leader in Kiangsi had explained the whole situation. Ordinary people who are not connected with the Nationalist Government are much less gullible, however, and they are openly showing their disapproval of the lack of honesty and frankness on the part of officials and politicos.

Facts such as these help to explain the loss of faith in the Central Government. They also help to explain the increasing credibility of claims and reports favorable to the Communists. "The Communists treated the people well after they took Tsinan [Jinan, capital of Shantung (Shandong)], a businessman said to me. "In fact, conditions improved remarkably after they took over." A weary pilot, on the train between Hankow (Hankou) and Canton, described the low morale of the unit he had just left in north China. He contrasted it with Communist morale. "The Communists," he said in partial explanation "take care of the families of their military men so that they don't have any personal worries." Statements such as these are made today by people who would have called them absurd propaganda a year ago.

I met very few people south of Nanking who would welcome the Nationalist Government with enthusiasm if it packs up and moves. The government's rear is psychologically weak and vulnerable. If an evacuation southward is made, the government will find itself in a region where people have already lost faith in the fight. It will encounter distrust. It may even encounter intense resentment and active opposition. With public morale at such low ebb, the job of mobilizing support and reviving a spirit of resistance against the Communists will be colossal—if it is possible at all.

11

American Exclusion Act, May 6, 1882

Since the recognition of Communist China and the reestablishment of diplomatic ties between China and the United States in 1979, Sino-American relations have ranged from mutual admiration to mutual recrimination. In many ways these developments have been consistent with the fluctuations in Sino-American affairs since the nineteenth century. Nineteenth-century American missionary accounts helped to shape popular perceptions of the Chinese as impoverished and pitiable souls in need of salvation. Poor Chinese laborers did migrate to California in the mid-nineteenth century, and many found work constructing the transcontinental railroad. But rather than foster mutual understanding, the presence of large communities of Chinese triggered a racial backlash that led to legislation outlawing the migration of Chinese laborers to America.

An act to execute certain treaty stipulations relating to Chinese.

Whereas, in the opinion of the Government of the United States, the coming of Chinese laborers to this country endangers the good order of certain localities within the territory thereof: Therefore,

Be it enacted by the Senate and House of Representatives of the United States of American in Congress assembled. That from and after the expiration of ninety days next after the passage of this act, and until the expiration of ten years next after the passage of this act, the coming of Chinese laborers to the United States be, and the same is hereby, suspended; and during such suspension it shall not be lawful for any Chinese laborer to come, or, having so come after the expiration of said ninety days, to remain within the United States.

SEC. 2. That the master of any vessel who shall knowingly bring within the United States on such vessel, and land or permit to be landed, any Chinese laborer, from any foreign port or place, shall be deemed guilty of a misdemeanor and on conviction thereof shall be punished by a fine of not more than five hundred dollars for each and every such Chinese laborer so brought, and may be also imprisoned for a term not exceeding one year. . . .

SEC. 8. That the master of any vessel arriving in the United States from any foreign port or place shall, at the same time delivers a manifest of the cargo and if there be no cargo, then at the time of making a report of the entry of the vessel pursuant to law, in addition to the other matter required to be reported, and before landing, or permitting to land, any Chinese passengers, deliver and report to the collector of customs of the district in which such vessel shall have arrived a separate list of all Chinese passengers taken on board his vessel at any foreign port or place, and all such passengers on board the vessel at that time.

Such lists shall show the names of such passengers (and if accredited officers of the Chinese Government traveling on the business of that Government or their servants, with a note of such facts), and the names and other particulars as shown by their respective certificates; and such list shall be sworn to by the master in the manner required by law in relation to the manifest of the cargo.

Any willful refusal or neglect of any such master to comply with the provisions of this section shall incur the same penalties and forfeiture as are provided for a refusal or neglect to report and deliver a manifest of the cargo.

SEC. 9. That before any Chinese passengers are landed from any such vessel, the collector or his deputy shall proceed to examine such passengers, comparing the certificates with the list and with the passengers, and no passenger shall be allowed to land in the United States from such vessel in violation of law.

SEC. 10. That every vessel whose master shall knowingly violate any of the provisions of this act shall be deemed forfeited to the United States, and shall be liable to seizure and condemnation in any district of the United States into which such vessel may enter or in which she may be found.

SEC. 11. That any person who shall knowingly bring into or cause to be brought into the United Stated by land or who shall knowingly aid or abet the same, or aid or abet the landing in the United States from any vessel of any Chinese person not lawfully entitled to enter the United States, shall be deemed guilty of a misdemeanor, and shall, on conviction thereof, be fined in a sum exceeding one thousand dollars, and imprisoned for a term not exceeding one year.

SEC. 12. That no Chinese person shall be permitted to enter the United States by land without producing to the proper officer of customs the certificate in this act required of Chinese persons seeking to land from a vessel.

And any Chinese person found unlawfully within the United States shall be caused to be removed therefrom to the country from whence he came, by direction of the President of the United States, and at the cost of the United States, after being brought before some justice, judge, or commissioner or a court of the United States and found to be one not lawfully entitled to be or remain in the United States.

SEC. 13. That this act shall not apply to diplomatic and other officers of the Chinese Government traveling upon the business of that Government, whose credentials shall be taken as equivalent to the certificate in this act mentioned, and shall exempt them and their body and household servants from the provisions of this act as to other Chinese persons.

SEC. 14. That hereafter no State court or court of the United States shall admit Chinese to citizenship; and all laws in conflict with this act are hereby repealed.

SEC. 15. That the words "Chinese laborers," wherever used in this act, shall be construed to mean both skilled and unskilled laborers and Chinese employed in mining.

Approved, May 6, 1882

12

Chinese Anti-Foreignism, 1892

Nineteenth-century Chinese perceptions of foreigners were often similarly inaccurate. Christian missionaries probably had the most extensive contacts with Chinese people, but this did not necessarily mean that they were better understood.

The Roman Catholic religion had its origin from Jesus, and is practiced by all the Western countries, and taught by them to others; it exhorts men to virtue. The founder was nailed by wicked men on a cross, and cut to death. His disciplines then scattered about the world to disseminate the doctrine. The Principal is called the Fa Wang Fu [the Kingly Father of the Doctrine]. Sexual congress without shame is called "a public meeting," or "a benevolent society." When they marry they use no go-between, and make no distinctions between old and young. Any man and woman who like may come together, only must first do obeisance to the bishop, and pray to Shangdi [God]. The bride must invariably first sleep with the spiritual teacher, who takes the first fruits of her virginity. . . . Two wives may not be taken, they say, because Shangdi created one man and one woman at first. In these countries therefore concubinage is not practiced, but no unchastity in other directions is forbidden. When a wife dies another may be had. When a father dies, his son may marry the mother who bore him. When a son dies, his father may marry the son's wife; and even his own daughter. Brothers, uncles, and nieces may intermarry promiscuously. Brothers and sisters of same parents also marry together.

Zhang Shoucai was a boat-tracker on the Hun river. A man named Liu informed him that by kidnapping little children and scooping out their hearts and eyes he could earn fifty taels a set.

A foreign devil at Canton went dropping poison down the wells at night. Every one fell ill of a strange disease, which could only be cured by foreign doctors. Untold numbers died. At last the Perfect found it out, arrested over thirty people, and put them all to death.

When these [foreign] devils open a chapel, they begin with their female converts by administering a pill. When they have swallowed it, they are beguiled, and allow themselves to be defiled. Then after the priest has outraged them, he recites an incantation. The *placenta* then is easily drawn out, and is chopped up to make an ingredient for their hocussing drugs.

At Tientsin they used constantly to beguile and entice away young children in order to scoop out their eyes and hearts. When the people discovered it, they tore down their tall foreign houses, and found heaped up inside bodies of kidnapped children, boys and girls.

All these facts should make us careful not to incur similar dangers. We should unite hands and hearts to keep out the evil before it is upon us.

His Excellency the Commander-in-chief for the Canton province.

Suggestions for Further Reading

Cheng, Pei-kai, and Michael Lestz. *The Search for Modern China: A Documentary Collection*. New York: W. W. Norton, 1999. This extensive collection of primary documents from the early Qing to the 1990s is clearly the best of its kind and an invaluable teaching resource.

Cohen, Warren I. *America's Response to China*. New York: Columbia University Press, 2000. The fourth edition of this classic work provides an up-to-date and historically grounded examination of the complex relationship between China and the United States.

De Bary, William Theodore, and Irene Bloom, eds. *Sources of Chinese Tradition: From the Earliest Times to 1600*. New York: Columbia University Press, 1999. Recently revised and updated, this landmark volume includes primary sources for premodern Chinese history, literature and religion.

Elvin, Mark, and Liu Ts'ui-jung, eds. *Sediments of Time: Environment and Society in Chinese History*. Cambridge: Cambridge University Press, 1998. This collection of essays by Western, Chinese, and Japanese scholars represents the latest scholarship on environmental change and its impact on Chinese society.

Friedman, Edward, Paul G. Pickowicz, and Mark Selden. *Chinese Village, Socialist State*. New Haven: Yale University Press, 1991. This well-balanced and highly readable study examines the impact of Communist policies in rural areas from land reform to the Great Leap Forward.

Hansen, Valerie. *The Open Empire: A History of China to 1600*. New York: W. W. Norton, 2000. Drawing on the latest archeological finds in China as well as other sources, Hansen's work takes an innovative and fresh approach to premodern Chinese history.

Huang, Ray. *1587: A Year of No Significance*. New Haven: Yale University Press, 1981. Written in a very engaging style, this book tells the story of the decline of traditional Chinese political institutions through biographical sketches of important historical figures of the late Ming dynasty.

Mackerras, Colin. *China's Minorities: Integration and Modernization in the Twentieth Century*. Oxford: Oxford University Press. This comprehensive look at Chinese minorities in the modern era introduces the complexities of ethnic identities and the politics of integration.

Mann, Susan. *Precious Records: Women in China's Long Eighteenth Century.* Stanford: Stanford University Press, 1997. This broad analysis of gender during the peak of the Qing dynasty (c.1683–1839) examines women's work, courtesan entertainment, and participation in ritual and religion.

Meisner, Maurice. *Mao's China and After.* New York: The Free Press, 1999. A standard work on the history of the People's Republic of China, the latest edition looks at events during the Deng era.

Mote Frederick W. *Imperial China, 900–1800.* Cambridge, MA: Harvard University Press, 2000. An absorbing panorama of late imperial history, Mote's work places special emphasis on conquest dynasties and Chinese adaptations to alien rule.

Pomeranz, Kenneth. *The Great Divergence: China, Europe, and the Making of the Modern World Economy.* Princeton: Princeton University Press, 2000. This path-breaking examination on Chinese economic history challenges standard "Euro-centric" approach to comparative economic history.

Schoppa, R. Keith. *The Columbia Guide to Modern Chinese History.* New York: Columbia University Press, 2000. This useful reference includes a narrative of modern Chinese history; a compendium of 250 short articles describing events, institutions, and important persons; annotated guide to print, video, and Internet resources; a chronology of key events; and primary documents.

Spence, Jonathan. *The Search for Modern China.* New York: W. W. Norton, 1999. Revised and updated, Spence's volume provides a comprehensive history of modern China from the late Ming dynasty to the post-Deng era.

Wills, John E., Jr. *Mountain of Fame: Portraits in Chinese History.* Princeton: Princeton University Press, 1994. In this engaging work Wills uses short biographies of important figures, such as Empress Wu, the Qianlong Emperor, and Mao Zedong, to explore Chinese history from earliest time to the twentieth century.

Websites

www.ukans.edu/history/VL/east_asia/china.html. Part of the World Wide Web Virtual Library, this metasite is an essential starting point for the geography and history of China. It provides many useful links to maps, historical maps, images, bibliographies, primary texts, and overviews of Chinese history.

Part 2

POLITICS

Edited by Bruce Dickson

INTRODUCTION
Bruce Dickson

The leader of China's Communist revolution, Mao Zedong, once said, "A revolution is not a dinner party, or writing an essay, or painting a picture, or doing embroidery; it cannot be so refined, so leisurely and gentle, so temperate, kind, courteous, restrained and magnanimous. A revolution is an insurrection, an act of violence by which one class overthrows another." By the time the civil war was over in 1949, China had suffered more than a century of decline, due to both internal problems and foreign encroachment. As Chairman Mao declared in Beijing in fall 1949, after the revolution was won, China had finally stood up for itself. But the problems the country faced after many years of war were numerous and severe. While Mao and the Chinese Communist Party (CCP) were committed to the eventual establishment of communism in China, upon taking power they had three immediate and more practical goals.

The first goal was *national unification*. After decades of disunion, China needed to reintegrate its fractured society. China had long been a unified country, but after being carved into sections occupied by the Japanese, Guomindang (Nationalists), and Communist armies, plus areas controlled by warlords, the first task was to create a unified country and system of government. Although the civil war had essentially ended in 1949, mopping-up operations in the south and western border areas lasted into the early 1950s.

The second goal was *transformation*. Mao and the CCP leadership were determined to carry out a revolution of the political and social system, which they viewed as the ultimate cause of China's backwardness. In some ways, the revolution only truly *began* in 1949, after the civil war had ended. During the 1950s, the CCP implemented land reform on a nationwide basis, overthrowing the traditional hold of landlords over the rest of the rural society and giving land to the peasants. It implemented a new marriage law that outlawed traditional arranged marriages. The marriage law was designed not only to enhance the rights of women, but also to break down the traditional power of clans and heads of families. It also banned opium and prostitution, putting addicts and prostitutes into rehabilitation centers where their medical problems were addressed and they were taught new skills. China's new leaders believed that political and social revolution was critical to successful economic modernization. None of these initial changes were distinctly socialist, however. Private property was still permitted and protected, the CCP cooperated with those outside the Party in setting policy priorities, and the CCP relied upon many of the former officials from the defeated Nationalist government to implement the new policies. The truly socialist transformation of the economy and society did not begin until the mid-1950s, when the other immediate goals were accomplished.

The third task was *modernization*. This entailed both economic recovery—especially ending inflation and restoring agricultural and industrial production to their levels before the Japanese invasion—and economic development, using the Soviet model of rapid industrialization and a centrally planned economy. Mao wanted China to be recognized as a great power among nations. But this could be realized only if the other two goals were accomplished first.

Oscillation between Economics and Ideology

Party policy in the Maoist period therefore oscillated between economic development and the ideological goal of creating a Communist society in which there would be no exploitation and an abundance of goods and services would be available for distribution to the population on a relatively equitable basis. When economic development was the primary goal, Party and state policies emphasized production goals and allowed a limited amount of private enterprise and market activity, permitting people to make a little money on the side which created incentives for more production. They emphasized technical skills in personnel matters and minimized the intrusiveness of political campaigns. In contrast, when ideological goals were paramount, Party-state policies prohibited or greatly constrained the markets, political campaigns became more coercive and dangerous, and economic growth suffered.

Mao was the champion of both sets of policies, and he shifted between the two as he felt national conditions mandated. Policy did not change without Mao's consent: his support was necessary for policy decisions, and in fact any change of heart he manifested could well trigger a change of goals or policies. As a result, China lurched back and forth between these divergent goals of development and ideological propriety as long as Mao lived. As time went on, Mao seemed to favor ideological goals above all else. He wanted to modernize

China, but for him, the means were as important as the ends. Mao was more concerned with questions of equity than he was with growth per se. His supporters often said it was better to be poor and Communist than rich and capitalist.

Key episodes in the post-1949 history of China are impossible to understand without appreciating Mao's central role in the political system. In fact, in 1953 the CCP's Central Committee passed a resolution that required Mao's personal approval on all decisions made by the Politburo and Central Committee. In 1987 the Central Committee passed a similar secret resolution, this time granting Deng Xiaoping, Mao's successor as supreme leader, the final say on all major decisions. Both resolutions violated not only democratic procedures but also the Party's traditional norms of consensual decision making. Nevertheless, they reflect the preeminent authority these two men held within China's political system.

During the Maoist period three major episodes occurred in which policy shifted from economic development to communist ideological goals. The first came with the collectivization of industry and agriculture in 1955. During the early years of the People's Republic, the CCP led a nominal coalition government (although the non-Communist members of the government were hand-picked by the CCP) and pledged to moderate its revolutionary goals. But by the mid-1950s, the CCP had consolidated power, eliminated its rivals, and restored the economy to pre-war production levels. It then decided to eliminate all remaining private ownership of land and capital, confiscate factories and stores (although the former owners were often retained as managers), and organize peasants into "agricultural production cooperatives" to farm larger plots of land in a collective fashion. This turning point was of major significance in Party policy: the CCP's basis for popular support had been its land reform policies, and now the land that had just recently been given to the poorest peasants was being taken away. The new policies on industry and agriculture also created a greater role for the Party: it had to coordinate production and make sure that its policies were implemented.

The Hundred Flowers Movement followed the collectivization of agriculture and industry in 1957. Mao invited criticism of the Party's performance from experts and intellectuals, confident that his policy successes so far had created considerable enthusiasm and support for the regime. He expected mild criticism of the bureaucratic work style of some Party and government officials, in line with his own view that the conservative nature of bureaucracies would inevitably slow progress toward the nation's development. Mao felt the government was composed of bureaucrats who, as he put it, behaved like women with bound feet, tottering along taking small steps, afraid to take bold strides. What he got instead was a stream of complaints about the fundamental

COLLECTIVES — HIGHLY EFFICIENT IN THEORY
BUT WITHOUT PERSONAL GAIN
DOOMED TO FAIL.

106 POLITICS

nature of the political system; about the absence of democracy, the rule of law, free expression, and free scientific inquiry; about Party interference in all areas of life, and, above all, about the intrusion of incompetent and illiterate Party ideologues into the work of the experts.

Mao seems to have been genuinely taken aback by the vehemence of the intellectuals' complaints. But rather than address their concerns, he labeled them "rightists," a term akin to counter-revolutionary and a very serious crime. He then launched an Anti-Rightist campaign to persecute them and replaced many of them with his own political supporters. The Anti-Rightist campaign alienated most of China's intellectuals and made them wary of voicing their political views again.

Following the Anti-Rightist campaign, a second episode promoting ideological goals began to take shape. After disregarding the concerns of China's experts, Mao decided to tap into the latent energy of the masses to create economic growth. The Party would encourage people to work harder, not with higher wages as incentive, but with propaganda and persuasion. This campaign became known as the Great Leap Forward (1958–1959), the period when communes were created. Communes were large-scale economic and administrative units, each combining ten or more villages. Work teams were sent out to mobilize the efforts of peasants and organize their work. Sometimes the peasants would be required to work twenty-four hour shifts of intensive labor. At first, the Great Leap policies appeared to be working: most communes reported a bumper harvest, and the counties and provinces began competing with one another to claim the highest production achievements, thereby proving that they were the most loyal to Mao, even though they knew their claims were false. Nightly dinners became banquets at the communes' mess halls as people tried to eat up the excess food, thinking there was too much to actually harvest and transport to urban areas. But in fact, the harvest fell far below projections. Much of the grain that would normally have been stored for the winter and for spring planting was eaten in the summer and fall. By 1959 it became clear that the country was in deep trouble. Economic forecasts were drastically downgraded. Reports of unrest in the countryside and general unhappiness with the mass mobilization tactics of the Great Leap Forward circulated among the Party leadership. The policy excesses and unusually bad weather created a crisis of huge proportions. During the "three bad years" of 1960–1962, close to 30 million people died as a consequence of the failed Great Leap policies.

The calamity of the Great Leap Forward resulted in a full-scale retreat from its policies and a period of recovery that lasted for several years. Once again, restoring order with careful central planning and increasing production through the use of financial incentives became official policy. Private plots, banned with the creation of the communes, once again were approved. These plots allowed farmers to grow a little extra fruit and vegetables for themselves and to sell for extra cash. Mao grudgingly tolerated these recovery policies, recognizing that they were necessary to relieve the severe crisis facing his country. But he was unwilling to accept them long-term, for fear they would restore capitalism to China and because they minimized the role of his supporters and, not incidentally, his own influence in central planning.

In 1966 Mao launched the Great Proletarian Cultural Revolution, the third episode of striving to achieve ideological goals. Mao had become convinced that the Party had lost its revolutionary fervor and had become hostile to him personally, as well as to his policies. He believed that many Party members, overly concerned with economics, including recovery from the Great Leap, had forgotten the goals and methods of revolution. Moreover, he felt that the younger generation of China, which had not been tempered in the furnace of revolution, would benefit from the struggle and chaos that revolution generates. He therefore encouraged young people, especially students, to form groups of Red Guards to attack, verbally and physically, representatives of the Party and state: local leaders, teachers, factory managers, and even high-ranking Party leaders and cabinet ministers.

The Red Guards did attack people who exercised or symbolized power, along with anyone else suspected of disloyalty to Mao. They fanned out over China bearing copies of the "little red book" of Mao's choice quotations, which they used to harangue people in lengthy propaganda sessions in factories, on farms, and out in the streets. They broke into Party and government offices where they found and published information that supposedly revealed the anti-Maoist activities of the officeholders. They held public "struggle" sessions, in which selected individuals were harshly criticized and subjected to beatings, imprisonment, even death. Some committed suicide. Targets included many who had fought in the civil war alongside Mao and whose involvement in the CCP went back to the 1930s. Deng Xiaoping, Mao's eventual successor, was publicly humiliated, removed from his high-ranking Party posts, and sent to work as a common laborer for several years. One of his sons was permanently paralyzed after he fell from a high window during an interrogation by Red Guards. Most schools and government offices closed down, and most regular activities ceased; all but one of China's ambassadors were called home. Economic production was disrupted for several years.

After being nearly destroyed between 1966–1969, the Party had to be rebuilt. Although weakened by intense factional conflict at all levels, from society's point of view the Party was stronger than ever. The Cultural Revolution had ensured that virtually every aspect of life had political implications, from opinions about Mao and the Party to the clothing one wore, hairstyles, and one's taste in books and music. Even owning a pet was considered a "bourgeois" affectation. It was a period of political correctness run rampant, with decisions about jobs, housing, access to food, and opportunities to travel or see a play determined by the local Party committee.

Just as the Great Leap Forward was an economic disaster, the Cultural Revolution was a political disaster. Many of China's best qualified and most experienced leaders were falsely accused of various crimes, removed from their posts, put in prison or sent to remote areas of China to perform menial tasks. Eventually many of these people were brought back to their old posts, but they were forced to work alongside the very people who had accused them and caused their suffering.

The Cultural Revolution was a turning point for many of China's citizens. By the time Mao died in 1976, a crisis of confidence was in process, a feeling that the Party and government were no longer legitimate. Many came to believe that the Cultural Revolution was not about revolutionary goals at all, but just a cynical struggle for power among Party leaders. Ironically, the Cultural Revolution also taught people that they should question the authority of their leaders; after all, Mao had told them to do so, and their own experience verified that many officials should indeed be criticized. This was not the result Mao had intended. Contrary to Mao's desires, many Chinese came to believe it was not necessary to assume the leadership always knew what was best, or that they had the best interests of society at heart. For a country ruled by a Leninist party, such ideas could only undermine the Party's ability to rule.

Each swing toward ideological goals enhanced the power of the Party and widened the scope of its jurisdiction. By the end of the Cultural Revolution, the CCP had assumed almost all the government's responsibilities, and no social organizations capable of challenging it existed. But at the same time, society had grown weary of the incessant political campaigns and frequent swings of policy. People had become disillusioned by a political system that seemed intrusive, arbitrary, inconsistent, and unresponsive to society's desire for a higher standard of living. With Mao's death in 1976, an opportunity arose to change the style and direction of policy fundamentally.

RETREAT FROM IDEOLOGY!

Politics in the Reform Era

Chairman Mao died in September 1976, and just a month later the main advocates of his ideologically motivated policies—a group known as the "Gang of Four," which included Mao's widow—were arrested following a brief succession struggle. A new consensus soon emerged: the ideological goals of the Maoist era had to be abandoned for the sake of economic development. This decision was reaffirmed at a historic Central Committee meeting in December 1978. Henceforth, the Party would abandon class struggle as its main task and the victims of past political campaigns would be rehabilitated. More importantly, the Party would concentrate its energies on economic modernization and adjust its policy choices and selection of personnel with this goal in mind. Throughout the post-Mao period, the Party's ability to foster economic growth, rather than its ideology or the charisma of its leader, has been the basis of its legitimacy.

In the 1980s Party leaders identified a series of problems inherited from the Maoist period and attempted reforms to remedy them, but with mixed results.

The first problem concerned the over-concentration of power. Most Chinese leaders agreed that Mao wielded too much power, so their solution was to create a collective leadership and prevent any one individual from dominating the political system. Although Deng Xiaoping was the paramount leader from 1978 until his death in 1997, he did not have the charisma that had allowed Mao to intimidate his fellow leaders. As noted earlier, in 1987 the Party secretly granted Deng authority to approve all major decisions, but he did not enjoy the level of authority that had allowed Mao to prevail even when most other leaders opposed him. Consequently, Deng had to work to forge and maintain a consensus behind his policy preferences, and he was forced to abandon some policies when faced with opposition from his colleagues. Although he never held the top post in either the Party or the government, symbolizing his commitment to collective leadership, he was nevertheless recognized as China's preeminent leader until his death in 1997. His successor, Jiang Zemin, had even less authority over his colleagues and had to work hard to build support among the Party, the government, and the military. The title of Party chairman was abolished because it was so closely identified with Mao and because there were no suitable checks on its power. Instead, the post of general secretary was created to provide an individual leader for the Party, but not one with unchecked authority.

At lower levels, efforts were made to distinguish the Party from the government more clearly. The Party was to limit itself to making major strategic decisions, allowing the government to devise and implement specific policies.

To this end limits were set on the number of concurrent posts top Party leaders could hold. During the Maoist period, for instance, the top Party leader in a province was also its governor, and the top Party leader in a city was also its mayor. Beginning in the 1980s, these posts were separated and held by different people. This produced mixed results. For one thing, all key positions, with rare and usually symbolic exceptions, were still held by Party members, and Party committees remained more powerful than their government counterparts. In fact, after the 1989 student demonstrations (for a detailed analysis of these, see reading 13), efforts to separate the Party and the government were rolled back because Party leaders believed the Party had become too weak as a consequence.

Another problem inherited from the Maoist era was the lack of formal institutions. Because Mao preferred to rule by virtue of his charismatic authority, formal government institutions became virtually meaningless during his regime. In the post-Mao period, reforms were implemented to emphasize collective decision making and restore the regular operation of those formal bodies. For instance, the Politburo, comprised of the top twenty to twenty-five leaders of the CCP, had fallen into disuse under Mao, but in the post-Mao era it began to meet regularly again. The National People's Congress, China's nominal legislature, which had been a "rubber stamp" parliament during the Maoist years, automatically approving whatever the Party decided, became rejuvenated during the post-Mao period, passing a variety of laws that it drafted, debated, and revised, and overseeing government operations. In addition, the decision making process has been opened up to a wider variety of people. A handful of people at the top still make the most important decisions, but now they consult with government officials, experts, local leaders, and others whose opinions are valued or who will be affected by the decision. Moreover, instead of making decisions in secret, top leaders hold regular conferences to share ideas and circulate drafts of major policies several times before making a final decision. However, the personal attributes of individual leaders, their connections with other leaders, and their reputations as revolutionaries remain more important than their formal posts. In fact, during the 1980s and 1990s, a group of "elders" constituted the true center of political power in China, even though they had formally retired from their Party and government posts. They continued to shape policy and personnel from behind the scenes and through their younger protégés. The clearest example of this was the 1987 decision giving Deng authority over all major decisions.

Another key task of the Party has been the rejuvenation of its own organization. At the end of the Maoist era, the Party had about 35 million members, up from fewer than 5 million in 1949. Fewer than 5 percent were under 25 years of age, compared with about 25 percent in 1949. The majority were still poorly educated: 45 percent had only a primary education, and 11 percent were illiterate. This educational profile was an improvement over 1949, when 95 percent were illiterate or had only a primary education, but it was hardly adequate to modern needs. Party members were not sufficiently educated to handle the technical matters of economic modernization. In addition, most Party members had been recruited during periods when the CCP was pursuing ideological goals rather economic development and therefore had dubious professional qualifications and political inclinations opposed to the new reform agenda. In short, by the time Deng Xiaoping took control, Party members on the whole were too old, too uneducated, and too radical. This state of affairs led to a change in recruitment policies. Although it came to power relying on the support of peasants, workers, and soldiers, the CCP today is a broad-based party, drawing its members from all walks of life. In particular the CCP began to target the young and educated, the new elites of the reform era. By 2000, the Party had grown to over 63 million members, which is only 5 percent of China's population but exceeds the population of many countries in the world. Almost half have a high school or college education (up from 27 percent in 1978), and over 22 percent are under thirty-five. Women constitute a higher percentage of Party members than during the Maoist years, but still account for less than 20 percent of all members.

These changes have led to inevitable conflicts. Veteran cadres resisted the reforms, recognizing that their political skills were taking second place to professionalization. There was strong ideological opposition to letting people formerly designated as "rightists" into the Party, especially the newly emerging class of private entrepreneurs. In 1989, after the imposition of martial law, the Party imposed a ban on the admission of private entrepreneurs into the Party and the appointment of entrepreneurs already in the Party to official positions. This ban was widely ignored at the local level, however, where local leaders appealed to successful entrepreneurs to join the Party. Finally in 2001, Jiang Zemin recommended lifting the ban, recognizing both that the Party needed them to fulfill its economic goals and also that the ban had proven ineffective. This change in policy reflected sweeping changes throughout Chinese society: the CCP no longer claims to represent just the workers and peasants, its traditional bases of support, but all those who are working for the economic, technological, and cultural modernization of China. Moreover, many in the Party, including top officials and their family members, are deeply enmeshed in the private sector, leading many outside the Party to complain that the benefits of economic reform are not being distributed equitably, but are being enjoyed mostly by the politically privileged. Although some die-hards continue to criticize the abandonment of the Party's traditional ideological goals for the sake of economic development, the change now seems irreversible.

Another challenge to rejuvenating the Party has been the lack of enthusiasm about joining it. Throughout the reform era, the CCP has continued to lose prestige, and many of its own members do not support it. Society as a whole has lost faith in socialist ideals and no longer responds to ideological appeals. Nevertheless, the Party remains an effective distributor of jobs, education, and travel opportunities and provides special access to loans, technology, and markets, along with other valuable goods and services. Party membership is still a valuable asset, even to those who do not believe in Communist ideology.

These various efforts to retreat from the excesses of the Maoist years were done to reconcile the Party with society. Party leaders recognized they had lost much of their prestige and public support during the Cultural Revolution by trying to micromanage all aspects of daily life. In the post-Mao period, they have tried to limit the scope of politics. For instance, the Party now allows the performance of a greater array of plays and music and publication of a broader array of literature. It is now possible to read traditional novels or listen to Western music without being accused of being a counterrevolutionary. Traditional festivals and customs have reappeared, especially in the countryside. New social organizations have been allowed to form as long as they are not politically oriented. In recent years, China has witnessed an explosion of chambers of commerce, sports leagues, hobby groups, professional associations for writers, teachers, and businessmen, and other types of civic and professional groups. The foundations of a civil society are increasingly emerging, albeit under the ever-watchful eye of the Communist authorities.

The more open political and social atmosphere has made Western ideas and products more readily available in China (reading 14). At the same time, a resurgence of nationalist ideas, often critical of the West and its treatment of China, has taken shape. As Andrew Nathan shows, many Chinese resent American criticism of China's human rights record, question whether the Western norms of human rights should be applicable to China's current level of development, and wonder if the West really cares about human rights or simply wants to meddle in China's domestic affairs (reading 15). The idea that China has suffered repeated humiliations at the hands of the West, going back to the Opium War and continuing today with the "demonization" of China is widespread, and has grown in popularity since the mid-1990s (reading 16). At times, the government stokes these nationalist feelings, but it is also wary of them. Several times in

China's recent history, anti-foreign protests turned into anti-government demonstrations when people decided the government was too weak to stand up to foreign pressures. The CCP wants to use nationalism to help legitimize its rule, but does not want nationalist sentiments to get out of control and become a challenge to its policies.

State-Society Relations in China

Several fundamental features characterize relations between state and society in China. First of all, China's one-party system allows no organized opposition. The CCP guards its political monopoly zealously. One of its primary goals has been to prevent the organization of any group outside its control. To this end the CCP operates a network of Party cells throughout the government, the military, and society to monitor compliance with Party policies. All labor unions, student organizations, professional associations, and even religious groups must be sanctioned by the government and its leaders are subject to official approval. Even China's so-called "democratic parties" have Communist Party cells. The Party proscribes autonomous trade unions, student groups, political parties, and religious organizations like the Roman Catholic Church, which is banned in China because its priests are loyal to the Pope in Rome, not to the leaders in Beijing. Any attempt to form these kinds of autonomous organizations is immediately squashed and its leaders punished with often lengthy prison sentences.

Because of this absence of autonomous social organizations, limited channels of communication exist between state and society. China developed the "mass line" concept during the early revolutionary period when the Communist Party competed with landlords and the Nationalist government for popular support: The state gets information from the masses in order to create correct policies, and it then communicates these policies back to the masses. But after 1949, the Party had clinched the competition for popular support, and the need to solicit public opinion as a guide to policy became less important. The concept of the mass line remained, but became ritualized. Citizens discovered the high price of offering opinions contrary to state policy, and instead learned to recite current slogans.

As in pluralist societies, individuals can write letters or visit newspapers or government offices to complain. Most papers have investigative departments to look into reports of official corruption, workplace problems, housing complaints, and so on. As long as people complain only about the improper implementation of policy, their grievances are likely to be resolved. However, they cannot question the merits of the policy itself or its general impact.

Moreover, the newspapers and other forms of media are themselves owned by the state, which obviously limits their effectiveness as a form of feedback on the state's performance. During the Maoist era, the media did not provide objective information, but only the Party's current propaganda line. By doing this, however, it imparted important clues about how to think and behave. Even today, Chinese media reports rarely break news of scandal, the abuse of power, poor governmental performance, or other exposés that people living in democracies have come to expect of their media.

Because the Chinese Party-state allows no organized opposition and imposes limits on the flow of information, it is largely free to decide for itself what policy should be. It makes decisions in secret, and its officials are not subject to voter approval. Nor are they held accountable to the population through such democratic mechanisms as citizen initiatives, referendums, and the recall of unacceptable office-holders. The results of policy cannot be assessed through citizen feedback because reliable information on public opinion is often lacking and the danger of punishment has stifled much public criticism of top Chinese leaders and their policies, although criticisms are quite common in private. But this does not mean that the state always gets what it wants: bureaucratic inertia, lower-level resistance, and outright evasion are common and prevent new policies from being implemented in a timely and proper fashion.

The law and the legal system play different roles in China than they do in a democracy. Democracies are based on the rule *of* law, and both state and society are bound by the same laws. Many of our laws are designed to restrict the ability of the state to interfere in our private lives. At least in theory, the courts enforce these laws, preventing the state from infringing on individual rights and civil liberties. This concept is very foreign in China, where the system is more aptly described as rule *by* law; laws are tools of governance, but they do not restrict the scope of the state's actions. A legal code was not adopted until the late 1970s, thirty years after the founding of the PRC, and many laws and regulations remain secret or are revised at the discretion of China's leaders to meet current needs. Moreover, there is no independent judiciary to mediate public and private disputes; the courts are an arm of the state, not an independent branch of government in a checks-and-balance system. For major cases, such as those against the student demonstrators in 1989 or against organizers of opposition parties and independent labor unions, the Party determines verdicts and sentences in advance. In short, individual citizens have little recourse if they become targets of state actions.

Nevertheless, relations between the state and society have generally improved during the post-Mao period. First, most victims of past political campaigns had their verdicts overturned; they were rehabilitated and assigned new jobs, and the old political labels of "rightist" and the like used to stigmatize them in the past were removed. People no longer receive punishment for actions that used to be considered political crimes, and many have regained their lost reputations and status. The use of mass campaigns as a way of implementing new policies has been drastically reduced in number and intensity. With a few notable exceptions, such as the "one child per family" population-control program and the campaign to eliminate the Falun Gong spiritual movement (reading 17), the Party uses less intrusive and drastic methods to implement its policies. Daily life has been "depoliticized," and a range of activities once prohibited or proscribed are now possible again. However, the boundary between the permissible and the prohibited is often unclear and subject to change. Finally, there are more opportunities for a lively cultural and social life without political overtones. This has stimulated an outpouring of new literature, the resurgence of traditional culture, and importation of many Western goods and values. In part this last is a product of the desire to make money and to provide a model for China's future. The result has been more color and variety, but also fears that China is losing its traditional identity and straying too far from Communist ideals.

In addition, Deng Xiaoping's economic reforms undermined the state's control over society. This effect was largely intentional. As noted earlier, Deng and other leaders had learned first-hand during the Cultural Revolution about the irrationality and arbitrariness of the political system they helped create. They recognized that the state had become too intrusive and only inhibited development rather than fostering it. With more goods and services available on the free market thanks to the reforms, with jobs being created in a small but growing private sector, and with expanding opportunities, even encouragement, to make money, citizens became less dependent upon the approval of local officials. During the Maoist period, housing, education, medicine, and welfare were all tied to the workplace; if you were fired, you no longer had access to any of these important goods and services. You therefore had to cultivate good relations with your superiors, especially the Party boss, to make sure you got your share of these scarce goods and services. But now the market gives people more options. The state cannot threaten to withhold things it does not control, and hence individuals have become less dependent upon it.

In fact, the reverse is now often the case. Many local officials are some-what dependent on local businessmen. Rewards and promotions are increasingly based on local economic performance, and the fastest-growing sectors are not the state-owned enterprises, but private and collectively owned enterprises. Local officials now cooperate with businessmen to help them succeed: they procure loans, find inputs and markets for goods, give tax breaks, protect local firms from outside competition, and carry out similar activities to promote economic growth in their communities.

Moreover, the CCP has sponsored the creation of numerous civic and professional associations both to liberalize social life and to promote economic development. As the state pulled back from micromanaging society and operating a centrally planned economy, it created new organizations to link it with key sectors of society. Even during the Maoist era, China had organizations for certain officially recognized groups such as workers, women, and youth, but these organizations were generally seen as "transmission belts" that monitored and enforced state policy toward these groups but had little ability to represent the interests of their nominal members or to influence policy. In the post-Mao era, the state has allowed new organizations to form and has even permitted the older organizations to represent their members more actively. China now has a great variety of associations for businessmen, for specific professions such as software writers, factory managers, lawyers, etc., for various religions and traditional practices, and many others. However, there are still no independent trade unions.

Most of these organizations have been created, or at least approved, by the state, and many are headed by government officials. For instance, local branches of the Industrial and Commercial Federation, whose members include the largest of China's manufacturing and commercial enterprises, are normally led by the government official in charge of "united front work," which handles relations between the CCP and non-Party individuals and groups. Their offices are often located in the government compound. In addition, only one organization exists for any given profession or activity. Where two groups with similar interests have sprung up in a community, local officials will force them to merge or will disband one in favor of the other. This practice prevents competition between the associations and limits how many are allowed to exist, making it easier for the state to monitor and control them.

Are these new associations like the transmission belts of old, or are they able to truly represent the interests of their members? The state's strategy in allowing them to exist is to provide a means for indirect leadership over the economy and society, in contrast to the direct Maoist penetration into all aspects of economic and social life. The state's goal is not to relinquish power, but to "give up control to gain power." Nevertheless, the associations are not simply loyal agents of the state. Business associations try to balance their mission of representing the state's interests with the desire of their members to have an organized voice that can address business-related problems. They even to try to influence the local implementation of policy. The leaders of these associations, though they are also government officials, often begin to identify with the interests of their members and use the associations to increase their own authority relative to other officials.

This growth of civic and professional organizations in China has created a great deal of excitement among outside observers. Many see them as forming the foundation of a civil society, which is a key component of liberal democratic government. The emergence and spread of such organizations in China may facilitate a transition from authoritarian rule to democracy, but democratization is not the only possible outcome. As Margaret Pearson describes, a key component of civil society is autonomy from the state (reading 18), and that element is missing in China. In fact, members of these associations do not seek autonomy, because they recognize that, in China's political system, being autonomous means being powerless and inconsequential. Instead, they want to be embedded in the state in order to increase their influence. The nongovernmental associations serve as links between the state and society: the state is unwilling to allow them autonomy, and the associations do not seek it.

But there have been few political changes comparable to the economic and social changes of the post-Mao period. Opportunities for political participation are still limited and the risks remain high. One reason is the legacy of the Cultural Revolution: every episode of mass political expression, whether the goals are greater government responsiveness or more citizen representation, has been categorized by Party leaders as resembling Red Guard activities and is therefore quickly repressed. All demands from society for political change have been met with a tightening of Party controls and a retreat from political reform. Although political reform has its supporters within the CCP, they have been on the defensive since the violent repression of popular demonstrations in 1989. Indeed, there is even concern among Party leaders and society at large that post-Mao reforms have created economic and social freedoms that will lead to political instability, and chaos is perhaps the greatest fear of China's traditional political culture.

Political Participation in China

In the United States and most democracies, political participation is primarily voluntary and spontaneous. People may join interest groups, donate time or money to a cause they support, sign petitions on various policy issues, write letters to their elected representatives or a newspaper, and take a variety of other actions to make their views known to policymakers and other influential observers. In nondemocratic countries, this kind of political participation is often risky or even illegal. Rather than allow spontaneous activities, authoritarian states often formally organize activities to support their policies and strictly limit society's opportunities to influence policymaking.

During the Maoist era, most participation was mobilized by the state. China underwent periodic mass political campaigns to both educate society on current policy and to promote proper implementation. Often a campaign occurred when policy changed suddenly, as when the Anti-Rightist Movement followed the Hundred Flowers Campaign, or when the Cultural Revolution began. People were expected to study the new policies and the propaganda that accompanied them, to learn the new slogans, internalize the new Party line, and change their behavior accordingly. They were not allowed to be passive: it was not enough to be quiet or to avoid politics. Instead, everyone was required to actively support the new policy in word and deed. However, people were *not* expected to question the new policy or its goals, to compare the results of the new policies with the past, or criticize their leaders for changing policy. The purpose of mobilization was to have people publicly affirm their support for a new policy, even if inwardly they do not agree with it.

In the post-Mao period, the campaign style of policy implementation has generally been abandoned, and the state has tried to be less intrusive in most aspects of social life. There are exceptions, of course: the state resorted to these old tactics after the violent end of the 1989 demonstrations and again beginning in the summer of 1999 against the Falun Gong spiritual movement. But the general theme of the reform era has been a state pullback from direct involvement in most activities, including the economy, social life, and even politics. People are no longer required to voice their approval of all policies, denounce the old policies and the leaders who promoted them, or refer to the ideology as the measure of correct policies. Instead, they have been encouraged to experiment to find the set of policies best suited to promoting economic development and improved standards of living.

In addition, there are now more opportunities for people to sound off on political issues spontaneously. Writing letters to national newspapers to report on local problems, such as corruption or the abuse of authority by local officials, is common. In the post-Mao period the state seems to have taken a greater interest in investigating these allegations than in the past. More recent forms of political participation include lodging complaints, relying on the courts, and voting for local leaders. Chinese citizens can now make certain kinds of complaints about local conditions to higher levels of government with some hope of having the situation corrected. Through the sheer process of lodging complaints, people are becoming better versed in official policy and using that knowledge to further their cause. A village may send a team to the county government, for example, to report on excessive taxation or misuse of government funds. They do not simply complain that taxes are too high; they complain specifically that local officials are demanding higher taxes than the central government allows. In other words, they seek to make local officials comply with the existing policies. Once deviations from policy are brought to the attention of higher level officials, they are very difficult to ignore.

China is trying to strengthen its legal system, in part to support the push for economic modernization (enforcement of contracts, protection of property, including copyrights, etc.) and in part to create more predictability by clearly spelling out what conduct is appropriate and what is not. This strengthening of the legal system gives people the power to defend their interests and protect themselves from capricious actions by their neighbors, other businesses, and even government officials. Private entrepreneurs have turned to the courts to force the government to honor its contracts or to compensate them for confiscating their property. Artists have been known to sue government-owned media for printing libelous accusations against them or for criticizing their works on political grounds. Such suits are not always successful; China's courts are still not independent of the state, nor are they neutral interpreters of the law. But enough such cases are successful to encourage others to follow their precedent. As businessmen, artists, and other groups in society are becoming better educated about the state's laws and regulations, they are increasingly using them to their own advantage.

China's villagers are now able to elect their local leaders. In the past, all local officials were appointed by higher levels of government, which made them accountable to their superiors rather than to the people the actually governed. Not surprisingly, this encouraged many local officials to act as petty tyrants, lording it over the local populace. Now villagers can use village elections to replace unpopular or abusive officials, as Tyrene White explains (reading 19). It is still common to hear stories in which higher government officials refuse to let an individual stand as a candidate, or throw out the results of elections they do not like, or even refuse to hold elections in the first place, but national law now requires periodic elections for village chief and village councils, and the Ministry of Civil Affairs has charge of publicizing and monitoring compliance with the law.

These conventional forms of participation are not always effective, and they are often risky. In a political system with only one political party and limited citizen's rights, the state does not have to be responsive to the wants and needs of society. Most Party and government officials are not accountable to the people, and they are used to protecting other officials against what are often seen as troublemakers and whistle-blowers. Those making complaints are often subjected to intimidation, arrest, job loss, and occasionally beatings and even death. Nevertheless, some people are willing to appeal to higher and higher levels. They will even travel to Beijing if necessary, in order to seek justice.

Other types of political participation are less conventional. Rural protest has become increasingly common. Incidents are usually due to government payments for grain with IOUs instead of cash, the confiscation of farmland for other uses, excessive taxation, or corruption. Even when policies are properly carried out, those unhappy with the consequences have been known to sprinkle broken glass in the officials' rice paddies (which are farmed in bare feet), set fire to the officials' houses, or physically assault them. Corruption of all kinds has become a prominent feature of Chinese life, damaging the state's reputation and triggering frequent protests from victims of financial scams and misconduct by local officials. James Miles examines the growing problem of corruption (reading 20).

While noting the changes in political participation that have occurred in the reform era, it is also important to understand what has not changed. Although the CCP is willing to allow experimentation with economic policies, complaints about improper policy implementation, and village elections, it is not willing to allow direct challenges to its authority or demands for changes in the basic political system. During the reform era, three occasions when Chinese demanded political reform and even democracy stand out. All three met with the same result: the movements were suppressed, their leaders arrested, and their demands ignored.

The Democracy Wall Movement, 1978–1979

In the immediate aftermath of the Cultural Revolution, a group of intellectuals and workers began putting up posters in an area of downtown Beijing that became known as "Democracy Wall." Initially, the protestors were supportive of Deng's efforts to replace the remaining Maoists in the Party and government. They called for criticism of the Cultural Revolution, of Mao, and of those leaders pledged to remain loyal to his policies. They sought the rehabilitation of victims of the Cultural Revolution and political reforms to loosen state controls over society. The movement led to the formation of politically oriented journals and inspired similar developments in other cities. Most of those writing the posters and contributing to the new journals portrayed themselves as loyal citizens seeking to reform and improve the political system, not to challenge or replace it. But some advocated positions more radical than even Deng and his allies were willing to permit. The best-known dissident to emerge in China at that time was Wei Jingsheng, who bemoaned the absence of democracy and rule of law in China (see reading 56 in Future Trends). He characterized Deng as just another authoritarian ruler who had not been chosen by the Chinese people and who would not be bound the public's interest. As the demands of the Democracy Wall protestors moved in this direction, the state initiated a crackdown, arresting leading figures, including Wei, and sentencing some to long prison sentences. It also moved the authorized site of Democracy Wall from a downtown street to a remote park. In 1980 the Party removed the right to put up wall-posters from the constitution, thereby eliminating one of the few avenues for public criticism of the government. China's leaders were still not willing to be accountable to public opinion.

Student Demonstrations, 1986–1987

During the early 1980s, with dramatic economic reforms taking place, political reform remained limited. Instead of opening the political system to new voices and groups, political reform focused primarily on administration and the bureaucracy. The number of government ministries, commissions, and offices was reduced (although the number of officials continued to grow), new criteria for appointing and promoting officials were put in place and mandatory retirement rules established for officials. Officials debated policy matters more extensively and drew upon feasibility studies and other technical considerations rather than ideological rhetoric, in making their decisions. These measures had important implications for how well the Party and government did their work, but they did not make the state more responsive to popular opinion. The state may have become more efficient, but it was not more democratic.

By the mid-1980s, many in China, especially in academic and intellectual circles, grew frustrated at the slow pace of political change. In December 1986, college students in Shanghai staged public demonstrations about poor living conditions on their campuses, but these actions soon included calls for more extensive political reform. Word spread to other campuses, and other areas of China began reporting similar demonstrations. Although the official media initially described the demonstrators as patriotic, the leadership soon changed its rhetoric and cracked down on the participants without offering any political concessions. Moreover, the general secretary of the CCP, Hu Yaobang, was forced to resign his post and to accept responsibility for the outbreak and spread of demonstrations. Hu favored conciliation toward the students, which put him at odds with Deng and other leaders, who feared the demonstrations might lead to increased instability if not handled forcefully.

The Tiananmen Crisis, Spring 1989

Hu Yaobang's death in April 1989 sparked the largest popular demonstrations in post-1949 China. The students, workers, professionals, and others who joined the growing demonstrations over the next few weeks were motivated by a variety of issues. As Andrew Walder describes it, some were concerned because double-digit inflation threatened to undermine their standard of living, wiping away the gains of a decade of reform (reading 13). Others grew alarmed at the rampant corruption that accompanied economic reforms. Both of these issues, in fact, mirrored the government's own concerns. But others used the opportunity these demonstrations provided to demand more fundamental changes in China's political system. They called for labor unions and student organizations free of government and Party controls; they even sought the removal of Deng Xiaoping and Li Peng, the unpopular prime minister who was widely viewed as an opponent of reform. China's leaders saw the demonstrations as an attempt to overthrow the government, and as such a serious threat to their hold on power. In the end, it was the form of these demands—popular demonstrations without government approval—more than their content that most frightened China's leaders and led to the tragic outcome. Martial law was announced on May 20 and imposed on June 4 with deadly force. Thousands of people were killed or wounded.

This outcome was not predetermined. It was the result of a long and divisive debate among China's top leaders about how to respond to the demonstrations. In fact, the perceived divisions among the elite fueled the demonstrations, creating expectations that the state might actually give in. The longer the state delayed its response, the more these expectations grew. Some of China's leaders were sympathetic to the demands of the protestors and sought a compromise to bring the demonstrations to a close. Others saw the dramatic surge of protest as a repetition of Red Guard activism, from which they had suffered earlier in their careers. They wanted to nip the movement in the bud. The swelling numbers of protestors and the diversity of people who joined in, including government officials and journalists connected with the official media responsible for conveying the official line to the public, embarrassed others.

The open display of discontent indicated a severe loss of legitimacy for the leadership in Beijing, which appeared incapable of controlling events even in Tiananmen Square, the political and symbolic center of China. For more than a month, demonstrators occupied the square and undertook a hunger strike to dramatize their cause. The willingness of these young idealists to march in defiance of the state's orders, to remain in the square after the declaration of martial law, and to persist in their food strike created sympathy and support among Chinese citizens and foreign audiences, who watched the drama unfold live on television. Foreign television crews had arrived in China to cover the visit of Soviet leader Mikhail Gorbachev, but his visit was quickly over-shadowed by the growing popular protests. The crews stayed in China even after Gorbachev departed, providing almost continuous coverage of the protests.

The failure of these demonstrations in Beijing and elsewhere in China to bring about lasting change was due to several factors. First and most important, the CCP refuses to recognize the legitimacy of any group it does not approve or accept demands for change from outside the limited channels of communi-cations. The political system was created to change society, not be changed by it. One consequence of the CCP's monopoly on political organization is that no mediating organizations exist with which the state could have negotiated a peaceful settlement. There is no equivalent of Poland's Solidarity or the church, which in various ways contributed to political change in Eastern Europe, Latin America, and elsewhere. For related reasons, the students, workers, and others who participated in the demonstrations had no organization to plan their protests and shape their demands. Organizations formed spontaneously during the demon-strations, but they had little interaction with each other or with the state. The protestors themselves were divided over their agenda, with some seeking the reform of existing policies and institutions and others who felt the system incapable of reform pursuing more radical ambitions. Ultimately, it was the CCP's past success in preventing autonomous organizations and its refusal to negotiate even with those whose demands echoed the state's own policies that led to the tragic outcome of these demonstrations. Ironically, in the years after 1989, most intellectuals and others in China came to believe that the Tiananmen demonstrations had been premature and too idealistic. As Stanley Rosen shows (reading 14), most Chinese—including university students—have less interest in promoting political change and a stronger desire to participate in the economic development of the country.

Although the CCP still enjoys a privileged status as the ruling party of China, this does not mean that it is monolithic or omnipotent. The history of CCP rule in China following the establishment of the People's Republic of China in 1949 has been marked by occasionally intense conflict over issues of power and policy. Party leaders do not always agree on the proper course of policy or even who should make those decisions. The central state often cannot get lower levels of government, whether on the provincial or local level, to comply with current directives. The economic and political reforms of the past twenty years have also reduced the state's control over the daily lives of most Chinese people, making it easier for them to switch jobs, change their place of residence, travel, and have access to ideas and sources of information not controlled by the state. But these changes have not challenged the CCP's preeminent position in China's political system.

POLITICS
Readings

13

The Beijing Upheaval of 1989

ANDREW G. WALDER

The demonstrations in and around Tiananmen Square in spring 1989 captivated a global audience and influenced perceptions of China in the years after. The demonstrations seemed to emerge without warning, but in fact they were the culmination of years of frustration about the consequences of reform. Students, workers, and professionals had different reasons for demanding change from their government, but found common cause in the popular demonstrations that began in April and spread throughout the country. By the time of the violent crackdown on June 4, the entire populace of Beijing seemed united in opposition to the government. This article outlines the motivations of the various protestors and the splits in China's top leadership that contributed to the outpouring of protests, the state's inability to find a satisfactory compromise, and the eventual massacre that brought an end to this dramatic political upheaval.

Bejiing's seven tumultuous weeks of popular protest marked a new stage in China's post-revolution political history. Student protest and elite power struggle, central to the events of this spring, are familiar features of the Chinese scene. But two new developments led from student protest to an unprecedented popular rebellion. First, the students received widespread and outspoken support from intellectuals in all fields, many of whom also organized protests of their own, while huge numbers of ordinary working people rallied to the demonstrations. Second, and perhaps more important, the party split internally over its response to the student movement, which prevented effective repression early on and which eventually led key elements of the capital's party apparatus and, most crucially, the mass media to support openly certain student demands. The combination of mass support and party fragmentation led rapidly to a massive, nonviolent rebellion that echoed in scores of cities throughout China, paralyzed the national leadership, and made the capital virtually ungovernable for several weeks. . . .

Changing Political Outlook

Only a decade ago, China's urbanites were still shell-shocked, demoralized by the ravages of the Cultural Revolution, and grateful for any change the party would make on behalf of their political or economic welfare. They were still largely unaware of the economic prosperity of their neighbors in East Asia, of life in Japan and in the West, and of the possibilities for change soon to be presented in the Soviet bloc. What has changed crucially in the Deng Xiaoping era is that the government has lost the ability to control the information that citizens use to evaluate their own circumstances, and thus to stem their propensity to conceive of their problems in political terms, to envisage alternatives, and to see the attainment of these alternatives as feasible. The opening to the outside world placed different ideals of governance into popular awareness, changed perceptions of the feasibility of democratic reform in China, and perhaps most importantly, provided models of strategy and tactics for public protest. Meanwhile, the 1980s consumer revolution and increased inflation and official corruption helped spread these changing perceptions beyond the intelligentsia.

Students and intellectuals

From the outset of this year's protests, China's students and intellectuals exemplified the profound changes that a decade of openness had wrought in public perceptions. . . .

. . . In the late 1970s, only a handful of students and visiting scholars had recently studied outside China, the foreign community was small and isolated, listening to broadcasts of the Voice of America (VOA) or the British Broadcasting Corporation (BBC) was a punishable offense, and contacts with foreigners were tightly restricted. By the beginning of this year, many tens of thousands of students and scholars had already been to the United States alone, Beijing's long-term foreign community numbered in the thousands, and tens of thousands of others visited China for scholarly or business purposes every year and enjoyed relaxed and easy contacts with their Chinese colleagues. VOA and BBC broadcasts, no longer forbidden, had a large and open audience. Western publications, in both their original languages and in translation, were readily available, and were not subject to systematic control at China's borders. China's national television news regularly employed footage from Western news agencies.

These changes helped create a student body and an intelligentsia that were highly cosmopolitan in comparison with their late-1970s counterparts. This year's student movement bristled with foreign symbols and allusions. Students

in both Beijing and Shanghai erected replicas of the Statue of Liberty in prominent public places. Wall posters and placards paraphrased or quoted Abraham Lincoln, Martin Luther King, and Patrick Henry, and they alluded to Mahatma Gandhi, Lech Walesa, Mikhail Gorbachev and *perestroyka*, the American civil rights movement, and Kent State. The student protesters wore the white headbands they had seen in films and photos of Japanese and South Korean student radicals; they flashed the "V" sign they had seen in news footage from the anti-Marcos movement in the Philippines. Although the mentality and style of the protesters in many ways remained characteristically Chinese, the ardent adaptation of foreign symbols and ideas was striking.

These long-run changes were unmistakable. But as long-run changes, they do not account for the striking difference in the strength and stridency of the student movement in 1989, compared with that of December 1986. . . .

Ironically, the crucial short-run cause of changed political perceptions was not influence from the West, but from the Soviet bloc. In the period after Hu Yaobang's ouster and the conservative backlash occasioned by the 1986 student movement, China's leaders reversed themselves on the political reforms promised in the summer of 1986 and began to draw back from further economic reform. However, in precisely this period political change accelerated in the Soviet Union and Eastern Europe. Gorbachev's *glasnost* received the rapt attention of educated Chinese. The 19th Conference of the Communist Party of the Soviet Union in 1988, extraordinary for its openly contentious debate, the stunning spectacle of the Soviet party's embarrassment in parliamentary elections early in 1989, and the subsequent parliamentary debates in mid-1989 have been the object of open envy among reform-minded Chinese. Equally crucial was the evident failure of martial law to solve Poland's political and economic crises, and the turn to a free press and partially contested parliamentary elections negotiated with Solidarity. Also important, but less dramatic, have been developments in Hungary, where a number of political organizations are now readying for promised parliamentary elections.

These developments have rapidly altered the standards by which educated Chinese judge their government, while they have undercut the main conservative objection to political reform. In the crackdown on the New Democracy Wall movement [1978–1979], right up through the backlash against the 1986 student protests, party orthodoxy has labeled calls for democracy "bourgeois" and inappropriate for "Chinese conditions." The emergence of coveted forms of socialist democracy in the Soviet Union and Eastern Europe directly undermines the conservative argument. On the eve of Gorbachev's visit to China, the political scientist Yan Jiaqi, a leading Beijing proponent of political reform (and now a dissident in exile), observed: "China used to be afraid of influence from the West. Now we are afraid of influence from the Soviet Union. . . . If we want to keep out Western influence, we can say we're against 'bourgeois liberalization' or against 'total Westernization.' But we can't use that pretext against Soviet influence . . . there is no ideological concept to resist it."

In effect, reform experiments in the Soviet bloc changed the terms of an implicit compact formed with China's intellectuals at the outset of Deng's reform program. Intellectuals in the post-Cultural Revolution period appear generally to have accepted Deng's argument against political reform in return for enhanced status and advisory influence, and as a price to be paid for the stability needed for economic reform and prosperity. Especially important in this acquiescence was the perception that no matter how far from the ideal, China's political situation in the early 1980s was infinitely better than in the recent Mao era and was the best that a citizen of such a party-state could hope for, at least in the immediate future.

The intellectuals' response to the student movement suggests that this political outlook had lost its viability by the late 1980s. No longer could Chinese intellectuals conclude that their political situation was the best they could hope for, nor could they be so readily convinced that democratic reforms or greater political openness were inappropriate for China or unrealistically ambitious goals.

In short, backtracking on reform in China, coupled with dramatic political developments in Eastern Europe, undermined the foundation of the intellectuals' consent to the political restrictions of the Deng regime and emboldened the students to act.

Blue- and white-collar workers

These factors were apparently less important to the broader working population than the high rate of inflation and the widely perceived upsurge of official corruption at all levels. After 1986, inflation became a serious problem for urban residents. After decades of extraordinary price stability, the last two years saw the real rate of inflation (much higher than the official rate) climb to an estimated 30 percent. Difficult as it is to measure inflation, it is even harder to assess the prevalence of corruption. Public perception of official corruption, however, does appear to have become more acute in recent years (a development not unrelated, as I shall note momentarily, to the upsurge in inflation).

The inflation of the late 1980s and the increased salience of corruption took place against the backdrop of a decade-long trend of increasing contention over wage matters. Three factors explain the increased wage contention. First, it was an inevitable outgrowth of the monetization of labor relations. Growth in real wages between 1979 and 1984 far outstripped increases in labor productivity. While the share of national income generated by urban workers rose by 9.3 percent, their total compensation more than doubled. From the late 1950s through the late 1970s, bonuses were either nonexistent or small and the material incentives that were offered were consistently linked to political evaluations of employees. By the mid-1980s, bonuses comprised almost one-fourth of the wage bill, and enterprises kept much larger percentages of their profits and distributed much larger percentages of these profits as incentive pay, as managers attempted to avoid labor conflict by "overspending" on bonuses and other benefits. Quotas and contracts proliferated on the shop floor, intensifying contention over standards of work and pay.

Second, the shift to light industrial production greatly increased the availability of consumer goods and purchases of key consumer goods increased by several orders of magnitude. In the late 1970s, the Chinese urban consumer aspired to own a wristwatch, a foot-powered sewing machine, a name-brand bicycle, and a transistor radio. By the mid-1980s, such items were commonplace, and the consumer could realistically aspire to own a color television (perhaps even an imported or foreign co-produced one), a washing machine, refrigerator, or a tape recorder/stereo with AM/FM/shortwave reception. . . .

During this same period, the housing stock doubled. Farmers' markets brought to cities fresh foodstuffs that had been tightly rationed or simply unavailable in the Mao era, but prices were much higher than in the reviled state stores. The consumer revolution in cities fed the workers' hunger for money, despite the sustained rise in living standards after the late 1970s.

Finally, increases in real wages, although rapid, had begun at a base more than 20 percent lower than the average real wage in the mid-1950s. Not until 1984 did the average real wage, according to official statistics, surpass the comparable figure for 1957. Urbanites, in fact, used the prosperity of the 1980s to recover from the depression of living standards they had suffered during the Mao era. During this process of recovery, workers were aware that peasants in suburban areas, who were now free to engage in private commerce, enjoyed much larger increases in income and could build for themselves much larger and higher quality housing than anything available to workers in cities. In short, a number of factors explain why workers' satisfaction might not increase along with their standard of living. . . .

. . . The inflation of 1987–1989 had a major impact on public perception. To an extent that we are as yet unable to gauge, real incomes began to fall for the first time in the post-Mao era. It is reasonable to suspect that such inflation would stimulate increased corruption among petty officials and clerks, whose wages are not high and who are also hit hard by price rises. Whether or not this hypothesis is true, corruption would certainly be much more sharply resented in an era of inflation: that of petty officials and clerks because it is visible and cuts further into worker incomes; that of higher officials—who are seen as responsible for inflationary policy—because their privileges protect them from the ravages of inflation. Whether corruption increased in fact or merely in public perception, inflation made corruption less tolerable.

Because Beijing's wage earners have been less articulate in their protests than the highly educated, changes in their outlooks are more obscure. But it appears that inflation had the effect of politicizing worker dissatisfaction in a way that made the student demands for democracy more appealing than a few years ago. Inflation and corruption appear to have fueled public protest primarily by enhancing the workers' sense of powerlessness and resentment at official privilege, thereby providing a long-missing link with student and intellectual demands for greater democracy.

As with the intellectuals, the implicit compact that the Deng regime had forged with the working class began to unravel after 1986. Workers now saw themselves as being made to sacrifice for a reform program of benefit only to the corrupt petty officials and clerks, and the privileged higher officials who set the policies in the first place. One worker from the Beijing Shoe Factory, while participating in the protests, told a reporter, "I cannot afford a decent life so naturally there is anger in me. . . . When I hear our leaders speak of 'reform,' I know that means the price of food is about to increase. . . . [Inflation and corruption make] rich men of party cadres and leave the masses behind. . . . The students have given all the people the courage to raise their voice."

Although workers' motivations were different from those of the students, many apparently felt that the protests would provide an avenue of expression, and perhaps redress, of their grievances. From the outset, the students sought to show sympathy and build ties with the broader public. In the massive and pivotal march of April 27, in which workers cheered openly from the sides, helped clear away police lines in advance, and swelled the student procession to several times its original size, one student banner read: "You work but you get nothing; your life is bitter.". . . Workers evidently felt that students provided an opportunity to influence the leadership on matters of concern to them. The more sustained the student protests, the more encouraged and emboldened workers became.

The Weakening of Political Controls

No matter how emboldened Beijing's workers became during this period, they never demonstrated a capacity to organize and sustain a movement of their own. Blue- and white-collar workers either participated spontaneously in student-led actions or formed themselves into small bands who left their offices and factories to march under banners naming their place of work. At least one autonomous organization of industrial workers, the "Capital Independent Workers' Union," publicly announced its formation, but we have little evidence to suggest that it was able to build a significant membership or to coordinate work actions in support of the student protests. Independent unions were more a result of the upheaval than a cause. In sharp contrast to Poland, where an organized labor movement, through superbly organized strikes and demonstrations, turned itself into a virtual opposition party, in China only the students and, to a lesser extent, the intellectuals, were able to form and sustain even loose-knit political associations.

But even this organizationally limited protest activity is significant in light of the heretofore remarkably effective institutions of grassroots political control inherited from the Mao era. China under Mao developed distinctive institutions of control centered in workplaces and neighborhoods. Even more so than in most Soviet bloc regimes, these controls made it very difficult for urban Chinese to change their jobs or place of residence, travel without workplace permission, obtain information other than from approved channels, or gather together outside official scrutiny. [During the 1980s] the framework of these controls was maintained but their exercise was relaxed. The intense workplace monitoring of behavior and thought characteristic of the past subsided, and rewards have been distributed increasingly based on performance rather than loyalty. In addition, a small urban private sector (some 6 million nationally) and a much larger sector of peasant entrepreneurs from the city's suburban rings have been released from such controls. The strict control over travel and information and means of communication characteristic of the Mao era has also been loosened, as a consequence of both the policy of openness and of China's rapid development. . . . These increases are due to the greater physical availability of travel and communication equipment, as well as to the fact that access to telephones, intercity travel, photocopy machines, and foreign radio broadcasts have in recent years all been subject to few or no political restrictions. . . . The rapid growth in these means of communication has clearly outpaced the capacity of the authorities to monitor them. Perhaps the most dramatic example of this fact is the ability of some hunted political activists to escape from Beijing, or from China altogether, in the weeks after the June 4 massacre.

The greater availability of these means of communication—many of which were in private hands—was much in evidence during the Beijing protests. A group of young motorcycle enthusiasts called the "Flying Tigers," employing a mode of transportation nonexistent ten years ago, rode throughout the city after the declaration of martial law to spread news of advancing troops and to bolster citizen defenses. Participants in the student movement communicated with their colleagues in North America and Europe via long distance telephones, facsimile machines, and electronic mail on computer networks. They received news, advice, and encouragement from Chinese students abroad via these same media; and the information on these networks helped inform news programs broadcast back to China on shortwave channels. As acknowledged by the resumption of jamming of foreign broadcasts on May 22, these news sources played an important role in spreading information about the protest's successes within China. Also, even in the midst of the rebellion, international travel was still unrestricted: people easily obtained visas and arrived from overseas with contributions of funds and supplies for the student strikers. Students from outlying areas easily made it to Beijing, periodically replenishing the ranks of protesters in the square. None of these advantages were available to the protesters of 1978–1979.

The Fracturing of Party Unity

The evident disintegration of party unity after the first week of May is perhaps the most important cause of the size and tenacity of the protest movement, especially its paradoxical growth after the May 19 declaration of martial law. The student demonstrators' invocation of the memory and progressive political legacy of former Party General Secretary Hu Yaobang drove wedges into an already divided party. Significant portions of the party-state apparatus openly supported the student campaign. Especially important was the defection of key organizations in the mass media that, on the eve of Gorbachev's visit, began to report openly and sympathetically on the growing demonstrations. This reportage helped to magnify public sympathy and involvement, and during a pivotal period, made it appear that the demonstrations might succeed in toppling the hard-line leadership.

It is apparent that the regime, beginning in the weeks leading up to martial law, was grappling with divided sovereignty in two respects. First, the Politburo Standing Committee itself found its powers usurped by Deng and members of the senior advisory group. This usurpation lasted a period of weeks, during which time there was no clear political center. Second, once these party elders, whose power rested not on formal position but on personal influence, forged an alliance with Premier Li Peng, President Yang Shangkun, and others, many of the personal followers of Zhao Ziyang and Hu Qili (as well as Hu Yaobang's former followers, among whom were many intellectuals), who headed key central and provincial institutions, including, apparently, part of the armed forces, contested the rule of premier Li Peng and the Politburo majority manufactured by Deng. In essence, key governmental institutions—such as the Foreign Ministry, research institutes, key newspapers, and others—reportedly refused to take orders from the Li Peng government. . . . A clearly divided party and state apparatus played a central role in feeding the popular rebellion. The population of Beijing was well aware of this division because of the mass media.

Beijing's mass media—local and national newspapers, the New China News Agency, local radio and television—also played a major role in mobilizing popular protest, initially through accurate and sympathetic reporting on the student demonstrations and the popular response, and later by openly challenging the party leaders who ordered martial law. As early as April 24, such newspapers as Shanghai's *World Economic Herald* and Beijing's *Science and Technology Daily* ventured sympathetic reports on the student protests, drawing the ire of officials. However, the official media remained hostile or silent on the student movement and followed the line enunciated in the *People's Daily* editorial of April 26, which attacked the students for engaging in a "planned conspiracy" aimed at overthrowing the party, until May 4, when, speaking at the reception for members of the Asian Development Bank, Zhao Ziyang declared that "the just demands of the students must be met" and that "we should solve the problem in a democratic and legal way."

During this time, the student demonstrations were massive and enjoyed clear popular support. In the demonstration of April 27, hundreds of thousands of students and their supporters marched through the streets for hours, repeatedly breaking through police barricades to fill Tiananmen Square. On May 4, hundreds of thousands of students and supporters again marched, and this time were joined by organized intellectuals and journalists under banners of their own, and by young workers who "easily outnumbered" the students.

Despite the enormous size of the demonstrations, they did not yet constitute a popular rebellion. They would become one only after the protesters came to see themselves as having the clear sympathy of one wing of the party and government apparatus and as helping this faction in its fight against the conservatives. This process began after Zhao's May 4 speech, which was followed by a series of conciliatory statements about "patriotic" students that continued up to May 17. Beginning on May 5, the official media began to run brief but objective reports on student activities and demands; by May 9, the reports had become longer and more detailed, leading quickly to actively sympathetic media coverage for a period of about two weeks, ending on May 25.

At two distinct points, the suddenly independent and assertive mass media played a pivotal role in the development of the popular rebellion. First, from around May 13 through May 19, the media's detailed and sympathetic reporting riveted the city's attention on the drama of the hunger strikers, building a huge groundswell of popular support, and openly seeking to pressure top leaders to reverse their intransigent stand against negotiations. This period was one in which, for the first time, protest marches swelled to 1 million or more (May 15, 17, and 18). White- and blue-collar workers, professionals, and cadres began to march under banners naming their workplaces (including at least eight agencies of the central government), and a force of several hundred thousand began to occupy the square continuously. During this period, the people of Beijing were told by their press and television that "hundreds of thousands" or "more than a million people" "from all walks of life" were going to the main square "to show their support for the students." They read detailed lists of student demands and heard reports that university presidents, teachers' organizations, leading social scientists, the staff of Beijing television, the head of the All-China Federation of Industry and Commerce, leading journalists and intellectuals, and the All-China Federation of Trade Unions had appealed to the government to negotiate with the students in good faith. Finally, they heard that citizens and organizations throughout the capital were sending aid and medical supplies to the hunger strikers.

Having so effectively mobilized public opinion for the cause of the students (and by extension for the cause of liberalization and reform), in mid-May, Beijing's mass media also laid the foundation for massive popular resistance to martial law beginning in the early morning hours of May 20. This second stage marked the start of an open popular rebellion against the Li Peng-Deng Xiaoping faction. Until troops moved into the compounds of broadcasting stations and newspapers on May 25, the mass media openly encouraged resistance to martial law, making it appear that practically the entire country was united in opposition against it.

During this week, hundreds of thousands of students and ordinary citizens continued to demonstrate in the square, while massive numbers of other demonstrators rushed to countless barricades throughout the city to block troop movements. People could read and hear in the official media that the masses were opposed to martial law, and that military officers were pledged not to attack the demonstrators. Photographs in newspapers showed citizens and soldiers fraternizing at the barricades. As Li Peng made speeches naming "turmoil" as the pretext for the military show of force, local papers reported that rates of crime and traffic accidents had gone down in the past month. *Science and Technology Daily* published an appeal, signed by twenty-four members of the Standing Committee of the National People's Congress, calling for an emergency session to repeal martial law. *People's Daily* printed on its front page an article quoting Hungarian Prime Minister Miklós Nemeth saying that his country had learned from sad experience that solutions to its problems did not come from military force, along with an article about the resignation of the Italian government. New China News Agency reports claimed that more than 1 million people marched in the streets to oppose martial law on May 23, when foreign observers put the number at 100,000, and the agency's interviews with citizens on the street directly refuted the rationale for martial law.

The evident division in the national leadership and the open defection of the mass media fueled an exhilarating sense of popular power. From the outset, the student protesters, in characteristic Chinese style, saw themselves not as dissidents but as loyal remonstrators. Their sense of insult at the April 26 editorial is evidence of this mentality; and a retraction of the accusation that they were "counterrevolutionary" became a key student demand. They saw themselves as patriots carrying out their duty as educated citizens to press the government even at personal risk. However, when it became apparent that their activities had sympathizers in the government, they began to feel a sense of direct participation in national politics; as the splits in the leadership widened, they and ever broader circles of the population came to feel that they were participating directly in a momentous historical drama. The disintegration of the party apparatus made victory seem possible and lowered the perceived costs of continued participation. Without this disintegration, it is hard to imagine a population united in rebellion against a party leadership that had already publicly committed itself to the use of military force.

Conclusions

From this perspective, the military assault upon Beijing should not be interpreted simply as a tough response to stubborn student protesters. The stakes were much higher by mid-May; by the time martial law was declared, the students were no longer the hard-liners' main problem. The entire population of Beijing was seemingly united in effective resistance against the hard-liners' refusal to negotiate with students, and broad sectors of party and government were in open defiance. Outside the capital, demonstrations had occurred in more than 80 cities. The crackdown was, instead, an act calculated to terrorize the entire population of Beijing, and the recalcitrant party-state apparatus, back into submission.

It is tempting, but misleading, to characterizing Beijing's popular rebellion as a movement by "society" against the "state." China's ordinary citizens did not organize to force themselves onto the political stage; they used an opportunity created initially by students, and then opened wider first by the rebellion of intellectuals and later by the defection of key parts of the government apparatus and the media. The events of this spring show, instead, how explosive is the mixture of popular protest and party disunity. The splits in the party were opened wide by the protests; but they were already deep. And while the protests showed extraordinary strength before the party's unity began to crumble, they would not likely have grown to such an extent had the party maintained internal discipline, as in 1986–1987.

14

1995

China Since Tiananmen Square

STANLEY ROSEN

In 1989, student demands for greater political reform and democracy were raised in China and broadcast live around the world. Most observers were surprised by the sudden emergence of this political movement and by the outpouring of popular support it received. After the tragic outcome of those demonstrations, the demonstrators and their supporters reassessed their goals and methods. Most young people in China have come to the conclusion that their country needs more economic development, not greater democracy. As this article shows, democratic ideals have often competed with nationalistic goals of a rich and strong country during China's modern era.

When Americans think of the People's Republic of China, certain indelible images inevitably spring to mind. Who can forget the spring of 1989, marked by student demonstrations for democracy, the hunger strike in Tiananmen Square, and the tragic denouement of the military crackdown on June 4? Since those dark days, as the Sino-American relationship has struggled to recover its pre-1989 momentum, the American press continues to document the enduring tensions between the two countries.

On global issues, there is the strong suspicion that in a variety of areas, including intellectual-property rights, trade policy, and nuclear proliferation, China is unwilling to play according to long-established international rules. On what China considers domestic issues as well, the regime has been repeatedly condemned for violating the human rights of its citizens, from prominent dissidents to disabled orphans to unborn fetuses.

While editorials and op-ed contributors debate whether MFN (most-favored nation) renewal should be tied to improvements in China's international and domestic behavior, there is remarkably little discussion beyond the broadest generalities of the changes in China since 1989 and the views of China's own citizens. Such information is crucial, at a minimum, if the United States is to avoid obvious missteps in its relationship with China; it is available through published survey research, public opinion polling, press reports, and discussions with a wide range of individuals in China. What these sources reveal is a China that has changed significantly from the late 1980s.

China Before and After 1989

Following the 13th Party Congress in October 1987 and prior to June 1989, China was a very lively place for intellectual discussion and contention. There was, by today's standards, a surprising amount of official tolerance toward those questioning China's past, present, and future. One of the clearest examples of this was a six-hour documentary shown on Chinese television in 1988 titled *River Elegy*, which attacked some of the major icons of Chinese civilization, including the Great Wall, the image of the dragon, and the Yellow River.

The message of the documentary was that a hopelessly backward Chinese civilization could only advance by following a Western model of development, and that only China's intellectuals were capable of serving as a bridge to link China with the West. The leader of the Communist Party at that time, Zhao Ziyang, was so taken with this documentary that he ensured that it was rebroadcast, thereby guaranteeing it a larger audience.

Conservative political leaders in China—and many Chinese abroad—were appalled by this frontal assault on Chinese civilization, but the policy at that time was to discourage the Communist Party from interfering in academic and cultural debates, so it could not be suppressed.

There were also debates in the press and before large audiences on university campuses over the best way for China to become democratic, whether a "neoauthoritarian" model à la South Korea, Singapore, and Taiwan or a more direct, Western-derived model best fit China's conditions. This openness, along with the self-imposed circumscribed role of the Communist Party, ended after June 1989.

Following Tiananmen, a decision was made to control political life and strictly limit academic debates that might have political implications. The overriding emphasis was placed on maintaining stability. Many intellectuals who had been tarnished in the eyes of the regime because of their "antigovernment" activities had their professional lives either sharply curtailed or ended completely. At the same time the regime knew that it had to restore its legitimacy and polish its own severely tarnished image.

The new policy had several components. One priority was to focus on raising the standard of living of the urban population, particularly those in the coastal cities who were best situated to take advantage of the state's new economic initiatives. Indeed, for the "tarnished" intellectuals, their only recourse was to engage in business, which many did with surprising success.

In addition to offering them more bread, circuses were provided in the form of a far more varied cultural life, albeit of a nonthreatening nature. Thus, China witnessed an explosion of tabloid newspapers and sensationalistic magazines, which was further fueled by the elimination of state subsidies and the necessity for all cultural organizations to adjust to the new requirements of the market.

Evening entertainment was enhanced with increased numbers of discos and karaoke bars and the importation of ten "blockbuster" movies per year, such as *Forrest Gump*, *True Lies*, and *The Fugitive*. A virtual revolution in consumer goods was spearheaded by the increasing penetration of cosmetics, toiletries, and other such wares of Western multinational corporations.

The government's strategy can easily be seen in the field of popular music. In place of the pounding rock music of rebellion that had been so important a part of the 1989 student movement, sentimental love songs from Hong Kong and Taiwan were encouraged and became dominant.

The Stress on Patriotism over Politics

Finally, indirectly acknowledging that heavy doses of obviously outdated political dogma had become counterproductive, the leadership has taken steps to promote patriotism while de-emphasizing politics. Thus, beginning in fall 1994, for the first time since university entrance examinations were restored in the late 1970s, students applying to study science did not have to take an examination in politics. Many educators expect the exemption to be extended to humanities and social science students in due course.

At the same time, however, there has been a sharp increase in "patriotic education," to teach students to be proud of being Chinese and to emphasize the achievements of Chinese culture, the Chinese people, and the role of the Communist Party in honoring and furthering these achievements. This is an astute move, because so few young people now believe in Marxism-Leninism-Mao Zedong's thought anyway.

The State Education Commission appears to have concluded that forcing students to memorize and regurgitate what they consider to be outmoded theories had created constant tension between the students and authorities. In its view, the periodic student protests of the mid- and late 1980s were in part a reaction against the hypocrisy the students felt these political education examinations and courses represented.

This new strategy thus far appears to have paid dividends. In addition to the absence of the type of demonstrations that marked the 1980s, surveys have suggested that the regime's message is getting through. Citing a recent survey conducted by private researchers based in Beijing, the *Far Eastern Economic Review* noted that 54 percent of urbanites agreed with the official line that economic development, not greater democracy, is the most pressing national need.

Moreover, many surveys have documented a resurgence in patriotism among Chinese youth. One of the most interesting is a survey of 698 youths in Shanghai and surrounding areas that compared the results to earlier surveys of a similar nature conducted in 1984 and 1990. Respondents were given a list of 18 values and asked to rank their top four and bottom four. Perhaps most striking was the fact that patriotism—which had ranked fifth in 1984—ranked second in 1994. Indeed, among workers, peasants, and science students, it was ranked first. Only a relatively low ranking by liberal arts students prevented patriotism from replacing "self-respect" as the most valued concept.

More detailed analysis, however, reveals that present-day patriotism is far different from its Maoist variant, that in significant ways it actually presents a strong current of individualism and a rejection of authority. To be more specific, surveys of groups as diverse as peasant youth and graduate students at the elite Beijing University all show strong support for patriotism in the abstract. When asked to evaluate a statement such as "defending the nation is every young person's sacred duty," around 85 percent of respondents would concur. But when asked to make sacrifices for the benefit of the country, the response is far different.

For peasant youth, politics is very practical and is associated with changes in their own village or the behavior of local officials. Most of them were only concerned about politics if it directly impinged on their own lives or the livelihood of their families. Only 10 percent in a recent survey agreed with the famous motto of Lei Feng, a model youth of the Maoist period, that one should serve the nation in whatever capacity one is needed, as a "rust-free screw" in the great machine of the state.

There were similar results in a survey on the meaning of patriotism under a market economy conducted among graduate students at Beijing University. Despite overwhelming support for patriotism as a cherished value, only 6.6 percent said they were willing to take a job assignment after graduation wherever the country needed them. Those who said they would "serve the people and make a contribution to society" were also a very small percentage.

Over 50 percent said that the old model of making selfless contributions was out of date, no longer credible, not sensible, unnecessary, and not worth the effort. Fewer than 7 percent said they still wanted to emulate this model, but even they felt they would be ridiculed and isolated and would not have the understanding and support of society. It is therefore not surprising that in the Shanghai survey cited above, the value ranked consistently lowest over the last decade—last at number 18 in 1984 and again in 1994—was "obedience to authority."

Chinese Youth and the Outside World

Some of the most riveting and moving moments for Americans who watched the coverage of the students in Tiananmen Square during the "democratic spring" of 1989 were the frequent references to American political history and political values. Six and a half years later, the United States and democracy more generally no longer have such a favorable image.

One public opinion poll published in early 1995 in the *Beijing Youth Daily*, which has arguably become China's liveliest and most widely read newspaper, attracted particular attention. Titled "Foreign Countries in the Eyes of Urban Young People in China," the poll was part of an annual survey of Chinese youth. What was unusual was the addition for the first time of four questions on foreign countries. Respondents were asked to choose (1) the country you like best; (2) the country you like least; (3) the country you believe is most friendly to China; (4) the country you believe is most unfriendly to China.

On all four of these questions, the United States ranked among the first three choices. In fact, 74 percent of Chinese youth said that the United States is the foreign country with the greatest influence on China. Still, the surveyors expressed their surprise at some of the results. While the United States was third (12. 1 percent) among the countries most liked, following only China itself (46.1 percent) and Singapore (14.1 percent), it was a clear first among the countries most disliked (39.8 percent), well ahead of Japan, Vietnam, and Russia, which were the next three choices.

Again, the United States was third among the countries considered most friendly to China (3.9 percent), but far and away No. 1 among those considered most unfriendly (71.9 percent).

To provide some context, it should be noted that North Korea was considered most friendly by a whopping 67.7 percent, followed by Japan at 8.4 percent. Following the United States as most unfriendly were Japan, Vietnam, and Great Britain. Even some youths who listed the United States as their favorite country felt it was the most unfriendly toward China.

To be sure, public opinion in China tends to be quite volatile and survey techniques are commonly less than state-of-the-art. Nevertheless, many Chinese youth have told me that they do not find these results particularly surprising. Indeed, as Liu Xiaobo, one of the country's leading dissidents and among the last four hunger strikers to leave Tiananmen, wrote recently in a Hong Kong publication: "History moves in such rapid cycles. Many an advocate of Westernization who clamored for 'democracy' and 'freedom' on or before June 4 have in an instant become nationalists rejecting Western hegemony."

It is important for those outside China to understand some of the reasons for the change in sentiment. One source of disillusionment is the lack of success the former Soviet Union and Eastern European countries have had in transforming and consolidating their new political and economic systems.

When I was in Beijing in August 1991 during and after the abortive coup attempt in the Soviet Union, many young Chinese intellectuals, told me excitedly that the final demise of communism in its homeland would have an immense, albeit not immediate, impact in China. Such palpable enthusiasm no longer exists. In fact, some openly suggest that, given the situation in 1989, China was fortunate to avoid the fate of the Soviet Union. This perceived failure of post-communist systems has given credibility to the government's continual stress on stability as the overriding value.

At the same time, the leadership appears to have been extremely successful in its presentation of the United States as the ringleader of those who seek to deny China its rightful place in the hierarchy of nations. The Chinese press consistently argues that American policy is premised on "containing" China, citing as evidence not only American policy during the Cold War years but recent articles in such premier publications as *Time*, the *Economist*, the *New York Times*, and the *Washington Post*.

The regime has been inadvertently aided and abetted by certain policy decisions emanating from the White House and Congress. A prime example is related to China's failed bid to host the Olympics in the year 2000. After Beijing barely lost out to Sydney as the host site, the Chinese press—on its best behavior on this subject until the decision was reached—unleashed a torrent of abuse against foreigners who were said to have bullied China before the communist victory, then sought to encircle, contain, and isolate the growing strength of the socialist nation. China's defeat on the Olympics issue was seamlessly tied to a consistent pattern of Western efforts to humiliate and perpetuate a weak China, neatly turning the setback into a lesson in patriotism.

Public opinion polls on college campuses revealed that the large majority of students were particularly incensed by the congressional resolution urging the International Olympic Committee not to award China the games because of human rights violations. Regardless of their views of the government or human rights issues, most students fervently supported China's Olympic bid and saw this resolution as blatant interference by a "superpower bully."

As if to reinforce such an interpretation in their minds, around the same period in 1993 the U.S. Navy shadowed and eventually searched a Chinese ship suspected of carrying chemicals to Iran that could be used to manufacture weapons. When no such chemicals were found the government-controlled press once again took the lead in excoriating the United States for groundlessly violating Chinese sovereignty and attempting to police the world.

Conclusion

China has changed significantly since June 1989. The regime appears to have willingly sacrificed many of its former socialist goals and offered its citizens an opportunity to make money and enjoy life in return for their political acceptance of the status quo. It has had many takers. Public opinion polls show one of the most popular slogans among youth today is "Money isn't everything, but without money you can't do anything."

At the same time, the authorities have used the media to portray a China on schedule to become a world power in the next century but being resisted by a resentful West, spearheaded by the United States, reluctant to share its hegemonic control. Considering the government's isolation back in 1989 and its estrangement from society, the current strategy to this point must be considered a singular success.

Whereas Chinese youth in the 1980s became obsessed with Western philosophical and political thought, embracing Sartre, Freud, Nietzsche, and many others one after another, there is much more interest now in the success of the East Asian economic miracle and China's prospects for replicating it. Singapore—authoritarian, rich, without corruption and willing to cane Americans—has become the most popular foreign country. Indeed, Singapore was rated first by Chinese youth among countries they most wanted to visit (26.8 percent), even outpolling the United States (21.8 percent).

The United States, of course, remains the foreign country of greatest importance to China's future. But the influence we exert is strictly limited and, when exercised unwisely, has led to counterproductive results. In future, we would do well to consider how our policy decisions will be interpreted by the Chinese people, particularly the younger generation, which combines a growing individualism marked by a pattern of conspicuous consumption with a desire to see a strong and respected China.

15

Human Rights in China

ANDREW NATHAN

Human rights have been one of the most contentious and sensitive issues in United States-China relations. In evaluating China's human rights record, it is important to consider both the international norms that the Chinese government has agreed to abide by and the standards that the China's government and society use to balance the state's interest against the rights of individuals and groups in society. In this article, Andrew Nathan describes the main points of contention and the areas where progress has been made.

The State of Human Rights in China

The international law of human rights centers on the Universal Declaration of Human Rights, adopted by the United Nations General Assembly on December 10, 1948, and on the two covenants—one on civil and political rights, the other on economic, social, and cultural rights—adopted by the UN General Assembly in 1966. Like all nations, China is bound by the Declaration. Although it has not acceded to the two covenants, they represent appropriate standards against which to evaluate any country's behavior. China has acceded to and is bound by nine UN human rights conventions, including the one against torture, and a number of International Labor Organization conventions related to workers' rights.

The international human rights regime requires individual liberty, but it does not require any particular kind of political or economic system. As the product of negotiations among all nations, the regime is not a weapon in the clash of civilizations. In light of Chinese fears of Western subversion it is important to separate human rights from democratization and treat it as the international idea that it is, not as a code word for Westernization.

Under Mao Zedong, and even more rapidly since the beginning of Deng Xiaoping's reform, China made progress in supplying its citizens with economic and social rights. Living standards have increased, compulsory education has been extended to nine years, adult literacy stands at 79 percent according to official figures, and life expectancy at 69 exceeds that of many middle-income

countries. Nevertheless, the record may not be as good as it is generally thought
to be: A recent World Bank study finds that more than 350 million Chinese live
in conditions of grinding poverty. But pending more research, the focus of
foreign concerns is appropriately on the deprivation of civil and political rights.

In this realm, pervasive and systematic violations occur, many of them
carried out as matters of government policy. The violations that should be of
central international concern are those that are conducted by government agents,
transgress China's international obligations, and are indefensible under even the
most culturally relativist standards. The fact that such violations are sometimes
carried out under the auspices of Chinese law should not mislead policymakers.
Many abuses transgress the clear language of the Chinese Constitution, the law
of criminal procedure, and other enactments. Governments apply their own
laws, but when they stretch the law beyond all sense they abuse, not interpret, it.
A good example is Wang Dan's* illegal pre-trial detention and the four-hour
show trial at which he was convicted.

Nor should the United States be dissuaded from recognizing rights
violations by the fact that many Chinese citizens have gained new liberties of
personal movement and of private political expression under Deng's reforms, or
by the fact that the victims of rights abuses are a minority. As in U.S. history,
rights are not rights when they are limited to actions the government chooses to
tolerate, or to speech by persons with whom the government agrees.

The major categories of rights abuses are as follows.

• *Imprisonment, arbitrary detention, or forced exile* of people who have not
used or advocated violence, but whose political beliefs counter those of the
government. The victims include democracy movement activists arrested for
such acts as writing articles and petitioning the National People's Congress,
Tibetans detained for verbally supporting independence, Mongols detained
for a cultural revival movement, people detained for protesting about
personal grievances, and people accused of divulging state secrets for
circulating publicly available information.

---

* Wang Dan was a leader of the 1989 Tiananmen demonstrations in Beijing and was
number 1 on the most wanted list after the June 4 crackdown. He turned himself in and
served nearly four years in jail. He was released in 1993, but re-arrested in 1995 and held
in secret detention for over a year. He was charged with "plotting to overthrow the
government" for critical writings published abroad while he was out of jail between 1993
and 1995. After a two-hour trial, he was sentenced to eleven years. In 1998, he was released
from prison on "medical parole" and forced into exile to the U.S., where he now lives.

• *Religious repression*, including the arrests and beatings of adherents of the autonomous Catholic and Protestant movements; detention of Tibetans for religious practices; the house arrest of a six-year-old child who was designated by the Dalai Lama as the incarnation of the Panchen Lama. Religious victims are often charged as counterrevolutionaries, yet in many instances they have carried out no political acts.

• *Violations related to criminal procedure*, including lack of procedural safeguards against police abuse, especially during the process of "shelter and investigation"; insufficient safeguards against unlimited detention without trial; failure to provide fair trials (no publicity, insufficient provision for notice to family and preparation of a defense, lack of a presumption of innocence); lack of independence of the judiciary; and the widespread use of "re-education through labor" as a form of imprisonment at police initiative without benefit of trial (as in the recent case of Liu Xiaobo).† The 1995 Judges Law and 1996 amendments to the 1979 Criminal Procedure Law addressed some of these issues, but they did not resolve them.

• *Torture and abuse of inmates of prisons and labor camps*, and imposition of forced labor on inmates. The Chinese government has signed the convention against torture, has intermittently campaigned against the use of torture by police and jailers, and reiterated the outlawing of torture in its 1994 Prison Law. But the practice remains prevalent. In the case of many political prisoners it is evidently condoned by the central authorities. Prominent political prisoners recently or currently mistreated in prison included Wei Jingsheng,‡ Liu Gang, and Xu Wenli; those denied adequate medical care included Chen Ziming and Bao Tong.

• *Forced resettlement*, suppression of dissent, and violation of labor rights in connection with work on the Three Gorges project.

---

† Liu Xiaobo is a veteran dissident and a leader of the 1989 demonstrations in Tiananmen Square. He spent about a year in jail, then was re-sentenced to "reeducation through labor" in the mid-1990s for his subsequent political activities.

‡ Wei Jingsheng is China's best-known dissident. He first came to public attention in the "Democracy Wall" movement of 1978–1979 (see his "Fifth Modernization" [reading 56] for a sample of his thinking). He was arrested in 1979 and sentenced to fifteen years in prison. He was briefly released in fall 1993, but re-arrested in March 1994. In November 1995, he was charged with plotting to overthrow the government and sentenced to fourteen years in prison. In 1997 he was released from prison on "medical parole" and immediately forced into exile. He now lives in the U.S.

• *Forced abortion and sterilization* as part of population planning practices. These acts violate declared central government policy, yet are carried out by local officials on what appears to be a widespread basis.

Other civil and political rights violations have been less noticed in the outside world but are also appropriate subjects of concern. These include denial of the right to strike, denial of the freedom of the Chinese and foreign press, mistreatment of homosexuals, eugenic practices, and state interference in the practice of Islam and Buddhism.

A number of issues that have drawn foreign attention are more debatable as rights violations. In dealing with them, Western policy should focus on the ways in which these actions clearly violate international law. Such issues include the following:

• *Capital punishment.* Its use is not against international or Chinese law. Yet China uses the penalty exceptionally widely and with grossly inadequate safeguards. Moreover, international law considers public execution, still widely practiced in China, to be a violation of human dignity.

• *Harvesting of organs from condemned prisoners for transplantation.* Organ transplant does not violate international law. But in China the need for organs reportedly leads to frequent violations of due process, and the authorities seldom obtain donor consent.

• *Kidnapping, trafficking and abuse of women and girls.* The government has campaigned against these practices, yet they continue on a widespread basis, and some analysts plausibly argue this is only possible with the cooperation of local officials.

• *Export of prison labor products to the United States.* This violates U.S. law but not international law. But when prison labor is compulsory, as appears to be the case in Chinese prisons and labor camps, it is prohibited by ILO conventions.

Human Rights as Realpolitik

It is often noted that human rights represent Western values, and that no China policy that ignores them can achieve stable public support. It is less widely realized that promotion of human rights serves Western interests. Humanitarian sympathy and moral outrage can drive human rights policy, but consistency of purpose and clarity of focus must come from thinking through human rights as realpolitik.

The United States has devoted increasing effort since the end of the Cold War to strengthening the international system of rules that benefit the West in such areas as arms proliferation, trade, and the environment. It should give equal attention to fortifying the international human rights regime, which was one of the earliest regimes the world started building after World War II. This regime provides the framework for countries to intercede peacefully against domestic abuses in other states that potentially have serious international consequences. It has growing utility in the post-Cold War world as part of an emerging new international order.

First, the theory of the "democratic peace" that goes back to Immanuel Kant remains a good guide to policy, even though it is not universally accepted by political scientists. The exercise of political rights by citizens is conducive both to reducing governmental misjudgments in foreign affairs and to creating a more peaceful, rational, and predictable foreign policy. Countries that respect the rights of their own citizens are less likely to start wars, export drugs, harbor terrorists, or generate refugees.

In China's case, respect for human rights is a precondition for peaceful resolution of the Taiwan issue and successful management of Hong Kong's transition to sovereignty by the People's Republic on July 1, 1997. The human rights gap is a source of Beijing's difficulties in both situations. [Former] Taiwanese president Lee Teng-hui cited human rights violations as reason for his government's reluctance to accept unification. Hong Kong citizens protested the Wei Jingsheng and Wang Dan trials; they were similarly horrified when China's foreign minister responded that their freedom of speech after 1997 would exclude the right to criticize mainland policy on dissidents. A blowup in either situation will involve U.S. and other Western interests. Besides its economic stake in both places, the United States is committed to peaceful resolution of the Taiwan issue by the 1979 Taiwan Relations Act, and to supporting Hong Kong's freedom and prosperity by the McConnell Act of 1992. In promoting human rights in China, the United States helps prevent these situations from exploding in its face.

Second, China's stability and prosperity have been declared interests of the West since the early 1970s when Henry Kissinger was Secretary of State and Richard Nixon was the first president to travel to Communist China. A stable and prosperous China will anchor a stable Asia and contribute to global prosperity through trade. A corrupt, unstable, economically stagnant China will contribute to regional disorder, pollution, and refugee flows, and in the extreme case could heavily tax outside resources for relief. China's rapid development has created such a mobilized and sophisticated population that the government can no longer legitimize itself without allowing a measure of political freedom and participation, and without legitimacy its political stability is at risk. The latest repressions testify to the fragility of the regime, which sees a handful of peaceful dissenters as an intolerable threat to its survival.

This is not to say that China should be pushed to adopt a particular model of political system. But long-term stability will elude it until it honors the political freedoms so wisely recognized in all four of its own Constitutions since the founding of the People's Republic. This argument has been propounded within China by party reformers since the mid-1980s. It is now being promoted by officials who are experimenting with village-level elections aimed at consolidating, not undermining, Chinese Communist Party power.

Third, it is sometimes argued that human rights violations are a necessary, temporary tradeoff to achieve economic development. But few Chinese rights violations (for example, mistreatment of prisoners or violations of due process) have any plausible link to development. The few that have—such as deprivations of freedom of speech and political action, which may be considered necessary to keep political order—more often lead to developmental mistakes than to developmental achievements. Others, such as coercive population planning practices, are shortcuts to achieve targets that could be achieved equally well or better by legal methods, and probably with more secure results. Meanwhile, the violations in themselves worsen the quality of life and constitute a form of underdevelopment unmeasured in gross domestic product (GDP) and other statistics.

The relationship between human rights and development is in fact the reverse. Systems that violate political rights tend to generate distorted communications and commit policy mistakes. Suppression of information contributed to a vast famine during the Great Leap Forward, devastation of forests, salinization of farmland, and a series of dam collapses in 1975. Repression need not be widespread to send a signal to all Chinese that they should remain silent. Rights violations throttle the channels of discussion that China desperately needs to manage its problems in the midst of rapid economic and social change. Enforced silence worsens corruption, removes checks to environmental damage, and clears the field for potential megadisasters like the Three Gorges Dam, which specialists think may do extensive ecological damage. Nor can China compete successfully in world markets in the age of information when it filters Internet access, tries to control financial reporting, censors the domestic and foreign press, and otherwise interferes with the flow of ideas.

Fourth, human rights diplomacy is often erroneously presented as standing in conflict with Western business interests. In fact, even at the height of the Most-Favored-Nation (MFN) debates in the United States, U.S.-China trade boomed. In 1995, placing orders for European-made Airbus Industrie airplanes, Premier Li Peng indicated that the Chinese government was penalizing the competing U.S. supplier, Boeing, for U.S. human rights pressure. But most observers believe the Airbus decision was made for business reasons, with the human rights linkage tacked on later. I know of no other case in which the Chinese government discriminated against a U.S. company because of U.S. human rights activism. Continued U.S. division over human rights, however, may encourage the Chinese to start enforcing such linkages.

So far, maintaining the human rights issue on the bilateral agenda seems to have strengthened the U.S. hand in a number of trade and other negotiations. After Tiananmen, the anti-China atmosphere weakened Beijing's negotiating position in talks over intellectual property rights and market access. In both negotiations, faced with a threat of trade sanctions made credible by the general U.S. willingness to be tough on China, Beijing made concessions to Washington's demands. The fact that China was on the defensive on human rights weakened its ability to block U.S. and French arms transfers to Taiwan, probably helped explain the replacement of a conciliatory Hong Kong governor with one who confronted Beijing on the issue of Hong Kong democratization,[§] and may have accelerated China's accession to the nuclear nonproliferation treaty (NPT). Western pressure on human rights did not prevent and may have facilitated progress over issues like arms proliferation, Korean denuclearization, and global environmental degradation, as China sought to improve its image and to escape international isolation.

Rule of law is essential to protect U.S. and other foreign interests (business and otherwise) in China. Today, those Chinese who make and enforce the laws (legislators, procurators, and judges) are chosen, promoted, and kept or fired at the pleasure of political authorities. They write, adopt, revise, and apply the laws under party supervision, with little independent input.

Enforcement of the laws is arbitrary and the courts have no autonomy. The lawlessness of the Chinese legal system is experienced as much by foreign business people as by Chinese dissidents. What happened to Wei Jingsheng has happened in different forms to the Australian businessman James Peng, International Monetary Fund official Hong Yang, Royal Dutch Shell employee Xiu Yichun, and others.

[§] This refers to Geoffrey Patten, Britain's last governor in Hong Kong before its reversion to Chinese sovereignty in 1997.

If the law is a system of rules that are known in advance and enforceable by appeal to independent arbiters, then China's legal system will become a rule of law only when it incorporates respect for human rights. Expanding the legal code will not solve the human rights problem. Rather, making advances toward a true rule of law and guarantees of human rights will solve the problems with the legal code. A human rights-neutral improvement of the Chinese legal system is impossible.

The community of nations has a strategic interest in improving the human rights regime in all countries, not just in China. But China's demographic and geographic size, its strategic and economic importance, its status as a permanent member of the UN Security Council, and its position of leadership in the developing world make international interest in Chinese human rights practices greater than interest in many other nations' practices.

The difference between a China and a Vietnam, a Zaire, or a Saudi Arabia—or even an Indonesia or an India—is not the international standards applied to it, but the country's potential impact on Western and global interests. China should be held to the same standards as other countries, but its international importance justifies giving its rights violations more urgent and sustained attention than the world can afford to spend on every offending country.

The United States is not alone in its concern for human rights in China. Strong NGOs focused on human rights can be found in Britain, France, Australia, and to a lesser extent in Japan and Germany. Paris and London have interceded intermittently on human rights issues; Bonn and Tokyo occasionally. The European Parliament has passed numerous resolutions and in 1996 awarded Wei Jingsheng the Sakharov Prize, an award that recognizes contributions to freedom. France, Britain, and Australia will no doubt take steps to defend human rights in China even if the United States does not, but their pressure can seldom be effective without U.S. involvement. Japan and Germany are less likely to act on their own, and even if they act in concert with the United States they will usually tailor their actions to be less conspicuous than U.S. actions. In this as in so many other areas, U.S. leadership is essential.

The outside world's interest in Chinese human rights presents no threat to Chinese interests, properly understood. The goals of the international human rights regime are consistent with China's announced internal goals of rule of law, prosperity, stability, and more open decision making. As a weaker power, China stands to benefit from strengthening international regimes that impose limits on stronger powers and buttress the prerogatives of sovereign states as regime participants and makers. China benefits from the norms of proceduralism and multilateralism that are embedded in international regimes. Only through active participation can China take a hand in shaping regimes further to serve its needs. All these arguments apply as much to the international human rights regime as they do to regimes in such areas as trade and nonproliferation of arms.

To be sure, the Chinese government fears it will be criticized and even overthrown when citizens are able to exercise freedom of speech. But repressing criticism is not a long-term strategy for stabilizing power, as many in the ruling party know. An old Chinese proverb says, "You can dam a river forever, but not the mouths of the people."

Shaping Policy

. . . The human rights agenda with China should include both immediate and longer-term issues. Certain goals deserve tactical priority not because they are intrinsically more important than other goals, but because of their human urgency; their importance at the center of the human rights idea; their conformity with development trends within Chinese reform; and their political, ideological, and cultural bases of support inside and outside China. Progress on these issues will open the way to progress on other topics. Priority issues include the following:

• *Release of political prisoners and international access to prisons.* Although progress on individual prisoner cases may seem to make for only superficial improvement in China's human rights situation, such cases (like that of Wei Jingsheng and Wang Dan) have crucial symbolic significance and must form a focus of Western human rights diplomacy if such diplomacy is to make sense to concerned publics in China and abroad. Because of their symbolic value, such cases should be viewed as involving more than the fate of individuals. Initiatives on individual cases should be pursued in concert with efforts to open the Chinese prison system to international humanitarian organizations such as the ICRC. This would help the central government in its goal of improving conditions of detention of all prisoners, political and otherwise.

• *Legal reform and institution-building.* The outside world can support and accelerate Chinese legal reform and the construction of Chinese legal institutions. The West should maintain a focus on key problems such as arbitrary detention, procedural safeguards in criminal trials, reform of provisions of the criminal code that violate international norms, and international access to trials. These issues touch on the basic nature of the Chinese legal system and reform in these areas already commands substantial support within China. Pressure from outside helps focus the minds of the leaders on proposals they are already receiving from internal sources.

• *Ending religious repression.* This is an area of deep concern to many Western publics, and the repression is out of proportion to any realistic threat to the interests of the Chinese state.

• *Guaranteeing the continuity of civil and political rights in Hong Kong after its reversion to Chinese rule on July 1, 1997.*

Western policy should combine negative sanctions with constructive efforts such as educational and technical assistance, exchanges of specialists, and institution-building. Both government agencies and nongovernmental foundations, universities, and exchange organizations can contribute. Promising areas of institution-building include deepening Chinese involvement in the UN thematic mechanisms, building the court system, reforming legal codes, training the legal profession, upgrading prison administration, and improving social welfare systems. Businesses and other nongovernmental actors in the West (foundations and universities, among others) should maintain and enhance educational and exchange programs that assist Chinese agencies in fulfilling the Chinese government's declared human rights policies.

A policy of economic engagement is an adjunct to, not a substitute for, a human rights policy. Economic development and the opening to the West have helped raise living standards in China. But by themselves they will not solve China's human rights problems. On some fronts, economic development makes things worse (consider, for example, labor conditions in some foreign-invested and locally owned factories, abuse of migrant labor, eviction of farmers from land needed for development, and victimization of ordinary people by rising corruption). In some areas, development helps improve human rights but it works slowly—too slowly, for example, to save prisoners now being mistreated in Chinese prisons—and on some human rights problems it has no effect; for example, lack of funds is not the cause of the high death rates in some Chinese orphanages.

Economic development did not alone bring human rights improvements in South Korea or Taiwan—this required a long political and diplomatic struggle—and it has done little so far to improve human rights in Indonesia. The linkage between development and rights is too loose, the threshold too high, the time frame too long, and the results too uncertain to make economic engagement a substitute for direct policy intervention on human rights. A policy of economic engagement is neither an alternative to, nor a substitute for, a human rights policy. The West can walk and chew gum at the same time: Participate in China's economic development while at the same time working to improve China's compliance with the international human rights regime.

The Western business community cannot respond effectively to the human rights issue by wishing it would go away. Western businesses encounter not only practical difficulties but also public relations risks when they work in an environment that is abusive of fundamental human rights. The need to manage the issue more actively will be all the greater to the extent that the Chinese government begins to link business dealings and human rights. The business community should help the Chinese government respond constructively to Western human rights concerns, especially in areas in which business has an interest, responsibility, and experience like child labor, prison labor, women's rights, social welfare, independence of the judiciary, media freedom, and due process. Business approaches need not be confrontational. Working through technical assistance, personnel training, institution building, and grants, businesses can encourage Chinese reform to move in directions that are good for the business climate.

For its part, the human rights community should encourage consumers to take some responsibility for the conditions under which the goods they use are produced. Consumers should learn to look at labels and ask about labor rights, forced labor, and child labor in the factories that produce the goods they buy. . . .

Conclusion

The Chinese government has succeeded in convincing many analysts that human rights pressure is counterproductive. Beijing has signaled that the subject cannot be part of normal diplomacy because of its need to save face, succession politics and the rise of the military, national pride in recovered sovereignty after a century of neocolonialism and exploitation, and the nationalistic "feelings of the Chinese people." Beijing has persuaded many that it cannot negotiate over human rights.

It is always useful for a government to convince its interlocutors that it is too rigid to bend on an issue. But in fact, in its human rights diplomacy as in other areas of foreign policy, China has behaved as a realist power, making those concessions it perceived as necessary to influence states with which it was interacting, and not making them when they were deemed unnecessary. Since the late 1970s, a Western human rights policy combining pressure and assistance has successfully supported an internal Chinese evolution toward improved human rights, achieving greater results when it was firm and lesser results when it was weak. The historical record suggests that the main obstacle to maintaining an effective human rights policy toward China is not Chinese intransigence but Western indecision.

China today understands the U.S. human rights policy as one of hostility, restriction, containment, and punishment. The policy should instead be articulated in a way that conveys that the United States accepts China's legitimate security and other needs but wants China to play by the international rules. It should also stress that the desire to build an international human rights regime is not a code word for subverting the Chinese system of government. At home, [the U.S. government] needs to articulate its strategic rationale and thus build a domestic consensus for including human rights in its China policy.

Of all the international regimes with which the outside world wants a rising China to comply—the missile technology control regime, intellectual property rights, the WTO, and others—the international human rights regime is the oldest and the best established in international and domestic Chinese law. Less real conflict of interest exists between Chinese interests and the international regime in human rights than is the case with other areas of dispute. Moreover, the human rights regime is easily grasped by the relevant domestic publics—U.S., Chinese, European, Japanese, and others—and it can serve as a symbolic anchor for the otherwise somewhat elusive idea that the West wishes both to acknowledge China as a great power and to insist on China's obeying world rules as a great power should. In dealing with a realist power like China, the West will do better in building the human rights regime if it acts as a realist itself and maintains a consistent stand on behalf of its own interests.

16

Chinese Nationalistic Writing in the 1990s

SUISHENG ZHAO

From the late Qing to the present, China has experienced periodic waves of Westernization and nationalism. Some have advocated rejecting Chinese traditions and embracing foreign ideas, goods, and technology as the only way to modernize China; others have seen foreign influences as the cause, not the solution, of China's problems. This article shows that in the wake of the 1989 demonstrations and the end of a period of relatively open political debates, the trend shifted back toward nationalism and criticism of the West, especially the United States.

The end of the Cold War has seen the revival throughout the world of nationalist sentiments and aspirations. In China, the rapid decay of Communist ideology has led the Chinese Communist Party (CCP) to emphasize its role as the paramount patriotic force and the guardian of national pride in order to find a new basis of legitimacy to sustain its role. However, nationalist sentiment is not the sole province of the CCP and its propagandists. One truly remarkable phenomenon in the post-Cold War upsurge of Chinese nationalism is that Chinese intellectuals became one of the driving forces. Many well-educated people—social scientists, humanities scholars, writers and other professionals—have given voice to and even become articulators for a rising nationalistic discourse in the 1990s. This nationalistic sentiment contrasts strikingly to the anti-traditionalism that once dominated Chinese intellectual circles in the 1980s, in spite of the fact that some advocates of this new sentiment are the same people who had a "pro-Western complex" and promoted anti-traditionalism earlier. . . .

Nationalistic Writing in the 1990s

The decline of anti-traditionalism after the Tiananmen Incident led to a "de-romanticization" of the West among Chinese intellectuals in the 1990s. This resulted in an image of Western countries, especially the United States, closer to the portrait in official propaganda. For years there was a marked gap between

159

official propaganda and the popular portrait of the West, and a mood of cynicism towards official propaganda among a large proportion of the Chinese people, including intellectuals. During the period of reform and opening, official propaganda warned that, while Chinese needed to learn Western technology and methods of economic management, they should beware of "spiritual pollution" from unenlightened and antisocial American values. However, this fell on deaf ears. Many Chinese were so disillusioned with the official propaganda that they assumed the truth must be just the opposite. By this principle, if the propagandists said the United States was bad, it must be good. However, when the Chinese people heard a lot of good things about the West and had their own sources of information from Voice of America (VOA) and the BBC, and even had chances to visit Western countries as contact increased in the 1990s, there was an apparent convergence of perceptions because many Chinese people found a West similar to that described in official propaganda. The Chinese people, including the best educated intellectuals, tended to concur with the official position that the failure of the Chinese bid for the 2000 Olympics was orchestrated by Western bullies, and the United States was a "black hand" behind the Taiwan and Tibet independence movements and a "liar" about China's human rights. This can be seen from the publication of a large number of books attacking the West by Chinese writers in the 1990s. Some of them were instant bestsellers. *China Can Say No*, a militant anti-American book written by a group of young Chinese intellectuals, sold more than two million copies in 1996. *Behind the Demonization of China*, a book written by eight Chinese scholars who studied in the United States (six returned scholars in China, one who still teaches in a major U.S. university and one who works in the United States as a journalist), revealed the so-called deliberate political bias of the American media against China, and became an instant bestseller in early 1997.

While concurring with the official portrait of the West, Chinese intellectuals rediscovered the value of the Chinese cultural legacy which the Party had so relentlessly attacked for so long. There was a new awareness among intellectuals of the need to articulate a more vivid sense of collective identity of the Chinese people. The authors of *China Can Say No* confessed that while at college they craved Western culture and things but they really began to think after Beijing's defeat in the Olympic site competition and, particularly, after the U.S. aircraft carriers were sent to defend Taiwan in March 1996. Before the Chinese could say no to the Americans, they had to say no to themselves, to their lack of nationalistic spirit and to their blind worship of the United States. Chinese scholars of social sciences and humanities found additional reasons to become frustrated and disappointed with the West. A "Nobel Prize syndrome" had afflicted Chinese literary and social science circles for years. In literary circles, Chinese writers were first hopeful, then disappointed, and finally angry and presumptuous. They could not understand why they were not qualified to win a Nobel Prize in literature. Chinese economists were also aggrieved. They believed that because China was on a unique path of economic development and would become an economic superpower soon in the next century, Chinese economists should be awarded a Nobel Prize for China's economic miracle and for their part in creating new economic theories.

One Western scholar noted that "in the broader context of Chinese society, since 1989 there have been numerous indications of a growing disenchantment with the West and its allies." At the core of the disenchantment was nationalist sentiment in the Chinese intellectual arena. Many social scientists and humanities scholars called for a paradigm shift. A conservative, nationalistic intellectual discourse emerged in this context. This supported the official version of state nationalism by arguing that a centralized power structure must be strengthened in order to maintain social stability and economic development. It also vocally promoted cultural nationalism or an "anti-Westernism" movement by advocating a nativist value system and exploring Western mistreatment of China in modern history and the contemporary era.

The nationalism that the CCP has pursued bears a statist feature as it portrays the Communist state as the embodiment of the nation's will, seeking for its goals the kind of loyalty and support granted the nation itself. State nationalism and its nation-building aspirations invest state policy with a nationalistic tone. Economic development becomes national cause and transformation into a powerful and modernized country is a collective effort led by the Communist state. Economic, political, and social policymaking and implementation are accompanied by or infused with official propaganda emphasizing national unity, goals, and accomplishments. The commencement of reform in the late 1970s brought challenges to state nationalism from two different sources. One was the decentralization reform which dispersed centrally controlled resources and hence weakened the CCP's ability to enforce state nationalism. The other was the call for liberal democratic reform which threatened the very basis of the CCP's legitimacy to carry out state nationalism. Beginning in the late 1980s, however, a conservative intellectual discourse, known as new authoritarianism, emerged, which, intentionally or unintentionally, provided an intellectual support to state nationalism as it urged for a strong and authoritarian state to enforce modernization programs. At the First National Symposium on Modernization Theories held in Beijing in November 1988, new authoritarianism was defined as an "enlightened autocracy" to enforce economic development. New authoritarianism argued that the economic miracle of the four "little dragons" in East Asia was created because they all shared Confucian collectivism, family loyalty and frugality as well as a patriarchal power structure. Before the Tiananmen Incident, new authoritarianism was only a heatedly debated topic. It was advocated mainly by some personal assistants of Zhao Ziyang, then the CCP General Secretary, and a few scholars, including Shanghai-based Xiao Gongqin and Wang Huning. Many liberal scholars, especially anti-traditionalist scholars, argued strongly against neo-authoritarianism by questioning the validity of the allegedly causal relationship between Confucianist authoritarianism and economic success. After the Tiananmen Incident, new authoritarianism became a nationalistic, perhaps even xenophobic, response to the dissolution of the Soviet Union and the Western sanctions against China and was known as neo-conservatism, dominating both intellectual and political circles.

Neo-conservatism emphasizes state capacity, order, and economic development above all else while intending to restore moral values based on the conservative elements of Confucianism. . . . In 1992 a group of politically ambitious intellectuals, backed by "crown princes" (that is, the grown-up children of CCP elders), published a widely circulated article, "Realistic Responses and Strategic Choices for China after the Disintegration of the Soviet Union," which soon became a banner of neo-conservatism. This article argued that Marxism-Leninism was no longer effective in mobilizing loyalty and legitimating the state. It was necessary to develop a new ideological vision that drew selectively from China's traditional culture. The CCP should base itself firmly on Chinese nationalism. It advocated strict polity in contrast to [policy that "spoiled" the citizens]. One of its extreme suggestions was to establish so-called Party-owned assets. In other words, the Party should directly own economic assets to strengthen its political capacity in the increasingly decentralized system. In early 1994 Wang Shan, a Beijing-based scholar, published a book, *Looking at China Through a Third Eye.* Its sweeping critique of Deng's reform policy and its call for a positive re-evaluation of Mao's legacy created a minor sensation among politically sensitive and educated Chinese and quickly attracted a wide readership among intellectuals. As one study indicated, "This book gains potency by tapping into the general angst over national identity . . . by opening up a new populist strain of thought not apparent in previous neo-conservative writings."

After 1994, some prominent scholars joined the orchestra of neo-conservatism in arguing for economic development first and a strong state power to ward off the possible break-up of the country and economy. Li Zehou and Liu Zaifu, two prominent humanities scholars who went into exile in the West after the Tiananmen Incident, presented a view of economic development first in *Farewell, Revolution*. This book targeted mass social movements, especially those during the 1980s, and proposed a four-period agenda for China's modernization: economic development, personal freedom, social justice, democratic reform. By advocating economic development first, the authors argued for the state nationalism that places national interest above personal freedom. In the meantime, Xiao Gongqin, the Shanghai-based historian who came to prominence in the late 1980s as an advocate of new authoritarianism, began to issue warnings about the dangers of weak central government control. Xiao saw no solutions in Western nostrums or in Communist ideology, but only in nationalism. Xiao's view was elucidated in his two articles, "Nationalism and Ideology in China in the Transitional Era" and "History and the Prospect of Nationalism in China." He worried about the possible disintegration of Chinese society resulting from the decline of the official ideology and argued that nationalism could play "the function of political integration and coacervation" in the post-Cold War era. Commenting on South Korean experiences, another scholar, Yi Baoyun, stated that "for nations lagging behind, the appropriate choice is not a renunciation of nationalism, but a revitalization of it so as to integrate and elevate people's loyalty on the national level. . . . Nationalism is an insurance [policy for] this national integration, and through a change of the system, the nation can be led to the road of self-strengthening and peaceful competition."

This point was confirmed by two Western-trained social scientists, Hu Angang and Wang Shaoguang, who published an in-depth study on this subject, *A Report on China's State Capacity*. Hu was a visiting scholar at Yale University before he went back to China to head a research center in the Chinese Academy of Sciences and Wang held a teaching position at Yale University. They argued that today's developing country could not repeat the model of "natural growth" followed by Western countries. Instead, a stronger role for government was needed in the economy and for the implementation of a "top-down" economic modernization program. In China this meant that the government should continue to rule with an iron fist especially in the areas of finance and economic planning. According to their report, the current central power in China was too weak and a stronger power was necessary. . . .

Nationalistic writing in the 1990s also promoted cultural nationalism, which took Chinese culture as a symbol against Western cultural hegemony and claimed the positive function of traditional culture in maintaining political order.

Liu Kang and Li Xiguang, two of the-authors of *Behind the Demonization of China*, stated that "in the 1990s, Chinese intellectuals ought to . . . liberate themselves from 'modern' Western speech and thought patterns, and acquire a new understanding of modern nationalism and nativism, to form a genuinely humane spirit and rebuild their 'academic lineage' and 'ethical traditions' with Chinese culture." Cultural nationalism argued that the dominance of Western culture in international cultural exchanges was threatening the cultures of developing countries such as China. Through these exchanges Western values and lifestyles were able to influence the social ethics of developing countries. Satellite and television broadcasts played a big role in this, when Western countries' military colonization gave way to "electronic colonialism" or "cultural hegemony." The advocates of cultural nationalism asserted that "the Western nations are wholeheartedly intent on turning China into a country such as India and Mexico. So we Chinese need to get conceptually free from the ideological and psychological 'Westernized mindset.'" Encouraged by China's rapid economic development in the 1990s, cultural nationalism predicted a Chinese cultural renaissance on the world stage in the 21st century. Guan Shijie, director of the International and Intercultural Communication Program at Beijing University, even stated that "the time has come for the West to learn from the East. The West should switch positions and the teacher should become a student. The Confucian concept of universal harmony will be dominant during the next century, which will be one of peace and development." . . .

Causes for the Rise of Nationalistic Discourse

Although nationalistic discourse developed by social sciences and humanities scholars overlaps, to a certain extent, the official ideology of the Chinese government, its emergence was largely independent of ideological propaganda. What was truly remarkable was that a great majority of intellectuals who promoted nationalism were trained in the West or were visiting scholars in Western academic institutions. Their intellectual background was not Chinese studies but Western social sciences and humanities. Some of them were the active advocates of anti-traditionalism in the 1980s. The dramatic change in their intellectual discourse does not prove the success of official propaganda. Nor is it mainly due to the repressive measures taken by the government against those advocating pro-Western and democratic views. Rather, some more complicated socioeconomic, intellectual, and personal reasons were responsible for the rise of nationalistic discourse.

At the socioeconomic level, the emergence of nationalistic discourse coincided with the end of the Cold War and China's rapid economic growth in the past decade. The West won the Cold War. However, many Chinese intellectuals discovered or concurred with the official propaganda that the West quickly supplanted the Cold War with a "Cold Peace." The post-Cold War transformation in Eastern Europe and the former Soviet Union was not as rapid or positive as expected. The West, its values and systems did not make that much difference to post-Communist countries. Although Russia adopted a Western-style democratic system, the Western countries still tried everything to weaken Russia's standing in international affairs and refused to provide Russia with sufficient assistance as it struggled internally with its reform program. For those who supported the 1989 student movement, there was the added realization that if China was to initiate the dramatic democratic reform promoted by the West, the nation could well [experience a disorder similar to Russia's].

In contrast to the former Soviet Union, China's incremental economic reform brought about rapid economic growth in the 1990s. Economic success transformed the nation's intellectual discourse and built up Chinese intellectuals' self-confidence in their tradition and awakened national pride and cultural identities. In a way, the lines between patriotism, nationalism, and China's pursuit of "modernity with Chinese characteristics" were blurred. Increasingly self-conscious with China's rising power status, Chinese intellectuals were fed up with the West that badgered them to change their own basic values, consisting of beliefs that were thousands of years old and shared by some other East Asian countries. They began to take a much more positive attitude towards their own past in a belief that traditional culture could play an important role in robust economic growth.

Vigorous economic development also encouraged China to push for the international rights it felt were commensurate with its rising power status (or "equal rights" in Chinese official terms). This drive inevitably involved a conflict of national interests with some Western countries. In the early years of reform and opening up to the outside world, China had very limited contact with the West and hence the conflict of national interests was not clear to many Chinese people, including intellectuals, who had a romanticized vision of the West. As noted earlier, anti-West sentiments among Chinese intellectuals developed after Beijing's failure to win its bid to host the 2000 Olympic Games and disputes between China and the United States regarding China's MFN trading status and its entry into the World Trade Organization. These events disappointed many Chinese intellectuals and made them believe that Western countries, especially the United States, were afraid of the emergence of a strong China. While just two years before, these same intellectuals were excited about the American punishment of Iraq in the Gulf War, they now felt that the West would use its power to prevent China from standing up. Coincidentally, after 1994, arguments supporting a policy to contain China appeared in the West. This lent credence to the new understanding of a conflict of interests between China and the West. Chinese intellectuals could hardly believe that these arguments to contain China were meant to contain Communism only. The West was aiming vindictively to contain China as a rising power. . . .

For Chinese intellectuals who went to the West, there was a huge gap between the Western model of modernization and the Chinese reality of history and culture. This led them to doubt the worth of modern Western values to Chinese society and the utility of mainstream Western theories for building a strong China. Some Chinese intellectuals turned to critical and peripheral theories in the West in an attempt to find intellectual inspiration for a new path of modernization that would fit the Chinese situation. Some others looked towards the Eastern civilizations and Chinese experiences to come up with a new modernity that, they believe, can resolve the problems that arose in the process of China's modernization. They therefore took a critical attitude towards the mainstream theories of modernity and advocated a paradigm shift in an attempt to establish a Chinese model of modernization.

The emergence of nationalistic writing was also related to the personal experiences of some Chinese scholars who traveled to the West and endured cultural shock and hardship. These personal experiences were expressed by a number of popular television series and books in the 1990s. The television series *A Beijinger in New York* became extremely popular with Chinese audiences, in particular with intelligentsia, in 1993. The series focused on conflicts between Chinese and Western culture, psychology, and concepts of values, and depicted a Chinese intellectual, Wang Qiming, who made his fortune after a train of failure and betrayals in the United States. One Chinese review of the series said that Wang's experiences would "help Chinese television viewers better understand American society and help those who entertain a rosy American dream to become more realistic." Other Chinese scholars' negative personal experiences were told in a bestseller of 1996, *Study in the United States*. The author, Qian Ning, is the son of Qian Qichen, [former] Chinese Foreign Minister, and a journalist who studied in the University of Michigan from 1989 to 1995." Although Qian presented some positive aspects of his own personal experience and American society, his book told many stories of Chinese scholars in their struggle to survive the cultural shock and fierce competition in the United States based on his extensive interviews.

Conclusion

This study shows that the intellectual quest for national greatness and modernization that began in the beginning of the 20th century has continued towards the turn of the 21st century, Despite ideological clashes and heated debates, Chinese intellectuals have pursued a similar [nationalist dream]: to make China rich and strong. China's reformist and revolutionary movements over the past century have essentially been born of the struggle to make the dream true. In their turbulent quest, Chinese intellectuals have progressed from hastily snatching ideas from the West and totally negating their own tradition to rediscovering the value of their own past and rejecting Western attitudes. The emergence of nationalistic writing in the 1990s was caused by complicated socioeconomic, intellectual and personal reasons. It took place when some Chinese intellectuals began a serious reassessment of their own past and Western values, particularly Western attitudes toward China's rise in the post-Cold War world. After a century of turbulence and Mao's social and economic experiments, the Chinese people, particularly the best educated intellectuals, have been inspired by the real possibility of rejuvenating the nation. The current rapid economic growth has fed national pride. They have become determined to eradicate all obstacles in their pursuit of prosperity and pride.

However, confrontation with the West has not only stimulated but also complicated the Chinese search for this dream. This development confirms Lucian Pye's observation that "between the two extremes of either nihilistically denouncing Chinese civilization or romanticizing it, most Chinese intellectuals and political leaders have consistently failed to do what their counterparts in the rest of the developing world have tried to do, which was to create a new sense of nationalism that would combine elements of tradition with appropriate features of the modern world culture." The dream of a strong nation may come alive only if it is constantly enriched through new realities. The American dream of independence was revised to take into account the increasing interdependence of the modern world. Chinese intellectuals have yet to find their way to forms of cross-cultural dialogue in which the Chinese and Westerners may more critically understand themselves in the light of each other.

17

A Quiet Roar: China's Leadership Feels Threatened by a Sect Seeking Peace

ERIK ECKHOLM

The sudden rise of the Falun Gong spiritual sect took China's leaders by surprise, and they have aggressively tried to stamp out the movement. Why are China's leaders threatened by a group of predominately middle-aged and elderly people who meet to do exercises and are critical of the corrupt and decadent practices of modern China? As journalist Erik Eckholm describes in this article, Falun Gong is more than just a group of people who meet for morning exercises, and even a group such as this poses a challenge to the Leninist state in China. The popularity and notoriety of Falun Gong reveals much about the political and social changes taking place in China as a result of economic modernization.

Has it come to this: that the Chinese Communist Party is terrified of retirees in tennis shoes who follow a spiritual master in Queens?

So it almost seemed here during recent days of bizarre scenes of arrests and flying invective against the Falun Gong movement.

As security forces worked frantically to round up believers who converged on Beijing to plead Falun Gong's case, the government left no doubt that it intends to wipe out all organized traces of the movement—even if that requires jailing thousands of people who never saw themselves as enemies of the state.

Behind closed doors in recent weeks many Chinese, from professors to cab drivers, have said the government has overreacted. Many say its blunt repression of a spiritual movement that attracted hordes of ordinary people seeking health and happiness will cause lasting social divisions and further erode faith in the party.

But many experts on Chinese politics say China's Communist leaders probably saw little choice.

Their first principle is preserving the rule of the party, which they equate with protecting social stability. And they have consistently tried to stamp out any competing loyalties. "Logically, they had to do this," said [Suisheng] Zhao, a Chinese-born political scientist at [the University of Denver; also author of reading 16]. "For the Communist Party, the greatest threat is a nationally organized force."

Since its founding in 1992, Falun Gong, a mix of cosmic healing theories, Buddhism, and Taoism that promises salvation in a corrupt world, had gained millions of followers—retirees, middle-aged women and even many officials and students, who gathered regularly in public parks to practice their mystical exercises.

"For the party this was a big problem," said Roderick MacFarquhar, a professor of Chinese politics and history at Harvard University. "The party cannot allow the existence of a rival mass organization with control over the hearts and souls of the ordinary people—and exposing their own ideological vacuum."

Although the group was outlawed on July 22, [1999,] unknown thousands of its believers have refused to fade away, creating an unexpected crisis and forcing the government to mobilize all its media and social organizations, even bosses in work places, to engage in ritual condemnations.

In the months since the ban, official vilification of the group and its elusive founder, Li Hongzhi, who moved to New York in 1998, has grown ever more shrill—a sign that the eradication campaign has not gone smoothly.

On Saturday senior Communist legislators described Falun Gong as "unprecedented in the 50-year history of the People's Republic in terms of its size of organization, influence, number of illegal publications as well as the damages it brought to society," the New China News Agency reported.

These were strong words for a group that had received little high-level attention before it held an unauthorized vigil in Beijing on April 25, when some 10,000 members from several provinces quietly gathered around the leadership compound to protest published critiques of their movement and to demand official recognition.

By its very existence, this gathering was the most serious challenge to Communist Party authority since the student-led demonstrations of 1989.

When they outlawed Falun Gong, the authorities charged that Li and a small cabal of leaders had a secret political agenda to subvert the nation, though no evidence was offered.

Li, who keeps in touch with an expanding global following through the Internet, insists he has no political aims. He has never advocated the overthrow of Communist rule, or even a more liberal policy on religion. And his believers insist they just want to be left alone to focus on their inner "cultivation."

But the believers have also been quick to mobilize in defense of their movement, in hundreds of smaller protests before and since the giant demonstration in April in Beijing. In China such defiance of authority is inevitably considered deeply political.

Although it has retreated from many spheres of personal and social life, the Communist Party still demands the stated allegiance of every organization. But as is evident in their willingness to face arrest, the more fervent followers of Falun Gong give their supreme loyalty to Li and what they consider his life-transforming theories.

When it banned Falun Gong, the government brought a variety of criminal charges against Li and arrested a number of top organizers. Thousands more who persisted in proclaiming their faith have since been detained or harassed in cities all around the country.

In Beijing over the last ten days, more than 3,000 protesters were rounded up as soon as they were detected, officials said. Many were bused back to the authorities in their hometowns for "reeducation," which may mean loss of jobs or time in labor camps.

But the police seem unable to mop up a core of believers, in Beijing and elsewhere, who say they are prepared to risk everything for their faith and have made smart use of e-mail, mobile phones and pagers to communicate with each other and with supporters abroad.

At the same time the effort to discredit and destroy Falun Gong, using the familiar scripts of Communist dictatorship, has shifted into high gear.

Last Thursday, in an effort to bolster the moral and legal case, the party's newspaper, *People's Daily*, featured a front-page commentary arguing that Falun Gong is an "evil cult" that any government would have to suppress.

The rank and file, it said, were mere dupes of Li's "sorcery." Small numbers of people continue to operate under Li's "remote control," it said, and are "unable to see the blood-soaked truth." Chinese authorities have blamed the group for at least 1,400 deaths of members who refused needed medical care.

On Wednesday another *People's Daily* editorial said, "Like all cults, Falun Gong is an antisocial, antihuman, antiscience, and antigovernment malignant tumor."

The group does have some cult-like features, including fervent devotion to one man's off-beat doctrines, obsessive secrecy, and often extreme reactions to criticism. Master Li, as followers refer to him, has been caught dissembling about aspects of his background, about his presence in Beijing just before the

April demonstration, and about some of his wilder claims of supernatural powers, among other things.

But the government offered no convincing evidence for its comparisons of Falun Gong to the Jim Jones cult, which committed mass suicide, and the Branch Davidians, who died while under F.B.I. attack in Texas.

Chinese who sampled Falun Gong in recent years, usually to see if it would improve their health and spirits, say that beyond the purchase of books, they were never asked to hand over large sums of money to the group. While differing loyalties to Falun Gong sometimes caused bitter divisions within families, followers were not asked to cut all normal social bonds. Nor, in contrast to the more notorious cults, was it difficult to leave the group.

The reported deaths of believers who refused medical treatment pose a far more complex issue than the official victim counts would have it, especially in a country where many people believe that cosmic forces influence health and rely on traditional treatments not always supported by modern medicine.

On Saturday the national Parliament, laying one of the final planks for coming show trials, adopted a stringent anticult law that was tailored expressly for prosecution of Falun Gong leaders.

The next day, in a step being strangely touted as progress toward the "rule of law," prosecutors charged four reputed ringleaders with major crimes under that new law—for actions supposedly taken months before it was adopted. Other indictments of lesser leaders around the country have also been reported.

In China's long history of authoritarian government, the danger to rulers from emerging national organizations has been repeatedly demonstrated, said Zhao, the political scientist . . . .

The lesson was not lost on Mao Zedong, Zhao noted. During his Cultural Revolution of 1966–1976, for example, Mao sent in army troops to disperse the Red Guards he had created as soon as local groups began to coalesce into broader entities. And in the 1950's, religious sects and secret societies were brutally crushed by Communist authorities undoubtedly mindful of how mystical movements like the Taiping rebels and the Boxers disrupted the country in imperial times.

. . . [W]ith rising unemployment, anger over official corruption and a slowdown in economic growth, the government feels insecure and vulnerable, many experts say. The authorities also worry about the long-term effect of new communications technologies—skillfully wielded by Falun Gong and democracy advocates—on the party's ability to monopolize power and public discourse.

Party leaders are only beginning to hint in public about the possible extent of their Falun Gong problem. Until this week, official statements about the crackdown stressed that while a small number of top leaders would be harshly punished, other adherents would simply need education about how they had been duped.

But an article Monday in *People's Daily* described for the first time the likelihood of "long-term resistance." Beyond the top leaders, it said, "second and third tiers" of leaders have been created.

"In a few areas, illegal meetings are still being held," the article said, the only clue for Chinese readers of the continuing subterranean struggle.

18

China's Emerging Business Class: Democracy's Harbinger?

MARGARET M. PEARSON

Many scholars and policymakers believe that economic reform will inevitably lead to political change in China. In a similar fashion, they believe that the private entrepreneurs will be primary supporters of democracy. But as Margaret Pearson shows in this article, most Chinese businessmen have little interest in promoting political liberalization. In fact, in many ways they are partners with the state in China, not potential adversaries. So far, China's entrepreneurs have been unwilling to perform the role that many foreign observers have assigned to them.

. . . Claims that democratization will emerge out of China's economic success have been muted recently because of the ripple effects from the Asian economic crisis, and the expectation that Prime Minister Zhu Rongji will deepen state-owned enterprise reforms that may lead to massive layoffs and, perhaps, instability. Yet the real problem with these claims is not that current economic difficulties will postpone democratization to the future: it is that the assumption of a link between the rise of new economic elites and democratization is logically flawed and not supported by empirical data. China's new business elite, while possessing relatively great autonomy and often holding politically liberal beliefs, has not emerged as a strong independent force. Rather, both the state's efforts to co-opt this group and its ability to navigate the business environment using nondemocratic means have denied China's new business elite the historical political significance many would wish for it.

Defining the New Business Elite

Members of China's new business elite work in the most advanced sectors of the country's economy. Two core segments of this group are owners of private enterprises and managers in foreign businesses operating in China.

173

These private and foreign business sectors were a creation of Deng Xiaoping's policies of domestic reform and "opening to the outside world," which were initiated in the late 1970s. Reversing a long-held antipathy toward markets and foreign capital, the post-Mao reformers encouraged private and foreign invest- ment with the hope of raising productivity and innovation, growing the economy, and attracting advanced technology and managerial skills from outside China. As a result of these reforms (and a favorable international economic environ- ment), China's economy has grown an average of 10 percent a year for the past two decades.

Although private firms in China tend to be small, they are growing in size and economic importance. Most have been established in the manufacturing, mining, transportation, and construction industries, but they have become a sig- nificant presence in the nascent professional-services sector, especially finance and real estate. In 1994 the government reported that there were 420,000 private enterprises, but the actual number is believed to be much higher. In the foreign sector, Sino-foreign joint ventures, wholly foreign-owned enterprises, and representative offices of foreign companies have emerged as important players in the economy, especially the export sector. As of 1997, over $200 billion in foreign capital, funding more than 300,000 projects, had flowed into China. About two-thirds of that investment originated in Hong Kong (now, of course, part of China) and Taiwan. Despite the dramatic growth in foreign investment, as of 1996 foreign capital—including that from Hong Kong—employed less than 1 percent of the entire Chinese workforce.

The foreign and private sectors have attracted an impressive group of people. The formal educational level of elites in these sectors tends to be high, although Horatio Alger stories are not uncommon, especially among those who were denied a university education during the Cultural Revolution and are now in their late forties. Elites in the foreign and private sectors command a relatively high income; they are paid many times the average manufacturing wage in China (which in 1996 was approximately $680 per year) and have a high standard of living. These attributes—position, education, and income level—have translated into considerable prestige in China's urban society, although recent corruption scandals involving elites have taken a toll. . . .

In Relation to the State

Not only have China's business elites taken on new economic roles, they have also carved out a new relationship with the socialist state. Their situation contrasts sharply with that of managers in government-owned enterprises. This latter group historically has been—and remains comparatively so today—tied to and dependent on the party-state. Their work is overseen by Communist Party cadres working within the enterprise. Their welfare, especially housing, medical care, and pensions, has been at the mercy of a system run by these cadres, one that rewards political loyalty as much as or more than managerial capacity. A dossier of employee activity is kept at the enterprise. In the absence of a labor market, these dossiers have been hugely influential in promotions or job transfers. The political, socioeconomic, and personal dependencies of state-sector managers have bound them tightly to the enterprise and the state.

This kind of dependency on the party-state has largely been severed in the foreign sector and, to a lesser degree, the private sector. The market orientation of these new business sectors, which are at least partially under the authority of foreign firms rather than party cadres, has translated into a significant degree of autonomy. This is especially true in southern China and Shanghai, where business elites find their more freewheeling ways unencumbered by state bureaucrats. The party presence in both sectors is minimal and ineffectual. Labor mobility is much greater; workers switch jobs at will in search of higher pay and more responsibility. Personnel dossiers are kept outside the enterprise; their contents are essentially ignored by foreign employers and have become irrelevant for private enterprise owners. . . .

Throughout post-Mao China, the private and foreign sectors have seen a resurgence of business associations. These associations are to be nongovernmental actors that facilitate economic growth at a time when the growing complexity of the economy dictates that the state devolve many functions it had previously carried out. Their nongovernmental status is to distinguish them from the mass organizations of the Maoist era, which were "transmission belts" for state policy and hence dominated by state interests. An important function of such associations is to act as advocates for newly legitimized business interests. They have helped businesses with arbitration and coordinated businesses' ties with government agencies. The associations claim to pass complaints of businesses upward to relevant government authorities, and in some cases they have successfully influenced the state's policy toward business, although usually in narrow areas and at the local level.

Playing It Safe

China's business elites hold political and economic views that are decidedly more liberal than those expressed in official policy. This is not unsurprising, given the general profile of the people attracted to the private and foreign sectors.

These elites view near-total use of markets and deeper privatization of the economy as necessary, although they believe steps in this direction must be carefully crafted so as not to produce social unrest. In addition, foreign sector elites in particular have been strongly influenced by their contacts with foreigners and often by their experiences abroad. They see virtually nothing in the workings of the international economy that they judge inappropriate for China.

In these elites' views of politics in China, the most notable sentiments are, at best, indifference and, at worst, hostility and disgust. There is a strong distaste for communism. Indeed, an important reason for choosing jobs in these two leading sectors is to escape politics. The elites favor political liberalization that will promote the freedom to live their lives and work as they see fit. Significantly, the freedoms they claim to value most are small ones, such as the ability to travel freely, rather than democracy writ large. Private enterprise owners tend to be somewhat less liberal than foreign-sector managers, moreover, believing that political change should be initiated and controlled by the state. They have been critical of the student-initiated demonstrations at Tiananmen Square in 1989, while foreign-sector managers have been considerably more sympathetic. Nonetheless, the views of both private entrepreneurs and managers in foreign firms are quite liberal.

China's new business elite has thus carved out a relationship with the state that diverges substantially from what existed under Maoism and from what exists for most of the urban population today. Members of the business elite in the foreign and private sectors have structured lives for themselves largely outside the purview of the state. They have strong opinions about the need for China to move away from its status quo—further away than is officially accepted by even reformers in the government.

But Civil Society?

Despite these changes, the question remains: Has this elite stratum, born of the economic reforms, created pressure on the state for political reform, and has it acted as a nascent force for democratization? Both types of entrepreneur enjoy considerable autonomy, and would seem to be better positioned than any other social group in China to generate civil society. And yet they disappoint those who would assign them this historic role.

To understand this failure, we must examine the expectation that the new business class will serve to promote democratization. This logic of the emergence of civil society proceeds in two sets of steps. It is posited, first, that for market reforms to succeed the state will have to devolve resources and decision-making authority to new economic actors. Moreover, new markets will provide an additional source of goods such as housing that previously have been the monopoly of the state. Once decentralization of the economy and the growth of market alternatives have created greater autonomy from the state, people will develop horizontal relationships within society (such as through business associations that lobby the government) and will understand themselves to have economic interests that, to a significant degree, diverge from those of the state.

If these changes are to translate into actual political reform initiated from below, a second set of steps involving consciousness and political behavior must occur. Strengthened horizontal relationships must lead to a group consciousness among new economic actors, and to a belief that they can determine their own economic fate. This realization must, in turn, stimulate involvement in political activity Not only must new economic groups act readily—they must also act toward certain ends.

New middle classes and business classes must have an interest in pressing for greater freedom from state controls. They must also be motivated to act by the belief that their interests will not be protected in their current situation. Ultimately, because political freedoms will be seen as necessary to protect economic freedoms, these new groups must press for extensive liberalization of the polity. The results of their efforts will be civil society.

The Limitations of Trickle-down Democracy

Even though economic reform may empower new groups, spur them to realize diverse interests, and create greater opportunity for autonomy from the state, these phenomena have not ensured the will to act or the desire to democratize. Although economic reform may create conditions conducive to democratization, the development of a liberal polity is multifaceted, extremely complex, and easily thwarted. For example, the interests of new economic actors may not actually support democratization but may instead lead them to collude with the state against labor, or simply remain apolitical. Moreover, scholars who observe transitions to democracy from socialist regimes emphasize that the key to a successful transition (as occurred in Poland) is the ability of societal groups and the state to organize within themselves, and then negotiate a pact with each other. But societal interests may not be able to organize themselves to push for liberalization, and the state may refuse to enter a pact-making negotiation, trying instead simply to smash any nascent opposition. A more subtle yet powerful strategy is to preempt the growth of organized political pressure from new economic actors, even while encouraging their economic dynamism.

With this logic in mind, we can observe what has happened in China. Most of the first set of steps toward civil society has actually occurred, as is clear from the previous description of the new business elite. The state has devolved authority to members of the elite, who are much less dependent on the state and are, ideologically, liberal. Yet while we must not ignore these inklings of civil society, we must recognize that the picture is decidedly more complex; these are just inklings. Indeed, the second set of steps has not occurred in China. Conditions that would seem to favor a democratic push by the business elite have been deflected by three factors: the actual perceived interests of most members of the business elite; the existence of alternative mechanisms for mediating with the state; and efforts by the state to preempt the business elite as an opposition force. Each of these counterforces can be considered in turn.

In terms of their perceived interests, although as a group members of the business elite oppose the current regime, most wish to avoid participation in politics. Though proud of their economic role, they are not, and do not wish to be, at the forefront of political change. They have not taken to the streets to protest policies, nor have they organized themselves to lobby or negotiate with the government for policy change. The apparent paradox of being antiparty but also apolitical can be explained in part by the personal experiences of these businesspeople. Having been forced into activism, particularly during the Cultural Revolution of 1966–1976, many tend to have a strong distaste for politics. Others have family members who suffered state discrimination during the Cultural Revolution or other campaigns. They do not readily distinguish between activism forced by the state on behalf of the state and more sponta- neous organization in their own interests. They prefer instead to immerse themselves in business. Members of the business elite also believe they are powerless to effect the changes they might want because they are too vulnerable to forge a new relationship with the state. Consistent with this perception, the business elite has not formed a strong network of horizontal ties or a strong group consciousness. . . .

The newly established business associations in the foreign and private sectors were intended to be legitimate advocates for economic interests that are independent of the state. And, as we have seen, they serve this function to some degree. Yet business associations also have a Janus-faced quality. The state's intention is to remain heavily involved in them and, ultimately, to use them to co-opt and influence business interests rather than be influenced by them. These associations represent an attempt by the state to unleash the power of business, but in a manner that directs it toward the government's goals and prevents the newly created forces from acting against state interests. The business associations have been organized and sanctioned by the state, and their leadership has been dominated by cadres dispatched from related ministries. Their legitimacy derives solely from having received state sanction. Members of the business class see them as state dominated and not especially useful except as vessels for clientelist ties.

Reasons to Remain Skeptical

. . . There is therefore ample reason for skepticism that the business elite will emerge as a catalyst for major political change in the People's Republic. The contemporary business elite will continue for some time to cooperate closely with officials (especially at the local level), and its business associations will remain, ultimately, dominated by the state. The segments of China's new business elite in which we are most likely to find greater independence from the state exhibit the behavior not primarily of civil society but of clientelism[*] and corporatism.[†] It is thus unlikely that other segments of the business elite that start out more closely tied to the state—such as officials-turned-entrepreneurs—will be at the forefront of significant political liberalization.

We can expect that other segments of the business elite will fit even more easily into the pattern that has emerged. And it is unlikely that actors in other key parts of the economy—the state-owned and collective sectors—will establish patterns of interaction with the state that are more independent and democratizing than what exists in the foreign and private sectors. It is true that, as the economic reforms deepen, individuals in these other economic sectors will increasingly rely on the market for jobs and the provision of other necessities. But these changes have not occurred at the pace or to the degree found in the private and foreign sectors, and clientelism and corporatism are equally, if not more, prominent there as well.

China's future will not be determined by its antidemocratic past. Nor will the future necessarily continue on the current path, no matter how functional that

---

[*] Clientelism refers to a set of personal relationships between patrons and clients that are based on exchanges of material goods, favors or other kinds of services. In the Chinese context, these vertical relationships are referred to as *guanxi*.

[†] Corporatism refers to a particular form of state-society relations, in which there are a limited number of organized interest groups, either created or approved by the state. The purpose is to maintain the state's control over organized interests and prevent competition between social groups, as occurs in a pluralist system like that of the United States.

path appears at the moment. Moreover, other noneconomic groups in China—dissidents, intellectuals, students—could prove successful at coaxing civil society. Yet, as with China's new business elite, the democratizing role attributed to these groups should be subject to close empirical scrutiny, and facile assumptions about the link between economic change and political liberalization should be avoided.

19

Village Elections: Democracy from the Bottom Up?

TYRENE WHITE

People who argue that there has been no political change in China should visit the countryside, as Tyrene White shows in this article. Based on her own observations and those of other scholars, plus reports of the Chinese government, she shows the logic that led to the implementation of grass-roots democracy in China's villages. The question now facing China's leaders is whether they can afford to extend democratic elections to higher levels of the political system without jeopardizing the CCP's grip on power.

. . . In the mid-1980s, when China's economic reforms began to take off, the country's rural institutions were breaking down. The reforms had begun to undermine the state's monopoly of economic and political power, and many local cadres saw more profit in working their own fields or starting sideline businesses than in carrying out difficult jobs such as collecting taxes and enforcing birth control. Peasants grew bolder in their resistance to authority, especially as price inflation, tax increases, and corruption began to erode the economic gains of the early 1980s and incomes began to stagnate or fall. Meanwhile, local governments sometimes ran out of money to buy peasants' grain and dared to hand out IOUs instead. Predictably, relations between peasants and cadres, and between cadres at higher and lower levels, grew tense, and skittish party leaders in Beijing began to worry about the prospect of rural unrest.

It was in this context that the foundation for village-level elections was established. In 1986 and 1987, heated debate took place on a draft law on grassroots organization called the Organic Law of Villagers' Committees. Adopted on a trial basis by the National People's Congress (NPC) in June 1988, the law attempted to address the problems of village-level organization and township-village relations by establishing a system of village autonomy and self-management.

The bill was designed to clarify the legal status of the village, which is not a formal level of government (the township, a level above the village, is the lowest official level of government), and to limit the rapacious tendencies of township and county governments to extract as much as possible from villagers to fund local development projects, pad budgets, and boost salaries. By declaring villages to be autonomous and self-managing, supporters of the bill hoped to establish a sound basis for village organization, and to temper the power of township officials by setting clear limits to their authority and defining village obligations explicitly.

If villages were to have any chance of achieving meaningful self-rule, however, they needed leaders who were empowered to defend village interests while still carrying out those unpopular and thankless tasks—collecting taxes, enforcing birth control—that villagers resisted but the state required. This legitimacy could come only through some form of popular representation or election. To that end, the trial law called for the creation of:

• Villagers' councils (comprised of all adults or a representative from each household),
• Villagers' representative assemblies (comprised of delegates nominated and elected by the villagers), and
• Villagers' committees (comprised typically of about five elected village leaders).

Despite intense opposition from conservative county and township cadres—who feared the new law would erode their power over village leaders— the bill took effect in 1988, only to be derailed by the 1989 democracy protests and crackdown. In the repressive climate that followed, conservatives tried to repeal the law, only to find that they were blocked by Peng Zhen, a conservative party elder who had been instrumental in navigating the law through the NPC. Peng was convinced that village autonomy would stabilize the countryside and thereby strengthen, rather than weaken, party rule. In late 1990, a party central directive endorsed the trial law, and in 1991 it began to be enacted in a variety of locations across the country.

The law's implementation over the intervening years has led to the establishment and election of village assemblies, the public posting of village finances, and the drafting of village compacts that cover rules and regulations on all aspects of village life and state policy. What has earned the law so much attention at home and abroad, however, is the practice of direct elections of village officials every three years. While the shadow of Tiananmen still hung over China in the early 1990s, few in or out of the country took much notice of the rural reform, assuming that the countryside was a conservative backwater that served as a brake on democracy, or that any elections under Communist Party rule had to be a sham.

Spreading the Word

The office in the Ministry of Civil Affairs (MCA) charged with the implementation of the village autonomy law, the Department of Basic-Level Government, worked steadily and methodically to establish model sites for villagers' autonomy in every province in the country, cultivating close ties with local authorities who were receptive to the program and attempting to win over those who were not. By 1992, contact with the Ford Foundation's Beijing office had translated into an initial cooperative agreement that allowed the MCA to bring foreign advisers and scholars to China, and to send members of the office staff to the United States for brief investigatory visits. That same year, the National Committee on U.S.-China Relations hosted an MCA delegation and introduced the visitors to the operations of local government in the United States. From this beginning the MCA office began to draw increasing media attention at home and abroad, as reporters started to investigate village self-government on their own, or with the assistance and cooperation of the MCA.

Throughout the early and mid-1990s, as international contacts, scholarly interest, and media attention escalated, the process of village elections became institutionalized in many areas. Although foreign observers, especially in the United States, were skeptical about how democratic the elections were, reporting on the topic began to shift as the shadow of 1989 receded and as more information about the electoral process became available. Chinese officials provided access to a wide variety of village election sites, including some that were exemplars of fair and competitive elections and others where elections had clearly been orchestrated by local party leaders. This gave outside observers the opportunity to gain a balanced view of the reform and draw their own conclusions. By the mid-1990s, officials who had confined themselves to the language of "villagers autonomy" after the Tiananmen crackdown began to speak more openly about "grassroots democracy," and foreign observers, while remaining circumspect and cautious in their appraisals, began to acknowledge that village elections showed real democratic potential, even if that potential was rarely fully realized.

As Sino-American relations plunged to their nadir in the wake of the Taiwan Strait crisis of 1996, and as conservatives in Washington and Beijing pressed to gain the upper hand in domestic policy debates, those on each side seeking to avoid a breach in the relationship began to marshall evidence to support a policy of constructive engagement. By 1996 and 1997 that evidence included documentation of progress in implementing rural elections in Chinese villages, documentation that was leading even skeptical observers to appreciate the Chinese effort, however imperfect and limited it remained.

It was by this path that village self-government made its way into the seemingly distant world of foreign policy and Sino-American relations. In a landscape littered with conflicts over trade, human rights, and security issues, the grassroots democratization project is a rare piece of terrain on which Chinese interests and American values seem to converge.

How to Think About Village Elections

Village elections may aid Sino-American diplomacy, but are they useful and meaningful to Chinese villagers? Answering that question requires critical examination of some of the claims made about village elections.

Village elections are conducted democratically.
Although the Chinese press consistently makes this claim, it is true only by the narrowest definition of democracy. If by democratic one means that China's villagers get the chance to cast a ballot, then the elections are indeed democratic. If, however, one means that the candidates for village leadership have been democratically selected in a transparent process that meets with villagers' approval, and that elections to each post are competitive, or at least potentially competitive, then many—perhaps most—village elections do not yet qualify as democratic.

There is no question that hundreds of millions of rural residents now have the opportunity to vote for their village leadership team, a group that usually consists of a village chairman plus several deputies. But specific election methods vary a great deal from place to place. All regions are supposed to conduct their elections according to the Organic Law of Villagers' Committees, but this still leaves ample room for provinces, municipalities, counties, and even townships to draft laws, regulations, or guidelines that specify local election procedures. In many regions local people's congresses have drafted laws or regulations, while local branch offices of the MCA have their own set of adminis-trative regulations. This process may eventually lead to a set of harmonized procedures in individual provinces (units equivalent in population to large European nations), but for now there continues to be substantial variety in how the elections are conducted.

The one feature most areas have in common is that the number of people on the ballot exceeds the number to be elected by at least one, thus creating a small element of competition. Villagers are asked to vote for a slate of leaders (for example, choosing five out of six or seven candidates), and may also be asked to indicate which individual on the slate they prefer as village chairman. A step beyond this is direct competition between two or more candidates for the post of village chairman, with the rest of the leadership team selected from a group of nominees that exceeds the total number to be elected by one or two. This type of competitive election first appeared in northeast China during the initial round of elections a decade ago, and was picked up quickly by other regions, such as Fujian and Hebei provinces, which have been leaders in implementing competitive elections.

Just as important as a competitive ballot is the issue of how nominees are selected. The Organic Law allows for several methods of nomination, including indirect nomination by a villagers' representative assembly, or direct nomination by any group of ten villagers. Because such public forms of nomination can intimidate villagers or be manipulated by local party officials, some areas have recently moved to a new method of nomination called *haixuan* (literally, election by sea), in which all villagers are allowed to write the names of candidates they would support on a secret primary ballot. Then a process of public winnowing occurs until the two or three most popular candidates have been selected for the final ballot.

No matter what method of selection is used, the test is whether villagers are satisfied with the candidates who emerge, and with the process that produced them. Some provinces and regions score better on this test than others, and there can be wide variation even within the same county on how the nomination process is conducted. Interference by party and government officials at the township and county levels, or unlawful manipulation of elections by corrupt village election commissions, has led some villagers to lodge formal complaints demanding the voiding of election results. If the complaints are a sign of continuing attempts to rig elections, they are also a sign of the growing sense of empowerment some villagers feel in the face of such abuses.

Village elections are designed to prop up a repressive regime.

It is true that the Chinese Communist Party turned to village elections in the hope that they would ease tensions and create the stability that would assure unchallenged party rule. But village elections cannot be labeled a sham merely because they serve the party; they are a sham only if they do not serve the interests of villagers by making local leaders more accountable. On this point the early evidence, although partial and incomplete, suggests that many villagers believe the elections give them an increased stake and a voice in village politics. According to MCA data, voter turnout is high, including participation by absentee ballot, and roughly 20 percent of incumbents are defeated in each round of elections.

Still, it is also true that where local party officials are determined to control an election they may succeed in doing so, especially if no one in the village complains or the officials have powerful allies at higher levels. As a general proposition for all of China, however, the statement that village elections are a sham is false. The fallacy here lies in assuming that the Chinese Communist Party is one uniform, monolithic authority, when in fact it is not. If China's economic reform has given us a strange, hybrid economic system, it has also given us a strange, hybrid communist system, one in which local power, prestige, status, and money are no longer monopolized by the Communist Party. If the party were monolithic, the villagers' autonomy law would not remain controversial in some quarters. Inland agricultural regions continue to drag their heels on implementing meaningful, competitive elections, while coastal areas in northeast and southern China work to improve the process by requiring campaign speeches, ensuring full secrecy in the balloting process, eliminating proxy voting, and providing absentee ballots for residents working outside the village.

The assumption that party power is inconsistent with meaningful elections underestimates the importance of local party sanction and support for getting the process right. Where elections have been successfully implemented and where nomination is fair and competition fully integrated, the county-level party secretary is usually a strong supporter of the process, setting the tone for township and village party leaders. So while it is true that party interference can crush all meaning out of the elections and turn the process into a sham in some locations, it is equally true that a supportive party leadership at the county and provincial levels can restrain township and village officials who might otherwise skew the election results their way.

The best indicator of a democratic process is the defeat of candidates who are party members.

This is one of the most common and most misguided assumptions that foreign observers make when evaluating village elections. Certainly it is important to know that non-party candidates can not only run for election, but sometimes win, turning out incumbents who are party members. This provides outside observers with added assurance that the electoral process is reasonably competitive and fair. Viewed from the point of view of China's villagers, however, the defeat of an incumbent who holds party membership may or may not be a good thing for the village, for several reasons.

First, what villagers want is what most people want in a local leader: someone who is honest, competent, capable of improving the local economy, and efficient and thrifty with tax money. They also want someone who will defend their interests in the face of pressures from county and township officials. Depending on local circumstances, local politics, and the merits of the candidates for village chairman, villagers may choose the candidate who is a party member as their best option. They may calculate that party membership will work in the leader's favor, or that his personal or family ties with township and county officials (or, even better, factory managers) will mean more jobs for villagers in township enterprises and greater economic development opportunities. Although party membership no longer carries the clout it once did, it can sometimes be seen as an asset, not a liability, where village interests are concerned.

Second, while party members voted out of office will learn one kind of democratic lesson, those voted into office may learn another. Assuming there is open and fair competition from nonparty candidates, party members who must stand for election and reelection may begin to experience in a new way the tension between their roles as party members and as representatives of their village interests. As a result, what the party gains in legitimacy from winning elections it may lose in internal discipline as village leaders resist the implementation of orders that cut against the grain of village interests. Conversely, but equally positive from the vantage point of villagers, local party branches filled with members who must stand for reelection may become more responsive to village needs and interests and less arbitrary in their rule.

Finally, in some rural villages, the party, whatever its limitations, may be the only force that can restrain the power of a strong local clan or village faction that has come to dominate village life at the expense of the weak and vulnerable. From abroad, the party is easily perceived as the only political bully on the block. But other bullies have emerged in recent years as the power of local party branches has declined. For example, complaints are already being heard about attempts by clans to dominate local elections by engaging in intimidation and vote buying. In villages where this is the case, a strong and uncorrupted party presence would be a welcome improvement, especially if it could eliminate clan violence and break up criminal gangs. In short, the diversity and complexity of contemporary village life and politics are easily overlooked by those who see the Communist Party as the only threat to China's prospects for liberalization and democratization.

China is another Taiwan . . . building democracy out of authoritarianism.

It is true that Taiwan's experience of first introducing elections at local levels has been noted and studied by Chinese officials, and that China's decision to begin at the grass roots echoes that experience. Yet the differences between the two are so great, and the trajectory of the People's Republic still so uncertain, that any attempts at comparison are entirely speculative.

One of the most important differences at this stage is the scope for elections in China as opposed to Taiwan. When the ruling Kuomintang (KMT) began to implement local elections in Taiwan in 1950 and 1951, it simultaneously introduced elections at the village, township, city, and district levels for positions on local councils. Like the Communist Party in China today, the KMT did not allow organized political opposition, and there was wide variation in the quality of the election process, with central and local KMT officials resorting to an array of methods to defeat, intimidate, or co-opt nonparty candidates.

The difference is that elections were not confined to the bottom of the political hierarchy, as they are in China today The result, for China's village leaders, is that they alone have been elected to serve, while the government leaders they must answer to are appointed, and then confirmed by local people's congresses. Meanwhile, county and township officials, who are not subject to electoral politics, and with their careers, incomes, and bonuses in the hands of other unelected authorities, find themselves increasingly at cross-purposes with village cadres who live in intimate contact with their electorate and are subject, to some degree, to public accountability. Their instinct is to resist village elections altogether, or to manipulate the process in their favor to ensure the election of compliant local leaders who will make their lives easier.

No Going Back?

In the run-up to the fifteenth party congress in September 1997, the issue of extending elections to the township level was debated at senior levels and tentatively endorsed by President Jiang Zemin. And on June 10, 1998 . . . a Communist Party Central Committee circular announced the party's intention to "make active efforts" to extend elections to the township level. The fears and uncertainties raised by this prospect, however, appear to have forestalled the creation of a timetable for implementation.

Yet unless China moves quickly to extend the electoral process upward to the township and county levels, forcing state officials to face the same public scrutiny beginning to fall on village leaders, the contradiction between the two political cultures will grow sharper. In the end, the fate of China's experiment in grassroots democracy may hinge on whether Beijing will commit itself to extending the process upward. The risks to the regime in moving forward will be tremendous. But after promoting grassroots democracy for a decade and allowing democratic elections to take root in the countryside, the risks of retreat might be just as high.

20

The Virus of Corruption

JAMES MILES

The economic reforms that characterize the post-Mao era in China have brought unprecedented prosperity and modernity to many areas of China. At the same time they have also triggered a surging wave of corruption among China's Party and government officials and their families, from the local level right up to the central leadership. Various leaders have described corruption as a "life or death" issue for the survival of the CCP because it damages the Party's reputation and undermines its legitimacy. So far, however, the state's efforts to crack down on corruption have not been able to address the problem. James Miles describes both the cause of the problem and the difficulties in eradicating it.

"Down with corruption" is a slogan that has been chanted by demonstrators and daubed on banners in almost every protest movement in modern Chinese history. Dissidents from KMT days to the present have tried to use popular anger against official corruption to goad the general public into revolutionary action. Communist historians identify corruption as one of the main reasons for the collapse of the Qing dynasty and of KMT rule on the mainland. As Jiang Zemin warned in 1991, "If we examine each dynasty in China's history, we see there existed corruption and struggles against it that were linked to the rise and fall and the life and death of a dynasty. . . . Historical experience tells us that if the anti-corruption campaign fails, China's society cannot achieve integrity."

Jiang, of course, had experience of the vehemence with which popular anger over corruption could express itself. In 1989, during the Tiananmen Square protests, slogans condemning corruption were more frequently seen and heard than those related to any other concern. One song particularly relished by the demonstrators was one that began with the words "*Dadao guandao* (down with profiteering officials), *dadao guandao, fan fubai* (oppose corruption*) fan fubai*," sung to the tune of the nursery rhyme *Frere Jacques*. Protesters said they felt corruption had become increasingly rampant since Deng Xiaoping launched his economic reforms, and although they did not openly attack the reforms themselves, some ordinary workers carried large portraits of Mao Zedong and his prime minister, Zhou Enlai, as a way of showing their contempt for what they saw as social and moral decay under Deng.

Corruption of course is a problem common to many countries, including industrialized nations, but in few is the problem as threatening to social and political stability as it is in China. Corruption is at least as rampant in the Indian bureaucracy, for example, as it is in China's. Yet India has mechanisms whereby the general public can vent their anger, ranging from the ballot box to their frequently exercised right to stage public demonstrations. In China, ordinary citizens can only bottle up their frustrations. When they do find a rare opportunity to air their grievances, as they did in 1989, the outpouring of rage is all the more likely to be politically destructive.

Speaking to top party leaders just a few days after the crushing of the Tiananmen Square protests, Deng decreed that between ten and twenty "major cases" of corruption should be publicly exposed "without delay" in order to "satisfy the people." Deng warned that failure to curb corruption could jeopardize attainment of the party's "strategic goals." But although in response to Deng's urgings the party declared its renewed determination to crack down, the problem refused to go away, not least because it affected so many people at every level of the government. . . .

Many ordinary Chinese complain that corruption was more the rule than the exception. Taxi drivers moan about police routinely extorting money or cigarettes as "fines" for nonexistent traffic violations. A friend of mine in the police force told me that even a murderer could be freed from jail on payment of the right bribe. He himself managed to secure the release of a relative suspected of political crimes by bribing his relative's guards. To get a telephone or a better apartment, admission to a good school for one's children or decent medical treatment more often than not requires handouts of cash or gifts to the right officials. Foreign businesspeople often complain about increasingly blatant demands by their Chinese partners for gifts, overseas trips, or even the sponsorship of education abroad for their children. The foreign tourist might see little if any sign of such corruption, but any foreign resident in China knows how important it is to provide at least cigarettes and imported soft drinks or alcohol for the plumber or electrician to make sure the job is done well and promptly.

Less visible but far more serious corruption is rife in the higher ranks of the bureaucracy, among those who have access to or control over coveted resources such as building materials, coal, oil, steel, fertilizer, or means of transport. The gradual freeing of prices in recent years has helped reduce

attempts to cash in on the difference between fixed and market prices, but profiteering remains rampant.

Much as he may have hoped to curb such practices, Deng only exacerbated the problem with his trip to the south in 1992.* His calls for bold experimentation and a risk-taking spirit encouraged economic practices that in many
countries would be illegal. In China, which only began to build up a legal
system after Deng came to power, the law still lags far behind the pace of social
and economic change. Officials and businesspeople who know next to nothing
about stock markets see nothing wrong with insider trading. Many civil servants
see nothing wrong with using state resources to generate some extra income for
themselves and their departments by doing private business on the side. Indeed,
many departments actively encourage it as a way of improving staff morale.
This is, after all, a country long used to operating not according to the law but
according to government or party dictate. Deng's instruction that officials should
dare to take risks and boldly explore new paths in reform therefore carried as
much if not more weight in the minds of many Chinese than any legal provision.
To communist officials confused and demoralized by political changes in the
former Soviet Union and Eastern Europe, Deng's words gave the green light to
feather their nests while the opportunity still lasted. In the minds of many
bureaucrats, the collapse of communism in Europe indicated that communism's
days in China were numbered as well.

More than a year after Deng's tour, Jiang Zemin admitted that "negative
and corrupt phenomena" had "seriously interfered with the work of reform and
opening" and that ordinary citizens were "rather dissatisfied." He said that unless
the party adopted "resolute measures" to curb these phenomena, "they will bury
the great cause of reform and opening and will finally lead to jeopardizing our
party's ruling position." But the damage had already been done, and to many
Chinese it appeared irreversible.

In the city of Shenzhen, the rapidly rising expectations of the general
public collided head-on with burgeoning official corruption in 1992, triggering
unrest that led to fears among reformist officials that Deng's new campaign
might grind to a halt in the face of renewed hard-line resistance. Given Deng's

---

* After the Tiananmen demonstrations in 1989 the Chinese government pulled back from
its ambitious economic reforms. Deng Xiaoping grew frustrated with these conservative
policies and embarked on a tour of economic hot spots in south China in 1992. During
this tour, he praised adventurous economic policies promoted by local governments.
Once his comments favoring economic reform and rapid growth were repeated in the
national media, a prolonged period of rapid growth began.

hopes that affluence would bring stability, it was particularly ironic that the trouble occurred in Shenzhen, the most prosperous area of China. The trigger was the city's stock market, an experiment with capitalism that Deng had defended during his southern tour. "We allow people to reserve their judgment [about stock markets]," Deng had said. "But we must try these things out. If after one or two years of experimentation they prove feasible, we can expand them. Otherwise we can put a stop to them and be done with it. . . . What is there to be afraid of?"

On August 9th, the Shenzhen city government began its annual sale of lottery tickets that would entitle those with winning numbers to buy shares due to be issued in the upcoming year. With huge numbers of investors chasing only a small number of shares on the Shenzhen and Shanghai exchanges—both formally opened in December 1990—there were fabulous profits to be made. Those who bought new share issues at the beginning of 1992 saw their investment increase more than seven times in value by the end of the year. The incentive to buy was made all the greater by low interest rates on bank deposits, which meant that, especially in years of high inflation, savers would effectively lose money by keeping their money in the banks. In 1992, interest rates were only about one percentage point higher than the national inflation rate, which meant that in big cities, where inflation tended to be higher than average, depositors lost money.

Even though only one in ten of the 5 million lottery tickets due to be sold would have winning numbers, investors poured into Shenzhen to buy them at 100 yuan apiece—the equivalent of a week's wages for the average factory worker. Officials estimated that a staggering 1.2 million people joined queues to buy the lottery tickets, of whom some 800,000 were from outside Shenzhen. Trains and planes bound for the zone were full to capacity, and vacant rooms at Shenzhen hotels were almost impossible to find. Some of those who flocked to Shenzhen were peasants who had brought with them stacks of identity cards in order to buy lottery tickets for their friends and relatives at home. Factory bosses and rich businesspeople paid workers to stand in line for them. Queues began to form two days before sales began, snaking for hundreds of yards in sweltering heat outside more than 300 banks and brokerages. Police used cattle prods, leather belts, and bamboo canes to keep the bad-tempered and impatient crowds in order. Dozens of people were injured in the crush, and many suffering from heat exhaustion were taken to hospitals.

The authorities had anticipated that the sale of lottery tickets would take two days. But within a few hours, almost all of the tickets were gone. The hundreds of thousands of people who continued to wait in line through Sunday night for the second day of sales realized on Monday morning that they had done so in vain. After three days and nights standing and squatting amid the spreading filth of human waste and discarded food containers, many investors could not control their anger. Simple arithmetic told them that even if everyone ahead of them in line had bought their full quota of ten tickets, there should still be enough left for at least some of those still waiting. Rumors spread rapidly that bank officials, police, and other civil servants hat kept many of the tickets for themselves or reserved places at the front of the queues for their friends and relatives. On Monday evening, August 10, tens of thousands of enraged investors rampaged through the streets in protest. Thousands of them gathered outside the city government headquarters shouting "Down with corruption!" Some carried placards and banners with slogans such as "fight corruption" and "fight for justice." The crowds overturned and burned several private cars and police vehicles, smashed shop windows, and attacked police. The authorities responded with water cannon, tear gas, and warning shots fired into the air. Aided by a heavy downpour of the rain, the police managed eventually to disperse the demonstrators.

In an attempt to pacify investors, the government put another 5 million lottery tickets on sale. To prevent further unrest while this was going on, police in riot gear patrolled the city in trucks, while officers on foot forced investors to wait in a squatting position rather than stand and shove. One report said policemen pulled young men seemingly at random from the waiting crowds and beat several of them mercilessly.

The rioting in Shenzhen was the most serious reported outbreak of urban unrest in China since the Tiananmen Square protests. Although the authorities were able to restore order relatively quickly, and with a remarkable lack of bloodshed, the violence was a sharp reminder of how suddenly public anger could erupt when ordinary people felt their economic interests were being threatened by a corrupt and callous bureaucracy. It was also an indication of potential danger ahead as Deng's economic reforms gathered pace, and corruption became increasingly rampant. The Shenzhen protesters' suspicions about the extent of corruption involved in the lottery ticket issue were borne out by the findings of an official investigation. A government report said the malpractice alleged by the demonstrators were "basically identical" to those discovered during the inquiry. It said ten of the eleven financial institutions authorized to sell the lottery tickets were involved in illegal practices. About 4,000 workers at these institutions appropriated an average of more than fifteen of the tickets each. Police and other officials took another 20,000 of them, and a similar number were given away by officials as gifts. One senior banking executive in the city took no fewer than 3,250 tickets for himself. "Government sources say the Shenzhen share incident has become a reminder of how much corruption has seeped into the well of economic reform," said the *China Daily* newspaper. . . .

A few months after the Shenzhen riots, these dangers became apparent in the capital itself when the authorities exposed a web of corruption surrounding the affairs of a privately owned firm in Beijing. The government declared that the enterprise, the Great Wall Machinery and Electronics Scientific and Techno-logical Company, was incapable of redeeming the high-interest bonds it had issued to some 200,000 small-time investors, many of whom had spent their life savings on the debentures. When the official media revealed in June 1993 that the company was being liquidated, hundreds of angry investors flocked to the company's headquarters on the northeastern edge of the city. When I arrived with a colleague to interview them, the police tried to stop us, saying we needed permission from higher authorities. As we argued with the officers, some people in the crowd jeered and hissed at the police. Dozens of investors followed us as we walked away and crowded round us once the police were out of sight. Then they poured out their anger, speaking with venom and bitterness not so much about the head of the company who had been accused by the official media of grave financial wrongdoings but about the government itself, which only a few months earlier had been praising the Great Wall Machinery and Electronics Company as an incarnation of the new reform spirit and encouraging people to invest in it. It was the first time I had heard members of a crowd in Beijing speaking with such heartfelt vehemence since Tiananmen.

In many other countries, the scandal surrounding the Great Wall Machin-ery and Electronics Company might have led to the resignation of a top leader or even a change of government. The Chinese authorities lamely tried to pin the blame entirely on the 39-year-old director of the company, Shen Taifu. The official media said Shen had issued bonds without the proper authorization and had violated government restrictions on the fixing of interest rates. It also accused him of embezzling funds from his company. But the official account was full of holes. The angry investors who gathered outside the company headquarters showed us copies of articles published only a few months earlier by the official media that had heaped praise on Shen and his enterprise. One clipping from the *Science and Technology Daily* included photographs of the deputy prime minister, Zou Jiahua, and the minister in charge of the State Science and Technology Commission, Song Jian, visiting Shen's company.

Another was a lengthy piece by a deputy chairman of China's parliament, Fei Xiaotong, which appeared in no less authoritative a newspaper than the *People's Daily* in January 1993. Fei, who is a well-known social scientist and a staunch defender of the party line, said in his gushing article that the company's techniques could "promote the development of the socialist market economy with Chinese characteristics as well as the market for science and technology." Fei said the company had grown in the space of a few years from a tiny operation owning just one bicycle to the biggest nonstate enterprise of its kind in the country, with its main product—"highly efficient, energy-saving electric motor" —widely used by Chinese industries. Fei said the sale of bonds by the company was being carried out "in accordance with relevant regulations issued by the State Council." He even suggested China should adopt the "Great Wall model" of bond sales in order to overcome its lack of funds for developing and marketing new technology and put to use the huge amount of money in personal savings. Fei also praised the company for "respecting old comrades" by hiring more than 160 former high-ranking officials. He said these old cadres were called on by the management to give their views on every major decision made by the company. This practice, Fei said, helped the company to avoid many problems and save a lot of time. No wonder, given this authoritative figure's ringing endorsement of Shen Taifu's enterprise, that many ordinary citizens rushed out to buy the company's bonds. Shen even had a certificate from the State Science and Technology Commission saying his fund-raising technique was legitimate. . . .

If Shen Taifu's operation was indeed illegal, the fact that he was able to sell his bonds so publicly amid so much positive publicity in the official media for ten months before the government decided to stop him suggests there was high-level complicity in his crime. The only top-ranking official indicted in the case was the deputy minister of the State Science and Technology Commission, Li Xiaoshi. Li was sentenced to twenty years in prison for allegedly accepting a 40,000-yuan bribe from Shen Taifu and other bribes from Hong Kong business-people as well as for embezzling public money. Eleven other state functionaries, including a middle-ranking official, four reporters, and three bank clerks were also prosecuted for taking bribes from Shen Taifu. Two of the journalists were sentenced to seven years and six years in prison, respectively, for accepting payment to write positive stories about Shen's company. The fate of the others was not made public, nor was that of another 120 officials who a Beijing-controlled newspaper in Hong Kong said were being investigated for their alleged dealings with Shen. It seems unlikely, however, that deputy minister

Li Xiaoshi really was the only top-level official involved in the case. Questions certainly deserve to be asked about how Fei Xiaotong, the senior parliamentarian, came to write his glowing account of Shen's operation in the *People's Daily*. The official media never mentioned Fei's dealings with Shen Taifu, nor did they explain why other top officials who visited his company, including Song Jian and Zou Jiahua, failed to point out any wrongdoings. One of Li Xiaoshi's fellow deputy ministers in the State Science and Technology Commission was Deng Nan, the daughter of Deng Xiaoping. Could she have been unaware of what was going on? Obviously there was far more corruption or at best incompetence involved in the Shen Taifu case than the leadership ever admitted. . . .

The publicity surrounding Shen Taifu's alleged crimes and his execution failed to put a complete end to ventures of a similar nature. Remarkably, given Shen's fate, a pyramid scheme of even greater proportions was revealed by the official press in July 1995. The case involved an apparently well-connected woman in the city of Wuxi in eastern Jiangsu Province who the media said had defrauded investors, including many government departments, to the tune of some $300 million by promising high interest rates. Her scheme had been running for five years—right through the Shen Taifu scandal—before it was halted by the authorities.

In early 1993 before Shen Taifu's problems came to light, the Chinese Academy of Social Sciences published a prediction that China would be plagued by increasing instances of rioting and other isolated "group actions" triggered mainly by "serious abuse of power among local officials" and the harming of peoples economic interests by such problems as factory closures. The report said corruption was being fueled by the increasingly widespread phenomenon of officials going into business without quitting their government posts. In 1992, as Deng's new reform campaign took off, more than 120,000 officials left their jobs to do business. A far greater number, however, preferred to earn money on the side while still enjoying the security and prestige of a civil service job. One estimate put the total number of officials doing business by the end of 1992 at 10 million. "Amid the pounding of the great wave of the market economy, the official class was the one most violently shaken up, with many of its members feeling a sense of loss or bewilderment about their future," said one Chinese commentator. In a market economy, wealth would become as important if not more so than power. Many bureaucrats felt they had to change their way of life in order to keep ahead. Their privileged positions gave them ready opportunity to do so. "It seems as if overnight, power, perks, and rank have plunged in people's estimation," said the commentator. With funds, labor, and materials all increasingly available through nongovernment channels, many official positions were becoming obsolete. The rich could now simply buy on the open market the coveted goods to which once only officials had access.

The Chinese leadership, determined to thin the ranks of the country's 35-million-strong bureaucracy, actively encouraged officials to go into business. In 1992, Deng's reform campaign suppressed the lingering misgivings of hard-liners about reforming the bloated, inefficient bureaucracy, which for decades had recruited its members on the basis of political loyalty and personal connections rather than any publicly assessed standard of competence. . . .

Inspired by Deng's southern tour, government departments leaped at the chance to generate more money and get rid of unwanted staff. "After news spread in the autumn of cuts in civil service departments and staff, even those cadres who were not interested [in doing business] before could no longer sit still," said the Chinese Academy of Social Sciences. "It was like adding oil to the fire. The heat went up and up, spreading to every town and village as far as the borders." In the northern province of Hebei alone, government units set up more than 5,500 businesses that year, employing some 50,000 former civil servants. In the first ten months of 1992, the number of real estate companies in China increased tenfold and the number of trading firms one hundredfold—most of them run by officials or former officials. Whereas long touted efforts to separate party and government functions were being pursued halfheartedly at best, the commercialization of the Chinese bureaucracy was carried out with revolutionary fervor.

This was not the first stampede by officials and government departments into business. As the economy boomed in the late 1980s under the guidance of Zhao Ziyang, there was a similar rush. Many turned to profiteering, a phenomenon that became one of the main complaints of demonstrators during the Tiananmen Square protests. In 1992, what the official media dubbed the "business fever" unleashed by Deng's southern tour was far greater in scope than anything experienced before in the course of reform. A Communist Party directive issued a few weeks after Deng's trip specifically allowed government departments to set up enterprises. Many local governments rushed to issue their own guidelines in order to encourage the trend. Local regulations allowed officials to keep their government ranks and perks while engaging in business. The only minor inconvenience they sometimes had to suffer was the loss of their government salaries. Not surprisingly, many bureaucrats were more than willing to make that sacrifice when they could earn many times as much money in the private sector.

Having whipped up this "business fever," the authorities appeared at a loss as to how to regulate it. The sophisticated legal framework that governs the market economics of industrialized nations simply does not exist in China. In mid-1993, several months into the drive to set up a "socialist market economy," Liang Guoqing, China's deputy attorney general, admitted that it was becoming harder to distinguish between crimes and acceptable business practices. "Problems involving the boundary between crimes of graft and bribery and noncriminal cases have increased," the *China Daily* quoted Liang as saying.

In July 1993, the central authorities belatedly tried to take action. The government issued a circular decreeing that party and government officials must not hold concurrent jobs of any kind in economic entities and must not moonlight. Enterprises set up by government departments to absorb excess staff must sever all ties with their parent organizations. The circular also banned government departments from deriving any kind of profit from enterprises they set up. In practice the new directive made little difference—the revolution Deng had unleashed proved unstoppable. One of my friends, a middle-ranking official in a state-run news organization, continued to run his own advertising and public relations company, exploiting the many contacts he had made in government and commercial circles while working as a journalist. One of his schemes was to act as an agent helping companies get endorsement from prominent high-ranking officials and other famous people. He said that normally, in order to invite a top official to attend an opening ceremony or the like, it was necessary to seek approval through a central department that schedules such activities. Approval, however, being very difficult to obtain, my friend hoped to make money as a middleman by using his extensive contacts with the secretaries of senior officials, which would enable him to bypass the regular channel. "These old men want some money to give their grandchildren," he said, "so they don't mind selling their calligraphy or other services." He said he had no choice but to do business on the side. His official salary of 400 yuan a month was not enough to cover his child's kindergarten fees, he complained. My friend and his associates showed not the slightest fear that the venture might be stopped. The government knew that to crack down effectively would dangerously undermine the morale of state employees. Its actions appeared largely confined to issuing stern-sounding but ineffectual directives.

Even official publications often drew attention to the abuses committed by bureaucrats-turned-businesspeople. One typical account told of how some Construction Department officials wanted to take over the management of a successful local restaurant. When the establishment's owner declined, the officials told him not to worry, and they would remain on good terms. A few weeks later, however, the construction began of a public lavatory opposite the restaurant. The owner, realizing his business was doomed, changed his mind and agreed to cede management of the restaurant to the officials. No sooner had he done so than work on the lavatory mysteriously ceased. Other reports in the official press told of how bureaucrats who had gone into trade would order enterprises to buy their goods. Anxious not to get on the wrong side of officialdom, the enterprises would buy them even if the products were of poor quality. Sometimes when organizing launch ceremonies for new companies, officials would send out invitations to big factories they had dealings with, indicating on them a bank account number to which guests could make donations.

Enterprises set up by officials were sometimes referred to in the press as "flipped nameplate companies" because of their easily interchangeable roles as businesses and government departments. A book on corrupt officialdom published by hard-liners in 1993 quoted an economist as saying of these new companies, "Overnight, we've turned the clock back more than a decade. This is a major step backward for reform." Many ordinary Chinese I met expressed similar sentiments.

The growing class of *nouveaux riches* officials made little secret of its wealth. In Beijing's most lavish restaurants, a significant proportion of the customers would usually be civil servants, wining and dining at the state's expense. Restaurant managers would complain quite frankly that anticorruption drives were bad for business. In Nanjing, the owners of about 20 percent of the city's privately run restaurants sold off their businesses at giveaway prices in the space of just three months in late 1993 because of a new campaign against graft. By early 1994, at least a third of Beijing's karaoke bars and nightclubs were on the verge of bankruptcy thanks to the campaign. But one official report noted that many club owners expected the situation to change, believing that "campaigns come and go, and everything would resume just as it had been before the crackdown."

Officials who preferred straight cash to lavish meals and entertainment could always buy fake restaurant and hotel receipts from black market receipt dealers who loitered around subway exits and other busy places in Beijing and other cities. These were particularly useful for the traveling official on expenses who could stay at the cheapest inn or with friends or relatives then use the receipts to claim much larger sums of money than he had spent.

In August 1993, the deputy attorney general Liang Guoqing admitted openly that corruption was worse than at any other time since the communists came to power. "Crimes of graft and bribery now involve larger sums of money and more party and government officials than previously," he said. "More and more officials working in judicial departments and economic management departments now participate in such crimes. . . . [Corruption] has spread into the party, government administrations, and every part of society, including politics, economy, ideology, and culture." . . .

Corruption has always been a way of life in China. The exchanging of gifts and lavish meals is an established part of business ritual. Chinese journalists think nothing of accepting gifts from interviewees. News conferences are often accompanied by lavish banquets and many Chinese companies even offer cash to reporters, handing it out in envelopes at the start or end of a briefing. In Taiwan, similar practices are common too. During the island's local and parliamentary elections in December 1989, officials handed out cameras to foreign reporters and hosted a banquet for them that included sharks' fin and abalone dishes—among the most expensive items of Chinese cuisine. What makes official corruption so destabilizing in China now, however, is that officials already have grossly disproportionate advantages in the race to set up a market economy. China may have given the go-ahead to engage in capitalism, but with land, property, and funds already concentrated in the hands of the state, the winners are bound to be those with bureaucratic connections. Japan and the "little tigers" of Asia began with somewhat more level playing fields. In China, officials can often take virtually whatever risks they like with the money at their disposal, knowing they would nearly always be protected by their positions and the party. They and not legal codes usually determine what is sound business practice. . . .

Suggestions for Further Reading

The Communist Revolution and Mao Era

Bianco, Lucien. *Origins of the Chinese Revolution, 1915–1949.* Stanford: Stanford University Press, 1971. A brief and insightful look at the domestic and international factors that influenced China's revolution and the ultimate victory of the Chinese Communist Party.

Chan, Anita, Richard Madsen, and Jonathan Unger. *Chen Village under Mao and Deng,* 2d ed. University of California Press, 1992. A very readable account of village life in China, covering both the impact of Maoist policies and the transformations of the post-Mao reforms, based on interviews with past and present residents of one particular village.

Li Zhisui. *The Private Life of Chairman Mao: The Memoirs of Mao's Personal Physician.* New York: Random House, 1994. Mao's former personal physician provides a revealing look at life among China's elites.

MacFarquhar, Roderick, ed. *The Politics of China,* 2d ed. Cambridge: Cambridge University Press, 1997. A definitive study of politics and policies in China, from the founding of the People's Republic in 1949 to the mid-1990s, including the Great Leap Forward, the Cultural Revolution, and the Tiananmen demonstrations of 1989.

Nathan, Andrew. *Chinese Democracy.* Berkeley: University of California Press, 1985. The best source for understanding how the Chinese have interpreted the concept of democracy and the obstacles to its practice in China.

The Reform Era

Baum, Richard. *Burying Mao: Chinese Politics in the Age of Deng Xiaoping.* Princeton: Princeton University Press, 1994. An overview of the post-Mao reform policies and the political conflicts they created.

Dickson, Bruce J. *Democratization in China and Taiwan: The Adaptability of Leninist Parties.* London and New York: Oxford University Press, 1997. Compares the democratization processes in China and Taiwan, suggesting why the Chinese Communist Party is unlikely to follow the "Taiwan model" of political change.

Fewsmith, Joseph. *China since Tiananmen: The Politics of Transition.* New York: Cambridge University Press, 2001. Examines how policy debates and

202

political conflicts among China's top leaders during the 1990s combine with intellectual trends to shape China's evolution.

Gilley, Bruce. *Tiger on the Brink: Jiang Zemin and China's New Elite.* Berkeley: University of California Press, 1998. An excellent biography of China's top leader and the interactions among China's political elites.

Goldman, Merle, and Roderick MacFarquhar, eds. *The Paradox of China's Post-Mao Reforms.* Cambridge: Harvard University Press, 1999. Covers a wide variety of political reforms and social changes that have accompanied economic reform and the problems that have arisen as a consequence.

Harding, Harry. *China's Second Revolution: Reform after Mao.* Washington, D.C.: Brookings, 1987. The standard source for understanding the initial economic and political reforms of the post-Mao era.

Lieberthal, Kenneth. *Governing China: From Revolution through Reform.* New York: W.W. Norton, 1995. The best textbook on Chinese politics, emphasizing historical trends, political institutions, and policymaking.

Nathan, Andrew, and Perry Link, eds. *The Tiananmen Papers.* New York: Public Affairs, 2001. This extensive collection of documents recounts debates among the central leadership about how to respond to the student demonstrations in 1989.

Schell, Orville. *Mandate of Heaven: A New Generation of Entrepreneurs, Dissidents, Bohemians, and Technocrats Lays Claim to China's Future.* New York: Simon and Schuster, 1989. One of the best accounts of the 1989 demonstrations in Tiananmen Square and their aftermath.

Weston, Timothy B., and Lionel M. Jensen, eds. *China beyond the Headlines.* Boulder: Rowman and Littlefield, 2000. Unlike most texts, this one is argumentative and lively, covering a variety of political and social issues that are often overlooked, and challenging the assumptions most American have about China.

Websites

www.chinaonline.com. A good source for business-related news and information.

www.insidechina.com. Inside China Today provides up-to-date information on political, social, and economic affairs in China, Taiwan, and Hong Kong.

www.taiwansecurity.org. A good collection of current articles and commentary on U.S.-China relations and related issues.

Part 3

SOCIETY

Edited by Martin King Whyte

INTRODUCTION
Martin King Whyte

Over the course of the twentieth century, the Chinese people were driven through an unusually wrenching series of social changes. While these changes have fundamentally transformed the nature of social life in China today, they have not entirely eclipsed the social structures and values of "traditional" China. Rather, China today is composed of a complex and seemingly contradictory amalgam of elements drawn from that country's Confucian tradition, the reformist but authoritarian Republican era of 1911–1949, Maoist socialism of 1949–1978, and the dynamically changing "open door" (but still very authoritarian) China that emerged under Deng Xiaoping's leadership after 1978. The readings in this section are designed to convey the complex and contradictory social patterns and customs that characterized China as it entered the twenty-fist century. This essay presents only a brief overview of the social transformations of the past century.

Late Imperial Social Order

Chinese society in late imperial times was shaped by a set of Confucian assumptions about the nature of the ideal society. The cement that held society together was supposed to be moral consensus rather than, say, law or police power, and the building blocks that were held together by this cement were human bonds and mutual obligations arrayed in a vast hierarchy. This hierarchy ranged from emperor and ministers down through local officials and village gentry and finally to the immediate family—through the bonds between father and son, husband and wife, brother and brother, and so on. It was assumed that a uniform, "correct" set of values and rules of behavior could be specified for all of the links in this vast human chain. In the ideal society, systematic instruction in the proper rules and group pressure to comply with them would produce social harmony and prosperity.

207

This conception produced a social order that was very different from the one that was emerging in modern times in the pluralist, individualistic West. Chinese officials were as much preachers as administrators, and they devoted great time and energy to encouraging proper thought and behavior. So, for example, they sponsored the drafting of codes of morality and essays extolling virtuous behavior, arranged for public lectures on Confucianism to be given on market days, and erected shrines in memory of righteous individuals. Nonetheless, officials and philosophers recognized that much of the population was poorly educated and could not be expected to behave properly simply as a result of such preaching. But they might conform to the expectations of their parents, their teachers, and their employers or other patrons. Thus an important task of Confucian statecraft was to try to ensure that everyone was bound tightly into the hierarchy of mutual obligations, so that there were no deviant groups or autonomous individuals.

At the base of this hierarchical social order was the Chinese family, and from the time of Confucius onward it was assumed that maintaining order in society at large depended in fundamental ways on ensuring that families were well regulated. The form of family life that evolved in China conformed to this image of strict, hierarchical role relationships and was thus different in fundamental ways from the family patterns of the contemporary West and even to some degree from the families of the pre-modern West. Individuals were born not simply into a family but a patrilineal kin group, and in some parts of China entire villages of several thousand souls belonged to a single lineage, sometimes called a Chinese "clan." Both patrilineages and the families that comprised them were organized hierarchically, with younger members and females expected to show deference and respect for older members and males. From infancy onward Chinese were instructed in obedience to the family and "filial piety," an ethic of worshipful deference toward one's parents and other elders. All members of the family were expected to defer to the will of the family patriarch who, as the representative of the patrilineal line and the head of the corporate family, was expected to make binding decisions that promoted the interests of the family as a whole.

Nothing better illustrates the strong emphases on group loyalty and the internal hierarchy of the Chinese family than the dominant set of marriage customs of late imperial China. Parents with the aid of hired marriage go-betweens arranged most marriages. In many cases the result might be termed a "blind marriage," since the bride and groom did not meet until the day of the wedding and had no say in the choice of a partner. Furthermore, since divorce was strongly discouraged, the perhaps poorly matched strangers were expected to make the best of things no matter how unhappy they were personally. These customs sound strange to Westerners oriented to romantic love, freedom of mate choice, and husband-wife companionship, but to most Chinese they made eminent sense. The new wife was not seen as a romantic partner for her husband, but as a new recruit for an existing, corporate family. She had important obligations to her in-laws that took precedence over whatever relationship she might develop with her husband. The same calculus applied to the new husband. If the bride was an intimidated stranger, he could be expected to fulfill his required role of helping to bring her into line so that she would become a dutiful and deferential daughter-in-law who would not upset the solidarity of her new family. In the great majority of cases the new bride moved into the family of her husband, rather than the couple setting up an independent household or going to live with her parents.

These distinctive features of Chinese family life created strong family bonds and a sense of security as well as indebtedness. Such sentiments could be a powerful force motivating individuals to work hard, study diligently, and take risks—all for the benefit of the family. But these features were achieved at some cost, particularly in the unhappiness and frustrated aspirations of individual members whose needs and feelings might be overridden by the demands of the family and its patriarch.

Family ties were not, of course, the only important social bonds in the late imperial social hierarchy. A variety of other kinds of social ties helped stitch society together. Many of these were vertical—for example, between teacher and student, employer and employee, sect leader and follower, and patron and client. Others were primarily horizontal—between former classmates, fellow villagers, members of temple associations, members of a craft guild, and city residents from the same native place. Observers often noted that most Chinese sought wherever possible to develop a wide-ranging network of personal "connections" (*guanxi*) of various kinds, rather than to have to depend on interactions with strangers on an impersonal basis.

The government's control over grass roots social life in late imperial times was minimal and largely indirect. The authorities did, over the course of most of the last millennium, attempt to institute a system of mutual responsibility groups in localities to assist the government in achieving its primary goals—maintaining order and collecting taxes. These groups were designed to make other families liable to sanctions if some members—their neighbors—did not pay their taxes or engaged in criminal or rebellious activity. The government also, as noted earlier, regularly made attempts at moral indoctrination of the populace and, through the examination system used to select officials, provided powerful incentives for local communities to organize their own efforts to tutor the young in Confucian values. In addition, imperial authorities were quite willing to use force to try to suppress forms of behavior or associational life that were deemed a threat to the state—heterodox religious sects, secret societies, feuding lineages, bandit gangs, and so forth. Still, the imperial bureaucracy was quite small in both numbers and resources, and it could not hope, nor did it attempt, to directly control grass roots social life. Instead, officials were generally content to allow social groupings to manage their own affairs as long as they did not challenge that state and its orthodoxy. As a result, well into the twentieth century, many activities that we associate with modern governments— running schools, caring for the poor, even organizing local police and fire protection—were often carried out by lineages, guilds, and other relatively autonomous social groups, rather than by the government.

Dilemmas of Reform in Republican China

In the nineteenth and early twentieth century, as China's weakness in competition with foreign powers became increasingly clear, voices in favor of reform and revolution were raised. Although the distinctive patterns of social organization sketched above might have helped promote stability in dynastic times, now drastic changes were seen as necessary. Critics could generally agree on what was wrong with the Chinese social order, but not on the solution.

China was weak, many argued, precisely because of the legacy of basing state power on personal ties and group membership. Individuals were socialized to be loyal primarily to their own family and kin group, and secondarily to local cults, guilds, groups of former schoolmates, and so forth. This form of social organization inhibited the development of national loyalty and made it difficult to develop general solidarities, such as class consciousness or an ethic of citizenship. Loyalty and kind treatment of those in one's network of mutual obligation went hand in hand with callous indifference or even vicious cruelty toward strangers or rivals. Early in the twentieth century Sun Yat-sen lamented that Chinese society resembled a "sheet of loose sand." In truth it was not simply that the grass roots groupings would not stick together, but that they were often at one another's throats.

The traditional social order was criticized on other grounds as well. The strong emphasis on obedience, deference to superiors, and reverence for tradition were said to foster a conservative or passive mentality that obstructed new ideas, technical innovations, and progress in general. The nepotism and personal favoritism that were fostered by Confucian values, it was argued, made it difficult to get Chinese organizations to select and promote the most capable individuals. And patriarchal family organization fostered a wide range of undesirable tendencies—for example, suppression of female talent, personal unhappiness of younger family members, and preference for a large number of sons.

In the Republican period (1912–1949), these criticisms of traditional social patterns coalesced into two rival agendas for change. Although it has been customary to refer to these options as reform versus revolution, those labels are somewhat misleading. As we shall see, the "revolutionary" solution, which came to the fore in 1949, was in some ways more "traditional" than the agenda offered by Western-oriented "reformers." So instead let us call these the "liberal" and "statist" options.

Those Chinese influenced by the Western liberal tradition advocated the development of a modern state machinery, a well-developed legal system, extensive reliance on markets, and the freeing of individuals from the excessive demands of, and loyalties to, their families and other social groups. The liberals argued that, as in the West, the liberation of individuals from traditional group bonds and obligations would not only produce greater personal happiness and fulfillment. It would also unleash much greater initiative and energy in all spheres of life that would benefit society in general. Simultaneously, the weakening of traditional bonds and the development of more modern forms of associational life, such as trade unions, professional societies, and voluntary associations, would also foster broader sentiments of citizenship and patriotism. Individual behavior would be regulated not so much by a hierarchy of personal obligations, but by a strong and impartial legal system, markets, commercial law, and other "modern" institutions. The liberals contended that this agenda would foster not chaos (the fear of the traditionalists), but a stronger state and an aroused citizenry.

A variety of changes in the nature of the Chinese social order occurred during the Republic era in response to these reformist efforts. A Civil Code and other legal instruments were enacted; chambers of commerce, professional associations, and other "modern" organizations emerged; and among some elements of the population (particularly the educated classes in the cities), new ideals of freedom of mate choice and divorce began to make some headway. Foot-binding for women, which had come under attack in the closing stages of the Qing dynasty, fell out of favor, while education for women and other departures from Confucian tradition were increasingly accepted. However, these changes were only partial, and the political and military chaos that consumed China after the 1930s prevented the liberal reform agenda from receiving a full test.

On the surface the "statist" solution, particularly as Chinese Marxists developed it, seemed to be advocating many of the same things as the liberals, such as freedom of mate choice in place of arranged marriages. However, in reality this agenda was quite different. The liberal option gradually lost favor as the Nationalist regime became increasingly authoritarian after the 1930s, and liberalism disappeared from the agenda after 1949 when the even more statist Chinese Communist Party (CCP) came to power. It was thus the statist approach that dominated the social change agenda in the Maoist era. What did this approach emphasize?

Social Transformations in Mao-Era China

The Chinese Communists shared with their dynastic predecessors the belief that the individual freedom from group obligations favored by the liberals would lead to chaos. If the demands of families and other personalistic groups constituted a major impediment to progress and national strength, the proper solution was not to free individuals from such demands, but to transform the nature of these groups so that they would systematically promote the interests of the larger society. In this sense the CCP could be said to have pursued the age-old dream of Chinese statecraft—to produce a unified and orderly social hierarchy. A crucial difference, however, is that the Chinese Communists had more power and greater resources than their dynastic predecessors to try to realize this dream.

What did this statist solution mean in practice between 1949 and 1976? It meant that the state made extensive and generally successful attempts either to gain control over, or to suppress and replace, existing grassroots groups. China's new rulers recognized that control of factories, banks, railways, schools, the military, the mass media, and other large institutions would not be sufficient to remedy the ailments of China's social order. The revolution would also have to transform grass roots social groupings in order bring them under state control.

In the Chinese countryside these efforts involved attacks on the power and property of lineages, temple associations, and other traditional forms, and the mobilization of rural residents into collectivist forms of agricultural organization similar to those in the Soviet Union. By 1956 this transformation had been substantially completed, with the resulting collectives subsequently consolidated into the commune system of the 1960s and 1970s. Chinese farmers and their families as a result became highly dependent upon local leaders installed and supervised by the CCP. Work assignments, family income, advanced educational opportunities, and eventually even permission to have a baby became subject to the power and restrictions of village cadres. This bureaucratic structure and associated state migration restrictions effectively confined rural residents to a lower caste position, an institutional feature that might appear to have more in common with feudalism than with socialism.

In urban areas much the same transformation occurred, although the specific organizational forms differed. As in the countryside, the aim was to eliminate any autonomous social groups. Some organizations, such as secret societies and religious sects, were attacked and suppressed, while others, such as trade unions, were co-opted or replaced by new organizational forms. The same socialist transformation completed by 1956 made urbanites heavily dependent upon two state-mandated organizational systems.

Work units (*danwei*) not only organized the daily work activities of their employees, but also often provided housing, nursery schools, health clinics, dining halls, and recreational facilities. They played an additional powerful role in social control over employees and their family members through mandatory political study sessions, supervised leisure time activities, household cleanliness inspections, mediation of family disputes, approving of marriages and divorces, and, by the 1970s, childbirth as well.

For those who did not have a work unit or did not reside in housing provided by such a unit, the second basic structure of post-1949 urban life—neighborhoods and their residents' committees—expressed state power. These are not voluntary associations, but obligatory structures established by the state in the early 1950s. Like work units, they have a dual role—to provide services for residents and to exert control. The residents' committee officers may establish nursery schools and first aid clinics, organize reading rooms for the retired and elderly, run small-scale sewing and bicycle repair workshops, mediate family disputes, and help keep an eye on local children after school lets out. In addition they are expected to organize mandatory political study sessions, report strangers to the police, organize local crime patrols, and pressure local families to accept the state's family planning targets. In this structure of work units and residents' committees, as in rural communes, individuals and families became highly dependent upon the resources and decisions controlled by the grass roots representatives of state power.

Where does the Chinese family fit into this complex bureaucratic system? Some observers claimed that the CCP was intent on destroying the family so individuals could be released to give their total loyalties to the Party and to Mao. Certainly the Confucian tradition, which had provided the ideological basis for China's patriarchal family forms, fell under concerted attack after 1949.

However, although there have been some instances of Party-mobilized conflict within families, that has not been the dominant approach. The post-1949 changes were designed not so much to destroy the Chinese family as to eliminate its autonomy. Mao and other leaders wanted families to be strong but compliant groups which would serve the interests of the state, rather than their own "narrow" or private interests. To this end state family policy was in some ways quite "conservative," as in the policy after the early 1950s of discouraging most divorces and in the legal stipulation that grown children must help support their aging parents.

In sum, in regard to grass roots social groups and even the family itself, the approach taken by the CCP after 1949 paradoxically reflected the Confucian tradition. The ideal society was one in which individuals would be tightly embedded in social groups arranged in a bureaucratic hierarchy, one that operated under the ideas and rules of an official orthodoxy. However, state control over this hierarchy, and therefore over all Chinese citizens, was strengthened immeasurably in comparison with the social order of late imperial China.

Flaws in the Mao-era Social Order

In many respects the social changes introduced after 1949 were quite successful. The nation was politically unified under a strong government that could stand up for China in world affairs. The new regime was able to mobilize human energies on a vast scale to confront the nation's problems, and local conflicts between lineages and language groups were kept largely under control. Crime, prostitution, drug addiction, and other "social evils" declined dramatically. The "sheet of loose sand" image no longer applied to China's body politic, and the authorities were able to gain an impressive degree of control over grass roots social life. As a result, sentiments of nationalism and loyalty to the regime and to Mao personally became widely shared.

Nonetheless, the new social order had a number of inherent flaws. These became particularly apparent during the Cultural Revolution decade from 1966 to 1976, when Mao and his radical followers tried to realize more fully their vision of solidary socialism. The radicals tried to eliminate all vestiges of private enterprise, market competition, material incentives, and pursuit of private interests, and to substitute a benevolent bureaucracy that would provide the population with their basic needs and reinforce their group and national solidarity. The premise was that by relying on the paternalistic state, people would experience security and rising living standards, leading to a sense of commitment to the system.

Most Chinese in Mao's final years saw their social environment in very different terms. They were locked into membership in state-mandated grass roots structures that tightly monitored all aspects of their lives. The time-honored ability of Chinese to leave and seek better opportunities elsewhere was effectively blocked. The bureaucratic structures had been repeatedly racked by political and class struggles, producing hatreds and fears of colleagues and neighbors from which there was no ready escape. Chinese were forbidden to have contact with most of the complex variety of China's traditional culture or the richness of the cultures of the outside world. They could only enjoy a narrow range of literature, art forms, styles of dress, and leisure activities that the state considered "proletarian." The failures and inefficiencies of the socialist economic system produced not abundance and a sense of a security, but the familiar maladies of socialist economies elsewhere—consumer shortages, long lines, stagnating or declining living standards, and a constant struggle to meet family needs. Those same economic failings made it necessary for individuals and families to cultivate personal ties and "back door" strategies in order to gain access to the basics of life. That necessity helped to undermine faith in the system, since it became increasingly apparent that high-ranking bureaucrats were in a much better position than ordinary citizens to deploy such personal connections for personal and family benefit. A social order that was intended to produce paternalistic welfare and popular gratitude increasingly had the effect of fostering social tension and popular resentment.

Chinese Society in the Post-Mao Years

The post-Mao elite under Deng Xiaoping's leadership was clearly aware of these flaws in the social order that they had helped build. Most of them had been victims of Mao's later political purges, and they became convinced that the path that China had taken since the mid-1960s was a dead end. China would fall further behind the dynamic capitalist economies of Asia and might even implode in political conflict unless dramatic reforms were introduced.

The years since 1978 have seen reforms in China so fundamental that many Chinese and outside observers consider them a new "revolution" at least as significant as the one that occurred after 1949. While no comprehensive account of these changes will be attempted here, the basic reform strategies employed by Deng and his colleagues can be summarized. They wanted to find ways to accelerate economic growth, raise living standards, and reduce political controls and tensions in the hope that these changes would restore faith in the leadership of the CCP. In the quest for these general goals, the CCP systematically introduced market reforms in place of bureaucratic allocation, opened the door for economic and cultural interchanges with the outside world, stressed the development of legal institutions, rehabilitated millions of victims of earlier campaigns, and relaxed state controls over popular thought and behavior. Curiously, the resulting strategy of substituting market and legal regulation for bureaucratic mobilization in many ways is reminiscent of the "liberal" option for remaking Chinese society that lost out in the struggle for influence in the 1930s and 1940s.

In the economic realm the post-1978 changes have produced a partial but nonetheless dramatic reduction in the degree of personal dependency upon the bureaucracy. In the countryside the collapse of collectivized farming and the revival of family farming, combined with the loosening of migration restrictions, has given rural families more autonomy to pursue a variety of strategies in their quest for prosperity. Managing the family's farming activities is in many places increasingly giving way to setting up family businesses, placing family members in jobs in village factories, and receiving remittances from the earnings of family members working elsewhere. While they are less subject to the daily orders and supervision of local cadres than in the Mao era, rural families also have to worry more about whether they can provide for their own needs, since the social safety net formerly provided by the collectivized system has been largely dismantled.

However, the bureaucratic state has not disappeared from the lives of rural residents by any means. The state's presence and control in the countryside are still much stronger than was the case in pre-1949 China. Village cadres beholden to the state still control access to farmland and, through their powers to tax, grant licenses, and approve construction projects, they maintain considerable influence over the ability of local families and the village as a whole to benefit from new opportunities. Rural cadres do not monitor and control the private lives of local residents as tightly as their predecessors did in the Mao era. However, on occasion and in certain realms, particularly in regard to enforcing state family planning targets, they can still mobilize considerable resources to demand compliance and punish locals who defy their authority (reading 24).

In China's cities the Deng-era reforms began somewhat later, generally after 1984, but there they also fundamentally altered the nature of the social order. Initially market reforms were aimed at providing more incentives and efficiency for enterprises rather than individuals. However, with the deepening of the reforms since 1992, the dependence of individual urbanites on their work units (and to some extent on their neighborhood organizations) has decreased. Lifetime work at fixed wages in a bureaucratically assigned job increasingly has been replaced by short-term labor contracts, freedom to seek and to change jobs, and variable pay based on complex incentive schemes. The "rehabilitation" of private enterprise and of foreign and joint-venture firms provides new employment options beyond the state and collective enterprises of the Mao era. As in the countryside, decreased dependence upon the bureaucracy is accompanied by increased competition and insecurity. Urbanites can no longer count upon the state and its bureaucratic appendages to supply them with a lifetime job, housing at nominal cost, free medical care, and the other benefits of a socialist economy. Revived labor markets produce competition for job opportunities (including increased competition from rural migrants), and once on the job, workers are likely to face a complex new array of rewards and fines as well as the prospect of being demoted, laid off, or fired. Reforms in other realms mean that housing, medical care, and other basics are no longer "free goods." Urban families are now required to pay costs that are increasingly influenced by market forces.

While it is sometimes argued that Deng Xiaoping's reform strategy involved an attempt to reform economic institutions while keeping political institutions unchanged, in truth the changes in the political realm have also been dramatic. The CCP continues to dominate the system and will not tolerate any organized opposition, but political rehabilitations and liberalization were central to the reform program. In many realms markets and laws are seen as preferable to bureaucratic allocation as a way of regulating popular behavior. With controls over allowed forms of behavior and thought substantially relaxed, although by no means eliminated, Chinese society has become much more varied and colorful. In the wake of these changes, religious activity, Confucian thought, lineage feuds, Western classical and world pop music, traditional Chinese operas, muckraking journalism, raising pets, employing household servants, wearing the latest Western fashions, and countless other formerly tabooed practices have all made a comeback.

China's leaders maintain that their system is still socialist rather than capitalist, since at least nominal state or public ownership of land and capital remains dominant over private ownership. But increasingly slogans about "building socialism" are seen as irrelevant by ordinary Chinese, and perhaps by the leaders themselves. More and more the Party bases its claim to legitimacy on its management of the economy and its defense of the nation, rather than on pursuit of a future socialist society.

Flaws in the Reformed Social Order?

In many ways the reforms introduced in China since 1978 have been highly successful, and certainly in comparison with the situation in the former Soviet Union and Eastern Europe. Income and consumption levels have been raised dramatically, poverty rates have declined, consumer shortages and rationing have been dramatically reduced, and China has captured the attention of the world for its successes in attracting foreign investment and selling its products overseas. China's leaders successfully defused many of the tensions that had built up during Mao's final decade in power. Millions of the victims of his campaigns were rehabilitated, broken careers and separated families were made whole again, and China ended its forced isolation from its own cultural heritage as well as the cultures of the outside world. In many ways China has become a more "normal" and even somewhat pluralist society.

Despite such successes, as China entered the new millennium it was by no means clear how stable the reformed social order would be. Party leaders, in their effort to keep the economic engine booming and retain control over an increasingly pluralistic society, seem to be, as one analyst put it, "riding a tiger." Deepening the reforms in the 1990s produced massive layoffs from failing state enterprises as well as Dickensian working conditions in many village and foreign-run enterprises. Individuals losing their jobs and facing cutbacks or rising costs in their housing and medical care look around them and see China's newly rich with their cellular phones, chauffeured limousines, and lavish private mansions. The pervasiveness of official corruption encourages a popular belief that the well-connected are monopolizing the fruits of China's reforms, rather than those who are most innovative or work the hardest. The resurgence in crime, prostitution, drug addiction, and other social problems feeds a popular perception that China's reforms have led to moral collapse. Some Chinese feel that China's Marxist leaders are presiding over the creation of the sort of unbridled capitalism that Marxism was designed to overthrow, while others recall Mao's prediction that China would face the danger of capitalist restoration after his death. The social tensions produced by political and class conflicts during the late-Mao years have not been replaced by social harmony and popular gratitude. Instead new resentments have been generated by widespread feelings that the current social order is inequitable and corrupt. Increasingly farmers, workers, and others are joining together to protest the injustices that they face and see around them.

The successors to Deng Xiaoping do not appear to have ready or effective answers to these problems. They have allowed an increasingly "normal" and
contentious society to emerge, but they appear quite uncomfortable with the
resulting pluralism and disrespect for official orthodoxy. While they feel they
have no choice but to continue to push the reform agenda forward in order to
keep the economy growing, they have been unable to come up with a new ideology and set of legitimating symbols to replace the widely discredited package of
Marxism-Leninism-Mao Zedong thought. Instead they repeatedly fall back on
slogans and practices of the socialist era, no matter how out of touch with reality
and ineffective these have become. Muddling through appears to be the order of
the day in managing China's increasingly contentious society.

The Complexity of Chinese Society Today

The reading selections that follow are designed to convey some of the
diversity and contradictions of reform-era Chinese society. Under the impact of
the reforms, social patterns stemming from the socialist era are in competition
with revived influences from China's own past as well as with new influences
and fads flowing in from the outside world. The relaxation of political and economic controls has made it possible for an underlying and formerly suppressed
diversity of customs and ways of life to become visible once again and for new
customs and trends to appear. Generalizations about social patterns have become
more difficult, as the standard template of socialist institutions has given way to
behavior and thought patterns that vary markedly depending upon local traditions,
Cultural Revolution experiences, recent economic fate, access to information,
closeness to China's coast, and other factors.

Readings 21–24 focus on contemporary family patterns. They present the
complex mixture of continuities with traditional family patterns and changes
stemming from the socialist and reform eras. It is also clear that contemporary
family patterns in rural (readings 22 and 24) and urban (readings 21 and 23)
China often diverge in important ways. Oversimplifying the contrast, the patrilineal family system is alive and well in most villages, producing, among other
results, a strong preference for sons over daughters that poses a challenge for the
state's family planning program. In contrast, in China's large cities family patterns
look less patriarchal and more like the "conjugal" patterns found in advanced
industrial societies, and this fact produces, among other things, an increasing
acceptance of divorce that contrasts with the situation in the countryside.

Readings 25–28 focus on the increased diversity in popular customs since 1978. Reading 25 vividly describes the Western-influenced consumption styles now visible in China's cities, as exemplified by the popularity of McDonald's restaurants. Reading 26, in contrast, describes the resurgence in rural areas of customs that stem from China's pre-1949 traditions, in this case involving the consultation of geomancy specialists to properly align new homes and gravesites and generally deal with life's problems. The revival described in reading 27 is more complex. Catholicism and other forms of Christianity of course had their origins in the efforts of Western missionaries in late imperial and Republican China. However, Catholic worship today is more influenced by the practices that took root in China prior to 1949 than by new foreign influences, a fact reflected in the continued use of Latin rather than Chinese in church liturgy. (The CCP's continuing ban on contacts between the Vatican and Chinese Catholics means that church practice is frozen in forms that predate Vatican II.) The revival of Christian worship is visible in both rural and urban locales in China. Finally, reading 28 deals with the revival of another set of indigenous customs, as observed in urban China—a set of mental and physical self-discipline techniques known as *qigong*. The resurgence of belief in *qigong* rituals and *qigong* masters described in this reading was a precursor to the rise of one particular *qigong* sect in the 1990s—the Falun Gong. In 1999 the mass following attracted by Falun Gong, and the willingness of this sect to challenge the authorities, caused an official panic that led the CCP to ban the group and launch a campaign to suppress it, a campaign that Falun Gong believers have resisted with surprising resilience. These two readings also illustrate the fact that revivals of traditions are not visible only in China's villages, while customs influenced by the West are not confined to the cities. Some of the revived practices, whether of domestic or foreign origin, cut across the rural-urban divide.

Readings 29 through 32 are all concerned with issues of inequality and inclusion or exclusion in Chinese society. Reading 29 conveys some of the debate occurring in the 1990s about the role of women in China and whether the dismantling of socialist institutions and the debunking of Marxist ideology have encouraged new or revived forms of gender inequality. Reading 30 deals with residents of a poor village who migrate to the city in search of manual labor jobs. To the extent that they are able to string together a series of daily jobs, they can earn more than they could back in the village. However, their higher wages and the money they can send back to their families are counterbalanced by the discrimination and harassment they face from urbanites on a daily basis. For a contrasting case of a village that has become so rich that they have to hire migrants from such poor villages to staff their booming factories, see reading 36.

Reading 31 deals with other forms of urban social life that are increasingly visible, if not fully accepted, in urban China today. It was sometimes claimed in the Mao era that China had no criminals or homosexuals, a claim that was dubious even at the time. In the reform era both groups are not so effectively suppressed and have become part of the social landscape. Recurring crackdowns have been launched against crime, but criminal groups and a criminal subculture are nonetheless increasingly visible. Homosexuals face a different situation. Official suppression has been relaxed, but China's gays still harbor considerable anxiety about whether they can enjoy the same increased tolerance as other groups.

Educational institutions are central to questions of inequality and inclusion or exclusion in any society. Schools play the key role in preparing China's youths for their places in society, as well as in preparing Chinese society as a whole to compete in the global economy. Reading 32 portrays the ways in which the lowest levels of schooling in one Chinese city have been affected by the post-1978 reforms. Schools reflect particularly vividly the consequences of a shift from bureaucratic mobilization to market competition. Children attending such urban schools enjoy a considerable advantage over their peers in the countryside, some of whom do not even complete primary school, and very few of whom can hope to get a college education. These disparities reinforce the great gulf in life opportunities between rural and urban China. That gulf was a product of the socialist institutions of Mao's China but persists today—as seen in the contrast between pampered urban children being treated to meals at McDonald's in reading 25 and migrant rural youths scrambling for menial day labor jobs in reading 30.

While these essays cover a diverse terrain, they barely scratch the surface of Chinese society today. Even so it should be abundantly clear that China enters the new millennium with a dynamically changing and increasingly diverse social order. The image of a vast social hierarchy operating under an official orthodoxy, an ideal stressed by Mao as well as his dynastic predecessors, no longer fits current social realities. But the liberal image of individuals competing in a society governed by markets and laws does not fit very well either. The current social order is a complex, often contradictory amalgam of market forces, outside cultural influences, legal regulation, personal networks, popular social movements, bureaucratic regulation, and other elements. It remains uncertain whether China's leaders can continue to "ride the tiger" by transforming this social order without further undermining their own political authority.

SOCIETY
Readings

21

Family and Household

CHARLOTTE IKELS

Chinese tradition produced patriarchal families and strong family obligations that differ in many ways from the family patterns of the contemporary West. But a century of revolutions, wars, and economic and cultural change have buffeted Chinese society and produced pressure for change. What is the mix of continuity and change in Chinese families today? Anthropologist Charlotte Ikels uses her fieldwork in Guangzhou (Canton) neighborhoods in the 1990s to sketch the basic patterns of family life in contemporary Chinese cities.

Courtship

Perhaps no aspect of family life is believed to have changed so radically as courtship. Visitors to Guangzhou, including former residents returning after an absence of as little as four years, express shock and dismay at the apparent loss of traditional virtue. One 1984 graduate of Zhongshan University reported that today's middle school students are very different from the middle school students of her day. When she was in middle school, even dating was unthinkable, but now, according to her friends and classmates who are teaching in middle schools, "Sixty percent of the girls are no longer virgins!" In her day there was so much pressure during the school year that it was impossible even to think of anything other than schoolwork (she had attended an elite prep school), but during the summer there were opportunities for recreation. A group of boys and girls who could talk easily together would arrange to meet at a park; they would chat together and get something to eat. There was no pairing off. Even when she attended the university, she knew her husband as a friend for the first three years, paired off with him only in the fourth year, and did not marry until three years after graduation. Now pairing off is common, and even though ten students might share a dormitory room, roommates arrange to be out so that a couple can get together privately.

Miss Mao, a 1991 graduate of Zhongshan, reported that although intense relationships between male and female students are officially frowned upon, dating and even having a special friend of the opposite sex are allowed. If students are suspected of engaging in sexual intimacies, however, they are likely to be dismissed from the school. Surely a good deal of discretion is involved here on the part of both the students and the authorities. According to a friend of Miss Mao's who was attending a university in Shanghai, the authorities had no choice but to take action against seven female students who occupied a room on the floor above her. These young women disappeared one by one in the course of the year—all allegedly expelled for prostitution.

Miss Mao proposed several explanations for the apparent increase in sexual activity among students. First, students identify sexual activity with modernity. They assume that the physical intimacy they see in Hong Kong- and Western-made movies is usual among "modern" people. Second, to behave otherwise may be to stigmatize themselves as tradition bound. Third, some students, mostly males, with little to do at the university expend their excess energy playing games with the opposite sex. Fourth, because playing around is less likely to affect one's marriage prospects if no one knows about it, some students develop casual sexual relationships with people from other parts of the country. After graduation, students from outside Guangdong are expected to return to their home areas. An affair in Guangdong between a student from Hunan and a student from Guangxi is unlikely to become public knowledge in either home community.

A young male faculty member at another university in Guangzhou stated that most students no longer take education seriously but instead spend their time fooling around. He opined that virginity is rare these days and estimated that 30 percent of the female students at his institution will have an abortion sometime or other during their university careers. The consensus is that unmarried women readily obtain abortions in ordinary health care facilities without the news getting back to their work units. As one woman explained, someone who is worried about her abortion becoming public knowledge simply goes to a facility where she is not known and pays for the procedure herself. Even someone who chooses to have an abortion covered by her work unit's insurance plan can save her reputation if the doctor is willing to write that the charge is for unspecified "treatment."

Other sources of data, however, suggest that perceptions of rampant premarital sexual activity among young people in Guangzhou might not be entirely accurate. For example, one day I asked an eighteen- or nineteen-year-old service worker I knew, who called herself Laura, whether I could talk with her sometime about the life of young people in Guangzhou. She agreed, but before we turned to this topic, she asked whether I knew much about psychology. She then explained that she thought that she was abnormal because when she did not know someone she would like him, but after she knew him for a while, she would want nothing more to do with him. She meant that as soon as a boy suggested getting physical (for Laura this meant no more than kissing), she would be repulsed and refuse to go out with him again. Her friends often commented on seeing her with different boys but never with the same one more than a few times. Laura said that normally she is very outgoing—when the workers have a complaint, she is the one bold enough to bring it up—but on this matter of boys, she could not figure out what was the matter with her. . . .

How does one account for these disparate images of young people: on the one hand sexually experienced, and on the other timid and foolish? Both pictures are correct, though they represent extremes; the behavior of many young couples falls on a continuum between them. The more modern image, however, is more readily noticeable and remarked upon. One couple rolling on the grass in Yuexiu Park makes a much bigger impression than 100 couples chastely sitting on benches eating Popsicles. The findings of a national survey of a random sample of 1,642 married males and 1,467 married females carried out from late 1988 to early 1990 offer a less impressionistic picture of urban sexuality.

According to this study both attitudes and behavior are (and have been) more accepting of premarital sex than either Confucian or Communist values would lead one to expect. Although they preferred that their spouse be a virgin, 41 percent of the males and 30 percent of the females "thought that pre-marital intercourse was not wrong and was entirely a private affair. When pre-marital intercourse occurs between fiancés, few think it immoral or unchaste." A more informal survey in Huhhot revealed that 64 percent (23 of 36) of "younger" male informants believed that if a couple is planning to marry, premarital sex is perfectly proper. As for behavior, the national study found that 19 percent of males and 15 percent of the females who responded to the question (2.5 percent failed to respond) reported engaging in premarital intercourse. Among those aged 20–35 the incidence of premarital intercourse had risen to 25 percent for males and 18 percent for females.

The Five City Family Study found that only 33 percent of the most recent cohort of young couples (those married from 1977 to 1982) had initiated their courtship—not surprising, given the shyness of many young people. The others had relied on friends to introduce them (50 percent) or on parents and relatives (16 percent). One percent claimed to have had arranged marriages. Still, these figures represent a major change from the experience of the cohort married prior to 1938, when 55 percent had arranged marriages and only 5 percent found spouses on their own.

According to the authors of the Five City report, young people fail to play the major role in their own courtship because they lack opportunities to meet; feudal thinking (the belief that males and females should have no contact) makes them shy; they have no confidence in their own decision making; and the person who introduces them, who serves as somewhat of a guarantor, makes the marriage more than simply a private matter and enhances its stability. To provide more opportunities for young people to meet and especially to help "over-aged youths" (women 27 or older and men 29 or older) find spouses, the authors recommend that adults provide introductions as part of their personal and social responsibility. They also suggest that introduction bureaus be opened and given serious support. Individuals should be encouraged to place personal advertisements in newspapers and magazines and even on the airwaves. Finally, work units should help their own unmarried young people find a mate by organizing social activities. Those with a heavily female labor force, for example, should organize activities with those whose labor force is heavily male. . . .

Marriage

The natural outcome of a successful courtship is marriage, and with marriage, in China at least, comes the rearing of children, or rather, in Guang-zhou, the single child. Before the child arrives, however, the couple must have a stable living arrangement in which to raise it. According to the Five City Family Study, 47 percent of couples in the most recent cohort to marry (between 1977 and 1982) lived with the husband's family after the wedding, 18 percent with the wife's. Only 32 percent established an independent residence, and just under 3 percent had to make other arrangements—for example, opting to live separately because of work assignments or overcrowding in their natal households that made the addition of even one more adult impossible. The figures for post-wedding living arrangements of the oldest cohort (those marrying before 1938) show a higher proportion (60 percent) living with the husband's family and a lower proportion (31 percent) living independently. What these figures conceal, however, is that from 1960 to 1965 more than half of all newly married couples lived independently. Even among those couples marrying between 1966 and 1976, 48 percent established their own household, whereas only 35 percent lived with the husband's family and 14 percent with the wife's.

It is critical to note, however, that the immediate postwedding residence is unlikely to be the new couple's long-term residence. Most couples are simply waiting for their housing assignment to be made. For example, a 1985 study of residence patterns in Tianjin revealed that 65 percent of young couples in stem families left the parental household in the first five years of their marriage; another 17 percent left within the next five years. Furthermore, according to a number of studies, most parents and adult children prefer living separately but, if at all possible, in the same vicinity so that they can continue to interact frequently. In fact the nuclear family is the most common family type in China's cities. According to the Five City Family Study 66.4 percent of urban families are nuclear, 24.3 percent stem, and 2.3 percent joint. An additional 2.4 percent are single-person households; 4.6 percent fall into the category of other.

These data reveal that although stem family living is a common experience in contemporary urban China, it is most characteristic of certain age groups: obviously those in their 20s and 30s (the newly married) but also those over 60 (the elderly). In the Guangzhou Family Study, in which all the elderly are at least 70 years old, 60 percent live in stem and joint families and 15.5 percent in nuclear families; only 8 percent live alone. Another 16.5 percent live in other arrangements, such as with an unmarried grandchild or with their long-term employer. A national study of the elderly carried out in 1987 presents the living arrangements of the elderly in a slightly different way, but the message (high rates of coresidence of the elderly and their children) is the same. Of the nearly 14,000 elderly living in cities (not including those living in rural townships) 61.8 percent lived in households made up of three or more generations, 26.9 percent in two-generation households, 7.5 percent as couples, 1.9 percent alone, and 2 percent in other arrangements.

Although the contemporary patrilocal stem family shares a common form with the ideal traditional family, its dynamics differ. The senior female of the household (the mother-in-law) generally controls the household budget, but this post is less powerful than is sometimes assumed. Both the Five City Family Study and the Guangzhou Family Study make the same observations on the significance of the household budget. Although others usually contribute a share of their income to a particular person in the household, this share represents the smaller part of their income. Furthermore, the household manager is not free to redistribute this money as she sees fit—for example, to those members in greatest need—but is expected to spend it on food. The junior couple retain the bulk of their income to pay children's educational and clothing expenses as well as their own transport, clothing, meals outside the home, and entertainment. Costly items such as electrical appliances or a new set of furniture are usually purchased by the younger generation, who take them along when they move to new housing.

The strict correlation between seniority and authority characteristic of the ideal traditional family is conspicuous by its absence. In the Guangzhou Family Study elders made it clear that by and large their adult children (even when still unmarried) make their own decisions about where to work, whom to marry, and whether their children (the eldest grandchildren) continue in school. Most of these elders have far less education than their children, are unfamiliar with the job market and the new strategy of locating work on one's own, and are intimidated by their own dependence (financial or physical) on the younger generation. Most freely admit they do not know how to advise on these issues and do not attempt to do so. Though they are happy to be asked their opinions, they usually concur with what the younger generation has already indicated it wishes to do. For its part the younger generation has already factored the elders' likely response into its own game plan. Families that are unable to develop a smooth working relationship usually divide the household if at all possible. . . .

The primary reason behind the space reallocation following the marriage of a household member is the belief that newly married couples are entitled to a bedroom of their own. Without this minimal requirement for privacy the arrival of the next generation would be delayed indefinitely. China, of course, is world famous (or infamous, depending on one's point of view) for the strictness of its population policy. During most of the 1950s the government's position on population growth was essentially "the more the better"; each additional person was seen, not as a mouth to feed, but as a pair of hands to build the new China. Though there was dissent from this position all along, until the early 1970s dissenters had too little power in the central government to reverse the pronatalist policies. Prior to this time the desirability of reduced fertility had been discussed primarily as a health benefit to mothers and infants, but thereafter the focus shifted to the need to keep down population growth to achieve economic growth. The state began in 1973 to promote the "*wan, xi, shao*" policy: delayed childbirth (*wan*), longer birth intervals (*xi*), and fewer births (*shao*). In the cities this policy was interpreted to mean intervals of at least four years between births and no more than two children per couple. Implementation relied primarily on persuasion, though more forceful measures were available to deal with the recalcitrant. Under this policy the Chinese birthrate dropped from 33.6 per thousand in 1970 to 18.3 in 1978.

This rapid drop, achieved even before any material incentives were explicitly made available, suggests that there was already substantial interest on the part of at least the urban population in reducing family size, probably for many of the same reasons as elsewhere: higher survival rates of children, higher costs in rearing them, more education and increased employment opportunities for women, and so forth. Again, comparisons with Chinese populations else- where in Asia are instructive. By 1987 the total fertility rates (average number of children born to women who had completed their childbearing) were 1.3 for Hong Kong, 1.5 for Singapore, 1.7 for Taiwan, and 2.3 for Malaysia. In none of these sites was the pressure to reduce fertility anything near what it was in China.

The pressure increased greatly with the introduction of the one-child family policy in 1979. When it was first announced, there was no consensus whether the policy positively limited couples to one child or set the one-child family as a goal. No national law was passed. Instead, individual provinces were left to formulate their own family planning regulations, and implementation methods (subject to provincial guidelines) were developed at the local level. Each administrative jurisdiction, such as a commune or a work unit, was assigned a quota of births by higher administrative authorities. Jurisdictions or units (or the cadres in charge) that kept births at or below the quota were to be rewarded; those exceeding it were subject to penalties. Given the government's traditional mobilization style, the "bold assault," it should not be surprising that coercion and other abuses accompanied the implementation of the one-child policy, particularly in rural areas, where resistance was greatest.

By 1990 the one-child family policy was understood to mean one child for urban families and up to two for rural families, particularly if a rural couple's first child was a girl. A rural couple may have a second child if one of them (1) is the single transmitter of the line for at least two generations (i.e., the only child of an only child), (2) is the only one in a set of brothers with the ability to procreate, (3) is the male who moves into the household of a woman who is an only child, (4) is an only child married to an only child, (5) is a disabled veteran, (6) is a woman married to a returned overseas Chinese, or (7) belongs to an exceptional hardship household in a remote mountain or fishing district. These exceptions directly address the concerns of rural families who view sons as critical for the continuation of the line and for their own physical survival. Even in the cities a couple may petition to have a second child under certain circumstances, such as having a child who will be unable to earn a living. In such a case a doctor has to certify that the child is disabled and that the disability was not caused by the parents. Some units require that the certifying doctor be from a level higher than a public health station.

Although there was some slippage in enforcement during the 1980s, by 1992, in the wake of tightening restrictions, the birth rate in had dropped to 13.1 per thousand overall and to only 10.9 in the city proper, indicating that compliance with the (modified) one-child policy is high but uneven. For example, although almost 96 percent of births were first births in two of the four core urban districts, in Haizhu district, the most rural of the four, the figure was only 87.8 percent. By contrast, in Guangzhou's four counties, 53–57 percent of births were first births. Such a narrow spread in the rural areas suggest both acceptance and vigorous enforcement of a two-child standard.

Authorities, attributing the excess births to the mobile population, by 1990 had targeted them for special attention. In 1991 the provincial government was requiring all people seeking employment to have a document specifying either that they were single or that, if married, they were in compliance with the one-child policy. Being in compliance means having no child or having one and practicing contraception. In China the officially preferred mode of contraception is the sterilization of one partner or the outfitting of the woman with an IUD before she returns to work. In the event that she is one of those few people who cannot tolerate an IUD and takes the pill instead, this must be stated on the document. Every year work units require a physical exam, to make sure that the IUD is still in place, as well as a urine test, to make sure that the women is not pregnant. Should she be found pregnant, an abortion is about the only alternative. A woman accidentally pregnant (i.e., with an IUD in place) is not considered blameworthy; her abortion is covered by insurance, and she receives full time off (normally fifteen rest days) An employer hiring people without the certificates takes a big risk because the state conducts periodic inspections. Anyone found to have violated the regulations by hiring someone without evidence of marital and parental status faces punishment. Furthermore, the self-employed must themselves be certified as in compliance before they can obtain a license to set up a business.

Giving birth to a child in Guangzhou requires official authorization. After registering one's marriage, one goes to the local street committee office, which provides newly married couples with a document known as a planned birth certificate stating that the female applicant is permitted to bear a child in the current year. By tradition, immediate childbearing is the rule, and surveys indicate that 65 percent of Chinese women still conceive within three months of marriage and that more than 85 percent conceive by the time of their first wedding anniversary. Should a woman experience a delay in getting pregnant, there is usually no problem extending the permit to the following year. When a woman goes to a hospital for a prenatal exam (or for any exam at which it is likely to be noticed that she is pregnant), she must present her pregnancy permit. If she does not have the permit, she is immediately called to account and pressured to have an abortion. For this reason women with unauthorized pregnancies frequently do not seek treatment for any health problems until after their baby arrives. If they are employed, however, their co-workers will notice their condition and press for an abortion. If they are not employed, they must stay in seclusion, for should they go out, the neighbors would notice the pregnancy and report it to the residents committee or the street committee. A couple's only hope is for the woman to flee the locality before her pregnancy is obvious. Even so, whether her unit or the local government office suspects that she has fled because of a pregnancy, it will be certain to visit both her parents and her parents-in-law to see whether she is hiding out with them. Officials might even chase her to the countryside if they know where she is likely to be. When she finally agrees to an abortion, the unit or government sends someone to escort her to the hospital—to make certain she actually has the abortion.

Every April each residents committee carries out an annual inspection of women of childbearing age in the neighborhood. A representative visits every household in which there is a married woman of childbearing age who has not been sterilized. According to one such representative, who "caught" a rural woman hiding out in her jurisdiction in the 1991 sweep, the inspection is nothing more than eyeballing the woman's abdomen to see if she looks pregnant. If she does, the residents committee pressures her and her family members to agree to an abortion. The residents committee also distributes contraceptives to the few couples with a child who have not been sterilized if the wife cannot tolerate an IUD.

When it comes time to deliver her baby, no hospital receives a woman, even if she is in labor, without the pregnancy permit. A woman under these circumstances either calls in a midwife for a home delivery or attempts to deliver at a public health station. Some such stations will accept her, but others will not, and in any event this delivery is not covered by her medical insurance. Furthermore, the hospital is the only legitimate source of a birth certificate for the baby, and without that the child cannot be officially registered as a resident of Guangzhou (or anywhere else, for that matter). Without registration as a city resident, the child (and thus the whole family) faces educational and employment disadvantages, though these are becoming increasingly less significant. Because these deterrents are well known, it takes a motivated person to buck public opinion and endure the penalties, which include fines and possibly dismissal from one's work unit. . . .

The success of the one-child policy in the urban areas is probably due to a coincidence of personal and official interests. Because pensions are available for most urban workers and those with no pensions and no descendants have a welfare safety net, people no longer perceive children as critical for survival in old age. This attitudinal change is reflected in a survey carried out in Shanghai that asked women why they wanted to have children. Urban women answered that they want children to achieve joy in life, avoid loneliness, have someone who will carry out their ideals, and enhance ties between them and their husbands. These sentimental reasons contrast with the more practical responses of rural women, who want to continue the line, gain security in old age, and increase labor power.

Chinese psychologists and educators worry endlessly about the upbringing of the only child. There is enormous concern that parents will make the child the center of their lives, with dire consequences for the child's development. Some fear the child will become a "little emperor," indulged, doted on, and lacking in self-discipline; others fear the parents will be overprotective, stifling the child; still others fear that the parents, having unrealistic expectations, will burden the child with unreachable goals. The CASS study found, for example, that 87 percent of parents hoped that their child would eventually attend a university.

22

Home-cured Tobacco—A Tale of Three Generations in a Chinese Village

DANIEL WRIGHT

A prime irony of the rural revolution led by Mao Zedong is the fact that the gap between Chinese cities and villages in customs and living standards is much larger today than it was in 1949. Dan Wright, Director of the Hopkins-Nanjing Center of Johns Hopkins University, spent two years (1998–1999) living in Guizhou, one of China's poorest provinces. In this vivid account of rural life in that province, Wright provides a picture both of contemporary family patterns in a particular village and of the difficulty faced by poor rural families in educating their children.

Chen Zhixian, a shy, modestly attractive 21-year-old woman from Big Nest Village, hasn't been the same since returning from Zunyi City four years ago. Her first time away from home as a would-be migrant laborer, Chen Zhixian found out she was different than most in the city: she was illiterate. In fact, when asked by potential employers to sign a simple contract, she couldn't even write her name—the minimum requirement. Chen Zhixian returned home in defeat, completely humiliated. The sad truth: Chen Zhixian has never attended a day of school in her life.

Within months of his sister's crushing experience, her brother Chen Dongfang, two years older and the eldest of seven children, returned from a distant vocational school to begin teaching at Big Nest Elementary School. Chen Dongfang says that his parents, poor farmers and illiterate themselves, could afford to send only one of their children to school. As the oldest son he received the privilege. After completing his primary education, Chen Dongfang went on to star as the number-one student at the township middle school and then studied elementary education at the vocational school.

Upon returning to Big Nest and a paying job, Chen Dongfang's first thought was his sister. He walked with Chen Zhixian down the hill to the elementary school and inquired if she could enroll. She'd have to start from the beginning—from first grade. School officials laughed. A 17-year-old sitting at a wooden desk in a room full of seven-year-olds? No way. The request was rejected; Chen Zhixian's trauma deepened.

Since then she has suffered from depression, expressed by lethargy and lingering sickness. The evening I arrived at the Chen village home I caught only a glimpse of Chen Zhixian. I found out later she had been sick and was taken that evening to a relative's home for "treatment." The distant cousin, I was told, would use "spirits" to attempt to cure her.

The following morning Chen Dongfang apologized to me in private: The chicken that the family was going slaughter for us as a welcome dinner was given to the witch-doctor relative as payment.

Chen Dongfang has one overriding concern in his life: that his younger siblings do not experience their older sister's misery. Besides Chen Zhixian, who stays at home, four siblings attend school and the youngest will begin first grade in September. Since he was 19 years old when he began teaching, Chen Dongfang has paid each of their tuitions. The second sister, Chen Zhifen, now 15 years old, is in fourth grade. She's the hardest working of the siblings, says Chen Dongfang. First brother Chen Zhihua, 13 years old, is in sixth grade. He's an introvert and has terrible grades. He'd much rather hole up in a room taking things apart and putting them back together. The second brother, Chen Liping, 12 years old, is in fifth grade. He's a peaceful boy, but his heart is not in his studies. The third brother, Chen Xiaobo, 11 years old, is also in fifth grade. He's smart and loves to talk. The youngest, Chen Chunfen, a playful 7-year-old sister, begins first grade this September. She's Chen Dongfang's favorite sibling. Chen Chunfen is courageous, he says. She'll do well.

Apart from their studies, the Chen children are part of a tightly knit household economy. Each child has daily chores: taking the water buffalo to graze along mountain paths, cutting wild grass for pig fodder, washing clothes by hand, sweeping the dirt-floor home and food preparation such as grinding chili peppers, washing vegetables, and peeling potatoes.

With big brother hovering over his siblings, they will all—with the exception of Chen Zhixian—learn to read and write. But that doesn't mean they enjoy it. Each of the children told me at some point during my visit that they do not like school.

"Why not?" I asked.

"My teacher doesn't care about me," was the common reply.

Little appreciated by villagers, elementary school teachers in this region's rural areas lack incentive to put their hearts into their work—unless they are exceptional, like Chen Dongfang.

During the four years he taught at Big Nest Elementary Chen Dongfang spent evenings visiting village families to stress the importance of education. He also pled with family heads to enroll their children in school. As a result of his efforts, which were completely of his own initiative, the number of students at Big Nest Elementary increased from 100 to 500.

I asked Chen Dongfang about his own dreams and plans for the future. "I have only one goal,' he replied without hesitation, "to continue to raise the money each of my five younger brothers and sisters needs to complete middle school." The 23 year old spoke with the seriousness of a parent.

This type of commitment would present a dilemma for most young people. Not for Chen Dongfang. Though his heart's desire is to remain in Big Nest to teach, and he is at the age at which most young men in his village marry, he has shelved all personal desires until he secures his brothers' and sisters' education. Because of expected tuition increases, Chen Dongfang is even considering going to China's coast after he completes his teachers program next summer to look for a construction job. If he could find employment, he would make possibly four times what he makes as a teacher. But it's a risk, he admits. Travel to the coast would mean forfeiting his guaranteed monthly teacher's salary. And plus, it's no sure bet he could find a job, especially with the economy as it is.

Chen Dongfang has the sharp, distinct facial features characteristic of someone from the mountains of Zunyi District. Add a Red Army cap to his head and some revolutionary fire in his eyes and he'd look like something from a poster of the 1950s. But this young man is a child of a different age. Education and travel outside his village have opened horizons not previously known in Big Nest, witness an uncle's sincere question as we sat around one rainy afternoon chatting with family and village friends: "Is China at the center of the world?" It was a fascinating question from someone who has never left his village. In response, Chen Dongfang patiently explained to his father's brother that the world is round.

Big Nest exists somewhere between centuries-old living conditions (wooden plows, cooking over open fire, smoke-cured ham and paraffin lamps) and urban values of the late 1990s as the village is pollinated by young people who travel back and forth from China's urban centers as migrant labor. The result is village life in which young and old, though living together, seem at times as if they belong to worlds that are shaped very differently.

During my four-day homestay with Chen Dongfang I began to sense the intriguing mix of continuity and change that exists in rural interior China. Most of my insights came as Chen clansmen and I sat on wooden benches in a small, barren room (used also as the eating area), chatting as we dodged drips from a leaking roof swatted pesky flies and shooed away scrawny chickens that kept sneaking into the room, convinced they would find grains of spilled rice.

Atmosphere was created by pipe smoking, an important activity in this tobacco country. Each man had a plastic bag stuffed somewhere in his clothes that contained chocolate-brown tobacco leaves. Each also had his own pipe made with a polished brass mouthpiece, a thin, five-inch-long piece of bamboo and a small brass bowl just large enough to hold the end of a rolled piece of tobacco leaf. These pipes are their prized possessions. As conversation circled the room, a man, empty pipe in mouth, would pull out a crumpled plastic bag from his pocket, remove a broad leaf of tobacco, carefully tear a strip about one-inch wide and six-inches long, roll it into a tight cylinder and then stuff one of its ends into the pipe's bowl. The men shared lighters or matches and when one of them had problems getting his pipe lit they would all laugh, joking that his lungs were not strong enough or that his tobacco (each grows his own) was inferior.

As we sat around, each man puffing away and enjoying conversation, Chen Dongfang's grandfather, Chen Daru, told some of his life story. Though he's almost deaf, his 80-year-old mind is lucid. He spoke as if the events of his life 60 years ago had happened just yesterday. No one I met in Big Nest is more thankful than Chen Daru that the past is history.

Grandfather

When Chen Daru was his grandson's age, destitute poverty, opium smuggling, warlords, salt monopolies and clan warfare strangled northern Guizhou Province. Besides the continual struggle to live off his land, Chen Daru enjoyed considerable standing in the Chen clan, some 1,000 families spread over five villages.

Chen Daru's social position was strengthened because his best friend, also from Big Nest—a dynamic, eloquent young leader—was recruited by the local warlord as his lead assistant. With his own army and political administration, the warlord controlled a piece of northeastern Guizhou Province equivalent in size to a present-day county. Like many warlords at the time, he entered into an uneasy alliance with the Nationalist government.

Within the warlord's stronghold, however, clan warfare was common. On the eve of the Communist takeover, sporadic hostility between the Chen clan and the neighboring Ye clan increased at an alarming rate. Chen Daru claims that the Ye clan was the aggressor and the Chen clan fought strictly out of self-defense.

The timing of the skirmishes could not have been worse. At the high-point of the Chen-Ye feud, the People's Liberation Army marched into northern Guizhou to "liberate" the area; that is, to mop up after their victory against the Nationalists and to consolidate power.

The new regime investigated the existing power structure and eliminated potential opposition. Chen Daru's best friend was summarily executed; Chen Daru was categorized as a counter-revolutionary, a label he would not shed for 30 years, until Deng Xiaoping rose to power in 1978.

"I never did anything wrong," 80-year-old Chen says quietly between puffs. "We were just trying to defend ourselves. I am *not* a counter-revolutionary."

Father

Regardless of what Chen Daru says about his innocence, among those who paid the heaviest price for his "crimes" were his children.

"Growing up was very difficult," says Chen Daru's oldest son, Chen Meixian. A man of few words, he enjoys the circle of conversation, but says little.

After learning more about his youth as the son of a "counter-revolutionary," I understand why he does not speak much. Born in the early 1950s, Chen Meixian grew to maturity through years of class struggle, communes, mess-hall eating, famine and tragic Cultural Revolution.

Because of his father's special status, other children were not allowed to play with him. He was not permitted to move freely around the village and he was denied the opportunity to attend school.

Toward the end of the Cultural Revolution a marriage was arranged for Chen Meixian to a young woman from a village three miles away They gave birth to their first child, Chen Dongfang, in 1975.

Life turned better in 1978 when his father was rehabilitated, but for someone—by that time in his mid-twenties—who had never known anything other than labels and class struggle, change was not automatic. Children are like wet cement. His personality had been formed; he had learned to mind his own business.

Though China's "one-child policy" was instituted in 1979, Chen Meixian and his wife gave birth to seven children by 1991. Villagers say that birth-control enforcement has not been strict in Big Nest until just the past few years.

Prior to that, clan mentality drove considerations of family size: the number of people relative to rival clans measured Chen strength. Village leaders, who are also clan heads, until lately encouraged families to have more children. The leaders, in turn, would falsify reports to township officials on the number of people in their village.

Today, Chen Meixian and his two younger brothers live in adjoining homes. His sister lives in a distant village with her family. According to custom, his father lives with the youngest son. And though their living space is separated, and they cook and farm according to their nuclear-family units, they share much of their lives in common as an extended family.

Chen Meixian is a gentle man. Though he appreciates the fact that his oldest son feels so strongly about education, his preoccupation in life is farming, and seeing that his crops (tobacco, corn, rice and potatoes) succeed. After all, he and his wife have a family to feed.

Son

Chen Dongfang is keenly aware of the profound changes that have occurred within his family in just three generations.

He is the first in his family to know how to read. The opportunity to study has clearly provided Chen Dongfang with new prospects and improved thoughts of how to care for his family. How else, he wonders, can his family and Big Nest Village ever break their isolation and cycle of poverty?

Chen Dongfang is also part of an increasingly mobile generation. Even those in Big Nest who have received little or no education now flow to China's urban and coastal areas, a reality made possible only since the 1980s when policies to restrict migration (through a combination of household registration requirements and rationing) were relaxed. In fact, an entire age group—those in their late teens through early 30s—is conspicuously absent from Big Nest.

One afternoon conversation included two brothers of about Chen Dongfang's age who work at construction in Kunming, the capital of inland Yunnan Province. They had returned for a brief visit with their wives and children. Though they come home only once or twice a year and have not lived at home since they were teenagers, they bring new ideas—and cash—every time they return. The result, as their experience is replicated millions of times throughout Guizhou Province and China's interior, is a pattern of increased interchange between China's urban and rural areas.

These brothers' absence and the absence of hundreds of others like them from Big Nest make Chen Dongfang's presence all the more meaningful. Though away at an education college most of the last year, he remains an inspiration for the village children.

Besides the young, Chen Dongfang also has the attention of Big Nest's older generation. To watch those his father's age sit like children as they listen to him tell stories of life in far-away cities and new-found information is quite a role reversal from what I imagine decades ago, when the young would sit wrapped in their fathers' stories about the production brigade or the latest clan skirmish.

But perhaps most interesting is the way Chen Dongfang and his family relate to each other. The respect he receives from both siblings and parents make it seem as if his siblings have two sets of parents: their mother and father who put food on the table, and Chen Dongfang who keeps pencils and notebooks in their hands. This dual, parent-like family structure demonstrates the ways in which education and mobility among young people in Guizhou's villages are influencing family relations.

Dramatic change has occurred in Big Nest since Chen Dongfang's grandfather was a young man, when this community, hidden deep in Guizhou's rugged mountains, was mired in 50 percent infant mortality, 30-year life expectancy and near-total illiteracy. Even so, Chen Dongfang is painfully aware—and he is reminded every day by his sister's suffering—that too much remains the same.

Postscript

One month after my visit to Big Nest Village, I met with Chen Dongfang at my home in southern Guizhou. Not having seen him since that time, I was eager to hear news of Chen's family. He shared the heart-breaking information that his youngest sister, Chen Chunfen was looking forward so much to beginning first grade, found out that she cannot go to school this year. Reason: This year's tobacco crop was damaged by flooding. There's not enough money, even with big brother Chen Dongfang's help.

"But can I go to school next year, Mother?" asks the disappointed seven-year old. "We'll just have to see," mother replies, hiding her fear.

23

How Come You Aren't Divorced Yet?

ZHANG XINXIN

During the 1960s and 1970s, both Chinese tradition and Party policy made divorce very difficult to obtain. In Maoist socialism, personal unhappiness or spousal conflict were things to be "mediated" and overcome in the interest of marital and social stability. Among the many changes initiated by China's reforms after 1978 was a more permissive attitude toward divorce. At the same time, many individuals who had had their lives disrupted by the Cultural Revolution wanted to turn a new page, and in not a few cases this involved a desire to leave unsatisfying marriages. The reassessments of marriage and personal happiness that became common in the 1980s and 1990s are portrayed in this account by Zhang Xinxin, a Chinese journalist who brought to China the oral history interview techniques pioneered by Studs Terkel.

"How come you aren't divorced yet?" I laughed aloud when I heard these words, and so did the friend who relayed them to me. They had been spoken by a college classmate of ours, and they represented him perfectly: shallow and cocky, yet somehow charming. He hadn't changed a bit! He was in Beijing now, doing a film about a soccer match that allegedly took place between foreigners and Chinese around the end of the Qing dynasty. He had invited some classmates to dinner, and naturally took the occasion to boast about his recent achievements as a film director. He also referred casually, and with great self-satisfaction, to his divorce "war." He went on to praise the beauty of his new wife, and then, with childlike sincerity, sprang that laughable question.

Unhappily, but unknown to him, each of the other three classmates at the table was secretly facing the problem of divorce.

Before the 1980s, divorce in China was a rarity—indeed, a scandal. In those days I had a childhood friend who decided to break off with her fiancé after getting a marriage license but before the wedding. Since the two sides agreed, they did not need a court; they just went to the office of the neighborhood committee and asked for a "divorce certificate." The people in the office warned the girl with brutal honesty: "When you got your marriage license it was as good as hopping into bed; who's going to want you now?" And sure enough,

242

people in the neighborhood and at her workplace began pointing and gossiping. Nobody could understand. Why would an honest-looking girl, with everything going her way—a good job, a fiancé in international relations at prestigious Beijing University—ruin it all by getting a divorce? People jumped to the conclusion that she must have some hidden flaw that the boy had discovered only after their marriage license allowed them to become sex partners.

The girl was forced to bow her head under the burden of the rumors in the neighborhood and at work. She was surrounded. by a prison of evil tongues until she was finally able to marry someone else, a young man who also happened to be a childhood friend of mine. His home had been ruined during the Cultural Revolution when his parents were held in solitary confinement for "political investigation." He had taken to the streets and become a hooligan, and was himself arrested in a knifing incident. After the Cultural Revolution, in acknowledgment of the unfair political treatment his family had received, the government reduced his sentence by ten years and released him. Out of prison, he, too, was beset by rumors, and found a companion in misery in my "divorced" classmate.

After the marriage, I asked my friend why she had left her first fiancé.

"Because we had nothing to say to each other . . . ."

In the late 1970s having nothing to say to each other would never be sufficient grounds for divorce. But by the late 1980s it had become a possibility. So had many other reasons. My girlfriend got divorced again in the 1980s, and then remarried again. She is no feminist activist, or even an intellectual in the habit of reflecting upon the course of life. She is just a busy clerk in the labor union office of a small factory.

According to statistics from China's Department of Civil Administration, 17.8 Chinese per thousand were married in 1987, and only 1.1 per thousand were divorced. But these are average rates, which obviously vary a great deal across different sectors of China's populace. For example, I have twenty college classmates, and fully half of them were facing either divorce or remarriage in early 1988. Among Beijing people in my age group (thirty to forty years), including both my acquaintances and the people I interviewed for my book *Chinese Profiles*, virtually everyone seemed to have encountered the divorce question.

These facts are, I have to say, intriguing to me. I can't help noticing how often it happens that, in conversations about people of my generation, someone casually says, "By the way, they're getting divorced." What's even more intriguing is the response of people in other generations—as young as twenty-five and as old as sixty—when I ask their views on this divorce trend. I get such strong and personal reactions! Nearly everyone admits that they, too, have had problems of this sort. People of other generations seem to differ only in the kinds of solutions they seek. Still, for the purposes of this chapter, I will concentrate on the group I know best: urban intellectuals aged thirty to forty.

A new player who has been responsible for many a broken home has appeared on the Chinese marriage scene. Divorce courts have begun to refer to "a third party stepping in," and the term *third party* has become common in the language of daily life. According to government pronouncements, the third party problem has resulted from the opening to the West and the influx of the sexual revolution into China. Some provinces and cities, in order to protect the stability of the family institution, have suggested that the work units of offending third parties punish them by placing administrative warnings into their personnel files. Third parties have also become key characters in the social commentary of Chinese writers and artists. They have appeared abundantly, and by no means always negatively in fiction, film, and television soap operas. . . . Most of the people who have discussed their divorces with me have had a third party involved.

Guo Yanjun, male, thirty-five years old, had gone to a May Seventh Cadre School with his father. Later he joined the army and was subjected to the hostility that soldiers from the country direct against those from the city. After that he worked in a prosecutor's office, where he handled some fairly important political, economic, and criminal cases. When I interviewed him he was a political columnist for a major journal that dealt with legal affairs. Along the way he had helped many people win their divorce cases. The most famous and mysterious of these was the divorce of a certain vice minister, who afterward married a well-known writer. The vice minister's attorney, a woman named Zhou Naxin, had been virtually unknown before the case, and afterward was already famous enough to be head of the Beijing Legal Affairs Institute.

Guo filed his own divorce case in 1986. Three years earlier it would have been impossible for him to do so, because of the pervasive public view that women need to be protected. Even when men could file for divorce in the !ate 1980s, it remained difficult. He said to me in the interview,

> God, am I miserable! What would I do without my motorcycle? First I have to take my girlfriend home from her office, then I have to deliver my son from nursery school to my wife's place, then I have to come back to my office—which doubles as my bedroom. My wife gets hysterical every time she sees me. This isn't my imagination—she herself says it. She says everything's fine until I show up. And my office gives me the creeps. It's in a building that also houses a top-security factory, so the whole building is locked and guarded from 8 p.m. to 8 a m. All night there's nobody in there except me and the rats.

In this big city, where human relationships have grown ever more cold and businesslike, where the pressure for survival grows with the population density, and where dust storms and monotonous gray buildings continue to spring up, Guo can be counted a modern hero. I got to know him, ironically, through a number of cases in which third party involvement was being used as a basis for divorce. Many people have asked me about divorce strategy, including how to play the third party card. I in turn have consulted Guo, who asks his friends in the district courts. Until Guo cleared them up, certain questions always puzzled me: How could all these people, who have good educations and plenty of life experience, be so ignorant of divorce procedures? And why don't they bring their questions to a court or a lawyer's office, instead of relying on hearsay and the back door? "Every lawyer has an endless pile of cases," Guo explained. "And the courts don't even have time for the formal lawsuits. Consultations? Out of the question!"

One incident, however, made me realize that extraordinary psychological pressures can impinge when a person tries to handle a marriage crisis through private channels. Zhu Weiguo, male, thirty-two years of age, was the son of a peasant from the hills of Fujian. After graduating from college with a major in literature, he went to work as a literary editor for a major press. . . .

> My leader at work called me in. My wife was besieging him with telephone calls—as many as six or seven a day—asking where I was living. My leader didn't know the answer, and was baffled by the incessant questioning. I didn't feel like explaining to him—or to any leader. The most I felt like saying was that she had a boyfriend, and that it was only after her affair that I got myself a new girlfriend. The problem is that she doesn't want to break up any more. I can't see why, though, because *her* new man's a good catch. He's a Chinese-American working in Beijing, and he could get her out of the country. . . .

Our conversation turned to the question of whether the third party problem, and the troubling stories it generated, could be attributed ultimately to undue pressures in the lives of Chinese intellectuals.

> Actually, my wife and I have *always* fought. It's never been over money, though we're hardly rich. She's a very caring person, really. Last fall, at the mid-autumn festival, she prepared a little banquet for me. I had been out to see some writers and just packed off some manuscripts to press, and I came home exhausted. All I wanted was to lie down. This made her angry. She said I didn't care a whit for her feelings, that I hadn't even glanced at her banquet table. It was true that I hadn't noticed it until she flew into a rage. Still, I told her I *had* seen it, and I was grateful, but I was just too tired. So why are we constantly fighting? I

have to admit she's right. If men and women are equal, women shouldn't have to tolerate things like this.

She later told me she had pursued her affair purely for revenge. When she said she was going on a business trip, actually she was going on a vacation with him. At the height of some of our arguments, she would even describe what went on between them. Then she would say that, of course, spiritually I was superior to that fellow, and that she still basically loved me, not him. Now, I admit that I am only the son of a peasant. But I couldn't forget the things she described to me, so I asked for a divorce.

Our child was not an issue. We both loved her, and custody with either parent was fine. We decided to have her stay with me, for fear that she might become an obstacle to remarriage for my wife. We were always careful not to fight in front of her. Whenever she appeared, we would stop fighting and put on smiles, so that there would be no harm done to her psychologically.

But deep down, my heart was bleeding, as if being ripped apart. Our situation was nothing like the one in that story of yours, where the couple manage to develop new feelings for each other as divorce draws near. Even as they are finishing the paperwork, they go out for lunch together. Not us! We were still yelling and screaming at each other right in front of the clerk who was doing our papers. Neither of us would give in. But deep inside I was almost paralyzed. Part of me wanted to beg her to come home and never mention the word "divorce" again. We had been classmates ever since junior high school, and it had all been quite natural that we should get together and eventually marry. All these years we had shared a kind of closeness that I didn't fully appreciate until I was in the divorce office. I was fighting with her and wanting her to stay at the same time.

A hitch in our paperwork suddenly seemed to bring reprieve. We were both supposed to hand in our marriage certificates, but mine was unacceptable because our little daughter had torn it badly. The office would not accept the shreds and insisted on a replacement certificate from my work unit before they would give their approval.

But my reprieve was short-lived, because I had to move out the next day anyway. My wife said that if I didn't move out, she would. She spent that very night in a crummy little hotel across the street, so the next day I just had to leave. I went to stay with a friend.

I couldn't go home to visit her, because when I did she would hold me and start weeping, asking for forgiveness. What could I do? My mind was changing every minute—no, a thousand times a minute! If I were to marry my new girlfriend, I knew that my wife, like the female characters in *Rebecca* and *Wuthering Heights*, would still not let go of me.

All this chaos and confusion brought me a pervasive sense of defeat. I thought of myself as a peasant boy fresh from college who had suddenly been thrown into the baffling fast-lane life of the big city. . . .

Wu Xiaojiang, male, thirty-five years old, was my college classmate. In college he was never much of an actor (people would laugh when he got up onstage, even before he opened his mouth), but later he became an outstanding theater director. In 1987 he was working on Eugene O'Neill's *Long Day's Journey into Night*; he also likes Tennessee Williams and Edward Albee. He is talented and highly civilized. In college I always had the impression he was low-key and level-headed.

He married the year we graduated, and I met his wife at the wedding. She seemed to me a mild woman—the kind who knows when to stop, and who can keep emotional surges under control. They seemed to be a couple made in heaven. Yet she asked for a divorce after only two years. His account:

> I moved to the theater house, into a little room without heat. I begged her to postpone the divorce until I could get a housing assignment from the theater troupe. But she thought I was saying this just to hold onto her, and to keep her from marrying her new boyfriend. Actually I felt fine being alone. All I had to do was learn how to light a stove. What's so hard about that?
>
> Later I came to realize that those two years of marriage had been the most exhausting and irritating years of my life—even in comparison to the years I had spent laboring in the Heilongjiang countryside. I wondered if I was just more suited to bachelorhood. Maybe my past had molded me to be this way. During nine years in the countryside, one year working in the city, and five years of college, I had always lived in a dorm. Whatever the environment, or the kinds of people in it, I would always find a little nest for myself, a nest that gave me my own psychological space. When I had to share the nest with somebody, maybe it just got too close and I couldn't adjust.

His self-analysis was calm and sincere. It seemed a pity that all the caring he gave to his friends could not be given to a woman who lived even closer to him.

All the people in these examples are from the generation that went through the Cultural Revolution and spent time in the countryside. All their marriages followed a period during which they had been at loose ends—fending for themselves as they labored in the countryside, returned to the cities, and then looked for work or sought entry to college. No matter how calm they were as they told their stories or did their self-analyses, they all felt uneasy inside. They felt strong desires to settle down—but in life had found this goal elusive. Their problems with third parties and fourth parties were clearly connected with their psychological longings for security and for order in their lives. As they told me their stories, they sometimes would hide some of the truth, or fail to face reality. Yet their introspection was sincere, and it covered the period not only of their broken marriages, but of all that had happened to them. . . .

There are a lot of women who knock on my door. Besides helping some them with the technical problems of divorce, I also counsel many divorced women who belong to my age group and now are raising their children on their own. I listen to all of their similar yet different stories.

One woman gets up at 6:00 every morning. She has to wash up and cook for herself and her daughter before her daughter gets up at 6:15. At 6:30 they leave the house together. The woman puts her daughter on the back of her bicycle and takes her to the bus stop, through side streets so the traffic police will not catch her carrying her daughter on the bicycle. Then, after helping her daughter elbow her way onto the bus, the woman pedals alongside the bus to make sure the girl safely reaches school. Only then does she go off to work. The daughter attends an important primary school very far from her home. In order for the mother to enroll her in this school, she had to pull a lot of strings to use her *guanxi* (connections). The problem of attending this school, however, is more complicated than just seeing that the child gets there safely.

Since the school does not cook lunch for the first-graders (because little children get sick easily and the school cannot take the responsibility), the mother, during her own lunch break, has to take her daughter's lunch to school. First she goes to a friend's house nearby to warm the food she prepared the night before and dropped off that morning. Then she has to take the food to school. Luckily, a few parents have started taking turns cooking and delivering the lunches.

In the afternoon the mother naps at her desk for a while, then returns to school to pick up her daughter. Again, she goes through the same routine: elbows her daughter onto the bus, follows the bus on her bicycle, and carries her daughter on the bicycle back home. In the evening, she reads while her daughter practices the piano. After her daughter goes to bed at 8:30, she writes letters under the desk lamp. Each Sunday, she takes her daughter to the piano teacher's place, paying 20 yuan every month for the lessons. Occasionally they go to a movie, a fair, or the amusement park together. At her divorce, the court decided that her ex-husband must pay 15 yuan a month for child support, but the average expenses for a child like hers in Beijing are about 60 yuan per month. Because she works for the government, she cannot get any kind of premium or subsidy and her monthly salary is merely 120 yuan. Her ex-husband has remarried; once in a while he takes their daughter to his place to spend some time with him. But every time she comes back, the girl asks her mother, "How come I don't have a dad like everybody else?" This woman's name is Wang Jiu and she's thirty-nine. She used to be a top student at an important girls' high school before the Cultural Revolution.

How should I explain all this to my child? Should I say, "Your dad is bad, he is irresponsible"? I'm the one who brought her up, but one visit with her father ruins everything I have tried to cultivate. Perhaps I should explain to her that her father's already got a new home and a new kid. . . . I don't know what a child thinks of the parent's divorce. Sometimes I try to imagine how my daughter feels. But I can't do it, because I didn't have this kind of experience when I was small.

I thought about my contribution to our marriage (which he ruined), my mistakes within it, and the reasons for its failure. I thought that maybe I had neglected my husband after our daughter was born. He needed a lot of love, but when we had our daughter, most of my love and care shifted to her. His temper grew worse and worse. In retrospect, I see it was a demonstration of his discontent. I let him go and, of course, he left. Sex may also have been a reason for the divorce. At first, everything was ok in the marriage. But later I always found myself too tired after a day's work to engage in sex. Also, the idea of having an abortion if I became pregnant scared me to death. He was horny all the time and he didn't like condoms. So I finally just said the hell with it and gave him whatever he wanted, yet he still left me. I know he felt that life was boring. He complained about everything. Actually, he is both intelligent and talented, but he was too bored to do anything. This is where I differ from him. But I can still understand him.

Everyone examines himself or herself at the time of divorce, but few share their reflections with others. . . .

The above narrators have all reached the halfway point of their lives. They feel there is a social reason for their broken marriages. But none of them choose to lead a single life. Instead, all of them long to settle down and are searching very hard for a way to do just that. I listened carefully to everyone and became surprised to find out that their standards kept becoming lower and lower. Of course, there were some stories of passionate love, but these affairs usually lasted for only a year. Then the fire burned out and new complaints popped up. . . .

This generation is still full of idealism. Their longing to settle down and their faith in higher aspirations are hovering in the air side by side, up and down, up and down. . . .

24

Human Rights Trends and Coercive Family Planning in the PRC

MARTIN KING WHYTE

China, with a population of over 1.3 billion, faces a serious challenge in adequately feeding, housing, and employing future generations. After initial neglect, Chinese authorities mounted an increasingly strict family planning program from 1970 onward. This program has been quite successful in keeping fertility in China much lower than it would otherwise have been. However, one of the ironies of this success is that since the launching of the "one child" policy in 1979, control over births has been pursued via coercive mass mobilizations reminiscent of the Mao era. As a result, while Chinese have more freedom in most areas of their lives than they did in the Mao era, they have significantly less freedom in regard to procreation. Sociologist Martin Whyte describes here the increasing disjunction between controlled fertility and most other areas of social life.

There are clear restrictions remaining on human rights in a number of realms, making Chinese observance of these rights less complete than in many other countries. For example, although individuals can more freely migrate to other places, they still in most instances cannot obtain the full rights of residence in their own locales, so that the two caste division between China's rural and urban populations persists. Similarly, even though Chinese can more freely engage in religious worship these days, they invite trouble if that worship occurs outside the supervised forms of religious expression allowed by the state. Legal protections are still weak at best, with no general presumption of innocence accepted, and most of one's fate already decided before trial. Despite these and other limitations that keep the general situation in China from meeting the standards of the Universal Declaration of Human Rights and other such norms, on balance the freedom of ordinary Chinese citizens has increased in most realms in comparison with the situation at the time of Mao's death in 1976.

However, there is one major exception to this generalization, an exception that raises a number of troubling questions. That exception concerns the exercise of reproductive rights in the PRC—the ability of Chinese citizens to decide how many children they will have without being subjected to state coercion. In the realm of reproductive rights Chinese citizens are much worse off today than they were in the late-Mao era. As a result of that deterioration, a number of other serious human rights abuses have increased sharply, with the most notable example being the heightened number of deaths of China's most vulnerable citizens, its baby girls.

This is not the place to review the overall trends in China's family planning program, but the main features are quite familiar. During most of the Mao period, the official line oscillated between promoting and dismissing the need for family planning. When state family planning efforts were launched they were initially voluntary. Prior to 1970 official policy and popular behavior were out of step with each other, with the sharpest drop in fertility occurring during a period of neglect of family planning (1959–61), and a "baby boom" occurring during a period of official promotion of family planning (1962–64).

This situation changed after 1970, when a sustained official family planning effort was launched, with persuasion increasingly backed by coercion. Up until 1979, the official effort focused on the slogan "later, longer, fewer" and aimed at promoting late marriage, longer intervals between births, and fewer births. The fertility goal at the time was generally to get urban families to stop at two children and rural families at three. During this period, many of the coercive tactics originated that were to be more systematically employed during the reform era—detailed monitoring of maternal menstrual cycles, confinement of "over-quota" pregnant women for "thought work," threatened penalties against family members, denial of household registration and private farming plots for an "excess birth," etc. Vigorous enforcement of such measures produced a marked decline in fertility levels and much closer synchronization of official family planning policy and fertility behavior.

Official coercion on behalf of family planning goals escalated further after the launching of the "one-child policy" in 1979. The prime motivation for the shift in policy was not, as is popularly believed, to reduce Chinese fertility levels from unacceptably high levels. The levels of enforcement and coercion of the 1970s "later, longer, fewer" policy had already done that, producing a national total fertility rate (TFR) that was extraordinarily low for a country that was still 70 percent or more rural—around 2.7 births. Instead, the shift to an even more draconian policy was the product of computer simulations of the demographic trends to be expected when China's "baby boomers" born in the early 1960s began to marry and produce children. In other words, the initial concern was to find ways to prevent China's fertility rate from jumping back up from the levels achieved in the late 1970s.

The "one-child policy" entailed a switch from multiple objectives, including promoting late marriage, to an overwhelming emphasis on directly monitoring and controlling the number of births. Furthermore, the policy mandated that families in large cities should be limited to one child, and that in the countryside while one child should be the ideal, more than one could be allowed in a variety of circumstances. Eventually during the 1980s the policy in many rural areas evolved into a de facto two-child rule, but toward the end of the decade and in the 1990s this rule has been combined with increasingly strict efforts to prevent third and higher order births. It is worth repeating the observation that this state-initiated control over popular fertility is not based on any traditional precedent.

The level of enforcement and coercion in pursuit of these family planning goals has fluctuated to some degree since 1979. It appears that an initial high tide of enforcement of the one-child policy peaked in a wave of abortions and sterilizations in 1983 and was followed by a slight relaxation (as the de facto rural two-child rule spread), which in turn was followed by a new high tide of enforcement at the end of the 1980s and in the early 1990s, with perhaps a slight loosening in mid-decade. The latest statements by Chinese officials . . . indicate a concern that too much tolerance is being shown in rural areas, and such statements may presage a new round of tightened enforcement of the policy.

Again, there is not enough space here to document systematically the variety of measures that have been adopted in pursuit of fertility control in the "one-child policy" era, and a number of treatments of this topic exist. In addition to the kinds of measures described for the 1970s, official enforcement in rural areas has involved imposing tight local quotas for the number of births allowed; making rewards and penalties for leading local cadres (and not simply family planning cadres) depend on keeping local births within these quotas; imposing large fines for disapproved births; promising nonagricultural jobs and other benefits for submitting to abortions or sterilization; requiring sterilization or at least IUD insertion while mothers are in the hospital recovering from their "last" permitted birth; threatening arrest for anyone removing an IUD without official approval; round-the-clock harassing of families in which a woman is pregnant without approval and particularly of the woman herself; and in widely reported cases the rousting of noncompliant families out of their homes, followed by the smashing of furniture and houses. In general, there is a systematic effort to try to subject families (and women in particular) to such unremitting threats and pressures that they will feel they have no way out except by submitting to an official demand for abortion and/or sterilization. . . .

Overall, one could say that this draconian family planning enforcement has been quite successful. China's fertility rate fluctuated somewhat after 1979, but by the early 1990s it had apparently declined further to a level at or below replacement, with demographers speculating on whether the TFR was 1.7 or 1.8 versus 2.0 or 2.1. Whatever the true figure is, women having two children or less during their lifetimes is a dramatic accomplishment for a still predominantly rural country.

The human toll of enforcement in rural areas can still be seen in a number of ways. After declining sharply from traditionally high levels to become relatively unimportant during the Mao era, female infanticide and abandonment of baby girls have risen dramatically once again. China's orphanages have had to cope with a vastly changed situation, as they have been swamped by the rising numbers of abandoned baby girls and have seen the proportions of "orphans" they care for who are female and who have no physical defect (unless one considers being female a defect) rise sharply. Untold numbers of such babies die without reaching an orphanage or adopting family, but with the death rate in China's poorly funded orphanages estimated at 50 percent, even those who make it to such an institution face an uncertain fate. Increasingly Chinese families are able to take advantage of the availability of ultrasound-B machines to determine in advance the gender of a fetus, precipitating a sex-selective abortion to avoid having to cope later with the birth of another daughter (although this practice is formally illegal). As result of a combination of such practices, the sex ratio at birth for China as a whole was reported to have risen to 120+ in the early 1990s, much higher than the level of about 106 expected in a normal human population. In response to such statistics, Chinese analysts seem to worry much more about how these excess males will eventually find brides than they do about the "missing girls" themselves.

Although newborn baby girls are the primary victims of this sharp deterioration in reproductive rights in China, adult women also are affected in multiple ways. As I have already indicated, it is pregnant women who are most directly the targets of harassment and penalties of family planning enforcers, who are often denied pre- and post-natal care for an "over-quota pregnancy," who at times resort to extreme measures such as binding their bodies or fleeing to other areas to conceal a pregnancy, and who are required to undergo a variety of medical procedures even when (as in the case of sterilization) the risk for a male would be significantly less. Whatever one thinks about the impact of reform era changes on the extent of sexual inequality in China generally, in this particular realm it seems clear that women have suffered.

At this point it is worth considering the kind of reaction one gets from Chinese officialdom to such generalizations about their family planning program. A typical response is to claim that official policy stresses voluntary compliance and opposes coercion, that the use of physical coercion constitutes a "deviation" from this policy by poorly trained and overly enthusiastic local cadres, and that in any case the revival of female infanticide is explained by the "feudal" sex preferences of Chinese peasants, since official policy stresses that a daughter is as desirable as a son. These claims are highly disingenuous, to say the least. Grass-roots enforcers are as zealous as they are only because the family planning enforcement system requires them to meet official quotas and penalizes them sharply if they fail to do so. It is the clear gap between official quotas and popular fertility aspirations that predictably leads to widespread coercion by grass-roots enforcers in pursuit of compliance when persuasion fails.

One can also reject the idea that Chinese peasant families want as many children as possible, or wish to have sons rather than daughters. Instead, they exist in a society in which there is no societal provision of reliable old-age support and no real effort to change the traditional custom by which daughters marry out into their husbands' homes and villages and transfer their obligations for old-age support to their in-laws. In this setting it is critical to have one son, and rural families are willing to take considerable risks to reach that objective if previous births have all been daughters. But at the same time they would like to have a daughter, even though this is not as absolutely essential, in terms of old-age support. Survey data show that a majority of rural parents would prefer to have one son and one daughter for their allowed two children. But the demographic odds are such that about one quarter of parents will fail to have a son in two tries. It is those who have a second daughter who are put in an impossible situation.

25

McDonald's in Beijing: The Localization of Americana

YUNXIANG YAN

China's reforms since 1978 have produced a major shift away from the spartan norms of the Mao era, and toward a new encouragement of consumerism and conspicuous consumption. China's "open door" policy has also made foreign goods and services increasingly available symbols of the new life styles. Anthropologist Yunxiang Yan describes how visits to McDonald's restaurants in Beijing have taken on a meaning and significance for Chinese consumers that are quite different from those they have in America.

On April 23, 1992, the largest McDonald's restaurant in the world opened in Beijing. With 700 seats and 29 cash registers, the Beijing McDonald's served 40,000 customers on its first day of business. Built on the southern end of Wangfujing Street near Tiananmen Square—the center of all public politics in the People's Republic of China—this restaurant had become an important landmark in Beijing by the summer of 1994, and the image of the Golden Arches appeared frequently on national television programs. It also became an attraction for domestic tourists, as a place where ordinary people could literally taste a bit of American culture. New McDonald's restaurants appeared in Beijing one after another: two were opened in 1993, four in 1994, and ten more in 1995; by the end of 1996, there were 29 outlets in Beijing. According to Tim Lai, the company's General Manager, the Beijing market is big enough to support one hundred McDonald's restaurants, and McDonald's plans to open six hundred outlets in China by century's end.

The astonishing growth of the Beijing McDonald's has to be understood in the context of recent changes in Chinese society. There is a new tendency to absorb foreign cultural influence and transform them into local institutions, a trend that Chinese political system resisted during the Maoist era (1949–78).

The Big Mac as a Symbol of Americana

On October 1, 1993, National Day in China, a couple in their early seventies had dinner at the McDonald's restaurant on Wangfujing Street. They had been invited to celebrate the holiday at McDonald's by their daughter and son-in-law, who spent almost 200 yuan for the dinner, an unimaginably large sum in the view of the elderly couple. The experience of eating in a foreign restaurant struck them as so significant they had their picture taken in front of the Golden Arches and sent it to their hometown newspaper, along with another photo they had had taken on October 1, 1949, in Tiananmen Square—celebrating the first National Day of the People's Republic of China. Their story was later published by the newspaper, with the two contrasting photographs. In the 1949 photo, the two young people appear in identical white shirts, standing slightly apart, their thin faces betraying undernourishment in hard times. In the 1993 photo, a portly woman proudly holds her husband's left arm, and the two are healthy looking and fashionably dressed. They took a taxi to McDonald's and, while crossing Tiananmen Square, they remembered how poor they had been in 1949 and realized how much China has changed in the interim.

At first glance, this news story reads like the typical propaganda skit that one still finds in official Chinese media, with its constant play on "recalling the bitterness of old China and thinking of the sweetness of the new society." However, in this case it is McDonald's—a capitalist, transnational enterprise—that symbolizes the "sweetness" of current life. What is even more interesting, the headline of the story reads: "Forty-four years: From *Tu* to *Yang*." The terms *tu* and *yang* have been paired concepts in the everyday discourse of Chinese political culture since the nineteenth century. In common usage, *tu* means rustic, uncouth, and backward, whereas *yang* refers to anything foreign (particularly Western), fashionable, and quite often, progressive. The juxtaposition of these common terms demonstrates how McDonald's and its foreign (*yang*) food have become synonymous with progressive changes that make life more enjoyable in contemporary China.

In the eyes of Beijing residents, McDonald's represents Americana and the promise of modernization. McDonald's highly efficient service and management, its spotless dining environment, and its fresh ingredients have been featured repeatedly by the Chinese media as exemplars of modernity. McDonald's strict quality control, especially regarding potatoes, became a hot topic of discussion in many major newspapers, again with the emphasis on McDonald's scientific management as reflected in the company's unwavering standards. According to one commentator who published a series of articles on McDonald's, the company's global success can be traced to its highly standardized procedures of food production, its scientific recipes, and its modern management techniques. As the title of his article ("Seeing the World from McDonald's") suggests, each restaurant represents a microcosm of the transnational, so much so that, according to another article by the same author, many American youths prefer to work at McDonald's before they leave home to seek work elsewhere. The experience of working at McDonald's, he continues, prepares American youth for any kind of job in a modern society.

Other news items associate the success of transnational food chains with their atmosphere of equality and democracy. No matter who you are, according to one of these reports, you will be treated with warmth and friendliness in the fast food restaurants; hence many people patronize McDonald's to experience a moment of equality. This argument may sound a bit odd to Western readers, but it makes sense in the context of Chinese culinary culture. When I asked my Beijing informants about the equality factor, they all pointed out that banquets in Chinese restaurants are highly competitive: people try to outdo one another by offering the most expensive dishes and alcoholic beverages. It is typical for the host at a banquet to worry that customers at neighboring tables might be enjoying better dishes, thus causing him or her to lose face. To avoid such embarrassment, many people prefer to pay the extra fees necessary to rent a private room within a restaurant. Such competition does not exist at McDonald's, where the menu is limited, the food is standardized, and every customer receives a set of items that are more or less equal in quality. There is no need to worry that one's food might be lower in status than a neighbor's. For people without a lot of money but who need to host a meal, McDonald's has become the best alternative.

During the autumn of 1994 I conducted an ethnographic survey of consumer behavior in Beijing. I discovered that the stories commonly told about McDonald's have taken on a surreal, even mythic tone. For instance, it is believed among a number of Beijing residents that the potato used by McDonald's is a cube-shaped variety. A twenty-year old woman working at McDonald's told me in all seriousness about McDonald's secret, cube-shaped potatoes, the key to the corporation's worldwide success. She was also fascinated by the foreign terms she had learned in the short time she had worked there, terms such as *weisi* (waste), *jishi* (cheese), and *delaisu* (drive-through). The first two are straight transliterations of the English terms, but the third is both a transliteration and a free translation: it means "to get it quickly." These half-Chinese, half-English terms are used by employees and customers alike, making their experiences at McDonald's restaurants exotic, American, and to a certain extent, modern. . . .

But what is it that the Beijing customers have accepted—the hamburgers or the ambience? My ethnographic inquiry reveals that whereas children are great fans of the Big Mac and french fries, most adult customers appear to be attracted to McDonald's by its American "style" rather than its food. Many people commented to me that the food was not really delicious and that the flavor of cheese was too strange to taste good. The most common complaint from adult customers was *chi bu bao*, meaning that McDonald's hamburgers and fries did not make one feel full; they are more like snacks than meals. . . .

It seems ironic that although people have reservations about the food at McDonald's, they are still keen on going there. Why? Most informants said that they liked the atmosphere of the restaurant, the style of eating, and the experience of being there. In other words, the attraction of McDonald's is that it offers, not filling food, but a fulfilling experience. Or, as a local writer says, it is the culture of fast food that draws Beijing consumers to these restaurants. . . .

For younger Beijing residents who have higher incomes and wish to be "connected" more closely to the outside world, eating at McDonald's, Kentucky Fried Chicken, or Pizza Hut has become an integral part of their new lifestyle, a way for them to participate in the transnational cultural system. As one informant commented: "The Big Mac doesn't taste great; but the experience of eating in this place makes me feel good. Sometimes I even imagine that I am sitting in a restaurant in New York City or Paris."

Throughout my fieldwork I talked with more than a dozen yuppies, all of whom were proud of their newly attained habit of eating foreign fast food. Although some emphasized that they just wanted to save time, none finished their meals within twenty minutes. Like other customers, these young professionals arrive in small groups or come with girl- or boyfriends and enjoy themselves in the restaurant for an hour or more. Eating foreign food, and consuming other foreign goods, has become an important way for these Chinese yuppies to define themselves as middle-class professionals. . . .

McDonald's experience in Beijing is a classic case of the "localization" of transnational systems. Efficiency and economic value—the two most important features of McDonald's in the United States—appear to be far less significant in Beijing's cultural setting. When Chinese workers load their families into a taxi and take them to McDonald's, spending one sixth of their monthly income in the process, efficiency and economy are the least of their concerns. When customers linger in McDonald's for hours, relaxing, chatting, reading, enjoying the music, or celebrating birthdays, they are taking the "fast" out of fast food. It is clear that McDonald's restaurants in Beijing have been transformed into middle-class family establishments, where people can enjoy their leisure time and experience a Chinese version of American culture.

26

The *Fengshui* Resurgence in China

OLE BRUUN

*Fengshui, or "geomancy," is a traditional system for divining the proper align-
ment of influences from the natural environment in order to benefit Chinese, both
the living (e.g., by selecting sites for homes, businesses) and the dead (gravesites).
Branded superstitious and suppressed during the Mao era,* fengshui *practices
have made an energetic reappearance since 1978. Danish anthropologist Ole
Bruun, who conducted fieldwork in several locations in rural China in 1992–1994,
describes here some of the ways in which Chinese villagers are once again
relying on these ancient arts.*

Customs related to *fengshui* (Chinese geomancy) were attacked by Confucianism
for centuries and restrained by consecutive regimes from the imperial throne to
the Kuomintang to the Communist Party. Throughout this century, attempts to
eradicate *fengshui* beliefs and practices were particularly harsh. *Fengshui*
customs were concurrently cursed as ignorance by Sun Yat-sen and as superstition by Mao Zedong. Today, such customs are nevertheless flourishing. In
virtually all rural localities in China proper, the *fengshui* of a site is now routinely
considered when a new house or grave is constructed. Far more bothersome for
the Chinese leadership, however, is the increasing authority that people grant to
fengshui in regard to disease etiology, mental disorders, accidents, the sex of
newborn babies, business affairs, and a host of daily occurrences. . . .

The ancient geomantic principles of *fengshui* (literally, wind-and-water)
have been used extensively by commoners through all times. The essence of
fengshui is that configurations of land forms and bodies of water direct the flow
of the universal *qi*, or "cosmic currents," which by the advice of a specialist can
be brought to optimum advantage for a person's wealth, happiness, longevity
and procreation; similarly, a malicious flow of qi may bring disaster. Despite its
roots on the mainland, *fengshui* has hitherto been associated by most scholars
with Taiwan, Hong Kong, Singapore and other overseas Chinese communities.
Its spontaneous re-emergence in the PRC, however, indicates the vitality there
of an undercurrent of alternative values, sentiments and ideologies. . . .

Beliefs and accusations phrased in geomantic terminology permeate Chinese history. *Fengshui* cosmology was applied to the siting of cities at least as early as the third or fourth century and was taken seriously by eminent thinkers such as Chu Hsi.

But Chinese geomancy was more potent in conveying rebellious sentiments than in supporting the state and formal power, especially in later Chinese history. Foreigners were often-resisted and repelled by peasants gathering around *fengshui* accusations—for instance, just before the Boxer uprising, when foreign churches and their missionary personnel were accused of having caused a natural disaster by their malicious *fengshui* influence. Machines, railways and telegraph lines were attacked under the pretext of the disturbances they caused to ancient tombs. Apparently, Chinese formal power was always aware of the threat posed to it by disorderly popular beliefs. As early as the Tang dynasty, imperial efforts were made to quell "unauthentic" geomancy and superstition.

At the outset of the PRC in 1949, *fengshui* was genuinely popular and used by all strata in Chinese society, albeit with varying degrees of refinement and classical learning. But after 1949, and especially after the Great Leap Forward, the struggle over *fengshui* became the spiritual parallel to class struggle in the material world. It was ironic, therefore, that the Communist regime itself employed *fengshui*-related forces, destructively so. In the hands of the Communist regime, it developed into a means of securing power for some by breaking the *fengshui* of others and included breaking their group confidence and uprooting their social identity. The Cultural Revolution witnessed a breaking of the peasants' links to their ancestors by wrecking graves and to their clans by demolishing ancestor halls, shrines and tablets. Although practising *fengshui* became a criminal activity, the authorities mounted attacks that suggested their own perverse belief in it. People of "bad class" background were punished by geomantic means—for instance, by publicly destroying their ancestors' tombs and burning the bones to wipe out their family lines.

It has been argued that the recent revival of traditional ritual in rural China is merely a reconstruction of cultural fragments, on the assumption that powerful state intervention for decades has destroyed the social basis for popular rituals and deprived them of their fundamental values and connecting ideology. In the case of *fengshui,* however, a high degree of continuity is evident. The actual techniques involved in divining good *fengshui* are largely unchanged, the objectives are similar, and most of the present practitioners had carried out their trade in the old days before the Communist crack-downs. . . .

Fengshui-related interpretations of daily events often lurk beneath the surface in China's urban areas today: a group of waitresses speculate that their restaurant has bad *fengshui* since they have had numerous divorces, many people believe that their bad fortune is due to family graves being destroyed during the Cultural Revolution, private businesspeople more and more openly play with *fengshui*-related principles and symbols, joint-venture hotels employ geomancers as a matter of course, and so forth.

Still, the attitude among many other urban Chinese is strongly unfavourable to traditional folk wisdom, in line with the modernizing ideals of the central government; as expressed by a loyal government official: "Don't collect folklore. We Chinese have only the future to be proud of!"

A Case Study

Given such qualms, even though popular books on *fengshui* have appeared in urban bookstalls and even though many city residents have an abiding belief in some of its premises, the revival of *fengshui* practises is primarily a rural development. My field studies in rural Sichuan and Jiangsu and observations in a number of other provinces reveal that almost anyone who had recently built a new family house, buried a deceased family member, or restored an ancestor's grave had consulted a *fengshui* specialist. My suspicion was that the few exceptions recorded were merely formal denials on political grounds, for instance by village heads, other Party members or fearful members of the elder generation. *Fengshui* specialists are employed by all groups: officials, the new rural entrepreneurs and ordinary peasants. I shall here report in some detail the findings of my Sichuan fieldwork.

The township of Longchuan is located approximately 30 kilometres southeast of Chengdu, the provincial capital of Sichuan, and close to the new city of Longchuanji. It lies where the fertile Chengdu plain borders the scenic Longchuan Mountains. The area used to be poverty stricken, but in recent years fruit growing for the urban markets has raised living standards considerably.

In the entire region the practise of *fengshui* was only briefly interrupted from 1965 to 1972. Local people frequently refer to *fengshui* (also termed *yin-yang*) as "the religion of this area." Due to its diverse landscape amidst rivers and streams and steep south-facing hills, this has been a famous site for the placement of graves since ancient times. A number of ancient grave sites are still to be found along with a few minor Buddhist temples which survived the Cultural Revolution.

Longchuan township consists of eighteen villages with a total of 28,000 inhabitants. Ten full-time *fengshui* practitioners carry on their trade within the township, and thus local people are always able to find a geomancer either in their own or in a neighbouring village. These local geomancers are all extremely busy and hard to find at home, and usually their wives or other family members receive the requests for them to perform *fengshui* inspections. Altogether the ten geomancers perform a total of at least 2,500 *fengshui* inspections per year. This means that the 5,600 households of the township average invite a geomancer approximately once every second year. In addition, people may drop by the geomancers' homes to ask for advice, to determine correct days for marriages and funerals or to ask them to write posters bearing fortune-bringing characters and symbols.

The *Fengshui* Specialist

When a specialist inspects a housing site, he "sees *fengshui*" (*kan fengshui*), scrutinizes his geomantic compass *(loupan)* and consults the traditional calendar. He determines the location of the White Tiger and the Green Dragon as represented by topographical features in the landscape. He usually calculates the birth data of the owner of the house to see if his elements correspond to those identified in the surroundings of the house. The actual techniques involved in rural *fengshui*-seeing are simple. Usually the specialists rely on experience and intuition more than on books of learning. Seeing *fengshui* also involves ritual, for instance the killing of a cock and the sprinkling of its blood on the building site.

The modern *fengshui* master is anything but a scholar. He is in every sense an ordinary member of the local community. He usually dresses in plain working clothes and lives in an unimpressive house that does not display his trade. He has the appearance of a craftsman, having acquired his skills through years of apprenticeship. His level of articulation will support the impression that he is not a scholar, although his vocabulary contains a large number of terms that commoners do not understand, usually drawn from Taoism and classical works on *fengshui*. The geomancer is usually supposed to guard a body of secret knowledge, which he is unwilling to pass on, unless to members of his own household. Thus, a number of the older geomancers, who had practised for a lifetime, expressed the view that a true *fengshui* master should be trained by his own father in a genealogical affiliation with their trade. Few of them, however, can point to such ideals being upheld for more than a few generations within their own families. It is only recently that circumstances have allowed the training of a new generation, usually grandsons or other closely related youths.

The tumultuous history of rural China finds expression in the older geomancers' life stories: in the convulsion between the social continuity expressed by ancestor worship and the modernizing aspirations of the Communist state. The great majority of geomancers are elderly men, trained before 1955 as apprentices to *fengshui* masters. Often persecuted by the party authorities, they were still requested by their fellow villagers to secretly continue their trade. A large number of them kept practising, as shown by the following example.

Fengshui master Luo, who is now 73 years old, was trained by his father from the age of 12. For many years he went out to work with his father, quietly watching his techniques, while at home he would study the old books under his father's tutoring. At the age of 18, he started doing smaller jobs on his own in order to gradually build up his skills and reputation. When his father died, he acquired the roles of *fengshui* master and head of household. He still lives in the same village and practises both here and in neighbouring villages. He has never in his entire lifetime had another job, except for spending his spare time taking care of his small orchard.

Even after the Liberation in 1949, when he was in his late twenties, he kept practising for a number of years without interference from the representatives of the new regime. At the time of the Great Leap Forward, however, *fengshui* came under attack and was prohibited, a fate it shared with all other practises branded as superstition. Luo never took part in the formal integration of the village into a people's commune and the organization of work teams and brigades. In fact he did not leave his home, a small dark house at the perimeter of the village, for a number of years. Yet the unfavourable political climate did not prevent him from continuing his trade. Clients would look him up at his home in order to seek his advice on *fengshui* matters, and even to ask for exact specifications when building houses and graves. They would draw maps on his small table with their fingers, and explain the distance and direction to major hills, groves and streams. At this time Luo still possessed the classical books on *fengshui* which he had inherited from his father. From such information he would determine the *fengshui* of the site in question and prescribe the correct layout for a new construction. The clients would pay him with a chicken, rice or a bit of money. In addition, relatives and neighbours would provide him and his family with basic foodstuffs.

After the calamities of 1960–62 more pragmatic policies were adopted and *fengshui* was again openly practised. But not for long. In 1966, when the

Cultural Revolution was launched, *fengshui* operations were again outlawed, and this time the ban was supported by a ransacking of people's homes. Luo saw his precious old classics burned at a huge sacrificial bonfire in the centre of the village, a fate he shared with most other rural geomancers. Only a few calendars survived: "The Red Guards did not find them because my house was in a mess." During 1965-72 Luo again hardly ventured from his home. People would still consult him, but less frequently than before. Fortunately his sons were then old enough to contribute to the support of the family.

After 1972, when the political campaigns subsided in the village, Luo again ventured out to do *fengshui* jobs on the spot. Some graves were quietly restored, though inconspicuously, and new ones were placed at auspicious sites in the hills. Toward the end of the 1970s, when Sichuan led the way to rural reform by dissolving communes, *fengshui* was again openly practised. The new opportunities for market-oriented production, which in a few years resulted in rapidly improving living standards in the countryside, became the foundation of the *fengshui* boom.

To assure that his knowledge is passed on within the family, Luo is now training his grandson to become a *fengshui* master. At eighteen, the grandson has already started to do simple jobs. To become a real *fengshui* master, however, he still has a long way to go. It is reckoned that three to four years is sufficient to train someone with a senior middle school education, but considerably longer is required for those at a lower level. Thus Luo considers seven to eight years to be the appropriate length of training for his grandson. . . .

Fengshui is routinely used for both *yang* dwellings (houses) and *yin* dwellings (graves). Although graves in Sichuan usually are humble in comparison with those of Guangdong and Fujian, newly established graves or old restored graves are growing in size and grandeur. For decades, family graves were restricted to inconspicuous plots in vegetable gardens or insignificant corners of fields. Through the 1980s, however, grave building followed the development in *yang* housing, with increasing demands on family savings. As was earlier the custom in this area, large engraved slabs of flagstone are again erected on the graves.

Local governments are everywhere confronted with an intensified public awareness of the *fengshui* around homes and businesses, partly due to the extraordinary building activity in recent years. When people living in the crammed centres of old villages want to build new houses, they must move to the outskirts of the villages where it is possible to build bigger. The local governments usually allocate land for such undertakings. But anywhere within the village confines, a new house towering above others is bound to influence other people's *fengshui*. Here, one person's good fortune in terms of *fengshui* becomes another's ill, as in the following example:

> The geomancer took great care to position the foundations and particularly the entrance of our house. There are reasons for this. The house is placed on a site allocated to us by the local government and it is very problematic in terms of *fengshui*. It is right in the courtyard of a low two-winged building that houses five families. That building used to have a large courtyard allowing all front doors to face directly towards the rolling hills beyond the village, but now people will feel that our new two-storey house will break their *fengshui*. They have complained both to me and to the local government, but there is really nothing they can do.
>
> A local government official responded to complaints with the comment that "you may want to build a new house yourself one day, and then you can move your house or build bigger."

Occasionally, news reports slip through the official ban on the topic, as when a notice placed in the *Shijiazhuang Daily* (Hebei Province) by municipal authorities stipulated that anybody wanting to place stone lions in front of buildings must apply for a permit. Commenting on this, a writer notes that:

> Battles have been fought over stone lions. One interior decorating company placed a pair of them before its gates so that they faced the salesroom of a nearby transportation company and a refrigerating plant. This made the sales staff angry. "The lions are trying to swallow us," they complained. "We have to smash them!" When a restaurant put two stone lions beside its entrance, the residents across the street sued. Some hung mirrors opposite the statues to reflect the evil effects. The manager of a printing and dyeing mill found that its gate was facing northwest, which was considered unlucky, so he put two lions in front of the gate to counteract the ill luck. But the residents in the complex opposite his became furious. Hundreds of residents, hammers in hand, threatened to shatter the lions because of the deaths that had occurred since they had been put there.
>
> Endless complaints have been lodged, enough to prevent the officials from doing their normal work. . . .

The *fengshui* specialists themselves see the four fundamental "concerns" taken from classical tradition as the aim of all *fengshui* work. They are wealth, happiness, long life, and new generations of offspring. These also represent the basic concerns of rural people.

The liberalization of the health sector meant that medical personnel no longer were assigned to work in rural areas. The fact that all doctors in Longchuan have moved to the cities may have contributed considerably to the rising prominence of geomancers. A local health clinic, on the facade of which is painted the World Health Organization slogan "health for all by the year 2000," has been abandoned. Rural people now have to travel to an urban hospital to see a doctor and they generally feel awkward in doing so. They also have little confidence in the intentions of city people, and they often claim they get cheated. Peasants have little knowledge of modern medicine and they have no frame of reference regarding payment. Furthermore, hospitals now tend to ask for considerable collateral before taking in any rural patient for non-ambulatory treatment. In the case of a retired cadre who was hospitalized for respiratory problems, the hospital asked for ¥3,000 before treating him because the doctors judged his condition serious. The family had to sell its two pigs. After two weeks of hospitalization the hospital asked for more money, which threatened to ruin the family, and so a geomancer was called in to inspect the house, but found nothing wrong.

In general people do not choose between a doctor and a geomancer; if they can afford it, they gladly consult both and do not see any conflict in the different approaches to disease and treatment. The doctor inspects the body, while the geomancer is in charge of external forces, including ghosts and ancestors. As noted by a farmer:

> Some time ago my daughter got a terrible pain in her stomach. I went to a *yin-yang* master, who specializes in driving out evil spirits. He poured water into a bowl and then stirred it slowly with his finger. Then he said, "you have pulled out a beam from the roof of your house and your ancestors are very unhappy about it. You must put it back in place and honour them properly." I remembered that shortly before I had pulled out one of the sticks supporting the thatched roof, because it was sticking out and I had bumped my head into it. I went into town and bought wine, food, candles, incense, and strings of coloured paper. When I came back the whole family gathered to pray to our forefathers. Soon after, my daughter recovered. We had also taken her to the hospital and got her some medicine. . . .

Popular attitudes to *fengshui* vary significantly with generation and gender. In general, however, everybody agrees that certain rules and principles regarding placement must be observed for everyone to prosper and stay healthy. An important distinction which was everywhere recorded concerns "use" and "belief." Whereas almost everyone will admit the use of *fengshui* as a matter of practical concern in all construction work, "believing in *fengshui*" (*xiangxin fengshui*) implies "believing in superstition," which, when expressed in public, will carry strong connotations of "backwardness" or, formerly, counterrevolutionary ideology.

In this respect, different attitudes toward *fengshui* may be observed between the sexes. In the teahouse, for instance, men will narrate stories of *fengshui* in a half-joking manner, while they maintain that "only the women believe." A traditional pattern of women being the caretakers of spiritual obligations and family ritual appears to have survived. Women make sure that paper money, food and drink are offered to the ancestors; similarly, women are far more likely to invite geomancers to inspect their homes than are men, whether or not they do so on behalf of their families. The women are also generally more secretive about spiritual affairs, usually discussing them only in confidential circles.

27

China's Catholics

RICHARD MADSEN

The combination of political liberalization and the "spiritual crisis" produced by the collapse of faith in Marxism-Leninism and socialism have fueled the search by Chinese citizens for alternative sources of meaning and solidarity. Many of the alternatives, such as the fengshui *arts described in the previous reading, are revivals of elements of the Chinese tradition. However, many Chinese are turning instead to non-Marxist influences from the West, and particularly to Western religions. Sociologist Richard Madsen describes here the revived worship in Chinese Catholic churches that he observed in the early 1990s.*

Early in the morning of August 15, 1992, I attended a Mass celebrating the Feast of the Assumption of Mary at St. Joseph's Cathedral (also known as Old Xikai Cathedral) in the northern Chinese coastal city of Tianjin. The Assumption is one of the "four great feast days" in the Chinese Catholic liturgical year (the other three being Christmas, Easter, and Pentecost), and the Catholics in Tianjin celebrated it accordingly. Even though August 15 fell on a Saturday, at the time a workday in China, the cathedral was packed to its thousand-person capacity for the 7:30 A.M. Mass; every seat was taken, and no standing room was left in the aisles. The participants were roughly equally divided between women and men (women only slightly in the majority), and about half the participants seemed to be younger than forty. The new bishop of Tianjin, Bishop Shi Hongchen, presided over a glorious solemn high Mass, with a degree of pomp and grandeur rarely seen in the West since the second Vatican Council of the mid-1960s. The bishop was assisted by a dozen altar boys (middle-school-aged, clad in red cassocks, with white and blue surplices) plus a full array of acolytes and deacons. Three stately processions occurred during different parts of the ceremonies; these processions were grand displays of hierarchical order: a cross bearer, row upon row of candle bearers, a deacon swinging a censer, the bishop with his miter and crosier followed by a half dozen other attendants. Each of the ministers wore a vestment appropriate to his station, the most spectacular being

269

that of the bishop, who wore a red robe with a ten-foot-long train, which was held up in the back by an acolyte.

Included in the ceremonies was the First Communion of more than a hundred children, most in the fourth and fifth grades, who had spent their summer vacation attending daily classes at the church in preparation for the event (despite government regulations forbidding religious instruction to persons under eighteen). The boys wore red cassocks, and the girls long white dresses with crowns of artificial red flowers on their heads. In the opening procession, the First Communion recipients each carried long-stemmed gladiolus; they solemnly placed these flowers in large vases on the ornate main altar, which was ablaze with candles and lights.

The behavior of the worshipers was in keeping with the splendor of the liturgy. Mostly dressed in their best clothes, men sitting on the left and women on the right side of the cathedral, the worshipers knelt and bowed in unison with what by American Catholic standards seemed like extraordinary attentiveness and devotion. Although the bishop and his ministers said the prayers of the Mass in Latin in virtually inaudible voices with their backs to the people, pre-Vatican II style, the worshipers in the pews participated enthusiastically in the liturgy by singing along with a twenty-person choir accompanied by an organ. The singing continued almost uninterrupted from the beginning to the end of the Mass. Most of the hymns were in Chinese, although there were some old Latin favorites like "Ave Maria." The singing was joyous, even triumphant, especially the opening processional, which was sung to the melody of the French national anthem. The thick stone wall of the church reverberated with the music. . . .

The scene at the Tianjin cathedral was part of a larger wave of religious revival that has been sweeping across China. Church members and leaders had been severely persecuted during the Cultural Revolution; most religious leaders were imprisoned or killed; all temples, churches, and mosques were closed and many were destroyed; and all public professions of faith were severely punished. But religious practice of all kinds has not only revived but has spread and flourished since the "reform and opening" of the post-Mao era. In the early morning, Buddhist temples resound with the sonorous chanting of monks, and throughout the day they are visited by crowds of worshipers placing thousands of smoking incense sticks in huge bronze receptacles and performing obeisance before restored images of Bodhisattvas. On Friday evenings newly rebuilt mosques are filled with Islamic worshipers, who are becoming an increasingly well-organized voice in Chinese society. On Sundays, burgeoning congregations of Protestants—which increased as much as twenty-fold from the early 1980s to the mid-1990s!—fill officially approved churches and unofficial "meeting points." And Catholics, whose members have increased from about three million in 1949 to about ten million today, crowd into churches or gather illegally for Mass in large open spaces or in the privacy of homes. Meanwhile, folk religious practices—ranging from ancestor worship to shamanism to the organization of out-lawed secret societies like the "Unity Way"—flourish throughout the countryside.

The spread of all this religiosity has confounded the expectations of most foreign social scientists who have studied China. Although anthropologists have documented widespread religious practice in Chinese communities in Taiwan and Hong Kong, most social scientists who studied mainland China did not imagine that religion would become an important factor in Chinese life after being so thoroughly suppressed during the Maoist era. The efflorescence of religion, in spite of its continued discouragement by the Chinese government, forces us to reconsider assumptions about the human need for faith and about the attractions of religious community. It also raises important issues about the significance of revived forms of religious solidarity for China's political future. . . .

Although I initially found the Tianjin Catholics' devotion moving, I gradually became uneasy about it. There was obviously a great deal of construc-tive religious energy here. In the way in which the Tianjin Catholics had organized their beautiful singing, in the way in which parents had educated their children in preparation for First Communion, in the familiarity and affection with which the Catholics greeted one another after Mass, one could sense an inspiring capacity for cooperation based on mutual trust. But as they approached the communion rail to receive the Body of Christ, with hands reverently folded, I was taken aback to see how they pushed and jostled each other to get to the communion rail first. Intertwined with the religiously inspired capacity for cooperation, there was a harsh, perhaps even dangerous, competitiveness. And over the self-regulating order of life in Church, there was a coercive framework of power. As people approached the altar for Holy Communion, some were firmly turned away by ushers, who scrutinized each member of the congregation to see whether he or she belonged in the church.

Upon leaving the church, the members of the congregation milled around in little clusters, chatting amiably with their friends, perhaps checking out the announcements of upcoming events or sampling the religious literature placed on tables in the courtyard; superficially they appeared like a typical congregation in the United States. Yet I soon found that the sociability covered histories of tragedy and prospects of danger that one does not expect in the United States. This distinguished looking man, chatting happily with his grandchildren, used to be a priest, renounced the priesthood under pressure from the Communists in the early 1950s, but nonetheless ended up being branded a rightist during the antirightist movement and spent twenty years in prison. That man over there is rumored to be a member of the secret police, sent to check on the political orthodoxy of the Catholics and perhaps even to undermine their community.

Then there is the underground Church. As I left the cathedral, on that Feast of the Assumption, some members warmly welcomed me and ushered me forward to take pictures of the first communicants and to meet the bishop. They were especially eager that I have my picture taken with Bishop Shi. It was not until over a year later, when I spent several months in Tianjin continuing my research project, that I learned why I had been welcomed so warmly. "You didn't realize it, but you were a great help to us that day," said a friend of mine from the church. "The underground Church was going to make a disturbance, but we told them, 'Hold off, there's a foreigner here taking pictures.'" The disturbance was averted, and nothing marred the First Communion day of the children from St. Joseph's Cathedral.

The underground Church consists of Catholics who refuse to accept the regulations concerning public religious practice imposed by the Chinese government on the Church. The underground believed that Bishop Shi had betrayed the faith by carrying out his ministry under terms set by the government. "This is not a matter of private feelings or personal ideas," said a pamphlet secretly distributed by the underground. "This is a 'line question'—a question of whether one does or does not believe in Jesus." While Mass was going on inside the cathedral, a group of more than a hundred underground Catholics knelt in the courtyard outside chanting the rosary in front of a statue of Our Lady of Lourdes. They steadily raised the volume of their insistent chanting in competition with the loudspeakers aimed at them, which conveyed the Mass taking place within the cathedral. Other underground Catholics stayed locked in their homes because of a rumor that on the Feast of the Assumption in 1992 the sky would darken and the world would end. . . .

The conflicted reemergence of the Catholic Church is one of many responses to a spiritual crisis facing China at the end of this century. A profound crisis of meaning indeed affects most societies in the world. Vaclav Havel puts it eloquently. "Today, many things indicate that we are going through a transitional period, when it seems that something is on the way out and something else is painfully being born. It is as if something were crumbling, decaying and exhausting itself, while something else, still indistinct, were arising from the rubble." Like other great moments of transition in human civilizations—the

Renaissance, for example—this is a period, says Havel, "when all consistent value systems collapse, when cultures distant in time and space are discovered or rediscovered. . . . New meaning is gradually born from the encounter, or the intersection, of many different elements.

Although all cultures today are unhappy, each is unhappy in its own way. The crisis of meaning in contemporary China bears the marks of that society's particular, traumatic twentieth-century history. The century began, for China, with the collapse of the old empire and, in the era of the May Fourth Movement, with an iconoclastic rejection by China's leading intellectuals of the traditional cultural system that had sustained the old order. Of course, similar rejections of traditional values, in the name of some combination of social revolution, anti-imperialist nationalism, and economic modernization, took place around the world. But China's rejection of tradition was particularly tumultuous and sweeping. The prolonged trauma of the Sino-Japanese war followed by a bloody civil war delayed the development of a new cultural synthesis. After the Chinese Communists won the civil war, they tried indeed to create a new, unified Chinese culture but in a way that only deepened the crisis.

Mao Zedong attempted to substitute a political ideology for traditional culture and to make himself the sole arbiter of that ideology's correctness. The result, as Jiwei Ci puts it, "was the building of morality on the most shifting of foundations. Political programs fail easily, and political beliefs sacrosanct today can look ridiculous tomorrow. People act on a politically grounded morality only when they subscribe to certain political beliefs, and these beliefs command allegiance only when the political program of which they are a part is thriving. It was thus a source of potential disaster that Mao's China relied on a political morality that could last only as long as Mao and his political program lasted."

The disastrous potential was realized in the most cataclysmic way when Mao's politics led to the Cultural Revolution. In that event the Maoists destroyed their credibility by destroying the lives of millions of people. So after the death of Mao a whole generation of Chinese had to come to terms with, as the dissident filmmaker Su Xiaokang puts it, "life made abnormal by fanaticism, by passion, naiveté, blindness, frankness, and even dedication." The need to "redeem ourselves" from the misguided, destructive zeal of the Cultural Revolution is, says Su, a matter of what "philosophers call 'ultimate concerns.'" Yet many of the cultural resources for dealing with these ultimate concerns had been obliterated by several generations of indoctrination in Maoist ideology.

Compared with most modern societies trying to find unifying meanings in times of transition, then, China's people today have ready access to fewer traditional cultural resources and must confront a recent past that poses excruciating questions. At the same time, explosive economic growth creates inequalities, forces dislocations, and engenders corruption—in short, poses urgent moral and political questions.

Under these circumstances, many people in China are earnestly searching for meaning and are renewing their affiliation with communities that carry such meaning. The revival of Catholicism is one small part of this. But it remains to be seen whether such quests will be conducive to public order or will improve Chinese society. Thirty years of isolation from the outside world—from the founding of the People's Republic of China in 1949 to the beginning of Deng Xiaoping's new policy of "reform and opening" in 1978—and almost fifty years of systematic indoctrination in socialist ideology have not led to a widespread belief in that political ideology, but they have inhibited the development of other forms of belief. When, for example, Catholics try to find in their theology a guide to a good life in an ideologically devastated landscape, they have, in many cases, only shaky memories of an outdated theology. Often these shaky memories are just those parts of the doctrine that have enabled small communities to hunker down against hostile attacks from outsiders, not those parts that would encourage ecumenical cooperation with a wide variety of outsiders. At the same time, many other groups—Protestants, Buddhists, Daoists, Muslims, practitioners of all sorts of folk religion, as well as intellectuals searching for secular answers to "ultimate concerns"—are engaged in their own confused spiritual quests, which sometimes emphasize the more rigid, exclusive parts of their traditions. The result of such a religious revival could easily be the breakdown of society into conflicting segments rather than the creation of a new public culture—"new meaning . . . from the encounter, or the intersection, of many different elements"—that could provide a constructive, common framework for a complex, diverse society.

28

Urban Spaces and Experiences of *Qigong*

NANCY N. CHEN

Another alternative source of meaning and belonging that has revived is the traditional practice of qigong. Qigong involves a set of rituals and disciplines concerned with control over the vital energies of the self and the body. Loosely connected to China's martial arts traditions, qigong practices are seen by some simply as fostering better physical health, but by others as curing disease, transmitting energy, and promoting personal and spiritual salvation. During the 1980s and 1990s a number of qigong *masters arose and competed for mass followings. Anthropologist Nancy Chen describes here the impact of the qigong revival on the urban scene in the early 1990s. More recently, in April 1999, one particular qigong sect named Falun Gong, whose charismatic master Li Hongzhi lives in exile in New York, staged a dramatic sit-in protest outside the residential compound of China's leaders in Beijing. Worried at the threat to their control, the Party leadership declared Falun Gong illegal in July of the same year and began a national campaign against the movement.*

In the years following initiation of the post-Mao reforms, the popularity of *qigong* practice (traditional breathing and health exercises) and healing in the People's Republic of China (PRC) grew to such immense proportions that many referred to the phenomenon as *qigong re (qigong* fever). Heated discussions, vivid testimonies, and folklore about the miraculous powers of *qigong* spontaneously developed on buses, at work units, even on university campuses. The popularity of *qigong* was fueled by martial arts films and pulp novels, as well as by official bodies of medical science and research institutes. Chinese government estimates in 1990 placed the number of practitioners at 5 percent of the total population (about 60 million persons); more recent estimates raise the number to nearly 200 million. But such figures cannot begin to capture the impact that the practice has had on personal experience and social groups.

As post-Mao urban spaces emerge from the structures of socialist planning to be more fluid in spatial and functional specialization, the practice of *qigong* also helps to negotiate former binary relations of rural-urban and public-private spheres into more meaningful ones. Work units were developed as key sites of urban control during Maoist years. In the face of urban expansion or "sprawl" even these centers have come to accommodate popular practices. During the late 1980s *qigong* practice took place not only in parks but also in work units. At the invitation of *danwei* officials, *qigong* masters held mass sessions including healing and altered states of consciousness. These *qigong* activities indicate how urban parks and work units could be simultaneously public sites and places of private experience. The inner experiences and social networks generated by such practices shape public arenas such as parks, gymnasiums, and buildings into zones of personal practice and cultivation. At the same time that individuals are aware of the physical landscape of the city, they are also producing mental spaces of an alternative order within this landscape.

The emotional texture of city life is expressed in sentiments ranging from anger to resignation or urban anomie. The bus is a microcosm of larger social issues in urban China today. . . .

Although buses are self-contained units of common experience, they traverse streets filled with dangerous intersections, traffic teeming with bicycles, and masses of humanity. Streets are noted for the chaos of urban life, in which violence is rife and madness is easily observed (in individuals who dance in the street only to be taken to mental hospitals). Floating populations of rural farmers, economic migrants, and tourists gravitate to cities, making the streets even more unruly and difficult to navigate. Occasionally islands of order appear where white-gloved police stand in the noxious fumes to direct buses, bikes, and cars. But streets remain disorderly and fearfully fluid; in times of protest, the streets become avenues of resistance (and suppression) where demonstrators block traffic and subvert the normal flow of directions and officialdom.

It is a long way from there to the parks, so I wish to convey a sense of the Chinese urban landscape barely visible to individuals who jam themselves into metal boxes on wheels sharing a square meter with thirteen other passengers. While less cramped than bus riders, bicyclists and pedestrians face the dangers of collisions, the inhalation of pollution and dust, and the wrath of the elements. For everyone who leaves the home the outside world remains treacherous and difficult to navigate. . . .

Upon entering an urban park, one immediately senses the relative tranquility and slower pace of activity. Grandparents stroll, sometimes while holding or pushing along young toddlers, lovers sit quietly in semiseclusion on benches and rocks, old men with bird cages gather to smoke or chat, students practice English, groups of people exercise or dance together. While the parks are public spaces, these sites are also arenas where urban dwellers seek refuge and attain a semblance of privacy in anonymity from work or home. Although public arenas such as Tiananmen Square resonate with political meaning, parks commonly remain areas where nonpolitical activity can take place. Compared to the concrete streets or cramped quarters of the bus, urban parks provide natural surroundings, with trees and fresh air.

Qigong practice in urban parks takes place in all weather and seasons, primarily in the early mornings "when the air is better," alongside other martial arts and exercises. The weekday practitioners are present from 6 A.M to 8 A.M., before working hours. There is a significant dropoff in the number of practitioners at 8 A.M., when workers return to official obligations at their work units. Those who remain in the park after this time are usually retired or unemployed persons with chronic disorders. Most people cite health-related issues as the main reason for taking up the practice. Sunday mornings are prime time, as most individuals enjoy the whole day off.

The social topography of parks correlates with different regimens. Disco dancers and enthusiasts of *taiji* and other martial arts also practice in the park, in addition to the babies in strollers and neighborhood members who visit in the mornings. Enthusiasts of all schools can be found in small groups or as individuals under trees. *Qigong* practitioners form "multiclass coalitions" whose members come from all ages, both sexes, diverse occupations, and a wide range of political backgrounds. Membership is quite fluid and can take various forms: practice in official schools recognized by the state, followers of private masters, or practice based on personal readings and instructions from popular literature. An individual might first practice in a large group and later move to a smaller group or private area for further practice. Official groups licensed with posted banners, membership rolls, and registered master coexist with unofficial autonomous associations in which individuals gather together simply to exercise and socialize. Daily practice is common to all groups. . . .

Although there are innumerable forms and schools of *qigong*, there are three basic forms of practice—as martial art, as meditation practice, and as healing ritual. The first type of *qigong* as martial art is often referred to as "hard *qigong*" (*ying qigong*). Masters of this form carry out incredible feats such as breaking rocks with the force of *qi* in their hands or moving opponents ten feet away by concentrating their powers of *qi*. The second type, *qigong* practice as meditation, is found more commonly in the early morning in the park, where individuals stand in prescribed stances or sit in lotus position under trees. These practitioners believe that trees have special powers of *qi* that can revive the *qi* in their own bodies. Many individuals can be seen hugging trees, rubbing their bodies around the trunk of trees, dancing in circles around trees, or sitting quietly before a tree. The third type, *qigong* practice and healing ritual, poses the greatest threat to the state, not only because of the immensely popular following that has grown since the early 1980s but also because of its growing resemblance to a spiritualist cult or millenarian movement. Individual masters of great charismatic authority visit the parks, instantly drawing waves of followers seeking relief or cures. Lineages and networks of followers emerge to reveal accumulations by such masters of political capital in *guanxi* (personal relationships) and power.

The formation of *qigong* associations can be viewed in a continuum from officially sanctioned bureaucratic organizations to popular revitalistic movements headed by charismatic masters. While the basis of their organization depends partly upon the practice being promoted (exercise, meditation, or healing), it is primarily economic and political interests that determine the type of alliances that develop. The four main categories of *qigong* associations are: (1) official bodies that are formed by the state and administered by bureaucrats; (2) legitimate and public groups that have attained official recognition but retain some autonomy in membership and practice; (3) popular, informal groups that are autonomous and exist in a "gray zone" of activities not necessarily sanctioned by the state; and (4) underground associations that are officially condemned or denounced as dealing in "false" or "superstitious" practices. All these associations face similar issues regarding legitimacy, funding, and recruitment. Some associations interact on both an official and an informal basis as members have multiple roles in various organizations. A *qigong* master, for example, may have a formally registered association while also, as sidelines, having patients seeking cures and training personal students to continue the lineage of knowledge.

Within the first category of official *qigong* associations are bureaucratic bodies such as the *qigong* Regulatory Bureau (established in 1989) and medical certification boards established for surveillance and regulation of the practice. These entities are responsible for defining "scientific" *qigong* and licensing *qigong* masters as officially recognized healers. State funded, their members consist primarily of medically oriented nonpractitioners. While such bureaucrats enjoy state sanction to define the boundaries of acceptable and rational practices, their legitimacy depends on countering and containing the popularity of masters whose bases of power exist outside official realms. Members of public, registered *qigong* groups work closely with bureaucrats, with whom they share vested interests. The administrative bodies monitor public groups regularly, while such associations depend on legitimization by the official bureaucracy for both financial and symbolic support. In most major cities, municipal *qigong* associations perform a variety of functions: registering licensed masters and official practitioners, holding regular classes, receiving delegations of visiting *qigong* enthusiasts, and the like. These associations have regular monthly meetings and publications funded by membership and municipal appropriations. The Beijing *qigong* association, for example, has been in existence for over ten years and regularly promotes classes for local citizens and even foreigners.

Other officially recognized associations include research units devoted to the study of *qi* phenomena and promotion of the "scientific basis of *qi*." The units are usually located in medical institutes or physics departments of major universities such as Qinghua or Beijing University. While municipal associations are composed primarily of *qigong* masters and devoted practitioners, intellectuals collaborate with masters in experimental research on *teyi gongneng* (paranormal abilities) or special powers of healing. Whole congresses have been held solely on the phenomenon of *qi*.

The two types of associations discussed above are heavily dependent on the state, whereas the third type, popular, informal *qigong* associations, reveals a hidden economy whose existence is public but autonomous of state recognition. Funding is based entirely on voluntary, personal monies, and is independent of state sponsorship; membership is fluid with individuals often entering into multiple associations. Sometimes an informal group may spin off from an officially licensed class or *qigong* master. The possibilities for such associations are vast, and meetings take place in a variety of urban arenas—parks, work units, temples, gymnasiums, even streets or apartments. The Thirteen Sisters, as the members of one such group call themselves, consist of women who range in age from the twenties to the sixties and meet every day to practice together.

Often after a group trance of fits and movements, some members break into vigorous disco dancing or share morning snacks. The Thirteen Sisters also meet outside their regular practice site for picnics in other parks or visits in homes.

Another group that congregates daily at the base of a large tree refers to its members by kinship terms such as Elder Sister Zhang or Little Brother Tang. Many assume *qigong* pseudonyms culled from Buddhist classics or Daoist lore. When *qigong* masters appear, members respectfully part or crowd about the master to ask for healing or advice. Such informal gatherings constitute a "gray zone" of activity, especially at times of impromptu healing sessions. Individuals contribute specific membership dues for regular *qigong* instruction (ranging from as low at 20 yuan/month to 50 yuan/session) or donate voluntary amounts of money or gifts in exchange for healing sessions. Communications among members take various channels—word of mouth, printed flyers and signs—affixed to public newsboards or street posts, or recommendations through friends.

Such popular and informal groups mushroomed between 1985 and 1990. Their proliferation was greatly aided by the official media, whose networks and major newspapers *(People's Daily, Guangming Daily, Beijing Evening News, Health News Daily, China Daily,* etc.) carried articles featuring the miraculous powers of *qigong.* This attention was viewed as encouragement by readers and practitioners. A vast offspring of popular monthly and weekly periodicals also flourished in this period. Articles focused on the sensational and phantasmagoric—a tree infused with special *qi* could heal various illnesses or induce trances; an individual once stricken with a chronic debilitating illness was now completely cured. Such narratives fueled the popular image *of qigong* masters as superhuman and capable of transmitting *qi* to heal individuals or throngs of people at once.

Before bans on large gatherings under post-Tiananmen martial law, it was common for hundreds, sometimes thousands, of people to gather in a mass healing session inside a crowded gym where a master would *fa qi* (send out *qi*) to the general audience. Members of the audience responded with uncharacteristic body movements of spontaneous twitching, shaking, even jumping, and dropped to the ground convulsing with the force of the *qi.* Others rocked back and forth in their chairs and laughed or cried uncontrollably. Such public events operated in a marginal zone; many practitioners claimed that because their exercises took place during leisure hours and were intended to promote healing, they were not at all dangerous.

By late 1990 the state regulatory bureau further enforced regulations concerning the strict licensing of masters and registration of practitioners. Such actions were carried out by public security in the name of social order to address the *luan* caused by "superstitious" activities. A fourth category of *qigong* associations, defined by the state bureaucracy, emerged in which "false" rather than "scientific" or "authentic" practice took place. Whereas previously people could move freely from group to group, they now had to submit to the watchful eye of the state or else risk being charged with illegal activity. Accordingly an underground network of communication, recruitment, and healing began to operate independently and even in defiance of the state bureaucracy. In 1990 Zhang Xiangyu, a female master in her thirties, was taken into custody by municipal authorities for "practicing and healing without a license." Zhang was an intensely charismatic person with a wide following. Her disciples and individuals practiced *da ziran gong* (great universal *qigong)*, a form marked by trance, possession, and speaking in tongues. . . .

The recent position of the Chinese socialist bureaucracy relative to *qigong* associations and masters indicates great concern over the revitalistic and political potential of such formations. Although *qigong* continues to be promoted by the state as a unique Chinese tradition, the social networks led by charismatic leaders present a latent danger. Popular *qigong* associations resonate with a long tradition of peasant uprisings and heterodox movements, such as the Boxers, who once practiced *qi* exercises to promote their visions of a utopian society. Regulation and intervention by the Chinese socialist state blames society, an ironic turn of events since people take up *qigong* because of disenchantment with official ideology and policy. The state's presence is inserted into everyday life through surveillance of public arenas such as the parks. Categories of "official" versus "false" *qigong* are created to permit practitioners of "superstitious" activities to be taken into custody for questioning. Those who continue to practice in parks do so under red banners and white certificates of legitimately recognized schools of *qigong.* Witch hunts of masters are carried out in the name of fighting corruption. And boundaries of normality are reestablished through creating a medical disorder called *qigong* deviation. . . .

In the early dawn at the Temple of Heaven park about twenty practitioners can be observed at the stone altar in various states of *qi* meditation. Some sit in lotus position while others stand to concentrate on their breathing or lie on the stone in a trance. Nearby, thirty other practitioners dance beneath trees or consult with one another on the best forms of practice, masters, and daily regimens. Occasionally deep primal sounds disturb the morning stillness. A few individuals communicate by speaking in tongues. They all appear to be ordinary people whom one might encounter throughout the day—storekeepers, street sweepers, free-market merchants, students, nannies. While *qigong* practitioners are visibly situated in public parks, their alternative states of consciousness imply a withdrawal from the confines of city and the state. As city life becomes filled with market reforms that bring dream factories of commercial images, the desire to inject personal meanings into such realms becomes even more pervasive. *Qigong* practitioners rewrite their identity through healing practices in search of personal balance rather than state order.

Many practitioners and masters in the PRC look forward to an apocalyptic ending of the present regime in the formation of a Great Universe. Within this yearning for utopian nature and cosmos are located important issues. The right to situate and define the individual body within an orthodox socialist state is being contested by an imagination that transcends official urban spaces. *Qigong* practice reveals how powerful and pervasive the Chinese tradition of healing and inner body cultivation can be. While remaining within the gates and walls of parks and city life, practitioners literally dissociate themselves from the state.

29

Chinese Women in the 1990s: Images and Roles in Contention

STANLEY ROSEN

In the Mao era there was an image created of Chinese women "holding up half the sky" and enjoying status equal to men, although the reality fell far short of this image. Nonetheless, the reform era brought in a new spirit in which the pursuit of gender equality and other social goals was made distinctly subordinate to the drive for economic growth. As a result, issues related to the status and treatment of women have become subject to much more contention and debate since 1978, as the following overview by political scientist Stanley Rosen reveals.

. . . China's accelerated transition to a "socialist" market economy, enshrined at the Fourteenth Party Congress in October 1992, is commonly viewed in restricted circulation Women's Federation publications as a potentially serious threat to the hard-fought gains women have achieved in the PRC. One typical report discussed three challenges women now faced. First, the elimination of the planned economy and the new power over hiring and firing given to enterprises have forced women to compete within the marketplace, where they are disadvantaged in several ways. Men were said to be physically stronger, to have more employment experience, and to be more willing to take risks and be innovative; women were burdened because of pregnancy, childbirth, and nursing responsibilities. Thus, men had two peaks in their employment lifecycle. Around the age of 35 they were most energetic; around the age of 50 they were most knowledgeable and mature. Women had only one peak, in early middle age, after which they were in gradual decline.

Secondly, the increasing prosperity of families, fueling a rapidly developing consumer society, was seen as a threat to the continuing efforts of women to make themselves strong and independent. It was tempting for a woman to drop out of the strenuous competition for individual success and simply look for a rich, successful husband, perhaps her boss. Thirdly, the use of women in the mass media, particularly to sell Chinese and foreign products, was perceived as a threat to women's consciousness. For example, the Nescafe coffee television commercial showed a "virtuous wife and good mother" solicitously holding a coffeepot with both hands, standing in front of her husband. When he says, "tastes great!" she looks as if a large burden has been lifted from her shoulders. In the Head and Shoulders shampoo commercial, a young woman in her late teens is sad when she sees a man frown but becomes extremely joyful, even smug, when he finds favour with her. . . .

The first challenge discussed above—employment difficulties for women—has surfaced in a variety of forms over the last decade. In the mid-1980s, the Chinese press featured discussions on whether women should take extended maternity leaves, whether they should have the same retirement age as men, and whether anything could be done about hiring units who rejected women applicants solely on the basis of their gender. By the late 1980s, as the reforms simultaneously increased the autonomy of state enterprises while putting more pressure on them to be profitable, there was a drive to optimize the labour structure and eliminate surplus personnel. The majority of those dismissed at this time were women. This was quickly followed by the movement to destroy the "three irons," particularly the iron rice bowl of lifetime employment, and the extension of the contract labour system, policies which many women also viewed as thinly veiled strategies to push them out of the labour force.

In one widely reported case in 1992, nine senior female engineers, aged 55 to 57, joined together and refused to retire as ordered, charging that their forced retirement amounted to sexual discrimination by their employer. They based their complaint on a 1990 circular from the Ministry of Personnel stating that high-level female experts could retire at age 60 instead of the fixed female expert retirement age of 55, so long as they were willing to work and were in good health. Leaders at the Shanghai Astronautics Bureau, where they worked, rejected the charge of sexual discrimination, arguing that their decision was based on two supplementary documents from the Ministry of Astronautics Industry. The documents said that senior engineers must retire unless they are given a contract appointment, which is to be decided by the employer based on the employer's needs. No female engineer over the age of 55 "happened to be" on the list of senior experts to be given contracts.

By 1993, the Chinese press was reflecting the effects of these earlier policies, as women were being eliminated at both ends of the labour force. In May, *Chinese Women's News* began a discussion forum after it became clear that many enterprises were compelling their women workers to accept "internal retirement" and pensioning by age 45, even though the legal retirement age for ordinary women workers was 50. Some fortunate women were able to retire, receive their pension and find another job, thus benefiting financially. Others accepted early retirement because they feared that if the enterprise's financial situation deteriorated they would be forced to retire anyway, but on even less favourable terms. One published dialogue between a forcibly retired worker and her factory manager presents a revealing picture of the pressure women were under, the indifference of factory management and, as in the case of the female engineers, the difficulties of attempting to use legal recourse in a system where laws often conflict:

> *Woman worker:* Back in the 1950s, the *Regulations of Labour Protection of the People's Republic of China* stipulated that women are to retire at the age of 50. Why did you make us retire earlier than that?

> *Manager:* The recently promulgated *Regulations on Changing over the Management Mechanism in Factories and Enterprises Owned by the Whole People* stipulate that enterprises have the right of decision in matters of employment.

> *Woman worker:* Look at this. Article 21 in Section 4 of the *Law of the People's Republic of China on the Protection of Women's Rights and Benefits* says "the state guarantees women the same rights to work as those enjoyed by men."

> *Manager:* The factory management hasn't ruled that retirees cannot work. Are you saying that you regard yourself to be working only if you are at your former job and not if you're doing something else?

> *Woman worker:* I hope the management will find some way of getting us organized so that we can work together.

> *Manager:* Why do you behave like a clinging bean stalk that has to twine around its pole? Women should learn to stand by themselves.

Organizations responsible for defending women's rights, such as the Women's Federation, found it difficult, given the new primacy of the market, to oppose directly the new retirement decisions. Perhaps recognizing these new realities, they instead often sought to encourage women to go into business or find another job, so as to alter the common mentality of "depending on their husband within the home and on their work unit outside of it."

This in fact reflects a debate among women's advocates themselves over the reasons women face such a difficult future under China's market economy.

On one side are those who stress psychological obstacles—women are unable or unwilling to compete because of low self-esteem, desire to sacrifice themselves for their families, and so forth—which contributes to their lack of education and technical skills. On the other side are those who recognize these problems but also see sexual discrimination as even more fundamental, reinforcing these other problems.

For example, a two-year study of 100 enterprises and close to 10,000 workers in seven provinces and major cities found the labour force marked by increasing social differentiation, including important differences between permanent, contract, and temporary workers. One major issue investigated concerned the differences between male and female workers. Although men made more money than women, this was not traced to gender differences but to other factors such as technical skills, age, occupation and so forth. Many other differences, such as power within the enterprise, concern with developments within the enterprise and so forth were, however, viewed as gender-related. Women were seen as less concerned with their social status than men and less willing to take risks. For example, women were more interested than men in moving to traditional iron rice bowl jobs in state enterprises or offices, or in commercial and service trades. Men were more interested than women in seeking riskier jobs in private enterprise or foreign-invested units.

This issue is particularly salient in recent studies of the employment problems of younger women in the labour force. Paralleling the situation of those who reach the age of 45, youth provides little protection as factories begin to downsize. For example, the results of a large-scale survey of 900,000 women working in 1,175 enterprises conducted in various provinces by the women employees' section of the All-China Federation of Trade Unions found that 21,000 women had left their jobs, 60 percent of all workers in those units who had done so. Those who left tended to be under 35 years of age, with limited education and weak technical skills, who were working on the frontlines of production. More than a third were reported to have left because their enterprises were unprofitable and needed to reduce their labour force. Another reason given was that for many years these enterprises had not taken into account gender differences so that, for example, in some heavy industries more than 35 percent of the workers were women, but such industries were unable to find suitable work for many of them (because of lack of physical strength or physiological reasons). But the most fundamental reason offered was the low quality of the workers and their inability to adapt to the requirements of the enterprise. Not all reports agreed with this assessment, however. When the women workers' section of the Shaanxi branch of the Trade Unions investigated 62 enterprises in 19 systems, their results also revealed that the large majority— over 80 percent—of those leaving their jobs were under 35 years of age. However, they discovered that the main reasons for women to step down included physical weakness, illness, pregnancy, giving birth, and the need to nurse their infants. This accounted for more than 50 percent of the cases. Those who left because of the poor quality of their technical skills, a lack of discipline, poor personal relations or the inability to become a cadre made up fewer than 10 percent of the cases.

Thus, whereas some reports specifically cite physiological differences and gender bias as secondary factors in the layoffs, the Shaanxi study sees these factors as primary. It cites four obstacles women face when confronted by the new labour market. First is the continuing traditional bias against women, so that an enterprise would rather employ an incompetent male than an outstanding female. Second is the fact that enterprises best suited to women, such as those in the tertiary economy, are still not well developed in China. Third is the lack of state-supported social welfare to support women who give birth and need child care facilities. Factories are unwilling to bear this burden. Only after enumerating these other causes is the lower educational quality of women in the labour force acknowledged. . . .

The disagreements over the causes for the removal of women from the labour force—e.g., the relative emphases placed on their own subjective weaknesses, the requirements of production and outright discrimination—are often addressed indirectly in the Chinese media, requiring some interpretive skills on the part of the researcher. Discussion of lifestyle issues tends to be much more direct. One topic extensively addressed in both the official limited circulation theoretical journals associated with the Women's Federation and the popular large circulation journals intended for women is the image of the strong woman, and whether it is positive or negative. Before the reform period, of course, there was little reference to strong women as such; at the same time, however, there had been a heavy emphasis on the achievements of model workers on the frontlines of production and on women who were political activists. During the Cultural Revolution, with Jiang Qing effectively in charge of cultural affairs, many of the leading heroes in model operas, films and literature would, by today's standards, certainly qualify as strong women.

Given the rather heavy-handed, didactic approach taken during much of the PRC's history to raise consciousness and create "socialist citizens," and to inform women of approved behavior, it is not surprising that the stereotypical images of the past are frequently ridiculed in today's popular journals for women. One typical article discussed a female Party member, model worker, and Youth League Committee secretary "who was so set on protecting her role image that she wore her work clothes even when she had dates with her boyfriend, insisted on maintaining a distance of 12 inches from him when out walking, and never indulged in any intimacies with him." As the author noted, "What man would want to marry a girl dominated by such a role stereotype?"

Many articles reported the cases of women who rose to high political positions or earned advanced degrees, which inevitably led to problems in their private life. One woman, for example, had effortlessly gotten into a top university and later became a department head in a provincial administrative office. Her husband was a "dashing" engineer. Because of her attractiveness and success, the husband was prey to conflicting emotions: he loved her, but could not endure so many other people liking her too; he wanted her to stand out among people around her but was unable to suppress feelings of inferiority when she outdid him; he was aware that life's struggles require certain sacrifices but could not bear the boredom of solitude. For reasons he could not explain, he deliberately sought an extramarital relationship. In the end, he told his wife that he did not want a divorce but that he "went with someone else only to have some fun, to dispel my loneliness. If I hadn't done so, would you be taking me so seriously now? What have I done? I merely want a wife who cares for me. Can't you give a bit of attention to your husband for a change?"

A brief list of just some recent articles in the popular press during the first half of 1993 should give a flavour of their contents: "Why Did a Woman with a Master's Degree Commit Suicide?"; "I Have a Wife at Home with a Ph.D."; "My Wife Is Not at Home." Nor were more "serious" publications, with a more "elite" readership, above taking a swipe at the image of the successful woman. For example, the Wuhan journal, *Research on Leadership Work,* reported the corrupt activities of the manager of a Beijing company under the title: "Why Did a 'Strong Woman' End up on the Execution Ground?" The answer was an insatiable desire for money and the lack of Communist ideals, although it was also suggested that her celebrated reputation as a strong woman had led to arrogance.

On college campuses as well, male students have been dismayed by the "co-eds" of the 1990s. A lengthy series in the popular magazine, *College Students*, began with a provocative article entitled "College Girls Are Not So Great." The author found college girls to have five major faults: they were arrogant, vulgar, absurd, sloppy and lazy, and they smoked. A few passages from his account are sufficient to present the tone of the piece. As to their arrogance, he noted: "They walk with their heads tilted slightly upward, sniffing through their little noses as though they would breathe fire and brimstone at the slightest provocation." He complained about their vulgarity: they always talk about money and the market economy, when they should be more pure and chaste. "Most boys are of the opinion that girls in their teens should be detached from worldly things and be more sentimental. . . ." As several male students put it, in criticizing one of the "bad habits" of college girls: "Dammit! It's not good that girls smoke. If nothing else it spoils their image. I don't want my girlfriend to be like me. That isn't good. To a certain extent, smoking is something for men. If girls appear to be highly motivated for that kind of thing, they'll lose that special bit of charm." The responses to this attack came from both men and women, with some of the women equally sarcastic about the lack of "he-men" on campus.

If the popular press has tended to stress the costs of being a strong woman, more theoretical journals from the Women's Federation have emphasized the *necessity* of being a strong woman in order to survive in a highly competitive society. While popular journals may ridicule or commiserate with strong women who need to "get a (family) life," the more lively of the Women's Federation journals in turn are likely to satirize society's (mis)conception of strong women. For example, the Beijing Women's Federation's house journal ran a discussion forum over three issues asking readers to evaluate the pros and cons of being a strong woman.

After informing readers of the term's use in the United States—and how it has come to refer to "superwomen" who do well both at their jobs and within their families—the provocative opening essay addresses the term's connotations in China:

> In our country, the so-called "strong woman" is conceived of or described by the following appearance: They're definitely not tender, and if you marry one of them, whenever you go home you should always be prepared to confront a jealous and shouting virago. Don't expect them to have the traditional womanly skills, the home will be a complete mess. Even more, don't count on them if you want to enjoy a good meal. They'll have a drab appearance and certainly won't be lovely or charming. They won't be sexy, even to the point that they'll certainly be. . . . Summing it up, they'll have no femininity at all!

Fully aware of the prevalence of this stereotype, Women's Federation journals and other groups engaged in women's studies rejected the argument that strong women inevitably would have no femininity and would be unsuccessful in their personal lives. Balancing the contradiction between family and job was seen as a problem which had existed since the founding of the PRC, not something new. In fact, with the one child policy, better social welfare and more husbands willing to help out at home, it was argued that handling this contradiction was currently less difficult than ever. It was also, however, commonly—and ruefully—noted in these journals that many women cadres had begun to "dress male," to "look down on feminine charms and qualities" and "over and over again to express a very negative, even nihilistic, attitude toward their own status as women. Such politically active women who sought to imitate the "machismo" of their male colleagues were therefore often taken to task. For example, one instructor at a women's cadre school wrote critically of a woman county director who was proud of the fact that "she could cuss with the best of the men . . . could drink anyone under the table . . . and even smoke circles around any of them," as well as of a deputy mayor who, on achieving that high position, immediately stopped associating with women comrades on the job.

After the effects of Deng Xiaoping's talks on his southern trip in January 1992 became clear, the Women's Federation with ever greater urgency stressed the importance of women adjusting to a highly competitive market economy. Journals, newspapers and books provided advice for women on how to "*xiahai*," or go into business. Not coincidentally, the Women's Federation itself was being pushed into the marketplace in order to survive. Their journals contained many articles advising local federation branches on how to raise funds. Structural reorganization had seriously cut their funding and staffing. For example, some counties and townships had amalgamated the Trade Union, Youth League, and Women's Federation into one office; others had simply eliminated all these organizations and set up a general mass organization office. Some counties had reduced Women's Federation cadres by a third and cut their budget by 20 percent, announcing that "after three years the Women's Federation would be entirely responsible for raising its own funds, its profits and losses, and its own development." . . .

In sharp contrast to earlier periods, China's reform process, with its secularizing tendencies familiar from other regimes which have undergone deradicalization, appears to offer a variety of role options for Chinese women. One manifestation of this new pluralism is the differing emphases one finds between the popular press and the less widely circulated Women's Federation publications. The Women's Federation has emphasized the successes achieved in politics and business through the competitive efforts of strong women. Thus, the recent appointment of the first female vice-governor in the history of Shandong Province was the lead story in *Chinese Women's News*. Moreover, they have used the positive examples of foreign women to stimulate Chinese women to be more aggressive in defending themselves. Anita Hill's resistance to sexual harassment has been employed to suggest that Chinese women "who suffer in silence, dare not protest, and are not even good at using the available legal weapons to defend themselves" could learn a great deal from the spirit shown by their Western counterparts.

The popular press has more often pointed to the *costs* of being a strong woman, of pursuing success outside the household. On the other hand, the popular press frequently reports on the now widespread vogue of beauty contests, which are even used by local Communist Party organizations to raise money, albeit often under more euphemistic names like "advertising model contests." Although the issue has been debated in their publications, one of the leading Women's Federation officials, Guan Tao, announced in July 1993 that her organization "neither approves, advocates, organizes nor participates in" beauty contests. The Ministry of Culture and the All-China Federation of Trade Unions have taken a similar stand, while the Central Committee Propaganda Department has set forth guidelines for localities to follow in holding such contests.

The new openness and diversity of the press has also led to the discussion of issues previously considered off-limits. Taking a cue from Western publications, which often reach Chinese readers via translation, "hot" new topics include sexual harassment and lesbianism. Unfortunately, the popular press commonly sensationalizes their accounts in an effort to titillate readers and expand their market, also in keeping with their Western counterparts. Some of the more serious treatments of sexual harassment, however, demonstrate how "the incidence of sexual harassment in the workplace has sharply increased in the wake of changing economic relations . . . as the personal power of enterprise administrators in economic entities grows and the personal benefits of employees are increasingly tied to such power relationships."

Ironically, if the Women's Federation has been less successful than the popular press in shaping women's views on questions of image and role, in a real sense, precisely at a time when they face staffing and budget cuts, the Federation has become more important than ever in defending women's rights. The withdrawal of state power from everyday life has often meant that abused women have few avenues available to redress their grievances. Spousal abuse is routinely considered by the public security bureaus to be an internal family matter. Nor are the courts willing to intervene, as several reports in the press have indicated. The Women's Federation has become the last resort for women with nowhere else to go.

Moreover, there are encouraging signs of a rise in "women's solidarity." The case of the nine women engineers cited above is one example. Another is the report from a township in Hunan province where a woman Party committee member lost her bid for re-election; as the organization department of the Party committee discovered, "once the results of the election were publicized, it was as if a bomb had been detonated among the women comrades." The charge was gender discrimination. It appears that concurrent with China's continued push towards a market economy, the country's women will continue to debate and forge new roles of their own choosing.

30

"Hey, Coolie!"
Local Migrant Labor

DANIEL WRIGHT

One of the most dramatic changes of China's reform era is the loosening of migration restrictions, a change that has enabled millions of villagers for the first time since the 1950s to leave their villages to seek greater opportunities outside. That same shift has meant that at any one point in time 80 million or more members of the "floating population" are flocking into prosperous villages and urban areas in search of employment. Despite their greater mobility, the members of the floating population do not enjoy equal rights with urban residents. They are subject to systematic prejudice and discrimination from urban residents and harassment by urban authorities. In this selection, Daniel Wright provides a portrait of the life of migrant laborers who have left a Guizhou village to seek jobs hauling loads on the streets of a small city in the same province.

Life is hard in Guizhou's countryside. That's the message my friend's three uncles communicate during a recent visit to their remote village home. No road, sheer mountains, shallow soil, no running water, backbreaking labor, stripped forests, too many mouths to feed and little money make life a constant challenge. Even so, their ability to live as well as they do—wood-beam houses built into abrupt mountainsides, terraced rice paddies, recently installed electricity and now even TV sets and rice cookers for some—amazes me every time I make the trek to Splendid Village.

Lack of food and clothes in this middle-class-poor community no longer poses a serious threat. The villagers say their biggest need is cash: the means to pay their children's school tuition, prepare daughters' dowries, purchase fertilizer and other needed items like cooking utensils.

As a result, 90 percent of the men and many of the women in their 20s and 30s have departed Splendid Village for the cities—the country's cash centers—as migrant laborers. Despite the strong attraction, however, urban areas stir apprehension in the hearts and minds of these rural folk.

293

One of First Uncle's daughters was deceived while looking for a job in coastal Guangdong Province; she ended up getting sold as someone's bride. She later escaped and found her way home, exhausted but free.

Second Uncle's sister-in-law, who stopped by while we were eating breakfast, lost her husband in a mining blast in neighboring Guangxi Province last year—yet another migrant-labor casualty.

Second Uncle says he would be working in a city somewhere, regardless of the risk, were it not for his wife's frail health. Because of chronic arthritis in her hips and knees, she is incapable of managing the affairs of their home on her own. Some days she cannot even get out of bed. So Second Uncle remains with his family. That neither of them is able to pursue cash outside the village has led to a painful family decision: Which one of the three children will drop out of school after Spring Festival next month?

Third Uncle works in nearby Duyun, the prefecture capital, pulling a pushcart from dawn to dusk. He happened to drop by while some of us were visiting at his brother's home.

Third Uncle speaks to me without raising his eyes. He says he has no other choice but to do this kind of beast-of-burden work. He seems ashamed. Yet after expenses he averages 500 yuan a *month,* almost as much as the average annual per-capita income for the township! Good money, yes, but he earns every fen of it through exhausting labor and the disdain of urbanites. I know—I've seen him around town.

Life is difficult in the mountains; but for farmers-turned-migrant laborers in the city, it is bitter, degrading and dangerous.

Many observers view China's labor migration as primarily a flow from the country's backward hinterland to the more prosperous eastern seaboard. Indeed, it looks this way from afar. But disparity in China cuts most deeply between city and countryside, not coast and interior. Labor on the move responds accordingly.

Most of the farmers I have spoken with in Guizhou Province say that more of their fellow villagers seek work in southwest China's urban areas than venture toward the better-known coastal destinations of Guangzhou, Shenzhen and Shanghai. Two-thirds of those who leave Splendid Village, for example, remain in Guizhou's cities.

China is not a country simply tilted east with all its labor sliding toward the coast. Rather, urban centers across the land—small, medium and large—are like raised magnetic points, attracting China's estimated 200 million redundant farmers from fields and mountains as if they were fine metal filings.

Little-heard-of Duyun, the city's 200,000 people squeezed along a river valley in the middle of southern Guizhou's mountains, is one of those points. Just ask some of the 2,000 pushcart pullers who run its streets each day.

Kao Huo [Warming by the Fire]

From a distance the parked pushcarts look like idle surfboards lined up on Malibu Beach. It had snowed twice in five days, so I wasn't surprised to see a group of porters huddled around a fire of old boards, warming themselves as they passed the frigid mid-January day.

Since returning from the visit with the three uncles just days before, I had become absorbed with the realization that the majority of "migrant" laborers in China probably never even travel beyond their province's borders. Compared with the stereotypical "Overland Chinese"—those laborers who work on the eastern seaboard and remit significant amounts of cash back to their homes in the hinterland—what distinguishes this lesser known but equally significant group of migrants? Why stay closer to home? Does one give anything up by not going to the more prosperous coastal cities? How do urban residents in the interior view this segment of the floating population? What are their pleasures, their hardships?

The next thing I know, I'm in the circle with these guys, chatting about their lives in the city. Surprised, but with typical rural hospitality, they respond warmly to my interest in them. The fire feels good.

It turns out they are part of a larger group of 30 that have come from the same home village about three hours from Duyun. Some are old-timers; one of the young ones has been in the city just three days. Most have been pulling pushcarts for three to five years. They average about 30 years in age.

Their huddle occupies a street corner toward the edge of the city. The intersection serves as the terminus for vans and transport trucks that arrive from outlying counties and Guiyang, the provincial capital. The city government has designated their gathering point as an "official" pushcart location—the sign says so. According to the guys, it simply means that if their pushcarts are not parked in a row they may get fined.

Besides their strategic location, the group has developed a clientele of sorts with a variety of nearby stores and factories and an auto-repair garage.

The porters haul anything and everything: construction materials, furniture, coal, bags of cement, lumber, sheets of glass, scrap metal, sacks of grain, even slaughtered hogs just off the bus from the countryside. If it can be loaded onto an eight-by-three-foot flat space, these guys can deliver it.

The porters average four or five yuan per load. The best haul they can remember is a job that paid 30 yuan; it was a heavy delivery that had to go a long way.

After expenses, which are minimal [30 yuan for rent and 100 yuan for food], each porter clears between 300 and 500 yuan a month. Compared to the cash available at home, this is a significant amount.

As we speak, an occasional request comes: "*Banche!*" [pushcart] But they may as well have been calling, "Hey, coolie!" One of the men hops up from around the fire and is off to the job. The circle tightens and expands as men come and go.

"Why did you all leave home in the first place?"

"We're too poor. There's no money back there."

"Who takes care of your fields and family while you are gone?"

"We have family members who look after things and do the work. If an emergency comes up, we are not far away."

"How often do you return home?"

"Spring Festival, planting, harvest, . . . about four or five times a year."

"Why didn't you go to the coast to work? Isn't the money better there?"

"The money's better, yes, but the risk is greater. It's much more dangerous there than here, and here is already bad enough. Plus, like we said, we're closer to our village and it's much easier to return home."

"What do you enjoy most about working here in the city?" I ask this to see their reaction to something they probably don't think about very often: pleasure.

No response. I don't fill the silence. Finally, one of them says, "Full stomachs."

"And the hardest thing?"

The answer comes more quickly:

"City people look down at us. We occupy the bottom of society."

"Why?"

"Because we're from the countryside. The work we do is dirty."

Among the circle, three do most of the speaking; the others just seem to take it all in. One man in particular, an older man of about fifty with a weathered, unshaven face, emerges as the group's spokesman. He's the veteran and has lived in Duyun some thirty years (when he was young his family moved from the countryside under special circumstances). He points to a shoddy two-story brick structure across the road. "That's my home. My wife, children and I live there."

But originally, he's from the same village as the others.

At some point in the morning conversation, a cute little girl runs up to him from across the street.

"This is my daughter. Actually, she's adopted."

"What's her name?" I ask as we squeeze her inside the circle so she can enjoy the warmth.

"Tang Lujuan. 'Lu juan' means 'flower by the road.' We found her as a baby, abandoned along the street in front of our house."

I switch the conversation back to the reason I first approached the group: "I'm quite interested in your work, both because it enables you to earn cash for your families back home and because of your contribution to the welfare of this city. How else would the city people transport their things—like furniture, new refrigerators and television sets—around town?"

Each day over the better part of one week, I frequented the porters' huddle. I'd sit for awhile, chat, warm up and then head on. I also walked the streets of Duyun, observing pushcarts and pondering this interesting segment of the local migrant labor population.

One day, I return determined to do more than talk. I want to experience a bit of their work firsthand. The fire's already warm by the time I arrive.

"What is the most effective way to find work as a pushcart puller?"

"You can roam or you can park yourself outside a store and hope that someone makes a purchase while you are standing there, but by far the best way to make money is to have a good relationship with a store owner or person at a factory who will direct work to you."

"What's the worse thing that has happened to you all out here?"

"We've had guys killed. Cars drive too fast and don't pay attention."
On this day there are just about six of us gathered around the fire. It's still quite cold. Someone walks up and asks for a porter to haul something down the street.

"How much?" asks Lao Tang.

"Two yuan."

The men laugh off the offer and turn back to the fire.

Fifteen minutes later another call comes—"*Banche*!" A man, with whom they seem quite familiar, dismounts his bicycle and says something about hauling scrap metal.

"How many of us do you need?"

"Three."

"How much per cart?"

"Twenty yuan for three carts."

"Fifteen per cart."

They settle on ten yuan a cart. Three men hop up; Old Tang is one of them. I follow.

We head toward an auto-repair garage that specializes in trucks. Several tons of rusted metal from wrecked trucks need to be hauled away to a man's scrap shop.

They load each pushcart piece by piece, occasionally checking to make sure the stack of strewn metal is balanced by lifting the cart's handles.

After about an hour, all three loads—about a half ton each—are maxed out and ready to go. We pull out of the factory compound and onto the main road. Even the slightest gradation requires all four of us to help: one in front pulling, three straining from behind.

Fortunately, most of the route is level. We arrive at our destination 45 minutes later.

I was struck by the sense of community experienced by the porters who had left the countryside (and their families) to pursue cash in the city. The relationships were especially strong among those from the same hometown or village.

At the same time, I was equally impressed by the extent to which urban dwellers look down on porters—for that matter, on all laborers who come from the countryside.

Every Grain of Rice . . .

"Dirty" is the first word used by a young urban woman when I ask her about migrant laborers in Duyun. "Of course, though, I don't feel that way," she adds when she sees the look on my face.

"When we were children," she explains, "our parents often told us that if we didn't study hard we would end up like them, working on the streets."

At the same time, urban kindergarten children, including my daughter Margaret, memorize a Tang dynasty poem called *Min Nong* [*Compassion for Peasants*]:

> *Weeding rice paddies,*
> *while the bright sun shines down from above;*
> *Sweat off their brow drips to the ground below,*
> *mixing with soil and seedlings;*
> *Who knows the toil*
> *that went into each grain of rice that sits on your plate.*

Memorized appreciation? Perhaps. But the longest 18-inch distance in the universe is between the head and the heart. Rural laborers construct their buildings, pedicabs cycle them around town, porters transport their burdens and women laborers polish their shoes, wash their plates and care for their children. But prejudice runs deep. In the eyes of most urban residents, rural folk are just, well, filthy.

Though the primary ways in which the urban-rural divide was institutionalized in the 1950s—household registration and migration restriction—have been eased or eliminated, they produced a two-caste mindset that remains until today. The result has produced perhaps China's greatest wall: little understanding or appreciation between its agricultural and non-agricultural populations.

Most rural people I have spoken with seem to have internalized this bigotry. A pervasive inferiority complex expresses itself in frequent self-diminishment, like the rookie porter who said I would lower my status if we had our photograph taken together.

Even so, as long as cash remains difficult to come by in many rural regions of the country and as long as the wage difference remains so unbalanced, millions of rural laborers will continue to migrate to the cities looking for work. How their urban bosses view them is among the least of their concerns.

31

Second-class Citizen

GE FEI

The reform era has changed the tenor of social life in China in many ways. The looser social controls of the Deng era have not only enabled many formerly suppressed traditional customs and Western influences to once again emerge. Social problems and deviant behavior of various kinds have also become more visible and worrisome to many. These selections from a reader by political scientist Michael Dutton give two examples of such behavior as published in the Chinese press—common criminals and homosexuals.

One summer's afternoon on a country road that lazily wove its way through the green curtain of tall crops like a stiff dozing snake in winter, there came a pair of newlyweds. The pretty and charming young woman opened her florally designed umbrella and, as the sunlight shone down on the nylon surface of the parasol, it projected a bright red-colored shadow which further heightened the alcohol-induced redness of this beautiful woman's face. This new bride was returning to her bridal home on a bicycle pushed by her new husband. Eager to show off his strength, he was determined to push the bike even up the steep inclines. The bride, however, saw how much effort it took her new husband and decided instead to walk with him.

Little did they realize that, even as they walked, disaster was about to befall them.

Suddenly, from behind the tall green curtain of grass sprang four evil bandits. Rushing out, they swamped the happy couple before they had a chance to turn around. Both were quickly bundled off into the maize field by the side of the road. The husband was beaten until he was unconscious, the couple's watches were stolen and all their money taken. After that, the four bandits gang raped the bride. They then stripped them both of their clothes and finally swaggered off. The bride, having suffered such a severe attack, never regained consciousness. The bridegroom, ashamed at their nakedness, dared not call for help. With the temperature reaching forty-odd degrees, it is unlikely that they would have ever been found had it not been for a peasant discovering them.

Analogous cases appear time and again in the city and suburbs. Such brazen criminal acts carried out in broad daylight are a challenge to society. But while such monsters climb one foot, righteousness is able to scale ten, and the long arm of the law always stretches out to catch such villains. In the end, the crime fighters were able to bring the seven thieves and rapists who organized and perpetrated this crime to justice. Four of them would pay the ultimate price. Nevertheless, it is worth noting that, of these seven criminals, six of them already had records, and five had already spent time in either reform-through-labor institutes or labor education centers for larceny and robbery.

In another city many miles from this, in a different and far off province, there was an even more cold-blooded case that would make one bristle with anger. This crime was also carried out blatantly in daylight and in full public view. A long-distance bus was stopped by scoundrels who stood in the middle of the road. After they got on the coach, two of their accomplices pulled out daggers and blocked the exits. While they did this, the other two criminals brazenly started to "clean up." Of the entire forty-odd passengers, not one was lucky enough to escape. In total, the thieves got away with over one thousand yuan. Only one young seventeen-year-old girl resisted this terrifying outrage. For her trouble, this brave girl was dragged off the bus, and had her clothes ripped from her body and there, by the side of the road, right before the eyes of the other passengers, was gang raped. The sun just hung in the sky.

Again it proved difficult for these four scoundrels to evade the wide net of the law. After being caught, two of them were sentenced to death while the other two received death sentences with a two-year reprieve. In the People's Court notice it was stressed: of the four, two already had records for larceny. In fact, in 1983, these two had spent three and four years respectively in prison. From the time of their release until their most recent crime only two years had elapsed.

On a train, nine men and one woman formed a "north east tiger" group and cleaned out four carriages, robbing over four hundred victims. One young woman who opposed them was sexually assaulted by having her breasts molested. One other young peasant was stabbed and badly injured. After their cases were heard, these ten "north east tigers" were executed. The remainder of their group received prison sentences that varied between life imprisonment and set term imprisonment. In the public notice of the People's Court accompanying this decision, it was written that, of the ten, three "tigers" already had records for train robbery. These sorts of evils are not restricted to the countryside, you even get them being perpetrated in large and medium-sized cities.

Desperados who busied themselves in one particular area were surrounded by police and tried to fight their way out. The police were worried about casualties and, because of a lack of experience in dealing with such situations, suffered four casualties. There were also two fatalities, one a police officer, the other an innocent bystander. With the loss of one of their number, the police's power to resist was affected. When they were brought to justice these criminals were given the death penalty. The court notice promulgating the sentence also revealed that two of the convicted criminals already had criminal records.

In the dead of night three murderers rushed into a bank, stabbing and seriously wounding two of the night security guards and stealing all the ready cash. After the case was brought to trial, three of the criminals were given the death sentence. The court notice in this case also noted that the principal criminal already had a record.

There is one case of a couple of infamous bandits who carried out robberies in more than ten provinces and, when they were finally brought to justice, were given a suspended death sentence with a two-year reprieve. Both of them had previous histories.

There was also a case of one couple using their place as a brothel for a number of prostitutes to practice their trade. After the case was cracked, they were both given the same sentence. It was discovered that the husband had once been imprisoned on robbery charges.

These sorts of serious criminal cases, which significantly and adversely affect social order would, if discovered even ten years ago, have been thought of as shocking. Today, however, they don't even raise a murmur let alone create a stir. These crimes are often undertaken in full view of the public. We have even reached the stage whereby people say they are "accustomed" to such things.

There has also been a tendency for criminality to increase in scope and take on new forms. Within criminal ranks, one discovers that secret societies and criminal armed gangs are once again being formed. These organizations are not only involved in traditional criminal forms, such as armed robbery, rape, and theft, but are also reviving prostitution, transnational drug trafficking, and smuggling. On the soil of mainland China, we now discover organized criminal gangs vying with each other for power, carrying out killings and openly enacting gang fights. They even surround and encircle the forces of law and order, carrying out violent armed struggle against them.

On the basis of statistics from a number of the larger southern provinces, in the ten-year period from 1978 through to 1988, the number of criminal cases of all types has increased six-fold. This includes property crimes (robbery, theft, embezzlement as well as other crimes carried out in the course of these crimes such as rape and murder), which now constitute something like 70 percent of all crimes. In the space of ten years, this type of crime has grown by 4.2 times.

The national campaign issued forth a "severe strike against criminal elements who seriously jeopardize social peace"—known simply as the "severe strike." Over the last three years, it failed to effectively keep within limits the black tide of wild crimes, leading the Chinese People's Republic, six years on, to relaunch the "severe strike."

Kind-hearted folk have expressed serious concerns regarding the severe public security situation, and their hearts are heavy with the dark cloud of crime that envelopes society.

In a number of northern provinces, a large-scale survey undertaken found that 95 percent of the people surveyed were unsatisfied with the contemporary security situation. Some large cities that conducted this type of research found 94.5 percent unsatisfied with the security situation.

The deteriorating security situation in contemporary China has important lessons and offers some previously unknown challenges to the law in the People's Republic. The economic reform process has inadvertently led to a crime wave casting a dark and evil shadow over the normally peaceful life of the citizens of the People's Republic. These crimes have shocked the People's Republic.

Social order has become the most talked about problem among the public and one of the "hot stories" of the media, not to mention the key concern of leaders in the social arena. Despite the severe strikes mounted by the public security and justice authorities against those criminal elements who seriously disrupt social order, and despite the fact that they often attach the big red tick to their notices of conviction [indicating a death sentence] we still read that the court officials are quite anxious about the situation. The problem of re-offence among those who are released from reform-through-labour or reform-through-education is a source of great concern. There are many serious cases whereby those released reoffend but who, upon discovery, not only don't give up but resist arrest, becoming desperados and sometimes murderers.

To be fair, the number of people released from these two forms of penal labor centers as a percentage of the overall population is very small. From the summer of 1983, when the "severe strike" campaign was launched through to the end of 1984, less than two million people were incarcerated, constituting a little over 0.1 percent of the population and, in recent years, the overall number of criminals of all types vis-à-vis the population as a whole doesn't even amount to 1 percent of the population.

Nevertheless, given the overall size of the population, even less than 1 percent of the population still means an awful lot of people. Quite apart from this though, it is important to note that it is the youth and the relatively youthful members of the population who are most represented among this group and that, within this group, the predominant gender is male. Moreover, this trend is continuing at an increasing rate.

There has been a ten-fold increase in the number of people released from incarceration in the two types of labor centers and the number of people released stands at about 10 percent of all cases. Not only this, but the majority of those who reoffend do so within three years of having been released. The number of those who reoffend within that time frame as a percentage of overall releases has grown every year at a quite significant rate. Nevertheless, while it has not reached 30 percent of cases in terms of overall population, there is more than a ten-fold chance of these people committing crimes rather than others.

Why are those who have already received some form of penalty more likely to reoffend than ordinary people? Within the household registration management system, there is a term known as the "special population." "Special population" refers to those people released either from reform through labor or education. Police records of the "special population" indicate what crimes they have committed, when they did it and what types of penalty they received.

Through the special population files those who are released from reform through labor or education are supervised and controlled by the police.

The masses really hate this criminal evil and detest these people released from the reform through labor and education centers, and pay a lot of attention to them—"the level of freedom" for criminals is much less than for ordinary people. People from the reform-through-labor and reform-through-education centers call themselves "second-class citizens" and this definition clearly shows their mixed emotions. While part of it is attributable to an inferiority complex, it also reflects that they have nothing to lose.

Nevertheless, it should be asked why they are under special controls, have special attention paid to them by the rest of the population, and why they have less freedom than other citizens. These factors contribute to the development of a feeling of inferiority as expressed in the term "second-class citizen" and easily lead these people back into crime.

Homosexuals In Beijing

JIN REN

For the vast majority of citizens of mainland China, homosexuality is quite alien. Nevertheless, one has to recognise that the endlessly increasing reports of homosexuality within the mainland probably means that people that are close to us, or even living within our midst, are that way inclined.

The first semi-public gay "salon" dance party was held on February 14, 1993 during the "sweetheart festival." This dance, organised in one of the many dance halls in Beijing's Xidan district, was called "men's world." In the soft glow of the dim light, the music lingered and the couples swayed, yet all of these lovers were male.

On the afternoon of the same day in the Dongdan Park in Beijing, there were even more homosexuals out celebrating the "sweetheart festival." Some people, recalling that day, said that it was like going to a fairground.

How many homosexuals are there in Beijing? No one is able to accurately calculate, but one gay guy who is pretty familiar with the scene and a frequent visitor to Dongdan Park, says he can recognise about 1000 regulars. The American scholar Alfred Kinsey, who conducted a survey on homosexuality in the United States, discovered something like 4 percent of the American population were homosexual. This figure seems to vary little between cultures.

Those "in the know" suggest that there are about 55 regular homosexual meeting places in Beijing and, of these, the vast majority are public toilet blocks. Most of the regular toilet block haunts are around public parks or greens. Another popular spot for gays in Beijing are the public baths. Hotels, bars, and dance halls also appear to be regular meeting places. In these latter establishments, the gay community is not the principal source of revenue. But by far the most famous site in Beijing is the aforementioned Dongdan Park—one does not need to buy a ticket to enter and so it is easy to come and go and this allows the visitor a certain anonymity. This fact, coupled with its relative proximity to the city centre, makes Dongdan Park a popular gay haunt 24 hours a day.

On the basis of one researcher's work on the gay scene, it is clear that homosexuality has always existed in Beijing. Nevertheless, there have been a number of recent reports about homosexuality, and this has brought it to the public's attention. In earlier times, the public lavatories on either side of

Tiananmen Square were pretty popular sites, and they were jokingly named the "East and West Palaces" by the gay community.

There is no way of telling the difference between a gay and straight person just in terms of appearance. Nevertheless, just about every gay man you talk to says that if you go into a public place, recognising another gay guy isn't difficult, although the secret to their success may be difficult for "straights" to fully understand. Gays will tell you it is easy to tell if you "look into their eyes and spot their desire" or if "you pay attention to someone and watch what they do." One gay guy told me that "when you meet another gay, actions speak louder than words and their eyes will do all the talking. This is true nine-tenths of the time. When one's eyes meet, it is such a charge and both men know what is going on." In public baths, for example, the first contact is often made by touching the other person with your foot. If they find you desirable, they will respond.

Within the gay community, activities in public places are quite often divided into what they describe as "social" (public) and nonsocial (private) activity. Their social activities consist of drinking together and chatting whereas their nonsocial activity often involves long-term, stable and relatively intimate relations with their gay partner. This can even go so far as to mean that they secretly live together. But it is very rare that they will only live this gay lifestyle. The homosexual, in choosing a partner, will pay particular attention to their lover's age, occupation, and education. Gay men from different backgrounds will find those differences reflected in their choice of partner.

Scholars in the fields of psychology, physiology, and sociology have all undertaken investigations into the causes of homosexuality. Some experts disagree that physiological explanations can tell us much about homosexuality. They emphasize, instead, its culturally acquired nature. Currently, the weight of academic opinion tends to suggest that cultural explanations are the most useful. This argument will identify childhood experiences and the confusion in gender identity that some suffer at an early age as one reason. Another explanation points to puberty and the way in which, at this time, sexual differentiation can lead to inhibitions developing. Still another points to the way in which homo-sexuals can lead the young into this type of activity. Generally speaking, most homosexuals do not subscribe to cultural explanations, believing instead that they were simply born that way.

One gay guy told me that even from a very early age he had a yearning for those of the same sex and was completely uninterested in the opposite sex. His first homosexual encounter was during a *pingju* performance—*pingju is* the local opera form of north and northeastern China—where he met a gay guy of the same age. After this initial experience, he longed to meet this person again. Later, when he was to leave Beijing for business, he met another homosexual man in a park who told him of the places where most gay men congregated. After he returned to Beijing, he really began to get into the scene and went to these places. These days though, he will only venture out a couple of times a month. The reason for this, he explains, is because he is in a fairly stable relationship.

In Beijing, gay men do not, to use a Western expression, "come out." There are some very famous figures within the homosexual community but even they do not "come out" but try, instead, to hide their sexual preference from relatives, family, and society. As far as gay men are concerned, to be exposed as homosexual in China would have dire consequences. The moral order of China is built upon the traditional values of Confucianism and the idea that there are three forms of unfilial activity but the greatest of them all is not bearing a son. Hence, every healthy adult male has to marry and give birth to a child. The pressure to marry is such that the vast majority of homosexuals end up getting married. They will find women who are willing to join in their activities but, all too often, such unions end in divorce. There are those who are bisexual, who love the same sex as well as the opposite sex. Pure homosexuality is a rarity.

Dr Li Yinhe, a famous Chinese sociologist, has undertaken a survey on the question of marriage and has been able to categorise the responses into three different models of behaviour. In the first, the man will have a guilty conscience and will do his best to fulfill his duty as husband. In the second case, the gay man will try to turn his wife around so she accepts his sexuality. The third case includes those who fail to change their ways and also to change their wife's views.

For the homosexual, getting married is equivalent to losing one's position. It will not only mean they will lose face among their homosexual friends, but it also means that certain restrictions will be placed on their life from that time forth. Naturally, there are many homosexuals who, after marriage, still frequent the old haunts and renew their homosexual acquaintances. Of the 51 homosexuals interviewed for Dr Li's report, some 31 men had been, or were, married. Fourteen of the men had higher education, fifteen were workers, fourteen were government cadres, five worked in technical or artistic affairs and seventeen were either peasants or had some other occupation. The oldest of the 51 men surveyed was 70, while the youngest was 22 years of age.

Perhaps the average person is unacquainted with homosexuality and we could even go so far as to say that, when they think about it, they feel sick. One survey undertaken into this found that 71 percent of respondents thought homosexuality an abnormality, or even a type of sickness, while 34 percent believed it to be illegal. Only 12 percent of those surveyed believed that it was a matter of free choice. After the "sweetheart festival" dance party, the manager of the Beijing dance hall where it was held lost his job. There was an obvious link between these two events.

The vast majority of homosexual men believe themselves to be little different from straight men in everything but sexual preference. Moreover, they do not regard homosexual behaviour as seriously antisocial. Professor Qiu Renzong of the Chinese Academy of Social Sciences points out that there is little reason for the public to view homosexuality as abnormal or illegal. From the point of view of the consequences of their actions, homosexual men may very well do some quite immoral and illegal things, but then, so do straight men. Immoral or illegal activities are the province of individuals rather than homo-sexuals generally. In terms of the morality and justice of their actions, there are many people who think, or could argue at least, that homosexuality is abnormal because it fails to promote procreation, hence it is abnormal and anti-life. But this is to presuppose that everyone wants children.

In mainland China at present, there are no clear regulations regarding homosexual activity. It, therefore, proves to be a rather tricky matter for the police. Under normal circumstances, the police do not interfere unless the homosexuals carry out their activity in public places or force someone to engage in homosexual sex. In October 1992, ten men were publicly engaged in homosexual acts in a number of bath houses in Beijing. These men were detained and fined by the police under provisions given in the "Regulations governing penalties for the security management of public spaces." At that time the police, in dealing with these matters, did not inform the work units of these people. Even today, only in cases where the people refuse to mend their ways will the work unit be informed.

There is no question that homosexuals are a high-risk group when it comes to the spreading of AIDS. It is not uncommon for one gay man to have quite a few partners, which makes them increasingly susceptible to the AIDS virus. A survey of 96 homosexual men discovered that, on average, every man had about seven partners. Some people say that AIDS is God's punishment on those who carry out abnormal sexual practices. The Chinese mainland had its first case of an HIV positive person in 1989, and while there has not been another such discovery, this has not stopped the general public from worrying about it.

From the homosexual perspective, AIDS is a very sensitive topic, and there is little agreement within the community about it. Some gay men are aware of the protective measures needed to combat the disease and are therefore not afraid of it. When they engage in homosexual activity, they take precautions.

Some research institutes on the mainland have been engaged in work among the homosexual community. The Chinese Health Education Research Institute began an "AIDS help hotline" in April last year and that has gained some headway. By the end of last year, the hotline had received a total of 1,126 calls asking for help and 15.2 percent of these calls were from self-proclaimed homosexual men. The hotline is operated by academically trained professionals in the area. The hotline also operates as a means by which to disseminate information on HIV/AIDS to the wider community. In places where homosexual activity is more frequent, information and advice services are also set up to try to alter the sexual practices of gay men so that they adopt safe sex practices. It was the hotline group that organised the "men's world" cultural salon last year. Since October 1992, when the salon was held, they have held six other meetings to try to get a stable means of communication going about the virus. There is an unofficial group operating within the homosexual community which aims at disseminating information about the virus and about ways of preventing its spread. In March 1993, one homosexual expert set up a social network in Beijing to help spread the word on AIDS and AIDS prevention. The Chinese Health Education Research Institute is about to open an advice line for gay males very soon.

Getting homosexuals together is a step toward preventing the spread of this disease, and it is principally from this perspective that such programs are being set up. As the director of the Chinese Health Education Research Institute, Chen Bingzhong, pointed out: "All human groups have health problems. Moreover, the health problems of one group can quickly become the health problems of all. The relationship between AIDS, homosexuals, and the masses is precisely this sort of relationship."

Professor Qiu thinks that, today, consciousness of homosexuality will increase along with concern for society and public health. Without some sort of clarification of homosexuality in China there can be no way forward.

32

Elementary Education

CHARLOTTE IKELS

China's success in modernization depends in a central way on the performance of its educational institutions, and those institutions have also been dramatically affected by the post-1978 reforms. In this selection Charlotte Ikels presents a portrait of the ways in which preschools and elementary schools in Guangzhou were organized and operated during the 1990s.

Preschool

Most Guangzhou children enter a preschool or kindergarten before elementary school. In 1989, for example, the enrollment rate for the municipality as a whole (eight districts and four counties) was 54.4 percent, but in the four central districts it was 98 percent. Preschools in China are primarily a phenomenon of the post-1949 period and provide day care to children of working parents as well as basic socialization. Nurseries provide care to infants and toddlers (those under three), whereas kindergartens normally serve children from three to six.

Although all kindergartens are expected to meet certain standards set by city and district preschool education authorities, there is considerable variation in the quality of the physical plant, the availability of equipment, the richness of the curriculum, and the qualifications of the teachers according to administrative body. A major cause of this variation among (and to some extent within) preschools is their source of financing. Most of the kindergartens are heavily subsidized by their governmental sponsors. The neighborhood preschools, however, rely almost entirely on the fees they take in, and consequently they can barely afford the basics and cannot afford frills.

The most highly regarded kindergartens tend to be those directly under the jurisdiction of the provincial Education Department, which accept primarily the children of workers from various (and multiple) government units,, for example, provincial schools, hospitals, and administrative offices. In some cases these preschool campuses can be quite elaborate, with multiple buildings, playing fields, and garden plots. City bureaus and enterprises, such as factories, sponsor preschools on their own premises that are primarily for their workers' children. Finally, street committees operate kindergartens for the benefit of the families living (or working) in their neighborhoods. They often have to squeeze the preschool into an old building in an already congested area. There are also some private preschools that must pass muster with the local authorities, but they are said to be a recent phenomenon, uncommon, and usually very small because they are operated out of people's homes.

Certain kindergartens are perceived as exceptionally desirable, and obtaining entrance to them can involve various strategies. The first, straightforward strategy is to meet the basic criterion for eligibility, that is, to be a parent employed at a qualified unit or living in the neighborhood. Even meeting the minimum employment qualification, however, does not necessarily qualify one's child for entry. There might be more children for a provincial or city-sponsored multiunit preschool than can be accommodated. One way of dealing with this is to give each qualified unit a certain number of spaces and leave further allocation up to the unit. The unit might then allocate the spaces on the basis of one per section or office. If this year in your office you are the only one with a child entering kindergarten, your child goes. Or allocation might be on the basis of rank or extenuating circumstances, for example, both parents are out of town a great deal on work-related matters.

A second strategy is to pay a onetime (legal) admissions fee to the preschool, generally 300 to 1,000 yuan (in 1991) but rumored to be as high as several thousand yuan for particularly desirable preschools. One mother cited a construction company working in her neighborhood that runs a kindergarten for its workers' children but will admit others (on a space-available basis) from the neighborhood for 600 yuan. This money, known as a "construction" fee, is supposed to be used primarily to upgrade the physical plant and equipment of the school. In addition, parents must pay the regular kindergarten fees. One reason the government allows the special admissions fee is to provide a means of educating children without local household registration, such as children of migrants. They may not attend unit or government-run schools, but they may attend schools operated by collectives, such as a street committee, if they pay the extra fee. Similarly, units with excess space may make it available to parents from other units. In some cases the parent's unit, lacking its own kindergarten, will "buy" space in someone else's. Alternatively a unit might provide a direct subsidy so that one of its workers can send a child to a kindergarten.

If neither the neighborhood nor either parents' work unit sponsors a kindergarten, parents can pursue a third strategy: to manipulate the household registration of their child from birth. Many women do not transfer their household registration on marriage and therefore register their child at their own parents' address. They do this primarily for their own convenience—they know that the maternal grandparents are available in emergencies and will pick the child up after school lets out. More important, since admission to elementary school is by neighborhood, an artful choice of household registration can make a child automatically eligible for entrance into a desirable elementary school. Many of my informants have used this strategy on behalf of their children.

And, as a final strategy, a parent can go through the back door, relying on personal connections to admit a child lacking proper qualifications. For example, if a relative or friend teaches at the desired school, the lack of proper qualifications could be overlooked.

Jiedao Kindergarten, a typical Guangzhou preschool, is located in Yuexiu district in an old congested neighborhood of shops, factories, and residences. A school has been on the site for many years, since before 1949. In 1958 the local street committee took it over, and the old building was used as a preschool until 1984, when it was torn down. A new five-story building, hemmed in on all sides by residences, was completed in 1986. There is a little concrete play space in front of the building and a small wading or swimming pool behind it. The pool is in use from May through September or October. An extension of the second floor provides a music/meeting room inside and a shaded outdoor area for play below. Above the second floor music/meeting room is another unroofed play space for the children as well as a pigeon coop with two or three pigeons. There are two classrooms per floor. Several children share a small table, and each classroom comes equipped with an attached bathroom (containing an L-shaped trench along two walls) as well as a sink for washing up. Individual towels are hung from hooks outside the classroom; each child is assigned a distinctive animal that is represented on a sticker next to his or her hook, so that these prereaders can readily identify their own towels. The children sleep either directly on the tables or on sleeping mats on the floor. Their quilts are kept in a closet off to one side of the room. At the entrance to the school there is an archway with benches on either side that provides shelter for children waiting to be picked up by their parents or grandparents. Off the archway on one side is the principal's office, with banners proclaiming various awards, and on the other side another office to take care of general inquiries. The week's menu is displayed on the wall for the benefit of parents.

Jiedao Kindergarten draws its students, or rather "little friends," primarily from residents of the neighborhood and secondarily from workers in the neighborhood. Kindergartens normally have three grades: *xiaoban* for three- to four-year-olds, *zhongban* for four- to five-year olds, and *daban* for five- to six-year-olds. With 440 students in nine classes Jiedao Kindergarten has an average class size of forty-nine with two teachers per class. Preschool officials interviewed in 1991 thought that 90 percent of parents would like their children to attend a kindergarten; the remaining 10 percent are those who preferred that the child stay with a grandparent and those who could not handle the expense. Fees (in 1991) were 22 yuan a month plus 1.5 yuan a day for the two meals and snack. (The provision of meals is one of the big differences between kindergartens and elementary schools. Kindergartens have children the whole day, whereas the elementary schools send most students home for lunch, wreaking havoc with the work schedules of adults unless their own offices have long lunch breaks.) The 22-yuan fee is set by regulations—Jiedao's staff would like to charge a higher fee and thus have a bigger budget to work with. In addition, each semester parents are charged a 5-yuan activity fee (for movies or trips) and a 6-yuan miscellaneous fee (to cover electricity, etc.). . . . Students at Jiedao do not wear uniforms. After a portion of Jiedao's budget is used to cover basic operating expenses, the rest is supposed to be distributed as follows: 30 percent for welfare (of the staff), 40 percent for supplies, and 30 percent for bonus money (discussed later in the chapter). All these budget items must come out of fees. Jiedao has no income-generating potential, so it must rely on its own resources or on donations. (The mirror and piano in the music room were both donated.) The teachers also do as much as they can themselves, for example, painting the chairs as well as colorful and imaginative designs on the building walls and doing maintenance.

The teachers are all women (as is the principal, who came here from the street committee office over ten years ago with no prior experience in education—she had worked as an accountant). They were quite certain that none of the schools training kindergarten teachers would even accept male students. Upon completion of lower middle school, would-be kindergarten teachers attend three years of a specialized upper middle school. Students trained at public expense in schools run by the government are subject to work assignment by the Education Department; students trained at their own expense find work themselves. Jiedao Kindergarten obtains its teachers from among those who have paid their own way. Whereas in the United States early childhood education is associated with young teachers, in China the preschool teachers are of all ages because until recently people seldom changed jobs. After serving a single trial or probationary year, the teacher is given permanent employment until retirement at fifty-five.

Wages in 1991 averaged 250 yuan a month, with a range from 210–220 for beginners to about 300. The lowest retirement wage they could receive was supposed to be 80 yuan.

The two goals of preschool education are modest: morality and culture. Under the rubric of morality children learn correct behavior (conduct and virtue), including courtesy, respect for the elderly, and self-control; under the rubric of culture they learn vocabulary and develop skills in singing and dancing. A typical day proceeds as follows:

6:45 Doors open—children begin to arrive and play freely
7:45 Doors close (no more arrivals allowed) and formal activities start
8:00 Breakfast served in classroom
8:40 First "class" of day (classes are of different lengths to accommodate the different attention spans of the age groups and are followed by activities and play)
10:00 Free play
11:00 Prepare for lunch and eat
12:00 Nap
2:45 Up from nap
3:00 Snack and play until picked up
4:15 Beginning of pickup time

The doors theoretically close at 5:30, but if there are still "little friends" who have not yet been picked up, some of the teachers stay behind with them. On Saturday the school closes at 12:00, immediately following lunch.

Elementary School

Unlike kindergartens, elementary schools are truly neighborhood schools, and all children from the designated catchment area must be accommodated before a school may consider how to fill any vacancies it might have. Vacancies would normally be made available to children in neighboring catchment areas or to the children of parents working in the general catchment area but living elsewhere. Prior to 1987 keypoint schools recruited their students from within a city district or even from the city as a whole. In Guangzhou elementary schools are normally assigned the responsibility of educating the children from the three or four residents committees (the administrative subdivisions of street committees) in their immediate vicinity. A distinction must be drawn, however, between those children living in the area who are legally registered residents and those who, although living in the area, are not. These children, who usually have rural registration, may not be admitted until all those with legal registrations have been placed. In 1990 less than 1 percent of elementary school students (but 2.8 percent of junior middle school students and 1.9 percent of senior middle school students) in the city proper fell into this anomalous category.

For years these irregular students were known as *jidu* ("mail study") students, that is, correspondence school students, although in fact they were physically present in the classrooms right along with the other students. They used to pay an extra 10 yuan a semester for the privilege of attendance, but around 1987 the city converted the charge to a onetime payment at entry of 300 yuan. As in the case of preschools, this payment, known as a "construction" fee, is supposed to be used for such things as extra equipment. Other than this there is no distinction between legally registered and improperly registered students. The authorities decided to allow these children to attend school because, practically speaking, if the parents are in Guangzhou, the children are not going to stay in the village. It was deemed better to accept them, regardless of registration, than to have uneducated youngsters in the city.

One of the more questionable practices currently affecting student admissions is the right of school principals to reserve up to four places per classroom (of forty-five to fifty students) for "selected" students. These are students who, though otherwise qualified, lack the proper residency requirement to attend the particular school but are nevertheless admitted for a fee at the discretion of the principal. Generally such students either have urban registration but live in the wrong neighborhood or have rural registration but come into the city for the superior education available there. The extent to which this student population might overlap with the urban-raised but rural-registered student population is not clear. This formerly backdoor practice, believed in the past to have relied more on connections than on money, has been legalized as a way of helping schools meet their expenses. The entrance fee charged these students is referred to as a "selected" student fee and not as a "construction" fee. In any case the fees are substantial—so substantial that in mid-1994 the municipal authorities laid down guidelines for the charges schools could assess entering "selected" students. The higher the level of education, the higher the maximum fee allowed. Thus, for example, students entering typical elementary schools in the fall of 1994 were to be charged a maximum of 2,500 yuan, whereas those attending more desirable elementary schools could be charged up to 3,000. These fees are dwarfed, however, by the 8,000-yuan maximum that provincial and city keypoint upper middle schools (academic and vocational) could charge their entering "selected" students.

Although students attending their rightful school are not subject to this onetime fee, even they have seen the cost of their supposedly free education soar because they are subject annually to a host of miscellaneous charges. At the beginning of each school year, parents are presented with a long list of all the fees they must pay. At one primary school in the urban area the fee list contained thirty-five distinct charges: ten fixed by the city, 1 by the district, fourteen by the school itself, eight on behalf of outside units (presumably supplying the school with services of some sort), and two by education authorities. To meet these as well as four additional special fees, parents had to expend between 500 and 600 yuan. What do all these fees ostensibly cover? According to one reporter, who obtained a township junior middle school's fee list with twenty-four separate charges, they cover essentially anything that the school administrators think they can get away with: health insurance, bicycle supervision, sanitation, registration, educational development, library, educational administration, and so forth. In short, these fees are simply a fund-raising device.

There is a national curriculum for elementary (and middle schools), but in addition, standards of student achievement are set locally (by city and district). Although technically rural and urban schools are supposed to meet the same minimum levels, they may be hampered by a lack of teachers and by financial constraints. Ambitious individual schools may set higher standards for their students, but even (former) urban keypoint schools do not necessarily exceed their locality's minimum requirements. In one Yuexiu district former keypoint school, for example, English is not started early but rather in fifth grade, as the city requires, because the school has only two English teachers. (Sometime in the mid-1970s Guangzhou was selected by the national government to specialize in the teaching of English, and no other foreign languages are normally taught at the elementary school level. Other cities also specialize— some in Russian, some in Japanese, and so forth.) In 1980 I had visited a non-keypoint elementary school in Haizhu district that required its third graders to take four English classes a week. The third grade class I visited at the very end of the school year was learning the difference between "some" and "any" while the fifth grade class was studying the verb form "to be going" as in "Is he going to plant trees?" Students were to match a particular pronoun subject with the correct form of the verb "to be."

Elementary school students in the same school work at basically the same pace; there is neither ability grouping within a class nor tracking or streaming of students of different abilities into different classes. Consideration is given, however, to these differences. For example, children with exceptional talent in music or art might be sent to the Children's Palace (a municipal-operated facility) to take special classes a few times a week, and there is an entire separate school specializing in physical education for children being groomed for national athletic competition. Similarly, each school offers a range of extracurricular activities, some of which amount to special classes for the academically talented. Students who take these classes are eligible for entry to the provincial Olympics School, a middle school attached to South China Teacher Training University. This school prepares students to participate in the biannual international academic Olympics. In the fall of 1994 to meet growing demand for this special training, the city opened additional Olympic classes at five junior middle schools. Their opening represented a concession to parents disappointed by the 1992 modifications to the system of assignment to junior middle school.

In elementary (and middle) school students are assigned to a particular classroom under the supervision of a single teacher, who also teaches one of their courses. Elementary school teachers in China's cities, unlike those in the United States, are subject specialists and teach only their specialties. Students remain in their own classroom while the teachers circulate. This pattern continues through middle school, though for such subjects as science, which requires special equipment, students venture to the teacher's laboratory. On the order of 10–20 percent of the elementary school teachers in a given school are likely to be male.

In contrast to practice in the United States, the 50 or so children in a particular first grade classroom will remain together throughout their six-year tenure at the school (or three-year tenure at junior middle school). This policy, intended to foster group ties and identification, is abetted by neighborhood stability: given the long-term housing shortage and low rates of parental job change, families seldom move out of their neighborhood. In addition, each classroom has its own quasi-administrative student organization of class head and class committee, responsible for serving as role models and helping to keep the class orderly and well motivated. In the middle school such class officers also take on tutoring responsibilities and organize extracurricular activities, such as athletic competitions.

The elementary school students of today are said to have somewhat different characteristics and needs from those of only ten or twelve years ago—changes viewed as resulting from their upbringing in one-child families and their access to television. At one school these differences were recounted to me so readily and precisely that it was clear the national debate in pedagogical circles on the "spoiled child" was one with which the school's administrators were thoroughly familiar. Today's students were described as "little emperors," used to being doted on and having their every whim met by adoring parents and grandparents who concentrate on this single child. They know only how to enjoy themselves and lack the discipline necessary to attend to things they do not want to do. Moreover, they lack independence in daily activities such as tying their shoes and putting away their blankets after naps because even though they have usually learned these skills in kindergarten, they are not required to use them at home. But they have a general level of knowledge higher than elementary school students of an earlier era because they have been exposed to much more through television and are smarter.

To overcome some of these problems, educators have sought parental cooperation. In addition to requiring an annual (or semiannual) home visit by teachers, schools also run classes for heads of households on how to help their child make the most of his or her education. Each grade holds these evening classes, meeting for an hour or so, four times each semester. Experts in child development are brought in to explain the child's needs and how the parents can best help the child. If for some reason the class has to be held in the daytime, work units are supposed to grant the parent leave to attend without financial penalty. Attendance by parents is mandatory. One mother, whose son was to begin first grade in the fall of 1991, had already been required to attend such meetings, even though the school year had not yet begun. She indicated that parents have to have a paper stamped certifying that they have attended such sessions; otherwise their child will not be allowed to enter the school. Parents are also responsible for certifying that their child has completed the day's homework assignments and must sign their name to each homework paper. Finally, twice a year, a parent or other senior household member must come to the school on Sunday to obtain the child's grades (on both scholastic achievements and correctness of attitudes) from the class supervisor.

If Jiedao Kindergarten is typical, Chaotian Road Elementary School, not far from the preschool, exemplifies the academic privileges of the former keypoint schools. This elementary school was founded in the Qing Dynasty during the reign of Daoguang (1821–50). The school is built in a U-shape around a large courtyard, which serves as a play area and outdoor gymnasium, and is shaded by two graceful banyan trees. The open end of the U faces the street but is separated from it by a high solid wall. Entrance to the school is possible only through a metal gate. During a tour of the school, I visited a computer class and found every one of nearly fifty students at a computer (an

Apple clone). There were also clones of IBM models XT and AT (only one or two of each) in another room for use by teachers or advanced students. Teaching students to use computers is certainly not the norm for elementary schools in Guangzhou. Out of fifty-odd elementary schools in Yuexiu district, only five have computer classes. Moreover, though all elementary schools in Guangzhou are supposed to reach English beginning in the fifth grade, Chaotian teaches spoken (not written) English in the second grade and has four teachers specializing in teaching English. In 1991 the school had 1,177 students, somewhat above average for an elementary school. There are six grades, with four classes to a grade. The average number of students per class is forty-nine; the range is forty-six to fifty-one. There is one teacher per class. There are sixty-five teachers at the school, including a few who have retired but continue to work—for example, one of the arts instructors who teaches (unfired) clay figurine making. In the past students entered elementary school at age seven, but legally one may now enter at six. In Guangzhou it is more typical for a student to enter at age six and a half because of a shortage of places. Chaotian Road Elementary School draws about 70 percent of its students from the three residents committees immediately surrounding it and 30 percent from elsewhere. Like other elementary schools, it may accept students from outside the immediate neighborhood only if it has spaces left over.

The traditional route to elementary school teaching has been to take the examination to enter a teacher training school following the completion of lower middle school. More recently prospective teachers have been urged (though not apparently required) to continue at a postsecondary specialized school for two years of college-level training. Elementary schools (including Chaotian) still have many teachers educated under the old standards. The Labor Department assigns teachers, forwarding the names of graduating students to the district Education Department. The Education Department notes which schools need replacements and discusses assignments with the school. Perhaps three candidates are presented as possible teachers; the school principal chooses the most suitable from among them. Apparently to encourage students who plan to teach, the Labor Department allows students graduating from teacher training schools to be placed two months ahead of those graduating from other types of schools. All but one of Chaotian's teachers are from Guangzhou. (In 1990 one teacher came from Wuhan with a spouse—not a teacher—who was transferred to Guangzhou.)

Teachers, considered state workers, are guaranteed a certain minimum basic wage and level of subsidies. Another portion of their income comes from bonus money (some generated by the school itself, some by the government). In

1991 the average monthly income of teachers at Chaotian was between 320 and 330 yuan. The range was from 270 yuan (for someone just out of teacher training school) to 450 yuan (for someone with many years of experience). Of the average monthly income about 200–230 is guaranteed by the state, and the rest is derived from bonuses. Chaotian Road Elementary School obtains its bonus money from several sources: a printing factory it owns and operates itself; arrangements with other commercial units that use its space, such as a light bulb factory that established a sales outlet at the school; and rental of the school for adult education classes or evening school.

Chaotian's doors open at 7 A.M., when students on athletic teams are likely to begin practice, finishing at 7:40. The school has swimming, soccer, and track-and-field teams (and possibly others) that participate in district-level competitions and, if they do well, higher level competitions. Classes begin at 7:50 and go to 11:30, with four class periods separated by ten-minute recess breaks, during which the students are free to run about and play. During the three-hour lunch break, from 11:30 to 2:30, most students return to their nearby homes. About four hundred students buy lunches at the school and either work on extracurricular projects or just hang around until classes resume at 2:30. The afternoon session extends to 4:00 and includes two 40-minute classes. Students are free to leave after 4 P.M. but many stay on for an hour of extracurricular (e.g., artistic, musical, or computer) activities. Thursday afternoon is entirely given over to extracurricular activities. In addition to regular classes in Chinese, English, math, and science, students also take physical education four times a week. (Two periods are devoted to actual physical activity and two to studying about physical education.) There are also music and arts classes.

One of Chaotian's vice-principals, during a trip in 1988, visited several schools in the United States, among them one in Hingham, Massachusetts. (Guangdong has a sister province relation with Massachusetts.) When I asked him about his impressions, he remarked that in the United States classes are small, with some fifteen to twenty students; that American teachers are casual, interacting with the student in a familiar conversational way; that students have great freedom to select what they study; that teachers are concerned about the students and do not, for example, yell at them or embarrass them; that a relatively high proportion of the government budget goes to education; and that teachers' salaries are good. These comments reflect the comparatively large size of Chinese elementary school classes, the more directive classroom style of Chinese teachers, the fixed curriculum, and the opinion of everyone in the field that education is seriously underfunded.

Suggestions for Further Reading

Baker, Hugh. *Chinese Family and Kinship*. New York: Columbia University Press, 1979. This is still the best available general summary of our knowledge about Chinese family life and kinship organization. It deals primarily with family patterns in urban and rural China in the late imperial and republican periods.

Bakken, Børge. *The Exemplary Society*. Oxford: Oxford University Press, 2000. A Norwegian sociologist examines the continuing efforts by China's post-Mao elites to apply moral emulation techniques to socialize and control their increasingly unruly population.

Banister, Judith. *China's Changing Population*. Stanford: Stanford University Press, 1987. A demographer examines multiple aspects of China's changing population for the entire period from 1949 up through the first decade of reform.

Bian, Yanjie. *Work and Inequality in Urban China*. Albany: SUNY Press, 1994. A sociologist examines how the system of getting jobs, promotions, and compensation works in contemporary China and particularly how this system has been altered by China's reforms.

Chan, Kam Wing. *Cities with Invisible Walls*. Oxford: Oxford University Press, 1994. A geographer examines the distinctive system of regulations and institutions constructed during the Mao era that produced a caste-like barrier between China's urban and rural residents.

Chen, Nancy N., Constance D. Clark, Suzanne Z. Gottschang, and Lyn Jeffery, eds. *China Urban*. Durham, NC: Duke University Press, 2001. This volume presents the work of several anthropologists examining a variety of aspects of urban social and cultural life in post-Mao China.

Cooper, Eugene. *The Artisans and Entrepreneurs of Dongyang County*. Armonk, NY: M.E. Sharpe, 1998. An anthropologist presents a detailed examination of how the life and work of woodcarvers and furniture-makers in a rural county in Zhejiang were transformed first by China's socialist revolution and then by the post-1978 reforms.

Davis, Deborah, ed. *The Consumer Revolution in Urban China*. Berkeley: University of California Press, 2000. This conference volume examines the post-Mao shift from a spartan ethic to one increasingly emphasizing conspicuous consumption.

Davis, Deborah, and Stevan Harrell, eds. *Chinese Families in the Post-Mao Era.* Berkeley: University of California Press, 1993. This conference volume examines many aspects of family life in the post-Mao era.

Davis, Deborah, Richard Kraus, Barry Naughton, and Elizabeth Perry, eds. *Urban Spaces in Contemporary China.* Cambridge: Cambridge University Press, 1995. This conference volume examines the impact of China's reforms on urban social life.

Davis-Friedmann, Deborah. *Long Lives.* Expanded Edition. Stanford: Stanford University Press, 1991. A sociologist examines how China's socialist revolution and subsequent market reforms have affected the elderly in rural and urban China and argues that the elderly have benefited more than they have suffered from the changes since 1949.

Dutton, Michael. *Streetlife China.* Cambridge: Cambridge University Press, 1998. Through a combination of translations, pictures, and original commentary, a political scientist provides a picture of the evolving nature of urban social life.

Eastman, Lloyd E. *Family, Fields, and Ancestors.* New York: Oxford University Press, 1988. This survey of existing research on the nature of the Chinese social and economic order and how they changed over the period from 1550 to 1949 provides a good introduction to the nature of China's social life and problems prior to 1949.

Entwisle, Barbara, and Gail E. Henderson, eds. *Re-Drawing Boundaries: Work, Households, and Gender in China.* Berkeley: University of California Press, 2000. This conference volume examines how the post-Mao reforms have affected households and their participation in work, with a particular focus on the impact of the reforms on women.

Friedman, Edward, Paul G. Pickowicz, and Mark Selden. *Chinese Village, Socialist State.* New Haven: Yale University Press, 1991. This collaborative effort sketches the tumultuous changes experienced by a village in southern Hebei province before and after 1949.

Guthrie, Doug. *Dragon in a Three-Piece Suit.* Princeton: Princeton University Press, 1999. A sociologist examines how a variety of existing firms in Shanghai and their managers have adapted to China's market reforms and dealt with the transition from socialist to capitalist methods of operation.

Honig, Emily, and Gail Hershatter. *Personal Voices: Chinese Women in the 1980's*. Stanford: Stanford University Press, 1988. Two social historians present a broad overview of the way the post-Mao reforms have affected Chinese women, with a primary focus on urban women.

Ikels, Charlotte. *The Return of the God of Wealth*. Stanford: Stanford University Press, 1996. An anthropologist examines how Guangzhou, a city at the cutting edge of market reforms, has been transformed since 1978. This study is based on local fieldwork in Guangzhou neighborhoods over many years.

Jiang Yarong, and David Ashley. *Mao's Children in the New China*. London: Routledge, 2000. Two sociologists present a collection of oral history accounts of the life experiences of former Red Guards confronting a society that is very different from the one in which they grew up.

Jing Jun, ed. *Feeding China's Little Emperors*. Stanford: Stanford University Press, 2000. In this collection a range of scholars use food and eating habits as a prism through which to view the changing nature of Chinese family life and society.

Judd, Ellen R. *Gender and Power in Rural North China*. Stanford: Stanford University Press, 1994. An anthropological examination of changes in three villages in Shandong province since 1949, with a particular focus on how women have been affected by these changes.

Lee, Ching Kwan. *Gender and the South China Miracle*. Berkeley: University of California Press, 1998. This is a sociological analysis of two factories primarily employing women which are run by the same foreign electronics company, one in Hong Kong, and the other just across the border in rural Guangdong. The author attempts to explain why the labor regime in the mainland factory is so much harsher than in its Hong Kong counterpart.

Lee, James Z., and Wang Feng. *One Quarter of Humanity: Malthusian Mythology and Chinese Realities*. Cambridge, MA: Harvard University Press, 1999. A historian and a sociologist systematically critique conventional views about traditional Chinese population behavior. Using detailed local historical records, mainly from the eighteenth and nineteenth centuries, the authors show that China was not more pronatalist than early modern Europe, although the ways in which population growth were limited were decidedly different.

Lü Xiaobo, and Elizabeth J. Perry, eds. *Danwei: The Changing Chinese Workplace in Historical and Comparative Perspective*. Armonk, NY: M.E. Sharpe, 1997. This collection explores the historical origins, in both pre-1949 China and in the Soviet Union, and recent evolution of the unusually enveloping and controlling urban workplace institution, the *danwei*.

Madsen, Richard. *China's Catholics: Tragedy and Hope in an Emerging Civil Society*. Berkeley: University of California Press, 1998. A sociologist operating in difficult fieldwork conditions describes the nature of the reemergence of Catholic churches and worship in post-Mao China.

Parish, William L., and Martin K. Whyte. *Village and Family in Contemporary China*. Chicago: University of Chicago Press, 1978. This comprehensive analysis of rural life under collectivized agriculture during the Mao era is based on interviews with informants from villages in Guangdong Province.

Pepper, Suzanne. *Radicalism and Education Reform in 20th Century China*. Cambridge: Cambridge University Press, 1996. This comprehensive study examines the tortuous changes that characterized China's educational system from before 1949 until the mid-1990s.

Perry, Elizabeth J., and Mark Selden, eds. *Chinese Society: Change, Conflict, and Resistance*. London: Routledge, 2000. This collection explores a wide variety of aspects of social conflict and popular resistance to the state in post-Mao China.

Potter, Sulamith Heins, and Jack M. Potter. *China's Peasants: The Anthropology of a Revolution*. Cambridge: Cambridge University Press, 1990. This detailed look at the changes experienced in a village in Guangdong village from 1949 up through the early reform period is based on detailed fieldwork and return visits in the early 1980s.

Solinger, Dorothy J. *Contesting Citizenship in Urban China*. Berkeley: University of California Press, 1999. A political scientist examines the nature of the massive flow of migrants from rural to urban China in the post-Mao period and the impact this migration is having on the nature of the urban system.

Tang, Wenfang, and William L. Parish. *Chinese Urban Life under Reform: The Changing Social Contract*. Cambridge: Cambridge University Press, 2000. Through a detailed analysis of several large-scale survey data sets, a political scientist and a sociologist explore the changes in the nature of urban social life in the post-Mao period.

Thurston, Anne F. *Enemies of the People*. New York: Alfred Knopf, 1987. A political scientist uses extensive oral history interviews to explore the experiences of intellectuals who fell victim to the tumult of China's Cultural Revolution in the late 1960s.

Walder, Andrew G. *Communist Neo-Traditionalism: Work and Authority in Chinese Industry.* Berkeley: University of California Press, 1986. A prize-winning sociological analysis of the way urban work organizations operated during the late Mao era, based primarily on interviews in Hong Kong with Chinese émigrés.

Walder, Andrew G. *Zouping in Transition.* Cambridge, Mass.: Harvard University Press, 1998. A team of China specialists of diverse disciplines presents the conclusions from repeated field visits to a Shandong village during the period from 1988 to 1993. The result is an examination of key institutional changes in one corner of rural China in the post-Mao era.

Whyte, Martin K., and William L. Parish. *Urban Life in Contemporary China.* Chicago: University of Chicago Press, 1984. Two sociologists present a comprehensive picture of the urban system in the Mao period and efforts to deal with its resulting maladies in the early reform era.

Yan Yunxiang. *The Flow of Gifts: Reciprocity and Social Networks in a Chinese Village.* Stanford: Stanford University Press, 1996. An anthropologist examines the changing nature of social networks and exchanges in a village in Heilongjiang. This work is the product of observations spanning more than twenty years, beginning when Yan was an urban youth "sent down" to the countryside, and continuing when he was a doctoral student and then a young academic.

———. *Private Life under Socialism: Love, Intimacy and Family Change in a Chinese Village, 1949–1999.* Stanford: Stanford University Press, 2002. In this second product of his unusually rich ethnographic research on a Heilongjiang village, Yan focuses on continuity and change in a wide range of aspects of rural family life.

Zhang Xinxin, and Sang Ye. *Chinese Lives: The Oral History of Contemporary China.* New York: Pantheon, 1987. Two Chinese journalists emulated Studs Terkel to produce this collection of more than sixty oral history personal accounts from diverse corners of reform-era China.

Zhao, Dingxin. *The Power of Tiananmen.* Chicago: University of Chicago Press, 2001. A sociologist presents a systematic account of the variety of social forces that produced the dramatic Tiananmen student uprising of 1989.

Part 4

ECONOMY

Edited by Barry Naughton

IN THE MIDDLE OF THREE TRANSITIONS
- RURAL TO URBAN ECONOMY
- PLANNED TO MARKET ECONOMY
- INFORMATION ECONOMY

Introduction

Barry Naughton

For the past two decades, China has been the world's most rapidly growing large economy. Recent spectacular growth has transformed China's appearance and standard of living, and given China a new prominence and importance in world affairs. China's dramatic growth has caught the world's attention and also attracted an inflow of foreign direct investment surpassing U.S. $40 billion annually. But recent rapid growth is in fact the culmination of an ongoing process of economic development that over the past fifty years has transformed China from a desperately poor, predominantly agrarian economy into a complex, semi-industrialized economy that is capable of bringing the majority of China's citizens a decent standard of living for the first time in history.

The economic transformation of China is very much incomplete. China is in fact in the middle of three different but interrelated transitions. The first transition is that from a predominantly poor rural economy to an industrialized and predominantly urban one. Half of China's labor force is still in agriculture, and two-thirds of the population lives in the countryside. Thus the structural transformation is only half complete, and China must be classified as a developing economy. Average per capita income is below that of Mexico, Brazil, or Thailand. The second transition is that from a government-planned economy to a market economy. China has dismantled the mechanisms of central planning and reduced government control over the economy. The role of the market and of private ownership in the Chinese economy has expanded rapidly, and Chinese economic growth accelerated with the onset of market transition. However, the legal and financial institutions needed to support a market economy have developed more slowly. They are only partly in place and are still shaky. The third transition is that towards a modern information economy. Today's developed economies, such as the United States, first developed an industrial base and only later evolved into economies predominantly based on services and information technology. In China, this last transition is occurring simultaneously with the later stages of industrialization. The Internet and the telecommunications revolution are having an impact on China nearly as great as they have had on the United States, even though China lags far behind in other areas. To a certain extent, the information technology revolution will permit China to skip stages of industrialization that developed countries passed through in the twentieth century.

These multiple, simultaneous transitions are the driving forces behind China's economic dynamism. None is complete: each has progressed to a different degree and each unrolls at a different pace. The result is an economy of mind-boggling complexity, in which subsistence farmers coexist with high tech enterprise and the Internet coexists with the oxcart (reading 33).

China's Traditional Economy

China had a sophisticated traditional economy. Although overwhelmingly rural, it supported a dense population. The agricultural system depended on intensive cultivation, on massive application of painstaking labor. As early as the Southern Song dynasty (1127–1279 A.D.), the lower Yangzi delta developed an extremely rich rural economy, based on three complementary elements of traditional technology. Early-ripening rice, imported from Southeast Asia, allowed farmers to plant two or more crops of grain annually on the same plot of land. Organic fertilizers—human and animal manure, but also pond mud, lime, and green algae—were applied to fields to maintain soil fertility. Irrigation systems permitted full control of water on fields. These three elements together formed a package, with improved irrigation, for example, allowing farmers to take full advantage of better crop varieties and fertilizer. Rice was sprouted in seedbeds, and the shoots were later transplanted to flooded fields. As the rice plants matured, fields were drained and the ripe plants were harvested. This system could produce very high crop yields per unit of cultivated land.

The densely populated countryside supported a thick network of markets. In areas that were suitable to the building of canals—particularly the lower Yangzi and Pearl River deltas—a highly developed system of water transport knit villages and farms into economically integrated regions. The major river systems, particularly the Yangzi, provided links between regions. The Grand Canal, dating back to the Sui dynasty (581–618), linked the rich lower Yangzi and the North China plain, site of the national capital. For places on the water transport network, even heavy and bulky commodities could enter into trade. China as a whole was highly commercialized for a pre-modern economy.

The sophisticated institutions necessary to support a complex network of transactions had evolved as the commercialized economy developed. Use of money was widespread, and commercial banks made it possible for merchants to remit money nationwide. People were accustomed to writing contracts to regulate transactions, including obligations to family and descendants. They were also familiar with large organizations, often kinship-based, and a national government. There were courts in which to resolve disputes, and guilds mediated and created support networks for merchants based on their place of origin.

Even given the sophistication of the commercial economy, nearly all production was undertaken by households, and almost always in the countryside. Textiles, leather goods, and iron tools and utensils—as well as food products such as wine, tea, sugar, noodles, and edible oils—were produced primarily by rural households which combined handicraft production and agriculture. Households then participated directly in the market on their own behalf, buying and selling small quantities of agricultural and handicraft manufactured goods. Thus, at the base of the Chinese traditional economy was a vigorous, household-based market economy. Millions of households engaged directly in production for different markets, which were, as a result, highly competitive. There was substantial social mobility in this extremely fluid, flexible economy.

Despite the sophistication and flexibility of the economy, most people were poor. The land produced a rich harvest per unit of land, but so much labor was required to wrest the bounty from the land that the return per unit of labor was low, and so was the average income of a worker. The intense competitiveness of markets often reflected the sheer struggle for survival of millions at the bottom of the social order. A significant portion of the farm population owned no land but rented from landlords and survived in crowded markets for handicrafts or petty commerce. Even in the best of times, life was hard for the vast majority of the population.

Crisis of the Traditional Economy

The traditional economy, it seems, ought to have been resilient. It should have responded well to contact with the West and to the new technologies that the West brought to China. But in fact, between the early 1800s and the mid 1900s, China plunged into a series of grave economic and political crises. At the beginning of this period, it was one of the largest economies in the world. According to estimates of world population and output compiled by Angus Maddison

(1998), China in 1820 accounted for about one-third of world population, and only slightly less than that share of world output, so Chinese output per head was within 90 percent of the world average. But after almost a century of disasters, China's share of world population and output had declined dramatically. In 1913 China accounted for one-quarter of world population, and only 9 percent of world output, so China's output per head was only 40 percent of the world average. These dramatic changes are partly attributable to exploding population and the beginnings of rapid economic development in the Western world, but they are also partly attributable to the stagnation of China's population and gross domestic product (GDP) over this period. Indeed, according to Maddison's estimates, per capita GDP in China in 1913 was lower than it had been in 1820.

It appears that China was undergoing major crises at the time when contact with the West accelerated in the nineteenth century. There is evidence that basic government jobs—such as maintaining irrigation networks and holding adequate stockpiles of grain—were not being done adequately by the early 1800s. The Chinese government at this time was apparently unable to do things it had done well in earlier centuries, much less develop a coherent response to the external challenge. In 1840 British gunboats inflicted a sharp defeat and imposed the importation of opium on China. They also forced the Chinese government to cede control over treaty ports to foreigners who would live and trade there. During the 1860s southern China erupted in the Taiping Rebellion, which lasted over a decade and devastated most of the Yangzi valley. Population growth ceased, and tens of millions were killed. Following on this catastrophe, the collapse of the last imperial dynasty in 1911 ushered in a period of warlordism and political division that lasted until the reunification of the country under the Guomindang [Nationalist Party] government in 1927. By the 1920s, foreign observers had begun to see China as a country in chronic crisis, the "land of famine." Despite the chaotic social and political environment, the early twentieth century brought the beginnings of modern economic development. The first modern civilian factories were created shortly after the turn of the century. After its unification of the country the Guomindang brought a decade of relative order to society (1927–1937). The Nationalists began to put government finances in order and drew up plans for economic development. Between 1912 and 1936, modern factory production grew at about 8 percent annually, a fairly rapid pace by the standards of the time. By 1936 a million workers were employed in mechanized factories. Responding to increased demand from the urban economy, farmers in some regions began to grow new, more commercial crops, including tobacco, peanuts, and vegetables.

This growth came from a tiny initial base. Even in the 1930s modern factory output accounted for only 2 percent of GDP. Industrialization had clearly begun, but it had not begun to fundamentally change the overall structure of the Chinese economy. Early industrialization was concentrated in two regions where foreign influence was particularly strong and shaped the patterns of development. The first pattern can be labeled "treaty port industrialization." It was concentrated in those cities where China had been forced to allow foreign-managed concessions in the decades after the Opium War of 1840. Shanghai was the preeminent center. The treaty ports provided a supportive environment for all kinds of entrepreneurship, native and foreign. Industrialization was concentrated in light industry, especially textiles and food products, and both foreign-invested and native Chinese firms played an important role. The second pattern developed in Manchuria, especially after Japanese colonization in 1931. Here industrialization was subordinated to Japanese strategic objectives. Coal, steel, and machine-building were the main industries, and they were dominated by Japanese corporations with close links to the government.

The beginnings of economic progress were interrupted by more than ten years of war and civil war. The Japanese invasion in 1937 devastated the Chinese domestic economy, although it paradoxically gave a boost to military-oriented industries in Manchuria and elsewhere in China. After the conclusion of the Pacific War in 1945, the Guomindang utterly failed to rehabilitate the economy. Hyperinflation raged, and the economies of Shanghai and Manchuria never recovered their pre-war prosperity. By 1949 and the Communist victory on the mainland, the economy had undergone over a decade of serious disruption. It was easy enough to look back over this decade of war, and the previous century of humiliation, and conclude that Chinese economic development before 1949 had been a failure. Although the reality is considerably more complex, there is no doubt that 1949 marked the initiation of a new period of accelerated growth under dramatically different conditions.

Socialist Industrialization, 1949–1978

The founding of the People's Republic of China in 1949 is certainly a political milestone, and it also represents an important economic turning point. The unambiguous beginnings of China's transition from the traditional, rural economy toward a modern urban economy occurred in the period immediately after the founding of the People's Republic. Within two or three years, China had begun its race to industrialize. In the fifty years since, China has consistently poured material resources and human effort into the building of a modern, industrial economy. During these fifty years, economic policies have sometimes swung wildly, and have ranged from centralized socialism all the way to market liberalization, but the commitment to modernization has been a constant. Industrialization would have occurred without the Chinese Communist Party (CCP), of course, but the actual pattern of industrialization has been shaped by CCP policies and by the political system created and controlled by the CCP.

After the establishment of the People's Republic of China in October 1949, China's economy was completely reoriented, wrenched out of its traditional framework. China's new leaders established a strong government and, turning their backs on China's traditional household-based, "bottom heavy" economy, set about to develop a massive socialist industrial complex. Planners neglected labor-intensive sectors suitable to China's vast population, and instead poured resources into capital-intensive factories producing metals, machinery, and chemicals. China's initial modern development—primarily a coastal enclave phenomenon open to foreign trade across the Pacific—was neglected in favor of an inward-directed strategy that accepted the Soviet Union as China's main trading partner and source of technology.

After a few years of economic rehabilitation, the Chinese government began to build the framework of a centrally planned economy during the 1950s. From this time through at least 1978, China operated a socialist planned economic system. Such a system is also called a "command economy," because market forces were severely curtailed, and government planners allocated resources directly according to their own preferences and priorities. In practice, those preferences gave overwhelming priority to rapid industrialization.

Individual economic decision-making was subordinated to the overall national development strategy. In the countryside, land was at first redistributed among households. But during the mid-1950s, as the other elements of the command economy fell into place, farmers were placed under increasing pressure to join agricultural collectives. By 1956 the pressures were too great to resist, and virtually the entire countryside was organized into collectives. Farmers surrendered their land and had to abandon many of their off-farm economic activities. They were organized into work teams to farm the land and had to sell their agricultural produce to the state commercial monopoly at a fixed price. Farmers gave up substantial income-earning opportunities, for which they received—at least in most years—more economic security in return. The poorest agricultural households benefited from subsistence guarantees and better access to the land. The collectives, moreover, gradually began to provide improved education and health services to rural residents. But the economic potential of rural households was drastically suppressed.

In an economy in which most people still worked on the farm, government control of farm output and farm prices was crucial to control of the overall economy. The government set up a system of monopoly purchase of the most important forms of agricultural output, especially food grains and cotton. By keeping farm prices low relative to industrial prices, the government was able to keep food prices and the wages of factory workers low as well. With cheap agricultural inputs and food supplies, state-run factories were virtually guaranteed to be profitable. The profits from state-run factories were then turned over to the government budget, which used them to fund a state-run program of investment. Under this strategy, the government controlled the bulk of national saving and pumped it into investments primarily in capital-intensive heavy industry. Investment was increased, and consumption was squeezed: personal services were neglected and ration coupons were required to buy many kinds of consumer goods. Predictably, this strategy produced rapid growth of industrial output. Between 1952 and 1978, industrial output grew at an average annual rate of 11.5 percent. Moreover, industry's share of total GDP climbed steadily from 18 percent in 1952 to 44 percent in 1978. Correspondingly, agriculture's share declined from 51 to 28 percent measured at current prices. Entire new industries were created—for example, those producing electric generating equipment, chemical fertilizer, and motor vehicles.

While this development strategy did produce rapid industrial growth, it also created serious problems and led to substantial waste. The most devastating failure came during the Great Leap Forward (1958–1960). A utopian scheme for social and economic transformation, the Leap led to an absurd intensification of the rapid industrialization strategy. Massive quantities of resources were transferred out of agriculture. Millions of workers were diverted to the industrial sector. Some went to the cities to work in the new modern factories just being set up, while others went to work in primitive "back yard" facilities. In order to feed these workers, planners confiscated a huge proportion of total agricultural output. Farmers were left with little to eat and little incentive to produce more for their urban bosses. The result was a collapse of agricultural production and consumption. During the three years 1960 through 1962, a massive famine ensued. According to the best estimates, up to 30 million people starved or succumbed prematurely to disease. It was a horrible indictment of the socialist system.

After the Great Leap Forward disaster, planners at first paid careful attention to rehabilitating the economy, but within a few years, economic policy was subordinated to utopian political objectives once again. As the post-Leap crisis eased, Mao pushed for the construction of the "Third Front," a massive construction program focused on China's inland provinces. The objective was to create an entire industrial base that would provide China with strategic independence. By building factories in remote and mountainous interior regions, Mao hoped to ensure that China's industrial base would not be vulnerable to American or Soviet military threats. Then in August 1966, Mao launched the so-called "Cultural Revolution." In contrast to the Great Leap Forward, the disruption of the Cultural Revolution was "managed" quite effectively: investment was curtailed in a relatively orderly fashion; agricultural production was only slightly affected; and while industrial production declined, the fall was moderate and production of vital necessities and priority projects continued. However, over the longer term, the Cultural Revolution had a deeply corrosive effect on China's economy. Although economic growth continued, all economic decisions were subordinate to political principles and struggles. Managers, engineers, and other skilled individuals were ignored and discriminated against. The universities were closed for years, and high school graduates were sent to the countryside where their city education was largely irrelevant. Human resources were wasted, skills deteriorated and administrative capabilities declined. More and more resources were tied up in misguided, never-to-be-completed investment projects. Growth gradually began to slow down, and living standards stagnated. By the time of Mao's death in 1976, pressures for dramatic change were building.

The Reform Era

After the death of Mao Zedong, economic policy vacillated under the weak leadership of Hua Guofeng. By the end of 1978, however, China's leaders had become convinced that a change of direction was necessary. As Chinese leaders struggled to free economic policymaking from the oversimplified political slogans of the Cultural Revolution, it became evident that a drastic rethinking of the principles of socialism would be required. China's first transition—toward an industrialized economy—had by that time passed through its initial phase, and planners were beginning to face new challenges as they attempted to guide a larger and more complex economy. Gradually, China's leaders, especially Deng Xiaoping, began to accept the need to adopt significant elements of a market economy. In the milestone Third Plenum in December 1978, the CCP decreed a shift in government policy away from political struggle and towards economic modernization. The initial commitments made during this meeting were vague and uncertain, but they touched off a period of experimentation and change that has continued to the present. China's second transition—the transition to a market economy—was launched at this important meeting, and has shaped more than two decades of economic development since then.

Initial reforms succeeded most quickly in the rural sector. At first, rural reforms were intended simply to ease the burden on farmers, by increasing the prices paid for grain, lowering the level of compulsory procurement, and giving farmers a greater role in the management of their cooperatives. However, once rural policy began to be relaxed, farmers increasingly pushed for more fundamental changes in the way their local communities were managed. Some villages began experimenting with the division of land to individual households. Premier Zhao Ziyang gradually accepted these experiments and presided over a further liberalization of rural policy that eventually led to the distribution of land to individual households through the so-called "contract responsibility system." Under this system, households leased land from the "collective," in return for payment of taxes and delivery of a fixed quota of agricultural produce. In response to these improved incentives, households increased their output of farm products and also economized on labor inputs into agriculture, freeing up labor for other income-earning pursuits. Many farmers went to work in so-called "township and village enterprises" (TVEs)—rural factories that sprang up, especially in villages close to urban markets. The result was that both farm and off-farm output soared in the early years of reform, through 1984. This dramatic success in the rural areas solidified Chinese commitment to the path of reform and launched a transition to the market economy.

One of the most distinctive features of this period was the dramatic role of the TVEs. TVEs were enormously diverse, but many of them were "collectively owned," which is to say, owned by the village community or government, or by the township government. This sector played a key role in introducing competition in industrial product markets, and the TVE sector grew much faster than overall output through the 1980s and most of the 1990s. This is somewhat ironic, because this rapidly growing economic form was not a type of private ownership—though some TVEs were de facto private—but rather a form of public ownership, managed predominantly at the local government level. This form of public ownership often involved interesting compromises between individual power and influence, government quest for resources, and the need to employ competent managerial personnel (reading 34). TVEs could be successful in part because they were operating in a market environment in which so many goods were scarce. After years of neglect of the consumer market by state-owned enterprises (SOEs), many simple types of production were quite profitable. The town of Wenzhou on the south China coast, for example, touched off an explosive phase of growth by specializing in buttons, ribbons, and plastic ID card holders which brought them unprecedented prosperity.

The success of the TVEs in the early stages makes it easier to understand some of the key characteristics of China's market transition. First of all, China's transition has been "institutionally conservative," that is, Chinese policy generally allowed existing organizations to take advantage of new opportunities. If the growth of markets created a business opportunity, then village governments, local schools, or existing firms might all be allowed to take advantage of the new conditions. Rather than dissolving existing organizations and trying to start anew with private firms and new institutions, Chinese policy tended to encourage the adaptation of existing organizations. The key features of the growth of markets were therefore "entry" of new market participants, rather than "privatization" of existing state-run enterprises (reading 35). One merit of this approach was that early reforms, during the 1980s, benefited an extraordinarily wide range of China's population. Farmers were the first to gain on a large scale, increasing income from both agricultural and nonagricultural production, and achieving much more autonomy to make their own business decisions. Urban workers followed, gaining access to a much broader range of consumer goods and wage increases at the beginning of reform, without being subject to the harsh discipline of the labor market. Even government officials gained, because they were often able to reap private benefits from the many new businesses that were springing up. Indeed, it has been argued that China's reform was initially a "reform without losers."

China was able to stumble into this happy situation because its approach to this transition was quite different from that of policymakers in the transition economies of Eastern Europe and the former Soviet states. Chinese reformers were always aware that the second transition—the move to the market—was taking place at the same time as the first—the transition to an industrial urban economy. It was never conceivable to Chinese policymakers that their economy would "mark time," postponing economic development until after an interlude of system transformation. It was always assumed that system transformation would have to take place concurrently with economic development, and indeed that the process of economic development would drive market transition forward and guarantee its eventual success. Indeed, sometimes completion of market transition was roughly equated with reaching a medium developed status: after

China had achieved more skills and a higher income level, it would be able to manage a sophisticated market economy. Measures taken before that time would have to be "transitional" both towards the market and towards a more developed economy. This is in contrast with the orientation of policymakers in Eastern Europe who implemented transition strategies in economies with substantially higher incomes. Those policymakers generally assumed that transition would have to interrupt economic growth, while institutions were drastically reshaped to resemble those they saw in Western Europe. Only after that restructuring, would growth be expected to resume.

Chinese policymakers believed that they did not have this luxury. Instead, they repeatedly tried experiments with partial system reforms and then judged them to be effective or not depending on whether they contributed to the goal of short-term economic growth. Inevitably this approach meant that many Chinese reforms created new distortions in the economic system. Indeed, Chinese reformers behaved as if the distorted allocation of resources they faced was both a challenge and an opportunity, in the following sense: Socialist systems were extremely wasteful, lavishing resources on industrial projects that were the priority of planners, while neglecting simple and easily satisfied demands of consumers. Although the overall system of planning was complex and hard to change, the unsatisfied needs of households and businesses were obvious and easy to see. So instead of trying to change the whole planned system, Chinese reformers simply starting allowing individuals—especially TVEs in the early period—to enter new markets and start addressing those unsatisfied needs. If, in the process, they had to be exempted from the rules of the socialist system, and earned higher incomes, that would be tolerated as well. Chinese reformers gradually opened up their system, using the opportunity to satisfy long-suppressed demands as a driving force both for economic development and for economic reform.

Early reforms almost never eliminated distortions. Instead, early reforms created pockets of unregulated and lightly taxed activity within the system. Reformers allowed such pockets to open up because they were seen as contributing to developmental objectives. A classic example of this general orientation was the creation of Special Economic Zones (SEZs). Almost immediately after the initiation of reforms, the Chinese government designated four SEZs along the south China coast, the largest of which was adjacent to Hong Kong. The SEZs were extremely controversial, because they seemed to more conservative Chinese to echo the treaty ports of the nineteenth century. Of course the SEZs have always been under full Chinese sovereignty, but it is true that they were used as experimental areas where policy could be quickly adapted to the needs of foreign investors. In the early years of reform, it would have been far too difficult to reshape the entire domestic economy to meet the requirements of foreign trade and investment. Instead, policymakers simply agreed to break off a chunk of Chinese territory and use it as a more highly marketized, lower tax zone where foreign businesses could begin to explore operations in China. SEZ policies were seen as contributing to growth by bringing in technology and investment, while not initially threatening the overall ability of the government to manage and direct the economy.

The policies permitted huge distortions to remain in the system, for example, the difference between the prices, taxes, and regulations that prevailed in the SEZs versus those that prevailed in the rest of China. However, these distortions, on balance, tended to encourage resources—people, money, initiative—to flow into these less regulated locations. Individuals or communities saw niches available that they could exploit. First movers made high profits. There was almost never equal and fair competition; rarely did one see a "level playing field." This approach was extended to state-owned enterprises (SOEs) when they were allowed to sell output above their plan quotas on the market. These "outside plan" sales took place at prices that were quickly determined by the forces of supply and demand. The result was that most products came to have two prices: a plan price and a market one. This "dual price" system grew up in the early 1980s and lasted into the next decade. The overall level of distortions in the system probably did not decrease very much in the initial stages of reform, but as dual price systems sprang up, distortions became more visible, because they could be measured by the difference between market prices and plan prices for the same goods.

Alert individuals began to move resources into unregulated "pockets of activity." Returns were higher, but so was risk. In the unregulated pockets, market forces set prices, but these prices were indirectly shaped by the planned economy as well. The planned economy devoured resources, creating inflationary pressures that kept market prices high. In addition, free market participants could often evade taxes, partially or completely. High market prices and low taxes were a recipe for high profits, so people and resources continued to be attracted to the market sector. The result was a kind of Swiss cheese economy, in which the old government-run economy provided the matrix for all economic activity, while holes were opened up to provide space for market activity. The state-run economy was gradually hollowed out, but the economy as a whole continued to grow. Agriculture, township, and village enterprises, foreign trade sparked by rapid growth of the SEZs —all these growth areas provided powerful arguments for the continuation and strengthening of reform.

Crisis and Reformulation, 1989–1993

Despite the successes of the first stage of reform, by the late 1980s China's reform strategy began to seem increasingly shaky. In part, this was simply due to short-term mistakes in economic policy. But in part, it was due to the exhaustion of the initial gains that the reform strategy had generated, and the difficulty the Chinese political system had in going beyond those initial reforms. During 1988–1989, serious economic difficulties fed a steadily unfolding political crisis that culminated in the bloody suppression of student demonstrators in Tiananmen Square on June 4, 1989. The political crisis derived in part from the perception that the economic gains from reform had been exhausted, at least temporarily. Inflation soared to unprecedented heights. In the countryside, growth of farm incomes slowed, and urban wage increases fell behind the rate of inflation. Meanwhile, corruption reached what at the time seemed to be intolerable proportions.

Moreover, the reform strategy seemed to have led to a continuous decline in the capability of government, and its ability to implement nationwide economic policy. Reforms had been successfully stimulated by a decentralization of power and resources to enterprises and local governments. The right to enter new markets had been used to stimulate the early phases of reform, but the terms on which different types of market participants had gained entry to the market was granted in very unequal fashion. Private firms were treated differently from state enterprises, which in turn were treated differently from TVEs or foreign-invested enterprises. This unequal treatment had seemed acceptable at the beginning of the reforms, but now there were increasing demands for equal treatment, and increasing doubts whether government was capable to adopting across-the-board rules that would apply fairly to all regions and all economic actors. The SEZs had sparked foreign investment, but now that meant the bulk of foreign investment went to the coastal provinces, which were not only wealthier than the inland provinces, but were also growing much faster. Regional disparities began to widen. Government budget revenues—as a share of gross domestic product—had been declining every year, as government resources were increasingly decentralized. This meant there was no money available to support the more backward, slower growing regions. Overall, the government's ability to provide crucial public goods seemed in question. Would the government be able to ensure the supply of electricity to feed the rapidly growing economy? Would there be enough new highways and railroads? The political fragmentation and paralysis around the time of the Tiananmen incident seemed to mirror the decline of governmental authority in the economic arena as well.

By the early 1990s, it was clear that new policies were needed. After the Tiananmen political crisis, conservatives opposed to economic reforms in general achieved a period of brief predominance. But their attempts to roll back reforms failed completely and have been largely forgotten. In early 1992 Deng Xiaoping gave the policy pendulum a forceful push back toward reform in his "Southern Tour" that took him to the SEZs and saw him give a ringing endorsement to accelerated economic reform. This was sufficient to tip the balance of political power in Beijing and restart the reform process. It was also one of Deng Xiaoping's last decisive personal interventions in Chinese policymaking. Shortly thereafter, a new, younger group of policymakers took over, and Deng and the other revolutionary elders passed from the scene. In economic policy, Zhu Rongji quickly emerged as the most important voice. Zhu established himself as the dominant player in mid-1993, while he was still vice-premier. He was elevated to premier in early 1998, but in fact policy from 1993 on shows his personal influence quite clearly. Zhu's strong, decisive personality helped him to shift to a new phase of economic reform.

Zhu Rongji first made his mark by initiating a period of macroeconomic austerity in mid-1993. A financial crackdown was clearly necessary, because after Deng Xiaoping's Southern Tour, wild, unbridled financial speculation and corruption had emerged. The sudden take-off of the economy tempted people at all levels with new visions of getting rich, and government officials were quick to pile on the bandwagon. The first thing Zhu Rongji had to do was to crack down on some of the worst cases of corruption and financial excess. But as it turned out, this crackdown signaled the beginning of a new macroeconomic policy regime. That is, policy changed so that state-run banks were much less willing to deliver cheap credit to state-owned enterprises. Fiscal policy remained reasonably conservative (budget deficits were generally not large), while monetary policy became much more conservative. The result was a slower growth of the money supply, and a gradual squeezing of inflation out of the system. In 1993–1994, inflation was running over 20 percent per year, but by the end of 1997, the inflation rate had dropped almost to zero. In 1998 the economy entered a period in which prices fell for over two years. Not only was inflation squeezed out of the system, it became clear that Chinese policy had shifted to a long-term policy of macroeconomic conservatism and had managed to deliver a significant degree of macroeconomic stability.

Zhu Rongji presided over a new, more regulatory approach to economic reform. The reforms were regulatory in the sense that they introduced new rules—and new prices—that at least in principle applied equally to all economic actors. There was more focus on creating and regulating competition as a force for economic change and less on direct government action in restructuring organizations and providing new incentives. Although this represented a real change of emphasis, it also reflected a natural movement from one stage of reform to another. Reform during the 1980s had introduced markets and incentives alongside the plan. But by the 1990s the nonplanned parts of the economy had been growing for a decade, while the planned parts of the economy remained constant, or even shrank. The result was that the economy had "grown out of the plan." It was now necessary to create a "level playing field" and reduce some of the most obvious distortions in the economy. As regulatory reforms proceeded, they led to a greatly enhanced emphasis on restructuring state enterprises. Restructuring meant converting state-owned firms into corporations with explicit, legally defined ownership, exercised by boards of directors representing owner-ship stakes. Over a thousand of the largest state firms were listed on the stock market, with minority shares of their equity sold to private parties. Tens of thousands of smaller state firms were privatized, sold off either to other firms (including private businesses), or to their own managers and workers.

Enterprise restructuring was coordinated with regulatory reforms that envisaged the creation of a legal framework that allows market forces to work. Such reforms were in harmony with the macroeconomic policies adopted. Regulatory reforms and the new macroeconomic policies both stressed the need to adhere to tough, objective rules; moreover, macroeconomic austerity made market conditions more difficult and thus tended to strengthen market discipline. Public enterprises—which had been used to support from the government and the state-run banks—suddenly found themselves caught between a demanding marketplace and less sympathetic government policies. Public firms that had always been able to sell their output suddenly found that they were competing much more intensely with other firms, including TVEs and foreign-invested firms, in an environment where downward pressure on prices was squeezing profit margins. The external environment increased the pressure on firms to restructure and on local governments to privatize those firms which they had previously owned and run.

Regulatory reforms have been promulgated in nearly every area of the economy. The most important were the foreign trade reforms of 1994, the fiscal and tax reform of 1994, and a number of important financial regulations covering banks (1995) and equity markets (1996–1997). The foreign trade reforms—particularly the devaluation and unification of the exchange rate on January 1, 1994—quickly brought about impressive results. China's exports surged, and China began to run a sustained trade surplus. The fiscal reform was an especially important turning point. As mentioned earlier, China's fiscal position had eroded significantly through fifteen years of reform. Government tax revenues slid, dropping from 35.8 percent of GDP in 1978 to only 11.2 percent at their low point in 1995. Fiscal decline was a logical result of an economic transition strategy that stressed decentralization of authority and benefits, and releasing resources from government control to the marketplace, but by the early 1990s, it was widely perceived that China had a serious fiscal crisis. Fiscal reforms in 1994 were designed to arrest this slide, by introducing new taxes, such as the value-added tax, which had relatively low rates, but applied them uniformly to all economic actors. Reforms took time to take effect, but fiscal revenues began to recover and by 2001 exceeded 17 percent of GDP. The change is highly significant because it represents a change in direction of a powerful, long-standing trend. In both banking and fiscal areas, the Zhu Rongji policies are associated with a stronger, more authoritative set of institutions.

The shift in transition strategy around 1992–1993 means that China's approach to transition is now somewhat less distinctive than it was previously. Economic policymaking in China now more closely resembles that in other transitional economies, such as Poland and the Czech Republic, and there is no longer a polar opposition between "big bang" and "gradualist" transitions. Both groups now focus on maintaining stable and consistent fiscal and financial policies and sound macroeconomic policies. Both groups focus on building a regulatory environment that can reduce corruption, support an advanced market economy, and protect fair and equal competition. The qualitative responses to the challenges of transition are now more similar.

In November 2001 China became a member of the World Trade Organization (WTO). Membership will create a whole new set of obligations for China to open its economy and lower trade barriers. Crucially, the agreement obligates China to permit greater access by foreign companies to a whole range of domestic sectors, particularly those involved in wholesale trade and distribution and services such as banking and telecommunications. These obligations typically phase in during a transition period of up to three to five years. They will create tremendous new opportunities but also new competitive challenges. WTO membership will also strain to the limit China's ability to provide fair and transparent administrative and regulatory resources that encompass both Chinese citizens and foreigners. At the same time, membership will lock in many of the most important reform commitments China has already made. It symbolizes a commitment to complete China's transition to a market economy.

The Third Transition: Towards an Information Society

During the 1990s, while the first and second transitions were still under way, China began the first tentative steps of a third transition, to an information economy. China has emerged as a major participant in the emerging global information economy. As an equipment manufacturer, it is an important presence in the computer and telecommunications industries. Foreign-invested firms do the majority of equipment manufacturing, and virtually all the exports from China are produced in foreign-owned firms, but domestic Chinese companies are coming up quickly in the field of electronics manufacturing. As a producer, China is being integrated into global production chains that cross national boundaries.

More importantly, the Internet and the telecommunications revolution have come to China. One sign of this change is the rapid spread of mobile telephones. China's fixed line telephone system is fairly typical for a less developed country, with only about ten telephones per hundred people, although the number is growing rapidly. However, mobile telephones have spread extremely rapidly through China in recent years. In 2001 the number of mobile telephone subscribers in China surpassed 100 million. China is now the second largest mobile telephone market in the world, after the United States. Sections of Chinese society have skipped a step in what used to be the regular pattern of development of telecommunications. Unable to obtain fixed-line telephone service in a timely fashion, consumers have simply jumped to the next stage in telecommunications service, and rely on their mobile phones.

The Internet has also become an important source of information and entertainment in China. While the total number of Internet users is not as impressive as the total of mobile telephone users, the Internet has nonetheless already emerged as an important source of information for young, well-educated urban dwellers. The Chinese government has aggressively developed websites with attractive layout and abundant content to try to attract Internet users and maintain its dominance over information flows within the society. At the same time, the government censors Internet content, both by blocking access to many websites and by demanding that authorized websites take responsibility for all postings. Despite these restrictions, the availability of information on the Internet clearly surpasses that available through other media, and Internet access is changing the nature of Chinese society, at least certain strata of that society. As in other countries, it remains to be seen exactly how the Internet will affect economic relations. While its potential impact is obvious, the appropriate business models for Internet commerce have so far remained elusive.

A China that is "wired" to the Internet, and in which robust networks of wireless communication thrive as well, will clearly experience economic development that differs from past patterns. At one extreme is the possibility that China will emerge in the next decade or two as one of the first "low wage, high tech" economies. China and India, because of their size and the sophistication of some segments of their work forces, will have a global impact in information technology industries that may be unprecedented for countries with still moderate average income levels.

Current Challenges

Despite rapid growth and institutional change over more than twenty years of reform, China continues to face serious economic challenges. Chinese policymakers used the first phase of market transition very effectively to build support for further reforms. As mentioned above, reform in the 1980s was a kind of "reform without losers," making some better off without significantly harming any major group. In a sense Chinese policymakers deferred difficult and costly measures as long as possible, but took the benefits of new kinds of producers and organizations as early as possible. This was a good strategy, but logically it cannot continue indefinitely. By creating a tough new set of rules that were to apply to all, policymakers were guaranteeing that a group of "losers" would be created, particularly among inefficient state-owned enterprises. Moreover, in agreeing to further market-opening measures—most crucially China's entry into the World Trade Organization—China's leaders have acquiesced in a process of increasing competition. As market competition intensifies, it will inevitably create an additional group of firms and workers who are unable to make the necessary adaptations. China's transition is no longer a reform without losers. State enterprise workers have most dramatically lost ground since the second half of the 1990s. Millions have been laid off and further millions have abandoned failing firms. Laid-off workers have experienced sharp reductions in their standard of living, notwithstanding various government programs that cushion the initial impact of unemployment. These workers have real grievances, based on their personal histories and their previous, relatively privileged position. This suggests a future for the Chinese transition process that may be somewhat more troubled than its past. As society experiences greater differentiation between beneficiaries and losers, the consensus in favor of reform and liberalization may become more difficult to sustain. Already, unemployment has grown, and it is undoubtedly becoming chronic. Hundreds of thousands of firms—under intensified market competition—have decided they can produce with far fewer workers and make greater profits if they do so. With this ongoing restructuring, demand for workers in urban areas is likely to be restrained for years.

One very important indirect effect of this phase of economic change is the impact on rural areas from changes in urban areas. China's rural areas, despite their rapid economic growth in the early 1980s, are still overly populated and capable of releasing millions of surplus workers to the urban economy. Indeed, during the mid-1990s, many millions of migrants left rural areas and came to work in the city. Large-scale migration is often viewed simply as a problem, and it is common to read about the potential problems created by China's "floating population." But this way of looking at the phenomenon is highly misleading. Migration needs to be seen as an enormous opportunity for many—and perhaps most—migrants (reading 36). Migration is one of the most effective ways for poor farmers to increase their income and move into the more dynamic sectors of the economy. Migrants not only increase their own income and contribute to the urbanization and development of the cities to which they migrate, they also contribute to the development of their home villages by returning with money, business skills, and new ideas which help break the cycles of poverty.

One of the greatest challenges to China's economy today is that migration is not large enough. With urban labor demand reduced by the lay-off of millions of workers from state firms, migrants became less confident at the end of the 1990s that they would find jobs in the cities. The pace of migration has therefore slowed somewhat.

At the same time the rural economy has been troubled by other factors that make for a more pessimistic outlook in the countryside. Since 1996 farm prices have been low in China and indeed worldwide. Simply put, there is quite a lot of food in the world, and prices have been declining over the long term. While this is good news for those worrying about global food security, it is often bad news for farmers, whose income suffers. In China's countryside, low and stagnant farmer incomes have been exacerbated by another, related problem. When the agricultural collectives were dissolved in the early to mid-1980s, there was no immediate institutional replacement to carry out their former functions. Local governments took over some of the tasks, but in order to fund these activities, they imposed a range of informal fees and taxes on farmers. Over the years, these fees have tended to grow, and, of course, some unscrupulous local officials have used the fees to enrich themselves. As a result, many farmers in China today find themselves with low incomes that are not increasing, with heavy and difficult-to-monitor fees and taxes, and with relatively few opportunities to move away and start a new career and life in the cities. This slowing pace of change in China's villages is one of the greatest challenges facing the Chinese economy today.

China's financial system still faces enormous challenges. Zhang clearly elucidates the foundation of the problem (reading 37). State banks for years made loans to state-owned enterprises, which were reformed, but not enough to bring their financial and corporate governance structures into conformance. The result is a severely weakened financial system and a huge burden of bad loans on the banking system. Increasing competitive pressures have forced many state firms into bankruptcy, frequently accompanied by default on their bank loans. A large proportion of bank loans are estimated to be "nonperforming," which suggests that banks may face a serious crisis of insolvency. At the worst, this may lead to a financial crisis, but even in the best scenario, the government will have to inject large sums of public money into the ailing banks.

As a member of the World Trade Organization, China will take on a whole new set of obligations to open its economy, lower trade barriers, and permit greater access to the domestic economy by foreign companies. Lower trade barriers will challenge China's agriculture to compete with grain imports from countries with abundant farmland. Industries will face unprecedented pressure to restructure and improve efficiency. In the short run, unemployment will rise as businesses adjust to the new competitive environment. At the same time, WTO membership will help guarantee continued access to developed country markets for China's exports, and expanded access for textile and garment exports. In the long run, entry by foreign firms will mean greater productivity in China's service sectors—including finance, trade, shipping, logistics and insurance—which will in turn improve China's competitiveness in world markets. WTO membership will increase the demand within China for impartial regulation and administrative services for the benefit of both foreigners and Chinese citizens.

Conclusion

China's economy at the beginning of the millennium presents a striking picture of dynamism and uncertainty. The rapid pace of change and the speed of economic development over the past decade certainly suggest that optimism for future prospects is well founded. At the same time, the breadth of change, the stunning fact that so much of the structure and institutional make-up of the economy is changing, suggests that potential for further development are still great. This is the primary message of the triple transition that China is undergoing. With new sectors emerging daily from the urbanization, marketization, and technological transformation of the economy, there is every reason to believe that the economy will continue to develop new sources of growth and new areas of competitive advantage. This should permit the economy to overcome the serious challenges it faces.

At the same time China faces serious challenges due to the underdeveloped capacity of the institutions that govern the economy. In part, this is because China is still a relatively poor, developing economy; in part, it is due to the still incomplete nature of its transition to a market economy. This institutional weakness will probably be overcome, but if it is not, it could lead the economy into a very difficult stretch. The enormous complexity and interest of the Chinese economy comes from these still incomplete processes, and the multiple ways in which the different processes of transformation interact with each other.

ECONOMY
Readings

33

China 2020:
Understanding the Present

THE WORLD BANK

This is the introductory chapter to a comprehensive report on China's economy produced by the World Bank in 1997. The report, which includes six sectoral reports and a summary volume, examines the forces that will shape China's economy through the year 2020. The chapter lays out the basic forces behind China's rapid growth in the last two decades of the twentieth century and projects them into the future. It provides an excellent overview of China's high-growth economy

China is in the midst of two historic transitions: from a rural, agricultural society to an urban, industrial one and from a command economy to a market-based one. The first transition would be unremarkable were it not for China's vast size, its past control of urbanization, and the unprecedented speed of its industrialization. Its population easily exceeds the combined total of Latin America and Sub-Saharan Africa, and its industrial growth is nearly an order of magnitude greater. Its transition to a market economy has also been unique, with a combination of experimentation and incremental reforms leading to rapid progress in some areas and slow progress elsewhere.

The interplay and synergy between these two transitions have sparked rapid growth. The Chinese economy expanded more than fourfold in the past fifteen years. Between 1978 and 1995 real GDP per capita grew at the blistering rate of 8 percent a year and lifted 200 million Chinese out of absolute poverty. Economic reforms, begun in 1978, have advanced China's integration with the world economy, maintained a strong external payments position, essentially privatized farming, liberalized markets for many goods and services, intensified competition in industry, and introduced modern macroeconomic management.

At the same time, the confluence of these two transitions has generated powerful vortices and cross-currents that are potentially destabilizing and always difficult to predict. Transition from command to market alone can be treacherous: witness the period of economic collapse in Eastern Europe and the former Soviet Union. Similarly, transition from a rural, agricultural society to an urban, industrial one also carries many risks. In the rich industrial economies this transition took centuries. In China the process is being telescoped into one or two generations.

So it is hardly surprising that China's rapid growth and structural change, while resolving many problems, have also given rise to new challenges: periods of macroeconomic instability stemming from partially complete reforms; increased employment and income insecurity; mounting environmental pressures, especially in urban areas; rising costs of food self-sufficiency; growing inequality and stubborn poverty levels; and a prickly, occasionally hostile world environment. These are formidable challenges. Unmet, they could undermine the sustainability of growth, and China's promise could fade.

This report argues, however, that China has the capacity to meet these challenges. While the difficulties ahead should not be underestimated, neither should China's strengths—relative stability, a remarkably high savings rate, a strong track record of pragmatic reforms, a supportive Chinese diaspora, and a growing administrative capacity. These strengths have driven China's impressive growth in the last two decades of the twentieth century. They will be equally necessary for rapid, sustainable growth in the first two decades of the next. To improve China's chances of success, these strengths will need to be supplemented by three other factors: skilled economic management, a supportive world economy, and domestic social stability.

Swift Growth

Measuring China's GDP growth is tricky. Official statistics show that per capita GDP growth averaged 8 percent a year between 1978 and 1995; other estimates suggest growth of 6–7 percent. Still, whatever the precise figure, China's growth has been almost unprecedented: only the Republic of Korea and Taiwan, China, have grown at comparable rates.

China's growth since 1978 is also outstanding in historical perspective. Performance during the nineteenth century and the first half of the twentieth century could hardly have been more disappointing: the country registered no improvements in living standards between 1820 and 1870 and only modest growth over the next three decades. During the tumultuous first half of this century per capita incomes actually fell as China saw the collapse of a 3,000-year-old imperial tradition, weathered a period of anarchy and warlordism, and survived foreign occupation and civil war. The rest of the world, though, managed respectable growth rates during this period despite the upheaval of two world wars. As a result, China's share in global GDP fell from a high of 30 percent in 1820—the largest economy in the world at the time—to barely 7 percent in 1950.

Since then China has been recovering some of this lost ground. Postwar recovery under communist rule saw a resumption in growth, although the Great Leap Forward and the Cultural Revolution caused considerable economic disruption and waste. By 1978, when China took its first tentative steps toward reforms, it remained a desperately poor, rural, and agricultural economy. Sixty percent of China's 1 billion citizens survived on less than $1 a day, the international poverty standard.

The rest, as they say, is history. The introduction of agricultural reforms was the first sprinkling that rejuvenated the parched economy, launching a growth process that has transformed the face of China. The torrid growth rate set over the next seventeen years helped the Chinese double their per capita income every ten years, faster than almost any country in recent history.

Three features of China's rapid growth are especially noteworthy. The first is its regional dimension. Despite concerns about regional disparities, the benefits of growth have been widely shared among China's country-size provincial economies. Although the coastal provinces grew faster than average at 9.7 percent a year, the other provinces also fared well. Indeed, if China's thirty provinces were counted as individual economies, the twenty fastest-growing economies in the world between 1978 and 1995 would have been Chinese.

The second notable feature is the sharp cyclical pattern of economic growth. Although the ups and downs of China's post reform business cycles pale in comparison with the wild swings in GDP growth seen during the Great Leap Forward and the Cultural Revolution, they nevertheless have been wide enough to concern policymakers. These growth cycles have been accompanied by similar fluctuations in the rate of inflation, revealing fault lines in macroeconomic management stemming from partially completed reforms in the fiscal, enterprise, and banking systems.

The third noteworthy feature of China's growth since 1978 is its reliance on productivity growth. Relative to other rapidly growing Asian economies, China's growth has been less dependent on volume increases in inputs of capital and labor. Consider, for example, growth in the stock of physical capital. In most countries growth in capital input exceeds GDP growth, often by a substantial margin. In China the reverse occurred, suggesting that factors other than capital accumulation have been important determinants of GDP growth.

In fact, a conventional technique to account for the sources of growth in China reveals that growth in capital inputs explains just 37 percent of growth. Another 17 percent can be attributed to improvements in the quantity and quality of the labor force. Thus nearly half of China's GDP growth—4.3 percentage points a year—is due to other factors. Data deficiencies . . . can reduce the absolute size of this residual component of growth slightly, as can differing methodological assumptions. But even after these adjustments, the fact remains that China's growth has come from much more than the mere accumulation of factors of production.

China's remarkably rapid growth since 1978 has been driven by four factors:

• A high savings rate, which has supported vigorous rates of investment and capital accumulation.

• Structural change, which has been both a cause and an effect of growth.

• Pragmatic reforms, which were well suited to China's unusual circumstances and enjoyed broad support.

• Economic conditions in 1978, which were especially receptive to reform; China's economy could be described as a dry prairie, parched by years of planning, awaiting the first sprinklings of market reform.

Each of these factors is considered in turn.

High Savings

The most striking feature of China's remarkable performance since 1978 is its savings rate. Savings, as much as growth, is China's real economic miracle. According to official statistics, China's savings rate averaged 37 percent of GDP between 1978 and 1995, although more conservative estimates place it at 33–34 percent. Even so, this rate is among the highest in the world.

No less important, the savings rate was remarkably stable, even as reforms and structural change were reshaping the economy. Contrast this with the collapse of savings in the transition economies of Eastern Europe and the former Soviet Union. In fact, the stability of the high savings rate was one of the primary successes of the reform path chosen by the Chinese.

Although China's savings performance sets it apart from other transition economies, it fits more comfortably in the mold of other dynamic Asian economies. All had rapidly rising savings rates in the periods immediately following takeoff, contributing to virtuous circles of high growth and high savings. China appears to be following this pattern, although its extremely high savings rate at a very low income level makes it an exception even within this select group.

What accounts for China's high savings rates? Under central planning high savings rates were engineered through the plan. Agricultural and raw material prices were kept artificially low and final goods prices artificially high. This concentrated profits in state enterprises, which invested them under the direction of the central and local planning apparatus. Between 1965 and 1978 savings remained at 33 percent of GDP, and investment strongly favored heavy industry. Household savings were of little importance, averaging just 1 percent of GDP.

Since reforms began in 1978, however, the roles of enterprises and households have been reversed. The household savings rate exploded from about 1 percent before reforms to 21 percent since then. Households now contribute half of total savings.

Why are Chinese households so thrifty? No single explanation seems adequate. Certainly, for many Chinese, rising incomes have brought an end to subsistence consumption. Rising incomes have also been accompanied by rising aspirations, as households set their sights on buying their own house or apartment, acquiring previously unavailable consumer durables, and giving their children a better education. Since households could not borrow much to finance these purchases, they saved more instead.

Another factor is China's changing demographics. Life expectancy today is ten years longer than it was in 1970, and it continues to rise. A typical Chinese baby can now look forward to living for more than seventy, years. Because city dwellers retire at fifty-five, they have strong incentives to save for their retirement, especially when they know that pension benefits may be inadequate. Furthermore, declining fertility has reduced the traditional form of support in old age—children.

Finally, institutional factors have also helped boost household savings. Of these, two stand out: the implicit public guarantee of deposits in the banking system and the proliferation of new ways to invest in China's fledgling securities markets.

Structural Change

With swift growth came rapid structural change. In this respect China followed the path of many other countries. Where China differed was in the pace of change: it compressed into a few years a process that has normally taken several decades. Consider employment patterns. In the eighteen years since 1978, agriculture's share of the workforce dropped from 71 percent to about 50 percent. It took the United States fifty years and Japan sixty years to achieve a similar structural shift.

"Push" and "pull" factors accelerated the flow of labor out of agriculture. Low incomes from farming and widespread poverty in rural areas encouraged farmers and their families to leave. At the same time, the demand for labor increased sharply in industry and services—especially among collectively owned enterprises-that had achieved rapid productivity growth.

The shift out of agriculture did not mean massive migration to cities. Cities' share of the population increased from 18 percent in 1978 to just 29 percent in 1995 (Box 4.1). Compared with the period before reform, however, urbanization was rapid. Between 1957 and 1978, when official policy discouraged urbanization, the share of the population living in urban areas climbed only three percentage points, from 15 to 18 percent.

The drift away from agriculture also facilitated a transformation in patterns of ownership, especially in industry. The first wave of industrialization took place after the establishment of the People's Republic and was concentrated in state enterprises. Since 1978, however, these enterprises have grown relatively slowly, so their share in aggregate output and employment has been falling swiftly. The second wave of industrial growth was in collectively owned and township and village enterprises. In the past few years a third wave of industrialization has been building: mostly privately and individually owned enterprises, supplemented by joint ventures and foreign-funded enterprises.

Box 4.1
HOW URBANIZED IS CHINA?

Despite the recent expansion of cities and towns, China's urban population—29 percent of the total, according to official statistics—is still below the 35 percent norm for countries with similar per capita incomes (calculated on a purchasing power parity basis). But China's urban population statistics are based on administratively defined boundaries, some of which include low population-density areas engaged in farming. At the same time, large tracts of coastal China's so-called rural areas are developing a new, dispersed pattern of urbanization. In three regions— the Pearl River delta, the lower Yangtze, and the Beijing-Tianjin-Tangshan metropolitan areas—industrial and commercial activities are transforming the landscape, forming urban and periurban corridors linking core cities. If regions with high population densities are considered urban areas, China's level of urbanization could be as high as 50 percent, significantly above that of the typical low-income country.

If anything, the size of the private sector is larger than official statistics suggest. Many private firms have reason to underreport their production and employment. Moreover, many collectively owned enterprises function as private enterprises in virtually every respect but find it convenient to operate under the banner of townships or villages—a practice known as "wearing the red cap." Doing so may help the enterprises obtain access to credit or licenses and avoid social or political stigmas that may still cling to private activity in China.

Structural change has given an extra boost to China's growth over the past eighteen years. Since a large portion of the agricultural labor force was underemployed, productivity leaped as workers moved from low-productivity agriculture to more productive employment in industry and services. Between 1978 and 1995 this process contributed about one percentage point a year to GDP growth. The changing pattern of ownership also contributed about 0.5 percentage point a year to growth, as employment shifted to the collective and private sectors, where productivity was higher.

The process of structural change varied across provinces, exacerbating interprovincial and especially rural-urban income differences. In provinces that industrialized faster, higher wages in urban and periurban areas opened a growing gap between urban and rural workers. Restrictions on rural-urban migra-tion helped maintain this gap, which was responsible for much of the sharp increase in income inequality over the past decade. Today urban incomes are as much as four times rural incomes, once subsidies enjoyed by urban residents are taken into account. Such rural-urban gaps are very high by international stan-dards. Evidence from thirty-six countries shows that the ratio of urban to rural incomes tends to be below 1.5 and rarely exceeds 2.0. In China the gulf between rural and urban residents explains 60 percent of overall income inequality. In contrast, regional income disparities have contributed relatively little to inequality.

Still, China is more egalitarian than most countries in Africa, Latin America, and even East Asia. But China's steep rise in inequality is exceptional in international perspective. In the early 1980s China's income inequality was well below average in a sample of forty countries for which data are available. By the 1990s it was above average.

Pragmatic and Incremental Reforms

China's economic reforms in 1978 were triggered by neither economic crisis nor ideological epiphany. The country had endured much hardship over the previous two decades, with the start of the Great Leap Forward and through the Cultural Revolution. Against this tumultuous backdrop the years leading up to 1978 were relatively tranquil.

The Chinese leadership was, therefore, eager to see improvements in living standards but had no appetite for dramatic changes in policy. Growth was important, but not at the expense of stability. The concern with growth initially focused on restoring incentives for agricultural production but soon broadened to encourage investment by firms, households, and local governments. These measures were introduced incrementally and involved decentralizing authority over capital spending. A favored approach was for the central authorities to experiment with new policies in selected provinces, prefectures, counties, and even firms. If the experiments worked, they were quickly replicated. If they did not, the costs of failure tended to be contained and limited. Reforms were occasionally reversed if the government believed that growth was not being served or stability was being jeopardized.

Pragmatism and incrementalism were also behind the government's evolving objectives. When the reforms began in 1978, it is not clear whether the authorities had reached a consensus on any final objectives other than high growth. New reform objectives emerged as old ones were achieved. In the first few years of reform the objectives were modest. With success, they became more ambitious. In 1979, for example, the government called for the development of "a planned economy supplemented by market regulation." By 1993 the goal had matured to the creation of a "socialist market economy with Chinese characteristics."

34

Is a Rich Man Happier than a Free Man?

CHENG LI

This selection provides a vivid and penetrating look at the development of township and village enterprises in a showcase village in the Yangzi delta region. It shows how successful businesses have grown out of the institutions of the socialist era, and how this growth has benefited virtually everybody in the village. At the same time, it shows that a few charismatic individuals have been able to dominate the growth process. The result has been the emergence of a corporate village that, in this case, is controlled by members of a single family.

The Richest Village in China

Huaxi village is located about 300 kilometers northwest of Shanghai. Huaxi occupies an area of 0.96 square kilometers, including about 600 *mu* of arable land. There are altogether 320 households and 1,475 residents, including 918 laborers, in the village. In recent years, the village has absorbed over 3,000 migrant laborers from neighboring counties or provinces.

Such a small village, of course, does not find its way onto the general map of Jiangsu Province, let alone the map of China. But Huaxi has recently received nationwide recognition and has been considered a model for China's rural development. During the past few years Huaxi has frequently appeared on the cover of many magazines in China, such as *Beijing Review* and *Rural World*. Top leaders of the country, Premier Li Peng, for example, visited the village in 1992. Li even wrote an endorsement for local officials, describing Huaxi village as "the place where the hope of rural China lies." Since the late 1980s, Huaxi has attracted thousands of visitors, both from within China and abroad. Many people came to study what has made this small town soar economically in such a short time.

What has made Huaxi village nationally famous is its rapid economic growth in the 1980s and 1990s. When it was founded in 1961, the village owned only 25,000 yuan collectively. But in 1992 Huaxi had amassed 230 million yuan of fixed collective assets, more than $40,000 per person, about 9,000 times the

1961 figure. The total industrial and agricultural output value of Huaxi in 1992 was 516 million yuan, 85 times that of 1982.

The living standard of the Huaxi people has improved dramatically in recent years. In 1993, average household savings were 87,500 yuan ($15,350) and per capita household fixed assets were 720,000 yuan ($126, 000). In 1994, the average output value per person was 1 million yuan and the portion of village revenue paid to the state per person on average was $10,000. Not surprisingly, officials in Huaxi have claimed that their village is the richest village in the country.

In both rural and urban areas of China today, a minuscule number of people own private cars. But in Huaxi, about 80 percent of families own Volkswagen Jettas, which each cost 175,000 yuan ($30,700). For Chinese workers whose annual individual salary was 3,000 yuan on average in 1993, 175,000 yuan is an astronomical amount.

"This is one of the most exciting events ever in our village," a village official told a Chinese reporter when the first 50 new Volkswagen Jettas, out of a total of 250 Jettas ordered, were delivered from a Changchun-based automobile factory to Huaxi. This event was widely publicized in the Chinese media. When I visited some homes in the village, I noticed many of the families cherished a photo showing these just-arrived Jettas, all the same red color, lined up in orderly fashion along the village square.

Villagers in Huaxi were also very enthusiastic about showing visitors their newly built homes. The previous single-story thatched-roof houses have all been replaced. About 80 percent of the families of Huaxi now live in three-floor, nine-room houses, all with kitchens, several bathrooms, garages, and balconies. Per capita living space in Huaxi is 35 square meters. . . .

Wu Renbao: "Huaxi's Lee Kuan Yew"

. . . Wu Renbao has been the "boss"—the Party secretary in Huaxi—since 1961, when the village administration was established. He is now concurrently general manager of the Huaxi Industrial Corporation (HIC), which handles all industrial, agricultural, and commercial affairs in the village.

A native of Huaxi, Wu Renbao was born to a peasant family in 1929. His father also worked as a cobbler when the farm work was not too heavy. At the age of seven, Wu Renbao started to help his parents in the field. With financial support from his relatives, Wu studied in an old-style private school for a couple of years. Because of his father's illness, Wu Renbao had to quit school and work as a migrant laborer in Wuxi. Later, he married a Huaxi girl who worked in a textile factory in Wuxi.

After the Communist victory in 1949, Wu returned to Huaxi, where he served as captain of the militia and head of the co-op, a Chinese commune organization. He joined the Chinese Communist Party in 1957. He was the first secretary of the Huaxi co-op (the predecessor of the village) and has held that post ever since. The Party Committee of Huaxi has five branches, with a total of 137 Party members. They account for 15 percent of the labor force in the village. Under Wu's leadership, Huaxi was known nationally during the early 1970s for its steady high grain yield. During the Mao era, Wu was selected as a deputy to the 10th National Party Congress. From 1975 to 1981, Wu served as Party secretary of Jiangyin County. He earned the title "National Model Worker" in 1989. During the recent National Conference of Rural Industries, Wu was selected as one of the top 10 heroes of township and village enterprises in the country. Now he is a deputy member of the People's Congress of China.

Although Wu is already in his late 60s, he does not intend to step down in the foreseeable future. In his recent talk at Qinghua University, he told the audience that he will not retire until he is 80. This seems highly possible, because in Huaxi no one can challenge Wu's authority.

Wu has four sons and a daughter. All of his sons and his son-in-law hold important leadership positions in the village. Just as Lee Hsien Loong, Lee Kuan Yew's son and currently the first deputy minister of Singapore, is expected to be the top leader of the country in the near future, Wu's oldest son, Wu Xiedong, currently the first deputy Party secretary of Huaxi and deputy general manager of the Huaxi Industrial Corporation, is a designated successor to Wu Renbao.

Wu's second son, Wu Xiede, also deputy general manager of the Huaxi Industrial Corporation, once headed the Huayuan Guest House, a 150-room hotel in Beijing run by the HIC. He is now general manager of Huahong Pipe Fittings Limited Company, a joint venture with Hong Kong. The third son, Wu Xieping, is general manager of Nanyuan Hotel, a high-grade 150-room hotel located in Huaxi. The fourth son, Wu Xie'en, a demobilized soldier, was in charge of industrial production supply in the village for a number of years. Now he is director of Huaxi Aluminum Products Factory. Wu Renbao's son-in-law, Miao Hongda, is deputy executive general manager of the Huaxi Industrial Corporation.

Wu Renbao and his "princes" are in firm control of political and economic power in Huaxi. Two sons and a son-in-law have occupied top leadership posts in both the Party Committee of the village and the executive committee of the Huaxi Industrial Corporation. Huaxi, in a way, can be identified as "Wu's family kingdom."

The phenomenon of strong family ties and nepotism is quite common in China's rural industries. In a recent article published by Township and Village Enterprises of Southern Jiangsu, an author used the term "power circle of relatives and friends" to describe the prevalence of nepotism in Jiangsu's TVEs. According to the author, this power circle has destroyed the incentives of a majority of workers in the enterprises and has not been conducive to the effort to fight against corruption. This phenomenon also raises the question of who really owns township and village enterprises. Many enterprises in Sunan claim to be collectives, but they are actually owned by directors of the firms, who are usually members of the same family.

Officials in Huaxi usually receive a large amount of money as bonuses because the village adopted a contract system for the distribution of profits in 1987. According to this contract system, 20 percent of the profits of an enterprise go to the Huaxi Industrial Corporation while the other 80 percent are distributed within the enterprises in a ratio of 1:3:3:3. this means that 10 percent of the remaining profits go to the director of the enterprise, 30 percent to other managers and technicians, 30 percent to workers, and the other 30 percent are saved as enterprise assets. In 1989, some directors of Huaxi received over 100,000 yuan as an annual bonus.

Wu Renbao once told the Chinese media that he was not, and would not be, the wealthiest person in the village. His salary was not the highest in the village. He claimed that he and his wife were among the last group of people in Huaxi who moved into new houses. But in 1994, a delegation of Hong Kong journalists visited the house of Wu Xieping, Wu's third son. They were surprised to find what a luxurious life his son lived. The dining room of Wu Xieping's house, where they had lunch, could accommodate five banquet tables with seats for over 60 people. According to Hong Kong journalists, the house was much better than the houses of the middle class in Hong Kong and Singapore.

I did not have a chance to interview Wu or any of his sons because they were all out of the village during my visit. Instead, I asked the villagers I met what they thought of Wu Renbao.

"He is great," a 50-year-old woman villager replied. "He has brought all these changes to our village."

"How?" I asked.

The woman did not answer my question right away, but instead looked at me for a while, making me feel that I had asked an absolutely dumb question, or the answer was too obvious for her to address.

Eventually she broke the silence. "You could not imagine how poor we were 30 years ago, or even 20 years ago."

"But Wu Renbao was also the 'boss' in Huaxi 20 or 30 years ago, wasn't he?" I asked.

"That's true," the woman answered, "but anyway, he was the leader who led us out of poverty in Huaxi."

Most people with whom I chatted in Huaxi seemed to share her view about Wu and other village officials. The satirical attitude toward officials and the resentment over corruption, which I had heard so many times in other parts of China, seemed not to exist in Huaxi. It occurred to me that corruption might not be a serious problem in Huaxi, just as it is not in Singapore. In addition, the dramatic improvement in the life of villagers over the past decade has been credited to local officials.

"When I was young, my entire family was crowded into one room, Hu Fenghu, a 54-year-old accountant at the village's steel strip factory, said to a Chinese reporter. "The annual individual income in Huaxi in the late 1960s and early 1970s was less than 100 yuan. We did not have enough grain and during those days we had to wear shoes made of straw."

But now his family lives in a three-story house with 400 square meters of living space. The house has modern facilities such as a telephone, air conditioner, washing machine, refrigerator, and hot water heater. His wife, son, and daughter-in-law all work in Huaxi's village enterprises. The family's annual income surpassed 70,000 yuan in 1994. His two grandsons attend the village kindergarten for free.

"Wu Renbao has required officials, at both village and enterprise levels, to follow two important guidelines," a 30-year-old factory director in Huaxi told me. "They are: one, 'to keep our hands clean' and two, 'to know our jobs well.'"

"Yes, I do receive 10 percent of the profits as a bonus," the director explained to me, "but according to our village's regulation, I must deposit the bonus in my account in the enterprise. The money will be reinvested. This means that the growth of the enterprise is as important as our personal development. We aim at collective prosperity rather than just individual wealth." . . .

From Huaxi Village to "Huaxi Inc."

The most impressive "job" that village officials have accomplished is, of course, the rapid development of rural industries in Huaxi. . . . [A] majority of people in the huge rural part of Sunan have experienced a fundamental change— an occupational change—in their lives during the past decade. Because of the rural industrial revolution, rural Sunan has become quite a diversified reality. Huaxi, like many other villages in the area, is no longer a traditional, agriculture-oriented village.

Laborers in the village are no longer necessarily peasants. As a matter of fact, 97 percent of the labor force in the village consists of nonagricultural workers. The percentage of Huaxi's agricultural output of the total declined from 23.1 percent in 1975 to 0.3 percent in 1989, and the industrial output increased from 50.4 percent in 1975 to 99.1 percent in 1989.

Only seven people, 0.8 percent of the total labor force in the village, are engaged in agricultural work. Huaxi has three characteristics of modern agriculture: (1) specialized production, (2) mechanized cultivation, and (3) merchandised grain. Although only seven people work on the farm, the total grain output has continuously surpassed 500,000 kilograms for nine years. During the harvest season, however, all the people in the village are available to help with farm work.

The village administration seems to understand the importance of grain production in a time of rural industrialization. The village has declared over 600 *mu* of grain fields a "protective agricultural area," which cannot be used for any nonagricultural purpose. In addition, 18 villagers in Huaxi, 2 percent of the total labor force, are engaged in sideline production. They have formed four groups, and each group specializes in vegetable planting, fish raising, domestic animal raising, or fowl raising.

The other 97 percent of the laborers work in industrial and commercial sectors. There are forty factories in Huaxi, among which five are joint ventures and ten state-collective affiliated enterprises. Their products include textiles, wool sweaters, metals, chemicals, aluminum goods, copper products, plastic decorating board, steel pipes and strips, and metal flange. These products are sold to almost all provinces in China and to twelve countries.

All these factories are under the administration of the Huaxi Industrial Corporation that Wu Renbao heads. Leading officials of the village are concurrently executive managers of the Huaxi Industrial Corporation. It seems appropriate to say that Huaxi village has now become "Huaxi Inc."

Huaxi did not have any industry until the early 1970s, when twenty villagers with a total of 6,000 yuan in capital established a hardware factory, which mainly repaired agricultural machinery. Village officials supported this experiment at the risk of being criticized for "taking the capitalist road." The factory made profits of 50,000 yuan in the first year and then more than 200,000 yuan annually in the following years. This experiment brought in both capital for further development and confidence in the industrial development of the village.

In the 1980s, the village not only set up many more factories, but also was engaged in a number of horizontal joint ventures with Shanghai, Beijing, and other regions. Huaxi Copper Products factory, Huaxi Aluminum Products factory, and Huaxi Cold-Rolled Belts steel plant, which were founded in 1985, 1986, and 1987, respectively, have had joint ventures with Shanghai factories. Huaxi Copper Products factory had an output value of 24 million yuan in the late 1980s. Joint ventures with foreign companies also emerged in Huaxi during the 1980s. Hua'an Flange Limited, which has an annual output of 5,000 tons of flange, is a joint venture with a hardware company in Singapore.

Since the beginning of the 1990s, Huaxi officials have made efforts to enlarge the size of village enterprises and have moved toward group consolidation on an extensive scale. For example, Shenhua Wire Rod factory, a steel-wire rod plant with a total investment of 60 million yuan and an annual capacity of 300,000 tons of wire rod, the largest wire rod factory in east China, was founded in 1993. More rural industries have taken an export-oriented approach. One enterprise in Huaxi has even established a branch company in Singapore.

Huaxi Industrial Corporation, which was established in 1992, has functioned as an enterprise group, coordinating the development of TVEs in the village. In 1994, Huaxi Industrial Corporation was ranked sixth in Chinas top 1,000 most efficient TVEs (HIC was first in Jiangsu Province). The HIC, with its thirteen branch companies and over forty TVEs, has become an economic giant in the region and is expected to "annex" neighboring villages and towns through "regional horizontal cooperation" in the years to come.

Huaxi's large-scale industrial enterprises have brought even faster economic growth to the village. Huaxi's total output value has increased from 516 million yuan in 1992 to 1 billion yuan in 1993, 2 billion yuan in 1994, and 3.5 billion yuan in 1995. Wu Renbao recently announced to the Chinese media that in 1996, when the village celebrates its 35th anniversary, the average household assets in Huaxi will exceed 1 million yuan.

"We've been pioneering our work step by step," Wu said proudly. "We've accomplished plans ahead of schedule before. Our aim is to give villagers happier lives."

35

How to Reform a Planned Economy: Lessons from China

JOHN McMILLAN and BARRY NAUGHTON

This selection was written during the period of maximum controversy over the contrasting approaches to transition taken by China, on the one hand, and certain Eastern European economies, notably Poland, on the other. At a time when orthodox economic opinion favored a rapid, "big bang" type transition, China's success with a more gradual approach seemed to cry out for explanation. The essay provides an intentionally one-sided view of China's transition strategy, emphasizing the way in which elements of a gradualist strategy interacted with features of the socialist economy to create a virtuous cycle of economic change. The selection provides one interpretation of China's policies during the first era of economic reform, when the most important challenge was to start dismantling the planned economy, without plunging the economy into a major post-transition slump.

Privatization Is Not Crucial; Competition Is

Many Western economists maintain that reform necessitates the rapid transfer of state-owned firms to private ownership; there are lengthy debates about the best way to achieve this. China's experience suggests that privatization is a red herring. Rapid privatization need not be the centrepiece of a reform policy. Scarce resources of economic and administrative expertise might better be directed into thinking about other problems. We see three reasons to delay privatization.

Entrepreneurs Set Up New Firms

Investment in new firms by profit-seeking entrepreneurs is the most potent force to be harnessed by reformers. China's most dynamic sector, particularly since 1984, has been non-state-owned industrial firms. These firms, mostly located in rural areas, have a range of formal organizational structures; but they are primarily profit-seeking firms. The non-state sector has grown since 1978 at an annual rate of 17.6 percent, such that in 1990 it accounted for a striking 45 percent of total industrial output. While the output of state-owned firms has also grown in absolute terms (7.6 percent annually from 1978 to 1990), it has shrunk dramatically relative to the non-state sector: state-owned firms accounted for only 55 percent of industrial output in 1990, down from 78 percent in 1978. China is growing out of the plan. Over time, the issue of how and when to privatize China's state-owned firms is becoming less important, as the state-owned firms weigh less and less heavily in the overall economy.

The scope for new entry in socialist economies is particularly great because of two fundamental characteristics of those economies. First, the size distribution of industrial enterprises is highly skewed towards large firms. In economies such as the Soviet Union or Czechoslovakia there were virtually no "small" industrial firms. While China was known for the large number of "small" firms in its pre-reform system, even these were relatively large, typically having over fifty employees. Rapid growth has occurred in "micro-enterprises," those with less than fifty employees. The size distribution of industrial firms in market economies, developed and developing, is quite consistent: small firms typically account for around 25–30 percent of industrial employment. There are numerous niches in both modern and developing economies that are best filled by small firms. Since those niches are empty in socialist economies, the potential rewards to entrepreneurs who arrive first are quite large, ensuring rapid entry and at the same time, holding the promise of efficiency gains for the economy as a whole.

Second, the price system of socialist economies is skewed in a fashion that raises profitability in manufacturing. Socialist governments maintain high prices for manufactured goods (except for a small number of items judged to be necessities). The purpose is to concentrate taxable revenues in the large-scale, state-dominated manufacturing sector (we return to this point below). This means that once barriers to entry are lowered, new entrants will be able to reap high profits in the initial phase. This effect is magnified by the presence of shortages of certain essential goods and services. Rural enterprises in China in 1978, before reforms, were earning an average rate of profit on capital of 32 percent. This very high profitability was not the result of superb efficiency on the part of these firms, but rather of the fact that they were able to share in a part of the monopoly profits created by state pricing policy. As entry has proceeded and the rural industrial sector has grown explosively, profitability has declined steadily, falling to below 10 percent of capital.

Lenin understood that the state's monopoly on production was essential for the survival of the planning system: he wrote "small production *engenders* capitalism and the bourgeoisie continuously, daily, hourly, spontaneously, and on a mass scale." Lenin foresaw what China illustrates, the corrosive effect of the entry of non-state firms. "The decisive thing is the organization of the strictest and country-wide accounting and control of production and distribution of goods."

The entry of new firms in China illustrates the vitality of market forces. Despite impressive impediments—little law of contract, weak property rights, underdeveloped capital markets—when the restrictions on the activities of non-state firms were loosened a huge amount of entrepreneurial investment occurred, such that by 1990 non-state firm were producing almost a half of industrial output. Because of the pre-existing distortions both in the size structure of industry and in industrial prices, the economic forces that propel entry are particularly strong. Entry looks to be a fringe phenomenon in the early stages of reform; but in fact it attacks the heart of the planning system.

State-Owned Firms' Performance Can be Improved

While shrinking relative to the rest of the economy, China's state-owned industry has itself achieved respectable productivity gains. This has been the result of liberalization measures that fall far short of privatization. China's state-owned firms are notoriously inefficient; press reports commonly describe them as "dinosaurs" and "terminally ill." But recent empirical studies show they are significantly less inefficient than they used to be.

China's state-owned firms have been commercialized: they have been given some market or market-like incentives. State-owned enterprises are now allowed to keep some fraction of their profits where before all profits had to be remitted to he state; enterprises now sell and buy in free market rather than selling and procuring everything at state-controlled prices; managers' pay is based on firm performance; and production decisions have been shifted from the state to the firm.

This commercialization has resulted in improved productivity. Under the system of enterprise contracting, state firms are required to deliver a certain fixed amount of profit to the government, and are allowed to retain a substantial fraction of any profits they generate beyond this fixed amount many firms now keep as much as 100 percent of residual profits.

The data show that, when firms' autonomy increased (in either of two senses: the firm's profit-retention rate was increased, or the responsibility for deciding output levels was shifted down from the state to the firm), managers responded by strengthening the discipline imposed on workers: they increased the proportion of the workers' income paid in the form of bonuses; and they increased the fraction of workers whom, since they were on fixed-term contracts, it was in principle possible to dismiss. The new incentives were effective: productivity increased significantly following the strengthening of worker incentives. Also, the extra autonomy was followed by an increase in productive investment by the state-owned firms.

Managers of state-owned firms are now paid according to their firms' performance: the data show a strong link between a firm's sales and its top manager's pay, and a weaker link between good performance. The data show that the careers of the managers of China's state-owned firms are in fact affected by how well or badly their firms do, so the prospect of promotion or demotion does work as an incentive.

Instead of auctioning off firms, the Chinese government has begun auctioning off top management jobs. Potential managers (including, often, the incumbent manager) vie for the right to be manager by submitting bids—promises of how the firm will perform in the future. This process has revealed information about the potential capabilities of both the firms and the potential managers. As a result it has put better people in top managerial positions than the old system, under which managers were simply appointed by government bureaucrats.

Firms in capitalist economies face discipline from their product markets. In order to survive, a firm must produce at a high enough quality and low enough price to persuade customers to buy from it rather than its competitors. As a result of both the entry of non-state firms and the fact that state firms have begun to sell on free markets, China's state-owned firms now face active product-market competition. This market-based discipline has given the state-owned firms additional incentives to improve their productivity.

Output per worker in state-owned industry rose 52 percent (in constant prices) during the reform years 1980 to 1989. China proves, then, that it is possible for state-owned firms to be induced to improve their productivity by measures that fall short of privatization. . . .

The State Must Monitor Firms during the Transition

Financial markets in modern market economies impose a variety of disciplines on firms, prodding managers to ensure firms operate efficiently. In the United States and the United Kingdom managers know that poor performance is likely to cost them their jobs: they will be dismissed by the board of directors; or their firm will be taken over and a new managerial team installed; or the firm will fall into bankruptcy, with blame attached to the manager. Further incentives come from the fact that their pay is linked to the firm's stock market performance. (Anecdotal evidence sometimes raises doubts about whether U.S. managers do face genuine incentives; but the data show that they do. A correlation, small but statistically significant, exists between poor firm performance and the manager's loss of job; and a correlation, also small but statistically significant, exists between a firm's stock market value and its top manager's pay.) In Japan and Germany the source of managers' incentives is different but the incentives are no weaker: banks with large stakes in the firm, both as creditors and as equity holders, monitor the managers' decisions.

An economy in the process of transition lacks financial markets. Fully operating financial markets will take years to develop. In the transforming economy, therefore, the usual capitalist managerial disciplines are absent. The only available substitute is the state. Government officials in a reforming economy must oversee the managers of state-owned firms, as they did when the economy was centrally planned. The incentives of the monitors thus become important (especially since, in the planned economy, government supervision used to produce grossly inefficient firms). Is it in the interest of officials in the reforming economy to maintain the right sort of supervision? Can the bureaucracy be relied on to induce managers to make their firms efficient?

China shows that officials' oversight of managers can generate managerial incentives that, while undoubtedly far from perfect, work in the right direction. State-imposed incentives have replaced state-imposed controls; and, as noted, these incentives have dramatically improved state firms' productivity. What induced China's bureaucrats to regulate for firm efficiency? The increased competition squeezed state-owned firms' profits; this meant that state firms' remittances to the government fell. State firms were the main source of government revenue (as we discuss below). To slow the drop in government revenue, the state was impelled in the mid-to-late 1980s to spur the state.

Financial discipline was tightened, so that firms faced greater financial risk but also steeper compensation schedules and stronger incentives. The need for increased financial discipline was created by the increased product-market discipline that resulted from entry and competition; financial discipline then reinforced the effects of the product-market discipline.

"Spontaneous privatization" is a problem that has arisen in Eastern Europe and the Soviet Union: with the breakdown of centralized control, some managers have extracted value from the firms for their own benefit. Preventing such plundering is an additional reason why state oversight of state-owned firms must continue during the transition. China's reforms replaced direct controls on firms with incentives. This relaxation of oversight resulted, as noted, in the firms' increasing their productivity; but much of this increase in productivity stayed within the firm. When a firm was granted increased autonomy, the incomes of managers and workers rose significantly, as did the firms' welfare funds. Despite the improved productivity, the amount of profits remitted to the state fell and the subsidies given to the firms by the state rose following the increases in autonomy. Perhaps this is evidence of some plundering; but it was not simply a transfer from the state to the employees of state firms, because other effects worked in the same direction. First, the lower profits were at least in part attributable to the increased competition that the firms were facing as a result of the reforms; and second, the increase in employees' pay reflected the improvements in productivity that followed the reforms. Evidence that autonomy did not lead to severe plundering comes from the fact that state-owned firms significantly increased their productive investments following increases in their autonomy. . . .

Agriculture Booms with Reform

Agriculture was the first area in which China implemented reforms. The commune system was replaced by the household responsibility system. Under the commune system, peasants were organized into production teams. Each team member was assigned work points, which attempted to measure both how many hours and how effectively he or she had worked. Income depended on the number of work points accumulated. Income was not perfectly related to effort, however, because it was impossible to observe how conscientiously each individual worked: this would have required each peasant to be continually monitored. Moreover, there was a tendency to spread the commune's earnings across the individual commune members: those with larger families were given more income, regardless of effort. Thus the link between individual effort and reward was weak. Under the responsibility system, in contrast, each peasant family is given a long-term lease of a plot of land. The household must deliver a certain quota of produce to the government each year, and may keep anything it produces beyond that quota. The household members consume it themselves, sell it to the government, or sell it in the newly instituted rural markets. With the exception of the special case of grain, they may decide for themselves what crops to sow and what animals to raise.

In 1978 and 1979 the government increased the prices paid for agricultural outputs, while leaving the structure of the commune system unchanged. Then, from 1980 to 1984, the commune system was gradually replaced by the responsibility system. The results were clear. Agricultural output increased by 67 percent between 1978 and 1985. In part this was caused by an increase in inputs. But mainly it was due to the strengthened incentives: productivity (measured as the amount of output for a given amount of inputs) increased by nearly 50 percent, compared with no increase in productivity over the previous two and a half decade. Over the second half of the decade, agricultural growth was slower but still respectable, averaging 4.5 percent annually. While land remains state-owned, each peasant family essentially has its own plot of land, and sells any output in excess of the fixed state quota on free markets. A household's income therefore depends on that household's efforts; this linking of effort and rewards has resulted in spectacular increases in the production of food. . . .

The increase in agricultural productivity in turn spurred the growth of rural industry, by generating a pool of savings and excess labour. Beginning from a small base, rural industry was allowed to grow with few of the restrictions that hobbled state-run industry. Rural industry expanded rapidly. The entry of these profit-seeking firms provided, as we have argued, the main ingredient in China's transition. Thus the transformation of agriculture was crucial to the overall success of the reforms. . . .

The Coherence of Evolutionary Reform

China's jumble of ad hoc reforms can be seen, with hindsight, to have added up to a coherent package. Ironically, certain key features of the old planning system eased the beginning of the reforms; and other key features of the planning system gave the reform process the momentum that made it self-sustaining.

State control of the price system ensured high profitability of manufacturing at the start of the reforms. This high profitability induced rapid entry of new firms once restrictions on non-state firms were removed. The profits earned elicited high levels of household saving, generating still more investment by non-state firms. Entry in turn subjected state enterprises to market discipline and reduced state-sector profitability. As a result, the government faced erosion of its revenue base. In an attempt to slow this erosion, the state intensified its monitoring of state firms, and increasingly provided them with incentive systems based on profitability. State firms responded by increasing their efficiency (which was abysmal to begin with), providing the economy with enough stability to encourage further growth, both inside and outside the state sector, while also providing essential producer goods. Faced with the erosion of its traditional sources of revenue, the state also sought to strengthen newly developing financial systems—the banking system and embryonic capital markets—in order to transfer private saving to productive uses.

Reform proceeds by a series of feedback loops: reform begets further reform. A microeconomic reform (resulting in competition for state firms) creates a macroeconomic problem (a squeeze on government revenue) which impels further microeconomic reforms (increasingly profit-oriented regulation of state firms). This positive feedback presuppose a series of constructive policy responses from government leaders; reform will not proceed without appropriate state action. But the dynamics of the process create opportunities for pro-reform leaders to push the reforms forward.

Gradualist reforms, it is sometimes said, will fail because they are not sustainable. A variant of this argument says that only a totalitarian government is strong enough to maintain its course of gradual change. Credibility ceases to be an issue, however, once evolutionary reform is properly understood. The government must only maintain its commitment to allow entry and competition. Beyond that commitment, there is only trial and error; no further promises are being made. Rather, the government is driven by its own need for revenue to create new fiscal institutions, and impelled by its need for popular support to create additional institutions to foster economic growth. Surely, the new democracies of Eastern Europe are at least as capable of sustaining this approach as is the Chinese gerontocracy.

36

Rural-Urban Divide: Economic Disparities and Interactions in China

JOHN KNIGHT and LINA SONG

Since the early 1990s, as the second phase of reform has begun to break down the barriers that separate the urban and rural economies, migration from the countryside to the city has naturally increased. In this sense China has begun to resemble other developing economies. Since rural-to-urban migration is a relatively new phenomenon in China, many city dwellers have expressed alarm about the rapid growth of the so-called "floating population." Inflated estimates of the number of migrants have also contributed to a tendency to view migration primarily as a problem to be managed. Knight and Song present a detailed case study of migration to a small city. By limiting the geographic scope of their study, they are able to provide a comprehensive view of the impact of migration. Though migrants sometimes challenge the ability of city authorities to provide facilities for them, and may compete for some jobs with city residents, migration also provides one of the most important channels out of poverty for migrants and their family members who remain behind in the villages.

The Surveys and the Data

The surveys were conducted in Handan, a municipality comprising a city and surrounding counties in the southern part of Hebei Province, over 400 km from Beijing. The survey of rural-urban migrants was conducted in Handan itself, a city of nearly a million people, and the survey of rural households was conducted in two (rural) counties falling under the authority of the municipality, Handan county and Wuan city. Handan city and its surrounding areas are fairly typical of a large part of central China. The city has a good deal of heavy industry and the surrounding rural areas have medium density of population and average agricultural resources. These counties are not particularly poor nor remote, and the province contains poorer rural areas more distant from Handan and other cities. The surveys were planned and supervised, and the questionnaires and sampling procedures designed, by the authors.

The Handan survey of rural-urban migrants (RUM) was conducted in October 1992. The survey covers individual migrants, both those who have arrived in the city and those who remain in the county but have decided to migrate and are on the Handan job waiting list.

The Handan rural household survey (RHH) was conducted in August 1993. The sample comprises one thousand households in seven administrative villages (previously brigades) within two counties under Handan municipality. A stratified random sample of villages was chosen. The two main criteria in selecting the villages were distance from cities and income level.

The RHH survey, by distinguishing migrant and non-migrant workers, and households with and without migrants, can help to explain the determinants of migration. It can throw light on the processes and facilitating factors, and measure some of the economic costs and benefits. It is also possible to analyse the relationships between migration and poverty or its alleviation. The survey is confined to out-migrants from the villages as in-migrants lived separately from the sampled village households.

Although the migration observed was of individuals leaving their households of registration temporarily, it is notable that respondents had their long-term sights on the city. If they found a satisfying job, nearly four-fifths of the migrants would want to stay in it as long as possible, and only a small number were target workers. While over a third of the migrants had a family member with them in the city, 90 percent of those without one wanted family members to join them, although frequently "not yet." The most important conditions were that the respondent should first have a well-paid and long-term job and suitable accommodation. More than half of the rural household heads, in answering a more hypothetical question, would want to move their family to the urban areas. Over two-thirds of respondents would like to get urban residence registration. Moreover, more than half of those who did not wish to acquire an urban *hukou* [residence permit] gave as their reason the high charge made for transferring their registration. When household heads in the RHH survey were asked the purchase price of an urban *hukou*, 51 percent of respondents said 5,000 yuan precisely. The mean value was 3,912 yuan, i.e., 136 percent of a migrant's annual wage. The sale of urban *hukous* has become a source of local government revenue.

This evidence that many rural people wanted to migrate on a long-term basis indicates the continuing disequilibrium nature of the Chinese labour market.

A major reason for the disequilibrium is the disadvantage of rural people without urban *hukous* in competing with permanent urban residents for jobs and resources as reflected in the market value of such *hukous*. Interestingly, the benefits of urban living were seen to be broader than income: the more frequently cited reasons were a convenient life, better education, and higher status. Income was the most important criterion for a job but the job was seen as only part of the urban package.

The Consequences of Migration

The consequences of migration are many and various. The Handan surveys enable us to explore two in particular. First, to what extent do rural households benefit from migration of their members through the receipt of remittances? Secondly, how far does migration of labour alleviate poverty and reduce income inequality in the rural areas?

The RHH survey contained data on migrant remittances, being the total income transferred in cash or kind to the rural household during 1992. Of the 232 households containing a migrant in the RHH survey, 206 received remittances and only 26 did not. The average remittance was 1,984 yuan per annum, representing 73 percent of the average migrant income. That migrants remit nearly three-quarters of their income suggests strongly that they remain an integral part of the rural household and promote its interests.

Table 4.1 shows the extent of income inequality among households as measured by the Gini coefficient. The value of the Gini for actual income (0.400) is fairly high. There is extreme inequality of migrant income as most households have none (0.824). It might appear, therefore, that migration increases inequality. That is not necessarily the case, however: much depends on whether poor or rich households send out migrants. Moreover, we know that the coefficient on household non-migrant income in the household migration equation is significantly negative: *ceteris paribus*, additional local income discourages migration. When the migrant households have their migrant income replaced by opportunity cost, the simulated income of households in the absence of migration has a Gini coefficient of 0.426. Thus the effect of migration is slightly to diminish income inequality: the Gini coefficient falls from 0.426 without migration to 0.400 with migration.

The second simulation assumes that the opportunities for migration improve dramatically, so that the number of households sending out migrants is doubled. The additional migrant households are selected as those most likely to produce a migrant . . . . Each of the additional 23 percent of households is assumed to send out one migrant and to forgo non-migrant income accordingly. The Gini coefficient falls front 0.400 to 0.347: again, migration is good for equality.

Table 4.1. MEASURES OF INCOME INEQUALITY FOR VARIOUS ACTUAL AND SIMULATED INCOME DISTRIBUTIONS

Income concept	Notation	Gini coefficient
Actual income	Y	0.400
Non-migrant income	Y_{nm}	0.448
Migrant income	Y_m	0.824
Income in the absence of migration	Y_1	0.426
Income with more extensive migration	Y_2	0.347

Not only does migration reduce rural income inequality but it also helps to reduce rural poverty. This we see by examining the proportion of households below possible poverty lines given the actual frequency distribution of household incomes and the two simulated frequencies. An ending of migration reduces mean household income by 19 percent, and raises the proportion of households with annual income below 1,000 yuan from 15 to 37 percent. A doubling of migration raises the mean by 6 percent, and reduces the proportion of households below 1,000 yuan to only 6 percent. . . .

Conclusion

The case study of Handan has enabled us to delve more deeply into the phenomenon of rural-urban migration than is normally possible, whether in China or in other countries. We were particularly helped by the pioneering juxtaposition of two research instruments, a rural origin survey and an urban destination survey. The particularities of this, or of any other, survey area make generalization a hazardous venture. Nevertheless, the powerful and readily explained regularities in the data have yielded many insights which are likely to have more general applicability.

Migration is a socioeconomic phenomenon which is not necessarily to be explained simply in terms of economic variables. For instance, migrants are more likely to be male, unmarried, and healthy. They are also disproportionately young, although the economic incentive to migrate increases with age. Life experiences are relevant: broadened horizons through previous army service or travel encourage labour migration, and access to local economic opportunities through Party membership or experience as a local cadre discourages it. College or professional high-school education encourages migration but education is little rewarded in the lowly jobs to which these rural-based temporary migrants generally have access.

The larger the household's labour force, the more likely it is to send out a migrant. More local income for the household decreases the propensity to migrate, probably by reducing the economic gain from migration. By contrast, more household wealth increases it. Wealth may have this effect by overcoming liquidity constraints on migration and reducing aversion to risk-taking. The powerful influence of the village on the propensity to migrate suggests that social networks are important in facilitating migration.

37

Development in Chinese Corporate Finance and Its Implication for Ownership Reform

WEIYING ZHANG

This selection does an outstanding job of linking changes in corporate finance and governance with changes in the overall economy. Zhang, one of the many excellent young economists who have emerged in China in recent years, shifts easily between microeconomic and macroeconomic perspectives. As the economy has moved to a market basis, saving and wealth have become increasingly private. The banking system has "succeeded" in collecting savings and loaning them to the corporate sector, ensuring continued growth. But the corporate sector is still dominated by publicly owned firms, with weak management and limited oversight and accountability. As a result, failing firms are propped up artificially far too long, and the financial system is weighed down by an increasing load of bad debt.

Introduction

Chinese economic reform, first introduced in 1979, has resulted in many significant changes in the organisational structure of economic activities and resource allocation. One such change has been taking place in corporate finance. . . . [A]lthough SOEs [State-owned Enterprises] are still tightly controlled by governments at various levels, debt finance from state banks has gradually taken over from state budget (equity) finance as the major financial instrument of SOEs. . . . The average debt-asset ratio of all industrial SOEs has increased from 18.7 percent in 1980 to 65.1 percent in 1997.

This change has mainly resulted from the fact that the distribution of national income has altered and households have taken over from the state as the major financiers of investment capital. Also, because direct financing markets have been very tightly restricted and underdeveloped, the state banks have become the dominant channel for funds flowing from households to enterprises.

382

The problem is that, although corporate finance has changed a lot, corporate governance has changed little: SOEs may be financed by households (through the banks) but they are still owned by the government. The government continues not only to hold full authority over the selection of SOE management but also to intervene considerably in SOE business. Since they do not bear financial risks, neither government officials nor management have adequate incentives to make enterprises under their control efficient. Because bank deposits are fully insured by the state and the state banks are fully controlled by the government, households as ultimate financial investors have neither interest in nor access to the monitoring of banks and SOEs. Similarly, it is impossible for the state banks as direct creditors to play any active role in the corporate governance of SOEs. This mismatch between the financial investors in the firm and the ownership of the firm has turned debt finance into a debt crisis.

The change in SOE financing has generated enormous impacts on the Chinese economy, both negative and positive. From the negative point of view, debt finance has driven almost all SOEs into financial distress. Many of them are unable to repay their due debts. As a result of SOE defaults, state banks as the major creditors are suffering because of substantial bad loans. A common estimate is that 20–25 percent of their total outstanding loans are unrecoverable. This not only hinders commercialisation of the state banks but also potentially threatens the stability of the macroeconomy, unless the debt problem can be solved within a reasonable period. On the positive side, the debt crisis has unveiled the deep-seated flaws of the state ownership system. It shows that more fundamental changes in corporate governance are necessary, and it has made privatisation of the SOEs more acceptable and feasible than otherwise. . . .

The reform of SOEs has been characterised by a continuously evolutionary process of shifting decision rights and residual claims from the central government to local governments, and from there to firm level. This has had a substantial impact on SOE corporate finance. First, although investment decisions constitute one of the rights that the central government has been very reluctant to give up, both state enterprises and local governments have acquired considerable autonomy in regard to such decisions as reform has proceeded. A recent study, by China Entrepreneur Survey System, indicates that the realisation of autonomy in investment decisions in 1993, 1994 and 1995 was, respectively, 38.9 percent, 61.2 percent and 72.8 percent. . . .

As a direct consequence of debt finance, the financial structure of SOEs has gradually changed. According to a survey by the State Asset Administration, the debt-asset ratio of state industrial enterprises as a whole was only 18.7 percent in 1980 and had increased to 67.9 percent by 1994. According to the 1997 *China Statistical Yearbook*, the average debt-asset ratio of 86,982 state industrial enterprises at the end of 1996 was 65.1 percent (61.1 percent for large enterprises, 72.4 percent for middle-sized ones and 72.4 percent for small ones). . . .

While the debt-asset ratio of 65 percent is already considerably high by international standards, official statistics seem to have underreported SOEs' real debt burdens. Numerous case studies show that actual average debt-asset ratios are much higher and that, in fact, many SOEs are 'zero-equity firms'. For instance, a survey of four industrial cities by the Debt Restructuring Research Group indicated that average ratios in 1994 were 77.5 percent (Chanchun), 81.3 percent (Xi'an), 74.4 percent (Ningbo) and 89 percent (Tanshan). In total, this means about two-thirds of SOEs with debt-asset ratios over 80 percent and more than a quarter with ratios over 100 percent. In other words, a considerable proportion of SOEs is technically bankrupt. This is the so-called 'over-indebted problem.'

As SOEs are more and more debt-financed, the bad loans of their major creditors (the state banks) have mounted dramatically and become a serious problem. A common estimate is that more than 20 percent of total outstanding bank loans are non-performing and unrecoverable. One rigorous study suggests that the figure in 1995 was 23 percent, which means that the absolute value of these bad loans reached 1,162.7 billion yuan (US \$141.8 billion), equivalent to 20 percent of the gross national product (GNP) of that year. It must be pointed out that bad loans are not normally written off; typically, they are recapitalised by the issuing of new loans.

In pre-reform China, as in other socialist economies, the government not only deprived state enterprises of the capacity to make investment and financial decisions, but also deprived households of choice between current and future consumption (and thereafter of their financial decisions). It did this by directly controlling the distribution of national income in various ways. It was the government that determined how much a household should earn. Zhang Chunlin (1997), a well-known Chinese economist, has identified 'taxation' and 'administrative pricing' as the two basic instruments that the state employed to control national income distribution and to finance state enterprises. Administrative pricing was particularly effective in controlling rural household income. By underpricing agricultural products and compulsorily purchasing them, the government transferred to the state sector much of the income that could otherwise have been saved by rural households, in the form of lower living costs for state employees and lower production costs. Through the underpricing of state employees' labour services, much of the income that could otherwise have been saved by urban households appeared in accounting statements as SOE profits, which were then completely handed over to the state treasurer. The government then used budget revenue to finance state enterprises and capital formation. . . .

The economic reform begun in the late 1970s has fundamentally changed the distribution of national income by liberalising both prices and entries of non-state enterprises (Figs. 4.1 and 4.2). In rural areas, as agricultural prices were raised in the late 1970s and eventually liberalised in the early 1980s, household incomes increased dramatically. For instance, per capita household income in

Fig. 4.1. Government share of GDP, 1978–97 (%)

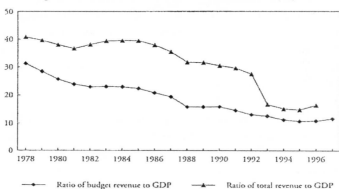

Figure 4.2. Distribution of national income, 1979–88 (%)

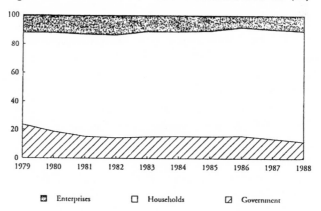

rural areas from 1978 to 1985 increased by 137.6 percent, in contrast to 75.4 percent growth in per capita GDP. This, together with the entry of non-state enterprises, eroded much of the profits previously earned by SOEs, by raising labour costs and reducing profit margins. In urban areas, as SOEs enjoyed greater autonomy over decision-making and retained profits, government administrative control of wages and bonuses was undermined, and more and more SOE revenue was distributed to employees. As a result, urban household incomes have also quickly increased, although not as fast as rural incomes in the earlier stages of reform. . . .

As the distribution of national income changed, the pattern of national savings also changed (Fig. 4.3). . . . Since 1983, household savings have been the largest source of investment funds; since 1985, households have provided more than half of total national savings. While households have taken over as the main financial investors, the enterprise sector has, since 1983, become the dominant physical investor (Fig. 4.4). Both the enterprise sector and the government have increasingly relied on household savings to finance investment, that is, they have become the net debtors and households the net creditors (Fig. 4.5).

The problem is not that enterprises should not use household savings for investment; it is normal in every modern economy. The problem is that the government failed to open capital markets to allow both households and enterprises to make their own choices among different financial instruments such as equity, bonds and mutual funds. Nor did the government try to privatise SOEs, as it should have, in response to the change in the savings pattern. Before the early 1990s, there was no stock market on which enterprises could raise funds. Enterprises were, and still are, tightly restricted in issuing bonds. Although rural area households can directly invest in township and village enterprises (TVEs) and private enterprises, urban households can only deposit their savings in state-owned banks, apart from buying treasurer bonds. As a result, banks have become almost the only channel for capital flow from households to SOEs.

Corporate Governance and the Debt Crisis

The debt crisis cannot be blamed solely on the shift to debt financing. If corporate governance were effective and efficient, debt financing might be good for a firm's value maximisation through disciplining management. . . The debt crisis has occurred because, although corporate finance has changed a lot, corporate governance has changed little.

Figure 4.3. Pattern of national savings, 1979 and 1988 (%)

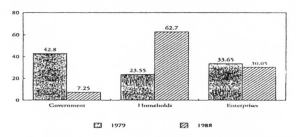

Fig. 4.4. Pattern of investment, 1979 and 1988 (%)

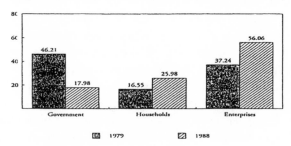

Fig. 4.5. Gap between savings and investment in each sector, 1988 (%)

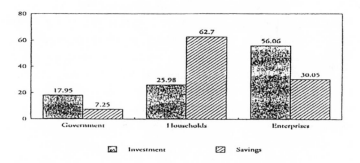

    First, the government as the only equity-holder has malfunctioned in both selecting and disciplining management because of agency problems on the bureaucrats' side. The feature of SOEs that most distinguishes them from capitalist firms is that, by definition, the role of principals in SOEs is played by the 'state' (government) rather than by natural capitalists: it is the government who appoints, motivates and disciplines the managers. . . .

Second, although reform has gradually shifted considerable autonomy to management in various ways, government can still intervene arbitrarily in SOE business.

Third, the state bank as the major creditor has failed to enforce the debt contract. In a market economy, debts play an important role in corporate governance through the threat of bankruptcy. China enacted a Bankruptcy Law in 1986, which became effective in late 1988. Theoretically, when enterprises become insolvent, the creditors take control and the threat of bankruptcy disciplines the management. However, this is not the case in China. Rather, bankruptcy has been widely used by enterprises and local governments as a way to write off debts, instead of disciplining managers (ICBC 1997). After bank-ruptcy procedures, either through reorganisation or through liquidation, most incumbent managers still run the firms as going concerns and probably the only major difference is that considerable debts have been cancelled (and, in some cases, the enterprises renamed). Because of this, managers are more than willing to file for bankruptcy. In contrast, state banks, as dominant creditors, have neither access nor incentive to execute their creditor rights. They have been very passive in dealing with distressed firms. Typically, when debtor firms default, creditor banks accommodate them, by, for instance, extending the loan payment period or capitalising unpaid interest, rather than pursuing their claims through bankruptcy or other active means. Indeed, the banks have filed very few bankruptcies.

The fundamental reason for creditor failure is that, when the government acts as the owner of both debtor-firms and creditor-banks, the debt is not a real debt in the legal sense, that is, a contract between debtor and creditor. When a debtor borrows from a creditor, the debtor fully understands the obligation to repay in due time or else face a bankruptcy penalty and the creditor fully realises that there is some risk of default by the debtor. The terms of the contract negotiated between the debtor and the creditor take into account all these foreseen considerations. Bankruptcy is a procedure that enforces the debt contract. In China, however, debts between the banks and the SOEs are very different. In the 1980s, when SOEs borrowed from the banks, they just took it as a new way of getting funds from the government and had little sense that the borrowed money would have to be repaid, and the banks simply understood it as allocating funds to state firms on behalf of the government and had little sense of risk of possible default. In fact, many bank loans were decided by the government through an administrative procedure, rather than negotiated between the firm and the bank. In this sense, the 'debts' of SOEs were more like equity than debts. Perhaps the only difference between debts and budget funds was a change of items in the balance sheets. Not until the 1990s, when the state banks had become burdened with enormous overdue bad debts and when both they and the SOEs had relatively independent entities with their own interests, was it recognised that bank money was different from budget funds. For this reason, I call the SOEs debts 'ex post debts'. Because of this ex post nature, the bankruptcy of SOEs is more like a bargaining process over the terms of new debt contracts rather than an enforcement of the existing debt contracts.

The second reason for creditor failure is that the incentive system of state banks is misstructured. Managers of state banks in China care only for accounting numbers, rather than for the real value of the bank asset.

For any proposal to be successful, therefore, it must simultaneously address both the over-indebted problem and the corporate governance problem. From this point of view, the privatisation of SOEs is not only desirable but also inevitable. Given that most of them need new equity funds and the state as the incumbent owner has none for injection, the problem can only be solved by introducing new, non-state shareholders. Privatisation is also more feasible now in China. Roughly speaking, with households the major suppliers of investment funds, the financial claims of SOEs have already been privatised. Now it is time to privatise SOE control rights. This can easily be done by transforming household investors from debt-holders of state banks into equity-holders of enterprises. In other words, China does not need to follow the Eastern European style of voucher privatisation; it can go its own way. This kind of privatisation will not only change the financial structure of SOEs but also restructure their corporate governance.

Privatisation has already begun. Observation suggests that the debt crisis has indeed been a powerful driving force behind this process. Many local governments are eager to sell the firms under their control, simply because they do not have the funds to ensure these firms' survival. A recent survey estimates that more than 70 percent of small SOEs in Shandong and a few other provinces have been fully or partially privatised (China Reform Foundation 1997: 35). The process has been further speeded up since the Chinese Communist Party's 15th Congress. Now, newspapers in China frequently carry a list of the large and middle-sized SOEs selected by local governments for sale. Three northeastern provinces are most noticeable for their recent public offer of SOEs for sale.

Suggestions for Further Reading

Lardy, Nicholas. *China's Unfinished Economic Revolution.* Washington, D.C.: Brookings Institution Press, 1998. Misleadingly titled, this book actually provides a penetrating analysis of China's banking system, with occasional reflections on the broader challenges and limitations of China's reform strategy. The book lays out the dimensions of the financial problems China faces and predicts a financial crisis.

Lin, Justin Yifu, Fang Cai, and Zhou Li. *The China Miracle: Development Strategy and Economic Reform.* Hong Kong: Chinese University Press, 1996. This lively work brings together long-run development patterns and strategic choices made during the economic reform process. It is good at relating the Maoist period to the subsequent reform period and providing an explanation for reform success.

Naughton, Barry. *Growing Out of the Plan: Chinese Economic Reform, 1978–1993.* New York: Cambridge University Press, 1995. This book provides a detailed description of reforms in industry and macroeconomic policy during the first reform era. It also describes and analyzes policy debates during the 1980s.

Nyberg, Albert, and Scott Rozelle. *Accelerating China's Rural Transformation.* Washington, D.C.: The World Bank, 1999. This study provides a comprehensive look at the many dimensions of economic change in China's countryside at the end of the twentieth century. It gives a clear-sighted view of the challenges faced, while always keeping in mind the incredible dynamism and diversity of the rural economy.

Perkins, Dwight H., ed. *China's Modern Economy in Historical Perspective.* Stanford: Stanford University Press, 1973. This collection relates various aspects of China's pre-1949 economy to post-1949 developments. The volume provides a broad perspective that is often missing in more recent works.

Rawski, Thomas G. *Economic Growth in Prewar China.* Berkeley: University of California Press, 1989. A vigorous and well-documented argument that China's economy was embarked on a self-sustaining growth path during the first half of the twentieth century.

United National Development Program, *China Human Development Report.* New York: Oxford University Press, 1999. This report provides a penetrating look at the many dimensions of China's human development record in the mid-1990s. It assesses, in an even-handed way, the complex tradeoffs brought by rapid economic growth that has increased incomes but also led to rapidly increasing inequality. It is also good on regional variation in living standards.

Walder, Andrew G., ed. *China's Transitional Economy*. Oxford: Oxford University Press, 1996. This collection provides comprehensive coverage of economic issues, with good articles on foreign trade, macroeconomics, and agricultural commerce.

Whiting, Susan H., *Power and Wealth in Rural China*. New York: Cambridge University Press, 2001. This book brings the story of China's township and village enterprises up to the eve of the twenty-first century. Whiting describes comprehensively and in detail the incentives faced by local officials and entrepreneurs. She also advances an ambitious argument about the interactions between local interests and national policy formation.

Websites

There is now an enormous amount of information about China's economy available on the web. Nearly all of China's ministries have websites, often very informative, although most of the information is in Chinese. Two of the best sites for English language content are:

www.tdctrade.com. The Hong Kong Trade and Development Council is a good source of up-to-date information about economic performance and policy in China.

www.moftec.gov.cn/moftec_en/index.html. Relatively abundant English information is available on the site of the Ministry of Foreign Trade and Economic Cooperation.

Part 5

CULTURE

Edited by Kirk A. Denton

INTRODUCTION
Kirk A. Denton

Tradition and Modernity

The term "culture" has undergone a radical re-appraisal over recent decades. No longer only associated with elite art forms and perceived as disconnected from the messy business of history, politics, society, and daily life, culture now encompasses television, advertisement, theme parks, websites, shopping malls, and pop music. Moreover, we have begun to see that culture has a complex relationship with social practice and political power. A more contemporary definition of culture might be: the diverse practices whereby a society negotiates meanings and identities for itself, allowing it to both cohere through shared values and to question and challenge those very values. I adopt this view of culture in the discussion that follows, looking at the culture of modern China as heterogeneous, multilayered, and closely intertwined with politics and shifting social identities.

In discussing Chinese culture of the past century, we must first come to grips with the thorny term "modern." What constitutes the modern in modern culture? What is modernity's relation to tradition? In the West, modernity has generally been understood, in both cultural and economic terms, as originating with Renaissance humanism and science and Enlightenment rationalism. These values then were reinforced in the nineteenth century with the industrial revolution and the rise of capitalism and its notions of progress and individualism. This model of modernity was adopted and adapted by many Chinese intellectuals and cultural figures beginning around 1895, with the resulting view of Chinese modernity as originating with the seminal Western impact. Chinese intellectuals defined modernity relative to a pernicious tradition that was, to some degree at least, manufactured to better justify appropriation of the new and the modern. That is, modern enlightenment values of progress and individualism became antidotes to a dark and oppressive tradition. Such artificial terms as "modernity" and "tradition" can blind us to the complexity of cultural practices

395

in modern China. The complex reality is that Chinese intellectuals and others involved in the promotion of culture from the late nineteenth century to the present have often behaved in very traditional ways, even as they made use of the discourses and cultural forms of the modern West. I do not want to suggest any kind of reductive view of absolute continuity between tradition and modernity—as we will see below, modern Chinese culture was in many ways radically at odds with that of premodern times. My point is that the linear "continuity versus discontinuity" model fails to account for tradition's ongoing presence within modernity.

In China, culture has been understood as a central part of the human fabric. Because of this, it has oftentimes taken on an instrumental role in the transformation of society. Traditionally, culture (*wen*) was understood as "patterns" of the human world, patterns that parallel and are connected to those of the cosmos itself. With such a cosmological basis, culture was perceived as integral to human existence, seamlessly interwoven with all aspects of what it means to be human—the personal, the social, ethical, political, and ideological. It was never taken as the embodiment of a monolithic, static set of values, although, as we will see, it came to be viewed that way in the modern period when intellectuals, under the influence of Western thought, attacked it as a barbaric force obstructing China's march toward modernity. Culture more often than not was conservative in its politics and morality, upholding a status quo form of Confucian ideology, yet it could also take on an antagonistic role in questioning, for example, the moral legitimacy of rulers. Furthermore, within the Confucian tradition there was much debate and intellectual discussion over the meaning of the classics, and literati with Buddhist or Daoist inclinations often critiqued mainstream Confucian thought. Modern intellectuals also used culture politically—to uphold the status quo or critique it. Like their traditional counterparts, they held faith in the power of culture to affect its intended audience.

Culture was an elitist affair in premodern China. Included in its domain were various forms of writing in the classical language (e.g., poetry, prose, history, and philosophy), painting, music, and calligraphy. Excluded were fiction and drama written in the vulgar vernacular, oral performance arts, folk art—forms of popular entertainment that were considered unworthy of attention because their language or techniques were unrefined and because they lacked moral seriousness—not to mention the culture of everyday life. Culture was the domain of the literatus, a highly educated member of a social elite. The successful literatus had a solid grounding in the Confucian classics, reams of poetry, and a great deal of historical writings. He could write in a variety of prose and poetic forms and styles. His educational training was intensive and involved years of rote memorization of classical texts, endless exercises in composition, and repetitive calligraphic training. The ultimate goal of such an education was moral self-cultivation, but also, more cynically, to pass the civil service examinations, which offered access to the state bureaucracy and usually guaranteed wealth and social prestige. Poetry was an important element of the examinations, so learning how to write it had a very tangible and practical benefit, but it was also a medium through which the literati class interacted with each other: "occasional" in nature, poetry was very often written for friends, family, or officials for specific social occasions, such as births, deaths, celebrations, and partings. Those who failed the examinations, or passed only the lower level, and never gained state sinecures—and there were many—often sought solace in literary and cultural pursuits. Paintings, antiques, rare books, and calligraphy were cultural objects whose function was not so much self-cultivation or social improvement as it was to demonstrate one's taste and sophistication. But literature and culture were not, of course, used solely for social advantage. The literatus often wrote poetry to express dismay at the bureaucratic world or to voice political and moral dissent, a dangerous pursuit in imperial China that often led to political exile. Some of China's greatest poetry was written by exiled literati lamenting injustices and longing for home.

Early modern intellectuals also came primarily from elite gentry back-grounds, many hailing from the Jiangnan area (which includes the provinces of Jiangsu, Zhejiang, and Anhui) that was the cultural center of China in late imperial times. Although, as we will see below, they attacked the elitism inherent in the Confucian scholarly tradition and promoted nonelite literary and cultural forms to reach a mass audience, they did so for the profoundly elite concerns of nation building and cultural rejuvenation. One might also see the highly Westernized culture they promoted as merely a new means through which to assert their tradi-tional status as cultural spokesmen, a status that had been severely undermined by the abolishment of the civil service examination system in 1905. Like their traditional counterparts, modern intellectuals also used writing and art for personal and political self-expression and, as in imperial times, this could be a politically dangerous undertaking. Not all cultural figures adhered to the decidedly political orientation of mainstream modern culture; like many of their traditional counter-parts, some modern intellectuals saw culture as the gentlemanly pursuit of taste.

Of course, beneath the elite culture in premodern times were forms of popular and folk culture, including local opera, oral storytelling, folk religion and arts, songs, etc. that were an integral part of everyday life in rural villages and small towns. The elite generally looked down on these forms, but some scholars tried to appropriate them for their own literati concerns. Novels in the vernacular, for example, which grew out of an oral storytelling tradition, were legitimized as serious literature by some scholars in the Ming (1368–1644) and Qing (1644–1911) as a vital antidote to an ossifying literary practice. Like their Ming and Qing counterparts, modern cultural figures embraced some of the very popular and folk forms so marginalized by mainstream Confucian elites. At the same time, however, they excluded new forms of popular culture, for example the entertainment fiction sometimes called Mandarin Ducks and Butterfly fiction, which didn't conform to their elite notions of the role of culture in social and national transformation.

These traditional values—the literatus as the steward of culture, culture as the vanguard of the moral transformation of society, and ambivalent attitudes toward popular culture, etc.—were very much at play in the formation of modern Chinese culture. The history of this culture, at least from one perspective, is a history of periodic attempts to radically refashion it so that it could in turn participate in the transformation of the social and political realms. And although the goal of these transformations was often the destruction of tradition, we should not forget that such a role for culture was fundamentally traditional.

Early Modern Culture (1895–1949)

By the late nineteenth and early twentieth centuries, the role of the literatus and traditional views of culture began to change. With the effects of Western imperialism and the disintegration of the social system in the final century of Qing rule (1800–1911), intellectuals began to question aspects of their tradition with an intensity and from a perspective never before undertaken. This questioning of tradition was not totally absent in the intellectual sphere before the nineteenth century, for the classics were always a source of interpretative negotiation, but rarely did the traditional scholar stand outside the social, ethical, and philosophical assumptions embodied in the classics. With the arrival of Western thought through translations and journalism in the late Qing (1895–1911), scholars began to look at their own tradition and their own cultural values from the outside— from the perspective of the Occident. Thus viewed, China looked tradition-bound, static, weak, and mired in an ancient and irrelevant set of cultural values. The West appeared by contrast dynamic, forward-looking, progressive, liberal, and powerful. The question for late Qing intellectuals became: How do we transform China into a more powerful nation-state, one that can compete on equal terms with the imperialist countries of the West and Japan.

For some, culture—not politics, society, or economics—was an important realm through which such a transformation could occur. To transform society, these intellectuals believed, the cultural realm had to be radically refashioned. Intellectuals of the late Qing, most importantly Liang Qichao (1873–1929), a Confucian-trained scholar who became one of the leading reformists of the 1890s, were the first to initiate this cultural regeneration. For Liang, this cultural regeneration could occur by promoting writing in a prose less abstruse and allusive than the various classical styles that existed at the time, raising fiction's status as a serious literary genre, writing poetry that responded to contemporary concerns, developing a commercial press, translating Western texts, etc. The May Fourth period (1915–1925), with its promotion of a radical break with tradition, intensified many of the concerns of late Qing reformists. Essential to their iconoclastic program was a cultural revolution that would replace the classical language and the conservative, outworn Confucian value system it propagated with a lively, modern vernacular language that would be the foundation of a new, socially engaged literature. This linguistic and literary reform would in turn transform the consciousness of the Chinese people.

Although not without a healthy skepticism about the possibility of such a transformation, Lu Xun (1881–1936) was surely its most profound proponent. Often considered the greatest Chinese writer of the twentieth-century, Lu Xun wrote short fiction, prose poetry, historical tales, and many volumes of essays. His dissection and critique of the failings of the Chinese "national character" is most obvious in his novella "The True Story of Ah Q." Poor and homeless, Ah Q ekes out an existence as a hired hand to his village's wealthy families. But the story is less a sympathetic portrayal of the downtrodden than it is an allegory of what is wrong with Chinese culture and the national psyche: Ah Q has an undeserved sense of superiority; he abuses those weaker than he just as he is abused by the powerful; he has no self-consciousness, nor does he grasp reality well. Through the voice of an ironic madman in his most famous short story, "Diary of a Madman" (1918), Lu Xun pronounces the Chinese tradition Ah Q seems to embody "cannibalistic" for consuming the individual and those who dare to differ—a chilling label that exerted a tremendous influence on the way Chinese have viewed their tradition. "Medicine" (1919) continues this representation of an ignorant and superstitious tradition as cannibalistic (reading 38). The story, set on the eve of the 1911 revolution that overthrew the Qing dynasty, recounts the Hua parents' efforts to save their son, who is dying of consumption. They purchase a steamed bun soaked in the blood of a recently executed revolutionary. The effect of the revolutionary's sacrifice is thus the prolongation of the very traditional values he opposed. Lu Xun's pessimism is profound: tradition is an "iron house" from which it is virtually impossible to escape, and efforts to change it (e.g., the revolution) are inevitably swallowed by it. This pessimism deepened in the mid-1920s as the promise of the iconoclastic May Fourth movement failed to pan out. Lu Xun's prose poem "Autumn Night" (1924) seems to capture some of the more personal effects of this pessimism (reading 39). Its lyrical mood, bizarre symbolism and imagery, and the concern with the unconscious mind mark a form of literature very different from the social orientation of "Medicine." It shows us that although social transformation was an important motivation for many writers in the early twentieth century, writers also wrote for deeply private reasons. "Autumn Night" may also point to Lu Xun's displeasure with the reduction of literature to a tool of revolutionary change, a chime that was beginning to be heard in the radical cultural camps of the time.

Other writers, for instance Yu Dafu (1896–1945), fought against tradition through a form of romantic literature of self-expression in which confession of one's dark sentiments and personal failings dominated. Women writers, such as Ding Ling (1904–1986) were an important part of the early modern literary scene, adding a personal and psychological dimension that was at odds with Lu Xun's form of cultural criticism. Ding Ling's "Diary of Miss Sophia" (1928) foregrounds through the diary form the complex consciousness and desires of a woman in a society in which women's roles were changing dramatically.

Urban Chinese in the late Qing and early Republican (1912–1949) periods were generally fascinated with the West. This fascination manifested itself at both the elite and popular levels. In his writings, for example, Liang Qichao introduced revolutionaries like George Washington and Guiseppe Mazzini. Western novels in translation—those of Charles Dickens and H. Rider Haggard were particularly popular—captured the imagination of the elite reading public. Translations of treatises on law (C. L. Montesquieu's *The Spirit of Laws*), capitalism (Adam Smith's *A Wealth of Nations*), and evolutionary thought (T. Huxley's *Evolution and Ethics*) helped intellectuals explain China's crisis. From this panoply of Western ideas, intellectuals formulated a Chinese discourse of modernity, consisting of such terms as democracy, science, individualism, enlightenment, nationalism, and progress. This discourse would be contested over the next few decades, but its iconoclastic assumptions and its acceptance of a Western-based model of modernity would remain largely in tact throughout the century.

Modernity—its values, technology, and exotica—was also all the rage at a more popular level, especially in China's coastal urban areas. Lithographic prints published in popular illustrated magazines introduced the exotica—or some imagined version of it—of the technologically advanced West (fig. 5.1). Cinemas, Western-style architecture, department stories, photographic images of the West, advertising, calendar posters, etc. were part and parcel of daily life in places like Shanghai, the most modern and westernized of China's cities. Calendar posters, scorned by high-minded intellectuals like Lu Xun, were advertisements, with images of exotic, modernized women, selling such products as cigarettes and wine. These images at once sexualize women and show them as modern and confident, in roles unthinkable a few decades earlier. Another fascinating avenue for the popular dissemination of modernity were illustrated magazines like *Companion Illustrated*, which featured, interspersed among its articles, advertisements (fig. 5.2) selling both native and foreign products and articles and photographs of the latest fashion styles (fig. 5.3). Wildly popular also among the urban population was entertainment fiction, known as Mandarin Ducks and Butterflies fiction—sentimental love stories, detective fiction, comedies, martial arts novels, etc. Unlike the elite discourse of modernity and its literary expression, which tended to be iconoclastic and in favor of radical westernization, these forms of popular fiction offered a space for readers to negotiate between traditional values and modernity. They also offered, of course, pleasurable escape from working drudgery, social problems, and the horrors of history. Butterfly fiction, and the entertainment films it so influenced, maintained throughout the Republican period audiences that far surpassed those for the works of progressive May Fourth writers like Lu Xun and Yu Dafu, and the literary and cultural fields of Republican China cannot be properly understood without recognizing its place in them. After the founding of the Peoples' Republic of China (PRC) in 1949, Butterfly fiction was banned for its dangerous lack of social conscience, and the Party promoted in its stead a highly sanitized and politicized version of May Fourth progressive writing. Butterfly fiction, as well as new forms of popular fiction, has reemerged strongly in the liberalization of the post-Mao period, attesting to the enduring lure of literature as diversion.

By the late 1920s Marxism had begun to exert a powerful influence over the cultural sphere. This political radicalism was an outgrowth of the May Fourth period—such iconoclasts as Chen Duxiu (1880–1942) and Li Dazhao (1888–1927) had gone on to become founding members of the Chinese Communist Party (CCP) in 1921—but it was also a response to several other factors: the rise of Japanese imperialism, the split between the Nationalists and the Communists (1927), and the failure of the Nationalists to solve social problems. Equipped with a Marxist materialist view of history, cultural figures began to question the idealism behind May Fourth culturalism. Real social transformation would occur through changes in the modes of production and the relations between economic classes, they felt, not by changing people's consciousness through culture. Yet, despite their Marxist materialism, these radicals continued to place a high degree of importance on the role of culture in historical development. This culturalism within a materialist framework is one of the hallmarks of the Chinese appropriation of Marxism.

By the late 1920s writers and critics began to promote "revolutionary literature," or a literature that would contribute to the goals of a proletarian revolution. Writers such as Mao Dun (1896–1981) tried to put these political ideals into literary practice; fortunately, their resulting works far exceed the political intentions invested in them. For example, Mao Dun's *Midnight* (1932) is a Marxist-inspired critique of capitalism, but its detailed and highly realistic description of Shanghai beautifully captures a sense of urban modernity of the time and presents a vivid panorama of social classes that cannot be reduced to any neat political formula. This leftist turn appeared not only in the literary sphere, but also in film and the visual arts. The woodblock print movement, promoted by Lu Xun, is one manifestation of this turn in the field of visual arts. Chen Tiegeng's (1908–1970) "Waiting," and, most famously, Li Hua's (1907–1994) "China, Roar!" (figs. 5.4 and 5.5) are visual emblems of the strong moral indignation favored by this leftist culture.

Modernist art, traditional style painting, Hollywood melodrama, martial arts movies, symbolist poetry, and experimental fiction were also part of the 1930s cultural field. The cultural field was heterogeneous, and by no means did all of its participants conform neatly to the nationalism/modernity paradigm formulated by the likes of Liang Qichao and Lu Xun and inherited by the leftists in the 1930s. Lu Xun's younger brother, Zhou Zuoren (1885–1967), for example, self-consciously reacted against this paradigm and asserted in its place local culture and continuity with tradition. Moreover, a neat dichotomy of leftist (socially engaged) and popular culture (apolitical entertainment) was not always clear, as filmmakers like Maxu Weibang (*The Song of Midnight*; 1937), for example, couched a leftist message in a popular Hollywood horror genre. Culture in Republican China was heterogeneous and its texts, such as this film, were often formally and thematically ambiguous and paradoxical.

During the war against Japan (1937–1945), culture was made to serve the interests of the war effort. Writers, filmmakers, and artists became, essentially, propaganda workers. To reach as broad an audience as possible, including the illiterate rural population, oral genres (street plays, storytelling, local opera, etc.) and visual forms (comics and posters) were promoted. This political role for culture was enshrined in Mao Zedong's "Talks at the Yan'an Forum on Art and Literature" (1942), lectures given to CCP cultural workers in Yan'an (reading 40). But as the war stalemated in the 1940s, writers and other artists balked at this subservient role and sought a return to a more active, critical role like that embodied in the writings of their May Fourth predecessor, Lu Xun. Some, like Zhang Ailing (1921–1995), who wrote in occupied Shanghai, seemed to reject both the Maoist and May Fourth literary models altogether. Her works are about the personal, not the national and the revolutionary. Her story "Sealed Off" (1943), however, even as it rejects any notion of literature becoming a "screw" in the revolutionary machine, as Mao put it, demonstrates brilliantly how history imprints itself on the individual psyche (reading 41). Other writers such as Shen Congwen (1902–1988) and Zhou Zuoren had also tried to buck the leftist tide, the former in apolitical lyrical sketches of his remote homeland of West Hunan, the latter in a nostalgic classicism. For this they suffered greatly after 1949 when the CCP attempted to impose its ideological vision on all writers and cultural figures.

The Maoist Period (1949–1976)

Mao's "Yan'an Talks" exerted a profound influence on the arts of post-revolutionary China, becoming the centerpiece of official Party cultural policy: culture should depict workers, peasants, and soldiers and be produced for that very audience; it is subservient to politics, and politics is determined by the CCP. Zhao Shuli's (1906–1970) stories were presented as models for other writers to follow. Although lacking the liveliness and humor for which much of Zhao Shuli's work is known, his postrevolutionary tale "The Unglovable Hands" (reading 42) is nonetheless typical of early socialist literature in China: it glorifies the nobility of hardworking peasants, their strong attachment to the land, and their willingness to work for the collective. Given the fact that this story was written in 1960, during the Great Leap Forward famine, Zhao's representation of the countryside rings false, especially since Zhao was aware of the problems and was himself a critic of the Party agricultural policies. With "The Unglovable Hands," we see how socialist literature idealizes reality.

Although much of the culture of the 1950s was trite, propagandistic, and not well received, the best of it was extremely popular and genuinely appealing to audiences. This was true of the film director Xie Jin's (1923–) comedies and melodramas, as well as of novels such as Yang Mo's (1914–1995) *Song of Youth* (1958). *Song of Youth*, about the revolutionary awakening of a young bourgeois woman, appealed to readers because it offered them a chance to participate in history vicariously. The novel conveys a clear revolutionary message, but it does so through a story of personal struggle and romance that allows for identification between reader and heroine. For young Chinese readers and audiences, socialist culture of the 1950s also offered optimism about the future and a sense of thrill and adventure, things that their everyday lives could not. Culture of the 1950s was strongly influenced by the Soviet model of socialist realism. Translations of Soviet literature were very popular and affected how Chinese writers depicted society and portrayed revolutionary heroes.

The Cultural Revolution (1966–1976) was, of course, primarily a political movement, an attempt by Mao to reassert control over the vast CCP bureaucracy, which had over the 1950s and 1960s gradually come under the sway of a more moderate, "pragmatist" faction. Yet like the May Fourth movement before it, it was also an attempt to entirely refashion a culture that had become, at least in the eyes of the radical leftists, conservative and not in the interest of the broad masses. In asserting a central role for culture within a political revolution, Mao was both acting in a fundamentally traditional way and carrying on the culturalism of the May Fourth. The reform of culture took many forms, one being the destruction of the "four olds," when Red Guards destroyed manifestations of "feudal" (i.e., traditional) or "bourgeois" (i.e., Western) cultures, including smashing temples, burning books, and torturing intellectuals. Writers associated with the pro-Western May Fourth were attacked—those who had died or were living outside the PRC were attacked in absentia—and their works were banned. Made into a poster boy for the radical leftists, Lu Xun (who had died in 1936) escaped attack, although everything he had stood for during his life—critical consciousness and autonomy for the intellectual—was in the process of being destroyed.

Two of the most important cultural forms during the Cultural Revolution were model revolutionary dramas and propaganda posters (for example, figs. 5.6 and 5.7). Both were ubiquitous elements of everyday life. The latter were posted in public places to advertise Party policy and keep people abreast of political shifts. They were also hung in private homes, where they demonstrated political loyalty and offered decorative color to drab apartments and dormitories. The model dramas were performed on stage throughout urban China, and distributed to remote rural regions in filmed versions. State radio stations broadcast productions and played arias from the operas, which every school child learned. Jiang Qing (1913–1991), Mao's wife, was directly involved in the development and production of these dramas in the form of Peking operas and Western-style ballets. She worked closely with scriptwriters, actors, and musicians. Whereas most commentators since the end of the Cultural Revolution have castigated Jiang Qing for creating a cultural wasteland by promoting these propaganda dramas to the exclusion of more sophisticated art, some see in them a sincere effort to fashion not only a revolutionary culture, but a feminist one as well. The most well known of these dramas is the ballet *White Haired Girl* (fig. 5.8), the story of which can be traced back to a folk legend that was made into an opera in Yan'an in the 1940s. It is the tale of Xi'er, a peasant girl who because of poverty is sold as a slave into the house of a rich and powerful landlord family. Xi'er escapes the oppressive household and makes her way to the mountains, living in a cave and surviving on berries (malnutrition causes her hair to turn white). The Eighth Route Army rescues her and her hair turns dark again. A ghostly life in the "old society" is made human through the intervention of the CCP.

The Post-Mao Period (1977–present)

When Mao died in 1976, radicals in the CCP who had promoted his leftist policies were arrested, and Deng Xiaoping (1904–1997) emerged from political purgatory to take over the reins of government. Deng instituted a remarkable change in the cultural sphere, reversing the Maoist view that culture is subservient to politics. Although there were periods when the state recoiled and cracked down on dissent, writers, artists, and filmmakers were freer in the 1980s than they had ever been in the history of the PRC.

Much as the May Fourth was viewed as liberation from an authoritarian tradition, the early post-Mao period has been portrayed as a kind of liberation from a repressive Maoist past. The Cultural Revolution was the primary target of this liberation; its radical politics were attacked, as was its revolutionary culture. Culture was the principal forum for this attack; and although by implication the critique sometimes seemed to undermine socialism itself, the Deng regime permitted it because it bolstered the regime's own political position, which gained legitimacy in vilifying its predecessor. Much of this early post-Mao culture—we see it in film, fiction, and visual art—sought to expose the "wounds" suffered primarily by youths and intellectuals during the Cultural Revolution. Kong Jiesheng's (1952–) "On the Other Side of the Stream" (1979) is a fine example of "wounds" or "scar" literature (reading 43). It tells the story of a brother and sister separated at a young age because of their parents' tarnished political reputations. They are reunited years later on a rubber plantation collective on Hainan Island but do not recognize each other. They fall in love. Only after they have made love do they discover each other's identity. To their great relief, they eventually learn that they are not related by blood, the sister having been adopted. The story demonizes the Cultural Revolution as the cause of incest and the complete disruption of normal family relations. Although these sorts of cultural products served an important cathartic function—purging the horrors of the Cultural Revolution and allowing people to get on with their lives—they also served the essentially conservative function of legitimizing the Deng regime. Their treatment of characters, moreover, is superficial and stereotypical, not far removed from that seen in the model dramas of the Cultural Revolution. As Perry Link describes, motivating stories like this—and much of the culture of the 1980s—is a deep-felt sense of moral and social responsibility, one that derived from a traditional sense of "anxious concern for national affairs" that was reinforced by socialist political engagement (reading 44).

As Party control over cultural workers relaxed, writers, artists, and filmmakers became increasingly radical in their experimentation. Visual artists experimented with expressionism, impressionism, and surrealism; writers with stream-of-consciousness, achronological plot lines, and multiple-perspective narrative modes; and filmmakers with flashback, camera angle, and non-narrative visual language. By the late 1980s China had developed a self-styled cultural avant-garde. In art, the avant-garde took many forms: performance art (in an infamous 1989 exhibition in Beijing, an artist walked into the exhibition hall with a gun and shot her own exhibit), conceptual art (Xu Bing's [1955–] series entitled "Book from the Sky" [fig. 5.9]), and ironic pop art images of the revolutionary past (Wang Guangyi's [1956–] "Great Castigation Series" [fig. 5.10]). A group of young filmmakers who graduated from the 1982 class of the Beijing Film Academy and later became known as the Fifth Generation of directors, sought to create a new cinematic language that rejected the literary and narrative emphasis of mainstream films like those of Xie Jin and tried, sometimes unsuccessfully, to avoid its use of melodrama. *Yellow Earth* (1984), directed by Chen Kaige (1952–), was the first such film. In literature, the avant-garde sought to develop a new literary language, purged of all Maoist influences. Stories such as Yu Hua's (1960–) "On the Road at Eighteen" also subvert the tropes of revolutionary culture (reading 45). The young man who sets out on the road of life in this allegorical tale is ill-equipped to face the radical contingencies of the world, a world that makes little sense and is filled with senseless violence. The implication is that ideology, particularly but not exclusively socialist ideology, cannot prepare one for an encounter with reality. In all of these art forms, we see once again an attempt to refashion culture for ultimately political purposes.

Artists and writers also pushed the limits of what kinds of stories could be told and themes pursued. Love and sex, considered bourgeois subjects in the Cultural Revolution, became common topics in post-Mao culture. The journalist Dai Qing (1941–) challenged Party versions of modern Chinese history in her reportage writing. Among the most controversial cultural products of the post-Mao era was the television documentary *Deathsong of the River* (also known as *River Elegy*), first broadcast in 1988, perhaps the most liberal period in the history of the PRC (reading 46). Very much in the May Fourth iconoclastic mode, the documentary glorifies the West as a means of criticizing Chinese tradition and the reappearance of traditional values in the socialist culture of the Maoist and post-Mao periods. The documentary was notorious for mocking revered cultural symbols, such as the Great Wall and the Yellow River, as emblems of Chinese isolationism and conservatism.

Perhaps the most far-reaching cultural transformation in the post-Mao era has been the return of urban popular culture. Existing only in underground "hand-copied" editions in the Mao years, popular literary genres like romance, mystery, science fiction, and martial arts have returned with a vengeance. Melodrama, thrillers, and martial arts are now popular film genres. Rock 'n' roll and pop music, much of it from Taiwan and Hong Kong, have captured the imagination of young people, offering forms of identification very different from any available in other cultural forms. Although the current popular music scene in China is varied and heterogeneous, one figure clearly stood out in the 1980s: Cui Jian (1961–) (fig. 5.11). His "I Have Nothing" became something of an anthem for angry, disaffected youth of the late 1980s, although it must be said that most Chinese continued to favor the saccharine love songs from Taiwan and Hong Kong over Cui Jian's raspy and angry sound (reading 47).

This same disaffected youth was also reading the novels of Wang Shuo (1958–). Subverting neat hierarchies of elite and popular literature, Wang's novels use popular forms (e.g., mystery in *Playing for Thrills*), but seem also to have a serious, politically subversive message, which Wang is at pains to deny (reading 48). His novels have been labeled "punk literature" because their main characters are irreverent cynics who are unemployed and often engaged in illegal activities; they drink, gamble, and womanize, and speak in a Beijing street language that mocks all authority and socialist moral values. Wang often parodies the official language of bureaucrats and other representatives of the state. Clearly, his tremendous popularity with young readers owes much to this satirical and mocking tone.

Wang Shuo's novels, and his marketing and promotion of them, also point to a broader phenomenon in the 1990s: the commercialization of culture. Over the course of the 1980s and especially into the 1990s, Chinese cultural institutions (film studios, television and radio stations, publishing houses, magazines and journals, etc.) have been gradually weaned of state subsidies and forced to largely support themselves. To survive, they have had to make products with a broad market appeal, and this has radically changed the shape of the cultural sphere. Evening newspapers, which focus less on hard news and more on lurid crime and entertainment, have overtaken their more serious daily counterparts in sales. Soap operas, sitcoms, and sports programming dominate the airwaves of state-run television stations. And, most significantly, advertising is omnipresent, although not yet to the degree it is in the United States. Serious and savvy Fifth Generation filmmakers like Zhang Yimou (1950–) and Chen Kaige produced such films as *Raise the Red Lantern* and *Farewell My Concubine* that, some say, were designed more for foreign consumption, with the hope of winning awards on the foreign film festival circuit, than for a domestic audience. And indeed, these films have perhaps had their greatest impact outside of China in shaping Western views of China.

This commercial tide has profoundly changed the role of culture in China. Intellectuals, writers, and artists struggle in this radically new environ-ment to find new roles for themselves. Some writers and artists struggle against it, retreating into purist views of literature as a transcendent realm apart from the crassness of the cultural marketplace. The very notion of cultural revolution, not just that of the Maoist era but even the more humanist May Fourth cultural revolution, is now openly scorned as idealist and utopian, a relic of former times. This commercialization of culture—and the larger consumer revolution—may prove, however, to be the most radical cultural revolution of all, one that has already changed the way individuals in China relate to each other and to the state. Contrary to the popular image conveyed in the Western mass media, the cultural scene of post-1989 China, as Geremie Barmé describes in his essay, is lively and heterogeneous (reading 49). The state has lost its ability to impose the kind of control over intellectuals it may have had in earlier times, and intellectuals are able to speak out quite openly, finding many ways of resisting the state and the onslaught of globalization and commercialization its economic policies have unleashed.

This global—some might say postmodern—culture is captured beautifully in "Fin de Siècle Splendor" (1990), a story by the Taiwan writer Zhu Tianwen (1956–) (reading 50). Mia, the story's main protagonist, is a fashion model living in Taipei. Her world and her life are defined by the constantly changing designer fashions from Japan, Milan, Paris, and New York. The story can be read as an allegory of the postmodern condition in which we are bombarded by a barrage of consumer signifiers—designer labels, trademarks, etc. This is the culture that is now shared, to a large degree, by Chinese in mainland China, Hong Kong, and Taipei, as well as those of us who live in Europe and North America. But behind this global postmodern culture of hybridity, one can also find nostalgic counter reactions like that expressed in the poet Yu Guangzhong's (1928–) "Homesickness" (1960s) (reading 51). Rather than celebrating cultural fragmentation, this poem expresses longing for a home and wholeness that Yu, who grew up on the mainland, moved to Taiwan, and has lived for extended periods in the United States and Hong Kong, perhaps never had in his life. Similarly, Chen Shun Chu's "Family Parade" (fig. 12), a work of installation art built on Taiwan's Penghu Island, suggests perhaps both the fragile state of the family in postmodern society and a longing for the stability and comfort family offers.

CULTURE
Figures and Readings

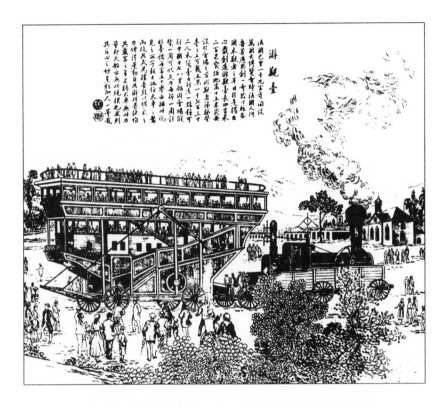

Fig. 5.1. Late Qing lithograph

Lithography was a new printing technology imported into China in the 1870s that quickly supplanted the woodblock printing industry. It was used by some of the emerging commercial presses in Shanghai to print, among other things, textbooks for candidates to prepare for the civil service examination, cheap editions of the Chinese classics, and dictionaries. The technology was also used by *Shenbao*, one of the leading Shanghai newspapers, in the production of their supplement, the *Dianshizhai Pictorial* (*Dianshizhai huabao*, 1884–1898), which presented illustrations (with commentaries) of current events, life in the emerging metropolis of Shanghai, world news, interesting inventions and exotica from the West, and all manner of oddities. This print shows the Mobile Observation Platform, which the accompanying text tells us was invented by a Frenchman for the 1890 International Exposition held in Paris and used for touring the exposition grounds. The late Qing was fascinated with things modern and Western, and these sorts of prints were an important means by which modernity, or an idea of the modern, was conveyed to a popular audience.

413

Fig. 5.2. Sun Sun Company advertising (1926)

This is an advertisement for Sun Sun (Xinxin) Company, Shanghai's third largest department store, after Wing On and Sincere. Sun Sun opened in 1926 and was located on Nanjing Road, the principal commercial thoroughfare in Shanghai. The modern department store, of course, offered a mode of shopping very different from traditional times, when shoppers would go to specialty stores or goods were brought by vendors to residences. The ad reads: "Sun Sun Company, with capital to spare, built this building seven stories high. We have products from around the globe, inexpensive and of high quality, and only the very best Chinese domestic products. Our banking facilities offer you high interest rates. You can give gift certificates to your friends and gain some face. The Sun Sun Hotel is arranged most exquisitely. It has both Chinese and Western food and drink, all prepared with great care. On the roof is a garden offering high-class entertainment. Our offerings are constantly changing. We have all that a department store should have."

414

Fig. 5.3. Republican Fashion (1926)

Fashions changed dramatically in the early twentieth century. Elite men began to abandon their scholars' robes and cotton shoes for Western suits and leather shoes. Footbinding for women was gradually eradicated, and the small silk and cotton shoes were replaced with pumps and high heels. The *qipao*, or cheongsam, a tight-fitting dress with a slit down one side, was all the rage in the early Republican period. Although it is now seen as a traditional Chinese form of dress, it was at the time modern and provocative. Magazines like *Companion Illustrated*, in which the above illustrations appeared, often contained sections on fashion, movies and movie stars, as well as more serious fare. The text reads, in part: "What Illustration A shows derives from, with modifications, the cheongsam. The outfit is green and adorned with a flowered border. Although its form is beautiful, it's not unconventional. What Illustration B presents is a motif based on the heart [*sic*] from poker cards to adorn the green. Most suitable for summer. The outfit's flowing quality makes for a very unusual look. What Illustration C shows is appropriate for a fashionable young married woman. The skirt is green, with black lines circling around. The sleeves are in a western style. The top part of the skirt and the blouse are decorated with black butterflies, the two calling to each other, giving the outfit an even prettier look."

415

Fig. 5.4. "Waiting" (1933, Chen Tiegeng)   Fig. 5.5. "China, Roar!" (1936, Li Hua)

The modern Chinese woodcut movement began in the 1930s. Stylistically, it was influenced by traditional Chinese and Japanese woodcuts, as well as Western modernist, expressionist styles (for instance, that of the German Käthe Köllwitz). The movement was closely associated with Lu Xun, who promoted it, and with leftist politics, but its origins were also in the avant-garde. Not all woodcuts were explicitly political. Some of the woodcut artists were more interested in self-expression and modernist experimentation. Chen Tiegeng's (1908–1970) "Waiting," for example, although it can be given a political message, is not explicitly so. What stands out is the more universal theme of anxiety. Li Hua's (1907–1994) "China, Roar," done on the eve of war against the Japanese, is clearly political, though it is done in a highly expressionist style. Here the Chinese people are shown in bondage, but with a defiant will to struggle and resist.

Fig. 5.6. "Destroy the Old World; Establish a New World"

Fig. 5.7. "In Following the Revolutionary Road, Strive for Even Greater Victory"

Political propaganda posters were an omnipresent part of daily life during the Cultural Revolution. These posters served to announce policy, encourage mass political participation, create models for emulation, give information, and, most importantly, to propagate the Maoist ideology of continuing revolution. The two posters here represent two very different styles. "Destroy the Old World . . ." is typical of the early Red Guard style of poster, which consciously harkened back to the woodcut prints of the 1930s. In the first poster, a Red Guard is smashing objects associated with the "old society": a Buddha, a Christ figurine, records, gambling die, etc. The second poster reflects the Maoist personality cult of the later Cultural Revolution. Here Mao is deified: transcendent, imperial, a disembodied head above the masses.

Fig. 5.8. The White Haired Girl ballet

White Haired Girl is perhaps the most famous of the Cultural Revolution model dramas (Peking operas and ballets deemed politically correct and disseminated nationwide to propagate a Maoist vision of the revolutionary past and the political present). Their ideological function was to divert attention away from the poverty, social problems, and political chaos of the day; construct a revolutionary past that was clear and meaningful and served to keep alive the revolutionary spirit in the present; and to portray history as a morality play in which there is a heroic victory of the forces of goodness and light over evil and darkness. Of course, they also were used as weapons in the political factionalism of the Cultural Revolution. *White Haired Girl* tells the story of Xi'er, sold into slavery by her father who is badly in debt. Xi'er escapes the cruel oppression of the evil landlord's family and flees into the mountains, where she lives in a cave and eats berries (thus turning her hair white). Xi'er is eventually liberated from her cave by members of the Eighth Route Army.

Fig. 5.9. "Book from the Sky" (1987–1991, Xu Bing)

Xu Bing, a PRC artist now working in the West, has been one of the most provocative and popular of Chinese avant-garde artists. His series entitled "Book from the Sky" are displays of meticulously carved woodcuts of non-existent Chinese characters printed on vast expanses of white paper. The installation above contains thousands of printed characters, all of which are fabricated by the artist and have no meaning. His work makes us think about the power of the written word and ultimately question the authority of those who use it to speak the truth and represent things

Fig. 5.10. "Great Castigation Series: Coca Cola" (1993, Wang Guangyi)

This oil painting is part of a large series by Wang Guangyi (1956–). The series combines Cultural Revolutionary imagery with icons and logos of contemporary consumer culture (*Elle* magazine, Hitachi, Disney, Adidas). This sort of political pop art was very popular in avant-garde circles in the 1990s. Artists had great fun with Mao's image. Wang's painting suggests at once a revolutionary attack on the global commodity culture symbolized by the Coca Cola logo and an analogy between radical politics and commodity culture.

Fig. 5.11. Rocker Cui Jian

Cui Jian was the king of Chinese rock 'n' roll in the 1980s.

Fig. 5.12. "House—Family Parade" (1995–1996, Chen Shun Chu)

Conceptual and installation art has been extremely popular among Chinese avant-garde artists. In this work, which was installed outdoors on his native Penghu Islands off the coast of Taiwan, Chen Shun Chu presents a decrepit, roofless stone house covered with framed photographs of his own family and friends, standing in formal poses. In effect, Chen's loved ones are inseparable from the foundation of the house and the house is inseparable from the barren landscape of his native place. Central elements of the Chinese cultural consciousness, family, home, and native place are tied together, although in a very tenuous and ironic manner, through the crumbling house, suggesting perhaps the fragile state of the family in postmodern Taiwan.

38

Medicine

LU XUN

Lu Xun (1881–1936), generally recognized as modern China's greatest writer, wrote two collections of short stories, Call to Arms *(Nahan, 1923) and* Wandering *(Panghuang, 1926). "Medicine," included in the former, is iconoclastic in tone, denouncing tradition and its backward and conservative values, and continuing the cannibalistic theme introduced in his earlier "Diary of a Madman." Although socialist critics have generally interpreted the final images of the story (the wreath and the crows) as positive signs pointing to a revolutionary future, the story as a whole shows us how tradition literally consumes the blood of the revolution—not a very optimistic view of the possibility of social change.*

1

It was autumn, in the small hours of the morning. The moon had gone down, but the sun had not yet risen, and the sky appeared a sheet of darkling blue. Apart from night-prowlers, all was asleep. Old Shuan suddenly sat up in bed. He struck a match and lit the grease-covered oil-lamp, which shed a ghostly light over the two rooms of the teahouse.

"Are you going, now, Dad?" queried an old woman's voice. And from the small inner room a fit of coughing was heard.

"H'm."

Old Shuan listened as he fastened his clothes, then stretching out his hand said, "Let's have it."

After some fumbling under the pillow his wife produced a packet of silver dollars which she handed over. Old Shuan pocketed it nervously, patted his pocket twice, then lighting a paper lantern and blowing out the lamp went into the inner room. A rustling was heard, and then more coughing. When all was quiet again, Old Shuan called softly, "Son! . . . Don't you get up! . . . Your mother will see to the shop."

Receiving no answer, Old Shuan assumed his son must be sound asleep again; so he went out into the street. In the darkness nothing could be seen but the grey roadway. The lantern light fell on his pacing feet. Here and there he came across dogs, but none of them barked. It was much colder than indoors, yet Old Shuan's spirits rose, as if he had grown suddenly younger and possessed some miraculous life-giving power. He had lengthened his stride. And the road became increasingly clear, the sky increasingly bright.

Absorbed in his walking, Old Shuan was startled when he saw the crossroad lying distinctly ahead of him. He walked back a few steps to stand under the eaves of a shop, in front of its closed door. After some time he began to feel chilly.

"Uh, an old chap."

"Seems rather cheerful. . . ."

Old Shuan started again and, opening his eyes, saw several men passing. One of them even turned back to look at him, and although he could not see him clearly, the man's eyes shone with a lustful light, like a famished person's at the sight of food. Looking at his lantern, Old Shuan saw it had gone out. He patted his pocket—the hard packet was still there. Then he looked round and saw many strange people, in twos and threes, wandering about like lost souls. However, when he gazed steadily at them, he could not see anything else strange about them.

Presently he saw some soldiers strolling around. The large white circles on their uniforms, both in front and behind, were clear even at a distance; and as they drew nearer, the dark red border could be seen too. The next second, with a trampling of feet, a crowd rushed past. Thereupon the small groups which had arrived earlier suddenly converged and surged forward. Just before the crossroad, they came to a sudden stop and grouped themselves in a semi-circle.

Old Shuan looked in that direction too, but could only see people's backs. Craning their necks as far as they would go, they looked like so many ducks, held and lifted by some invisible hand. For a moment all was still; then a sound was heard, and a stir swept through the onlookers. There was a rumble as they pushed back, sweeping past Old Shuan and nearly knocking him down.

"Hey! Give me the cash, and I'll give you the goods!" A man clad entirely in black stood before him, his eyes like daggers, making Old Shuan shrink to half his normal size. This man was thrusting one huge extended hand towards him, while in the other he held a roll of steamed bread, from which crimson drops were dripping to the ground.

Hurriedly Old Shuan fumbled for his dollars, and trembling he was about to hand them over, but he dared not take the object. The other grew impatient, and shouted, "What are you afraid of? Why not take it?" When Old Shuan still hesitated, the man in black snatched his lantern and tore off its paper shade to wrap up the roll. This package he thrust into Old Shuan's hand, at the same time seizing the silver and giving it a cursory feel. Then he turned away, muttering, "Old fool. . . ."

"Whose sickness is this for?" Old Shuan seemed to hear someone ask; but he made no reply. His whole mind was on the package, which he carried as carefully as if it were the sole heir to an ancient house. Nothing else mattered now. He was about to transplant this new life to his own home, and reap much happiness. The sun too had risen, lighting up the broad highway before him, which led straight home, and the worn tablet behind him at the crossroad with its faded gold inscription: "Ancient Pavilion."

2

When Old Shuan reached home, the shop had been cleaned, and the rows of tea tables were shining brightly, but no customers had arrived. Only his son was sitting at a table by the wall, eating. Beads of sweat stood out on his forehead, his lined jacket was sticking to his spine, and his shoulder blades stuck out so sharply, an inverted V seemed stamped there. At this sight, Old Shuan's brow, which had been clear, contracted again. His wife hurried in from the kitchen, with expectant eyes and a tremor to her lips.

"Get it?"

"Yes."

They went together into the kitchen, and. conferred for a time. Then the old woman went out, to return shortly with a dried lotus leaf which she spread on the table. Old Shuan unwrapped the crimson-stained roll from the lantern paper and transferred it to the lotus leaf. Little Shuan had finished his meal, but his mother exclaimed hastily:

"Sit still, Little Shuan! Don't come over here."

Mending the fire in the stove, Old Shuan put the green package and the red and white lantern paper into the stove together. A red-black flame flared up, and a strange odour permeated the shop.

"Smells good! What are you eating?" The hunchback had arrived. He was one of those who spend all their time in tea houses, the first to come in the morning and the last to leave. Now he had just stumbled to a corner table facing the street, and sat down. But no one answered his question.

"Puffed rice gruel?"

Still no reply. Old Shuan hurried out to brew tea for him.

"Come here, Little Shuan!" His mother called him into the inner room, set a stool in the middle, and sat the child down. Then, bringing him a round black object on a plate, she said gently:

"Eat it up . . . then you'll be better."

Little Shuan picked up the black object and looked at it. He had the oddest feeling, as if he were holding his own life in his hands. Presently he split it carefully open. From within the charred crust a jet of white vapour escaped, then scattered, leaving only two halves of a white flour steamed roll. Soon it was all eaten, the flavour completely forgotten, only the empty plate left. His father and mother were standing one on each side of him, their eyes apparently pouring something into him and at the same time extracting something. His small heart began to beat faster, and, putting his hands to his chest, he began to cough again.

"Have a sleep; then you'll be all right," said his mother.

Obediently, Little Shuan coughed himself to sleep. The woman waited till his breathing was regular, then covered him lightly with a much patched quilt.

3

The shop was crowded, and Old Shuan was busy, carrying a big copper kettle to make tea for one customer after another. But there were dark circles under his eyes.

"Aren't you well, Old Shuan? . . . What's wrong with you?" asked one greybeard.

"Nothing."

"Nothing? . . . No, I suppose from your smile, there couldn't be," the old man corrected himself.

"It's just that Old Shuan's busy," said the hunchback.

"If his son. . ." But before he could finish, a heavy-jowled man burst in. He had over his shoulders a dark brown shirt, unbuttoned and fastened carelessly by a broad dark brown girdle at his waist. As soon as he entered, he shouted to Old Shuan:

"Has he taken it? Any better? Luck's with you, Old Shuan. What luck! If not for my hearing of things so quickly. . . ."

Holding the kettle in one hand, the other straight by his side in an attitude of respect, Old Shuan listened with a smile. In fact, all present were listening respectfully.

「老栓彷彿得了神通，有給人生命的本領
似的，跨步格外高遠。」

「喂！一手交錢，一手交貨！」

吃下去罷，病便好了。

你看！——看這是甚麼呢？

Fig. 5.13. Feng Zikai illustrations to "Medicine" (1954)

The old woman, dark circles under her eyes too, came out smiling with a bowl containing tea-leaves and an added olive, over which Old Shuan poured boiling water for the newcomer.

"This is a guaranteed cure! Not like other things!" declared the heavy-jowled man. "Just think, brought back warm, and eaten warm!"

"Yes indeed, we couldn't have managed it without Uncle Kang's help." The old woman thanked him very warmly.

"A guaranteed cure! Eaten warm like this. A roll dipped in human blood like this can cure any consumption!"

The old woman seemed a little disconcerted by the word "consumption," and turned a shade paler; however, she forced a smile again at once and found some pretext to leave. Meanwhile the man in brown was indiscreet enough to go on talking at the top of his voice until the child in the inner room was woken and started coughing.

"So you've had such a stroke of luck for your Little Shuan! Of course his sickness will be cured completely. No wonder Old Shuan keeps smiling." As he spoke, the, greybeard walked up to the man in brown, and lowered his voice to ask:

"Mr. Kang, I heard the criminal executed today came from the Xia family. Who was it? And why was he executed?"

"Who? Son of Widow Xia, of course! Young rascal!"

Seeing how they were all hanging on his words, Mr. Kang's spirits rose even higher. His jowls quivered, and he made his voice as loud as he could.

"The rogue didn't want to live, simply didn't want to! There was nothing in it for me this time. Even the clothes stripped from him were taken by Red-eye, the jailer. Our Old Shuan was luckiest, and after him Third Uncle Xia. He pocketed the whole reward—twenty-five taels of bright silver—and didn't have to spend a cent!"

Little Shuan walked slowly out of the inner room, his hands to his chest, coughing repeatedly. He went to the kitchen, filled a bowl with cold rice, added hot water to it, and sitting down started to eat. His mother, hovering over him, asked softly:

"Do you feel better, son? Still as hungry as ever?"

"A guaranteed cure!" Kang glanced at the child, then turned back to address the company. "Third Uncle Xia is really smart. If he hadn't informed, even *his* family would have been executed, and their property confiscated. But instead? Silver! That young rogue was a real scoundrel! He even tried to incite the jailer to revolt!"

"No! The idea of it!" A man in his twenties, sitting in the back row, expressed indignation.

"You know, Red-eye went to sound him out, but he started chatting with him. He said the great Qing empire belongs to us. Just think: Is that kind of talk rational? Red-eye knew he had only an old mother at home, but had never imagined he was so poor. He couldn't squeeze anything out of him; he was already good and angry, and then the young fool would 'scratch the tiger's head,' so he gave him a couple of slaps."

"Red-eye is a good boxer. Those slaps must have hurt!" The hunchback in the corner by the wall exulted.

"The rotter was not afraid of being beaten. He even said how sorry he was."

"Nothing to be sorry about in beating a wretch like that," said Greybeard.

Kang looked at him superciliously and said disdainfully, "You misunderstood. The way he said it, he was sorry for Red-eye."

His listeners' eyes took on a glazed look, and no one spoke. Little Shuan had finished his rice and was perspiring profusely, his head steaming.

"Sorry for Red-eye—crazy! He must have been crazy!" said Greybeard, as if suddenly he saw light.

"He must have been crazy!" echoed the man in his twenties.

Once more the customers began to show animation, and conversation was resumed. Under cover of the noise, the child was seized by a paroxysm of coughing. Kang went up to him, clapped him on the shoulder, and said:

"A guaranteed cure! Don't cough like that, Little Shuan! A guaranteed cure!"

"Crazy!" agreed the hunchback, nodding his head.

4

Originally, the land adjacent to the city wall outside the West Gate had been public land. The zigzag path slanting across it, trodden out by passers-by seeking a short cut, had become a natural boundary line. Left of the path, executed criminals or those who had died of neglect in prison were buried. Right of the path were paupers' graves. The serried ranks of grave mounds on both sides looked like the rolls laid out for a rich man's birthday.

The Qing Ming Festival that year was unusually cold. Willows were only beginning to put forth shoots no larger than grains. Shortly after daybreak, Old Shuan's wife brought four dishes and a bowl of rice to set before a new grave in the right section, and wailed before it. When she had burned paper money she sat on the ground in a stupor as if waiting for something; but for what, she herself did not know. A breeze sprang up and stirred her short hair, which was certainly whiter than in the previous year.

Another woman came down the path, grey-haired and in rags. She was carrying an old, round, red-lacquered basket, with a string of paper money hanging from it; and she walked haltingly. When she saw Old Shuan's wife sitting on the ground watching her, she hesitated, and a hush of shame spread over her pale face. However, she summoned up courage to cross over to a grave in the left section, where she set down her basket.

That grave was directly opposite Little Shuan's, separated only by the path. As Old Shuan's wife watched the other woman set out four dishes and a bowl of rice, then stand up to wail and burn paper money, she thought, "It must be her son in that grave too." The older woman took a few aimless steps and stared vacantly around, then suddenly she began to tremble and stagger backward: she felt giddy.

Fearing sorrow might send her out of her mind, Old Shuan's wife got up and stepped across the path, to say quietly, "Don't grieve, let's go home."

The other nodded, but her eyes were still fixed, and she muttered, "Look! What's that?"

Looking where she pointed, Old Shuan's wife saw that the grave in front had not yet been overgrown with grass. Ugly patches of soil still showed. But when she looked carefully, she was surprised to see at the top of the mound a wreath of red and white flowers.

Both of them suffered from failing eyesight, yet they could see these red and white flowers clearly. There were not many, but they were placed in a circle; and although not very fresh, were neatly set out. Little Shuan's mother looked round and found her own son's grave, like most of the rest, dotted with only a few little, pale flowers shivering in the cold. Suddenly she had a sense of futility and stopped feeling curious about the wreath.

Meantime the old woman had gone up to the grave to look more closely. "They have no roots," she said to herself. "They can't have grown here. Who could have been here? Children don't come here to play, and none of our relatives have ever been. What could have happened?" She puzzled over it, until suddenly her tears began to fall, and she cried aloud:

"Son, they all wronged you, and you do not forget. Is your grief still so great that today you worked this wonder to let me know?"

She looked all around, but could see only a crow perched on a leafless bough. "I know," she continued. "They murdered you. But a day of reckoning will come, Heaven will see to it. Close your eyes in peace. . . . If you are really here, and can hear me, make that crow fly on to your grave as a sign."

The breeze had long since dropped, and the dry grass stood stiff and straight as copper wires. A faint, tremulous sound vibrated in the air, then faded and died away. All around was deathly still. They stood in the dry grass, looking up at the crow; and the crow, on the rigid bough of the tree, its head drawn in, stood immobile as iron.

Time passed. More people, young and old, came to visit the graves.

Old Shuan's wife felt somehow as if a load had been lifted from her mind and, wanting to leave, she urged the other:

"Let's go."

The old woman sighed, and listlessly picked up the rice and dishes. After a moment's hesitation she started slowly off, still muttering to herself:

"What could it mean?"

They had not gone thirty paces when they heard a loud caw behind them. Startled, they looked round and saw the crow stretch its wings, brace itself to take off, then fly like an arrow towards the far horizon.

April 1919

39

Autumn Night

LU XUN

This prose poem, a genre Lu Xun helped to develop in China, was one of twenty-three poems included in a collection entitled Wild Grass *(Yecao, 1927). Marxist critics in China have had a tough time with these poems, for their tone is pessimistic, their style lyrical and imagistic, and their focus deeply personal—in other words, they are not in the combative, iconoclastic style for which Lu Xun was respected. They have often been given, therefore, rather forced readings that draw more from Lu Xun's life than they do from the texts themselves. These poems show us that even for a figure like Lu Xun, who had done more than anyone to formulate a discourse of nation and modernity, the individual psyche and its conflicts and struggles continued to be important literary concerns.*

Behind the wall of my backyard you can see two trees: one is a date tree, the other is also a date tree.

The night sky above them is strange and high. I have never seen such a strange, high sky. It seems to want to leave this world of men, so that when folk look up they won't be able to see it. For the moment, though, it is singularly blue; and its scores of starry eyes are blinking coldly. A faint smile plays round its lips, a smile which it seems to think highly significant; and it dusts the wild plants in my courtyard with heavy frost.

I have no idea what these plants are called, what names they are commonly known by. One of them, I remember, has minute pink flowers, and its flowers are still lingering on, although more minute than ever. Shivering in the cold night air they dream of the coming of spring, of the coming of autumn, of the lean poet wiping his tears upon their last petals, who tells them autumn will come and winter will come, yet spring will follow when butterflies flit to and fro, and all the bees start humming songs of spring. Then the little pink flowers smile, though they have turned a mournful crimson with cold and are shivering still.

As for the date trees, they have lost absolutely all their leaves. Before, one or two boys still came to beat down the dates other people had missed. But now not one date is left, and the trees have lost all their leaves as well. They know the little pink flowers' dream of spring after autumn; and they know the dream of the fallen leaves of autumn after spring. They may have lost all their leaves and have only their branches left; but these, no longer weighed down with fruit and foliage, are stretching themselves luxuriously. A few boughs, though, are still drooping, nursing the wounds made in their bark by the sticks which beat down the dates: while, rigid as iron, the straightest and longest boughs silently pierce the strange, high sky, making it blink in dismay. They pierce even the full moon in the sky, making it pale and ill at ease.

Blinking in dismay, the sky becomes bluer and bluer, more and more uneasy, as if eager to escape from the world of men and avoid the date trees, leaving the moon behind. But the moon, too, is hiding itself in the east; while, silent still and as rigid as iron, the bare boughs pierce the strange, high sky, resolved to inflict on it a mortal wound, no matter in how many ways it winks all its bewitching eyes.

With a shriek, a fierce night-bird passes.

All of a sudden, I hear midnight laughter. The sound is muffled, as if not to wake those who sleep; yet all around the air resounds to this laughter. Midnight, and no one else is by. At once I realize it is *I* who am laughing, and at once I am driven by this laughter back to my room. At once I turn up the wick of my paraffin lamp.

A pit-a-pat sounds from the glass of the back window, where swarms of insects are recklessly dashing themselves against the pane. Presently some get in, no doubt through a hole in the window paper. Once in, they set up another pit-a-pat by dashing themselves against the chimney of the lamp. One hurls itself into the chimney from the top, falling into the flame, and I fancy the flame is real. On the paper shade two or three others rest, panting. The shade is a new one since last night. Its snow-white paper is pleated in wave-like folds, and painted in one corner is a spray of blood-red gardenias.

When the blood-red gardenias blossom, the date trees, weighed down with bright foliage, will dream once more the dream of the little pink flowers . . . and I shall hear the midnight laughter again. I hastily break off this train of thought to look at the small green insects still on the paper. Like sunflower seeds with their large heads and small tails, they are only half the size of a grain of wheat, the whole of them an adorable, pathetic green.

I yawn, light a cigarette, and puff out the smoke, paying silent homage before the lamp to these green and exquisite heroes.

September 15, 1924

40

Talks at the Yan'an Forum
on Art and Literature

MAO ZEDONG

It may seem odd that Mao Zedong (1893–1976), head of the CCP, would give lectures on art and culture to cultural workers in Yan'an in the midst of the war against Japan (1937–1945) and an on-going conflict with their erstwhile allies, the Nationalists. But just as Mao developed during the war his major ideological writings that would become known as Mao Zedong Thought, he also felt a need to forge a cultural policy. The "Yan'an Talks," given in the spring of 1942, although not original or sophisticated literary theory, would become the theoretical basis for the rigid cultural policy implemented by the CCP after the revolution. It is as such among the most important texts in the cultural history of the PRC. Even today, in the free-wheeling atmosphere of the PRC cultural market, the "Talks" serve as a keenly felt reminder of more oppressive times. The "Talks" were given as part of the Yan'an Rectification movement, aimed at bringing in line wayward writers, intellectuals, and political cadres, and clearly part of Mao's strategy of gaining absolute control over the Party membership. Mao's central idea is that literature should serve political interests, interests determined by the Party.

Comrades! Our forum has met three times this month, and several dozen party and non-party comrades have spoken up in our search for truth. Heated debates have taken place, bringing problems into the open and making them concrete; I believe that this will prove beneficial to the whole movement in literature and art. . . .

Well then, what is the central issue facing us? In my opinion, our problem is fundamentally one of serving the masses and how to do this. If we do not solve this problem, or if we do not solve it properly, then our workers in literature and art will not be attuned to their circumstances and responsibilities and will come up against a string of problems both internal and external. My conclusion will consist of some further explanation with this problem as the central issue and will also touch on a few other problems related to it.

1

The first question is: who are the people our literature and art are for? . . .

There is in truth such a thing as literature and art that serve exploiters and oppressors. The literature and art that serve the landlord class are feudal literature and art, that is, the literature and art of the ruling class in China during the feudal era. This kind of literature and art still has considerable influence in China to this day. The literature and art that serve the bourgeoisie are bourgeois literature and art; although people like Liang Shiqiu, who was criticized by Lu Xun, talk about some kind of literature and art that transcends class, in practice they uphold bourgeois literature and art and oppose proletarian literature and art. The literature and art that serve imperialism, represented by people like Zhou Zuoren and Zhang Ziping, is called slave culture or slave literature and art. There is also another kind of literature and art, which serves the Special Branch and may be called "Special" literature and art: it may be "revolutionary" on the surface, but in reality it belongs with the three categories above. For us, literature and art are not for those groups mentioned above but for the people. As we have said before, the new culture of China at its present stage is an anti-imperialist, antifeudal culture of the popular masses under the leadership of the proletariat. Whatever genuinely belongs to the masses must now be under the leadership of the popular masses, and what is under the leadership of the bourgeoisie cannot belong to the masses. New literature and art, which are part of new culture, are naturally in the same category. We do not by any means refuse to use the old forms of the feudal class and the bourgeoisie, but in our hands these old forms are reconstructed and filled with new content, so that they also become revolutionary and serve the people.

Well, then, who are the popular masses? The broadest section of the people, who constitute more than ninety percent of the total population, are workers, peasants, soldiers, and the petty bourgeoisie. Therefore, our literature and art are in the first place for the workers, the class that leads the revolution. Secondly, they are for the peasants, the broadest and firmest allies in the revolution. Thirdly, they are for the workers and peasants who have taken up arms, namely the Eighth Route Army, the New Fourth Army, and other popular armed forces; these are the chief strength in war. Fourthly, they are for the petty bourgeoisie, who are also allies in the revolution and can cooperate with us on a long-term basis. These four kinds of people constitute the largest sector of the Chinese nation and the broadest popular masses. We should also make alliances with the anti-Japanese elements in the landlord class and bourgeoisie, but they do not support democracy among the broad popular masses. They have a literature and art of their own, while our literature and art are not for them and are in any case rejected by them. . . .

2

. . . Reaching a wider audience and raising standards are both worthy activities, but from what source do they arise? Works of literature and art, as conceptualized forms on whatever level of operation, are the result of the human mind reflecting and processing popular life; revolutionary literature and art are thus the result of revolutionary writers' minds, reflecting and processing popular life. Rich deposits of literature and art actually exist in popular life itself: they are things in their natural forms, crude but also extremely vivid, abundant, and fundamental; they make all processed forms of literature pale in comparison; they are the sole and inexhaustible source of processed forms of literature and art. They are the sole source, because only this kind of source can exist; no other exists apart from it. Someone may ask whether works of literature and art in book form, classical, or foreign works aren't also a source. Well, you can say they are a source, but a secondary and not a primary one; it would be a distorted way of looking at things to regard them as primary. In fact, books and other works already in existence are not the source but the flow, they are things that the ancients and foreigners processed and fabricated from the literature and art they perceived in popular life in their own time and place. We must absorb these things in a discriminating way, using them as models from which we may learn what to accept or what to reject when we process works of literature and art as conceptualized forms from the literature and art in popular life in our own time and place. It makes a difference to have this model, the difference between cultured or vulgar, crude or refined, high or low, fast or slow; therefore, we certainly may not reject the ancients and foreigners as models, which means, I'm afraid, that we must even use feudal and bourgeois things. But they are only models and not substitutes; they can't be substitutes. Indiscriminate plagiarism, imitation, or substitution in literature and art of dead people or foreigners is extremely sterile and harmful literary and artistic dogmatism of the same basic nature as dogmatism in military, political, philosophical, or economic affairs. Revolutionary Chinese writers and artists, the kind from whom we expect great things, must go among the masses; they must go among the masses of workers, peasants, and soldiers for a long time to come, without reservation, devoting body and soul to the task ahead; they must go into the heat of battle; they must go to the sole, the broadest, and the richest source, to observe, experience, study, and analyze all the different kinds of people, all the classes and all the masses, all the vivid patterns of life and struggle, and all literature and art in their natural form, before they are ready for the stage of processing or creating, where you integrate raw materials with production, the stage of study with the stage of creation. Otherwise, your toil will have no object, since without raw materials or semiprocessed goods you have nothing to process, and you will inevitably end up the kind of useless writer or artist that Lu Xun in his will earnestly instructed his son never to become. . . .

3

Since our literature and art are for the popular masses, we can now discuss two further questions, the first concerning the relationships within the party, i.e., the relation between party work in literature and art and party work as a whole; the other concerning relationships that go outside the party, i.e., the relation between the party and non-party work in literature and art—the question of the united front in literature and art.

Let us start with the first question. In the world today, all culture or literature and art belongs to a definite class and party, and has a definite political line. Art for art's sake, art that stands above class and party, and fellow-travelling or politically independent art do not exist in reality. In a society composed of classes and parties, art obeys both class and party, and it must obey the political demands of its class and party, and the revolutionary task of a given revolutionary age; any deviation is a deviation from the masses' basic need. Proletarian literature and art are part of the whole proletarian revolutionary cause; as Lenin said, they are "a screw in the whole machine," and therefore, the party's work in literature and art occupies a definite, assigned position within the party's revolutionary work as a whole. Opposition to this assignment must lead to dualism or pluralism, and in essence resembles Trotsky's "Politics— Marxist; art—bourgeois." We do not support excessive emphasis on the importance of literature and art, nor do we support their underestimation. Literature and art are subordinate to politics, and yet in turn they exert enormous influence on it. Revolutionary literature and art are a part of the whole revolutionary cause; they are a screw, which naturally doesn't compare with other parts in importance, urgency, or priority, but which is nevertheless indispensable in the whole machinery, an indispensable part of the whole revolutionary cause. If literature and art did not exist in even the broadest and most general sense, the revolution could not advance or win victory; it would be wrong not to acknowledge this. Furthermore, when we speak of literature and art obeying politics, politics refers to class and mass politics and not to the small number of people known as politicians. Politics, both revolutionary and counterrevolutionary alike, concern the struggle between classes and not the behavior of a small number of people. Ideological warfare and artistic warfare, especially if they are revolutionary, are necessarily subservient to political warfare, because class and mass needs can only be expressed in a concentrated form through politics. Revolutionary politicians are professional politicians who understand the science or art of revolutionary politics; they are simply the leaders of millions of mass politicians, and their task is to collect the opinions of mass politicians, distill them, and return them to the masses in an acceptable and practical form; they are not like the kind of aristocratic or armchair "politician" who acts as if he had a monopoly on brilliance—this is the difference in principle between politicians of the proletariat and the propertied classes, a difference that also exists between their respective politics. It would be wrong not to acknowledge this or to see proletarian politics and politicians in a narrow or conventional way. . . .

Since we must join in the new era of the masses, we must thoroughly resolve the question of the relationship between the individual and the masses. Lu Xun's couplet should become our motto:

Stern-browed I cooly face the fingers of a thousand men,
Head bowed I'm glad to be an ox for the little children.

The "thousand men" are the enemy; we will never submit to any enemy no matter how ferocious. The "children" are the proletariat and the popular masses. All Communist Party members, all revolutionaries, and all revolutionary workers in literature and art should follow Lu Xun's example and be an ox for the proletariat and the popular masses, wearing themselves out in their service with no release until death. The intelligentsia must join in with the masses and serve them; this process can and definitely will involve a great many trials and hardships, but as long as we are resolute, these demands are within our grasp.

Translated by Bonnie MacDougall

41

Sealed Off

ZHANG AILING

When Zhang Ailing (Eileen Chang, 1921–1995) was publishing her short fiction (later collected into a volume called Legends *[Chuanqi]) and essays (collected into a volume called* Gossip *[Liuyan]) in occupied Shanghai in the 1940s, she was extremely popular. However, painted as a purveyor of smut and vilified by Marxist literary critics for her anti-Communist novels of the early 1950s, Zhang was removed from the literary canon until the post-Mao cultural liberalization, when she was "rediscovered" and exerted a tremendous influence on contemporary writers who admired her exquisite language and nonpolitical orientation. Recent scholarship has tended to portray Zhang's work as representative of an "alternative modernity," one that self-consciously reacted against the literature-as-social-transformation paradigm of mainstream writers like Lu Xun. This view is justified, to a point. Zhang wrote in a 1944 essay: "I can't write one of those works often called a 'monument to the era,' and I don't plan to try, because it seems that such objective, concentrated subject matter is not yet available. Things are even to the point where I only write about trivial things between men and women. There are no wars or revolutions in my works. I believe people are more free and unadorned in love than in war or revolution. Because of the very nature of their events, war and revolution often more urgently require the support of intellect over emotion, and the reason works describing war and revolution often fail is that their technical aspects are superior to their artistic aspects." Much of Zhang's fiction does indeed deal with relationships between men and women, but the best of it, such as "Sealed Off," also shows us how the private realm of the psyche and the relations between men and women cannot avoid being influenced by history, in this case war.*

The tramcar driver drove his tram. The tramcar tracks, in the blazing sun, shimmered like two shiny eels crawling out of the water; they stretched and shrank, stretched and shrank, on their onward way—soft and slippery, long old eels, never ending, never ending . . . the driver fixed his eyes on the undulating tracks, and didn't go mad.

If there hadn't been an air raid, if the city hadn't been sealed, the tramcar would have gone on forever. The city was sealed. The alarm-bell rang. Ding-ding-ding-ding. Every "ding" was a cold little dot, the dots all adding up to a dotted line, cutting across time and space.

The tramcar ground to a halt, but the people on the street ran: those on the left side of the street ran over to the right, and those on the right ran over to the left. All the shops, in a single sweep, rattled down their metal gates. Matrons tugged madly at the railings. "Let us in for just a while," they cried. "We have children here, and old people!" But the gates stayed tightly shut. Those inside the metal gates and those outside the metal gates stood glaring at each other, fearing one another.

Inside the tram, people were fairly quiet. They had somewhere to sit, and though the place was rather plain, it still was better, for most of them, than what they had at home. Gradually, the street also grew quiet: not that it was a complete silence, but the sound of voices eased into a confused blur, like the soft rustle of a straw-stuffed pillow, heard in a dream. The huge, shambling city sat dozing in the sun, its head resting heavily on people's shoulders, its spittle slowly dripping down their shirts, an inconceivably enormous weight pressing down on everyone. Never before, it seemed, had Shanghai been this quiet—and in the middle of the day! A beggar taking advantage of the breathless, birdless quiet, lifted up his voice and began to chant: "Good master, good lady, kind sir, kind ma'am, won't you give alms to this poor man? Good master, good lady . . ." But after a short while he stopped, scared silent by the eerie quiet.

Then there was a braver beggar, a man from Shandong, who firmly broke the silence. His voice was round and resonant: "Sad, sad, sad! No money do I have!" An old, old song, sung from one century to the next. The tram driver, who also was from Shandong, succumbed to the sonorous tune. Heaving a long sigh, he folded his arms across his chest, leaned against the tram door, and joined in: "Sad, sad, sad! No money do I have!"

Some of the tram passengers got out. But there was still a little loose, scattered chatter; near the door, a group of office workers was discussing something. One of them, with a quick, ripping sound, shook his fan open and offered his conclusion: "Well, in the end, there's nothing wrong with him—it's just that he doesn't know how to act." From another nose came a short grunt, followed by a cold smile: "Doesn't know how to act? He sure knows how to toady up to the bosses!"

A middle-aged couple who looked very much like brother and sister stood together in the middle of the tram, holding onto the leather straps. "Careful!" the woman suddenly yelped. "Don't get your trousers dirty!" The man flinched, then slowly raised the hand from which a packet of smoked fish dangled. Very cautiously, very gingerly, he held the paper packet, which was brimming with oil, several inches away from his suit pants. His wife did not let up. "Do you know what dry-cleaning costs these days? Or what it costs to get a pair of trousers made?"

Lu Zongzhen, accountant for Huamao Bank, was sitting in the corner. When he saw the smoked fish, he was reminded of the steamed dumplings stuffed with spinach that his wife had asked him to buy at a noodle stand near the bank. Women are always like that. Dumplings bought in the hardest-to-find, most twisty-windy little alleys had to be the best, no matter what. She didn't for a moment think of how it would be for him—neatly dressed in suit and tie, with tortoiseshell eyeglasses and a leather briefcase, then, tucked under his arm, these steaming hot dumplings wrapped in newspaper—how ludicrous! Still, if the city were sealed for a long time, so that his dinner was delayed, then he could at least make do with the dumplings.

He glanced at his watch; only four-thirty. Must be the power of sugges-tion. He felt hungry already. Carefully pulling back a corner of the paper, he took a look inside. Snowy white mounds, breathing soft little whiffs of sesame oil. A piece of newspaper had stuck to the dumplings, and he gravely peeled it off; the ink was printed on the dumplings, with all the writing in reverse, as though it were reflected in a mirror. He peered down and slowly picked the words out: "Obituaries . . . Positions Wanted . . . Stock Market Developments . . . Now Playing . . . ." Normal, useful phrases, but they did look a bit odd on a dump-ling. Maybe because eating is such serious business; compared to it, everything else is just a joke. Lu Zongzhen thought it looked funny, but he didn't laugh: he was a very straightforward kind of fellow. After reading the dumplings, he read the newspaper, but when he'd finished half a page of old news, he found that if he turned the page all the dumplings would fall out, and so he had to stop.

While Lu read the paper, others in the tram did likewise. People who had newspapers read them; those without newspapers read receipts, or lists of rules and regulations, or business cards. People who were stuck without a single scrap of printed matter read shop signs along the street. They simply had to fill this terrifying emptiness—otherwise, their brains might start to work. Thinking is a painful business.

Sitting across from Lu Zongzhen was an old man who, with a dull clacking sound, rolled two slippery, glossy walnuts in his palm: a rhythmic little gesture can substitute for thought. The old man had a clean-shaven pate, a reddish yellow complexion, and an oily sheen on his face. When his brows were furrowed, his head looked like a walnut. The thoughts inside were walnut-flavored: smooth and sweet, but in the end, empty-tasting.

To the old man's right sat Wu Cuiyuan, who looked like one of those young Christian wives, though she was still unmarried. Her Chinese gown of white cotton was trimmed with a narrow blue border—the navy blue around the white reminded one of the black borders around an obituary—and she carried a little blue-and-white checked parasol. Her hairstyle was utterly banal, so as not to attract attention. Actually, she hadn't much reason to fear. She wasn't bad-looking, but hers was an uncertain, unfocused beauty, an afraid-she-had-offended-someone kind of beauty. Her face was bland, slack, lacking definition. Even her own mother couldn't say for certain whether her face was long or round.

At home she was a good daughter, at school she was a good student. After graduating from college, Cuiyuan had become an English instructor at her alma mater. Now, stuck in the air raid, she decided to grade a few papers while she waited. The first one was written by a male student. It railed against the evils of the big city, full of righteous anger, the prose stiff, choppy, ungrammatical. "Painted prostitutes . . . cruising the Cosmo . . . low-class bars and dancing-halls." Cuiyuan paused for a moment, then pulled out her red pencil and gave the paper an "A." Ordinarily, she would have gone right on to the next one, but now, because she had too much time to think, she couldn't help wondering why she had given this student such a high mark. If she hadn't asked herself this question, she could have ignored the whole matter, but once she did ask, her face suffused with red. Suddenly, she understood: it was because this student was the only man who fearlessly and forthrightly said such things to her.

He treated her like an intelligent, sophisticated person; as if she were a man, someone who really understood. He respected her. Cuiyuan always felt that no one at school respected her—from the president on down to the professors, the students, even the janitors. The students' grumbling was especially hard to take: "This place is really falling apart. Getting worse every day. It's bad enough having to learn English from a Chinese, but then to learn it from a Chinese who's never gone abroad . . ." Cuiyuan took abuse at school, took abuse at home. The Wu household was a modern, model household, devout and serious. The family had pushed their daughter to study hard, to climb upwards step by step, right to the tip-top . . . A girl in her twenties teaching at a university! It set a record for women's professional achievement. But her parents' enthusiasm began to wear thin and now they wished she hadn't been quite so serious, wished she'd taken more time out from her studies, tried to find herself a rich husband.

She was a good daughter, a good student. All the people in her family were good people; they took baths every day and read the newspaper; when they listened to the wireless, they never tuned into local folk-opera, comic opera, that sort of thing, but listened only to the symphonies of Beethoven and Wagner; they didn't understand what they were listening to, but still they listened. In this world, there are more good people than real people . . . Cuiyuan wasn't very happy.

Life was like the Bible, translated from Hebrew into Greek, from Greek into Latin, from Latin into English, from English into Chinese. When Cuiyuan read it, she translated the standard Chinese into Shanghainese. Gaps were unavoidable.

She put the student's essay down and buried her chin in her hands. The sun burned down on her backbone.

Next to her sat a nanny with a small child lying on her lap. The sole of the child's foot pushed against Cuiyuan's leg. Little red shoes, decorated with tigers, on a soft but tough little foot . . . this at least was real.

A medical student who was also on the tram took out a sketchpad and carefully added the last touches to a diagram of the human skeleton. The other passengers thought he was sketching a portrait of the man who sat dozing across from him. Nothing else was going on, so they started sauntering over, crowding into little clumps of three or four, leaning on each other with their hands behind their backs, gathering around to watch the man sketch from life. The husband who dangled smoked fish from his fingers whispered to his wife: "I can't get used to this cubism, this impressionism, which is so popular these days." "Your pants," she hissed.

The medical student meticulously wrote in the names of every bone, muscle, nerve, and tendon. An office worker hid half his face behind a fan and quietly informed his colleague: "The influence of Chinese painting. Nowadays, writing words in is all the rage in Western painting. Clearly a case of 'Eastern ways spreading Westward.'"

Lu Zongzhen didn't join the crowd, but stayed in his seat. He had decided he was hungry. With everyone gone, he could comfortably munch his spinach-stuffed dumplings. But then he looked up and caught a glimpse, in the third-class car, of a relative, his wife's cousin's son. He detested that Dong Peizhi was a man of humble origins who harbored a great ambition: he sought a fiancée of comfortable means, to serve as a foothold for his climb upwards. Lu Zongzhen's eldest daughter had just turned twelve, but already she had caught Peizhi's eye; having made, in his own mind, a pleasing calculation, Peizhi's manner grew ever softer, ever more cunning.

As soon as Lu Zongzhen caught sight of this young man, he was filled with quiet alarm, fearing that if he were seen, Peizhi would take advantage of the opportunity to press forward with his attack. The idea of being stuck in the same car with Dong Peizhi while the city was sealed off was too horrible to contemplate! Lu quickly closed his briefcase and wrapped up his dumplings, then fled, in a great rush, to a seat across the aisle. Now, thank God, he was screened by Wu Cuiyuan, who occupied the seat next to him, and his nephew could not possibly see him.

Cuiyuan turned and gave him a quick look. Oh no! The woman surely thought he was up to no good, changing seats for no reason like that. He recognized the look of a woman being flirted with—she held her face absolutely motionless, no hint of a smile anywhere in her eyes, her mouth, not even in the little hollows beside her nose; yet from some unknown place there was the trembling of a little smile that could break out at any moment. If you think you're simply too adorable, you can't keep from smiling.

Damn! Dong Peizhi had seen him after all and was coming toward the first-class car, very humble, bowing even at a distance, with his long jowls, shiny red cheeks, and long, gray, monklike gown—a clean, cautious young man, hardworking no matter what the hardship, the very epitome of a good son-in-law. Thinking fast, Zongzhen decided to follow Peizhi's lead and try a bit of artful nonchalance. So he stretched one arm out across the windowsill that ran behind Cuiyuan, soundlessly announcing flirtatious intent. This would not, he knew, scare Peizhi into immediate retreat, because in Peizhi's eyes he already was a dirty old man. The way Peizhi saw it, anyone over thirty was old, and all the old were vile. Having seen his uncle's disgraceful behavior, the young man would feel compelled to tell his wife every little detail—well, angering his wife was just fine with him. Who told her to give him such a nephew, anyway? If she was angry, it served her right.

He didn't care much for this woman sitting next to him. Her arms were fair, all right, but were like squeezed-out toothpaste. Her whole body was like squeezed-out toothpaste, it had no shape.

"When will this air raid ever end?" he said in a low, smiling voice. "It's awful!"

Shocked, Cuiyuan turned her head, only to see that his arm was stretched out behind her. She froze. But come what may, Zongzhen could not let himself pull his arm back. His nephew stood just across the way, watching him with brilliant, glowing eyes, the hint of an understanding smile on his face. If, in the middle of everything, he turned and looked his nephew in the eye, maybe the little no-account would get scared, would lower his eyes, flustered and embarrassed like a sweet young thing; then again, maybe Peizhi would keep staring at him—who could tell?

He gritted his teeth and renewed the attack. "Aren't you bored? We could talk a bit, that can't hurt. Let's . . . let's talk." He couldn't control himself, his voice was plaintive.

Again Cuiyuan was shocked. She turned to look at him. Now he remembered, he had seen her get on the tram—a striking image, but an image concocted by chance, not by any intention of hers. "You know, I saw you get on the train," he said softly. "Near the front of the car. There's a torn advertisement, and I saw your profile, just a bit of your chin, through the torn spot." It was an ad for Lacova powdered milk that showed a pudgy little child. Beneath the child's ear this woman's chin had suddenly appeared; it was a little spooky, when you thought about it. "Then you looked down to get some change out of your purse, and I saw your eyes, then your brows, then your hair." When you took her features separately, looked at them one by one, you had to admit she had a certain charm.

Cuiyuan smiled. You wouldn't guess that this man could talk so sweetly— you'd think he was the stereotypical respectable businessman. She looked at him again. Under the tip of his nose the cartilage was reddened by the sunlight. Stretching out from his sleeve, and resting on the newspaper, was a warm, tanned hand, one with feeling—a real person! Not too honest, not too bright, but a real person. Suddenly she felt flushed and happy; she turned away with a murmur. "Don't talk like that."

"What?" Zongzhen had already forgotten what he'd said. His eyes were fixed on his nephew's back—the diplomatic young man had decided that three's a crowd, and he didn't want to offend his uncle. They would meet again, anyway, since theirs was a close family, and no knife was sharp enough to sever the ties; and so he returned to the third-class car. Once Peizhi was gone, Zongzhen withdrew his arm; his manner turned respectable. Casting about for a way to make conversation, he glanced at the notebook spread out on her lap. "Shenguang University," he read aloud. "Are you a student there?"

Did he think she was that young? That she was still a student? She laughed, without answering.

"I graduated from Huaqi." He repeated the name. "Huaqi." On her neck was a tiny dark mole, like the imprint of a fingernail. Zongzhen absentmindedly rubbed the fingers of his right hand across the nails of his left. He coughed slightly, then continued: "What department are you in?" Cuiyuan saw that he had moved his arm and thought that her stand-offish manner had wrought this change. She therefore felt she could not refuse to answer. "Literature. And you?"

"Business." Suddenly he felt that their conversation had grown stuffy. "In school I was busy with student activities. Now that I'm out, I'm busy earning a living. So I've never really studied much of anything."

"Is your office very busy?"

"Terribly. In the morning I go to work and in the evening I go home, but I don't know why I do either. I'm not the least bit interested in my job. Sure, it's a way to earn money, but I don't know who I'm earning it for."

"Everyone has family to think of."

"Oh, you don't know . . . my family ."A short cough. "We'd better not talk about it."

"Here it comes," thought Cuiyuan. "His wife doesn't understand him. Every married man in the world seems desperately in need of another woman's understanding."

Zongzhen hesitated, then swallowed hard and forced the words out: "My wife—she doesn't understand me at all."

Cuiyuan knitted her brow and looked at him, expressing complete sympathy.

"I really don't understand why I go home every evening. Where is there to go? I have no home, in fact." He removed his glasses, held them up to the light, and wiped the spots off with a handkerchief. Another little cough.

"Just keep going, keep getting by, without thinking—above all, don't start thinking!" Cuiyuan always felt that when nearsighted people took their glasses off in front of other people it was a little obscene; improper, somehow, like taking your clothes off in public. Zongzhen continued: "You, you don't know what kind of woman she is."

"Then why did you . . . in the first place?"

"Even then I was against it. My mother arranged the marriage. Of course I wanted to choose for myself, but . . . she used to be very beautiful . . . I was very young . . . young people, you know . . . ." Cuiyuan nodded her head. "Then she changed into this kind of person—even my mother fights with her, and she blames me for having married her! She has such a temper—she hasn't even got a grade-school education."

Cuiyuan couldn't help saying, with a tiny smile, "You seem to take diplomas very seriously. Actually, even if a woman's educated it's all the same." She didn't know why she said this, wounding her own heart.

"Of course, you can laugh, because you're well-educated. You don't know what kind of—" He stopped, breathing hard, and took off the glasses he had just put back on.

"Getting a little carried away?" said Cuiyuan.

Zongzhen gripped his glasses tightly, made a painful gesture with his hands. "You don't know what kind of—"

"I know, I know," Cuiyuan said hurriedly. She knew that if he and his wife didn't get along, the fault could not lie entirely with her. He too was a person of simple intellect. He just wanted a woman who would comfort and forgive him.

The street erupted in noise, as two trucks full of soldiers rumbled by. Cuiyuan and Zongzhen stuck their heads out to see what was going on; to their surprise, their faces came very close together. At close range anyone's face is somehow different, is tension-charged like a close-up on the movie screen. Zongzhen and Cuiyuan suddenly felt they were seeing each other for the first time. To his eyes, her face was the spare, simple peony of a watercolor sketch, and the strands of hair fluttering at her temples were pistils ruffled by a breeze.

He looked at her, and she blushed. When she let him see her blush, he grew visibly happy. Then she blushed even more deeply.

Zongzhen had never thought he could make a woman blush, make her smile, make her hang her head shyly. In this he was a man. Ordinarily, he was an accountant, a father, the head of a household, a tram passenger, a store customer, an insignificant citizen of a big city. But to this woman, this woman who didn't know anything about his life, he was only and entirely a man.

They were in love. He told her all kinds of things: who was on his side at the bank and who secretly opposed him; how his family squabbled; his secret sorrows; his schoolboy dreams . . . unending talk, but she was not put off. Men in love have always liked to talk; women in love, on the other hand, don't want to talk, because they know, without even knowing that they know, that once a man really understands a woman he'll stop loving her.

Zongzhen was sure that Cuiyuan was a lovely woman—pale, wispy, warm, like the breath your mouth exhales in winter. You don't want her, and she quietly drifts away. Being part of you, she understands everything, forgives everything. You tell the truth, and her heart aches for you; you tell a lie, and she smiles as if to say, "Go on with you—what are you saying?"

Zongzhen was quiet for a moment, then said, "I'm thinking of marrying again."

Cuiyuan assumed an air of shocked surprise. "You want a divorce? Well . . . that isn't possible, is it?"

"I can't get a divorce. I have to think of the children's well-being. My oldest daughter is twelve, just passed the entrance exams for middle school, her grades are quite good."

"What," thought Cuiyuan, "what does this have to do with what you just said?" "Oh," she said aloud, her voice cold, "you plan to take a concubine."

"I plan to treat her like a wife," said Zongzhen. I—I can make things nice for her. I wouldn't do anything to upset her."

"But," said Cuiyuan, "a girl from a good family won't agree to that, will she? So many legal difficulties . . ."

Zongzhen sighed. "Yes, you're right. I can't do it. Shouldn't have mentioned it . . . I'm too old. Thirty-four already."

"Actually," Cuiyuan spoke very slowly, "these days, that isn't considered very old."

Zongzhen was still. Finally he asked, "How old are you?"

Cuiyuan ducked her head. "Twenty-four."

Zongzhen waited awhile, then asked, "Are you a free woman?"

Cuiyuan didn't answer. "You aren't free," said Zongzhen. "But even if you agreed, your family wouldn't, right?"

Cuiyuan pursed her lips. Her family—her prim and proper family—how she hated them all. They had cheated her long enough. They wanted her to find them a wealthy son-in-law. Well, Zongzhen didn't have money, but he did have a wife—that would make them good and angry! It would serve them right!

Little by little, people started getting back on the tram. Perhaps it was rumored out there that "traffic will soon return to normal." The passengers got on and sat down, pressing against Zongzhen and Cuiyuan, forcing them a little closer, then a little closer again.

Zongzhen and Cuiyuan wondered how they could have been so foolish not to have thought of sitting closer before. Zongzhen struggled against his happiness. He turned to her and said, in a voice full of pain, "No, this won't do! I can't let you sacrifice your future! You're a fine person, with such a good education . . . I don't have much money, and don't want to ruin your life!"

Well, of course, it was money again. What he said was true. "It's over," thought Cuiyuan. In the end she'd probably marry, but her husband would never be as dear as this stranger met by chance—this man on the tram in the middle of a sealed-off city . . . it could never be this spontaneous again. Never again . . . oh, this man, he was so stupid! So very stupid! All she wanted was one small part of him, one little part that no one else could want. He was throwing away his own happiness. Such an idiotic waste! She wept, but it wasn't a gentle, maidenly weeping. She practically spit her tears into his face. He was a good person—the world had gained one more good person! What use would it be to explain things to him? If a woman needs to turn to words to move a man's heart, she is a sad case. Once Zongzhen got anxious, he couldn't get any words out, and just kept shaking the umbrella she was holding. She ignored him. Then he tugged at her hand. "Hey, there are people here, you know! Don't! Don't get so upset! Wait a bit, and we'll talk it over on the telephone. Give me your number." Cuiyuan didn't answer. He pressed her. "You have to give me your phone number."

"Seven-five-three-six-nine." Cuiyuan spoke as fast as she could.

"Seven-five-three-six-nine?"

No response. "Seven-five-three-six-nine, seven-five . . . " Mumbling the number over and over, Zongzhen searched his pockets for a pen, but the more frantic he became, the harder it was to find one. Cuiyuan had a red pencil in her bag, but she purposely did not take it out. He ought to remember her telephone number; if he didn't, then he didn't love her, and there was no point in continuing the conversation.

The city started up again. "Ding-ding-ding-ding." Every "ding" a cold little dot, which added up to a line that cut across time and space.

A wave of cheers swept across the metropolis. The tram started clanking its way forward. Zongzhen stood up, pushed into the crowd, and disappeared. Cuiyuan turned her head away, as if she didn't care. He was gone. To her, it was as if he were dead.

The tram picked up speed. On the evening street, a tofu-seller had set his shoulder-pole down and was holding up a rattle; eyes shut, he shook it back and forth. A big-boned blonde woman, straw hat slung across her back, bantered with an Italian sailor. All her teeth showed when she grinned. When Cuiyuan looked at these people, they lived for that one moment. Then the tram clanked onward, and one by one they died away.

Cuiyuan shut her eyes fretfully. If he phoned her, she wouldn't be able to control her voice; it would be filled with emotion, for he was a man who had died, then returned to life.

The lights inside the tram went on; she opened her eyes and saw him sitting in his old seat, looking remote. She trembled with shock—he hadn't gotten off the tram, after all! Then she understood his meaning: everything that had happened while the city was sealed was a non-occurrence. The whole of Shanghai had dozed off, had dreamed an unreasonable dream.

The tramcar driver raised his voice in song: "Sad, sad, sad! No money do I have! Sad, sad, sad—" An old beggar, thoroughly dazed, limped across the street in front of the tram. The driver bellowed at her. "You swine!"

1943

Translated by Karen Kingsbury

42

The Unglovable Hands

ZHAO SHULI

"The Unglovable Hands" was written by Zhao Shuli (1906–1970), a Shanxi native of peasant origins who was an important writer in the CCP-controlled areas during the war. In the 1950s, Zhao was constructed by the Party cultural apparatus into a "model peasant writer" who successfully put into practice Mao's literary ideals. Even as a model writer, though, Zhao was not without political problems under the postrevolutionary state. He was attacked for his criticism of Party agricultural policy of the late 1950s, and his fiction was seen to promote "middle characters"—characters who were neither fully good nor absolutely evil. In the Cultural Revolution, Zhao was the object of bitter attack; he died in 1970 as a result of harsh treatment. "The Unglovable Hands" nicely conveys the glorification of poor peasants as the embodiment of pure class consciousness that was an important part of Maoist ideology.

The training corps of the Big Millstone Mountain Brigade, the White Cloud Ridge Commune, had been established when the brigade was still an advanced agricultural cooperative, and its goal was to teach skills to people who joined farm production for the first time. During that period of the advanced cooperative in 1956, a number of women and young students who had never participated in farming joined the work force, but their work was below standard. Hence Director Ch'en Man-hung proposed that a training corps be established, that two old farmers of high productivity serve as instructors, that some low-yield land be set aside as the training fields to train the unskilled. After the proposal was approved by the Administration Committee, a few scores of low-yield *mu* on top of the Big Millstone Mountain and several parcels of orchard land in the gulch on the southern side were designated as such; Ch'en Ping-cheng, father of Director Ch'en Man-hung, and old orchard-hand Wang Hsin-ch'un were selected as instructors. Ch'en served as coordinator and Wang as vice-coordinator, and the corps' members were assigned to various villagers as coaches. When commune members encountered unexpected difficulties with their work or when their coaches could not help them, they would then seek the advice of Ch'en or Wang. Even though the purpose of the corps was to train new workers, there were exceptions: (1) workers who had trouble with certain tasks might register for the classes when those tasks were taught; (2) those who could not perform certain tasks well or those recommended by the Evaluation Committee because of bad work attitudes were also included. Those in the last category, during this training period, would be denied full credit for each workday, which would be calculated on a 60 percent basis. It was a sort of token punishment for those who could have performed better but didn't.

Coordinator Ch'en Ping-cheng was already a man of seventy-six. In general, most men of his age should not participate in any major physical labor, but he was especially hale and hearty. As a young man, he could do the work of a man and a half; now in old age, he was the better of most young men in terms of strength. In the winter of 1958, when communes were established, the Big Millstone Mountain was classified as a brigade, and its leader was Ch'en Man-hung. The brigade soon had its Respect-Old-Folks Home, and the Evaluation Committee recommended that Ch'en Ping-cheng retire and live in the home. After three days in the home, the old man felt that light tasks such as stripping hemp stalks and picking cotton were not demanding enough to deplete his energy, so he asked to leave the home and to resume his job as coordinator of the training corps.

Old man Ch'en Ping-cheng's skill as a farmer was considered first rate, not only in the Big Millstone Mountain but also in the whole White Cloud Ridge area, which had cited him as an exceptional, exemplary worker. The stone dikes that he helped build never collapsed; the fire in the smoldering fertilizer pile that he had helped stack up never went out; and he was second to none in common tasks such as ploughing, seeding, hoeing, and harvesting.

When he taught in the training corps, he insisted not only on standards but also on proper style, claiming that if the style were not correct, the work would be below standard. For instance, in second-hoeing, he stressed that the tiller must bend his body to a certain degree, slant his body and feet to one side, and hold his feet steady. Also his hands must tightly hold on to the hoe, firmly strike the ground, and not allow the hoe to shake in any way. The standard was that the hoe must strike close to and around the seedling but not cover up any area yet undug. In piling dirt around the seedling, the tiller must, to the utmost extent possible, make a small mound with no more than three strikes of the hoe, and the top of the mound must be flat rather than pointed. As he lectured, he demonstrated to the trainees; sometimes he repeated the instructions more than ten times before he would allow them to do any work. Because of his many rules and regulations, they would remember one rule and forget another. Sometimes they stood too straight or moved forward incorrectly. Sometimes they hoed haphazardly, complicating simple chores. Old man Ch'en Ping-cheng kept reminding one trainee, then another; he also frequently interrupted their work by giving another demonstration.

A man named Ho Ho-ho had spent half of his life hoeing without ever bending his back. When he hoed, the hoe itself bounced around wildly; if it happened to bounce onto the weeds, then he cut the weeds, but if it happened to hit the seedlings, then the crop was damaged. After the founding of the training corps, the brigade's Evaluation Committee wanted him to have some training in the corps. When he came, Coordinator Ch'en Ping-cheng, as usual, taught him the proper hoeing style. The problem was that this man—nicknamed "Ha-ha-ha"—was indolent by nature. After bending down a little for hoeing, he would immediately straighten his back again. Old man Ch'en Ping-cheng had his ingenuity. Next day he brought a spare hoe from his own home and shortened it to a length of three feet, telling Ho, "Your habit of not bending down can only be cured with this short-handled hoe." Once he had a new hoe, his problem was corrected. He had to bend his back when using this three-foot hoe, otherwise, he could not touch the ground. Later other teams heard of this new method; they all prepared a number of short-handled hoes for those not accustomed to bending their backs.

When the trainees became tired from style exercises, Coordinator Ch'en gave them a break. Eight or nine terraced paddy-fields below, Vice-coordinator Wang Hsin-ch'un taught his class the planting of seeds. During the break the two groups met; the two old men smoked tobacco and chatted; the trainees read their newspapers or had a good time together. When the two old men met, Ch'en would extend his hand for a handshake, and Wang would always try to avoid it. Though younger than Ch'en by more than ten years and friendly with Ch'en, Wang abhorred shaking Ch'en's hand, because when Ch'en shook his hand, he felt as though he were being squeezed by pliers.

One day during the break Chen invited Wang for a smoke. Ch'en had a flint. Wang said, "How nice it would be to have a fire!" A new trainee, a high school student, quickly proceeded to look for twigs. But all he could find were two dry, two-inch-long persimmon twigs. Wang smiled and said, "You don't have to look for firewood. Grandpa Chen has some." Puzzled, the trainee looked around him but could not see any. Old man Ch'en added, "Yes, I have some." Leisurely he put down his flint; without looking he scratched the dirt around him for a while and, lo and behold, found two big handfuls of bark and twigs. Wang lit a match, while old man Ch'en scratched around and got more wood, which he put on top of the pile. The trainee exclaimed in amazement, "This is very good," and began to do likewise. Old man Ch'en tried to stop him: "Wait a minute; don't." But it was too late. The young man's middle finger had been pricked and he quickly withdrew his hand. Wang said, "Son, what kind of hands do you have? What type of hands does he have? His are like an iron-rake; brambles or thorns—nothing could hurt them."

While rubbing his middle finger, the student looked at Ch'en's hands, which were different from those of ordinary people. The palm seemed to be square in shape, the fingers short, stubby, and bent; the back and the palm of the hands were covered with calluses; and his round fingertips resembled half cocoons with nails attached to them. The hands looked like two small rakes made of tree branches. The student looked at the hands with contempt instead of admiration, as if he were saying, "How can you call them hands?"

The two old men sensed the young man's scornful attitude. Ch'en ignored him. Looking proud, Ch'en picked up his pipe to smoke. Old man Wang, after lighting his pipe, said to the young man, "Young fellow, don't you slight his hands. Without them, the present training field would still remain uncultivated. This land belonged to landlord Wang Tzu-yü. According to old folks, these ten and more sections of land on top of the Big Millstone Mountain were left uncultivated since the third year of Emperor Kuang-hsü [1877] until the third year of Emperor Hsüan-t'ung [1910]. In those days neither his family nor mine had any land; he was a field hand working for Wang Tzu-yü, and I was a herd boy. Later he came here to cultivate the land; after I grew up, I was elevated from herd boy to field hand and followed him to plant rice seeds in the marsh. All these fields were cultivated by him and our present brigade leader, digging them hoe by hoe and building dike after dike. Without his hands, this whole area would still be wasteland."

Even though the student was a little sorry that he had despised Ch'en's hands, he was unwilling to acknowledge his mistake openly. Instead, he said in a mocking tone, "No wonder we are such slow learners; it is all because we don't have his hands."

In a serious voice, Ch'en lectured the young man, "We want your hands to learn to work like mine, not to be like mine. If I wasn't the first one to dig these fields for planting, my hands wouldn't be like this. Now, folks of the older generation have already plowed the land with their hands; soon everything will be mechanized, and your hands won't have to become like mine."

Even though old man Ch'en did not wish others to have hands like his, he, nonetheless, was proud of them. His hands were not only firm and tough but also dexterous. He loved weaving and frequently wove thorn vines into all types of farming tools and sometimes made children's toys out of stalks of kaoliang. When he made tools out of vines, he did not have to use an oxhorn wedge in splitting them. He divided a vine into three and used his index finger as the splitter—chi, chi, chi—the vine was split, and his hand was not even scratched. Yet he also did work of a very delicate nature. No one would guess that it was done by the same hands. The katydid cages that he made out of kaoliang stalks featured a door, windows, upstairs and downstairs rooms, and on the two-inch-square windows he made many decorative patterns from different angles, with holes so tiny that even bees would have difficulty crawling through them.

After the periods of land reform, mutual assistance teams, and cooperatives, communes were established. Old man Ch'en Ping-cheng's family income increased. In the winter of 1959, his children and grandchildren bought him a pair of knitted gloves to protect his hands. Upon receiving the gift, he said, "My hands have never enjoyed such luxuries before." As he tried them on, he found the palm not big enough, the fingers too tight and long. He barely drew them on before he stretched the palm into a square, stuffed the lower part of the fingers full and left the upper part of the fingers empty. His son Ch'en Manhung said, "After a while, they will fit you nicely." He put them on, opened and closed his hands a couple of times, then took them off and gave them to his daughter-in-law. "Please keep them for me."

"Dad, Please wear them. Don't your hands get cold when you work in the field?"

"We are building a storage shed in the gulch and it's not convenient to move stones with them on." As soon as he said this, he left his gloves and walked away. Not long afterwards, the work at the gulch was completed but other work followed—cutting hay, cleaning sheep-pens, storing turnips for winter, and thrashing corn, none of which went well with the use of gloves, and he soon forgot he had them.

One day the White Cloud Ridge held a goods exchange fair. His daughter-in-law said to him, "Now they don't really need you to teach them these odd skills, why don't you take the day off and visit the fair?" The old man agreed. He changed into his new cotton-padded jacket and tied a new sash around his waist. She then said, "This time you must wear your new gloves," and brought him his gloves. He drew them on and left.

The Big Millstone Mountain was a small village and had no consumer co-op. As the neighbors heard he was going to the White Cloud Ridge and saw him walking down the street in his new jacket and gloves, they asked him to buy things for them. One family wanted three ounces of oil; another family wanted two catties of salt. All those purchases would be more than his hands could carry, so he borrowed a basket from a neighbor. When he reached the White Cloud Ridge, he walked past half a street block and arrived at the consumer's co-op and purchased what he had been asked to buy. Then he walked to the commune and saw a carload of pitchforks being unloaded by a salesman. For two years new pitchforks had not been available in the area, and what the different brigades had was not enough to go around. He felt he could not miss the opportunity. Having no money, he remembered that his son, who was attending a meeting at the commune, might have some. So he went and told his son about the pitchforks. Man-hung said, "Yes, by all means. They are very precious. Go buy them quickly," and gave him fifty dollars. With the money he went to the mountain-goods section and looked over the pitchforks. Fastidious with tools, he could not bear to see any blemish on them. Removing his gloves and tucking them inside his sash, he picked up one pitchfork, put it on the floor to see if its three prongs were even and strong, and whether its head and handle were straight. Before he finished looking at one, more than ten people had gathered, everyone holding and examining a pitchfork. In no time, many more people came; even the brigade leader, who was conducting a meeting at the commune, temporarily halted the meeting to come over to buy some. No one was as fastidious as the old man; they merely asked the price and paid. Old man Ch'en Ping-cheng saw the situation getting out of hand. Forgetting his high standards, he chose five pitchforks at random, and the rest were grabbed by others. He paid, tied the pitchforks together, put them on his shoulder, carried his basket and jostled his way out of the congested market section. With his hands full, he had no interest in wandering around the other half of the street block and went home by the same road he had taken.

Once outside the White Cloud Ridge village, the congestion was gone, and the road was much wider. Then he felt for his gloves. He could only find one. He put down his basket, the pitchforks, loosened his waist sash, but he could not find the other glove. He knew he must have lost it at the market. He thought, "All right, so be it. I don't use the gloves much anyway." He tied the sash back around his waist, carried the pitchforks on his shoulder with one hand and his basket with the other, and walked toward home. After he had taken a few steps he thought, "The kids bought them especially for me. Now that one glove is lost, and if I don't go back to look for it, I am not being nice to them." Turning back he returned to the fair at the White Cloud Ridge. Fortunately, the salesman had found his glove and kept it on the counter. He returned it to him.

Some time later, old man Ch'en Ping-cheng was selected as the model worker of the year by the Evaluation Committee, and he had to attend the Convention of Model Workers at the county seat. It was another opportunity for him to wear his gloves. Besides his new cotton-padded jacket and his new sash, he wore his gloves.

The Big Millstone Mountain was about forty *li* from the county seat. Winter days are short, so Ch'en, after breakfast, left home and reached his destination at dusk. It was the registration day. Once in town, he registered for the convention, received his attendance permit, and started looking for a place to stay. He had not been in town for more than six months, and it had changed— the streets had been widened, the roads were smooth, the dilapidated place where he had stayed while attending the meetings before was replaced by rows of newly built brick and tile houses. It was dark when he entered the hostel. Rows of rooms in the rear section by the passageway were lit, indicating their occupancy; some of the rooms on the first three rows were lit also. He went to the reception desk, registered, and the receptionist took him to Room 5 of West Row Two. When he reached West Row Two, he saw that the only light came from Room 6, while the rest of the rooms were dark. He stepped on some objects, some of which were hard and others soft; he had no idea what they were. The receptionist told him, "Be careful. This row of rooms was just completed, no more than a week ago, and there are still a few things here and there. Walk on this side; the other side is a lime pit. Walk by the wall; there's some loose lumber around." As they got to Room 5, the receptionist snapped on the light before letting him into the room. What came into view were a clean room, a good fire in the fireplace, a table by the window, two chairs, a stool, two beds on each side of the room, an unpainted door and windows, and recently whitewashed walls. The walls smelled damp as they were heated by the fire. Looking at the beds, he asked, "Four in each room?" The receptionist replied, "Yes."

Will you have all the rooms occupied during the convention?"

"Almost. Some participants from far places have not yet arrived. Take a little rest. Let me bring you some water to freshen you up." A while later the receptionist brought in the water. The old man washed his face, and people streamed in steadily, occupying all the rooms on West Row Two. Besides the old man, Room 5 had three young men. The four of them introduced themselves to one another.

The convention lasted for three and a half days. The old man either listened to reports or prepared to make his own; like everyone else, he was kept busy until the morning of the fourth day, when the County Party Chief made a summary report. In the afternoon those who lived nearby went home; those who lived some distance away had to stay one more night. Ch'en's home was forty *li* away—neither too far nor too near. A young man could probably cover the distance and reach home shortly after dusk. Since he was old, he did not want to walk in the dark and planned to spend an extra half day in town.

After lunch those who would stay the night all wanted to take a walk around town. The old man returned to West Row Two, Room 5, where his three roommates and another young man from Room 4 were playing poker. He said, "Don't you want to look around town?" One young man replied, "Grandpa, you just go ahead. We'll go later." The old man tied the sash around his waist, put on his gloves, and left. Since the courtyard was partially blocked by two big logs, he had to walk close by the wall of Room 3 after he passed the door of Room 4. He thought, "If only I could roll those logs aside, but to where?" Squatting by the door of Room 4, he sized up the situation, concluding that it would be best to roll the logs southwards to face the lime pit. Once he made up his mind, he took off his gloves, put them on the steps and proceeded to roll one of the logs. Cut off from both ends, this one log's middle section was unshapely, thick, short, bent, and flat. It was not easy to roll at all. It took him considerable strength to prop it up, but it turned over only once and was flat on the ground again. Seeking help, he first knocked on the door of Room 4, but no one answered. So he returned to Room 5 and said to the young people, "Comrades, would you please help me move the logs in the courtyard so people can walk more easily?"

"Surely, I tried to do that yesterday, but the logs won't budge," a young man replied, putting down his cards. The other three young men got up and stepped outside. The old man took off his new cotton-padded jacket, left it on his bed, and stepped out of the room.

The old man helped them move the logs. One young man said to him, "You just rest; let us do the work." The four young men took all the room around one short log. Unable to lay his hands on the same one, he started to move the other log. After they had moved the short log, they saw him struggling with the other one. One young man stopped him. "Grandpa, please don't. We can do it." A second young man helped the first one lift it up. This log was a little longer than the first, and one end was thicker than the other. Though the person holding the thin end had no trouble lifting it, the man supporting the thick end did, murmuring continuously, "No, no." Then he let go. The young man at the other end was also about to drop the log when the old man said, "Let me do it." Immediately he bent down. Using his hands to support the log, and with his legs apart as if he were riding on a horse, he stiffened his shoulders and lifted it up. When the first young man saw the second one sticking up his thumb in admiration of the old man, he joined his friend, saying, "Grandpa, you are really marvelous. But you are an old man. Let us do it."

A receptionist carrying a kettle of hot water came by. When he saw what went on, he hurriedly said, "Thank you all. Let us do it."

"It's nothing."

"Before the convention started, the only cleanup work remaining was the courtyards of the first three rows of rooms. During the convention we had no time. We're waiting for tomorrow morning to start cleaning up when all the guests will have moved out. The few of us can finish the work in just a couple of days." Old man Ch'en Ping-cheng said, "Why must you wait until we leave? The convention has ended. Isn't now a good time to help you clean up?"

"No, no, that would be too much trouble to impose on you all."

Old man Ch'en and the young people all said that they didn't mind, and comrades from other rooms, who had not left for town, all came out of their rooms saying that they too would like to help in the cleanup. Seeing this, the receptionist hurried to consult the manager. Even before the receptionist returned, everyone looked for cleanup tools. Since the first two rows had not been thoroughly cleaned up, the tools were piled up in the courtyards between the west-east rows. They found shovels, brooms, open baskets, and poles, and they immediately started to work. Old man Ch'en wanted to haul the baskets for them, but everyone, upon seeing his white beard, insisted that he not do that type of heavy work. So he could only use a broom to sweep the courtyard along with the others. Model workers were truly model workers. When the people from the first three rows of rooms saw that the people on West Row Two were busy cleaning up, they immediately joined in the operation. In a short while, the receptionist and the manager came back. The manager advised everyone not to bother with the work; however, since he could not convince them, he called every staff member, including his assistant, the accountant, the receptionists, to join in the task.

Everyone used shovels to remove left-over bricks or tiles, bark, wood shavings, and other miscellaneous items; old man Ch'en followed and swept after them. He started from the southwest corner of the courtyard in West Row Two and swept northwards. When he reached the window of Room 6, he saw that there were mud cakes and wood shavings on the windowsill; he reached for the dirt with his broom. Because the windowsill was rather small, the broom was less than efficient; he put down his broom and brushed off the dirt with his ironlike hands. Then, looking toward the east, he saw every windowsill was similarly dirty. He started from Room 6 to Room 5, then to Room 4, and cleaned every windowsill before he returned to the west side to clean the courtyards.

Since there were many people, the work was done quickly. Within two hours, the six courtyards had been cleaned, and the garbage stood by both sides of the passageway; materials that could be used were left at the rear entrance of the storage room, to be hauled away by a truck that came by at night. After all the work had been completed, old man Chen felt satisfied, knowing that people could walk a lot more easily from then on.

The manager, his assistant, the accountant, and all the receptionists went to get water for the model workers to clean up. After that, some went into town; old man Ch'en once again put on his new cotton-padded jacket, tied the sash around his waist and planned to put on his gloves—only to realize that they had been lost again. He casually asked his young friends, "When you cleaned, did you see my gloves?" One man answered, "No, we didn't see them. Where did you leave them?"

"On the windowsill of Room 4." Another man said, "Yes, I seemed to remember one glove in a pile of wood shavings, all smeared with mud, and I thought it was someone's discarded old glove."

"Yes, probably when I pulled down the wood shavings of Room 4 the shavings covered them and you didn't see them and threw them in with the garbage pile." The old man went to look for his gloves in the garbage pile by the passageway, but the garbage from the row of West Two alone filled up more than several dozen baskets. How could he find his gloves right away?

When a receptionist saw him, he asked, "Grandpa, what are you looking for?"

"My gloves."

"Are you sure they are in there?"

"Yes, I am."

"Then you go into town and have a good time. We will find them for you."

"Don't bother; they are not of much use to me," the old man said firmly.

The old man strolled around several blocks in town. Other than admiring some new buildings, he had little interest in anything else, thinking, "I don't buy or sell. Why must I linger by the stores?" So he returned to the hostel. It was not yet dusk, and his roommates had not yet returned. A receptionist opened the door for him and told him that his gloves had been found. He entered his room;

the fire in the quiet fireplace was still strong; and his gloves had been washed by a receptionist and put on the back of a chair to dry.

He returned home the next day. After changing his clothes, he returned the gloves to his daughter-in-law. "You'd better keep them. My hands are unglovable."

Translated by Nathan K. Mao and Winston L. Y. Yang

43

On the Other Side of the Stream

KONG JIESHENG

This story is an example of Wound, or Scar, literature, which was extremely popular from 1979–1982. Wounds literature exposed the social and psychological devastation wreaked by the radical politics of the Cultural Revolution. "On the Other Side of the Stream" demonizes the Cultural Revolution by showing how it destroys a family and perverts normal human relations, causing "brother" and "sister" to have an "incestuous" relationship. Wounds fiction served an important social function in confronting the horrors of the Cultural Revolution, but it also implicitly legitimized the new Deng regime, thus serving a conservative political function.

> Dedicated respectfully to those whose lives are still in darkness. May
> they soon be set free to enjoy the pure, fresh air of day and the clean,
> brilliant light of the sun.

Grim clouds were enveloping the mountain ridge and generating thunderclaps. As the sheet of misty rain gradually disappeared, the streams overflowed with roily water.

On the mainland, there is seldom rain after the Mid-Autumn Festival; but on the island, Hainan Island, the rainy season follows its own whim; it couldn't care less when the Mid-Autumn Festival comes. Just as stubborn, the tropical sun is equally hot in summer, fall, winter, and spring.

Yan Liang, a worker on a state farm, a little over twenty years old, waited for the rushing stream to quiet down a little. Then he put on his old straw hat, picked up his satchel, left his thatched hut, and followed the twisting grassy path that led to the farm headquarters.

One crossed a stream eight times to get to the headquarters, though in fact it was the same stream each time. The stream wound its way back and forth through the hills, obliging people to cross and recross it. Nobody knew the name of the small stream, any more than the names of the innumerable hills and mountains of the Wuzhi range. The Li and Miao tribesmen who had lived here

463

for generations had never thought to name the stream. People didn't even know
where the stream came from or where it disappeared to.

When Yan Liang arrived at the headquarters, he scrunched his straw hat
down over his eyes, so that he wouldn't be recognized by anyone he knew and
walked into the cramped little farm store. Even though it had then been almost a
year since the overthrow of the Gang of Four, this little shop, along with the rest
of the state farm, hadn't changed a bit. Outdated political slogans hung everywhere, and, the shelves were loaded with books that would never be sold. Out of
simple ignorance, they were still selling that Gang of Four poster called "The
Moonlight Sentry." The place was just like the legendary Land of Peach
Blossoms, so remote from worldly strife that people didn't even know when
dynasties changed. Yan Liang finally found something new—an envelope with a
picture of the enchanted lady Chang'e flying to the moon. He bought a few cans
of food, cigarettes, and some other things. Then, since the illustration of Chang'e
had been printed so nicely, he bought a few of those envelopes, too, and carried
them home.

Passing back over the stream eight times, he returned to his solitary hut
just as the sun was going down in the west. When he took out the envelopes to
admire them, he couldn't help a little sad smile. He was all alone in the world,
with no family or friends. It seemed everyone else had just forgotten him. To
whom could he write a letter?

1. A Solitary Soul Deep in the Mountains

In the famous words of Tolstoy, "Happy families are all alike, unhappy
ones are unhappy in their own ways."

Yan Liang had been born into a cadre family, and had originally been
known as Gu Yanyan. His father had been a cadre who came south with the
People's Liberation Army, and his mother had done underground work in a
southern city. At the start of the Cultural Revolution, his father had been the
head of a government office and his mother the assistant head of a section in the
People's Bank. He also had a sister called Gu Ganggang, to make a family of
four. To look at this family from the outside, one would assume it was happy,
but in fact this was not so.

From the time he was old enough to understand such things, Yanyan
could see that there were problems between his parents. Yanyan received a great
deal of affection from his parents, but found that his father did not care at all for
his sister. From the time she was small, his sister had been left with an aunt in
the suburbs, and his father would not let her back into the house. Once when his

father was away on business, and Yanyan himself was on summer vacation, he stole away to see his sister. Brother and sister caught crickets in the tall grass, dug clams at the riverbank, and flew a kite by running through the fields. The happiness of their two hearts flew with the kite into the blue heavens. What happy days, but all too short! As soon as their father returned from his trip, he brought Yanyan home in his jeep. Yanyan caught sight of his sister, running along behind the jeep, wiping the tears from her eyes; the tears came rolling down his own face too.

So it was that Yanyan could see his sister hardly once or twice a year. Even then, their meetings had to be secretly arranged by his mother. Every time his sister came, she brought him a little present; sometimes it was a little bird, sometimes a couple of crickets. Yanyan couldn't understand it: such a wonderful sister—why couldn't his father let them all live together?

Yanyan found out that his mother, though she deferred to his father on the subject of his sister, often put up an argument with him on other questions. These were "Party" questions, or questions "of a political nature," and Yanyan didn't understand them very well. Yanyan hadn't had time to sort all this out before the Cultural Revolution was upon them. At that time, he was in the first year of junior high school, and his sister was in the same year in a suburban school. Yanyan threw himself into every kind of "revolutionary activity" of his juvenile comrades in the Red Guards. They broke into many people's houses, burned tons of books, paintings, and calligraphy, and smashed the display windows of department stores that exhibited perfume and cosmetics.

But soon Yanyan's own family was overclouded by the great wings of fate. His mother was found to be a "false Party member" and was thrown into a "cow shed." When this happened, Yanyan's father took his chance to get a divorce as fast as he could. Yanyan was assigned to the custody of his father, while his sister remained "the daughter of a false Party member." All this shocked Yanyan very deeply, but like the true little revolutionary general he was, he accepted it as an unpleasant fact. Besides, how could he defend his mother when his father had so clearly gone along with the accusation that she was a false Party member?

Yanyan was still one of the "five red categories," after all. But when he and his revolutionary comrades were attacking the "cow ghosts" and "snake spirits," he couldn't help thinking of what had happened to his mother; when he was vilifying the "seven black categories" among his schoolmates, he couldn't help thinking that at another school, his sister was among the "bastards" being accused.

Yanyan began to wonder a little.

His father very quickly got the Party to find him a pretty young nurse as a new wife. He constantly bragged to her that he was the comrade of a certain important cadre's secretary, and was always hinting that he would soon move on to better things. Yanyan wondered who was really the better Party member, his mother or his father.

In the fall of 1968, his father really did become one of the influential people in the military control commission. Yanyan didn't want to be any hindrance to his father's career, so he volunteered to be sent to the countryside, to Hainan Island. He felt no reluctance at leaving his family. But before he left, he did go to visit his aunt and sister in the suburbs. He was shocked to find that, after only two years, the house was an empty shell. His aunt had died, and nobody knew where his sister had gone. "Sister! Where are you?"

Yanyan went to his military production brigade in Hainan, and was assigned to the region of the Wuzhi Mountains: he wrote a letter to his sister's school, but never got a response. The two remained out of touch from that time on, and Yanyan's feelings of nostalgia also gradually faded away. The two of them had not, after all, spent much time together. Yanyan wrote to his father, but after a few letters found he had nothing much to say. He began to realize that, among his family members, it was his mother to whom his thoughts returned, for she, after all, had given him the most love. Should he write to her? But who knew what kind of trouble she was in now?

Yanyan's doubts did not prevent him from reading and rereading Chairman Mao's "Three Classic Articles" in the time left over after chopping wood and clearing land. He learned twenty or thirty "Quotations of Chairman Mao" in song form, and wholeheartedly took part in "Seeking directives in the morning and reporting accomplishments in the evening." He even paraded along mountain paths holding torches aloft to celebrate the proclamation of the "latest instructions" from the top—even though those instructions were usually unclear and hopelessly ambiguous. After he had been in Hainan for about half a year, Yanyan joined the Communist Youth League. He was put on the local branch committee (at that time, there was no need to be elected to such posts) and conducted the special sessions on "practical application." It never occurred to him that the favorable wind blowing him along the road of life had come from his father, who held important positions on both the provincial and the municipal revolutionary committees, and whose career was rising like a rocket.

Right after Yanyan's application for Party membership had been voted upon, China underwent an enormous change. And Yanyan's fate underwent a similar change. It was just after the Lin Biao affair of 13 September 1971 that the Party branch formally notified Yanyan that the Party committee of the Youth League had rejected his application. From then on, it was also forbidden that he write to his father. The reason was that his father, as a sworn follower of Lin Biao, had played a shameful part in the illegal move by "Lin's family dynasty" to set up an alternative Party central.

The treacherous winds of life had dashed Yanyan's little boat against the fearsome shoals that surrounded him. He was now classified as a "child of the black gang" and from morning to night was shunned on all sides. The stench of his father's bad name carried more weight than his own revolutionary conduct, and he could not forgive his schoolmates for that. At a mere nineteen years of age, Yanyan had already shouldered the black mantle of his father's sins, and could not see when the day of redemption might come.

In the spring of 1973, Yanyan finally managed to get permission to return home for a visit. The first thing he did on this visit was the paperwork to renounce his relation with his father officially. Then he went to ask his mother's whereabouts at the administration department of the bank where she had worked. The answer was so freezing that it made his heart clench.

Mother was dead! They said she had "died from disease." She had been a little over forty, and had never been sick. What was the real reason she died?

"Lin Biao persecuted a great number of respected cadres. I hope the Party can reopen my mother's case," said Yanyan.

"First of all, you are no longer her son," replied the political officer. "Second, she was not only a false Party member, but also an important undercover agent. We have indisputable proof of this. When she was in school, she was trained by the [KMT] government in telegraphy. That is spy training."

Since when had white become black, glory become shame? Yanyan had often heard his mother talking about that part of her past. The Party underground, during the war with Japan, had *directed* her to take those training classes in order to learn telegraphy. But to Yanyan, already familiar with the fate of an outcast, it was clear that nothing useful could be accomplished by further pleas. And so he quietly walked away. This meant that the only person in the world he could call his family was his sister. But where was she? Yanyan no longer was able, or even wanted, to look for her.

On board the steamer, Yanyan's listless gaze fell upon the mist-softened form of the great southern city. It occurred to him that he was bidding eternal farewell to his childhood home. He had spent the happy years of his youth here, but would never in this life be able to return.

Back on Hainan Island, he became a completely different person. No smile crossed his face. He took to smoking cigarettes, and his fingers turned yellow from the tar. He also took to drinking. At twenty-one, he was acting like a broken old man. He hated his father and he hated his own unjust fate. He renounced his father's family name of Gu and took the name Yan Liang, meaning "Forbidding Cold," to show his lack of warmth toward people and his disillusionment with the world.

The months and years slipped by. In their militia unit, famous for being "revolutionary," life was as dull and monotonous as could be. Each day was only the day before come back again. But one cannot be completely cut off from the world, high as the Wuzhi Mountains might be. People returning from home leave spoke of the turbulent political changes on the mainland. These reports only made Yan Liang recall his buffetings at the hands of fate. He felt cheated, toyed with. At one time, he had supported the doctrine that children must answer for their parents' crimes; now that very doctrine had become a heavy chain around his own neck. How dirty could politics be? How rotten the world? Were ideals merely dreams?

Yan Liang longed to take leave of this dusty, clamorous world. Just one mile from the company headquarters, there was a nursery for young rubber trees. It was protected from storms by a growth of Taiwan acacia. Someone had to take care of this nursery. This is what led to Yan Liang's putting up his thatched hut not far from the small stream. Except for coming in once or twice a month to draw his pay, grain, rations, fertilizer, and tools, his only contact with the outside world was a transistor radio. Time flowed by like the water in the brook. The radio reported to him the mad stampede of the outside world, but this in no way affected the cold indifference in his mind.

Finally, the air waves carried the news of the fall of the Gang of Four. Yan Liang's first thought was that this was the same old political game as before, but the radio continued to bring novel and refreshing news. It finally seemed his country was moving in the right direction, and that the nightmare that had been haunting him for the past few years might disappear.

His militia unit was reorganized as an agricultural brigade. This caused the brigade members, as always, to produce a new round of cheers and then relapse into silence. Yan Liang soon realized that the disappearance of these devils [the Gang of Four] was glad tidings only to people in the mainstream. Outcasts like himself would always live in a shadow. And sure enough, all the other urban youth, one by one, got transferred back to jobs in the city. Finally Yan Liang was the only one left.

Yan Liang concluded that he would pass the rest of a long life right at this nursery. His life would be like this nameless stream: it would hum along, day and night, murmuring to itself. No one would hear the plaint in its mournful song. It would twist and turn continually, coursing day and night, yet no one would know where it was going.

Truly, little stream, where are you going?

2. On the Other Side of the Stream

During those years in the agricultural brigade, Yan Liang even forgot what Mid-Autumn moon-cakes tasted like. At Mid-Autumn Festival he just opened a can and heated up his holiday banquet. Then he lit a cigarette, sprawled on his bed, and gave himself over to Cantonese songs coming from the radio— things such as "Rosy Clouds Pursuing the Moon" and "Bright Full Moon"—all of which seemed very familiar, yet at the same time, in this place, quite alien.

The end of the last song, which was called "Enchanted Evening," prompted Yan Liang to go down to the stream to wash up. Stripping to his undershorts, he grabbed a towel and left his hut. He raised his head to admire the moon just as it dodged behind a strip of thin clouds. How radiant and enchanting the moon of his childhood had been, and never crisper or purer than at Mid-Autumn Festival. But here in Hainan, even on the most clear and serene autumn nights, there would always be a few clouds. Was this due to the luxuriant tropical foliage, or to the maritime climate? Yan Liang had forgotten what his school text had said about the formation of clouds. There were, in fact, many things he had forgotten; and there were some things he could not forget if he tried.

Leaning against a betel nut palm, Yan Liang raised his head and waited defiantly for the full Mid-Autumn moon again to show itself from behind the cloud layer. When at last it did, its cool silver rays imparted a glow to the ranks of mountains, and the colors of the night were tender as a dream. As if possessed by a perverse spirit, Yan Liang pointed out to himself that even the bright moon has its perpetually dark side, just as the most just of societies will always have its injustices. His lighthearted mood suddenly turned sour.

Just at that moment, in the midst of a chorus of cicadas, there came and then disappeared the sound of a soft, casual song. Yan Liang turned to see if the radio in his hut were still on, then reproached himself for imagining things. There must be something wrong with his hearing. He went on toward the stream, but the closer he got, the clearer the sound of the song became. Yan Liang stopped and listened carefully. It was the melodious voice of a woman singing a song Yan Liang himself had also once known:

> The bright and clear moon hangs high in the sky,
> Bathes the great earth with its brilliance:
> The silver light everywhere makes me long for home, . . .

Yan Liang quietly walked to a steep part of the bank. He was suddenly so taken by surprise that he forgot to breathe. There on the other side of the stream was a young woman, washing her clothes in the clear, silver waves. Who was she? Why had she come to this deserted place?

When the moonlight threw his reflection onto the water, the girl sprang to her feet and looked directly toward Yan Liang on the opposite bank. In the moonlight, he could see her eyes flashing this way and that. The clothes she was washing started to drift downstream. Yan Liang suddenly realized he was not properly clothed, and hurriedly turned to leave. In a moment, he heard a loud splashing in the stream, which must, he thought, have been the sound of a terrified girl making a frantic escape. But in another moment, her song again issued from the other side of the stream, for her splashing had only been to retrieve the clothes that had drifted away. It was he who had yet to recover from fright. He knew that another state farm had a tree nursery about ten minutes' walk across the stream in the other direction, and that there was another thatched hut there. But the other state farm had not designated any particular person to look after its nursery, and those people who did come never slept in the hut overnight. Even their daytime visits happened only a few times per month. Occasionally, the banks of the lonely stream would reveal some Li tribesmen, shouldering their muskets and leading their hunting dogs. But where had this girl come from?

Yan Liang went to sleep that mid-autumn night with the sounds of a throng of crickets and of rustling treetops all around him. But all he heard was that comely voice echoing in his ears.

As the sky turned blue, and the first rosy clouds of dawn appeared, Yan Liang stepped across the morning dew down to the river to wash his face. The sound of song floated up again, this time "The Sun Comes Out from Behind the Mountain," and following the joyous song the image of the girl he had spied the night before flashed forth from a grove of wild bananas. She was carrying a towel, plunging through the horsetail ferns, coming down to the stream. Catching

sight of Yan Liang, she stopped her song and greeted him with perfect composure: "Good morning."

Somewhat at a loss, Yan Liang looked at the girl and blurted out a good
morning—a phrase he found strangely unfamiliar because it is so seldom used in
the countryside.

She was small and slender, her skin deeply tanned by the sun, her clothes
patched, her russet feet bare. She was quite ordinary-looking. Perhaps Yan Liang
could not appreciate the looks of a woman; they all seemed alike to his
indifferent eye.

"We're neighbors," the girl said with a beaming smile. "We drink from
the same stream." She laughed. "Are you the only one in that hut? What's your
name? How long have you been here?"

"My name is Yan Liang, and I've been here alone for four years," Yan
Liang replied. Then, noticing her accent, he asked, "Is your family from Haizhou?"

"Why yes, how did you know? Where is yours from?"

"Same as yours."

"Hey, you speak Mandarin very well. What school did you go to? What
class were you in?"

"I went to . . . High School Eighty-one, class of '68." Mortification
overcame Yan Liang as he spoke. His alma mater was a special school for the
children of high military officials.

The girl looked him over quizzically. "Senior high or junior high?" she
asked.

"Junior high."

"Then you're the same year as me! You certainly don't look it! I thought
you were thirty years old. Why don't you get a haircut? Or try shaving? If you
go home looking like that your own father'll disown you."

Another stab of pain in Yan Liang's heart. One mention of his "stinking"
father and the girl would certainly turn hostile.

Just as she was dipping her washcloth into the water to wash her face,
she suddenly cried out, "Oh my, look at that! Look right now!" He followed
where she was looking and saw a little bird with bright red feathers skimming
and twittering through the morning air. It landed in a bush by the stream,
looking like a red flower in full bloom. This exotic tropical bird, which the Li
tribes considered to be magical, had never been caught or caged. In fact, it was a
rare thing even to see one.

"Oh, how beautiful! This is a wonderful place!"

The comment caused Yan Liang to recall that she had called herself a
"neighbor." Could it be that she had moved into the hut across the stream? He
wanted to ask, but dared not. When he had washed and was ready to leave, she
broke the silence again. "What's your rush, Yan . . . uh, what did you say your
name was?"

"Yan Liang."

"Look, you haven't even asked me mine! It's Mu Lan—'Mu' as in Mu
Guiying and 'Lan' as in Hua Mulan. From now on well be seeing each other
across the stream," she laughed. "I thought I was the only one living here, but
when I saw that betel nut palm yesterday, I felt better."

That betel nut palm was one Yan Liang had planted himself after he
arrived. It is a strange tree, for it grows only where human beings have settled. In
the Wuzhi Mountains, a betel nut palm always signals the presence of a nearby
village.

"What are you doing here?" Yan Liang finally asked out of curiosity.

"Oh, you and I are in the same business. Our brigade's tree nursery was
almost overgrown with weeds and grass, so they made me come down here to
look after it."

Yan Liang couldn't understand why they would send a girl to look after
the nursery, but he didn't want to ask any more questions. By this time, the sky
was completely light. Yan Liang could feel Mu Lan's intense gaze curiously
scrutinizing his every move, and this made him feel somewhat ill at ease. He
went up from the bank of the stream.

After that, Mu Lan's song often floated over from the other side of the
stream. And Yan Liang encountered her at the bank of the stream a few more
times. When this happened, Yan Liang seldom spoke, while Mu Lan chattered
away like a little sparrow. Yan Liang learned from her that almost all the urban
youths once stationed at her farm had already returned to the city. In her brigade,
she was the only one left.

Mu Lan was peppery and forthright, and often used words that normally
only boys use. Once she said, "What do they think they're talking about—'grasp
the key link of class struggle and bring great order to the brigade'? Bullshit! The
head of our farm, a 'double stand-out' cadre is a real little bastard. He worked
his lousy tail off for the Gang of Four, but the next thing you know he was hot to
'smash the Gang of Four,' too. What a little pile of dogshit! And because this
turd was in charge, our whole brigade lost its shirt. And then they talk about
modernization!" Yan Liang was about to say that his farm was also on the brink
of bankruptcy, but didn't quite dare.

At dusk on he eve of the October First National Day, Yan Liang was down by the stream washing his bedsheets when Mu Lan started singing again. She noticed a few lush, ripe papayas on a tree at the stream bank; slipping off her sandals, she pushed aside the spiky leaves of the underbrush and made her way to where she could shake down some papayas. She casually tossed a couple toward Yan Liang, who scrambled over barely in time to catch one of them, while the other fell into the water and bobbed away. This made Mu Lan laugh until she lost her breath, and even Yan Liang couldn't help smiling. Mu Lan shouted, as if she had just discovered something, "Oh ho, your face is always so wrinkled up like a pickle that I didn't think you even knew how to smile! Ha, ha . . ."

Yan Liang smiled again, something of a wry smile, and didn't reply.

Mu Lan went on, "Yan . . . Yan Liang. You know, it really doesn't sound very nice to call yourself a name that means "forbidding and cold." You might as well call yourself Yan Luo, the King of Hell. Ha ha, don't get mad! What's so bad about the King of Hell? I'd really love to be the King of Hell some day. What I'd do is I'd send my deputies—those cow-headed horse-faced messengers like the ones in the pictures in the old Buddhist books—and chase all the goddamn bastards of the world right into hell! Then they'd get a taste of what it's like to shinny up hills of knives and get dunked in boiling oil. But Yan Liang, what I really wanted to ask you was why you never went home to Haizhou."

"I don't have any family there," Yan Liang mumbled evasively.

Mu Lan, keenly observant, quickly withdrew her smile. "I think maybe there's some other reason. C'mon, tell! Look, I don't have a family either. My mother was hounded to death by the Gang of Four and hasn't been exonerated, even though it should happen pretty soon. The reason I can't get transferred back is that I'm a 'counterrevolutionary'!"

"You?" Yan Liang shivered.

"Sure. A few years ago, some people put up a wall poster calling for a more democratic system. Did you hear about it? I wrote a letter supporting it, and—bang!—was stuck as a counterrevolutionary and paraded around to be struggled by all the work teams. Those apes! They beat the hell out of me! It was half a month before I could stand up straight again. But they better think twice if they think they scared *me*!"

Yan Liang looked at her in amazement. He never would have imagined that her delicate body could have undergone such a fascist beating. And how could such a young girl already be a counterrevolutionary? That was something that normally took a lifetime! After a moment of reflection, Yan Liang said, "Your problem will be settled sooner or later. But mine is different. My father was one of Lin Biao's right-hand men, and nobody can live that down. For me there's no way out."

Mu Lan looked at him sympathetically but said nothing. After a moment she said, "It won't be easy for me to remove my counterrevolutionary label, either. They make you a counterrevolutionary in a matter of minutes, but God knows how many years it takes to prove they were wrong. And in my case, the problem is not something the agricultural production brigade can handle—it has to go up to certain big officials. But I couldn't care less who it goes to—I'm not scared!"

After another pause, Mu Lan asked, "Are you going back to your brigade headquarters for National Day on October first?"

"No," Yan Liang answered, without thinking. "Are you?"

"Do you need to ask? Tonight I'll come to your place to pay my respects. May I?"

" . . . certainly . . ." Yan Liang didn't quite know what to do.

3. An Evening Chat in the Thatched Hut

Yan Liang had just finished tidying up his thatched hut inside and out. In the distance, the peaks of the Wuzhi Mountains reflected the last blood red light of the sunset. He busied himself building the fire for his evening meal. By the time the food was ready, the sky was filled with cloudy moonlight. Outside, Mu Lan's song started up again; this time it was "The Hawthorn Tree":

Song floats lightly on the waters of the golden dusk . . .

Hey!" called Mu Lan from outside the hut, "Here comes the honorable guest!" In a moment she had followed her laughter into the hut.

"Heavens, why the droopy face? You cooking dinner? Forget it, make it into fried rice in the morning. I've brought you some steamed rolls, and they taste just the way they do back in Haizhou." She laughed.

Mu Lan was not a bad cook, and her steamed rolls stuffed with beanpaste were delicious. Yan Liang sat by the side of the bed, leaving the only bamboo chair for Mu Lan. But Mu Lan kept walking around, humming a tune, inspecting his low-ceilinged kitchen and turning the pages of his few books.

"You sing pretty well," said Yan Liang, searching for something to say.

"Me? Nah! I only sing because of you, because I'm afraid of embarrassing you. I bellow it out when I go down to the stream bank, just to warn you that a woman is around." Having said this, Mu Lan lost herself in laughter, and the crisp sound of that laughter penetrated into the night outside. Yan Liang began to realize that Mu Lan, despite her very open and outgoing manner, took pains to be considerate.

Mu Lan sat down and without the least awkwardness said, "I don't know how it is, but I keep thinking that I've seen you somewhere before."

Yan Liang found it awkward to meet her gaze, but thought for a moment and replied, "Back when I used to be so red I was almost purple, I used to go over where you were to hold 'practical application' sessions. You probably saw me up on the platform making a fool of myself. My goodness—'practical application' sessions! Now it all sounds pretty ridiculous."

Mu Lan laughed icily. "No, it couldn't be that," she said. "I never listened to a word of all that hot air, so that wasn't where I had the honor of making your acquaintance!"

"So that makes me a hot air artist, a bullshitter?"

"No, we were all victims, but some people woke up earlier than others . . . Oh, now I remember! It was the last time I went to the shop at your brigade . . . the same day volume five of Chairman Mao's *Selected Works* came out, that day it was so crowded. I saw a guy with long ratty hair, sunburnt and skinny. *That* was you. I don't know why, but you made a special impression on me."

Yan Liang reflected uneasily that, if he had really been so conspicuous in those days, he had been risking considerable trouble. Mulling over his regret, he started to fish out a cigarette, but then stopped awkwardly with his hand in mid-air. Mu Lan's gaze was fierce. "If you're going to smoke, give me one too." Clumsily, he lit one for her.

Yan Liang's inhibitions gradually dissipated with the cigarette smoke. He heaved a sigh. "You were talking just now about how some people 'woke up' earlier than others," he said. "I saw through their tricks as early as anybody. But it was like waking up from a nightmare and finding you're still in the dark."

Mu Lan's glistening black eyes darted up and down Yan Liang once again, and she laughed. "Did you join the Youth League?"

"I almost joined the Party! But I got kicked out of the Youth League right when I turned twenty-five."

"Then you believe in communism?"

"To tell the truth I had my doubts. But not any more, of course. Ideals are like the sun in the sky, and reality like the shadows on the ground. When the Gang of Four fell, almost everybody could enjoy the sunshine again. But I've been unlucky enough to stay under a cloud. It's just like the Wuzhi Mountains. Other people can see that there are actually five peaks, but from our vantage point we can see only three. And that's because of the angle were looking from, that is to say. . ."

"I know what you're talking about," Mu Lan chuckled. "You're something like the decadent poets and the nihilist philosophers."

Yan Liang was startled. He hadn't realized that Mu Lan knew so much. "I guess you don't agree?" he ventured.

"Why not? Everything you said is true." Mu Lan changed her cheerful expression and continued solemnly. "After all, I'm the daughter of one of the 'seven black categories,' I never joined the Youth League, and later I got stuck with political labels. But I never really doubted communism, and still think it's going to come true some day. The communism I believe in is one that can make a person happy. Aren't we always saying that the proletariat can liberate all of humanity? How come not all citizens have the same rights? Why does everybody have to be divided into 'red categories' and 'black categories'? What right do they have to drive people to death so recklessly? What right do they have to call me a counterrevolutionary? Where's the legal distinction between 'revolutionary' and 'counterrevolutionary'? Take you, for example. Why should it make any difference whether your father is 'rotten? Why should a son have to carry around a father's bad name for the rest of his life?"

Mu Lan's suntanned face had now turned red, and Yan Liang realized from her impassioned talk that she felt even more deeply than he about these things. He sighed helplessly. "Maybe when your kind of communism arrives, we can get out of the fix we're in," he said.

"Why wait? Why should we wait?" Mu Lan's eyes were glowing like the flame of the kerosene lantern. "I didn't bow my head for one minute to those savage bullies! I'll appeal my case level by level to the Ministry of Agriculture, to the courts, to the Provincial Committee, to the procurator-general . . . and if all that doesn't work, I'll write to Uncle Deng himself. I'll denounce them, denounce every one of those damn bastards right into the ground!"

Yan Liang was staggered by Mu Lan's gall and her stubborn courage. But then he reflected that he had not, after all, been publicly labeled a counterrevolutionary; how could he make a formal appeal to higher levels?

Mu Lan sighed and her voice became husky. "Our country has gone through a massive disaster these last ten years, and why did this happen? If it was only because of Lin Biao or the Gang of Four, then tell me how all those other opportunists got to the top! Did anyone ever ask the people if they wanted them or not? Okay, so they got kicked out this time—but if the people can't have democracy, then what's to stop a 'Gang of Five' or a 'Gang of Six' some year bringing another big mess? So I'm making my appeal not just for myself. It's also for my martyred mother, and for everyone who's been hounded to death, hoping that we'll never see a bloody tragedy like this again!"

A long and deep silence. The only sound was the hiss of the kerosene lantern. Yan Liang had always blamed the outrages of those ten years on the evil Lin Biao and Gang of Four. He had never considered the flaws in the social system. Now he sat pondering this question intensely.

Mu Lan fixed Yan Liang with her gaze. "You ought to write to the *People's Daily* and tell them just what's happened to you. Why not? Afraid? Afraid of what? The *People's Daily* is starting to speak for the people these days. I never used to be very brave, but when I lost everything, I lost my fear too. What the hell is there for an 'active counterrevolutionary' to be afraid of?"

Yan Liang laughed coolly, for he knew that the normal way of handling letters from readers was to refer them back to the leaders in one's own work unit, and that only made things worse, much worse.

The night was getting late, and they began to hear the sound of the autumn dew dripping from the leaves of the trees onto the parched underbrush. Mu Lan said it was time for her to go. She broke off a switch of thorny bamboo from the crudely bound broom that stood behind the door. "Lot of snakes around here," she said, whipping the switch on the ground a couple of times.

"I'll see you home," said a concerned Yan Liang.

Mu Lan chuckled. "Don't bother. I'm not afraid of snakes. Are there wild boars around here? I'm not afraid of them either."

But Yan Liang insisted. When they got to the bank of the stream, Mu Lan gave Yan Liang a gentle shove, took a few running steps, and jumped over the stream. On the other side, she turned back to face him. "I don't need you to see me home, but there is something I'd like your help with. That rickety hut of mine is nice and near to the tree nursery, but it's too far from the stream—not very convenient. I think I'll build another little nest for myself, and I'll have to use a little cost-benefit analysis to choose the location! Ha-ha . . ." Mu Lan didn't wait for Yan Liang to reply, but ran laughing up the hill.

4. Companions in Adversity

The next day, which was National Day, Yan Liang and Mu Lan did a whole day's work under the steaming sun, finally completing a sturdy little reed hut for her. They built it behind a grove of wild banana trees on the other side of the stream. Yan Liang scattered sulphur around the cottage to ward off snakes.

When he had finished, Mu Lan said nothing to thank him; she only grinned and said, "You're pretty handy."

Yan Liang later taught Mu Lan everything he knew about grafting young rubber plants. He explained that if she cut her hair and scattered some of it around the nursery, the wild boars would be turned away by the human scent and not trample the plants.

In the evenings, the two of them would get together to read and chat. Mu Lan was well informed on a wide range of subjects, and they talked about everything under the sun. But Mu Lan, ever ready to say or do anything, showed she was also very solicitous of other people's feelings. She never asked about Yan Liang's family, just as he never asked about hers. Neither wanted to open the other's wounds.

Yan Liang lost his melancholy; Mu Lan's refreshing candor was like a ray of sunshine in his somber life. He felt as if he had known this girl for years. Perhaps because he had been living alone too long, a cozy feeling grew in Yan Liang's heart in no time at all.

Once when Yan Liang was squatting at Mu Lan's side, showing her how to graft rubber shoots, he found himself shifting his gaze toward her sweat-lined face.

"What are you doing?" Mu Lan suddenly asked.

" . . . What?"

"What are you gaping at? If I did something wrong you wouldn't even notice."

Yan Liang's face turned red, and he lost his composure.

That evening Yan Liang did not go to the other side of the stream. He was sorting through his confused thoughts when Mu Lan appeared, singing her usual song. As if nothing had happened, she said to Yan Liang, "Say, from now on, don't cook your own food, okay? We're such close neighbors—why cook separately? Besides, you're a terrible cook."

After that they were together even more. Even though Yan Liang did everything he could to repress the thoughts that were coming into his mind, he couldn't help noticing that Mu Lan's eyes often quietly followed him, and that, when she happened to meet his perplexed gaze, she calmly blinked her eyelashes without looking away.

They were companions in adversity; fate had been their only matchmaker. Love sprang up in two hearts that were more used to the bitter than the sweet.

Hainan has no autumn. October is the typhoon season. When number thirteen typhoon in 1977 assaulted the Wuzhi Mountains, its center passed directly through Yan Liang's and Mu Lan's area. After the first violent onslaught of the storm, there was actually an interval of clear sky as its eye passed over. Before the stream rose too high, Yan Liang found a wooden staff to help him wade through the rushing water and go see if he could reinforce Mu Lan's hut. He had just patched a few leaks when the wind suddenly blew up again. It savagely drove pellets of rain, like insistent darts, into the groaning forests of the mountain. Mu Lan brewed up some ginger sugar water to ward off the cold. When the two had finished it and chatted for a while, the sky was already very dark. Wrapping his raincoat around his shoulders, Yan Liang made his way out the door, but hadn't gone more than a few steps when he stopped in amazement. The swollen stream had almost exceeded its banks, and the rushing water made a terrifying roar as it hurtled forward. Through the curtain of rain, he could see on the other bank the betel nut palm snapping back and forth crazily in the violent wind. Crossing over was out of the question.

Mu Lan dashed out and pulled Yan Liang back into the hut. Her eyes sparkled as she wiped the rain from her face. "Don't go," she said evenly, looking straight at Yan Liang. "You can't get across anyway. Stay here."

Yan Liang jumped as if delivered an electric shock.

"Are you some kind of Confucian moralist?" asked Mu Lan. "You believe all the classics of morality?" She was laughing, but it was a brittle laugh that was actually a cover for the inner excitement she also felt.

Yan Liang still couldn't say a thing. Mu Lan began to help him remove his raincoat. "You're shivering, look, you're soaked through!" Yan Liang suddenly grasped Mu Lan's warm hands . . .

Some time later, a gust of wind blew out the guttering flame in the kerosene lantern. They didn't light it again.

This pair of lucky—and yet also unlucky—young people: had they been too hasty? They had known each other only two months! Yet they felt as if they had been fated for one another in some previous existence. In this deserted outpost, on this night of the fierce typhoon, it had been their common fate that had brought them together.

If certain leaders of their state farms had known what they were doing, the consequences would have been terrible. Although most people generally do acknowledge certain moral prohibitions, they do not like to see the enforcement of those prohibitions placed in the hands of cold-hearted bullies. Heaven only knows whether this pair of young lovers, who intended to swear themselves to one another, had done anything wrong. The Lord of Heaven certainly did seem to be enraged, to judge from the roaring fury of the typhoon. Magnificent crashes, from great trees snapping in the wind, continued to sound from time to time. The maddened wind and driving rain shook the little thatched hut angrily. Was Heaven trying to punish someone?

Nonetheless, inside the lovers' hearts, all these noises of heaven and earth seemed far, far away.

5. Whose Fault?

The sky lightened. The typhoon had passed. The muddy stream was carrying its burden of splintered branches, blasted leaves, and half-submerged papayas and coconuts down to the sea. Yan Liang took Mu Lan by the hand and led her across the stream to see how his own hut had come through the disaster.

The storm of emotions had also passed. The sweetness of their love seemed to hang in the gentle winds and tear-soft rains as they cuddled together and talked about the future.

"Let's get married tomorrow," said Yan Liang.

"Whatever you want. My gosh, what sorts of paperwork will we have to go through? It'll probably be a pain."

"I have no idea. I guess we'll have to fill out some forms."

"What shall we put on them?" She giggled. "You'll put that your 'family background' is 'anti-Party element,' and I'll put that my 'class' is 'active counterrevolutionary.' Blacker and blacker! Ha ha! . . . But wait, we'll still have to put down our family and residence, and neither of us has any family."

Yan Liang sighed. "Well I do have a sister, actually, but don't know where she is."

"Oh, really? Why not?"

"When we were small, they never let us be together. My father didn't like her. When my parents got divorced, she went with my mother. By the way, my mother's maiden name was also Mu!"

Mu Lan turned white and suddenly grabbed Yan Liang's hand. "What was your sister's name?" she blurted out in extreme apprehension.

"Gu Ganggang."

As if struck by lightning, Mu Lan threw aside Yan Liang's hand and leapt to her feet. Two terror-filled eyes stared straight at Yan Liang.

Mu Lan's whitened lips began to tremble. "You . . . you're Yanyan?" she whispered.

Yan Liang's head began to spin. Everything grew foggy.

"Ma . . . no!" Mu Lan let out a jolting scream, covered her face with her hands and ran crazily from the hut. Yan Liang followed her without quite knowing what he was doing, only to see Mu Lan plunging recklessly down the hill. She tripped and fell headlong into the stream, then got up, dripping from head to toe, and rushed on, leaving a trail of shrill cries along the way.

Yan Liang suddenly realized that she . . . she was . . . oh, no! Yan Liang's knees buckled. He stumbled forward a few steps, threw his arms around the trunk of the betel nut palm, and slipped listlessly to the ground. There he sat in the mud, trembling all over, feeling like vomiting.

Somehow he found his way back to his hut and flopped down on his bed. Soon he began to get chills. Yan Liang had once caught malaria, which was common in this tropical area, and he had the usual recurrent bouts of it even after he seemed to have recovered. Now the fever came in waves, causing him to writhe on his cot in pain; it alternated with spells of shaking, which made the cot creak and groan. Hallucinations appeared in his muddled mind. Suddenly he would see himself and his sister flying kites and running gleefully through the fields; then his mother, locked in her "cow shed," would flash before his eyes, calling in despair to her children; next the shameful events that had occurred the night before on the other side of the stream would reappear. How shameful! How evil! But wait—where were these dazzling gold stars coming from? No! It was all dark again. Where are you, Mother? Can't you save me?

He didn't know how much time had passed. He struggled upright to swallow some quinine, and sat crouched for a while, his head lolling on his knees. Heartless fate had cuffed him once again, destroying everything he had left. Whose fault was this? Whose?

These two late-blooming flowers had borne a bitter fruit. Everything was quiet on the other side of the stream. At dusk a few days later, Yan Liang was at the bank of the stream and saw . . . his sister. How thin she seemed, how ashen her face. Yan Liang cast his eyes downward uncertainly, and said nothing. Mu Lan did not lift her eyes either, but furtively filled her pail with water and slipped away.

Yan Liang came to realize that, from now on, each time he and his sister met would be a kind of torture for both of them. A chilling thought occurred to him . . . .

One day when Yan Liang was propped on his cot with that chilling thought in his mind, his sister slipped quietly into his room. She sat down woodenly, but

Yan Liang jerked upright with a shudder. A glance told him that some deep contemplation lay behind his sister's bloodshot eyes.

After a silence, Mu Lan spoke. "Yanyan, since I'm the elder sister, I have the responsibility to think things through for both of us. What we did was not our fault. Forget about what we did. Don't think about it ever again!" Mu Lan almost broke down, and took a moment to recover. "Yanyan, listen. I went to the farm office this morning, and found out that Mother's unit had sent a letter saying she's been exonerated. They're planning a memorial service and want me to go back for it. The Party secretary in our office is such a stinking bastard he didn't want anybody to tell me. The deputy manager of the farm told me in secret. I think you and I should go back together . . . what's wrong? Don't worry! Mother's spirit would forgive us even if she knew."

Yan Liang silently nodded his head. He was near to choking. His clogged throat could not produce a word. Mu Lan stood and put her hand gently on his shoulder. Yan Liang quivered.

"Don't be that way, Yanyan. Wipe all that out of your mind . . . You're my brother; stand up and call me sister." Mu Lan's tone of voice had changed.

" . . . sister."

"All right. I'll come back this evening," Mu Lan, who also could hardly hold herself together, darted out of the hut.

Yan Liang's heart hurt as if a knife were twisting inside it. He lay his head on the table and sobbed.

6. Toward the Light

Yan Liang knew that the farm would never approve a leave for him. But he had already put everything else out of his mind. Luckily, there are many more good-hearted people in the world than evil ones. Even though neither of them had documentation for a trip home, they managed to board a steamer for Haizhou without mishap.

Late that night, the half-moon left a rippling trail of silver on the sea. The hot faces of this brother and sister felt comforted by the salty sea breeze. They leaned over the railing of the ship, peered at the boundless sea, and shared their thoughts.

Yan Liang learned many new things about their past from his sister. After their mother's divorce, she and her daughter had moved to the company quarters of the bank. But within half a month, their mother had been put into the "cow shed," and his sister had been forced to vacate their room. A kind-hearted old man who worked as doorkeeper at the bank had taken her in. One morning, this old man anxiously informed her that her mother had had her collarbone broken and was running a high fever. In her delirium, she had called out for Ganggang and Yanyan. Mother had been so nearby yet so inaccessible. There had been no way to see her. Mu Lan had bought medicine, written a note to go with it, and asked the kindly doorkeeper to find some way of getting these to her mother. She had gone to High School Eighty-one to find her brother and tell him about their mother, but had been surprised to learn that one had to report one's class background in order to get through the school gate. When it had been learned she was a "bitch's daughter," she had been refused entrance. At that point, she had written a letter home to her brother, but had never received a reply. (Yanyan had never even heard of this letter; needless to say, the pettiness of their worthless father had been at work.) This had made her despise her brother completely and feel he was just as much a beast as her father. From then on, she had banished the thought that she had ever had a brother. In 1968 her school had assigned her to go to the countryside, but she had not gone. Within six months, her mother had died in prison without her even having had a chance to see her mother's face. Afterwards, she had joined the old doorkeeper's daughter and this girl's classmates from High School Five in an assignment to work on Hainan Island. She had changed her name, and had said only that she was with High School Five. From then on, she had had no family to turn to, and had floated aimlessly for eleven years until she had come across her equally ill-fated brother. Now it all seemed to belong to another world . . .

At the memorial service, which was held in the cemetery for revolutionary martyrs, the steely Mu Lan melted into tears, while Yan Liang, normally the weaker of the two, stood implacable as a statue. He gazed dumbly at the casket that held his mother's ashes. He could not believe that his mother, who had been a solid, loyal member of the Communist Party, could be packed into such a little box. He began to doubt that it did hold her remains at all.

Who had killed our mother? Who had brought every conceivable suffering upon us, her children?

Yan Liang shook off his timidity. He went along with his sister to the public complaint offices of the departments concerned, and there they stated their case. They also filed an appeal with an Intermediate People's Court, and joined in writing a lengthy wall poster that criticized the leadership of their state farms. They furiously denounced the malevolent toads who took pleasure in persecuting people and the heartless bureaucrats who could only behave like cogs in a machine. Mu Lan's problems were eventually cleared up, thanks to the full support of the Party committee at the People's Bank. The Intermediate People's Court directed Mu Lan's state farm to exonerate her, and the People's

Bank deputed someone to accompany the brother and sister back to Hainan so that they would not be prosecuted for having taken leave without authorization. The bank even said that it would bring both of them back the following year and arrange jobs for them.

There was no way to "exonerate" Yan Liang, because he had fallen victim to no law, but merely to the *policy* of denying certain rights to people like him. Yan Liang had come to understand that freedom and democracy were not tasty pastries that others would hand to you on a platter; the more one lived in darkness and adversity, the more one needed to stand up and fight. He and his sister wrote letters to the newspaper demanding that the rule of law be strengthened and that all people be equal before it.

There are still little tyrants around, who feel that "the mountains are high and the emperor is far away," leaving them absolute power to make their own little laws in their own little kingdoms. But their day is coming to an end! The sunlight of the Party will eventually break through the dark clouds and shine into every corner. The Party committee on Mu Lan's state farm had already been reorganized, and a Party work team at Yan Liang's was in the process of reorganizing the leadership there.

Who says the Wuzhi Mountains must swelter all year round? Throw up your arms and shout, for the spring breeze is coming!

7. The Parted Lovers Reunite

The banks of the stream had often echoed with the sounds of song and laughter from brother and sister. What a pity that complete happiness is so elusive. There still remained that one incident, the painful memory of which haunted them both. Each had privately sworn never to marry. Their only wish was to be together, never again having to part.

Oh, if only the leadership everywhere were as benevolent and effective as it was this one time. Yan Liang received a letter from the Party committee at the bank: "Comrade Yan Liang, recently we have come across something your mother left you when she died. Tucked inside the cover of her *Quotations of Chairman Mao,* we found this letter addressed to you. There obviously should be a letter to Comrade Mu Lan as well, but we have been unable to find it. We feel most apologetic, but could you inform Comrade Mu Lan . . ."

Yan Liang hurriedly unfolded this parting letter from his mother. It was written on a very thin piece of paper, with tiny words crowded everywhere. The flimsy paper rustled in his hand. He was shaking as he smoothed it out on his table. The words danced and jumped before his tear-filled eyes:

Yanyan—

I do not have long to live, and I have a few things that I must tell you. Your father is an evil person with a mean soul. You must never follow in his footsteps. When I am dead, you must seek out your sister Ganggang. There is something I have always kept from you both, because you were too young to understand. Toward the end of 1951, I was doing land reform work in the Shiwan Mountains of Eastern Guangdong. At that time, bandits had still not been wiped out in the area, and the mountain districts were extremely poor. Once, in a small hamlet, a destitute woman asked me to hold her baby girl for a moment while she went to the outhouse. She left and never came back. Afterward I found out that her family was so poor that she had been intending to give this female child to somebody. This was your sister Ganggang. I think she's about six months older than you.

Good-bye forever, Yanyan. Don't weep for me. Stand up proud and straight, and live! My last wish is that you and your sister be reunited and stay together always. Look after each other, encourage each other. I'm writing these last letters to you and your sister from a dark prison cell, and I have no way of knowing if they will ever get to you. When I eventually am exonerated by the Party authorities, you and sister must come and report to me in my grave. I know I will hear you.

—Mother

By the time he had finished reading, Yan Liang felt as if arrows were piercing his heart. His tears gushed as if from springs. He sat in a daze, reading and rereading his mother's letter. Suddenly, as if there had been a flash of lightning, he saw the whole world in a different way. Snatching up the letter, he ran out of his straw hut and bounded across the clear little stream . . .

Oh, little stream—people do know your source now. You come from every cloud in the sky, from the dew on every leaf in the forest; you are crystal clear about the human world, its loves and hates, the sweetness and the terror.

Oh, little stream—people do know your destination now. Traveling your nine bends and crooks, you witness all manner of human suffering as it is washed before you into the great sea, in just the same way that our road through the world is bumpy, our lives are full of twists and turns, and the brightness of our future disappears and reappears.

Oh, little stream—people do understand you now, as you murmur along night and day. You are telling us: "May the dead achieve eternal life; may the living achieve eternal love. May the sun forever bring light and warmth, may humankind forever enjoy its warmth and solace."

February 1, 1979

Translated by Charles W. Hayford

44

Responsibility

PERRY LINK

This essay nicely conveys the powerful sense of social responsibility often felt by modern Chinese intellectuals. This sense of responsibility is a legacy of Confucian notions of loyalty and service, which were inherited by modern intellectuals and transformed into concern for the fate of the nation. Even in the 1980s, as they sought to break with the Maoist notion that they be subservient to politics, intellectuals continued to worry over the fate of the nation. Only in the 1990s, a product of radical market reforms and commercialization, did intellectuals self-consciously react against this tradition, seeing in it the seeds of authoritarianism.

The Worrying Mentality

Youhuan yishi [worrying mentality] is, first of all, related to patriotism in the sense that China, one way or another, is always the main object of worry. The entire mentality is couched in the big question "What can we *do* about China?"—a question that often takes on a despairing tone. In its pessimism and self-doubt, *youhuan yishi* stands apart from the chauvinistic or jingoistic varieties of patriotism. In fall 1988 an investigative reporter published a review of the large body of "literary reportage" that had recently appeared on problems such as inflation, overpopulation, the housing shortage, the brain drain, low educational standards, and even the "unmentionable" ones—prostitution, abortion, and begging. Yet his overall point was to praise the *youhuan yishi* and "the sense of mission and responsibility" of the authors of the reviewed works. Never celebratory in its mood, *youhuan yishi* dwells on "the dark side" of society, on the very facts that undermine chauvinistic claims.

Yet the intensity with which Chinese intellectuals undertake this self-examination rests upon their fierce conviction that China can and should be an exemplary culture and society. This pride undergirds the whole spectrum of complaints about the dark side of society, creates an especially sharp contrast between social ideals and reality, and impels the demand that China, certainly *China*, must do better. But even this underlying pride—an essential component

487

of *youhuan yishi*—is not exactly the same as ordinary patriotism, because in the end it aims at a morality that is fundamentally human, not just Chinese. It holds that in a proper world, China should exemplify the best way to conduct human affairs. Other societies should—and would, in a proper world—emulate China.

Youhuan yishi is, in one form or another, pervasive among Chinese intellectuals in all fields, localities, and even generations. The young, to be sure, exhibit it less, although it remains to be seen whether they will articulate it more as they mature. Intellectuals in Beijing, close to the political and intellectual centers, seem somewhat more smitten than their colleagues elsewhere. Natural scientists are usually as deeply affected as humanists and social scientists, differing only in that they can generally maintain a clearer borderline between *youhuan yishi* and their professional work.

In winter of 1989 a professor of Chinese at Beijing University published an interview on the roles of contemporary intellectuals, distinguishing three main types: first, those who "taint" themselves by engaging in commercial activity or compromising with the state by accepting official posts; second, those who bury their heads in their own scholarly work, usually living in poverty and virtual anonymity; and third, those who dedicate their work to improving society. All three types, the professor argued, exhibit *youhuan yishi* and deserve sympathy and respect. Those who fall into the first category do not really want to taint themselves; they are driven to do so and feel guilty about it. Those who bury their heads still hope that their scholarly results will be broadly useful in the end. Yet they often find that their labors of love are ignored and that they have become "separated from the times." Those who work to improve society, whether they succeed or not, represent the courageous ideal of the Chinese intellectual in its fullest form. A literary scholar commented that events such as the Tiananmen demonstrations in spring 1989 show that *youhuan yishi* is latent in the first two categories of intellectuals and emerges in times of crisis: many scholars apparently wedded to their desks began to march and sign petitions in spring 1989; others tainted by moonlighting jobs donated both time and money to the demonstrators.

Most Chinese I spoke with attributed the origins of *youhuan yishi* to traditional conceptions of the intellectual's moral duty to "take responsibility for all under heaven," to "be the first in the world to assume its worries," and so on. Stories of courageous intellectuals such as Liang Shuming, Hu Feng, and Wu Han, who had championed these virtues even under the Communists, helped to maintain the vitality of the ideal. But whether speaking of the origins of *youhuan yishi* or of its contemporary practice, most people regarded the attitude as distinctively Chinese. In the spring of 1988 Liu Zaifu observed, "In America, if a writer or an intellectual went around all day shouting about 'the duty of the writer' or 'the mission of the intellectual,' he might seem a bit ridiculous; but in China, to be a writer or intellectual and not speak of responsibility and mission seems equally ridiculous." I sometimes commented to my Chinese friends, in an effort to cheer them, that I admired their concern for the large issues, and wished that we in America showed the same sort of commitment. On one occasion a senior historian, a man who understood recent American history well, rebutted me in an illuminating way.

"You say our big concerns are admirable; I say they're pitiable. Where do they come from? From traditional Chinese virtues? Only in part. Do you remember the 1960s in your country, when students and intellectuals were questioning 'the system'? Those were 'big picture' worries, were they not? And why were people worrying? Because of *crisis*. They asked the big questions about 'the system' because of a fear that something was fundamentally wrong. But China, our China, has been in crisis almost constantly now for about 150 years, ever since the Opium War. We've had no choice, really, but to keep asking the 'big picture' questions—over and over again. Is that admirable or pitiable? I just hope a time will come in China when we don't need this 'admirable worrying' any more. It seems ironic, I know, but the 'admirable' Chinese intellectuals identify with China more strongly as China gets more and more badly off. If China were suddenly to do better, their commitment would go down. And that would be fine."

Another historian, while agreeing with her colleague's argument that a "crisis mentality" had much to do with *youhuan yishi*, was unwilling to overlook its distinctively Chinese component. "Isn't it true," she asked, "that the American antiwar movement in the 1960s was stimulated by the military draft? If the American questioning of 'the system' came about because people were worried about their own fates, then it's still different from *youhuan yishi*, whose aim is to set things right as a matter of principle, even at the cost of one's personal fate." This comment elicited a counterriposte from a younger historian. "I have a friend who is an entomologist," he said. "He worries a lot about China. I am a modern China historian, but I don't worry about bugs. Why does he worry about my field and I not worry about his? Because he *has* to worry about China. The sorry reality of China affects his life every day; if bugs bothered me that much, I would worry about bugs, too. So I'm not so sure *youhuan yishi* is purely idealistic."

Even considering its more mundane causes, there is much to admire in *youhuan yishi*. I felt this admiration most strongly when going to visit friends in their homes. On these visits I would generally walk down a chilly, unlit street, pick my way through the rubble of the Beijing street-repair projects that seem never to end, enter a barren cement-framed doorway, carefully ascend a dark— sometimes pitch-dark—stairwell cluttered with bicycles, garbage receptacles, and an occasional scurrying rat. Knocking on the door, and listening as a series of locks was undone, I would then enter a cramped apartment modestly decorated with a few prized possessions—perhaps a painting, a television set, an antiquarian piano, and always some books. In these surroundings, my friends would worry about China, the obligations of *youhuan yishi* their only surplus.

More than once on these visits, I was made to think of the Buddhist metaphor of the lotus, its blossom floating on the river surface as its roots extend into the muck at the bottom. Chinese intellectuals themselves sometimes remarked upon the incongruity between their high-minded concerns and their dreary surroundings, often finding humor in the irony. Liu Zaifu, even while pleading the case for *youhuan yishi*, referred to it as the "prevailing malady" of Chinese intellectuals. A young sociologist, in declining his relatives' offer to emigrate to the West, facetiously characterized his motives for staying: "Leave China? Like everybody else? Not me. I will stay till the bitter end, until only the smartest person—me—and the stupidest people—my government—are left here."

Youhuan yishi was itself one of the issues that Chinese intellectuals worried about. They wondered whether this kind of constant, depressing concern was useful. Did it constrict their vision and prevent them from functioning in more enlightened and productive ways? They were especially concerned that events in the last century and a half had seemed to transform *youhuan yishi* from its broadly humanistic grounding in Confucian tradition into more narrow, set views that could stifle independent thought and aid dictators. The transformation seemed to have two stages. First, the shocks of nineteenth-century Western imperialism and twentieth-century Japanese aggression had seemed to reduce *youhuan yishi* to a relatively simple imperative to "resist the invaders" and "save China." Then, in the 1950s, it was reshaped again, when the new Communist government introduced a heavy emphasis on loyalty to itself as the representative of "the people."

In its demands for loyalty, the new government sought to conflate all of the several aspects of *youhuan yishi*. Duty to country or society became coterminous with duty to the party; opposition to China's enemies was equated with support of the party; patriotism came to mean loyalty to China's current political system. By the late 1980s the rapid decline in the prestige of the party had led, especially among young intellectuals, to a rebellion against responsibility in every form. "We don't want *anyone* laying duties on us any more," said a young writer. "We've been told what to do, what to think, ever since we were born. And there has always been a big *moral* overlay to it. 'If you don't obey, you're immoral.' This has always been the government's attitude. Now our intellectual leaders like Liu Zaifu and Liu Binyan are also telling us about our social responsibilities, and also add their big moral overlay. We don't want it! We don't want any talk of responsibility." Said another, "The older generations were so preoccupied with 'saving China' in the 1930s and 1940s that they froze their own critical judgment and were easily manipulated in the 1950s. They can't see how they were trapped by their own 'responsibility' ideas. And they want us to follow them?"

To the older generations these attitudes were irritating but not easily dismissed. Many sympathized with the young in their strong desire to be free from party control, but they were pained by the rejection of basic ideas of social responsibility. "Some youth," as Liu Zaifu saw it, "have developed an 'anti-social consciousness'—the attitude that, since society is hopeless, I will care only for myself. This is the very opposite of *youhuan yishi*. It's too bad. The young don't realize that prior generations of Chinese intellectuals also faced some very hard times earlier in this century. One of the most valuable things to come out of May Fourth times was the idea of *resisting despair*. Lu Xun's story called 'The Passerby' shows it well: a man traveling along a road stops to rest at a roadside stand. He doesn't exactly know what his destination is or how he will get to it, but after a short rest he *keeps going*. He won't give up just because things seem hopeless. In fact, you might say he keeps going *just because* things seem hopeless. This determination to 'resist despair' could be found in Lu Xun's generation; I wish I could find it among our young people today." A younger writer who was listening nodded his head and said, "The Communist Party has given responsibility a bad name."

45

On the Road at Eighteen

YU HUA

Yu Hua is part of a group of avant-garde writers that emerged in the late 1980s, a group that includes Ma Yuan, Can Xue, Su Tong, and Ge Fei. These writers self-consciously sought to purge from their writing all traces of the Maoist political discourse. But the avant-garde were no literary purists. They pushed the limits of acceptable subject matter (graphic violence and grotesque descriptions of the human body are hallmarks of the avant-garde) and subverted much of what socialism holds dear. Yu Hua's story has been read as an allegory about the inadequacy of political ideology in dealing with the chaos and senselessness of the real world.

The asphalt road rolls up and down like it's pasted on top of ocean waves. Walking down this little highway in the mountains, I'm like a boat. This year, I turned eighteen. The few brownish whiskers that have sprouted on my chin flutter in the breeze. They've only just taken up residence on my chin, so I really treasure them. I've spent the whole day walking down the road, and I've already seen lots of mountains and lots of clouds. Every one of the mountains and every one of the clouds made me think of people I know. I shouted out each of their nicknames as I walked by. So even though I've walked all day, I'm not tired, not at all. I walked through the morning, now it's the tail end of the afternoon, and it won't be long until I see the tip of dusk. But I haven't found an inn.

I've encountered quite a few people along the road, but none of them has known where the road goes or whether there's an inn there. They all tell me: "Keep walking. You'll see when you get there." I think what everyone said was just terrific. I really am just seeing when I get there. But I haven't found an inn. I feel like I should be worried about that.

I think it's weird that I've walked all day and only seen one car. That was around noon, when I'd just begun to think about hitchhiking. But all I was doing was thinking about hitchhiking. I hadn't started to worry about finding an inn—I was only thinking about how amazing it would be to get a lift from someone. I stood by the side of the road waving at the car, trying my best to look casual.

492

But the driver hardly even looked at me. The car or the driver. They hardly even looked at me. All they fucking did was drive right by. So I ran, chasing the car as fast as I could, just for fun, because I still hadn't started to worry about finding an inn. I ran until the car had disappeared, and then I laughed at myself, but I discovered that laughing too hard made it difficult to breathe, so I stopped. After that I kept walking, happy and excited, except that I started to regret that I hadn't picked up a rock before I started waving at the car.

Now I really want a lift, because dusk is about to fall and I can't get that inn out of my goddamned head. But there haven't been any cars all afternoon. If a car came now, I think I could make it stop. I'd lie down in the middle of the road, and I'm willing to bet that any car would come to a screeching halt before it got to my head. But I don't even hear the rumble of an engine, let alone see a car. Now I'm just going to have to keep walking and see when I get there. Not bad at all: keep walking and see when you get there.

The road rolls up and down from hill to valley, and the hills tempt me every time, because before I charge up to the top, I think I'll see an inn on the other side. But each time I charge up the slope, all I see is another hill in the distance, with a depressing trough in between. And still I charge up each hill as if my life depended on it. And now I'm charging up another one, but this time I see it. Not an inn, but a truck. The truck is pointed toward me, stalled in the middle of the highway in a gully between two hills. I can see the driver's ass pointing skyward and, behind it, all the colors of the approaching sunset. I can't see the driver's head because it's stuffed under the hood. The truck's hood slants up into the air like an upside-down lip. The back of the truck is piled full of big wicker baskets. I'm thinking that they definitely must be packed with some kind of fruit. Of course, bananas would be best of all. There are probably some in the cab, too, so when I hop in, I can eat a few. And I don't really care if the truck's going in the opposite direction as me. I need to find an inn, and if there's no inn, I need a truck. And the truck's right here in front of me.

Elated, I run down to the truck and say, "Hi!"

The driver doesn't seem to have heard me. He's still fiddling with something under the hood.

"Want a smoke?"

Only now does he pull his head out from under the hood, stretch out a black, grimy hand, and take the cigarette between his fingers. I rush to give him a light, and he sucks several mouthfuls of smoke into his mouth before stuffing his head back under the hood.

I'm satisfied. Since he accepted the smoke, that means he has to give me a lift. So I wander around to the back of the truck to investigate what's in the wicker baskets. But they're covered, and I can't see, so I sniff. I smell the fragrance of apples. And I think: Apples aren't too bad either.

In just a little bit, he's done repairing the truck, and he jumps down from the hood. I rush over and say, "Hey, I need a ride." What I don't expect is that he gives me a hard shove with those grimy hands and barks, "Go away!"

I'm so angry I'm speechless, but he just swings on over to the driver's side, opens the door, slides into the cab, and starts the engine. I know that if I blow this opportunity, I'll never get another one. I know I should just give up. So I run over to the other side, open the door, and hop in. I'm ready to fight if necessary. I turn to him and yell: "Then give me back my cigarette!" The truck's already started to move by now.

He turns to look at me with a big, friendly smile and asks, "Where you headed?"

I'm bewildered by this turnaround. I say, "Doesn't matter. Wherever."

He asks me very nicely, "Want an apple?" He's still glancing over at me.

"That goes without saying."

"Go get one from the back."

How am I supposed to climb out of the cab to the back of the truck when he's driving so fast? So I say, "Forget it."

He says, "Go get one." He's still looking at me.

I say, "Stop staring at me. There's no road on my face."

With this, he twists his eyes back onto the highway.

The truck's driving back in the direction I just came from; I'm sitting comfortably in the cab, looking out the window and chatting with the driver. By now, we're already the best of friends. I've found out that he's a private entrepreneur. It's his own truck. The apples are his, too. I hear change jingling in his pockets. I ask him, "Where are you going?"

He says, "I just keep driving and see when I get there."

It sounds just like what everyone else said. That's so nice. I feel closer to him. I want everything I see outside the window to be just as close, just as familiar, and soon all those hills and clouds start to bring more friends to mind, so I shout out their nicknames as we drive by.

Now I'm not crying out for an inn anymore. What with the truck, the driver, the seat in the cab, I'm completely at peace. I don't know where the truck's going, and neither does he. Anyway, it doesn't matter, because all we have to do is keep driving, and we'll see when we get there.

But the truck broke down. By that time, we were as close as friends can be. My arm was draped over his shoulder and his over mine. He was telling me about his love life, and right when he'd got to the part about how it felt the first time he held a woman's body in his arms, the truck broke down. The truck was climbing up a hill when it broke down. All of a sudden the squeal of the engine went quiet like a pig right after it's been slaughtered. So he jumped out of the truck, climbed onto the hood, opened up that upside-down lip, and stuffed his head back under it. I couldn't see his ass. But I could hear the sound of him fiddling with the engine.

After a while, he pulled his head out from under the hood and slammed it shut. His hands were even blacker than before. He wiped them on his pants, wiped again, jumped down, and walked back to the cab.

"Is it fixed?" I asked.

"It's shot. There's no way to fix it."

I thought that over and finally asked, "Now what do we do?"

"Wait and see," he said, nonchalantly.

I was sitting in the cab wondering what to do. Then I started to think about finding an inn again. The sun was just failing behind the mountains, and the hazy dusk clouds looked like billows of steam. The notion of an inn stole back into my head and began to swell until my mind was stuffed full of it. By then, I didn't even have a mind. An inn was growing where my mind used to be.

At that point, the driver started doing the official morning calisthenics that they always play on the radio right there in the middle of the highway. He went from the first exercise to the last without missing a beat. When he was finished, he started to jog circles around the truck. Maybe he had been sitting too long in the driver's seat and needed some exercise. Watching him moving from my vantage point inside the truck, I couldn't sit still either, so I opened the door and jumped out. But I didn't do calisthenics or jog in place. I was thinking about an inn and an inn and an inn.

Just then, I noticed five people rolling down the hill on bicycles. Each bike had a carrying pole fastened to the back with two big baskets on either end. I thought they were probably local peasants on their way back from selling vegetables at market. I was delighted to see people riding by, so I welcomed them with a big "Hi!" They rode up beside me and dismounted. Excited, I greeted them and asked, "Is there an inn around here?"

Instead of responding they asked me, "What's in the truck?

I said, "Apples."

All five of them pushed their bikes over to the side of the truck. Two of them climbed onto the back, picked up about ten baskets full of apples, and passed them upside down to the ones below, who proceeded to tear open the plastic covering the top of the wicker and pour the apples into their own baskets. I was dumbstruck. When I finally realized exactly what was going on, I made for them and asked, "Just what do you think you're doing?"

None of them paid the slightest bit of attention to me. They continued to pour the apples. I tried to grab hold of someone's arm and screamed, "They're stealing all the apples!" A fist came crashing into my nose, and I landed several feet away. I staggered up, rubbed my nose. It felt soft and sticky, like it wasn't stuck to my face anymore but only dangling from it. Blood was flowing like tears from a broken heart. When I looked up to see which of them had hit me, they were already astride their bikes, riding away.

The driver was taking a walk, lips curling out as he sucked in deep draughts of air. He had probably lost his breath running. He didn't seem to be at all aware of what had just happened. I yelled toward him, "They stole your apples!" But he kept on walking without paying any attention to what I had yelled. I really wanted to run over and punch him so hard that his nose would be left dangling, too. I ran over and screamed into his ear, "They stole your apples." Only then did he turn to look at me, and I realized that his face was getting happier and happier the longer he looked at my nose.

At that point, yet another group of bicycles descended down the slope. Each bike had two big baskets fastened to the back. There were even a few children among the riders. They swarmed by me and surrounded the truck. A lot of people climbed onto the back, and the wicker baskets flew faster than I could count them. Apples poured out of broken baskets like blood out of my nose. They stuffed apples into their own baskets as if they were possessed. In just a few seconds, all the apples in the truck had been lowered to the ground. Then a few motorized tractor carts chugged down the hill and stopped next to the truck. A few big men dismounted and started to stuff apples into the carts. One by one, the empty wicker baskets were tossed to the side. The ground was covered with rolling apples, and the peasants scrabbled on their hands and knees like ants to pick them all up.

It was at that point that I rushed into their midst, risking life and limb, and cursed them, "Thieves!" I started swinging. My attack was met with countless fists and feet. It seemed like every part of my body got hit at the same time. I climbed back up off the ground. A few children began to hurl apples at me. The apples broke apart on my head, but my head didn't break. Just as I was about to rush the kids, a foot came crashing into my waist. I wanted to cry, but when I opened my mouth, nothing came out. There was nothing to do but fall to the ground and watch them steal the apples. I started to look around for the driver. He was standing a good distance away, looking right at me, and laughing as hard as he could. Just so I knew that I looked even better now than I had with a bloody nose.

I didn't even have the strength for anger. All I could do was gaze out at everything that was making me so angry. And what made me the angriest of all was the driver.

Another wave of bicycles and tractors rolled down the hill and threw themselves into the disaster area. There were fewer and fewer apples rolling on the ground. A few people left. A few more arrived. The ones who had arrived too late for apples began to busy themselves with the truck. I saw them remove the window glass, strip the tires, pry away the planks that covered the truck bed. Without its tires, the truck obviously felt really low, because it sank to the ground. A few children began to gather the wicker baskets that had been tossed to the side a moment before. As the road got cleaner and cleaner, there were fewer and fewer people. But all I could do was watch, because I didn't even have the strength for anger. I sat on the ground without moving, letting my eyes wander back and forth between the driver and the thieves.

Now, there's nothing left but a single tractor parked beside the sunken truck. Someone's looking around to see if there's anything left to take. He looks for a while and then hops on his tractor and starts the engine.

The truck driver hops onto the back of the tractor and looks back toward me, laughing. He's holding my red backpack in his hand. He's stealing my backpack. My clothes and my money are in the backpack. And food and books. But he's stealing my backpack.

I'm watching the tractor climb back up the slope. It disappears over the crest. I can still hear the rumble of its engine, but soon I can't even hear that. All of a sudden, everything's quiet, and the sky starts to get really dark. I'm still sitting on the ground. I'm hungry, and I'm cold, but there's nothing left.

I sit there for a long time before I slowly stand up. It isn't easy because my whole body aches like crazy every time I move, but still I stand up and limp over to the truck. The truck looks miserable, battered. I know I've been battered too.

The sky's black now. There's nothing here. Just a battered truck and battered me. I'm looking at the truck, immeasurably sad, and the truck's looking at me, immeasurably sad. I reach out to stroke it. It's cold all over. The wind starts to blow, a strong wind, and the sound of the wind rustling the trees in the mountains is like ocean waves. The sound terrifies me so much that my body gets as cold as the truck's.

I open the door and hop in. I'm comforted by the fact that they didn't pry away the seat. I lie down in the cab. I smell leaking gas and think of the smell of the blood that leaked out of me. The wind's getting stronger and stronger, but I feel a little warmer lying on the seat. I think that even though the truck's been battered, its heart is still intact, still warm. I know that my heart's warm, too. I was looking for an inn, and I never thought I'd find you here.

I lie inside the heart of the truck, remembering that clear warm afternoon. The sunlight was so pretty. I remember that I was outside enjoying myself in the sunshine for a long time, and when I got home I saw my dad through the window packing things into a red backpack. I leaned against the window frame and asked, "Dad, are you going on a trip?"

He turned and very gently said, "No, I'm letting you go on a trip."

"Letting me go on a trip?"

"That's right. You're eighteen now, and it's time you saw a little of the outside world."

Later I slipped that pretty red backpack onto my back. Dad patted my head from behind, just like you would pat a horse's rump. Then I gladly made for the door and excitedly galloped out of the house, as happy as a horse.

Translated by Andrew F. Jones

46

Deathsong of the River

SU XIAOKANG and WANG LUXIANG

Deathsong of the River was, and continues to be, one of the most highly controversial television documentaries ever broadcast in the PRC. It was first aired in 1988, but was banned, on and off, through the 1990s. The documentary attacked Chinese tradition as conservative and oppressive and saw Maoism and Chinese socialism as inheritors of that tradition. Images of a free and open West (symbolized by the vast blue oceans) were used throughout to contrast with a closed and authoritarian China, represented by such national symbols as the Yellow River and the Great Wall. The documentary was attacked by some for its essentialist—some said superficial—portrayals of both Chinese and Western cultures. Others have shown how its absolutist discourse was but a tool with which to make political critiques.

This venerable yet frightening old image was once the embodiment of our ancestors' nightmares. Do we still want to use it to focus our current feelings of sorrow and longing for the past?

Dragon worship would seem to prove that the soul of our nation is still deeply attached to the atmosphere of that ancient culture born from the Yellow River and still stuck fast in the dark shadow of our ancestors. This soul seems to be living in a dream. Yet today the time has come to bring it fully awake.

Maybe we should not mind other people coming to raft on our Yellow River. River rafting is after all but a sport, and risking one's life to do something out of spite is not an expression of strength. Someday when we finally rediscover the real meaning of sport, and then go rafting on their Mississippi, that will be a very elegant and refined sport.

We don't have to pound our chests and stamp our feet to express our regret at losing a ball game or several championships. Olympic gold medals cannot prove we are a strong nation. Our thousand-year old dream of empire already came to an end long ago in the time of Emperor Kangxi [1662–1722]. Now the most important thing is not to cheat ourselves any more.

Our civilization has declined, but we don't have to feel sad. Without exception, all the river valley civilizations in the world have declined. The British historian Toynbee has estimated that out of twenty-one civilizations in human history, fourteen have vanished, six are in decline, while only ancient Greek civilization has been transformed into industrial civilization and has overwhelmed the entire world. We should face history bravely.

History has proven countless times that the decline of a civilization is not caused by attack from external forces, but rather by the degeneration of its internal system.

Toynbee said that the greatest role of an outside enemy is to strike a final blow to a society that has already committed suicide, yet not drawn its last breath.

For thousands of years, the Yellow River civilization was under constant attack from the outside but never fell. We have always appreciated its great power to assimilate other cultures. But today at the end of the twentieth century, even though external attacks are no longer accompanied by cannons and iron hooves, our ancient civilization can no longer resist.

It has grown old and feeble.

It needs a transfusion of new blood for its civilization.

Oh, you heirs of the dragon, what the Yellow River could give us has already been given to our ancestors. The Yellow River cannot bring forth the civilization that our ancestors once created. What we need to create is a brand-new civilization. It cannot emerge from the Yellow River again. The dregs of the old civilization are like the sand and mud accumulated in the Yellow River, they have built up in the blood vessels of our people. We need a great tidal wave to flush them away.

This great tidal wave has already arrived. It is industrial civilization. It is summoning us!

. . . In direct contrast to the now-forgotten Great Wall of the Qin, the Great Wall of the Ming which retreated a thousand *li* backwards, has been the object of incomparable reverence. People pride themselves on the fact that it is the only feat of human engineering visible to astronauts on the moon. People even wish to use it as a symbol of China's strength. And yet, if the Great Wall could speak, it would very frankly tell its Chinese grandchildren that it is a great and tragic gravestone forged by historical destiny. It can by no means represent strength, initiative, and glory; it can only represent an isolationist, conservative and incompetent defense and a cowardly lack of aggression. Because of its great size and long history, it has deeply imprinted its arrogance and self-delusion in the souls of our people. Alas, O Great Wall, why do we still want to praise you?

Scholars have already discovered that the Great Wall which meanders ten thousand *li* lies pretty much along the boundary line of fifteen inches of rainfall. This rainfall line also signifies the natural boundary between agriculture and the lack of it.

Today on the Great Wall at Hongshi Gorge in Shaanxi, we can still see the stone tablet left by our ancestors to designate the "natural barrier between Chinese and barbarians." This truly is the last frontier of an agricultural civilization. Everything is extremely clear: our ancestors would never be able to go beyond the bounds of the soil and of agriculture. Their greatest feat of the imagination and most courageous act could only be to build the Great Wall!

. . . For approximately twenty-odd years in the middle of this century, China once again faced a good opportunity for economic development. And yet locking our country's door and blindfolding our eyes we set off to "surpass England and America," never ceasing to engage in one great political movement after another, swearing that on Chinese soil "*we would rather grow the weeds of socialism than the sprouts of capitalism*," so that in the end our national economy was on the brink of collapse. Once again History cold-heartedly passed us by.

Let us open our eyes and see our people's situation on this planet! The World Bank's annual reports reveal the following figures: Out of one hundred twenty-eight nations in the world, China's average per capita GNP ranks about twentieth from the bottom, in company with poor African countries such as Somalia and Tanzania. China's rate of increase in per capita GNP, the structure of her export commodities, her investment in education and public health all fail to match those of Asia's "four little dragons." In 1960, China's GNP was equivalent to Japan's; by 1985, it was only one-fifth of Japan's; in 1960, U.S. GNP exceeded China by 460 billion U.S. dollars, but by 1985 it exceeded China by 3 trillion 680 billion dollars. Though we always thought we were making great strides towards progress, how little we knew that others were making far faster strides than us! If this gap should continue at present rates, some people have made a frightening comparison: that in another fifty or sixty years, China will once again be in the situation of the Opium War: that foreigners will possess foreign guns and cannon, leaving Chinese with only long knives and spears. No wonder then that someone has made an even louder appeal: that if things go wrong, China's global citizenship will be revoked. . . .

In this hospital famous for the treatment of goiters, there isn't a single doctor whose income surpasses that of the old lady selling baked sweet potatoes at the front gate. *"Those who cut open the head are not as well off as those who shave it"*; *"piano players are not as well off as piano movers"*; mental and physical labor are in an inverse relationship, so that those who *"put the problems of the world first"* will be those who *"get rich last."* The source of all this unfairness is that society lacks a competitive mechanism for ensuring equality of opportunity, it lacks a common yardstick—the market. Only when we can develop a healthy market can we ensure that opportunity, equality, and competition will start to link up; yet this is precisely the thing that our people with their ancient civilization know the least about.

As long as competition exists without the prerequisite of equal opportunity, then the loosening of price controls, which would seem to be appropriate to the rules of a commodity economy, can actually create economic disorder and dislocation; the friction between the old structure and the new one will cancel out the positive elements on each side; the many evils such as "bureaucratism," "feudalism," the use of public power for private ends, and so forth will all seem to find their "common yardstick" and reflect themselves in society in the form of commodity prices. In a country with a long tradition of egalitarianism, the loss of control over prices will necessarily make the people apprehensive, even to the point of fomenting social unrest. And if for this reason we lose the support of the majority for economic reform, then China will once again be mired in stagnation. . . .

The restless blue waves of the Pacific were always silently calling to that ancient people stretched out on the continent and from time to time aroused it to action, leading its ships to the Persian Gulf and the Arabian peninsula. Yet in the end the attraction of the blue sea was no match for that of the yellow earth.

The hidden reason why the "'yellow" civilization had such an enormous cohesive power was that Confucian culture had gradually attained a position of sole dominance in this land.

The Confucian system of thought expressed the norms and the ideals of land-based civilization and in the mature period of oriental feudal society was clearly rather reasonable. But this monistic ideological unity weakened the development of pluralistic thought, and so the various rich strands of seafaring civilization in ancient life, just like a few thin trickling streams flowing out onto the yellow soil of land-based civilization, vanished quickly without a trace. . . .

As the land-based civilization daily increased in power in China, a "blue" sea-faring civilization was gradually arising in the Mediterranean Sea.

. . . Even today in the 1980s, in the midst of our great debate stirred up by the "passion for studying Chinese culture," people still continue the century-old inconclusive argument over the strong and weak points of Chinese versus

Western culture. No matter whether it is the fantasy of "wholesale Westernization" or the fervent wish for a "third flowering of Confucian civilization," it all seems to be going over the same ground as before. No wonder some young scholars say with a sigh that their tremendous cultural wealth has become a tremendous cultural burden, that their feeling of tremendous cultural superiority has become a feeling of tremendous cultural inferiority; and this we cannot but admit is a tremendous psychological obstacle standing in the course of China's modernization.

. . . Chinese history did not create a bourgeoisie for the Chinese people which could hasten the victory of science and democracy; Chinese culture did not nurture a sense of citizenship. On the contrary, it taught a subject mentality. A subject mentality can only produce obedient people who meekly submit to oppression on the one hand and madmen who act recklessly on the other. But History did give the Chinese people an entirely unique group: its intellectuals.

It is very difficult for them to have economic interests in common or an independent political stance; for thousands of years they have been hangers-on. Nor can they become a solid social entity that employs a steel-hard economic strength to carry out an armed critique of the old society.

Their talents can be manipulated by others, their wills can be twisted, their souls emasculated, their backbones bent, and their flesh destroyed.

And yet, they hold in their hands the weapon to destroy ignorance and superstition;

It is they who can conduct a direct dialogue with "sea-faring" civilization;

It is they who can channel the "blue" sweet water spring of science and democracy onto our yellow earth!

Translated by Richard W. Bodman and Pin P. Wan

47

"I Have Nothing" (1986)

CUI JIAN

Cui Jian was China's first and most notorious rocker. His raspy, guttural voice, ironic and transgressive stage costumes, and provocative lyrics were a reaction against the sappy Hong Kong/Taiwan love songs and insipid political folk songs that dominated the music scene in the 1980s. Originally a trumpet player in the Beijing Philharmonic Orchestra, Cui Jian formed his first band in 1984, with performances limited to college campuses. But in 1986, he performed "I Have Nothing" at the One Hundred Pop Stars concert at the Beijing Workers' Stadium and became an overnight national sensation. Since then, Cui's reputation has risen and fallen with the political times. During the 1987 anti-bourgeois liberalization campaign, he performed a rock version of the revolutionary folk song "Nanniwan," for which he was publicly criticized. In the liberal climate of 1988, his reputation soared and he received his first recording contract. Cui performed for student protestors during the 1989 Tiananmen movement, and "I Have Nothing" became a sort of anthem for the movement. During his Asian Games Tour (1992), he performed the song with red bandana over his eyes. Although some would say that the current Chinese rock world has left Cui Jian in the dust, he continues to be active, most recently working on the sound track of Jiang Wen's film Devils on the Doorstep *(Guizi laile).*

I've asked tirelessly, when will you go with me?
But you just always laugh at my having nothing
I've given you my dreams, given you my freedom
But you always just laugh at my having nothing.

Oh! When will you go with me?
Oh! When will you go with me?

The earth under my feet is on the move,
The water by my side is flowing on,
But you always just laugh at my having nothing

Why haven't you laughed your fill?
Why will I always search?
Could it be that before you I will always have nothing?

Oh! When will you go with me?
Oh! When will you go with me?

(Suona [horn] solo)

The earth under my feet is on the move
The water by my side is flowing on

I'm telling you I've waited a long time
I'm telling you my very last demand
I need to grab both your hands
Only then will you go with me
That's when your hands will tremble
That's when your tears will flow
Can it be that you're telling me you love my having nothing?

Oh, only then will you go with me
Oh, only then will you go with me

(Guitar solo)

The earth under my feet is on the move
The water by my side is flowing on

Oh, only then will you go with me
Oh, only then will you go with me

Translated by Andrew F. Jones

48

Playing for Thrills

WANG SHUO

In the late 1980s and early 1990s Wang Shuo, who has written numerous novels and many scripts for television and film, was closely associated with "punk literature," which portrays the seamier side of Beijing society. Playing for Thrills *is a kind of postmodern mystery. Its first-person narrator is suspected in a murder that took place ten years before the novel opens. He spends the bulk of the novel trying to find out if he did or did not commit the crime. Along the way, we are presented with an array of Wang Shuo's notorious "punk" characters, layabouts who spend their time gambling, drinking, and womanizing and who scorn conventional values and mock socialism. They speak in a hard-edged, slangy Beijing dialect. This excerpt is taken from early in the novel, shortly after the narrator has learned that he is suspected by the police.*

Fat Man Wu was playing cards when I walked into my apartment. "My wife came home," he announced, "so we decided to move the Party group meeting to your place." He pointed to a stranger with large features. "We dug up a new member," he said. "Since we can never count on you to attend meetings, and you're always behind in your Party dues, we decided to place you on probation for the time being."

"You can take my place if you want," the stranger said.

"No, I don't feel like it," I said. "I accept the Party's decision."

"What's up with you?" Liu Huiyuan asked. "You look like you just crawled out of a latrine."

"It's just possible," I said as I sprawled on the sofa, "it's goddamned possible that I'm a murder suspect."

Fat Man Wu took the cigarette out of his mouth, glanced at his cards, then looked up. "Lucky you," he said. "What trick did you use to turn yourself into a celebrity?"

"Don't think you're such hot shit," someone else said with a chuckle. "I advise you to hold on to those two ounces of meat down there. I doubt you could even give it away."

I laughed. "What's there to say to dumb fucks like you?"

"What can we say to a dumb fuck like *you*?" They laughed.

"Who knows what you're up to. You're like someone heading into the wind for an eight-*li* trip with a hard-on that'll be gone when you need it. Just you wait and see."

"Oh, right, you've got guests in the bedroom. They're not cops, and my guess is they're the darling couple Mingsong sent. When you didn't show up, they hoofed it over on their own."

"Go on, get in there," Fat Man Wu urged me. "The bride's a real looker, tender as a fresh clam."

"Don't give me that," I said with a laugh as I stood up. "I know you're making it up. If she was everything you say, you'd be hanging around her like a pesky fly instead of sitting here playing cards."

I went into the next room. The newcomers jumped to their feet. I'd expected a lot worse. Except for their gaudy clothes, which they assumed gave them a sophisticated look, but actually made them look foolish, they had the airs of southern gentility. Story time: I told them I'd passed out on the way to meet them the day before, and some good Samaritans had rushed me to the ER. I was an epileptic, I said. Impossible to predict when a seizure might hit. But I apologized for missing them at the station. The guy said that was OK. The card players had already told them about my illness, so they weren't upset. The groom was real tight with Mingsong, who had sent them to me, since Mingsong was real tight with me too, and had them bring me a couple of pounds of mooncakes. I was so hungry I started in on one of them and asked how Mingsong was doing, if he'd had a windfall, if he and his wife had divorced, and who'd been given custody of the kid. The guy said that Mingsong was doing fine, that there was no windfall, and that his wife hadn't divorced him, since they'd talked a lot about getting married but had never actually gone through with it, and as for the kid, the one you saw was probably his brother, since Mingsong had a kid brother but had never actually raised a kid of his own, though his girlfriend had miscarried several times. I cleared my throat and said who cared if he had a kid or not since it had nothing to do with me, and so what if they were two different kids. Since you're so far from home and have no kin around here, you can count me as family. So tell me, what are you up for? The groom stammered that they didn't have anything in mind, they just wanted to have some fun. Since there was no one to meet them the day before, they'd spent the night at the home of some relative of the girl. But the place was too cramped, with a *kang* that filled up half the single room, which the relative let them use; she slept on the floor. "That was too much for us." I could see that, so I told them that if they wanted to see where Chairman Mao was residing, I couldn't get tickets, but I could put them up, if that's what they wanted. No meals, but you can turn handstands in the place, if you feel like it. The bride and groom grinned from ear to ear and even peeled the paper off a piece of candy and stuck it into my mouth. Enough of that. I'm not big on etiquette of any kind, it makes me uneasy. I've never been coddled, not even as a child, so when you give me such a warm reception, out of the blue and everything, I can't help thinking that maybe I ought to be a little more wary. There's nothing wrong with that candy, I swear. It's from the wedding. From now on, we're going to be great friends. I can't think of anything better than having a friend like you, since we have so much in common, like age and all. If you ever need anything back home, just say the word. "Enough already." I extricated myself from their enveloping presence. "Where does that friend of yours live? You can move into my place tonight." They giggled and buttered me up a while longer before taking off. I went back to join the card players, and sat there with a silly grin. I'd completely forgotten what it was I was supposed to be doing, so I asked the guys sitting around the table. "Any of you remember what I was going to do?" Out came one raunchy, midsection comment after another: "Propping up the wall with one hand to free the other for something else," and stuff like that, which brought some laughs, and that loosened my brain just enough to remind me that I had to make a phone call. The telephone rang and rang, until someone picked it up and a female voice asked who it was. The police, I said. Xu Xun's at work, she replied, so why was I calling his home? I hung up and dialed the police station. The duty cop asked who it was. I said I was calling from Xu Xun's house. He picked up the phone, and when he heard it was me, he told me to hang up. "I'm busy now. I'll call you back." He did, after a little while, this time from a different telephone. His voice was barely audible as he said he couldn't talk over the phone, and he told me to come to his place the next morning. "Make sure you're alone." "Are things that bad?" I was still treating it all as a joke, but he slammed the receiver down.

I must have looked pretty bummed out, the way everyone was gaping at me. "What's wrong?" Liu Huiyuan asked as he dealt a new hand. "Something bothering you?"

"It's nothing." I forced a smile. "Just making things hard on myself, that's all."

"Whatever it is, you can tell us," Fat Man Wu said without looking up from his cards, a cigarette dangling from his lips. "Bottle it up inside, and it'll only get worse."

"Really, it's nothing. Besides, I wouldn't let it bother me, not me."

"Don't tell us if you don't want to," Liu Huiyuan said before Fat Man could open his mouth again. "Let's play cards, guys."

There was a knock at the door, and I went pale. The others, seeing the worried look on my face, exchanged hurried glances. They asked me who it was.

"How should I know?"

"Who but our darling couple, back already." Liu Huiyuan threw down his cards and got up to answer the door. Following some confused noise, the new-comers appeared, sweaty-faced and loaded down with luggage. "Here we are."

"So you're here. Is that any reason to carry on like that?" Then I smiled, got up, and pointed to the bedroom. "It's a cozy room. You could walk around naked and never catch cold."

"Oh, let me introduce you. This is Li Jiangyun, my wife's cousin. She's the one who put us up last night."

"Pretty," I commented as a lovely young thing followed them into the room. "If I were you, I'd rather squeeze in with her than move over here."

"They like a good joke," the groom said with a laugh. "A great bunch of guys."

"Hah," Li Jiangyun said with a smile. "I've seen more guys like this than you have. The place is crawling with them. If you don't need me anymore, I'll be on my way. Let me know if something comes up."

"Can I let you know if something of mine comes up?"

"No," Li Jiangyun said with a little laugh as she shook her head.

"Where do you live? Far from here?" Liu Huiyuan asked her.

'No, not far," the groom said. "She lives on the next street over."

"What's your hurry then? Sit down, take a load off. It's not every day I meet someone like you." I moved out of the way to let Liu Huiyuan shepherd Li Jiangyun inside.

"Maybe you'd better go home, Yun." The bride didn't like the look of things; I could hear it in her voice.

"She's safer than you are," Liu Huiyuan said. "Yun knows her way around. See that smile—she's not worried. But you'd better look out for yourself. Before the week's out, your factory-equipped model here won't have anything to do. It's your own resolve you'd better concentrate on stiffening."

That broke us up. "Take it easy," the guy said to his wife. "Just some friendly banter. We're among friends."

"Not so fast. Friends don't count at a time like this, do they, Fang Yan?"

"That's right." I nodded. "Every man for himself."

Li Jiangyun confidently let herself be escorted into the room, smiling and nodding at Fat Man Wu and the others. Liu Huiyuan introduced her around, then poured tea.

"Did you say Li Jiangyun?" Fat Man lowered his cards, took a drag on his cigarette, and laughed. "Couldn't call you famous, since I've never heard of you."

"And who might you be?" Li Jiangyun replied laconically. "One of those people who couldn't make people hear of him if his life depended on it?"

"Ever hear of him?" Fat Man pointed to me with his cigarette hand.

Li Jiangyun turned to look at me. Didn't I see you on a wanted poster a while back?"

"A wanted poster, she says." We all laughed. "Our pal here's a writer," Fat Man said. "You must have read his stuff. The only book with a larger print run is *Selected Works of Chairman Mao*."

"Is that so?" She looked at me again. Keeping my eyes lowered, I nodded.

"What have you written," asked the bride.

"Not so fast," Fat Man broke in. "You'll answer your own question as soon as I tell you his pen name: Qiong Yao."[*]

That always got a big laugh, even from people who had heard it before. But this time I didn't laugh. I had some more tales in my bag.

"He does more than write books. He's an actor and he's made movies. What you call a Renaissance man. But he's better known in Europe than here in China."

"Who have you played?" The empty-headed little bride was falling for it, hook, line, and sinker.

"A young Gorky and a young Zhou Shuren[†]—before they grew moustaches."

"Really?" The bride *and* groom both eye me cautiously. By then I was smoking a cigarette, and I raised my head, as if posing for a portrait.

"You *do* look like them."

---

[*] A writer of popular fiction in Taiwan. Her novels were enormously popular in China in the 1980s.

[†] The real name of Lu Xun (1881–1936), modern China's most famous writer.

"His newest film is a joint-venture deal with the Czechs. It's called *The Mole's Story*. He plays the male lead. Also premoustache period."

The laughter this time was loud and hearty. And it included Li Jiangyun, who turned to the empty-headed bride. "Haven't you figured out yet that they're pulling your leg?"

"You married?" Fat Man Wu, suddenly a model of seriousness, asked Li Jiangyun.

"No." She smiled. Then she turned back to us and pouted.

"You ought to get married," Fat Man said with mock seriousness. "You're not a kid, you know. You're OK-looking now, but that'll go soon enough."

"Thanks, but I actually am married, so you can stop worrying." Li Jiangyun laughed.

"Glad to hear it," Fat Man said. "Now you should be thinking about taking a lover. Once you've fulfilled your marital obligation, it's time to think about yourself, about hooking up with somebody you really like."

"You've got an answer for everything, haven't you?"

"That's the primary aim of our party. If you were a member, we'd have to expel you, but since you're not, it's our duty to prepare you for membership. The one thing we can't do is let you remain idle."

I burst out laughing, my shrieks sending me sliding out of the chair and into a kneeling position on the floor. Everyone was staring at me. Li Jiangyun said to Fat Man Wu, "What makes you think I'm so eager to join your party?"

"Ah, now that's covered by party bylaws, which say: Whether or not someone asks to join the party, if members find that someone pleasing to the eye, that person becomes a member, and that, as they say, is that."

"Then how come he's laughing?" Li Jiangyun said. "You guys are just looking for someone to be the butt of your stupid jokes, is that it?"

"No, not at all." I stood up, still laughing. "A funny line from a Shandong skit just popped into my head: Anty fanties, arty farty, let me into your panties, and you can join my party. In the skit that's what the party secretary says to girls who are just aching to join up."

I doubled up laughing again.

Li Jiangyun turned to Fat Man Wu. "Do you think that's funny?"

He shook his head. "No, I don't."

"It sounds pretty raunchy to me. Why do you think that is?"

"Well, you're right," Fat Man said. "And we've already petitioned the local judiciary to take him into custody and punish him properly."

"With people like him, what else can you do?"

"Not so fast. With us it's instinct. Sooner or later every member of our party cools his heels in jail—that's how we keep things jumping politically."

Engulfed in waves of laughter, Li Jiangyun finally realized that there was no way out of her predicament, so she smiled and held her tongue, letting Fat Man Wu and the others carry out their performance without reacting to anything they said, thus shielding herself from further attack. As soon as they saw they could no longer get a rise out of her, they went back to playing cards. "You'd better go now," they said dismissively. "You'll tarnish our reputation if you hang around after dark."

"Are you always like this, sending your adversary off when you see victory slipping away?" You couldn't help admiring her spunk. "You guys are great at letting the situation dictate your actions."

"You're a smart girl, and if there's anything we dislike it's smart girls. Smart girls are dumb where it counts."

"It seems to me you'd like all guys to be gymnasts and all girls to be soft pads for you to bounce around on."

"I've never seen a virtuous man who's the equal of a lustful one."

"That's it, time to go." I picked up Li Jiangyun's scarf and gloves and forced them on her. "I've had enough ridiculous talk for one day. Impatient guys don't get started unless there's something in it for us. We prefer to snare the white wolf without lifting a finger."

"I'm leaving." Now all bundled up, she gave us one of those looks, then walked out the door grinning.

"Don't be angry, just pretend we never met." I closed the door behind her and walked back to where the stunned couple was sitting. "Off to bed with you two," I said. "No sense waiting up, since we're not sleeping together."

"If you ask me," Liu Huiyuan said after the couple had left the room, "that old maid wasn't bad."

"She sure wasn't, so how come our pal here didn't like her?" Fat Man Wu, his eyes reduced to slits, asked. "I joked around with her as much as I could. Feeling any better?"

"A lot better." I laughed.

We went back to our card game, but my attention was caught by a silver-gray Naugahyde bag hanging by its shoulder strap from a peg on the bookcase. Its natural luster was gone, covered by a layer of dust. Bags like that had been popular some years back. The game was heating up, and luck was with me—whatever I needed seemed to leap off the deck into my hand, and I swept the table. Even when I played the wrong card I won. That was not a good sign, since luck in cards usually means rotten luck elsewhere. That's a tried and tested, axiomatic law of probability. Then I got a phone call from some woman. She said a girl named Ling Yu was in bad shape in the hospital. Her lupus was in the final stages, and she was asking for me. I tried but couldn't place the name. The woman asked if I was coming. I said no, I had to be on a flight for the U.S. early the next morning. I said I was sorry. After a pregnant pause, she hung up. I went back to the game, and my luck went straight into the toilet.

Translated by Howard Goldblatt

49

The Revolution of Resistance

GEREMIE R. BARMÉ

This text, by one of the leading Western observers of contemporary PRC, Geremie Barmé, shows us a diverse and open culture in the 1990s that belies Western images of an omnipotent socialist state silencing intellectuals and artists. The economic reforms initiated by the Party in the 1980s and intensified in the 1990s have created a free-wheeling cultural field that is beyond the power of the state to macromanage as it could even in the 1980s. Within limits, intellectuals and artists are surprisingly free to experiment, debate, and voice opinions. Barmé's text also shows us, however, that "resistance" by intellectuals and artists in the 1990s was often intertwined with the state's interests, as well as with the flourishing mass media and culture industry. So a binary opposition of state oppression and intellectual resistance is not a tenable model for understanding China's complex and heterogeneous cultural field.

The post-1976 period of the officially sponsored 'movement to liberate thinking' from Maoist strictures was a time during which social ideology underwent a transformation that freed the authorities from past dogma while also providing a rationale for economic reform and new directions for social growth. In a retrospective analysis of the intellectual developments on the mainland over the two decades from 1978 to 1998, Xu Jilin, a leading scholar of twentieth-century intellectual history based in Shanghai, observed that the party's previous reliance on a utopian political program was gradually replaced by theoretical justifications for the 'secular socialism' of the economic reforms.

The next phase in this process—or rather the continuation of it—was a complex intellectual and cultural mutation that extended far beyond the earlier limited aims of pro-party revisionists. From around the middle of the 1980s, the mainland experienced a cultural effervescence that was called by some 'another "May Fourth" movement', a 'Chinese Enlightenment'. Like that earlier period of cultural and political debate and furor during the 1910s and 1920s, this post-Cultural Revolution 'New Enlightenment' was supposedly witness to an initial period of broad agreement among thinkers who rejected the old state ideology and propounded instead various alternative models for modernization; there was an active reappraisal of political systems and cultural paradigms that emphasized economic growth, as well as potential political and cultural freedoms. It was a period in which intellectual traditions were invoked, invented and reclaimed as part of intellectuals' attempts to define themselves within the Chinese polity and claim a role in its evolution. This supposed consensus, however, also contained within it a critical response to the various international discourses that were being introduced piecemeal through translation projects, young scholars studying overseas, conferences, seminars and a wealth of publications; and it was a response that carried also the seeds of a major reassessment of China's 1980s and 1990s fascination with the West (or global commercial and political culture) itself.

Moreover, the debates of the 1980s were influenced by an intermittent series of cultural and political campaigns, or purges, in particular the nationwide attacks on 'spiritual pollution' and 'bourgeois liberalization' in 1980–81, 1983–84, 1987, and 1989–90. These administrative and ideological condemnations included attacks on official Marxist-style humanism and the efforts by loyalists to construct a new rationale for the party beyond the confines of its economic program. The purges more often than not had the effect of silencing establishment intellectuals and critics who stepped out of line, or resulted in their isolation within or banishment from its ranks. In conjunction with economic reform and more general social transformations, however, a semi-independent sphere of intellectual activity gradually blossomed, and found outlets in the deregulated publishing market. At the same time, a revival of the educational sphere and academic standards saw a rapid increase in tertiary enrolments and a college-trained urban stratum that enjoyed unprecedented (in post-1949 terms, at least) access to information and a range of media. As a consequence, they provided a ready audience for the products of the *Kulturkampf*.

The period of the 1980s New Enlightenment was, to use Xu Jilin's description,

> A major historical turning point for Chinese intellectuals in that through cultural debate they gradually withdrew from and, in some cases, entirely broke free of the politico-ideological establishment and the state system of specialized knowledge production [that is, the strictures of official academia]. This enabled them to create intellectual spaces and attain a new cultural independence.

It was a kind of autonomy more akin to the situation that had existed prior to the founding of the People's Republic in 1949.

Although they avoided direct confrontation with the official ideology, these intellectuals in effect began to challenge its dominance in every field of thought. The public realm for intellectual debate was to flourish in the 1990s although the consensual environment shared by different schools of thinkers and cultural activists was ruptured first by the 1989 protest movement and the subsequent purge of élitist activists, and then again by the effects of the economic boom that followed in the wake of Deng Xiaoping's 1992 'tour of the south.'

In the 1980s, intellectual contestation had generally centered on debates about abstract ideas and theoretical issues; there was a renewed belief that it was through cultural and national transformation that China would be revitalized. Educated urbanites long excoriated under Maoist cultural policy presumed that this new 'Enlightenment project' was their responsibility, and members of the intelligentsia were anxious to play the role of patriot-savant supposedly central to the identity of the traditional educated caste. Following the successes, and excesses, of the economic reforms during the 1990s, however, engaged intellectuals related their disagreements more directly to economic and political programs, as well as to class or caste differences. In an age during which much of the 'capital accumulation,' that is, superficial economic prosperity, that had been the goal of earlier reforms and revolutions seemed to have been realized, the nature of this affluence and the inequities it presented now came to the fore as issues of pressing importance. The intelligentsia had, throughout the twentieth century, argued bitterly over the merits of a dizzying array of developmental theories, political programs, economic systems and cultural paradigms. Now, at the century's end, debates and intellectual programs began to revolve around not simply how to achieve power and prosperity, but the dilemmas of power and prosperity per se.

In this environment ideas were not mere abstract formulations; economic wealth and the vision of a strong and prosperous China—or even the reverse, the looming menace of an economically imperiled, crisis-ridden and socially divided nation—made the debates about the history of modernity in China and the future it faced both relevant and urgent. Although past controversies had been launched from a common ground, and a general wariness of monopolistic party rule had existed among diverse cultural and intellectual worlds from the late 1970s, now questions were disputed on the basis of vastly different, even mutually exclusive, academic and theoretical frameworks, as well as social experiences.

While open intellectual debate in the style of the 1980s was quelled for a time after 4 June, the broader cultural sphere was witness to considerable resilience. During 1990 the pall of the Beijing Massacre still hung over artistic life in the capital in particular as well as much of the rest of the country. It was, however, also a time of considerable ebullience for alternative culture. For example, the rock 'n' roll scene enjoyed unprecedented activity and growth. Similarly, in 1989–91, independent painters developed on the diversity of the 1980s arts scene and began creating work that would gain an international audience and, through high-profile exhibitions and reviews, came to represent more than any other aspect of mainland culture the face of the new 'New China' overseas. Despite a number of bans on authors directly involved in the 1989 protests, controversial and younger novelists and poets who were not aligned with the establishment, along with essayists and cultural critics, continued to publish in leading provincial journals or, when the opportunity arose, in the pages of Hong Kong and Taiwan publications. . . . Beijing TV aired *The Editors*, a sitcom set in a magazine editorial department that lambasted the official overculture with unprecedented, and ill-concealed, glee. Zhou Lunyou's *A Stance of Rejection* itself appeared in a samizdat poetry journal that subsequently ceased publication because its contributors found they could readily get their works into mainstream literary magazines.

The growth of these popular market spaces was not as revolutionary vis-à-vis the ordained cultural order as many observers would claim. Nonetheless, the rise of a local rock and pop (dubbed by some 'Mandopop'—that is, Mandarin rock pop) scene, the mass publishing market with its plethora of entertainment and lifestyle journals, mainland commercial and party advertising, and so on, did constitute an active response by local culture producers, both mainstream and alternative, to the incursion of off-shore cultural forms and capital. However, in the years following Deng Xiaoping's 1992 tour, during which he openly criticized 'leftist' thinking (that is, political opposition to the accelerated market reforms, the privatization of state industries, the 'outsourcing' of state functions, and so on), the most vocal and concerted attacks on the Communist Party's reformist agenda and its sociopolitical impact came not from the semi-independent intelligentsia, or fringe cultural figures, but from within the party itself.

The hostility of the official left, a group of establishment thinkers and writers who were derided by their public critics as 'red fundamentalists,' also found expression in a number of public forums that had been created following 4 June. As they were routed by policy shifts and marginalized during the 1990s, many of the true believers decamped to institutions and publications on the fringes of power. Their journals covered both cultural and ideological issues and, throughout the decade, they produced a constant stream of criticism—and in many cases vitriol—aimed at the most divisive elements of the party's program. They also launched attacks on an array of ideological soft targets, in particular individuals whom they regarded as being dangerous revisionists, the chief object of their spleen being Wang Meng, the writer and former Minister of Culture (1986–89).

In 1995, the Australian-based Chinese journalist and oral historian Sang Ye questioned one retired high-level cadre about his views of the degeneration of the revolution and his opposition to the reform policies. He said that,

> . . . starting with the Third Plenum of the Eleventh Party Congress in 1978, we have pursued a dangerous rightist policy. We've now gone so far to the right that we've abandoned the basic principles of Marxism and the objective rules of social development. [W]e still talk about revolutionaries being people who struggle valiantly their whole lives for the cause of liberation, and no matter what difficulties we encounter we should just tough it out. But things have reached a point that anyone with a conscience, anyone who cares about the fate of our nation, just has to weep at the dire predicament we are in.

Retirees like this former government minister muttered glum condemnations in private while some of their colleagues memorialized the Central Committee through secret petitions, but from the mid 1990s a number of writers chose to speak out publicly against the market reforms that they believed (or at least argued) were undermining what remained of both the ethos and the rationale of the revolution.

Their protests were aired in a media debate about what was called the 'humanist spirit' and 'kowtowing to the vulgar.' The burgeoning of mass-market popular culture led to despair among people who had only recently regained their faith in (and affirmed their identification with) the tradition of the Chinese literati-scholars, the political and cultural mandarins of the past. It was a self-identification reinforced by an abiding belief in the socialist dogma of the artist as prophet. Having borne witness to the decay of the cultural welfare state over the past decade, they now saw their own influence waning. They felt that writers who profited from the tide of commercialization were prostituting their talents and betraying the cause of a revived literati culture.

Among the most outspoken critics of the new marketplace and its advocates were two ex-Red Guard novelists, Liang Xiaosheng and Zhang Cheng-zhi. They issued dark warnings about the effect that mass commercial culture was having 'on the soul of China.' As Zhang wrote in an alarmist hyperbole partially inspired by Samuel Huntington's writings on 'the clash of civilizations':

> I've been thinking. After the war of the civilizations, they should at least find in the rubble of the defeated a few bodies of intellectuals who fought to the death. I

despise surrender. In particular, in this war of civilizations, I loathe intellectuals who have made a vocation out of capitulation.

Appeals for a moral rearmament that would find its ordnance in the Maoist past were part of a strategy used by writers like Zhang to carry out their critique of contemporary social, political and artistic realities. To question the status quo, the incursion of capital and the consumer tendencies of the society was a shrewd tactic in an avowed 'war of resistance.' Opponents to this approach, however, were deeply suspicious of the presumption of intellectuals to harangue their fellows. Of these the most noteworthy was the novelist and essayist Wang Xiaobo (d. 1997), an important figure who perhaps, more than any other 1990s writer, represented the urbane scepticism of people both weary and wary of intellectual afflatus. 'I respect your high-sounding ideas,' he wrote, 'but I'm less than anxious to have them shoved down my throat.' Or as he remarked on the habits of the educated caste: 'Chinese intellectuals particularly enjoy using moralistic paradigms to lecture others.'

Indeed how useful or reliable were the tainted resources of high-socialist 'leftism,' ones that were by the very nature of their place in contemporary Chinese life unreliable, compromised and disingenuous? Or was 'leftist' political and cultural history being adapted with the help of various theories that authorized the use of a past that was fragmentary, piecemeal and ad hoc, to serve élites in their creation of an expansive critical unanimity in the mainland? Was the objectivization of the past simply distorted and clouded by the subjectivist caste of those who lived it/remember it, or needed to use it to justify themselves in the 1990s? Again, a number of writers were equivocal about intellectual grandstanding and instead turned their attention to the detail of the past and attempted, through the writing of local histories for a general readership, to fill in some of the gaps of public knowledge.

Not all critics of either the moral revivalists or the 'new leftists,' however, were as phlegmatic as Wang Xiaobo. The ideological control of the party had been such that many had suffered, or continued to suffer, directly from its manipulations, or at the hands of the people's democratic dictatorship (the main organs of which were the police, the penal system, the armed police, the army and the judiciary). There were those who had been arrested for their unorthodox activities or views, denied publishing opportunities, or chances to travel, or refused improved housing conditions and promotion, as well as those who had been jailed, harassed by the police, and placed under surveillance. They were emotionally and intellectually determined to see the one-party state weakened and undermined no matter what the cost. For them the marketplace was a welcomed ally in their quest. They would prefer an enfeebled party-state that permitted direct resistance even if it meant that the new dominant market might well make that resistance little more than cosmetic.

For some publishers and editors the sense of trepidation about the continued ability of the CCP to maintain national integrity, as well as to shore up its ideological and cultural hegemony, was virtually on a par with fears about the inundation of overseas capital and the multinational corporations that were energetically expanding into the Chinese cultural market. As one publisher remarked to me in late 1998: 'If you are a responsible intellectual you have to consider whether you are willing to live with the consequences of your opposition to the relatively free-wheeling status quo.' Such an opposition could see local cultural institutions (publishing, the media, the sports entertainment industry, cultural activities, and so on) overwhelmed by foreign capital, know-how and new forms of commercial and capital repression that could well prove to be more insidious than those typical of the chaotic environment of late-socialism. Individuals like my interlocutor contemplated a future ruled by the kind of Great Leader that the American journalist P. J. O'Rourke encountered during his late 1990s 'worst of both worlds' sojourn in fin-de-siècle Shanghai,

> . . . omnipresent amid all the frenzy of Shanghai is that famous portrait, that modern icon. The faintly smiling, bland, yet somehow threatening visage appears in brilliant red hues on placards and posters, and is painted huge on the sides of buildings. Some call him a genius. Others blame him for the deaths of millions. There are those who say his military reputation was inflated, yet he conquered the mainland in short order. Yes, it's Colonel Sanders.

Modernization and prosperity had been central to the aspirations and public discourse not only of the Chinese intelligentsia but also to the concerns of the broader population throughout the twentieth century. When, during the 1990s, the economic reforms created a version of modernization as well as its attendant problems in the urban centres of the nation, the debates about it took a new turn.

As we noted earlier, the 1980s saw intellectuals and broad segments of the population gradually breaking away from the thrall of the socialist nation-state to articulate visions of the society and its future at variance with the official world. In the 1990s, a gradual reformulation of controversies and issues that had first resurfaced in the intellectual and cultural worlds (resurfaced in the sense that they found a lineage in pre-1949 cultural debates, as well as being a reformulation of issues directed by the state since the founding of the People's Republic) took place. The topics of political reform, Enlightenment values and modernity were now interrogated in more comprehensive terms and in relation to the history of modern Chinese history, conventionally dated from the Opium War of 1840.

A number of the key intellectual critics of the 1990s—as well as some of the most controversial participants in the debates—were themselves historians, or specialists in aspects of intellectual history. Their number included academics like Xiao Gongqin, Lei Yi, Wang Hui, Xu Jilin, Qin Hui and Zhu Xueqin. They were thinkers who constantly shifted between their studies of sociopolitical issues of the past, the development of historical narratives during the century, and an engagement in contemporary polemics. Although these individuals were attracted to different academic schools of thought, from the early 1990s they were all active as media cultural commentators. Writers like Xu Jilin recognized that even though the intelligentsia no longer enjoyed its previous prominence, there was still a place for the socially engaged cultural commentator: "One can take on the role of observer, a person who from their particular intellectual and cultural standpoint attempts an independent critique of various social phenomena. You try to participate actively in the cultural evolution of your world . . . and try to use the mass media to give voice to one's conscience." . . .

Intellectuals debating these issues in the pages of learned journals, often employing the guarded language required by an environment of official censorship, was one thing. But change would not necessarily come from the refined 'wonking' of the chattering classes or *trahison des clercs*. Dissidents felt that only popular agitation would allow disparate social forces to have a say in the direction and protection of their own lives, as well as in national politics. Other nonaligned intellectuals and social activists attempted in a myriad of ways—through private, small-scale charity projects, covert foundation activities and so on—to engage actively in civic actions that would benefit their fellows. However, for those imbued with the ideologies of national salvation and participation, to be materially well-off but politically dispossessed, a member of the underclass or itinerant labour force, or being engaged but compromised within a system that would allow the acquisition of capital but maintained electoral disenfranchisement and political impotence, was deeply frustrating. The hope, follies and failure of 1989 and the quest for systemic change and political reform that was central to the concerns of thinkers, cultural activists, progressive politicians and people of conscience at the time remained issues central to the political agenda ten years on. Enforced political impuissance and the internecine warfare obsessed the intelligentsia, and for moderate thinkers like Xu Jilin and his fellows, it was increasingly evident that when major changes did come the niceties of political discussion could once more be overridden by restive mass sentiment.

At the end of the millennium, as the People's Republic celebrated its fiftieth anniversary, here was the dilemma that the intelligentsia and cultural activists faced once more. Was the role of the independent critic or feisty artist enough to satisfy participants in the bitter debates about the state of the nation and its future? Was the 20th-century tradition of political agitation and commitment to remain obscured by the Communist Party's purges of the early 1950s, the repression of the Hundred Flowers, the 'mass democracy' of the Cultural Revolution, the crushing of the Democracy Wall dissidents, and the purges of the 1980s, as well as the bloodshed of 1989, and the quelling of dissidents in late 1998? Would élite intellectuals who proffered analyses of the nation's woes find fellowship with dissidents who were willing to confront the government, or workers and peasants whose outrage at exploitation increasingly led them to rebel? Or was the reconstitution of the intellectuals' mission something that encouraged circumspection and inactivity? This 'cult of transgression without risk' found adherents at all points of the political spectrum, while a cult that did not really transgress, like that of the Buddho-Daoist Falun Gong meditational sect that was outlawed in mid-1999, did ironically pose risks for its adherents.

In his 1991 manifesto, *A Stance of Rejection*, Zhou Lunyou had advocated cultural disengagement and disobedience. In the following years, market reforms as well as expanding areas of civil debate and social agitation blurred the simple cultural antagonisms of the past. By the end of the decade, the romance of resistance may still have appealed to observers of the mainland arts scene (both Chinese and foreign), but for prominent participants it was often easier to ignore the state than to resist the discreet charms of offshore capital. In the revolution of resistance, outspoken members of the intelligentsia found themselves variously on the defensive and on the offensive, participants in and opponents to the reforms that had given them a new lease on life. At the *debut de siècle*, the domain of intellectual politics on mainland China was quickened not by an overlapping consensus, but by issues and debates that divided and confronted at every turn.

50

Fin de Siècle Splendor

ZHU TIANWEN

Zhu Tianwen, daughter of writer Zhu Xining, is one of the most well-known writers in contemporary Taiwan. She and her sister, Tianxin, established themselves as leading authors in the early 1990s. Zhu Tianwen has edited various literary magazines and won prizes for her short stories and filmscripts (she has had a very close collaboration with the director Hou Hsiao-hsien, having written most of his film scripts). Her novel Notes of a Desolate Man *(Huangren shouji), told from the perspective of a gay man, has recently been published in English translation. "Fin de Siècle Splendor" captures, through the figure of a fashion model in contemporary Taipei, life in a postmodern commodity culture.*

This is Taipei's unique city skyline. Mia often stands on her ninth-floor terrace, observing the skies. And when she is in the right mood, she lights some sandalwood in her flat.

The roofs are covered with illegal structures built with corrugated iron; the thousands of structures extend like an ocean of trees to where the sun sets and where the sun rises. We need lightweight building material, Duan, Mia's lover, had once said. Duan used lightweight perforated tin plate to solve the problem of sun glare from skylights and French windows in some villas. On Mia's sun terrace there is also one such awning, where all sorts of dried flowers are hanging upside down.

Mia is a fervent believer in the sense of smell; her life is dependent on memories evoked by different smells. The fragrance of the sandalwood brings her back to the spring fashion show of 1989, when she was drowned in chiffon, georgette, crêpe, sari tied, wound, wrapped, and hanging in the sweeping Indian trend. In such a perfect collection the Sikh turban was of course a must. To complement this collection the decor was of the style that dominated Viennese architecture and paintings at the end of the last century. Kamali, with his heavy use of beads and sequins, was the leading figure.

Mia is also dependent on memories evoked by color. For instance, she has always been looking for a particular shade of purple. She cannot remember

523

when or where she had seen it, but she is absolutely certain that if she were to
come across it again it would not get away; of course everything loaded onto
that shade of purple would reappear, too. However, compared with smell, color
is much slower. Smell, being shapeless and intangible, is sharp and accurate.

The structures of corrugated iron bear witness to the fact that Taiwan is
fighting for space with earth itself. Of course we can also see in this our
predecessors' solution to the problem of heat and leaking related to flat roofs:
they invented this semi-outdoor space. Our predecessors' accumulated life
experience has given us a building style that copes well with Taiwan's climate:
lightweight. It is different from the West and again different from Japan; light in
form, in space, and in visuality, it provides a breathing space for the crowded,
sunbaked cities of Taiwan. According to I. M. Pei, style emerges from problem-
solving. If Pei had not had a group of technicians to help him solve the
problems, the glass on his pyramid at the Louvre would not have had that
glittering transparency, said Duan.

These words of Duan's were mixed with the scent of peppermint in herb
tea. They were chatting under the awning, and she went in and out to make tea.

The fresh taste of peppermint herb tea recalls for her the pale seaside
colors of the 1990 summer show. Those were not the colorful prints of the
Caribbean, but of the North Pole shores. Several icebergs from Greenland
floating in the misty North Pole seas; every breath was ice-cold. All was snow-
white, with hints of green or traces of emerald. The details were a continuation
of the 1989 autumn/winter trend—lace was given new life with mesh patterns or
braided with motifs of fish fins and shells.

When Mia and Duan are not talking, they watch the metamorphosis of
the city skyline in the sunset like impressionist painters. Just as Monet, that great
master who captured time on canvas recorded, with clocklike precision, the
shimmering lights on the river at Giverny on a single day, they too are entranced
by the subtle changes in their surroundings caused by the shifting hours. Prawn-
red, salmon-red, linen-yellow, and reed-yellow; the sky turns from peach to
emerald. Before the curtain falls it suddenly lights a huge fire on the horizon,
torching the metropolis. They indulge themselves aesthetically, so much so that
either their energy is exhausted in the process, or their spirit shattered by the overwhelming spectacle, and very often they do not even do what lovers are supposed
to do. This is what Mia wants; this is the lifestyle she has chosen. In the
beginning this was not what she wanted, but finally it became her only choice.

Her girl friends—Ann, Joey, Wanyu, Baby, Christine, and Ge; at twenty-
five she is the oldest. Ann with her beautiful suntan is always trying to make

herself a shade tanner, so that she will really stand out in psychedelic red, green, and yellow. Ann does not need men; Ann says she has her vibrator. And so Ann has chosen as her lover a forty-two-year-old married man with a successful career. Married, so that he would not bother her. Ann is busy as a beautician, and even when she has time, she only sees him if she feels like it.

As for the young bachelors, deficient in both money and patience, Ann has absolutely no interest in them.

Because of her profession Ann exudes a cold smell of scrub creams. Actually it's a cold fragrance reduced to a very low temperature and pressed into a thin blade—that's Ann.

In Japanese there is a shade of gray called "romantic gray." A fifty-year-old man with a full head of soft black hair, white at the temples, arousing in a young girl the dream of romance—the gray of life, of experience. Mia had come out of childhood very early. Nevertheless she was attracted to Duan by his "romantic gray," and by his smell—it was the smell of sunlight unique to Duan.

In those days, Mia had seen clothes hung out to dry on bamboo poles stuck between a willow tree and a wall. Those were the days before fabric softeners. After a whole day in the sun, the clothes became hard and rough. When she put them on, the distinct difference between cloth and flesh reminded her of the existence of her clean body. Mother folded the family's clothes up for easy storage; women's clothes had to be put under the men's, just as she insisted that men's clothes had to be hung in front of the women's. Mia fought openly against this taboo; her young mind wanted to see whether this would bring a natural disaster. After the willow tree had been cut down and the land repossessed by the government for public housing, her elder sisters got married and her mother grew old. All this became gentle memory, with the smell of clothes washed in white orchid flakes and baked in the July sun.

The smell of a husband. Mixed with the smell of aftershave and cigarettes, that's Duan. A husband provides security. Although Mia can support herself and does not have to take any money from Duan, when Duan takes her out of the city for a pleasure trip, he gives her a wad of notes with which she pays their expenses throughout the journey; there is always some left, which Duan tells her to keep. Mia is happy with the way he spends money, treating her like his wife, not his lover.

How the times have changed! Even Comme des Garçons has made a clean break with the asexual look that made her name and has joined the camp of sheer femininity. Layers of thin gauze and an irregular cut emphasize a gentle softness. The wind of change had come much earlier, in early 1987, when the fallen angel Gallianno returned to purity. A collection of pre-Chanel suits for the Nineteenth-Century New Woman, and for the evening low-cut, tight-fitting dresses with crinoline, and the colonial white beloved by royal families, all came onto the stage.

Ge has discarded her three-piece suits with heavy shoulder pads. The career women's stiff outfit is just like a housewife's apron; wearing it constantly equals giving up your rights as a woman. Ge dons the body-hugging fifties style: narrow-waisted, three-quarter sleeves. In the flash of a second it dawned on her: Why not? She fully intends to take advantage of the fact that she is a woman, and the more feminine a woman is the more she can get out of men. Ge has learned to camouflage her vicious designs with a low profile, and since then success has come with much less effort on her part.

The hang of the fabric has taken over from clear-cut lines; silk is in, linen out. Washable silk and sand-washed silk have brought the fabric to the modern age. Rayon is made from wood paste; it has the feel of cotton but is more absorbent and hangs better. Besides, rayon chiffon is just a third the price of silk chiffon. On Christmas Eve that year, during a cold front, Mia and Wanyu had a photo session modeling spring fashions for a magazine. It was a collection of cutwork rayon creating the image of the flying goddesses of the Dunhuang cave paintings. Mia agrees with Wanyu: earning money and supporting themselves is a matter of pride; spending the money of a man they love is happiness. These are different things altogether.

In damp, drizzling weather rayon turns moldy easily. Mia worried over the jars and bunches of dried flowers and dried reeds in her house, and Duan bought her a dehumidifier. Wind and rain darkened everything. Mia looked at the city skyline where black moss seemed to have grown. To counter the damp, she either drank hot ginger tea or put lots of powdered cassia into her cappuccino.

The smell of cassia and ginger was dissipated in the wind. The sun came out to shine on a purple ocean of Rococo and Baroque in the streets. That was the result of the film *Amadeus*. Mia looks back to the long summer and long autumn of 1985, when classical music cassette tapes topped the pop charts.

After the Irises broke a world record at auction, yellow, purple, and green became the main colors. Van Gogh led the way to Monet, and the brilliant blues, reds, and purples reflected in the waters of the twenty-four Giverny paintings came to life again in the form of clothes. Tahitian flowers and orange shades were also a hit; that was Gauguin. There was a retrospective exhibition of Gauguin in Paris with over 300 paintings; Duan and his younger son Weiwei happened to pass through there on their way back from the World Cup held in West Germany, and he gave her the painting "Jacob Wrestling with the Angels."

Because Gauguin was from Europe, he hesitated over the use of colors and spent a long time trying to decide. In fact it was simple: all he had to do was follow his will and paint the canvas with patches of red and blue. In the streams time flowed like glittering gold, so enchanting. Why hesitate? Why not pour the joyful gold onto the canvas? Plagued by his European habits, he dared not. It was the shyness of a regressive race, said Gauguin of his Tahitian period. Duan told her the story as though it were about an old friend.

Duan and Mia belong to two separate circles; the sections that overlap seem to occupy a very small amount of their time, but the quality is high. It is the time when they discard all worldly concerns, and one day is as good as a thousand years in crystallizing the essence of their relationship—it is like frankincense, a kind of resin originating from eastern Africa or Arabia, an expensive perfume.

Frankincense brings Mia back to 1986, when she was eighteen. She and her boyfriends made love with Nature. That was the year when Taiwan took a giant step forward and caught up with Europe, the center of high fashion. Mia's group signed up for a Madonna look-alike competition, which started her on her modeling career. She became keenly aware of her figure and gave up loose, long tops, favoring short and tight-fitting ones instead. The trend of sporting underwear as outer clothing started by Madonna had swept over Europe, and Mia, too, had several of these lovely things—in satin, see-through silk, linen, and lycra. She wore them with suede miniskirts in the daytime; at night she changed into a sequined skirt and went dancing at KISS.

Like the expensive frankincense she acted as a cohesive force binding her boyfriends together. She was always the one to call for a gathering, and everyone came. Yang Ge, Ah Xun and his wife, Ou, "Ant," Kai, and the Yuan brothers. Sometimes she would call for a gathering at midnight while dancing wildly away; sometimes they were the last table to go after Yeru Restaurant was closed in the wee hours—they had paid their bills and as soon as everyone was there they were on their way. Kai had a car, so did Ou, and they drove to Mt. Yangming. First they bought all the food they needed at the Seven Eleven at the crossroads, then they headed for the mountain.

In the bamboo groves mid-way up the mountain they lay down side by side. A bottle of Chinese liquor was passed around and drained, and the lighted marijuana cigarette was an eerie red glowworm, which they inhaled in turn. After they had inhaled they relaxed and lay down, waiting. When their eyelids slowly closed from exhaustion, they no longer heard any heavy breathing; all sound had been vacuumed away and their surroundings expanded infinitely. In silent space the wind in the bamboos was like a bellows emitting, from the remotest distance, a mist that congealed into sand that swept together as waves. Dry, powdery, and cool, it approached from far, far away to cover them, and then—swoosh—it completely receded. In the naked, cool vacuum, the sky was suddenly filled with bird song. Frankincense floated in the air; bird song fell like rain to cover them. We're making love with Nature, Mia sighed sadly.

She definitely did not want it to end just like that. She was in love with Kai; he had caught her eye before June that year. That June, the magazine *Men's Non-no* brought out its first issue, and the young women of Taipei and Tokyo simultaneously found their Prince Charming—Abe Hiroshi. Since then she had collected twenty-one issues of *Men's Non-no*, all with Abe Hiroshi on the cover. Kai has the same manly eyebrows as Abe Hiroshi, the same guileless face sweating from exercise, the same clear, deep-set eyes born for romance. The only thing Kai lacked was a *Men's Non-no* and an agency to turn him into a star, Mia thought indignantly.

And so Mia and Kai developed a sense of comradeship; they were the best partners for magazine fashion features. Kai donned the heavy rebelliousness of London boys; a manmade leather jacket flung across one shoulder, she wore a high-waisted mini pencil skirt with a zip splitting her belly, and on either side of the zip two rows of eyelets going right down to the hem and tied together with two chains shoelace fashion right up to her ribs. It evoked the sound of motorbikes; the universe was on fire. Kai was so handsome that he loved only himself, and he treated Mia as his beloved brother Narcissus.

Mia was in love with Yang Ge, too. After the birdsong had stopped, they had rested for a while before the dampness of the heavy dew awoke them. They scrambled up and headed for the cars. Yang Ge held her hand as they wove through dead bamboo trees and sharp bamboo shoots, his warm, fleshy hand letting her know his intention. Mia did not want to make up her mind about anyone yet, despite her fondness for Yang Ge dressed in his perennial Levi jeans and khaki cotton shirt with its tail hanging out, and for the way he stuck his hands in his pockets, looking so bored that you expected him to vegetate. She was so infatuated with this air of nonchalance created by his old blue jeans and faded khaki that she would have impulsively married him. But Mia never answered the inquiring look in Yang Ge's eyes, never gave him any hint or any chance. They all got into the cars and drove up to the observatory.

The vapor and the clouds hung heavily in the air, like a river. The head-lights courageously broke through the waters and worked uphill to the peak. A long wait. Ou took out a slip of paper the size of a fingernail and gave her half of it. She put it on the tip of her tongue where it slowly dissolved, and as it did she became so excited that she shook with uncontrollable laughter; even when the laughter turned to tears she still could not control herself. Ou took an army coat from the trunk and wrapped her up tightly from head to legs, and then thrust her under the arms of the Yuan brothers so that she could stand steadily. She loved it when Ou pulled the doors of the car wide open and turned the music to its loudest: in the mist and vapor Billy Jean started dancing to the tune of Michael Jackson's "moon walk."

At last, look! What they had been waiting for is here. In the valley in front of them a mirage rose up. The water vapor was a mirror, reflecting in the darkness before dawn some part of the Taipei basin, a somber castle, quite clearly outlined.

Mia's eyes filled with tears. She vowed to the people sleeping soundly in that castle that she would have nothing to do with love. Love was too wishy-washy, too degrading—like Ah Xun and his wife, forever engaged in a mean-spirited tug-of-war. She did not even have time enough to feast her eyes on the world's many splendors; she decided that she'd create a brilliant future for herself whatever it might take. Material girl—why not? She'd worship things and she'd worship money. Youth and beauty were on her side; she worshipped her own beautiful body.

As they came down from the mountain they decided to have a bath at the hot springs. The headlights surged through the mist and falling petals, and soon it was dawn. Since they hadn't slept at all they could not stand the sunlight. Everyone put on sunglasses—the old-fashioned Franklin variety—and called themselves vampires. The vampires lay sleeping on the rocks after they had had their bath. Sulfuric vapor rolled upstream from the bottom of the valley, and the sun on their sunglasses looked like a metal biscuit. Mia pulled the reel out of the cassette tape and held it up against the wind; like a snake it whooshed out towards the sun. She held onto the reel, and the brown string became a trail taking her through the muddy yellow sky directly towards the metal biscuit. She felt that she was standing there alone, surveying all living things and the whole universe in a grand sweep of history.

From 1986 to the autumn of 1987, Mia and her boyfriends were absorbed in this kind of game, unaware of the brevity of youth. In October Pierre Cardin came to Taiwan to see how his products were doing. In the same month Abe

Hiroshi wore a rose-red cashmere V-neck pullover and a turquoise necktie on the cover of *Men's Non-no*; he also starred in a film with Minamino Yoko playing a fashionable girl. For some reason all this seemed to have deprived Mia of something.

Overnight, she discovered that she was no longer in love with Abe Hiroshi. Her collection of his photos ended in February 1988—that was number 21. In a vast expanse of snowy plain Abe Hiroshi wore a white hat and a white outfit, hugging a white Japanese dog and smiling to show his healthy white teeth; so childish! It was an unfair relationship: one-way traffic. Even if she were to die for the love of Abe Hiroshi he belonged to the public; he would not even give her the hint of a smile. She was surprised that she had been tricked. Abe Hiroshi was a narcissistic fellow who was so full of himself he had no room for anyone else. A narcissistic woman may be lovable, a narcissistic man is just unmanly.

Mia did not want any more games. Without her acting as convener, her boyfriends all dissipated like the mist to fight for their own careers. Quite a few of them became homosexuals, maintaining sisterly relations with Mia.

That was the watershed. The fear of AIDS led to a new fashion trend: feminine clothes for women and a gentleman's look for men; unisex clothes all disappeared. Mia, too, said goodbye to her hermaphroditic dress code, which had passed through phases of David Bowie, Boy George, and Prince.

Years ago when she changed out of her school uniform she wore an army style outfit: khaki or beige, with badges. She walked around the West Gate district and the school girls all swooned over her. At fifteen she had led the way in the beggary trend, wearing clothes with huge holes on the shoulders; her mother was no longer in a position to raise any objections. Although she did not know it at the time, she had always been ahead of her peers in following the trend set by Yohji Yamamoto and Issey Miyake. In 1984 Kou Kanuko created a new, country look with floral prints and layers of frills, but Mia just told her friend Baby to wear it. She herself donned a metal gray riding jacket, bark-colored culottes, and a pair of cloth shoes on her unstockinged feet. The two of them went to McDonald's for the Valentine menu. Baby wore a gold-plated bracelet with Mia's name on it. They had a pair of moon and star earrings: one was on Baby's right ear, the other on Mia's left. That was the year when 31 Ice Cream came on the market—thirty-one different flavors in the form of colorful, solid little balls. Baby was an Aries, and on her birthday the two of them invited each other there. It was an icy cold place, but bright and airy like a greenhouse. Together they mapped out their dream-plan of opening a shop some day.

In the twenty-some years of her life, she owes Baby too much. When she for the first time wore a denim bra instead of a blouse under her jacket and a tight-fitting cotton skirt to show off her figure to her playmates, Baby was extremely displeased. In her overreaction she gave Mia a harsh scolding. Baby became more and more like Mia's mother, and the more she objected the more Mia rebelled. She was the one who led her playmates into the Madonna whirlwind. During the competition finals the mass media turned up in strength to take photographs of them. Afterwards she saw a local MTV splicing shots of their group of Madonna lookalikes in with the publicity van of Wu Shuzhen, who was running for the Legislative Yuan on behalf of her husband, and with the yellow ribbons of Corazon Aquino's people-power revolution. In her red-hot circle there was a new group of people—her boyfriends. Baby drifted further and further away. When she occasionally looked back, she would see that from beyond where the ripples ended, Baby's lonely eyes were looking at her accusingly.

At twenty she was tired of fooling around. She became cruel like a queen bee; her only purpose was to make money. Romeo Gigli took the scene by storm; this Italian designer had great admiration for ancient Pompeii and used fabrics tightly wrapped around the body to conjure up a sense of nostalgia. Mia parted her curly hair in the middle and coiled it up at the back, showing her forehead, her shoulders, and her swanlike neck, like a nymph resurrected. She met Duan.

Baby asked her out for a long talk. She had heard that Mia was living with a married man and actually thought that she'd persuade her to leave him. Mia haughtily refused, treating Baby's sincere words as part of her selfish designs. Baby tried so hard to convince her, as if her life depended on it, but Mia just watched her as if she were some badly conceived character in a play who did not realize that her designs had been totally exposed. The air was filled with Baby's usual scent—Amour, Amour. What a moldy smell! It constantly reminded her of that dull, sweaty afternoon: outside the window the red blossoms of the cotton tree squatted on the branches like so many plastic bowls. Baby cried from sorrow; she left in a suppressed rage.

Soon after that she received a wedding invitation from Baby. The envelope was in her handwriting, but the card inside contained nothing but printed words. It was a most ordinary card with a cheap fragrance, an unknown name for the bridegroom, and common, a-penny-a-dozen names for the groom's parents. This was Baby's way of getting back at her. She was infuriated that anyone should sink so low, and refused to go to Baby's wedding.

They lost touch. Two years later, during the French Revolution bicentenary, she heard that Baby was staying at the maternity ward of the Veterans' Hospital. She went to Evergreen to get a box of "Revolution Candies" wrapped in the blue, white, and red of the tricolor flag, thinking that she would go and visit Baby, but then so many things happened and she never got round to it. Then she learned that Baby was divorced and had opened a flower shop; her daughter was just three.

The winter collection of '92 was still dominated by the Empire style: a flowing cape or poncho with tight trousers or thick stockings, or even a pair of knee-length boots. It is true that long boots are not suited to the Taiwan climate, but they can effectively correct the proportion of legs and torso and create a long, cranelike look. In the last three years "Revolution Candies" had ceased production and had therefore become antiquated editions, rare items.

It turned out that the flower shop also sold food. Baby was sitting on a black rattan stool; from the back her mature figure looked as stable as a huge piece of rock. She tip-toed in and covered Baby's eyes from the back, saying: this is rape. She had learned that years ago from some blue film and had done it to give Baby a fright; this had then become an intimate greeting between them. Baby struggled free and half hid herself behind the flower display unit, glad to see her and yet angry at the same time, saying that she should not have turned up unannounced and deprive her of a chance to make herself more presentable. At that moment Mia wished she had looked older, less glamorous, instead of looking as though she had cheated the years. Should she wait in the shop while Baby went home to do her hair and change, or should she come back some other day? Baby preferred to meet on another day. So instead of catching up, she blew a goodbye kiss at Baby, just as in the old days.

Now the flower shop has become the rendezvous for her girlfriends. It is in an expensive area, and all the shops along the lane are small boutiques. Mia can smell the shops; sometimes the smell is evoked by colors, sometimes by the decor and the use of space. Every time she walks down the lane it is like traveling through the world's ancient civilizations. The flower shop with its complex mixture of scents is like a Byzantine tapestry; the aroma of coffee wafts in the air, recalling the ancient age of handicrafts. Joey is responsible for the food served in the flower shop: homemade fruit cakes, cheese pie, oatmeal biscuits, and flower-petal puddings.

Mia had just made a decent sum and given it to Baby to invest in the shop. Baby only holds a third of the shares. The other two shareholders are her ex-husband and a potter friend, and they both declined Mia's offer because they did not know her. Though rejected, Mia felt happy. It seems that on the scales of her friendship with Baby, her side has gained back a little weight because of this.

By this spring the nostalgic trend had turned licentious. It was the licentiousness of the Orient, that of wearing embroidered jackets inside out. Mia had done that for years, so Paris and Milan were trailing behind her. She stood in front of the Christian Lacroix boutique opposite the flower shop: the display window shows a single Moroccan-style coat, its surface of rough ivory raw silk blends with the ivory-colored deco under the window lighting and turns into an expanse of desert sand—a color of sparsity. A corner of the flap is turned up to reveal the brocade lining of Damascus red with embossed patterns of purple and gold thread, which is also visible through the wide cuffs. Mia could smell the mysterious scent of musk.

Indian musk-yellow. Purple silk flings open to show a musk-yellow lining; dark blue cloth blows apart to reveal a scarlet blouse; emerald-colored satin is lined with a delicate pink. India boasts of a sense of mystery in its licentiousness, while China's is well-controlled. As for Japan, everything is formalized; its is a stylized licentiousness.

Nostalgic splendor is just one side of the coin, the other is a repentant return to nature. In autumn and winter 1989 Christian Lacroix introduced his leopard hats, Moschino his leopard trimmings, and Ferre his coats of a combination of animal-fur patterns—tiger, zebra, giraffe, and snake. All this is reminiscent of the old British Empire two centuries ago; the stuffed animals they imported from their colonies swept through Europe like a wild fire.

These are fake furs, of course. Ecological protection is the byword now, so wearing the real thing will not just arouse public rage but is also unfashionable. Don't be a slave to fashion, be yourself; those are Moschino's famous words. That's a lie; Mia can almost see Moschino winking at her in his Milan workshop as he confesses.

Fake furs were the rage in the winter 1990 collections. They could pass for the real thing, and they did not violate the animal protection laws. But what's the point of imitating the real thing? It's just foolish. Much better for the fake items to be self-mocking, which is in line with the modern spirit, somewhat witty and quite cute. Even the three-tier string of manmade pearls Mrs. Bush wore, priced at $150, set a trend for pearl necklaces in the winter of '89. Mia's '91 anti-fur show, with its variations of fake furs dyed red and green, was cute and trendy.

Ecological consciousness began in the spring of '90, pale beach colors or soft desert tones. The subdued shades and cheerful grays are different from the neutral colors of the eighties: eggshell white, pearly gray, oyster black, ivory yellow, and seashell green. Natural is beautiful. Mia discarded her eyeliner with its clear definitions; eyeshadows are no longer the focal point. One should emphasize personal characteristics: the natural shape of the face, high or low cheekbones untouched by blusher. Almond colored or *café au lait*; the contrast of light and shadow disappears, and so do boundaries. All is clear and transparent. Foundations of the nineties are pear colored, as opposed to the olive complexions of the eighties.

Mia has become quieter because of Duan; she is leaving behind her exaggerated queen bee stage. Slightly hanging breasts and a smooth curve at the waist are in line with the logic of environmental protection and are said to have real sex appeal.

Having become single again, Baby goes to her ex-husband's place to pick up her daughter every Saturday. The flower shop closes at 8:30 P.M., and a bronze candelabra with dark blue candles lights the place after closing; they sometimes have a night snack there with Mia. Sometimes they go to Mia's place to try her new concoctions of herb tea, and Duan is left sitting in a corner listening to music; there is no way he can break into their endless small talk. Baby's daughter is a Scorpio with a sting in her tail, a difficult child. When the three of them go out, Baby drives, and Mia either holds Baby's daughter on her lap or leaves her to play in the back seat with Baby keeping an eye on her in the mirror. Mia can foresee that this is the way of life Baby will choose for herself.

Christine proclaims herself a pajamas woman, one of a stubborn group who refuses to wear any kind of uniform such as the three-piece suits sported by successful career women. They cannot stand the pressure of a collar against their neck, and so they choose to wear the French-styled "Most Beloved"— long T-shirt-like dresses, or cotton-knit V neck, boat neck, and collarless blouses with lace trimmings.

Wanyu, on the other hand, is the pathetic woman of action. She is expert in fulfilling other people's dreams—her husband's, her lover's, her son's. She is constantly busy either because of a spirit of self-sacrifice or because she does not want others to be disappointed. They have great sympathy for Wanyu, this woman of action. She should leave some space for herself: have a good cry, go on a shopping spree, or just sit and stare; all this will do her good.

As for Mia, she's probably a witch. Her flat is filled with dried flowers and herbs, like a pharmacy. Duan often has the illusion that he is with a medieval monk. Her bathroom is planted with Chinese orchids, African violets, potted pineapples, Peacock coconuts, and all sorts of nameless ferns. On top of all that there are scores of different bath salts, bath oils, soaps and shower gels in glaring, poisonous colors; the room is like a magician's distillery. All this started with Mia's sudden wish to retain forever the delicate pink color and fragrance of roses imported from Holland. Before the flowers were in full bloom, she took them out of the vase, tied them in a bunch and hung them upside down in the draft from the window; she looked helplessly at the pink color as it faded day by day. She had just moved out of her elder sister's home after they had a big row, escaping her sister's career-woman, two-income-family lifestyle and her mother's supervision. Like a goldfish suddenly set free, she was faced with the immediate pressure of fending for herself in the open sea, and she grabbed every opportunity to make money. On some occasions when she was hard up and could not afford to join in the fun, she put on a stern face of having seen through it all and said with an air of superiority that she had to go home to bed. And it is true that she had tried her best to build a warm nest. It was during this period that she developed a hard-times friendship for the bunch of dried roses.

She was witness to how the flowers lost their fragrance and how their colors darkened, until they turned into a different kind of matter altogether. That's fate; but there is still a chance, and her curiosity was aroused. She hung up a bunch of serissa for observation, and that was followed by cornflower, high mallow, field mint. So the experiments started.

The first time Duan visited her place, there were no table and no chairs, no coffee and no tea, just five stunning cushions lying anyhow on the floor, several bunches of ferns and flowers hanging at the windows, a clay bowl filled with dried yellow rose petals, and a rattan tray containing the dried peel of lemons, oranges, and mandarins. They sat on the floor drinking 100 percent pure orange juice; Duan had a clean yogurt cup in one hand, which he used as an ashtray, and smoked and talked away. He asked her whether she had bought her cushions in three different places; Mia, surprised, replied in the positive. The two wax-dyed ones were bought as a pair, the two made of imported floral prints with tulip patterns were another pair, and the one with an embroidered elephant and little round mirrors was Indian; these two mugs were rather postmodern. Mia was glad that these household items, which she had selected with such care, had all been appreciated, and thought that maybe she should buy a good ashtray for the house. The next day she was also glad that her flat had no clear boundaries between the eating, sitting, and sleeping areas, for this made it natural for them to become lovers.

Duan had left the Soviet-made Red Star watch in her place. The next day he came back for it, only to forget again. He came again, and forgot again. For three whole days this man and this woman left their work unattended to; Mia almost missed an Armani autumn show at Sincere. They couldn't go on like that; they both said that it was right to break up. The Red Star watch was given to her as a memento; he had to resume working, too.

Mia's flat was filled with the sour-sweet taste of passion fruit; like golden-red larva it seeped through the cracks in the windows and the door and poured down from the balcony and the lift, until it filled the whole building. Just in case Duan might still phone her or come round, she sat there the whole day and finished a whole basketful of passion fruit. She dug at them with a spoon and fed herself mouthful after mouthful; by nightfall both the spoon and her teeth seemed to have been corroded by the sour juice. Only then did she stop. She buried her head in the pillow and fell sound asleep. The cleaned-out passion fruit shells were put on the balcony to dry—they're also called arhat fruit—the black shells look like rows and rows of arhat heads. Mia was extremely depressed. The next morning she took a large bag and left, having decided to ignore the notice for shooting a commercial that day even if it meant losing her job. She just would not sit around like a fool waiting for him to call; she would not turn into a worm gnawing at bitter fruit.

She bought a ticket and boarded a train, not caring where it was heading. When the train emerged from the railway station she was shocked by the ugliness of the streets along the railway: she had never seen Taipei from this angle. The train headed south, which was as strange to her as a foreign land; even the trees seemed unfamiliar. Her ticket was for Taichung, where she got out. She walked around till evening and then boarded a public bus. The bus was full, and she seemed an extraterrestrial among the passengers. The bus was bound for somewhere called Taiping Village. It was growing dark, and the wind carried a strange fragrance—a desolate foreign country. She got off, ran across the road, and found the stop for the return bus. She couldn't wait to get back to that city of indulgence and vice—her home. If she were to live away from the city, she would wither like an uprooted plant. She woke up in the express bus to see the huge display windows of Mitsukoshi Department Store and the clothes and accessories stands that lined the sheltered walkways. The bus turned into Chungshan North Road, where lights in the shops shone and glimmered through the camphor and maple trees. The bus went up the flyover, and she saw wall-size neon signs all around her. Like a fish back in water, Mia came alive again.

She went to see the Yuan brothers. Their father had a piano bar in a basement. By law they were not allowed to have a shop sign, so they hired a small truck, which they decorated as a shop sign and had it parked in front of the building every evening. A display board covered by neon lights; set against the background of silver and red lights are these golden words: Riddle in a Riddle. The elder of the Yuan brothers had the rotten luck to be called up for military service. When the younger Yuan saw Mia, he was elated, and proceeded to teach her a new way to have fun: he detached the electric wires connecting the neon lights to the building, switched them to the truck batteries and told her to get on. Decked out like a Christmas tree, their truck speeded over the overpasses, took a detour to the East Gate and the Chiang Kai-shek Memorial before they turned back. Mia proudly showed Yuan her Red Star watch, took it off, and said he could wear it for a few days.

This is her homeland: a city-confederacy of Taipei, Milan, Paris, London, Tokyo, and New York. She lives here, steeped in its customs, well-versed in its artistry, polished by its culture, ready to emerge as one of its preeminent representatives.

Faced with the trend toward femininity, Issey Miyake gave up his three-dimensional cutting and shifted his attention to the use of fabrics. Patterns are pressed onto silk and chiffon to create a stiff feel quite different from their original texture: giving a hard edge to soft femininity. Patterns of fish fins, seashells, palm leaves were pressed onto the fabric, creating a three-dimensional effect that replaced three-dimensional cutting. This effect is enhanced with criss-cross stitching. The result is futuristic, typical of the willful genius of Miyake.

When the Seoul Olympics was broadcast all over the world, Yves St. Laurent and Gianni Versace both frankly admitted that they had adopted for their day and evening wear the flamboyant Gravache's tight lace trousers and his cutting that allowed free athletic movements.

As a child Mia had seen Prince Charles and Princess Diana's wedding of the century. Everyone copied the Princess's hair style. It is sad that the fairy tale did not end there, that the story continued on, sad indeed.

Duan came to see Mia again. Mia ran up to him joyfully and clung to his neck; he was caught unawares and almost fell down laughing. She left her door wide open, hanging onto him in the elevator lobby like a baby monkey hanging onto its mother. Duan, a little overcome by her passionate behavior, had to quickly carry her into her flat. Mia loved to try lifting Duan, to see if she could get him one inch off the ground. Or else she would stand on his feet and they'd walk round the flat in an embrace. All this made Duan feel clumsy and embarrassed. They're lovers, but she's young enough to be his daughter.

When she gets married, Duan said, she could use his gold credit card to sign for everything, sign till he's broke. Mia listened quietly, saying nothing.

The next day Duan made haste to correct himself: he should not have talked about her getting married; if he had kindled this idea in her, when the disaster came it would be his Achilles' heel, for Mia was his. Soon after that he corrected himself again: he's older than her and would probably die first. What would she do with the rest of her life? Better take things as they come. Mia listened to all this with the loving look of a mother, as if Duan was just a chattering child.

Just as summer wear is always replaced by autumn wear, passion cools and is replaced by a warmth like that of jade worn close to the body. Mia started with dried flowers, and continued her observations and experiments with herbal teas, bathroom accessories, pressed flowers, and handmade paper. All this was just to develop her reliance on the sense of smell, and to try desperately to retain the brilliant colors of the flowers.

Duan's company arranged for a tour to the national forest reserve for employees and their spouses, and while he was there he gathered a whole bag of pine cones, pine needles, and fir needles for her. She mixed two teaspoonfuls of cinnamon with half a spoonful of cloves, cassia, two drops of scented oil, some pine oil, and some lemon oil, and brushed a layer of the pine oil on the pine cone. Eucalyptus leaves, cork leaves, rose petals, and geranium leaves were tossed into this mixture, and dried red chilies, berries, and poinsettia were added. All this was put into a pine-colored, oval-shaped bowl: a festive bowl of fragrance reminiscent of Christmas for Duan's workshop.

Recently we have started using stones for corner areas. In the past it was all pebbles, but now we hope to use 30 percent Yilan stones. This way we can give a new look to old techniques and also overcome the shortage of tile workers. It was a development for DINKs and "single aristocrats." Duan had wanted to reserve one for Mia, but Mia prefers her own top-floor flat with the corrugated-iron structure on the roof. Here she can put her flowers, leaves, and peel out to dry, and she can stand against the railings to observe the sky, wearing a plain blue blouse that the wind blows open to reveal a bright red lining.

She is two years older than Duan's eldest. She has met the second son, Weiwei, who takes after his mother. The castle of clouds on the city skyline tells her that she will live to see Weiwei have a successful career, get married, and have children, but that Duan might not. And so she must learn to become independent of emotions, and she has to start now.

She put shredded waste paper into water to dissolve the gluey substance and then transferred the paper into a food processor. The paste, mixed with water, was blended and poured onto mesh and pressed dry. Then the mesh was placed between white cotton cloth sandwiched between newspaper and wood boards, pressed repeatedly with a rolling pin, and then put under some heavy object for several hours. The sieve was then removed, and the cotton cloth with its contents was pressed evenly with a warm iron. A week ago Mia produced her first sheet of paper, paper she could write on. To prevent ink from penetrating it, she brushed a layer of alum on the sheet. This week she added some purplish rose petals into the food processor, and produced her second sheet of paper.

The castle of clouds is being blown apart, revealing a lake of Egyptian blue. Rosemary.

When she is old and her beauty has faded, Mia will be able to support herself with her handicrafts. The abyssal blue of the lake tells her that the world men have built with theories and systems will collapse, and she with her memory of smells and colors will survive and rebuild the world from here.

1990

Translated by Eva Hung

51

Four Stanzas on Homesickness

YU GUANGZHONG

Written in the 1960s, by Yu Guangzhong (1928–), a poet who grew up on the mainland, moved to Taiwan and who lived for extended periods in the United States and Hong Kong, this piece expresses a kind of nostalgic longing for home and wholeness that is in some sense typical of older generation writers working outside China. This nostalgia is both a reaction to modernity and a product of it.

Give me a scoop of the Yangzi River, oh, the Yangzi
    River like wine
    The taste of drunkenness
    Is the taste of homesickness
Give me a scoop of the Yangzi River, oh, the Yangzi

Give me a red hibiscus, oh, red hibiscus
    Hibiscus as red as blood
    The scalding pain of seething blood
    Is the scalding pain of homesickness
Give me a red hibiscus, oh, red hibiscus

Give me a white snowflake, oh, white snowflake
    Snowflake as white as a letter
    To wait for a letter from home
    Is to wait feeling homesick
Give me a white snowflake, oh, white snowflake

Give me a fragrant plum blossom, oh, plum blossom
    Plum blossom as fragrant as Mother
    Mother's fragrance
    Is the fragrance of my native soil
Give me a fragrant plum blossom, oh, plum blossom

Translated by Michelle Yeh

Suggestions for Further Reading

Andrews, Julia F., and Kuiyi Shen. *A Century in Crisis: Modernity and Tradition in the Art of Twentieth-Century China.* New York: Henry N. Abrams, 1998. A collection of articles on key trends in modern Chinese art that focuses on the People's Republic. This volume was produced as a catalogue for the modern section of a 1998 Guggenheim exhibition of Chinese art. Topics include the Shanghai School, the Lingnan School, the woodcut movement, history of oil painting, socialist realism, modern calligraphy, and contemporary art.

Barmé, Geremie. *In the Red: On Contemporary Chinese Culture.* New York: Columbia University Press, 1999. This lively and readable account discusses culture in the People's Republic in wake of the 1989 Tiananmen protests. It has chapters on T-shirt culture, the filmmaker Zhang Yuan, Wang Shuo, the exiled dissident movement, advertising, Maoist nostalgia, and so forth. Barmé lets readers know how he feels about things.

Chang, Sung-cheng Yvonne. *Modernism and the Nativist Resistance: Contemporary Fiction from Taiwan.* Durham: Duke University Press, 1993. This is a book-length general study of Taiwan's literature, constructed around the debates and literary practice of the Western-inspired modernists and the *xiangtu* nativists who promoted realist literature.

Chen Xiaomei. *Occidentalism: A Theory of Counter-Discourse in Post-Mao China.* New York: Oxford University Press, 1995. This book looks at the role of Western culture and literature in the formation of a "counter-discourse" aimed at the official state discourse in the post-Mao period. Its primary focus is post-Mao drama, but it also contains chapters on *River Elegy* and Obscure poetry. This is an important book in cross-cultural studies.

Chow, Tse-tsung. *The May Fourth Movement: Intellectual Revolution in Modern China.* Cambridge, MA: Harvard University Press, 1960. This is an exhaustive historical study of the May Fourth New Culture movement.

Clark, Paul. *Chinese Cinema: Culture and Politics Since 1949.* Cambridge: Cambridge University Press, 1987. The volume provides an overview of the development of film in the People's Republic from 1949 to the advent of Fifth Generation in the mid 1980s. It looks primarily at the political and social functions of film and at important film genres (minority films, revolutionary films, musicals, May Fourth adaptations, history films). Clark structures his view of Chinese film around a tension between Yan'an cultural bureaucrats and Shanghai filmmakers.

Dai, Jinhua. *Cinema and Desire: Feminist Marxism and Cultural Politics in the Work of Dai Jinhua*. Eds. Jing Wang and Tani Barlow. London: Verso, 2002. Dai is one of the leading voices in cultural studies of the People's Republic. This book contains essays on film, mass and consumer culture, and so forth.

Denton, Kirk A., ed. *Modern Chinese Literary Thought: Writings on Literature, 1893–1945*. Stanford: Stanford University Press, 1996. A collection of translations of writings about literature from Liang Qichao to Mao Zedong, including seminal texts by Wang Guowei, Lu Xun, Hu Shi, Chen Duxiu, Guo Moruo, Lu Xun, Liang Shiqiu, and Ding Ling. It includes a long scholarly introduction and an annotated glossary.

Goldman, Merle. *China's Intellectuals: Advise and Dissent*. Cambridge, MA: Harvard University Press, 1981. In this general book about intellectuals in China and their difficult relation with the state, Goldman argues that Chinese intellectuals have wanted to both serve the state and assert their independence.

Goldman, Merle, ed. *Modern Chinese Literature in the May Fourth Era*. Cambridge, MA: Harvard University Press, 1977. This seminal collection of essays on modern Chinese literature includes studies of Yu Dafu, Lu Xun, Ding Ling, Mao Dun, and Qu Qiubai.

Hockx, Michel, ed. *The Literary Field in Twentieth Century China*. Honolulu: University of Hawaii Press, 1999. This collection introduces a sociology of literary production to the study of modern Chinese literature, examining such topics as literary societies, love letters, literary journals, networking among writers, and so forth.

Hsia, C. T. *A History of Modern Chinese Fiction*. New York: Columbia University Press, 1971 [1961]. The first—and still useful—English language history of modern Chinese fiction, although it is heavily biased against leftist literature.

Hung, Chang-tai. *War and Popular Culture: Resistance in Modern China, 1937–1945*. Berkeley: University of California Press, 1994. This volume studies journalism, theater, posters, cartoons, etc. during the War of Resistance Against the Japanese.

Huot, Claire. *China's New Cultural Scene: A Handbook of Changes*. Durham: Duke University Press, 2000. This book provides a general overview of the radical transformations that have taken place in the literature, art, film, music, theater, and popular culture in 1990s China.

Jones, Andrew. *Like a Knife: Ideology and Genre in Chinese Popular Music.* Ithaca: Cornell East Asian Program, 1992. This first book about Chinese rock music is structured around the tension between a subversive rock 'n roll (*yaogun*) and popular state-sponsored (*tongsu*) music. It contains much on Cui Jian.

Landsberger, Stefan. *Chinese Propaganda Posters: From Revolution to Modernization.* Amsterdam: The Pepin Press, 1995. An overview, with many lavish examples, of Chinese propaganda posters, especially those of the Deng era.

Laing, Ellen Johnston. *The Winking Owl: Art in the People's Republic of China.* Berkeley: University of California Press, 1988. This good general introduction to art in the People's Republic of China emphasizes the post-Mao era.

Lee, Leo Ou-fan. *Voices from the Iron House: A Study of Lu Xun.* Bloomington: Indiana University Press, 1987. This excellent general study of Lu Xun's fiction, essays, and poetry has a detailed discussion of his relationship with the leftist culture movement of the 1930s.

———. *Shanghai Modern: The Flowering of a New Urban Culture in China, 1930–1945.* Cambridge, MA: Harvard University Press, 1999. In this two-part study of Chinese modernism, the first looks at the rise of urban culture in the 1920s and 1930s and the second presents readings of literary texts by such "modernist" writers as Mu Shiying, Liu Na'ou, Shi Zhecun, Shao Xunmei, and Ye Lingfeng.

Link, Perry. *Mandarin Ducks and Butterflies: Popular Fiction in Early Twentieth Century Chinese Cities.* Berkeley: University of California Press, 1981. In this sociological study of popular urban entertainment fiction from the 1910s to the 1940s, Link sees "butterfly" fiction as offering its urban readership solace in the face of the decline of tradition and the onslaught of modernity.

———. *The Uses of Literature: Life in the Socialist Chinese Literary System.* Princeton: Princeton University Press, 2000. In this detailed scholarly study of China's literary system, especially the early post-Mao period (1978–1981), Link focuses on the multifaceted contexts surrounding the production, dissemination, and reception of literary texts rather than the texts themselves.

McDougall, Bonnie S., and Kam Louie. *The Literature of China in the Twentieth Century.* London: Hurst and Co., 1997. The best English language "history" of modern Chinese literature, this book is at once a reference work and a narrative description of literary development through three major periods.

Sullivan, Michael. *Art and Artists of Twentieth-Century China*. Berkeley: University of California Press, 1996. This is an excellent general overview of twentieth-century art in China.

Wang, David Der-wei. *Fin-de-Siècle Splendor: Repressed Modernities of Late Qing Fiction, 1849–1911*. Stanford: Stanford University Press, 1997. Wang discovers in the fiction of the second half of the nineteenth century an "alternative" modern Chinese literature "repressed" by the hegemony of May Fourth realism and Marxist socialist realism.

Wang, Jing. *High Culture Fever: Politics, Aesthetics, and Ideology in Deng's China*. Berkeley: University of California Press, 1996. This excellent introduction to the intellectual and literary trends of the 1980s includes chapters on *River Elegy*, Wang Shuo, avant-garde fiction, the question of subjectivism, and culture fever.

Yeh, Michelle. *Modern Chinese Poetry: Theory and Practice since 1917*. New Haven: Yale University Press, 1991. The best introduction to modern Chinese poetry, including that of mainland China, Taiwan, and Hong Kong, this book takes a refreshing formalistic approach.

Zha, Jianying. *China Pop: How Soap Operas, Tabloids, and Bestsellers Are Transforming a Culture*. New York: The New Press, 1995. A breezy and personal look at popular culture in the People's Republic, this book has chapters on the television soap opera *Yearnings*, Beijing architecture, the film-makers Zhang Yimou and Chen Kaige, the erotic novel *Abandoned Capital* by Jia Pingwa, and pop music. One drawback is its Beijing-centered view.

Zhang, Yingjin, and Zhiwei Xiao, eds. *Encyclopedia of Chinese Film*. London: Routledge, 1998. This is an excellent reference for the study of Chinese film.

Websites

For an extensive bibliography of modern Chinese cultural studies, see Modern Chinese Literature and Culture [MCLC] Resource Center:
http://deall.ohio-state.edu/denton.2/biblio.htm.

Part 6

FUTURE TRENDS

Edited by Bruce Dickson

Introduction
Bruce Dickson

Now that the People's Republic of China (PRC) is more than fifty years old, what remains of the founders' goals for the country, and in what direction are the current leaders taking it? The original goals of the revolution have all been abandoned—and generally for good reason—for the sake of economic modernization. The main remnant of the communist revolution in China is the Chinese Communist Party (CCP) itself, and it prefers to focus on the promise of the future rather than its own messy record.

During the past twenty years the key policies and institutions that had defined the Maoist era were abandoned. Collective farming has been discontinued and the communes dismantled, both replaced by the return to private farming. State ownership of industry and commerce is being whittled away in favor of private entrepreneurship. The CCP is now crafting new laws to protect private property and the rights of private entrepreneurs. Ideological indoctrination has been toned down considerably; while not totally abandoned, the state's monopoly on information has been lost to the multiple sources of information now available via the Internet, satellite television, and the burgeoning media market within China. State penetration into society has been withdrawn, replaced in part by an explosion of private groups and civic organizations that have led many to announce the emergence, or reemergence, of civil society in China. While some of the old stalwarts in the Party have been disillusioned by this wholesale abandonment of the goals of the revolution, the rising standards of living and relaxed political atmosphere satisfy the vast majority of China's people.

In short, most of the hallmarks of the Communist state and its policy goals have disappeared during the past twenty years of reform. Mao's slogan "never forget class struggle" must seem hopelessly outdated to a generation responding to Deng's advice that "to get rich is glorious." It is increasingly apparent that the policies of the late Maoist era were an aberration that knocked China off the path of economic and social development it had been on for over a century before the beginning of the Communist era.

What remains of the founding moment of the PRC is, of course, the continued rule of the CCP. While Marxist and Maoist goals of class struggle and collectivism seem irrelevant in today's China, the Leninist aspirations of the CCP remain intact. Although there is a complex network of new and old organizations that link state and society, they exist at the mercy of the state. The Party initially created many of these organizations, even if some of them have taken on a life of their own and no longer are loyal agents of the state. Although policymaking has become more consultative and more incremental than under Mao, most consultation and deliberation occur among Party members. Non-Party groups have little access to decision-making arenas and little recourse if policies harm their interests. For instance, although local officials work closely with local businessmen to spur economic development, business associations are not allowed to actually shape policy and have little influence over its implementation. Despite important modifications to the policy process in the China, there is still no accountability for the state when policies go wrong or officials go bad.

Above all, the Party still zealously protects its monopoly on political organization. It persecutes those who attempt to form any group that may have political goals, whether that organization is a political party, a labor union, or a church or religious group that is not sanctioned by the state. The continued crackdowns on organizers of the Chinese Democratic Party and Falun Gong are reminders of the strict limits on groups that desire autonomy from the state in order to influence or challenge the state. Such autonomy is unacceptable to a Leninist party. The CCP resists alternate visions of politics, insisting on obedience to its leadership. It cannot claim to be infallible or to have a monopoly on virtue: it has already admitted the mistakes of the Maoist era and each day brings new revelations of corruption by its current officials. However, it does still insist that it alone is qualified to identify and correct its shortcomings. This refusal to tolerate external criticism has been a key element of the Party's history.

The Party itself has undergone tremendous changes in these past twenty years. The original generation of revolutionaries—both those reviled as "capitalist roaders" who returned to power after Mao's death and the Maoist ideologues who tormented them—have gradually died off. China is currently governed by a "third generation" of leaders, and a fourth generation is now being groomed for high office. Susan Lawrence profiles some of these leaders (reading 52).

With this generational change has come a remarkable improvement in the professional backgrounds and educational standards of new members and top officials. Roughly 90 percent of the CCP's Central Committee members now have a college education, and the Party has set an unofficial quota of having two-thirds of new recruits have at least a high school education. In addition to reaching out to China's educated elites, it is also creating links with the country's newly emerging economic elites. Many officials have left their posts and gone into business for themselves. Of greater interest are the successful businessmen the Party targets for recruitment. The CCP is actively courting the largest and most successful entrepreneurs, particularly those who convert their economic success into political influence by winning local elections. Ironically, both Party officials and entrepreneurs believe those who win village elections should join the Party if they are not already Party members. To refuse admission to the Party is to be "outside the system." Autonomy from the state may be the goal of business leaders and interest groups in the West, but it is the definition of political impotence in China.

Although there is little evidence that this new class of entrepreneurs has political ambitions or will seek to transform China's political system the way it is transforming the economic and social environments, many observers continue to look to them as a potential source of political change. As Margaret Pearson observes (reading 17), this is probably wishful thinking, but the growing ranks of entrepreneurs may prove to be "kingmakers," able to tip the balance between those who want to maintain the status quo and those who want to challenge it. It is this concern that has led the CCP to co-opt them as much as possible, turning potential opponents into allies. Whether this strategy will be effective in the long run may help determine China's political future.

Because of the continued political constraints imposed by the CCP, it does not reap the rewards of policy success. The Party has tried to rewrite the social contract in China. It is not interested in being judged according to whether it is moving the country toward the communist utopia. Instead it hopes that as long as the standards of living continue to rise, the CCP will be seen as legitimate. But while the CCP is generally accepted as the only game in town, it does not benefit from much popular support. Many question what the Party stands for, what role it plays in China's modernizing economy and society, and whether it can keep its own house in order, much less the country intact. The fear that the CCP is the only thing keeping the country together may be more important for keeping it in power than gratitude for its reform policies. It is often said the voters in democratic countries vote according to their pocketbooks: as long as the economy is good they will support the incumbents. It is unlikely that a similar logic would apply in the PRC.

The political and economic liberalization of the post-Mao era means that the state is no longer the obstacle to modernization it once was. It no longer tries to push the country along an unnatural path of economic and social development that denies the self-interested behavior of farmers, workers, managers, and entrepreneurs. This was the fundamental flaw in the Maoist logic of collectivism. The heroes of today—the successful farmers, the innovative businessmen, the former state officials and employees who have taken the plunge into the private sector—are the class enemies of the past. The state now encourages the reemergence of groups it previously persecuted into extinction. The fact that a new generation is returning to their families' traditional line of work in manufacturing, commerce, trade, or food service is one of the many ironies of the recent years. It is also a tangible reminder of the missed opportunities and wasted years of the not too distant past.

If we look at the PRC today as a single snapshot, without reference to the past, we have an image of a country with a host of economic and social problems, an unresponsive leadership, and an obsolete political system increasingly out of synch with its dynamic economy. All that is true, and yet it is not the whole story. It is only by comparing the problems of today with the even more severe problems of the past that we can have hope for China's future.

Political Stability

Although economic modernization has been the preeminent goal of the post-Mao era, China's leaders have been nervous about signs of potential unrest and instability. There are frequent reports of strikes, protests, and other demonstrations of popular dissatisfaction. Many of these have been the consequence of the state's economic policies. Many workers are being laid off from state-owned enterprises, and others often face delays getting paid because their firms are saddled with debt and cannot pay wages on time. In the countryside, funds allocated to local governments to buy grain from farmers are often diverted to construction projects or spent on cars, housing, trips, or banquets for officials, and farmers have protested being paid in IOUs instead of cash for their grain. Local officials have often confiscated property for new development projects, triggering protests demanding compensation for lost property. Local officials also often impose excessively high taxes and fees on individuals and enterprises, and these have been the cause of repeated conflicts. Protests are directed not only at local governments, but also at local privately owned and joint venture enterprises for not following official labor policies. In light of these repeated outbreaks of protest activity, Beijing has ordered local governments to be on the lookout for signs of instability and to be vigilant at maintaining order.

The relaxation of state controls over society has also allowed the reemergence of so-called "feudal" influences in many areas of China. Clan-based lineages are once again influential in many rural areas. They often enjoy wide support locally and can be involved in criminal activity, such as drugs, smuggling, or kidnapping. In some areas, they have reportedly replaced the Party as the center of power, and in others Party and government leaders are themselves clan members. The decline of the CCP at the local level has also contributed to the spread of religion, both the resumption of traditional religions, such as Buddhism, Daoism, and ancestor worship, and also to renewed interest in Christianity. Here again, the state has tried to prevent the spread of churches and similar organizations outside its control. It has closed many Buddhist monasteries and nunneries in Tibet and surrounding areas, as well as Islamic schools. The ongoing crackdown against Tibetan Buddhism and Islam reflects both the state's concern about the teaching of unsanctioned religious doctrine as well as separatist tendencies in Tibet and among the Moslem Uighurs in the western province of Xinjiang. While the state allows Protestants and Catholics to worship in officially recognized "patriotic" churches, it has closed many so-called "house churches," small congregations that are not part of the official hierarchy.

Central policy toward religious practice has varied considerably in recent years, tolerant when the overall political environment is relatively open but repressive when the state tightens its control. The attitude of local leaders is also important. Some see these trends as a threat to the state's and their own personal authority and try to clamp down. Reports of repressive measures seem to be most prominent in the interior, less developed areas, especially those with a tradition of religious-based political unrest. In the more developed coastal provinces, especially in the south, there are reports of local leaders taking more conciliatory measures. Rather than try to stop the spread of clan influence and churches, some local leaders try to forge alliances with clan and church leaders in order to preserve the peace and to implement mutually beneficial policies, especially the provision of medical and welfare services to the poor, elderly, and disabled. Some even see increased religious activity as an opportunity to make money, by renting unused office space to churches or lending money for the building of new churches. Even in the more relaxed areas, however, local leaders cannot totally ignore central directives, and restrictions against some groups can spill over to others. For instance, when the central leadership decided to crack down on Falun Gong, other religious groups also felt the heat. The

Western media and political activists often present a one-sided portrait of repressive religious policies in China, but the reality is more diverse.

One of the most important forms of political participation in China is political dissent. Those who protest missed paychecks, IOUs instead of cash, excessive taxation, and other problems do not seek a change in the government; instead most want local governments to abide by central policy. Political dissent points out the failings of the political system itself. Dissidents promoting democratic progress and respect for human rights face not only government opposition but also the skepticism of broad segments of Chinese society. Without better public opinion surveys, it is impossible to know the current beliefs of Chinese citizens, but most observers agree that fears of political chaos are quite strong. Correctly or not, many Chinese fear that the promotion of individual liberties and free speech that are the basis for international norms of human rights are not consistent with Chinese traditions and more importantly pose the risk of political instability in the here and now that threatens continued economic development. Like many authoritarian governments, China's leaders have argued there is a tradeoff between the goal of economic development and international norms of human rights, which they insist would threaten the nation's stability and slow its growth. In order to maintain stability and promote growth, they argue, dissent must be held in check. This rationale seems to resonate with many of China's citizens. Some have wondered why the Western nations, and the United States in particular, seem so interested in the fates of the few thousand political prisoners when the living standards of hundreds of millions of Chinese are improving. While there need not be such a tradeoff between human rights and stability, the debate in China often is oversimplified that way. Political dissidents in China therefore have to confront not only potential repression by the state but also deep-rooted cultural norms (for more details on the human rights issue in China, see reading 15 by Andrew Nathan).

Efforts by China's dissidents to mobilize popular support are hampered by the CCP's monopoly on political organization, which it guards zealously. For instance, there is no group like Charter 77 in Czechoslovakia or other Eastern European associations that organized the activities of and spread information among dissidents before the collapse of communism. Beginning in the summer of 1998, groups of dissidents around the country began trying to form local branches of a Chinese Democratic Party, but its leaders were quickly arrested and some sentenced to prison terms of ten to fourteen years. Repeated efforts to register this party have been repressed.

"Virtual networks" of dissidents may be spreading throughout China via the Internet. The Chinese government has tried various measures to monitor and regulate the flow of information on the Internet in China, but the versatility of the web makes this difficult, as John Pomfret describes (reading 53). It also makes it difficult for outside observers to assess the scope or efficacy of such communications. But Internet bulletin boards and chat rooms have been convenient and popular ways to criticize the government, whether its reputation for corruption or its response to the accidental bombing of the Chinese embassy in Serbia by U.S. planes in 1999. Groups like Falun Gong are also known to communicate with its widespread network of supporters via email.

The absence of organized opposition makes political protest unpredictable in China, and explosive and prone to excess when it does occur. The "rules of the game" are a bit clearer than in the late 1980s, the last period of political ferment, but the boundaries of the permissible are still shifting. Journals and publishers are always uncertain regarding how far is too far. While groups with varying degrees of autonomy do exist, such as local chambers of commerce, they have not been used a vehicles for political protest or opposition.

Maintaining Growth

After a period of rapid growth, China now faces the challenge of fighting a downturn. The economy continues to grow, but not as rapidly as before, and perhaps not fast enough to provide jobs for the people who are being laid off from the state sector or joining the labor force every year. For a regime that bases its legitimacy on its ability to promote economic modernization and boost living standards, this is a worrying sign.

Beginning in the late 1990s, the rate of growth began a slow but steady decline, from around 10 percent to close to 6 percent. The government increased spending to try to boost the growth rate. While this was partially successful, the spending was generally wasteful and inefficient, providing a one-time boost without solving the economic and financial problems that threaten the long-term health of the economy. Most people in China, especially among the leadership, understand the nature of the problem, and what needs to be done about it. Many of China's state-owned enterprises are old, inefficient, and saddled with antiquated technology, mounting debts they have no hope of repaying, and an excessive number of workers. All this makes the cost of production high. But the solution to these problems will be costly and painful to the many people who will lose their jobs and the benefits that come with them.

The state is faced with having to reform its state-owned enterprises to make them more profitable. This entails closing down many of the money-losing enterprises that are a drain on the government's resources, or at least forcing them to merge with more profitable enterprises. The reform of state-owned enterprises is also adding to China's growing unemployment problems. As China's barriers to foreign competition are also lowered through the reduction of tariffs and other restrictions on foreign companies, many of China's state-owned and even privately owned enterprises are likely to fail, adding to the employment problems. Because China does not have much of a public welfare system, people who are laid off are also cut off from medical care and do not receive unemployment insurance. The measures, designed to improve the long-term prospects of the economy by improving efficiency through increased competition, are likely in the short-run to be very painful steps. To make matters worse, growth in the private sector has also slowed. For many years the private sector has been the main source of economic growth and new jobs, but it is no longer able to absorb both the people who are leaving the state sector and the young people who are looking for their first jobs. Finding ways to provide good, high-paying jobs while promoting the efficiency and profitability of enterprises will be a major challenge for China's leaders in the years to come.

In the post-Mao era, economic growth has been the primary goal, and equity has been de-emphasized. Deng in particular was a fan of rapid growth at any cost. But he was forced to compromise with those who were more concerned about order and stability and who feared that the negative consequences of reform required a slower pace of reforms, and even a periodic rollback. Advocates of continued reform among China's current leaders, in particular Jiang Zemin and Zhu Rongji, still face these same challenges. The more orthodox or conservative leaders feel that economic equity cannot be totally abandoned, because rising resentment against the regions and individuals who are getting rich faster than others may also threaten political stability, and ultimately the legitimacy of the CCP. Despite these negative and generally unintended consequences, the benefits of reform—a more dynamic economy, rising standards of living, a flourishing cultural life, greater access to an increasing variety of goods and services, opportunities for entrepreneurship and innovation, improvements in transportation and housing, etc.—have created tremendous popular support for further economic reform.

Although incomes have generally risen, they have not risen evenly. There is a growing gap between urban and rural areas and between coastal and inland areas. This has led to a large-scale migration of people from the countryside to the cities in search of jobs. This "floating population" is estimated to number 100 million. These workers often find low-paying jobs that urban residents are unwilling to perform, such as construction, repair work, and housework for young women (see reading 30). Because they live on the outskirts of the cities and are not well connected to the established urban society, they are often blamed for rising crime and other problems. On the other hand, the conspicuous consumption of China's *nouveau riche* has created resentment among the less fortunate, be they established locals or migrant workers.

Rising income levels have combined with relaxed political controls and the collapse of both traditional Confucian and Communist value systems to let crime flourish. Social ills, such as gambling, drug use, pornography, and prostitution have reemerged after being eliminated in the early 1950s. Reports of violent crime, kidnappings, and blackmail have become common. Women in particular have encountered problems during the reform era. They receive lower wages than men for the same work, are often the first to be laid off from state-owned enterprises, and face physical and sexual harassment in the workplace. Women who migrate to urban areas for factory work or are recruited from rural villages with the promise of urban jobs are occasionally kidnapped and sold as wives to men in other rural areas. The government tries to deal with these problems, but as incomes rise, so too does the magnitude of the problems. Ironically, some people in China are nostalgic for the Maoist years when these problems were much less pronounced, even though Maoist policies brought other kinds of suffering to most Chinese.

Decentralization and its Consequences

The economic reform initiatives of the post-Mao era entailed a reduction of central control over both economic and social activity. There are two related trends at work here. First, the central government has granted more authority to local governments to manage their own affairs. This decentralization of authority contributed to the rapid growth of China's economy, but has also made the center less able to mandate and monitor the behavior of local leaders. Local leaders now control a greater share of the economic resources, and they do not have to be loyal agents of the center to be successful. The center must therefore cajole, persuade, and negotiate with local leaders to get its way. For example, there has been widespread resistance to new tax policies, new limits on unbudgeted investment, and efforts to fight local protectionism. The second type of decentralization involves the reduction of state controls over the economy and society. The emergence of markets in the post-Mao era has provided the ways and means for workers and farmers to attain the necessary goods and services for daily life. It has reduced their dependence on factory managers and Party and government officials. In short, by reducing the center's control over lower level officials and the state's control over the economy and members of society, the reform policies of the post-Mao era may have also reduced the stability of the political system itself.

Declining central authority has created concern in some observers that China is on the brink of collapse or a return to warlordism. This concern is over-blown, because there are off-setting stabilizing factors, most prominently the centuries' old tradition of a unified China and the dominance of the Han nationality in most areas of the country. Decentralized authority can also moderate the swings of political sentiment at the center, as when central leaders tried to roll back reforms in the early 1990s, but were forced to give up after encountering resistance from local governments. But decentralization of authority does contribute to fears of political instability if the center cannot coordinate and implement effective responses to recurring episodes of local protest over the economic and social changes now underway.

One consequence of weakened central authority has been the explosion of corruption among Party, government, and military leaders at all levels. The unchecked spread of corruption is a clear manifestation of the center's inability to monitor and control the behavior of provincial and local officials. At the same time, it reflects the dilemma noted by Plato long ago: Who will guard the guardians? The Party has been reluctant to create independent organs with suf-ficient authority to tackle corruption meaningfully, out of fear that such indepen-dence would threaten the Party's own authority. Although the level and scope of corruption is hard to measure accurately, media reports suggest that the number of investigations and punishments grow with every passing year. Apparently, the benefits of corruption still outweigh the risk of exposure and punishment. The institutions created to handle this problem—the Central Discipline Inspection Commission, the Ministry of Supervision, and their local offices—do not have the manpower, the resources, or the elite support needed to turn this problem around. In fact, corruption has gotten so severe that some speak nostalgically of the days of Nationalist China or the Maoist era. Such sentiments reflect how frustrated people have become with the current situation, and the situation shows no sign of improving.

At the local level, corruption has various consequences. As is often noted, corruption can be beneficial. It is grease for the wheels of an imperfect and undeveloped market, allowing enterprises to avoid market-distorting regulations and get the inputs, licenses, access to loans, transportation, and markets they need to conduct business. There is also reportedly popular support for petty corruption to provide a little extra income for underpaid local officials, as long as they promote local well-being. But corruption threatens political stability when instead of contributing to economic growth, it contributes primarily to private gain. The threat is not so much protests directed against corrupt officials, but the steady gnawing away at the legitimacy of the political system and support for it as a whole. Cases of high-level corruption, involving real estate and foreign trade deals, for instance, undermine popular support for the regime even when individual citizens are not personally damaged. Resentment against corruption contributed to popular support for the 1989 demonstrations, although by itself was not enough to trigger the protests. When the public perceives that the benefits of growth are being unfairly eaten up by unproductive and unaccountable leaders, corruption diminishes respect for authority and adds to the list of grievances against the state. This fuels the fire when protests do break out. Whether corruption leads to direct protests or simply the continued deterioration of popular support, it poses one of the major problems facing central and local governments in maintaining political order.

The Environment

Balancing needs of growth with the welfare of the environment is a dilemma that confronts all countries. In China, the emphasis on growth over the environment has been particularly stark and is starting to create domestic and international pressures for cleaner growth policies. Environmental degradation in China is extensive and severe. For instance, acid rain affects between 30 to 49 percent of China's territory. China is the second largest contributor of greenhouse gases, and within ten to twenty years it will have the dubious distinction of being number one. Particulate matter in the air in most large cities is six to ten times the international standard. Indoor air pollution is worse in the countryside than in the cities, due to use of coal and organic material for cooking and heating. As a result, rates of respiratory disease, the leading cause of death, are about 65 percent higher in rural areas than in towns and cities. More than three-quarters of river sections near cities are polluted and unfit for use as drinking water. Fifty-two of 135 urban river sections are so polluted they cannot even be used for irrigation. Between 70 to 80 percent of the shallow underground water layers are polluted, as are 30 percent of the deep layers. More than a hundred cities are seriously short of water. The water table under Beijing is so low that the city is actually sinking. China is losing land to industrialization and desertification, largely because trees have been cut down to open land for farming, industry, or other development. As a result, an estimated 178,000 people die prematurely due to respiratory diseases caused by pollution. The total cost of air and water pollution in terms of health problems, clean-up, etc. is 8 to 10 percent of GDP. In other words, environmental costs may be as large as or even exceed total economic growth.

The causes of China's environmental problems are clear. Above all, the state's emphasis on growth makes the environment of secondary importance. Rapid industrialization has created increased energy demands and resulted in untreated air and water discharge. Energy prices are kept below international prices in order to facilitate growth. This discourages more efficient use and ignores the costs of pollution associated with excess energy consumption. China's energy efficiency (GDP/energy consumption) has actually improved by 50 percent over the past twenty years, but the absolute level of consumption has also increased.

Rising standards of living have led to increased demand for interior heating, air conditioning, and electricity. Rapid growth in car ownership in China's cities—one of the most visible signs of rising standards of living—has exacerbated the problem of air pollution. A ban on leaded gas went into effect in Beijing in the late 1990s and in 2000 for the rest of the country. China's per capita energy consumption is still roughly half that of the global average, and less than one-fifth that of Japan, but the total size of China's population means that the country's aggregate energy consumption is still massive.

China's pollution problems are compounded by its reliance on coal. China has extensive coal reserves, limited supplies of natural gas and oil, and few nuclear plants. Seventy-five percent of its energy comes from coal. Sulfur content in some parts of China, such as Sichuan and Yunnan, is five times international averages. Coal is also a primary cause of airborne particulates.

So far, there has been little social pressure to protect the environment. Public opinion polls suggest that society does not see the connection between rapid growth and pollution and is primarily aware of noise and other types of pollution in their immediate vicinity. Demands for environmental awareness came at state's initiative without societal pressure via environmental interest groups. In fact, because China does not have such interest groups, and because the media does not play an independent, watchdog role in China, the state is largely free of outside pressure to deal stringently with pollution problems. And because the state's top priority has been growth, enforcement of environmental laws and standards has often been lax. This is no different from most countries: business interests normally have top priority.

But pollution is now starting to be so severe that it can no longer be justified as an acceptable cost of modernization. New environmental organizations are being allowed to form, but they have mostly an educational function, to inform people about the severity of the problem and what individuals can do to help. Foreign countries, especially the United States and Japan, are now working with China to protect its environment. They have begun providing new technology to reduce the discharge of industrial pollutants into the air and water and have signed several agreements to monitor pollution levels. China's production of greenhouse gases has actually declined, at least temporarily, although the expected increase in car ownership in the near future may lead to new increases. Many in China also argue that being selected as the site of the 2008 Olympics will lead the government to impose and enforce tougher environmental protection laws, at least around Beijing.

China's record of increased energy use and pollution is no different from that of other countries during the phase of rapid industrialization, and it has been reluctant to bear the entire cost of cleaning up its environment. It may be a major producer of greenhouse gases today, but industrialized countries created the problem originally. China argues, with some justification, that it should not be expected to slow its economic development just because it is adding to the environmental problems created by other countries. With pressures to maintain high rates of growth, China's environmental problems, with all their international implications, will likely get worse in the years to come.

Integration

China's post-Mao leaders abandoned Mao's efforts to isolate the country from international influences, which he believed were harmful to his revolutionary goals. During the past twenty years, the degree of China's integration into the global community has expanded rapidly. Foreign trade, foreign investment in China, diplomatic activity, tourism, foreign study have increased at a remarkable pace. Although China's integration into the international system has led to concerns that it may play a disruptive or even threatening role, especially in military and security matters, for the most part this integration has been mutually beneficial for both China and for the world. Michel Oksenberg,

Michael Swaine, and Daniel Lynch discuss the implications of China's future in reading 54.

Within China, the trend of increased integration has renewed the old debate about the costs and benefits of these foreign influences. How much of China's traditions can be—or should be—preserved during its drive for modernization? This is a question all countries undergoing rapid development face, and there is no easy answer. The dilemma seems particularly salient for China with its long history and proud traditions. Since the nineteenth century, a debate has raged in China regarding whether its traditions are an obstacle to economic, political, and social progress, or whether they should be preserved as a crucial link to the past and to the nation's identity. Should the solution to China's problems be found in the experiences of other countries, or does exposure to foreign ideas and ways of doing things simply compound those problems? This remains a point of often-bitter contention, especially among the leadership.

Taiwan

The most sensitive issue in China's international relations undoubtedly concerns Taiwan. Although Taiwan today is a thriving democracy with extensive economic and cultural ties with the international community, China considers Taiwan rightfully part of its territory. It is the last remaining symbol of foreign interference in China's territorial integrity at the end of the nineteenth century. Hong Kong was returned to China in 1997 after more than a century as a British colony, and Macao was returned to China in 1999 after being a Portuguese colony. Taiwan was surrendered to Japan after it defeated China in a brief war in 1895. It was returned to China after Japan's defeat in World War II, but at that time China was in the midst of a protracted civil war. The Western allies recognized the Nationalist government of Chiang Kai-shek, which was fighting the Communists. After Chiang and the Nationalists lost the civil war in 1949, they retreated to Taiwan, hoping to regroup and retake the mainland. After the outbreak of the Korean War in 1950, the United States announced it would prevent a Communist takeover of Taiwan. Both the Nationalist government on Taiwan and the PRC government on the mainland claimed to be the sole legitimate government of all China and forced other countries to have formal diplomatic ties with one or the other, but not both. Unlike the two Germanys before their unification in 1990 or the two Koreas, China and Taiwan do not allow "dual recognition." China demands that other countries accept its "one

China" principle that there is but one China and Taiwan is part of it as a precondition for diplomatic relations.

This is the origin of today's Taiwan issue. Taiwan today desires to maintain the status quo, leaving open the possibility of future unification, but China is worried about signs of "creeping independence" that would make permanent the current separation of Taiwan from the mainland. Although Taiwan now has diplomatic ties with only about thirty countries, mostly small states in Central America, the Caribbean, Africa, and the Pacific Islands, Beijing remains adamant that other countries not have political or military ties of any kind with Taiwan, and that Taiwan be excluded from most international organizations, especially those that require independent sovereignty as a condition of membership, such as the United Nations, the International Monetary Fund, and their subsidiary organizations. It harshly criticizes actions or statements in support of Taiwan as interference in China's internal affairs.

With the consolidation of Taiwan's democracy, the rising tide of Taiwanese nationalism, and above all the 2000 election as president of Chen Shui-bian of the Democratic Progressive Party, which is formally committed to Taiwan's independence, China's leaders have become increasingly anxious about the prospects for unification and impatient with the refusal of Taiwan's leaders to negotiate the terms of unification. China has repeatedly claimed it hopes for a peaceful resolution of the Taiwan issue, but has also refused to renounce the use of force as an option. In the spring of 2000, just before Taiwan's presidential election, Beijing announced three conditions under which it would use force against Taiwan: if Taiwan declared independence, if it was invaded and occupied by a foreign country, or if it refused to negotiate over an indefinite period of time. China has also been mobilizing its military forces near Taiwan, increasing the number of its ballistic missiles capable of hitting the island, and holding regular military exercises along the coast. These actions have increased tensions in the region, creating fears of a potential future international conflict.

The United States, for its part, has been reluctant to get directly involved in resolving the Taiwan issue, either as mediator in the dispute or by favoring one side over the other. Officially, the United States is committed to a "one China" policy and does not have formal diplomatic ties or a defense treaty with Taiwan. But the implicit policy of the United States has been described as "strategic ambiguity": the United States is likely to defend Taiwan if it is attacked without provocation by China, but is not likely to defend Taiwan if its government precipitates an attack by unilaterally declaring independence. Washington refuses to say whether it prefers unification or independence as the eventual outcome, but insists that the resolution of the Taiwan issue be peaceful and acceptable to the people on Taiwan. In recent years, however, U.S. strategy toward Taiwan has become less ambiguous. The Clinton administration sent two aircraft carrier groups toward the Taiwan Strait during a period of heightened tensions and Chinese military exercises in 1996. This action was intended to deter China from actually attacking Taiwan or miscalculating U.S. resolve to defend Taiwan's *de facto* independence. In the early months of his presidency, George W. Bush told a reporter that the United States would do "whatever it took" to defend Taiwan from a Chinese invasion. Whether this reflected an actual change in official policy or simply the president's own predilections, it left little doubt that the United States was committed to Taiwan's security. The Taiwan Relations Act passed by Congress in 1979 committed the United States to helping Taiwan defend itself. China is understandably bitter about this commitment and sees continued arms sales to Taiwan as the main reason that unification has not yet been accomplished. China has consistently said that the Taiwan issue remains the main obstacle to improved United States-China relations, and its actions have matched its word. With no resolution in sight, the Taiwan issue will likely remain a vexing one in China's diplomacy and a source of periodic crises in the years to come.

Prospects for Political Change

One of the key questions about China's future, and one of the goals of U.S. policy towards China, concerns the prospects for future democratization, which Martin Whyte assesses in reading 55. Many of China's political institutions are not compatible with democracy. The rule of law, as described in the "Politics" section, is not protected; the courts and even the constitution are political tools of the state and strongly influenced by the changing preferences of the leadership. They do not act as constraints on the state's own actions. The leaders are not accountable to the people, except at the grass-roots level where village elections provide some accountability. And even there, the record on the ability of village elections to provide accountability over village leaders is still spotty. There are no similar elections in the urban areas. China also lacks elites committed to democracy in numbers large enough to influence decision-making. China certainly does have leaders who favor political reform, even including democratization, but they are wary of being too open in their beliefs for fear of losing their jobs. Ironically, the leaders who were instrumental in promoting village elections were not supporters of democratization: instead, they were concerned with maintaining political order in the restive countryside. Supporters for reform had a potential window of opportunity in 1989, but were outmaneuvered by hard-liners. Obviously, the state itself is the main obstacle to democratization in China.

Economic reform, however, is bringing about changes that may increase pressures from below for democratic change. For more than two decades, China has experienced rapid growth in its national wealth. Its GNP topped $1 trillion by the late 1990s, though its per capita income remained quite low (around $750). This new wealth has been accompanied by other changes that are more intriguing. The growth of private enterprise in China has reduced state control over the economy and society, and most people are less dependent on the state than at any time since before the Communist revolution. The number of private enterprises continues to grow, and most new jobs and economic growth are created by the private sector. However, private entrepreneurs themselves do not seem interested in promoting democracy, at least not now. As in some other authoritarian countries, especially in East Asia, private entrepreneurs are partners of the state and benefit from many of its policies. They are indifferent, or even opposed, to calls for political change, a reality strikingly inconsistent with the common supposition that private enterprise generally fosters democracy.

But the growth of China's private sector may have indirect effects on potential democratization. It may, for example, give rise to a middle class and a civil society that will be more supportive of democracy. Here, too, however, the evidence thus far is limited. China's growing middle class is closely tied to the state and remains generally passive in its political behavior, another reality at variance with Western expectations. Its civil society is still undeveloped, largely because the state suppresses efforts to organize groups independent of its control. The state has pursued an authoritarian neocorporatist strategy of setting up business and trade groups to link economic and political elites. Some have hoped that these business associations will develop their own identity and stake out a more independent position and influence policy, but so far their efforts have been focused on narrow business and commercial interests, not on more fundamental political issues. Meanwhile, there are no independent trade unions that might represent the labor force in tripartite neocorporatist negotiations.

Attitudinal issues are also important. Many people—including Chinese intellectuals—have argued that Chinese political culture, with its emphasis on hierarchy and order and its lack of emphasis on individual rights and interests, is not compatible with democratic ideals. According to this perspective, only after an extensive period of economic growth, rising levels of education, increased freedom of information, and greater interaction with the outside world, will China's political culture be suitable for the establishment of democratic institutions. Literacy levels have been rising, allowing people to absorb more information, and the state is no longer able to control the flow of information as completely as it did in the past. Ironically, the new communications technologies not only allow for more diverse sources of information, the commercialization of information also allows people to avoid politics more than ever, diverting their attention to other areas of interest.

Not all aspects of this argument stand up to scrutiny, however. The success of village-level elections suggests that people can participate in government even before a democratic culture is created. The gradual democratization of Taiwan—where traditional Chinese values were even more officially encouraged than on the mainland—shows that the democratization process itself helps create democratic values. So even though those values may be necessary for democracy to survive, they may not be necessary to get the process started. One of China's best-known political dissidents and advocates of democracy, Wei Jingsheng, argues that immediate democratization is needed to ensure and protect the other benefits of modernization (reading 56).

Roughly 92 percent of China's population belongs to the Han nationality. However, minority groups, though few in number, occupy strategically important areas of the country. The largest such areas are Tibet, the Buddhist nation that was forcibly annexed in 1951; the western province of Xinjiang, whose native Muslim population is now outnumbered by Han Chinese following the state's policy of in-migration, and inner Mongolia. The periodic activity of independence movements in these areas has provided the Chinese government with a rationale to keep them under control. It denies them autonomy and cracks down on political restiveness, at times quite severely. Thus China's ethnic and religious heterogeneity works against democratization.

The international environment is an ambiguous factor. Clearly, many countries, including the United States, would like to encourage China's democratization. But the very willingness to initiate political change makes the international environment seem threatening to China's leaders. They recognize that foreign governments would prefer that China not remain communist, a direct threat to their hold on power. They see the foreign promotion of "peaceful evolution" toward liberal democracy and a market-based economy as an attempt to undermine their political system.

These attitudes cannot help but create difficult choices for the world's democracies in their policies towards China. The debate in the United States on approving China's admission into the World Trade Organization is a case in point. The Clinton administration, adopting a policy of "engagement," approved its entry into the WTO in 1999 in hopes that integrating China more fully into the global trading order will promote its democratization over the coming years. Critics of this strategy opposed bringing China into the WTO or granting it other benefits until it democratized or, at the very least, ceased flagrant human rights abuses such as the exploitation of labor. Though the opposing positions may differ as to the *means* of promoting democracy in China, both favor democracy as the ultimate goal. Both sides are motivated not only by concerns about the civil rights of China's vast population; many advocates of democratization also believe that a democratic China will be a peaceful China. The Communist government's current efforts to strengthen its nuclear arsenal and its occasionally bellicose statements regarding Taiwan provide continuing cause for concern about its military intentions in the Pacific region.

The PRC's leaders are suspicious of foreign motives and critical of efforts to meddle in their internal affairs. Mistrust of foreigners has deep historical roots in China, and any attempt by outside powers to manipulate the Chinese people or its government invariably strikes a raw nerve, evoking bitter memories of past exploitation. China's pride was fully evident during the celebrations in July 1997 that greeted its assumption of sovereignty over Hong Kong, which reverted to the PRC upon the expiration of Britain's 99-year "lease." But Chinese sensitivities were also on view during the Kosovo conflict in 1999 when U.S. warplanes hit the PRC's embassy during a bombing run over Belgrade. Washington quickly apologized for the incident, insisting it was an accident. In Beijing, thousands of angry protestors surrounded the U.S. embassy for weeks, chanting anti-NATO slogans; relations between the two governments remained chilly for several months. As a general rule, the Communist authorities have tried as much as possible to suppress foreign influences regarding democracy and political change. Thus far, efforts to promote democratization from the outside have in fact had the opposite of their intended effect.

Perhaps the most striking phenomenon thus far with regard to democratization is the failure of economic growth and the emergence of a large private sector to stimulate more intense pressures for political change. Nevertheless, as the spontaneous student demonstrations of 1989's "Democracy Spring" showed, events can take a sudden turn. Hopes for democracy may still lie just beneath the currently placid surface of Chinese society. The events of 1989 also showed, however, that if democracy is to take hold, it must have the support of key elites, both in the government and in society. So far, China lacks sufficient numbers of those kinds of elites.

Final Thoughts

As China enters the twenty-first century, many of the most important issues it faced at the beginning of the twentieth century are still unresolved. Is the West the cause of China's problems, or part of their solution? Which Chinese traditions and values are appropriate for the modern world? Is democracy suitable to China, given its traditions, distinctive characteristics, and current level of economic and social development? These questions are fundamental ones, and no definitive answer may be possible any time soon. Nor are these questions unique to China: many developing countries face the same dilemmas. Given China's size and potential for future development, however, the way China answers these questions is likely to affect not only its future, but the future of its neighbors and perhaps even the international community of nations as a whole. For that reason, China's future is worth watching.

At first glance, China seems exotic, difficult to understand, and an exception to many theories developed on the basis of the experience of Western countries. Indeed, China prefers to portray itself as exceptional and argues that conventional theories cannot capture its complexities. But it is only by comparing and contrasting contemporary China with its own past and with other countries that we gain a clearer understanding of what is truly distinctive and what fits more general patterns of behavior. All countries are unique to some extent, and China no more so than many others. Its ultimate fate will surely tell us a great deal about democracy's potential as a universally applicable system of government, about the proper balance between market forces and state regulation in promoting economic development, and about the capacity of societies to change their political order. For centuries, China has captured the imagination of scholars and policymakers, and it continues to do so today.

FUTURE TRENDS
Readings

52

The New Guard: Five Younger Officials Make Their Way to the Top

SUSAN V. LAWRENCE

The future of China will largely depend on its top leaders. Their priorities, reputations, and ability to get local officials and society at large to support their policies will shape the course of future events. In this article, journalist Susan Lawrence profiles five men who are widely expected to emerge as top leaders in the years ahead.

Chinese officials have long bridled at the Western media's cynical sobriquet for their country's leadership: a "gerontocracy." It was a label prompted by the large number of elderly Red Army veterans who wielded power and influence, even after their official retirement from party and government posts. Typifying the gerontocracy was Deng Xiaoping who was treated as China's highest leader until his death [in 1997] at 92, even when his only official titles were honorary chairman of the obscure Soong Ching Ling Foundation and most-honorary president of the association for his favourite card game, bridge.

But as the '90s [wore] on, many of the veterans . . . died and the Chinese leadership has grown younger—and, party propagandists say, more vigorous. At the vanguard of the group of up-and-coming leaders is Hu Jintao, who joined the Communist Party's most senior body, the seven-man politburo Standing Committee, at the relatively tender age of 49 in 1992. Today, of the 22 men on the full politburo, five are younger than 60. These 50-somethings could remain major figures on the political scene for a decade or more to come. In the past year, several have taken on some of the party's most challenging portfolios. All are worth watching.

These new leaders are united in their commitment to ensuring the primacy of the Communist Party and to implementing market-oriented economic reform. Trained as engineers (or, in one case, as a geologist), they have reputations as good managers and operate primarily as party bureaucrats. Only one, the new party boss of Guangdong Province, has displayed anything approaching populist

569

flair. Although older party ideologues have warned that this generation could throw up a Chinese Gorbachev—someone who opens up the political system and in the process brings down the Communist Party—none of these rising stars shows signs of being a radical political reformer.

The up-and-comer who has risen highest is Hu, now 55. In addition to his post on the politburo Standing Committee, where his brief is party affairs, Hu was appointed vice-president of the People's Republic of China in March. He may take over as party general secretary when Jiang Zemin completes his second term in that position in 2002.

Trained in hydroelectric engineering at the prestigious Qinghua University, Hu rose to national prominence through the ranks of the Communist Youth League, first in the poor and remote northwestern province of Gansu, where he was sent to do labour during the political campaigns of the Cultural Revolution, and then in Beijing. He later did two stints as a party chief in the regions, first running poor Guizhou Province in central-south China, then fractious Tibet. Cynics in Beijing see those postings as resume-padding exercises. Hu was in Guizhou for just two years. And while the Tibet job lasted four years, he never got used to the altitude and climate on "the roof of the world," as Tibet likes to call itself; he spent much of his time in Beijing.

Looking toward the hurly-burly of any leadership succession struggle, some observers see gaps in the mild-mannered Hu's preparation. He hasn't handled economic portfolios and he has had few opportunities to build up a strong power base. As president of the Central Party School since 1993, he has met thousands of senior party cadres from across the bureaucracy and the country who have attended training courses at the school. But he can't necessarily count on their loyalty or support. And while Hu sits on a party Central Committee body in charge of personnel assignments, he doesn't head it.

Some observers also suggest that Hu's Tibet tenure might be a handicap in building relationships with foreign leaders—China's security forces crushed demonstrations there while he was in charge.

Although Hu is the only one of these younger leaders on the politburo Standing Committee, he's no longer the only one on the political horizon. The 15th party congress in September 1997 installed on the politburo three other leaders born in the 1940s. (A fourth was already a member.) Arguably the brightest of the five younger leaders is Li Changchun, 54, the party boss of wealthy Guangdong, the province that borders Hong Kong.

Li, an electrical engineer, spent most of his first five decades in the northeastern province of Liaoning, climbing the local Communist Party ladder.

He served as mayor and then party chief of Liaoning's capital city of Shen-yang—a centre for heavy industry—and later as governor and deputy party chief of the province. Along the way, Li oversaw a number of popular projects. The best known is the expressway linking Shenyang and the Liaoning port of Dalian. The first expressway in all of China, it boosted not only the Liaoning economy, but also the economies of neighbouring provinces.

Li was reportedly reluctant to leave Liaoning, but party leaders in Beijing had bigger plans for him. In 1990, they dispatched him to run Henan, a mid-ranking agricultural province in the centre of the country with very different economic needs than coastal Liaoning.

In [1998] the party leadership threw Li a new challenge: Bring wealthy and wayward Guangdong, where market-oriented economic reform started 20 years ago, back firmly under the control of Beijing. In a speech quoted in Guang-dong papers on September 8, Li said that in recent years leaders in the province had run into trouble because they relied too much on experience to guide their actions, and too little on "theory." Some cadres, he said, have cynically "even passed off their own incorrect understanding as the original intention and important spirit of Deng Xiaoping theory." The speech made frequent reference to Guangdong being "under the leadership of the party centre with comrade Jiang Zemin at its core" and in it Li pledged that Guangdong would "comprehensively carry out every task given at the 15th party congress."

Party appointees before Li have tried to rein in free-wheeling Guangdong, and failed. While top posts in Shanghai are a sure route to power in Beijing, cadres assigned to Guangdong have often seen their once-promising national careers founder. Li is shaking things up at all levels of Guangdong government, but it's too early to tell how successful he will be. If he manages to bring the province to heel, Li will be a strong candidate to succeed Premier Zhu Rongji in 2003.

China's other young star these days, Wen Jiabao, 56, isn't new to leader-ship circles, but has recently risen to new heights and taken on what may be the most diverse and demanding set of portfolios of any top party leader.

Wen first entered Zhongnanhai, the Chinese leadership compound, in 1985 as deputy director of the party's Central Committee General Office. He was, in effect, deputy chief of staff for then party chief Hu Yaobang. Hu was purged in early 1987, the first of Deng's chosen successors to fall. But, in what is widely seen as testament to his unobtrusive geniality and general air of competence, Wen kept his job, and was even promoted. He ran the General Office through the two-year tenure of Hu's successor, Zhao Ziyang. Then, when Zhao was also purged in 1989, Wen stayed on in the post for another three years, serving Jiang.

In [1998] Wen became both a politburo member and a vice-premier. A geologist, Wen oversees a raft of big issues including agriculture, poverty relief, forestry and water resources. In summer 1998, as the Yangtze, Nen and Songhua rivers burst their banks, Wen became a familiar face on evening television news broadcasts in his role as "commander-in-chief" of the flood-relief effort. Also during this period, Zhu named Wen to head the party's new Central Work Commission on Finance. In that position, Wen is leading a critically important overhaul and recapitalization of China's troubled banks, working to clean up and stabilize the country's volatile securities markets, and supervising a far-reaching reorganization of the Ministry of Finance.

Wen's plate has been piled so high because "he has a very good track record as a manager," says a Western economist in Beijing. "He is collegial. He works well with people. He has a good grasp of the overall situation." Indeed, Jiang appears to have a special trust in Wen. The Chinese leader's constant travelling partner on trips outside Beijing is his chief of staff, Zeng Qinghong, 59—but Wen often goes along too.

When the party established the Work Commission on Finance, it set up a parallel body to oversee state-enterprise reform and appointed Wu Bangguo, 57, to head it. While Wen has won high marks for his work in the financial sector, foreign observers have been less impressed with Wu's stewardship of state-enterprise reform. "It is a nightmare," says the Western economist in Beijing, "he is not in control." The economist concedes, though, that state-enterprise reform would be "a huge nightmare for anyone." Wu has been at his most ineffectual in attempting to mediate disputes among the many industrial fiefdoms that see their interests threatened by the reform programme.

Wu, a former Shanghai party chief, studied radio electronics at Qinghua University, and later worked for a dozen years in the Shanghai No. 3 Electronic Tube Factory. As a deputy party chief of Shanghai from 1985 to 1991, he served for a period under then party chief Jiang, and alongside, and then under, Zhu, who took over as party chief from Jiang. For Jiang and Zhu, Wu is thus a familiar colleague whom they know to be loyal.

The fifth rising leader on the politburo is Jia Qinglin, 58, who also serves as mayor and party boss of Beijing. The least dynamic of the five, Jia, too, is a Jiang loyalist. An electrical engineer, he spent his early career at the First Ministry of Machine-Building Industry. Jiang worked at the ministry during the same period. Most recently, Jia was party chief of coastal Fujian Province, across the strait from Taiwan.

Jia was named Beijing mayor in February [1997] and took over as party boss in the following August. He has announced plans to spend $14.5 billion on infrastructure projects in the city before the 50th anniversary of the founding of the People's Republic on October 1, 1999. Projects include a subway extension, bringing natural gas into Beijing by pipeline from China's northwest, and expanding the city's airport. He also plans to develop between 10 and 15 hi-tech industry groups in fields such as electronic information, biotechnology and new medicines.

But there's no guarantee any of China's middle-aged turks will remain at the highest levels of leadership. The lessons of the 1980s still apply: High office doesn't mean a secure future, and aggressive politicking can still make or break careers. Moreover, any large discontinuity in Chinese politics has a habit of throwing up new and surprising faces as candidates for leadership. When the Chinese military crushed pro-democracy demonstrations in 1989, leaders in the capital reached for someone untainted by the bloodbath in Beijing and settled on the then party secretary of Shanghai, 63-year-old Jiang. Although he had been a politburo member since the age of 61, he had never been identified as a possible candidate for China's top job.

53

Chinese Web Opens Portals to New Way of Life

JOHN POMFRET

What impact is the Internet having on China? Much attention has been focused on its potential for promoting political dissidence and organizing opposition activities. But for most Chinese, the Internet has more mundane purposes: finding new jobs, meeting new people, and buying new things. Nevertheless, even at this level, the Internet is transforming China, breaking down barriers that formerly existed. But it is also dividing China into discrete groups of haves and have-nots, just as economic modernization is increasing income gaps more generally. The government is ambivalent about the Internet, intrigued by its benefits for commerce, trade, and scientific exchange, but wary of its potential for creating political and social unrest.

NANJING, China—Wang Siping is not your average Chinese "Web worm." For starters, she's a woman and from Qinghai Province, one of the poorest regions in China. But the 25-year-old former soldier and bar hostess, who never attended high school, shares a common characteristic with many of China's Internet enthusiasts: She wants a new life.

"It's new and it's fun and it got me out of Qinghai," she said.

The search for a man brought Wang to the Web. She posted her face on a Chinese personals Web site and met a Hong Kong businessman who moved her to the leafy southern metropolis of Nanjing, where she now works in his company as a secretary.

"If it wasn't for the Web, I'd still be back in the desert," she said with a laugh.

Wang's story is emblematic of a quiet revolution in China being driven by the Internet. From children's books to online dating services to chat rooms in which almost anything goes, from pricing information for apple farmers to the latest tips about bars, brothels and billiards, the Internet is transforming lives across the country.

While Westerners may be focused on the Internet's potential to roil Chinese politics, its most profound effect has been to promote broader changes in the way people think, grow up and buy things in the world's most populous country.

The Internet start-up boom has become a magnet to draw Chinese students educated in the United States back to China, a homecoming of potentially great social, economic, and political significance considering that only an estimated 3 percent of the 300,000 students who have left China since the late 1970s have returned.

It is connecting parts of China that, because of geography and history, have never really been united, a development as meaningful as the campaign that has laid more than 150,000 miles of road in China in the past six years. And it's happening at an incredible pace: Internet use has jumped from an estimated 620,000 Chinese in October 1997, the first time it was measured by the government, to 8.9 million people during the most recent survey [in January 2000].

The government's view of the Internet has been deeply ambivalent. While encouraging foreign technology investments—and attempting to reap profits from them—Beijing [in January 2000] banned discussion of "state secrets" on the Internet in the latest attempt to harness a medium that is fast spinning out of the Communist Party's control. A party circular also said that all Internet content and service providers based in China must undergo a "security certification" process.

While the Internet is bringing people together in China, as it is worldwide, it is also pulling them apart and escalating the country's split into haves and have-nots. So far, about 80 percent of China's "Web worms" are centered around China's richest cities, and almost 80 percent are educated and male.

Wang Siping illustrates the split in Chinese society. In November, she competed in the Miss Internet China beauty pageant after beating out only six other contestants from Qinghai. By contrast, hundreds of women competed to represent the cities of Beijing, Shanghai, Guangzhou, and Hangzhou.

"Where I come from, the only net people know about is a tennis net," Wang said, "and that's only because people watch TV." Qinghai accounts for only 0.08 percent of China's Internet users.

"The Internet has created a new man and a new society in China," said Li Xiguang, the director of the Center for International Communications Studies at Beijing's prestigious Tsinghua University. "With the explosion in the number of Internet users, a new species of human being has come into being in China."

The American Influence

"Awesome!"

Joseph Chen, Nick Yang and Zhou Yunfan use the word nonstop, with varying fluency. They meet a fellow graduate of Stanford University: "Awesome!" They discuss the potential of the Internet in China: "Awesome!" They confide their feelings about returning home to help build a young industry: "Awesome!"

Chen, 30, Yang, 25, and Zhou, 25, met at Stanford. Backed by several million dollars from American investors, they started Chinaren.com last year—an Internet "portal" that hopes to bring what Chen calls an "e-lifestyle" to China.

China's Internet revolution has an American look, taste and feel. Internet entrepreneurs spice their Chinese with American computer lingo. After a Chinese box lunch, they repair to one of Beijing's five Starbucks outlets for a java infusion. Although the state tries to block access to many foreign sites, including washingtonpost.com, Internet users share ways of getting around the restrictions. Many Chinese Web sites are modeled after American successes. And China's Internet dreams are powered almost solely by American investment—an estimated $200 million so far from firms including GWcom Inc., Citigroup Inc., Intel Corp., Yahoo! Inc., Dell Computer Corp., Dow Jones & Co. and IDG Books Worldwide Inc.

"The Beijing minute is faster than the New York minute right now," said Chris Mumford, a former New York investment banker who co-founded an Internet start-up, Yaolan, which plans to sell baby-care products throughout China. "If you leave here for a month, you always notice something new. The environment is constantly changing."

In an economic system in which promotions and success are traditionally tied not to ability but to seniority, the youth of China's Internet entrepreneurs is another reflection of their American models. The oldest employee at eLong.com and Chinaren.com, two Chinese start-ups, is 35.

Even fashion mimics the laid-back look of Silicon Valley. Charles Zhang, who returned to China with a Ph.D. from MIT to start Sohu.com, a popular portal, favors Nikes and bluejeans over business suits. Zhang, thanks to relentless publicity, has become something of a sensation in China.

"Are you a Ping-Pong star? An athlete?" gushed a waitress at a British-style pub a few blocks from Zhang's Beijing office one recent night. "No," Zhang replied, "I'm on the Web."

Beijing Is Watching

But freewheeling Web culture goes only so far in China. Police have installed monitoring equipment on all of China's major sites. Shanghai authorities last week shut down 127 unregistered Internet cafes, and a few Chinese have been arrested for posting politically sensitive material on the Web. And all Chinese Internet portals employ people to weed out politically incendiary statements from China's raucous Internet chat rooms.

China's economic policymakers also have tried to limit foreign participation in Web ventures. In 1999 they tried to stop foreign investors from buying pieces of China's Internet industry, but that effort failed. Now, foreigners can own up to 50 percent of China's Internet firms. In the latest twist, Beijing announced that private Chinese Internet firms will need government approval to list their shares overseas. But that battle isn't over yet.

China's Internet entrepreneurs have tried to accommodate the government without scuttling the appeal of the Web. Chen, the co-founder of Chinaren.com, is developing a special software to monitor its chat rooms automatically—weeding out buzzwords that could offend the country's leadership.

"We think our self-censorship should be up to government standards," said Chen, who is an American citizen. "We want to be cool and patriotic—at the same time."

Even so, the talk on the Web is some of the freest in China. Many Chinese know about the $10 billion smuggling scandal unfolding in the southern city of Xiamen, for example, because they read about it on the Web; Chinese papers have been banned from reporting about it. The need for political reform is a common topic in Chinese chat rooms but so are demands that China stand up to the United States.

Some liberal Chinese aren't comfortable with the polemics churned out in various chat rooms. Since NATO's bombing of the Chinese Embassy in Belgrade on May 7 [1999], much of the chat has taken on a strong nationalist bent. A campaign launched on the Web blasted President Jiang Zemin for not reacting more strongly to NATO's attack.

Wang Xiaodong, a writer and self-described nationalist, thinks China's liberals are foolish to be concerned. "The thing you see on the Web is the real face of China," he said, referring to the mix of jingoism and democracy.

But many Chinese welcome the cacophony of Chinese sites.

"The Internet will affect China more deeply than other societies because China is a closed society and the Internet is an open technology. It will force

China to open more," said Guo Liang, a researcher at the Chinese Academy of Social Sciences and one of the premier writers on the Internet in China today. "In 1989, I was in Tianamnen Square. We failed then. The Internet won't fail."

In some ways, Chinese Internet companies play fast and loose with rules that in the United States are taken more seriously. 8848.net, for example, is marketing itself as China's foremost e-commerce site and claims $1.4 million in sales a month. But Chinese sources said the firm inflated its e-commerce figures by getting businesses to "route" purchases through the site, even though the goods were bought or sold by traditional means. "Their real figures were much lower," said a Chinese investment banker. Company officials did not respond to numerous telephone messages asking for comment.

Still, e-commerce is growing in China. Turnover jumped 400 percent last year—from $8 million in 1998 to more than $40 million, according to government figures.

Overseas, the Internet has sparked an enthusiasm for the China market reminiscent of turn-of-the-century traders who dreamed of selling every Chinese an American toothbrush. Chinese call American venture capitalists "crazy" capitalists for their enthusiasm for almost any Chinese firm.

John Harris, the chief executive officer of CBQ Inc., a Texas-based e-commerce firm, recently put down $150 million to buy a Chinese software company and then invested an additional $15 million for an Internet service provider.

"It's coming in a wave that's as tall as this hotel," he said, speaking in the tony confines of the 16-story Beijing International Club Hotel. "If you're not ready, you're dead."

An example of the power of China's Internet buzz is Etang.com, a Boston-based e-commerce firm started by a native of Shanghai who got an MBA from Harvard. In less than six months the firm has raised $43 million even though its chief executive officer, Tang Haisong, doesn't know what it wants to sell.

"We're working on that," he said.

54

The Chinese Future

MICHEL OKSENBERG, MICHAEL D. SWAIN, and
DANIEL LYNCH

*In this wide-ranging article, the authors survey recent developments in China
and the potential for the future. They look at ongoing political changes within
the Chinese state, the politics of selecting the next generation of leaders, social
changes, challenges to continued economic growth (including issues of the
environment, energy, and education), the rise of nationalism, military modernization, and China's integration into the world. They address two central questions:
will China remain politically stable, or will devolve into chaos and disunity? And
will China's rise pose an economic and military threat to its neighbors?*

China's leaders are preoccupied with a daunting list of domestic concerns and
issues, many of which arise from the sheer size and complexity of their country.
National security and foreign policy concerns are subordinated to these domestic
issues; indeed, foreign policy choices are evaluated primarily in terms of their
domestic implications.

Consider these basic imperatives in the governance of China:

- The leaders of China cannot take the unity of their country for granted.
The huge nation is geographically and culturally diverse, and disunity and
civil war have plagued China through much of its history.

- Never in history has a single government attempted to rule so many people
within a single political system. China consists of 31 provinces, 160
prefectures, 2,500 counties and cities, nearly 100,000 townships and urban
wards, and over a million rural villages. Seven layers of government separate
the rulers at the top from the populace. Bureaucracy is inevitably enormous
in such a vast setting, and the loss of information is considerable as data
passes through the several layers of government.

- The leaders of China must ultimately bear responsibility for feeding nearly
five times the population of the United States on roughly 60 percent of

America's cultivated acreage. And the population is growing, though at substantially slower rates than many other developing countries. Fifteen million additional laborers enter the urban and rural workforce annually. Since 1972 and Nixon's opening to China, the country's population has increased by over 400 million people—more than the entire population of North America, or South America, or Africa south of the Sahara, or the Middle East, or the former Soviet bloc. As this number was absorbed into the economy, the absolute number of people living in poverty fell dramatically and employment opportunities for rural dwellers expanded rapidly.

• The leaders must respond to rising expectations for an improved standard of living, greater geographic and social mobility, and increased opportunity to participate in the decisions that affect peoples' lives. Meanwhile, income disparities are increasing both within and among regions in China, as some benefit more swiftly from the country's growing involvement in the international economy than others.

• Severe environmental problems press upon the populace. Water and air pollution, soil erosion, and inadequate water supply north of the Yangzi are beginning to pose serious health problems and to constrain growth rates.

• Additional problems are posed by an aging population, by the need to import technology, equipment, petroleum, and agricultural commodities in order to sustain high growth rates and meet popular aspirations, and by the inefficiencies resulting from the many legacies of the previous command, state-controlled and -planned economic system.

• The leaders of China deserve empathy and some respect as they attempt to cope with this complex agenda. Both their accomplishments and deficiencies merit acknowledgement.

Political Change

Conventional wisdom holds that during the Deng Xiaoping era (1978–1997) China reformed economically but not politically. Foreign observers frequently contrast Deng's approach to reform with the Gorbachev-Yeltsin model, which gave pride of place to political reform over economic reform. This "wisdom" is actually incorrect. In fact, China's political system today differs considerably from that of the late Mao era. To be sure, the rate of political change is slower than the rate of economic change, and the instruments of totalitarian control—the public security apparatus, labor camps, severe limits on the freedom of assembly—remain in place, ready to be activated in case of need.

Indeed, since the brutal suppression of the spring 1989 demonstrations, a whole new apparatus of internal control—the People's Armed Police—has been expanded to quell domestic unrest.

Nonetheless, the change is significant. People are no longer mobilized in an endless series of political campaigns. They need not affirm their adherence to Maoist ideological precepts on a daily basis. They enjoy the right of geographic and occupational mobility—freedoms denied in the Mao era. Individuals can withdraw from political life and pursue private interests—as long as these do not challenge the right of the leaders to rule.

Perhaps even more significant has been the enormous extent of administrative decentralization. Previously, the entire nation had to respond to the dictates of a single individual: Mao Zedong. He literally set the national agenda. And, on most issues, the lower levels of government responded with alacrity to Beijing's commands. Indeed, many of the nation's key industries were directly controlled by ministries in Beijing—even if they were located in far off Guangdong or Sichuan provinces.

Today, all that has changed. Authority is dispersed. Provinces, counties, and even townships control significant portions of government revenue. Personnel appointments now reside in the main either within the administrative level or one level above; in the past, all key appointments were made two levels above. Almost every Party, government, or military unit runs its own enterprises and has its own sources of income. Agencies at every level have a sense of entitlement to their revenue, the land under their control, and even the activities for which they are responsible. Authority is fragmented.

This means higher levels have a tough time getting lower levels to obey their orders. Higher levels cajole, bargain, and entice lower levels to obey the directives that emanate from above. Admittedly, some hierarchies—such as the public security system—are more centralized than others. And the top leaders unquestionably retain the capacity to direct lower levels to achieve a limited number of objectives (such as the implementation of the family planning program). But in other areas—for example, collecting central government revenue—higher-level leaders must exert great effort to secure the compliance they seek. The system is not as efficient and disciplined as communist countries are often imagined to be.

Succession Politics

China's leaders are in the midst of succession politics. Jiang Zemin, who heads a collective leadership, made significant strides at the September, 1997 Fifteenth Party Congress to become China's paramount leader, but he continues to face many challenges and obstacles in his quest for pre-eminence. In any case, he is unlikely to emerge with the power that Deng Xiaoping possessed, just as Deng did not enjoy the power Mao held.

Since Deng Xiaoping's death in February, 1997 and indeed before, Jiang's strategy has encompassed four dimensions:

- To cultivate support in the military;

- To place loyal subordinates in key positions throughout the government and Party bureaucracies;

- To enunciate a vision or the direction he intends to lead the country that is relevant to the Chinese condition and mobilizes support both within the Party and among the populace more generally

- To demonstrate an ability to shape and move a consensus effectively and to reveal, therefore, that he can energize the authoritarian system to his advantage.

As Chairman of the Military Affairs Commission, Jiang at least nominally presides over the military. He presumably has been involved in the massive changes in command positions of the last few years, thereby generating some sense of obligation toward him among the younger and more professional officer corps. The military has also enjoyed rapid increases in its budget in the past five years, and its voice in the conduct of foreign policy has also increased. Two of its leaders—Minister of Defense Chi Haotian and Vice Chairman of the Military Affairs Commission Zhang Wannian—are on the new Politburo. While it is unclear whether these developments result more from Jiang's efforts to win support within the military or reflect the military's ability to extract rewards from him, the net result seems to be that Jiang has made progress in mastering this key dimension of power in Chinese politics. Perhaps as a result, no PLA general was promoted to the Standing Committee of the Politburo. At the same time, the PLA retains its presence on the important Politburo and Secretariat, giving it veto power on critical issues relating to its primary responsibilities. . . .

Since coming to Beijing from Shanghai in June, 1989 and being designated as the leader of the Party "core" under Deng's tutelage, Jiang has promoted numerous officials who previously served either under him in Shanghai or with him in the several economic ministries where he worked from the 1950's through the early 1980's. Indeed, Jiang allegedly has been criticized for promoting too many of his Shanghai group at the cost of having a geographically representative set of leaders on the Politburo.

Jiang remedied this situation at the [1997] Party congress by broadening the provincial representation on the Politburo. Moreover, he engineered significant personnel changes at the Party congress. One of his potential rivals for supremacy, Qiao Shi, lost his position on the Standing Committee, Politburo, and Central Committee. [Soon after, Qiao also lost his post] as Chairman of the National People's Congress (NPC) Standing Committee when that body [met] in spring of 1998. Qiao had used that position to expand the role of the NPC and to argue that the NPC—not the CCP—was, the supreme organization of state. Jiang also . . . prepared the ground for additional changes: the transfer of Li Peng from the premiership to the NPC Standing Committee chairmanship and the selection of Zhu Rongji as China's next premier. The new Politburo contains few people who can be easily identified as "liberals" or "hard line ideologues." The over-all cast of China's top twenty-five to thirty-five leaders now seems to be cautious, pragmatic, centrist in the Chinese political spectrum. The new Politburo members include trained engineers with long careers in the provinces and economic bureaucracies.

Perhaps more noteworthy are the massive changes in the Central Committee, where a wholesale retirement of older officials occurred in favor of younger, better educated bureaucrats. The political significance of this change will become evident in one to three years, as the newcomers begin to influence policy through their semi-annual conclaves and as the top leaders have to elicit support from them. This group, ranging in age from 45 to 55, seems somewhat bolder, more attuned to the outside world, and more eager to undertake political and economic reform than their elders.

Although Jiang made considerable progress on the personnel front, his vision for the Chinese future remains vague. At the Party congress, he did set a national goal of more than doubling the gross national product by the year 2010, a further improvement in the subsequent decade so that the people will enjoy an "even more comfortable life," and by the mid-21st century, "China will have become a prosperous, strong, democratic, and culturally advanced socialist country." But he gave little specificity to these terms, especially what he meant by "democratic" or "culturally advanced."

As he himself stresses, Jiang continues to cling tenaciously to the vision of Deng Xiaoping: China's overwhelming task is economic development; economic reform and opening to the outside world are necessary for that objective; so too is political stability, although some political restructuring is necessary to make the system more honest, efficient, and responsive to the needs of the people.

Jiang envisions Marxist-Leninist ideology to be a flexible doctrine that permits a wide range of practices (such as public ownership of formerly state owned corporations through sale of stocks). But one aspect of the system must be preserved at all costs: the supremacy of the Chinese Communist Party. Although a China under the rule of law is part of Jiang's articulated vision, he thus far has provided little indication that he understands what this slogan really means. The notion that the Communist Party and its leaders should be subordinate to the law and to an independent judiciary that enforces it is still alien to his thought. As a result, Jiang does not repeat a slogan that his predecessor Zhao Ziyang enunciated at the Thirteenth Party Congress in 1987: "Separate the Party from the government." Jiang advocates an integrated Party-government apparatus, with the army an instrument of the Party charged with helping the Party to remain in power. Even when speaking of the reformed enterprises, he advocates that their Party organizations be their "political nuclei."

This vision may appeal to the Party faithful, but it is unlikely to galvanize the nation. Indeed, Jiang's own assessment of China's current political situation merits repeating:

> The work style of the Party and the government, current social behavior, and public order still fall short of the expectations of the people; corruption, extravagance, and waste and other undesirable phenomena are still spreading and growing; and bureaucratic style of work, formalism, and deception constitute serious problems.

Jiang's appraisal also appropriately notes the many positive aspects of the current scene, but his relative lack of attention to the means for remedying this harshly-appraised political situation is noteworthy.

The conclusion of the Fifteenth Party Congress means that the fourth aspect of Jiang's strategy—demonstrating his ability to shape and move a consensus—is now at the forefront. Jiang has announced the agenda for the coming two to three years against which his own performance can be measured—namely a concerted attack upon the inefficient state owned enterprises. The reasons for assigning priority to this task are outlined below.

Jiang's call has been preceded by numerous experiments in transforming the ownership and management systems of these firms, and in some areas of the country, the reforms are well underway. But many problems predictably will arise in the course of these reforms—rising urban unemployment, the need to install effective capital markets, the need for transparency and strengthened regulatory, capabilities.

If the process goes smoothly, Jiang can claim the credit, as Deng did with agricultural reform even though much of the initiative for those reforms was attributable to local leaders. But if the transformation stalls with a banking crisis or is accompanied by increasing corruption and social disorder, Jiang and the leaders he has gathered to assist him—especially Li Peng and Zhu Rongji—will be in a difficult position. In this sense, Jiang's quest to become China's paramount leader and to place China irreversibly on the course of sound, well regulated economic growth has just begun. Whether he can do this without embarking on major political reform remains open to question, as does the success of this new stage in China's economic reform.

Contradictory Social Trends

Chinese society today is characterized by a bewildering array of contradictions. Its people exist in a spiritual vacuum and succumb to crass materialism, but simultaneously demonstrate a growing interest in Buddhism, Christianity, and Daoism. They both yearn for an involvement with the outside world and are repelled by the foreign influence upon China. Cosmopolitanism and nativism, internationalism and nationalism, and regionalism or localism are all increasingly evident and coexist in an uneasy tension, even within most individuals. The populace is increasingly diverse in its lifestyles, avocations, and aspirations, and yet elements of a new national popular culture are being shaped by television, advertising, and increased geographic mobility.

Society clearly enjoys more autonomy vis-à-vis the state than in the past. In many respects, the people keep the "tiger world" of Chinese politics at arms length as they seek to earn a living. Increased geographic mobility means that tens of millions of Chinese citizens are no longer enmeshed in the control mechanisms that had been perfected for a stationary populace. Chinese people seek to evade the predatory behavior of police, market regulators, and other officials in the collection of endless fees, fines, and taxes. On balance, the domain of the state is shrinking and that of society is expanding. Voluntary associations are forming, many of them illegal and subject to repression (such as unofficial churches or trade unions). While the state retains tight control over the organization of religion and other non-governmental institutions, the populace enjoys an increased capacity to worship in the officially-sanctioned churches, mosques, and temples. And the number of licensed non-governmental organizations is increasing rapidly. But at the same time, local governments—urban wards, neighborhood committees, villages, townships, and counties—have grown considerably in the past two decades, with local budgets (and personnel ranks) swollen as a result of revenues earned from the enterprises they have spawned and the bank credit at their command.

Leaders at all levels of the hierarchy recognize that the Chinese people seek greater participation in the making of decisions that affect their lives. There is a clear yearning for greater political freedom. But at the same time, the people demand order and security. There is little desire to risk the many gains of the past 20 years. The populace particularly resents the corruption, nepotism, and unaccountability of their leaders. They seek the rule of law, but not necessarily a rapid transition to democracy if the transition were to be accompanied by chaos and economic recession.

These contradictory trends both increase and decrease stability. The benefits that so many people have derived from the rapid growth of the past 20 years mean that they have much more to lose from political experimentation, and most people still remember the chaos, fear, and poverty of the recent past. Yet at the same time, aspirations, income disparities, and discontent with the rapaciousness of high officials are all growing—fueling the demand for political reform.

The Improved Human Condition

The horrors of June, 1989—when the leaders ordered the People's Liberation Army (PLA) to occupy Tiananmen Square by force—remain indelibly imprinted in the minds of many Americans, for whom the brave soul who defied the column of invading tanks captured the moment of a regime crushing its own people. With that searing image still so fresh, many Americans are naturally inclined to believe the worst about the Chinese regime and its treatment of the Chinese people.

Yet the fact is that since that tragic moment, the human condition of most Chinese has continued to improve, as it had done from the end of the Mao era in 1976 until 1989. And we are not just speaking about improvements in per capita income and the availability of consumer goods. China's leaders have undertaken a number of measures to expand the political rights of citizens:

  · They are attempting to introduce the rule of law. The leaders have instructed local governments to inform the populace about the laws that the national government has enacted and that local agencies are responsible for implementing. When local agencies disregard, exceed, or violate these laws, citizens in some locales are now able to request the local court to annul the action. Lawyers are being trained in modest numbers and law offices are being established to assist plaintiffs to bring suit against the state. However, the courts do not have the right of judicial review to examine whether laws and administrative regulations are in compliance with the constitution. And introduction of the rule of law will be hampered by the wide administrative discretion that local officials enjoy and the dependence of the courts on these officials for funding and personnel appointments.

· Village elections have been introduced and monitored to enable villagers to participate in the selection of their leaders. Many non-communists have been elected. To be sure, the electoral process in most areas remains firmly under the control of the communist Party, and the village Party organization still plays a major role in running village affairs. But the idea of democracy is being introduced at the grass-roots level.

· Citizens have the right temporarily to migrate without first securing permission of their superiors. Peasants can lease out land that the village has assigned to them and that they choose not to farm themselves.

· The populace clearly enjoys a wider range of choice in the cultural domain. The number of magazines, newspapers, and books being published is increasing dramatically. Even in rural areas, videocassettes of Hong Kong and Taiwan movies, contemporary and classical foreign novels in translation, and traditional Chinese novels are widely available.

Arguably, most Chinese enjoy a greater degree of freedom than at any time in the past century. And yet most Americans would find the human rights situation in China intolerable. Freedom of speech and assembly do not exist. The government's treatment of Tibetan Buddhism is undoubtedly oppressive. Torture, arbitrary arrest, and indiscriminate application of the death penalty are wide-spread. The state interferes in the most cherished moments of life's passages—birth, marriage, and death, dictating the number children a couple may have, the age of marriage, and burial practices. High-level officials whom the government-controlled media have identified guilty of corruption go untried in court, their misdeeds not clearly explained to the public, while lower-level officials convicted of seemingly lesser crimes are sentenced to death. Although in private Chinese are quite willing to express their political views to close friends or foreigners whose discretion they trust, individuals who publish views or undertake actions that oppose the regime or denigrate specific leaders are arrested. The regime does not tolerate organized political dissent.

In short, although China's human rights record is improving, it still is unsatisfactory by most standards, including those held by most Chinese. To improve the human condition and to create a social setting that will truly sustain a regime committed to human rights require the strengthening of such norms as respect for the rule of law, trust in and a sense of obligation toward people outside one's own circle of family and friends, and tolerance of diversity. These will take many years, perhaps decades, to inculcate.

Moreover, the weakness of these norms should not be attributed to Communist rule, though the past forty years greatly eroded them. While precedents can be found in the pre-communist past for the rule of law, tolerance, and individualism, or a widespread social consciousness, these attributes were not dominant aspects of traditional culture. Certain practices that many foreigners find odious—such as widespread use of the death penalty—are deeply ingrained in Chinese culture. As pre-communist Chinese novels, short stories, and anthropological studies make clear, life for the vast majority of Chinese has long been brutish. As a result, although arbitrary rule and constraints on freedom undoubtedly generate discontent, cynicism, and political apathy, they do not immediately lead to political opposition and rebellion. Rather, the human condition produces widespread grievances toward the regime that people seem willing to endure—unless an opportunity or desperate need arises to act upon them.

The Political Quandary

To varying degrees, top officials realize that their political system is antiquated and lacks broad-based popular support. Their speeches in fact openly discuss the difficulties they face in recruiting and retaining high-quality, active Party members. They know the ideology on which the Party is based lacks popular appeal. They are well aware that the trend in the Asia-Pacific region is toward democracy, and they believe that their populace desires increased opportunity to participate in the decisions that affect their fate. And in private conversations, several of the highest leaders—though with differing degrees of explicitness—acknowledge the many virtues of democratic rule. From the highest levels to the lowest, many officials appear to recognize that their regime can only regain popular support through sweeping political reform: strengthening parliamentary bodies, placing the military and police more firmly under civilian control, relaxing controls over formation of nongovernmental organizations, strengthening the judiciary, improving the civil service system, and granting the populace more meaningful avenues of political participation.

But the leaders fear political reform even as, increasingly, they recognize its necessity. They worry that the loosening of control will unleash a sequence of events even worse than what occurred with the dissolution of the Soviet Union or Yugoslavia. If the current structure of authority in China were suddenly to collapse, independent national governments at the current provincial levels would not be the result. Nothing in Chinese history would sustain such a notion. Rather, the likely result would be anarchy, chaos, and civil war to determine who would be China's next unifying ruler. All the leaders fear this chaos. None wishes to put at risk rule by the Communist Party, without which they believe China would cease to be unified. Recognizing the need for political change, they are deeply divided over the speed and manner in which political reform should be undertaken. Given the consensual decision-making process that exists among the top decision makers, they have only been able to agree on the circumscribed political reforms listed above.

In short, if the leaders could acquire a map charting a safe path for a peaceful transition to an openly competitive political system with the Communist Party remaining the dominant or ruling party at the end of the journey, some would probably choose to embark on that path. But no such map exists. And in its absence, the leaders cultivate popular support in other ways: maintaining high economic growth rates and unleashing popular nationalistic aspirations.

The Challenges to Economic Growth

Conventional wisdom now holds that the Chinese economy is on a trajectory of rapid growth likely to last for many more years, perhaps decades. Expectations of continued rapid growth undergird the predictions of China as a looming world power and rival to the United States. And, indeed, many underlying factors are likely to continue to propel the Chinese economy forward in robust fashion: a high savings rate; an industrious and entrepreneurial population; a demographic profile conducive to growth; the spread of science and technology that enables the populace to become more productive; the financial, managerial, and technological assistance provided by ethnic Chinese from Hong Kong, Taiwan, Southeast Asia, and North America; a generally propitious external setting that at least tolerates rapidly growing Chinese exports, invests capital, provides technology, and poses no military threat; and a leadership that has repeatedly demonstrated more acumen than the leaders of many other developing countries in guiding the economy well. Lending further credibility to optimistic assessments of China's economic strength has been its extraordinary export performance, its accumulation of over a hundred twenty billion dollars in foreign currency reserves, the low level of domestic government indebtedness, and the maintenance of a foreign debt level (approximately a hundred billion dollars) that can adequately be sustained in light of China's export performance.

Yet China's economy is still only half-reformed: The state-owned banking system dominates the financial sector. Other state-owned enterprises (SOEs) dominate capital-intensive industrial production, and they employ the vast majority of urban workers. The government relies on SOEs to keep the urban peace by providing workers with social benefits such as housing, health care, and pensions because the fiscal system at present is far too inefficient to allow the government itself to fund a large-scale social welfare system. What is needed is a simultaneous reform of China's capital markets, industrial ownership structure, social welfare system, and fiscal system, since each constitutes an integral component of the total political-economic system.

Consider first the reform of the inefficient SOEs. These industrial behemoths employ two-thirds of the industrial workforce and consume two-thirds of China's investment resources, but produce only one-third of total societal output. It is, to be sure, an important one-third, consisting of the bulk of capital-intensive production. SOEs thus massively waste China's scarce societal resources. Their liabilities to banks as a percentage of assets increased from 11 percent in 1978 to 95 percent in 1995; many thus are technically insolvent, but are kept afloat by a politicized banking system forced to use the savings of China's hard-working population to fund the low interest rates—because stock and bond markets are underdeveloped. Yet, until recently, the government has permitted only a miniscule number of SOEs to cease their operations and go bankrupt. The leaders cannot abide the thought of tens of millions of urban workers suddenly being tossed out onto the street.

Because SOEs and the banks that prop them up need not face the threat of bankruptcy, they ultimately have very little incentive to use the factors of production efficiently, with the result that, as long as the current system remains in place, scarce societal resources will continue to be wasted on a grand scale. They will be siphoned away from their socially-optimal uses, which in China typically means the uses to which they are put by the private, collective, and foreign-funded sectors. Moreover, partly because the state has historically depended on SOEs to supply it with most of its revenue, the rise of the non-SOE sector and SOEs' great inefficiency have produced a sharp drop in government revenue as a percentage of gross domestic product (GDP), from 31 percent in 1978 to 11 percent in 1995. The resulting political-economic profile is highly inconsistent with the pattern of the typical developing country, and implies that the Chinese government will face a serious shortage of both funds and political support as it tries not only to reform SOEs and the financial system, but also to tackle a set of severe ecological problems.

Environment

China's rapid rate of industrialization has involved a thoroughgoing assault on the environment—air, water, and soil. The Chinese people now live in a dangerously polluted milieu. Their health is at risk on a daily basis. Air quality in most rural areas does not meet minimum World Health Organization standards, for example, and over 80 percent of rivers are seriously polluted. The population is suffering from alarming increases in respiratory ailments in both the big cities and the rapidly-industrializing countryside. Governments at all levels of the political system are now beginning to address this problem, but the primacy of economic development inevitably renders offices charged with environmental protection weak and hamstrung in bureaucratic competition with the more powerful industrial ministries. The result is exceedingly slow progress in cleaning up the environment or, in many cases, no progress at all.

Energy

China's energy supply exacerbates its environmental problems. China's thirst for petroleum exceeds its domestic supply; its dependency on petroleum imports—largely from the Middle East—is growing rapidly. Its hydroelectric potential is primarily located in the western regions of the country, far from population centers. Its natural gas reserves are modest. Its nuclear power industry is still in its infancy and still dependent on foreign technology, which is, however, quite accessible from Russian and European suppliers. Alternative energy sources are not available in large quantities. That leaves coal as the main resource to meet China's rapidly growing energy needs, and coal reserves are available in abundant supply. At present, coal supplies roughly 75 percent of China's energy needs; roughly 80 percent of its electricity comes from coal fired power plants. These figures will persist long into the future.

China's coal, however, is not high grade. Most has high sulphur content and contains other impurities. The net result is the emission of sulphur dioxide and acid rain affecting many areas of China and its neighbors. Moreover, China's increasing use of energy, its reliance on coal, and the inefficiencies in Chinese energy use result in rapid increases in emissions of greenhouse gases. Within a decade or two, China will join the United States as the largest source of carbon dioxide emission. To alleviate these problems will require billions of dollars to increase energy efficiency and reduce emission of pollutants.

Education

China's economic growth also will be constrained by inadequate human resources. In fact, China has become a major importer of human talent. According to some estimates, as many as 50,000 Hong Kong citizens and 200,000 from Taiwan are serving in managerial, professional, and technical positions on the mainland. In part, this situation reflects Beijing's inability to attract over 150,000 Chinese graduate students sent abroad who have yet to return home. But China also is now plagued by years of neglect of education at all levels. For decades, China's per capita expenditures on primary schools have ranked among the lowest in the world, and the dissolution of the communes has inadvertently led to an erosion in school financing and attendance in substantial numbers of villages. Meanwhile, universities have still not fully recovered from the battering their faculty suffered during the Mao years, and as is true of other agencies dependent on government funding, they are now expected to launch their own enterprises and secure foreign support to sustain their educational offerings.

The result is an inadequate supply of technically proficient men and women to serve the nation's managerial, engineering and scientific needs. The shortages are particularly evident in the brain drain from rural and impoverished areas, where skilled labor is particularly needed but wages and working conditions are not competitive, and in the difficulty urban firms have in retaining skilled personnel. Eventually, a free labor market and expanded higher education will overcome these difficulties, but for the foreseeable future, China's growth rate will be adversely affected.

All of this suggests that the Chinese economy has many vulnerabilities. Recent economic difficulties in Japan, Korea, Malaysia, and Thailand are reminders that the Asian strategies for rapid growth—strong states guiding the economy, pursuing export-led growth, and encouraging high rates of capital investment— have their vulnerabilities. Straight-line projections that China will continue to grow at nearly 10 percent a year are unwarranted. Yet the factors stimulating growth are probably sufficiently powerful to sustain it at rates substantially higher than those prevailing in most other developing countries. An annual growth rate of 6–8 percent seems attainable to most experts for the foreseeable future if the leaders can implement their plans to reform the SOE and financial sectors. (On the other hand, failure to implement these reforms could cut the growth rate in half.) If China could sustain a growth rate of 6–8 percent for three or four decades, the country would emerge with one of the world's largest economies, although per capita income would still be well below the average in developed countries. But a 6–8 percent growth rate is substantially less than that achieved in the last two decades and may not be sufficient to meet the aspirations of the populace for employment opportunities and a rapidly improving standard of living. And the leaders have generated support for their rule by fulfilling these expectations.

Popular Nationalism

China's opening to the outside world, along with the telecommunications and transportation revolutions, has enabled "public opinions" to form outside state control. The leaders must struggle both to manage and to satisfy these opinions as they seek to maintain political stability and effective governance. Satisfying popular demands is one reason that the government encourages the proliferation of radio and television "hotline" programs, letters-to-editors in newspapers, and public opinion polling.

Nationalistic sentiments also rally the people behind the rulers. Popular nationalism has been evident in anti-foreign demonstrations following victories over foreign sports teams, the resentment over not being awarded the Olympic Games, and the popularity of the anti-American diatribe *China Can Say "No"*. Chinese attribute China's current predicaments and poverty to its century of invasion and exploitation by the Western powers and Japan. Many still harbor bitter memories toward Japan as a result of the atrocities it committed during its brutal occupation of Manchuria and large parts of core China from 1931 to 1945. All this contributes to a sense of grievance toward the outside world.

The leaders have clearly decided to appeal to these nationalistic sentiments in the absence of a convincing ideology. Nor is the use of nationalism simply an exercise in cynical manipulation of popular opinion. Most of the leaders clearly share these sentiments themselves. The deliberate use of the return of Hong Kong as an occasion for a national celebration exemplified this somewhat contrived but genuinely felt national pride and patriotism. Clearly, a nation that had been humiliated and scorned seems to be regaining its rightful place in the world. But the leaders can overplay their hand, arousing or unleashing anti-Japanese or anti-American sentiment that could engender a backlash in Tokyo or

Washington. After all, in the final analysis, China needs Japan and the Untied States to fulfill its developmental plans.

Nowhere are the dilemmas posed by a resurgent Chinese nationalism more evident than in Beijing's policies toward Taiwan, Tibet, and Hong Kong. The essence of the leaders' nationalistic—some would say patriotic—appeal at home is that they are restoring China's greatness. And in the minds of most Chinese, the moments of greatness coincide with the moments of maximum unity, strength, and national territorial integrity. The great leaders in Chinese history are those who brought all the rightful parts of the domain back into the fold. The despised rulers are those who contributed to China's fragmentation and penetration by foreign powers.

From Beijing taxicab drivers to Shandong farmers to Sichuan intellectuals, the refrain is the same: Taiwan, Tibet, and Hong Kong are all parts of China. They can enjoy considerable autonomy within a Chinese framework, but the residents of those places cannot deny their heritage any more than a family member can deny his ancestors. As one Shandong county official explained his sentiment: "If Taiwan tries to deny it is part of China, we will have to kick their butt." And as a Beijing taxicab driver put it, after expressing deep disenchantment with China's top rulers: "Look how incompetent they are! Over 40 years have passed and still they haven't gotten that little island of Taiwan back. Why do they deserve all the money they are getting?" This is not official rhetoric artificially implanted in the minds of the populace. It is popular opinion with which the leaders must reckon now that their other tools for managing the populace—the household registration system, total control over the media, and a high level of bureaucratic discipline—are breaking down.

In short, public opinion somewhat constrains China's leaders in their approaches toward Taiwan, Tibet, and Hong Kong. The leaders believe they would be condemned in some fashion if they were seen as surrendering Chinese territory. But it is by no means clear that the Chinese public demands the sometimes hard line policies that the rulers have adopted toward these locales. For example, it is doubtful that popular nationalistic sentiments demanded the 1995–96 outcry over Taiwan President Lee Teng-hui's foreign travels, the opposition to the 1994–95 Dalai Lama's involvement in identifying the reincarnation of the Panchen Lama, or the strict limits Beijing placed upon the number of Hong Kong's Legislative Council members to be democratically elected.

In these and other instances, it appears that China's leaders deliberately sought to convey a nationalistic message. Through rhetoric and public posturing, China's leaders have stimulated emotions among their people in their dispute with Taiwan, their handling of their territorial claims in the East and South China Seas, and their policies toward Tibet. They have castigated the Dalai Lama, President Lee Teng-hui of Taiwan and the leader of Hong Kong democratic forces, Martin Lee, for allegedly seeking to "split" China and serving the interests of foreign powers. This rhetorical nationalism is a two-edged sword. The use of nationalistic appeals appears to rally the populace behind the leaders. But it makes the leaders captive of the sentiments they have cultivated, probably reduces their own flexibility on these issues, and surely alienates the objects of their wrath.

The net effect is to reduce the prospects for resolution of these issues in, ways that accommodate the desires of the local populace.

The Military

Eight years ago, before the PLA's quashing of the Beijing demonstrations, the United States was in the midst of selling military equipment to China: an advanced avionics package to the air force for its jet fighters, improved artillery shells to the army, and advanced turbine engines to the navy for its destroyers. Following the Tiananmen tragedy, the United States halted those sales, and ever since, America's contacts with the PLA have been sporadic at best and always viewed skeptically by the U.S. Congress. Many Americans view the PLA as a prop for the dying communist regime; the source of China's disturbing supply of advanced weaponry and technology to Pakistan and Iran; a prime source of corruption through its economic activities at home and abroad; and the prime force behind China's muscular behavior in the South China Sea and Taiwan Strait. According to this negative view of the PLA, the military has successfully pressured the civilian leaders to pursue an assertive foreign policy and rapidly to increase defense expenditures. In short, adherents of this view consider the PLA to be malevolent and increasingly important in Chinese domestic politics, with the inevitable consequence that China will pose a military threat to the United States in a relatively short period of time.

This view cannot be dismissed, but it is misleading:

• The PLA was not the instigator of the June 1989 suppression. Civilian leaders, including several Party elders, were the chief architects of the debacle. Substantial evidence exists that many retired PLA marshals and generals opposed the dispatch of the PLA into the streets of Beijing, and many of those who obeyed the commands of their Party chieftains initially did so without enthusiasm.

• The PLA as a whole is not the source of Chinese xenophobia. Elements of the officer corps have been at the forefront in seeking increased contact with the outside world, in part to secure the technology necessary for military modernization.

• Chinese military expenditures, although growing, have not been skyrocketing upward. The Chinese defense budget is one of the most opaque aspects of the Chinese scene, but even the highest of the well-founded estimates of Chinese defense expenditures judge the defense budget to be about equal to Japan's defense spending. Indeed, China's military expenditures as a percentage of total defense expenditures by all Asian countries have been decreasing steadily since the mid-1970s.

• The United States possesses overwhelming military superiority over China and will do so for decades into the future, providing the United States retains the will to keep its own defense budget at current levels. China remains vulnerable to devastating attack from American forward deployed forces in the western Pacific.

• The Chinese military is complex, and should not be treated as a coherent and integrated whole. There is a core of professional military, consisting of strategic forces, army (with central, regional, and local units), air force, and navy—with their own internecine bureaucratic battles; a military-industrial complex that is converting to production of civilian commodities; and a portion that is engaged in politics.

. . . Generalizations are not easy to make about an institution as complicated as the PLA. Portions are corrupt, and others honest; portions are nationalistic, and others seek PLA participation in international peacekeeping efforts; portions are intellectually ill-equipped for the modern world, while others are extremely sophisticated and among the most enlightened people in China; portions are resistant to change, and others progressive.

Thus, as with other aspects of the China scene, a balanced appraisal is required, and historical perspective is needed. The PLA is neither evil incarnate nor a knight in shining armor. The foreign invasions and the massive peasant uprisings that affected China from the mid-1800s to the mid-1900s led to the militarization of the polity and society. The military became an important avenue of social mobility and a crucial actor on the political stage. And in many ways, communist rule has not fundamentally de-militarized the polity and society. The military remains an important part of the Chinese state; no person can emerge as the paramount leader against the concerted opposition of the military and leaders must enjoy support from at least a portion of the military. A substantial segment of China's heavy industry has intimate links with the military. A major effort was made in the 1950s to demilitarize the polity, to establish a professional military and to keep them in the barracks, but the military once more assumed civilian roles during the chaos of the Cultural Revolution. The Deng era again saw an effort to create a professional military and to delineate a clear boundary between it and the civilian sector, but that process is far from complete. Further, the PLA is an instrument of the Party; one of its stated tasks is to keep the Party in power and its chain-of-command is from the military Chiefs-of-Staff to the Party's Central Military Commission (CMC) and, ultimately, to the Party Politburo. Under these circumstances, with this historical background, it is difficult to disentangle the military from the rest of the Chinese state, and this condition is likely to persist for the foreseeable future.

However, the influence of the military does not explain China's commitment to modernization. Modern Chinese history is the relevant factor: China's military weakness invited foreign aggression; its ineffective and fragmented internal security forces yielded disorder and civil wars. And since 1949, partly as a result of their own menacing and seemingly unpredictable behavior, China's leaders have experienced threats of nuclear attack and amassing of awesome might deployed against them. Against this background, the acquisition of military might has been a central objective of China's rulers not only in the communist era, but ever since the Opium War. China's leaders—no matter who they are—will surely seek to build a modern navy, air force, and army as their technology and economic resources permit. The differences among the leaders both in the military and outside it have involved, and will continue to involve, issues of priority and sequence: whether to postpone weapons research and acquisition in favor of constructing a firm, broad-based economic infrastructure; what are the most dangerous threats confronting China; what technologies are most important for acquiring strength; what strategies are appropriate to modern warfare and therefore what the force structure and weapons should be.

Thus, there can be no doubt that as China's economy grows, its technological and scientific resources will expand, and its government budget will increase. And although it is unlikely that the rate of increase will enable China to pose a greatly expanded direct threat to the United States (it currently can strike at U.S. territory with only a small number of ICBMs), almost assuredly

China will accrue greater military strength. But there is considerable doubt as to how rapidly this will occur. And, almost assuredly, China will obtain increasing capability to affect the military balance on its periphery, especially vis-à-vis Taiwan. Indeed, in recent years, as a result of markedly greater tensions over the Taiwan issue, many areas of China's military modernization have become focused precisely on improving the credibility of Beijing's long-standing threat to use force against Taiwan. This new development poses the most serious near-term threat to U.S. regional interests deriving from China's military modernization program.

Deep Versus Shallow Integration into World Affairs

Put succinctly, the key question confronting China's leaders is: Do they believe their national interests will be served by a deeper integration into the international and regional security, economic, and value systems? Or do they believe China's interests require limiting the nation's involvement to the relatively shallow extent that has been attained thus far? Certainly they have publicly proclaimed a commitment to deep integration, but will they implement these promises? In no small measure, the answer to these questions will determine whether China emerges as a threat or partner in the region and globally in the years ahead.

In the security realm, on the whole, China has yet to enter into agreements that significantly narrow its foreign policy choices. It has yet to make commitments in the arms control and weapons development areas that constrain its future military development. China's leaders demonstrate particular ambivalence over the existing security arrangements in East Asia that are undergirded by America's alliances with Japan and Korea and its forward military deployments. China's leaders recognize that the U.S.-Japan Security Treaty in some respects contributes to stability in the region by anchoring Japan in an alliance system, but they do not acknowledge that an American military presence in the western Pacific would continue to contribute to regional stability after tensions on the Korean peninsula have ended. In fact, its assertive claims in the South China Sea and its posture toward Taiwan have provoked regional security concerns that, over the long run, China is going to be a troublesome neighbor.

In the economic realm, China has yet to commit itself fully to the opening of its markets and to its full integration into the international financial and commercial systems, though it has applied for admission to the World Trade Organization (WTO) and committed to making at least some important adjustments to its domestic economy. The current negotiations over China's entry into the WTO concern precisely what sorts of adjustments will be made. Is China prepared to restructure its domestic economy to the deep extent necessary to make it congruent with an increasingly open international economic system?

And in the realm of culture and values, will the leaders of China continue to assert that, because of China's distinctiveness, certain internationally-accepted standards of governance are not applicable to China? Clearly, the issues at stake concern human rights, democratization, and the rule of law. Are China's leaders prepared to accept the notion that their performance should be judged by the same standards that are applied to other countries, particularly when China has pledged to adhere to certain international treaties and agreements? Do China's leaders somehow intend to wall their people off from international cultural currents? Is this even possible, given rapid advances in communications technologies and their dissemination throughout China?

In all of these areas—security, economy, and culture—both the leaders and the citizens of China are deeply divided. Some vigorously advocate a deeper integration into world affairs, arguing that unless China participates fully in the global system it will be unable to develop economically and attain for its people the benefits of modernity. Others believe further integration risks loss of China's cultural heritage and threatens the country's unity. Localities that are success-fully incorporated into global and regional affairs will drift apart from those less integrated. Thus, deep integration risks the primary achievement of the communist revolution—the reknitting of China. The vigor of this debate demonstrates the extent to which China's future orientation toward the Asia-Pacific region and the world as a whole has yet to be determined. . . .

55

Prospects for Democratization in China

MARTIN KING WHYTE

Many people, including China's political and even many intellectual leaders, have argued that democracy will not work in China because of its Confucian traditions, low level of economic and cultural development, absence of an established legal system, and other obstacles. But as Martin King Whyte shows here, most of these arguments are simplistic and ignore a variety of more promising features and changes underway that may make a transition to democracy more feasible.

Barriers to Democratization

A variety of powerful arguments have been raised to explain why democratization is difficult, if not impossible, under Chinese conditions. The first and perhaps most important barrier concerns China's history and traditions. This argument is obvious and familiar. China does not have significant historical experience with democratic institutions, and, in fact, has a long bureaucratic-authoritarian tradition that is profoundly antagonistic to democratization. China being China, this tradition goes back farther and is more continuous than is the case with other former imperial systems, including Russia. This lack of historical precedent for democracy involves more than simply the fact that Chinese emperors and bureaucrats ruled without benefit of popular consent. China's imperial system involved several elements that could be seen as "proto-totalitarian." For example, in state Confucianism, a single set of orthodox ideas was supposed to bind the entire society together under a moral consensus, and numerous indoctrination procedures were carried out among the populace to foster this "one-mindedness." Ideas and groups that seemed to elites to threaten this moral consensus were branded heterodox and suppressed. Intellectuals were closely tied to the state and tended to work within the system to achieve their goals, rather than outside of or against it. The reality of social life in late imperial China was far different from these "proto-totalitarian" ideals, with substantial autonomy from the state found in local communities and organi-

600

zations, but the ideals of the system nonetheless promoted continual striving for unity and orthodoxy.

With the decay of the imperial system after the mid-19th century, elements of a more democratic order gradually emerged in China—political parties, voluntary associations, mass media with some autonomy, new legal codes and courts, and so forth. However, these changes were partial and fragile, and, after the 1930s, first the turn of the Nationalists toward greater authoritarianism and then wartime conditions created an environment inhospitable to further democratization. Moreover, even the most ardent advocates of democratization prior to 1949 continued to see things in terms that were more "statist" than "pluralist." Even the democratic reforms that were initiated were intended to mobilize popular ideas and energies and thus strengthen the state by providing it with a broader popular consensus. They were not designed to protect individuals and groups from the state or to institutionalize group differences and foster the competition of ideas. The precedents for democracy in China thus were largely foreign in origin, adapted to emasculate any pluralistic emphasis, and fairly fragile.

A second and related barrier to democratization concerns the absence of a number of prerequisites. Here the argument is more sociological than historical, and is based upon generalizations from the European experience. The claim is that even though democracies as we know them today did not exist in premodern Europe, a number of elements had developed that made subsequent democratization possible. The exact prerequisites listed by those who make this argument generally include:

• a well-developed legal tradition with an emphasis on the rule of law, rather than of men;

• a highly commercialized society and money economy with private property rights, fostering a conception of equality before markets as well as before the law and some personal autonomy vis-à-vis the state;

• the existence of independent sources of power and autonomous sources of values and beliefs, embodied in a variety of social forms—a separate church hierarchy, a system of competing small states, institutionalized estates, chartered cities, and so forth;

• a large and growing bourgeoisie and/or middle class and conflict between landed and commercial classes ; and

- a conception of universal citizenship, the existence of autonomous associations promoting various causes, and a variety of other precursors of "civil society."

Whether one uses this list or some variant, the conclusion reached from such arguments is that China in late imperial times lacked most of the prerequisites for democratization. There was, to be sure, a highly developed commercial economy with private property rights and some elements of a legal system (although not much stress on the rule of law per se). However, most of the other elements listed were totally lacking or only weakly developed, and changes since the fall of the Qing dynasty have done little to promote the development of such prerequisites for democratization.

A third and compounding barrier working against democratization in China is the transformations of the social order that took place under Mao Zedong after 1949. The Chinese Communist Party (CCP) leaders extinguished the fragile elements of democracy that had developed over the previous half century, and, in doing so, realized "one-mindedness" much more thoroughly then their imperial predecessors. All independent associations, mass media organizations, and private enterprises were suppressed or taken over. An extreme version of the Leninist/Stalinist organizational form was implanted in China, a form that was in some ways even more hostile to personal autonomy and individual choice than the Soviet version. In particular, after the mid-1950s, China made more thorough attempts to destroy markets as a principle of distribution, virtually eliminating the labor market and making individuals dependent upon bureaucratic allocation for most of the necessities of life Although initially some autonomy and diversity in lifestyles and culture were permitted within this system, in Mao's later years, and particularly after the Cultural Revolution was launched in 1966, an extreme intolerance toward anything that deviated from orthodox "proletarian" culture was enforced, making politically risky not only deviant political views, but even such innocuous behavior as wearing colorful clothing, enjoying traditional Chinese operas, or raising goldfish. By the time Mao died in 1976, even the partial steps toward democratization visible in China before 1949 were no more than a distant memory. They had become completely alien to the ways people had to operate to survive within the Maoist order.

Both the immediate and longer-term historical precedents in China thus appear profoundly hostile toward democratization. To this list of barriers we must now add a fourth barrier: China's poverty, low level of education, large territory, preponderance of peasants, and huge population. A number of familiar arguments can be made in regard to these factors:

- the task of holding the country together and launching modernization in a world filled with richer countries requires a strong central government capable of mobilizing all national resources;
- democratic forms and procedures are slow and unwieldy and tend to produce rancorous debates and regional animosities at a time when tight national unity is needed;
- democracy requires a well-educated and informed citizenry, and if the population is too poor and illiterate, they will be unable to make informed decisions about political matters and thus will be vulnerable to mobilization by demagogues and other enemies of democracy;
- peasants care about little apart from feeding their families, and they may prefer strong leaders who rule by the knout rather than the ballot;
- to control population growth and deal with other pressing crises, a government has to adopt and maintain harsh measures, and thus democratic forms are unsuitable for countries facing such problems.

Such arguments can be seen as another version of the "prerequisites for democratization" argument (now involving current socioeconomic conditions rather than historical experiences). They imply that democratization is unlikely to occur except in relatively rich and well-educated societies. Critics of such arguments often point to India as an exception to these generalizations. However, the usual response to such critics is that India is the exception that proves the rule. Democratic forms were imposed from the outside by British colonial rule, and recurring political turmoil in India and the difficulty of pursuing population control policies there illustrate quite clearly, so the argument goes, the liabilities of a democratic system in a large and poor country. . . .

A fifth barrier to democratization in China might be called the "no Gorbachev" argument. In all of eastern Europe, except for Albania and Yugoslavia, state socialism was imposed after World War II through Soviet military occupation, and the shaky legitimacy of the resulting regimes depended upon Soviet backing. Soviet military force and the threat of such force served to maintain compliant regimes in power, most dramatically in Hungary in 1956, Czechoslovakia in 1968, and Poland in 1980–81. When Gorbachev assumed power in the USSR and repudiated the "Brezhnev doctrine" (which pledged Soviet military support whenever socialism was endangered), the critical prop sustaining Leninist regimes in Eastern Europe was removed, and they rapidly crumbled.

Here the contrasts with China are clear. China's socialist revolution was indigenous, rather than imposed via Soviet occupation. The Sino-Soviet split after 1960 reduced any Chinese economic and military dependence upon the USSR to essentially zero. China's leaders in 1989 were still, for the most part, representatives of the generation that fought in the hills to bring their Leninist system to power, not successor *apparatchiks* dependent upon Soviet support. Withdrawal of Soviet backing and even the collapse of the Leninist system in the USSR itself would not knock the foundation out from under the system in China, as the events since 1989 have shown.

A final barrier, in terms of the prospects for democracy in China, is the state of the economy in the early 1990s. China is a very poor country facing daunting economic problems. However, these economic problems do not appear to be as crippling as those that faced the Soviet Union and Eastern Europe in the 1980s. Many would argue that severe economic crises and the inability to solve them within the existing system were the critical factors paving the way for dramatic changes in other Leninist systems. If that is so, then this critical factor is lacking in the Chinese case. China's economy is in considerably better shape than it was when Mao died. Even though China's economic reforms are no longer producing the buoyant growth they did in the early 1980s, most economic trends are still positive. Indeed, since the 1989 crackdown, the inflation rate has decreased and China's trade surplus has grown dramatically. Those in China who would like to argue that only system-transforming changes will solve the country's economic problems have a more difficult "sell" than their counterparts in Eastern Europe and the Soviet Union.

This listing of obstacles to democratization in China is not exhaustive, but it encompasses the most important arguments usually raised. If we stopped at this point we would have to conclude that it is hardly surprising that China's 1989 democracy movement failed. However, before we accept such a conclusion we need to consider the other side of the question. What are the factors that might work in favor of democratization in China?

Forces Favoring Democratization

The first set of positive forces requires us to qualify the "lack of a democratic tradition" argument. Even though in many respects China's historical tradition was not democratic and can even be seen as proto-totalitarian, as discussed earlier, the picture is not entirely bleak. There are a number of elements of China's historical tradition that are compatible with democratic ideals and institutions. Beginning with Kang Youwei in the late nineteenth century, Chinese reformers have argued that democracy is not entirely an alien Western import. Proto-democratic elements can be derived from the paternalistic ethos of state Confucianism. Rulers and officials were not seen as simply having a divine right to their power, but as obligated to promote the welfare of the population. Intellectuals and officials could and did "remonstrate" the ruler when they saw his actions and policies deviating from what they felt would produce harmony and prosperity, although such actions risked dismissal and even death. Under extreme circumstances, when the dynasty had become hopelessly corrupt and oppressive, the "mandate of heaven" concept could be used to justify overthrowing rulers and establishing a new regime. Even though there were no elections, periodic protests and rebellions made it clear to China's emperors that in some form the consent of the governed was both necessary and problematic.

A related set of ideas concerns human perfectibility. Although at any point it was recognized that some individuals were better educated and more capable of behaving properly than others, and that therefore "mean people" had to be supervised and controlled, the Chinese still had an abiding faith in the power of education and moral example to guide any individual toward the proper path. Unlike in feudal Europe or Japan, not to mention India, there were only small and marginal groups who were seen as fundamentally inferior and not capable of aspiring toward the moral standards of the Confucian gentleman. There was no assumption that peasants, illiterate people, or other large groups were inherently inferior or that they could not be brought to an awareness of moral and political propriety. To be sure, notions comparable to modern citizenship did not exist in imperial China, but these traditional conceptions of the educability and perfectibility of virtually all Chinese provided some potential basis for notions of democratic citizenship.

To these potentially democratic elements of the traditional legacy must be added the consequences of the substantial de facto autonomy and self-regulation of local communities and associations mentioned earlier. Even though there was a recurring effort to foster compliance with orthodox ideals, in fact the imperial bureaucracy was pitifully small, unable to reach further down into society than the county magistrate's office. Below this level there were some official efforts to shape local community organizations (through such mechanisms as *baojia* and *lijia* semi-official groupings), but these were never very successful. To a substantial extent, Chinese organized their own social lives through such forms as lineages, clan associations, guilds, secret societies, temple associations, and native-place associations. Some of these organizational forms were run quite autocratically, while others involved substantial degrees of member involvement. Whatever the case, the important point here is that at the bottom of Chinese society in late imperial times the principle of organization was nonbureaucratic. Chinese have a long tradition of organizing their own local affairs without waiting for official guidance.

A further important point about traditional influences involves the changes that occurred after the late Qing, and particularly during the first decades of the twentieth century. Institutional forms and ideas that promoted autonomous associational life strengthened during this period. Even though, as noted earlier, these developments were fragile and after the 1930s faced increasing danger from the authoritarian Nationalist state, they constituted an important departure from the practices of imperial China. Many analysts have pointed to occupational associations, trade unions, privately owned mass media, political parties, local assemblies, literary clubs, and other developments of these years as signs of growth of a relatively new Chinese "public sphere" or, to use a related concept, a "civil society." Even though Chinese living today have had little experience with the formal institutions of democracy, many of them grew up in a China in which there was much more autonomy at the grass roots than has existed since 1949.

Because this period was more recent than in the case in the Soviet Union, and because more of the leading figures in such pre-1949 associations have survived in China than in the USSR (as a result of both this time difference and Stalin's purges), notions of getting things done in local communities without relying totally on state guidance are not so alien as my earlier discussion implied. If we think not in terms of whether democratic institutions existed in the Chinese tradition, but of whether certain elements developed that are compatible with democratization, then the influence of China's historical legacy is not as negative as many have argued.

A second set of potentially positive forces concerns China's population composition. The sheer size of China's population may be considered an obstacle to democratization, but certain other aspects of that population work in the other direction. The first aspect I have in mind is China's substantial ethnic homogeneity. Approximately 92 percent of China's total population is Han Chinese, whereas only about 50 percent of the population of the former Soviet Union is Russian. Ethnic differences and nationalistic sentiments make it difficult to develop shared power in democratic institutions, and democratization may be resisted by elites when it threatens to lead to the breakup of the state. Not only developments in 1991 in the Soviet Union and Yugoslavia, but also intense conflicts in Lebanon, Northern Ireland, and many other parts of the globe illustrate the dangers involved. To be sure, these problems are not absent in China. China's minorities occupy disproportionate shares of the country's territory and have often been mistreated by their Chinese overlords, and democratization might well lead to secession of Tibet and perhaps some other areas. Animosities among the various linguistic and regional groupings that make up the Han Chinese (e.g., between Cantonese and Mandarin speakers) are not trivial either. However, on balance, China's long history of territorial unity despite such conflicts and the sheer preponderance of the Han Chinese make the "ethnic problem" less of an obstacle to democratization in China than in many other places.

Some other aspects of China's population composition may also be seen as positive. Democratic institutions work best when status and economic differences among the population are modest. Not only religious cleavages, but large differences in incomes and wealth, constitute obstacles to democratization. The principle here is simple—elites resist the devolution of power into the hands of the population if they fear that the result will be the poor using their greater numbers to mount class warfare and seize elite wealth. Within communities, sharing of power is difficult if groups sense that the things that divide them are more basic than what they share in common. China's current rulers may have monopolized power quite thoroughly, but they have not amassed great wealth, and official policies and the pattern of economic development in China since 1949 have resulted in distributions of income and wealth that are more equal than in most of the third world. Insofar as substantial income equality is a prerequisite for democratization, China stands on the positive side of the ledger.

Another aspect of population composition concerns China's educational level. Access to education and literacy levels have been rising fairly steadily throughout the 20th century, and currently virtually all Chinese children (more than 95 percent) attend school at least long enough to become minimally literate. Even though Chinese urbanites and intellectuals continue to look down upon peasants as ignorant and illiterate, such sentiments are based more on prejudice than on reality. General educational levels in China today are certainly much higher than in 18th-century England or America, and they are also higher than in contemporary India. Insofar as general literacy and the potential for an informed public are important to the operation of a democratic system, China today can be seen as a positive, rather than a negative, case.

A similar argument can be made about China's level of urbanization. It is often assumed, as noted earlier, that the fact that 70–80 percent of all Chinese are peasants represents a formidable obstacle to democratization. However, if we consider where pressure for democratic change might come from, it is not clear whether it is the relative or the absolute size of the urban population that is important. China's urban population may be small proportionately, but at the same time, China has more urbanites than America or Russia has people! The conditions of modern life (large concentrations of people with access to mass media; standards of living above a bare minimum; at least a moderate degree of education, civic concern, and awareness of the outside world; etc.) help lay the groundwork for democratic change, and China has a very large urban sector that can play this role. The fact that the 1989 demonstrations spread to hundreds of towns and cities beyond Beijing, and that apparently the students aroused considerable sympathy for their cause, seems to indicate that Chinese cities can generate very substantial pressure for democratization, despite the fact that the majority of the population is rural.

A third set of potentially positive forces for democratization involves some of the legacies of the Mao era, and of the Cultural Revolution decade in particular. That this period should have contributed to the potential for democratizing change is ironic. At the time, the mass rallies of Red Guards who sang the praises of the Great Helmsman seemed as far as you could get from a breeding ground for democratic sentiments. How did this era foster democratization?

A critical feature of the mass-movement phase of the Cultural Revolution (1966–69) was that all the bureaucratic structures of authority, with the exception of the People's Liberation Army, fell under attack and ceased to function normally. This development meant that normal Leninist grassroots social-control structures and indoctrination activities were immobilized, and large numbers of people had opportunities to roam around the country, engage in unsupervised activities and conversations, and think deeply about the turmoil that enveloped their society. In this relatively unsupervised atmosphere, many people had to deal with very unpleasant realities about Mao's China. Some became targets of mass struggle or were forcibly shipped off to the countryside; others had family members or friends lose housing, be deprived of needed medical care, or commit suicide. Many learned the seamy details of the corruption and hypocrisy of their leaders and of the poverty and superstition prevailing in China's villages. All had to struggle to comprehend how the combination of a supposedly wise leader and loyal followers produced vicious factional fighting that killed thousands and tore society apart. The combination of release from organizational discipline and confrontation with suffering and violence led to a shattering of faith in the system for many Chinese, and a groping for alternative ideas. Paradoxically then, a movement that appeared to be leading to a hysterical form of "one-mindedness" produced in its wake critical thinking and spreading alienation. Perhaps the impact of these developments was greatest on Red Guards who were shipped off to the countryside after 1968. But many intellectuals, ordinary citizens, and even some leaders (those who survived purges and rehabilitations) began to believe that basic changes in the political system were required.

Mao tried to re-impose organizational discipline and reinforce "proletarian" indoctrination in the years after 1969, but the damage to the system was too extensive to be remedied by customary Leninist tactics. Then, after Mao's death in 1976, and the repudiation of Cultural Revolution policies and the launching of the reform program that followed in its wake, those who had lost faith in the system began to make their feelings known. During the 1980s, it became increasingly possible to share grievances and critical ideas with other like-minded people and even get such ideas published in the mass media. Large numbers of individuals who had been victims not only of the Cultural Revolution, but of earlier struggle campaigns, and particularly of the anti-rightist campaign of 1957, were "rehabilitated" and given positions as writers, teachers, film-makers, journalists, and editors—positions from which they could spread their critical ideas to the literate public and particularly to China's young people. Repeatedly during the decade, media discussion and popular debate spread beyond economics to address China's need for political reforms. The sense that China's Leninist state had become a stultifying and barbaric relic blocking further progress was increasingly shared by many critical intellectuals.

. . . What impresses me about the period prior to 1989 is that despite periodic crackdowns and even arrests of critical intellectuals, democratic "surges" kept reappearing, particularly in the student demonstrations that erupted more or less annually starting in 1985. These developments indicate that the situation had changed fundamentally from the Mao years. An official crackdown, with its use of the age-old Chinese tactic of "killing the chicken to scare the monkey," no longer had the intended effect. Rather than respecting and fearing the power of the party-state, educated Chinese kept sharing their sentiments that the political system had to be changed, and they acted on those sentiments when the opportunity to do so appeared. Of course, the crackdown launched in 1989 was much more severe and prolonged than such 1980s predecessors as the "anti-spiritual pollution campaign" of 1983–84 or the "anti-bourgeois liberalization" campaign of 1987. However, there is not much sign that the current round of tightened discipline and heightened political indoctrination is enjoying more success than previous attempts to inoculate China's body politic against future democratic surges. . . .

A fourth force with some potential to foster democratization concerns the [deaths of "revolutionary elders" like Deng Xiaoping and Chen Yun and the rise of a new generation of leaders to top party and government posts.] I take it as a hopeful sign that relatively few of the officials promoted into leading positions during the reform years prior to 1989 have been purged. I do not assume that most of China's middle-aged party leaders are closet Jeffersonian democrats, but they are, at least, not totally identified with the wartime struggles to create the revolution. Many have varying degrees of commitment to reform ideas and a desire to adopt measures that would restore some of the dynamism that characterized China prior to the events of 1989. If a sufficient number of such leaders, or a few particularly powerful ones, become convinced that major political reforms are required for China to deal with its problems, then they may launch such changes. The example of the Soviet Union shows that post-revolutionary leaders who have come up through the party are, under certain circumstances, able to launch and protect even system-transforming political changes. Whether China is likely to produce the likes of a Gorbachev or a Boris Yeltsin is, of course, impossible to say, but the [passing of the old generation of leaders has left] China with leaders quite different from those who presided over the 1989 crackdown.

A fifth potentially positive force that may foster democratization is the linkage between economic reforms and political trends. Even though China's gerontocrats at times sound as if they want to turn back the clock, they in fact maintain a considerable commitment to the economic reforms introduced after 1978. As long as this commitment is sustained, economic reforms will foster trends that work against the reassertion of strict Leninist political controls. A complex set of phenomena lie behind this simple assertion, and there is not enough space here to go into the matter in the detail it deserves. Let me instead list a number of trends connected to the economic reforms that have had and will continue to have some erosive impact on the party's ability to exert total control over society.

Economic reforms have weakened the power of the central state bureaucracy over Chinese society and produced a growing awareness that people's economic fate is tied to their local enterprises and governments, rather than directly to a unitary system controlled from Beijing. By the same token, reforms have put funds and decision-making power in the hands of provincial and local governments, work organizations, entrepreneurs, and individual families, and in some cases, these resources have been used to flout the messages coming from the party center and to organize to promote particular interests. In the first half of this paper, I noted the claim that the personal autonomy provided by distribution through markets rather than through bureaucratic allocation is a vital prerequisite for democratization. If that is the case, then the fact that market reforms in China have progressed much further than those in Eastern Europe prior to 1989 or in the former Soviet Union even at present counts strongly in China's favor. Reform policies also give greater authority and prestige to experts, entrepreneurs, and intellectuals; hard line political leaders know they cannot treat these people too nastily without threatening the health of the economy. For this reason, intellectual as well as economic autonomy advances. The maintenance of the open-door policy also means that the Chinese will continue to have access to news and ideas from other countries, and this outside cultural influence will continually threaten official claims that China is following the only proper road. Perhaps the most basic implication of the reforms is that China under Deng Xioaping has adopted a form of "goulash communism." Increasingly, the system is justified not by reference to messianic political goals, heroic national struggles, and the construction of a more perfect society, but by its ability to produce and deliver goods and raise living standards. With this shift, the party loses its monopoly over questions of morality and value, and public opinion emerges and plays a heightened role. China's leaders become to some extent accountable—they have to worry about popular sentiments and whether consumption difficulties are creating growing resentment toward officials and their policies. Even though China's leaders have considerable resources that they can use to persuade the population that things are fine and getting better, there are limits to how successful official public relations campaigns can be. If the economic situation takes a serious turn for the worse, China's leaders now have to worry very much about their loss of popular support, worries that Mao Zedong never had to face in the wake of the regime-induced economic debacles of the 1950s and 1960s

A sixth potentially democratizing force concerns events taking place in the outside world. China in the 1990s faces a very different world from the one that existed less than a decade ago. The main change is simply the downfall of the system in the Soviet Union and Eastern Europe. China now stands alone (or alongside of North Korea and Cuba) in trying to preserve the Leninist system in the face of democratizing changes elsewhere in the socialist world. Another set of influences come from Asia, where the "people's revolution" in the Philippines and democratizing reforms in Taiwan increase the sentiment that China is

out of step with modern trends. The changes in Taiwan are particularly important in this regard, since they demonstrate that a formerly Leninist party (the
KMT) operating in a Chinese cultural context can abandon its monopoly on power
without (so far, at least) chaos resulting. In today's world, external influences
fostering democratization have become more important than in the past, making
internal preconditions less salient.

To be sure, in the short term, the effects of some of these changes elsewhere have worked against democratization. Seeing the Ceauescus executed, for
example, did not heighten the ardor of Deng Xiaoping, Li Peng, and others for
democratic changes. Also, nationalistic strife in Yugoslavia, the Soviet Union,
and even in Czechoslovakia is likely to encourage China's leaders to resist
major moves toward democratization. However, in the long run, the more positive consequences of the democratizing trend occurring in so many other parts of
the world is likely to impress the Chinese. As noted earlier, the maintenance of
the open door means that many Chinese will be quite aware of how out of step
China is with trends elsewhere, and there is little enthusiasm for solitary socialism.

A seventh and final force that may foster democratization is the effect of
the Tiananmen massacre itself. One very important new grievance has been
added to the set of criticisms of the system existing prior to 1989—China's
leaders, and China's army, now have the blood of many of their citizens on their
hands. To be sure, Chinese communism had produced many victims in earlier
years and campaigns. However, for the most part, these earlier episodes either
were less visible or involved people the regime could stigmatize as "class
enemies." The Tiananmen massacre was very different. The sight of peaceful
young people demonstrating to reform the system being slaughtered by the army
to preserve the power of the party leadership had a traumatic impact on popular
consciousness, at least in urban areas. Many who were reluctant critics were
transformed into bitter enemies of the regime. China's hard-line leaders hope
that time and perhaps good economic results will heal all wounds, and that
eventually the brutality that the Tiananmen Square massacre illustrated will fade
from memory. So far, I see little sign of this happening.

Conclusions

I began with a number of powerful arguments why democratization is
unlikely in China. I then listed a series of other arguments why at least some
democratizing changes are likely. How are we to judge between these contend-
ing arguments? I have no ready answer to this question. My main purpose in this
exercise has been to persuade readers that the absence of meaningful democrati-

zation in China is not inevitable and eternal. If the ideas in the second part of this article have any value, they indicate that the odds against democratizing changes in China are not so long as many doubters have assumed. . . .

At this point those who remain skeptical about the chances for democratization in China usually fall back on statements about the bureaucratic/collectivist tradition stretching back millennia and the low level of economic development in China, along with the general distance of the middle kingdom from Western culture and democratic ideals (all factors bearing more on the Chinese than on the Soviet case). Lurking behind some of this skepticism, I suspect, is a certain ethnocentrism—democracy is fine for us, but it is not to be expected of people raised in such a different tradition. I remain unconvinced that under contemporary world conditions, democratization requires a Western cultural grounding. People in any cultural tradition may want to have some role in managing their own affairs and some say in picking the leaders who will exercise control over them, especially when they hear of people in other societies who are gaining such power. Some would even contend that experience in a Leninist system is the best "school" for learning democratic values. Only when you have learned what life is like in a political order where you are totally dependent upon the whims of distant and unresponsive leaders will you acquire a visceral hunger for democracy.

Furthermore, the arguments about China's backwardness bring to mind the patronizing program of "political tutelage" that Sun Yat-sen advocated in the early 1920s. Sun's argument was that the poorly educated Chinese people were not yet ready for democracy, and that they had to be led by strong leaders until they became ready. The subsequent history of Sun's Nationalist Party suggests that this sort of political tutelage argument was a convenient rationalization for indefinitely postponing any meaningful changes. Even the democratizing reforms occurring in Taiwan more than 60 years later were grudging concessions of the KMT to social forces, not enlightened ceding of power after the successful completion of democratic tutelage. The fact that the doctrines of "new authoritarianism" were being advocated by some of China's leaders prior to 1989 suggests a similar effort to forestall meaningful democratization. In response to such "not ready" arguments, I tend to side with Mao Zedong, who pointed out that the only way to know how a pear tastes is to eat one. Similarly, democratic procedures should be learned by actual experience, rather than by tutelage from authoritarian leaders.

For several reasons, then, I feel that the odds are not stacked hopelessly against democratization in China. Similar sentiments lead me to conclude that the failure of the Beijing Spring of 1989 was not inevitable. My sense is that this outcome was rather a close call, and that if a few developments had occurred slightly differently, the outcome might have been very different. Social theorists often argue about the relative roles of system determinism and historical contingency in explaining events. Given the arguments reviewed in the preceding pages, I believe that contingency played the greater role in deciding the outcome in 1989. If that is the case, then may it not also be true that there is plenty of opportunity for historical contingency to operate in determining China's future, perhaps producing a more democratic order in the next round?

56

The Fifth Modernization

WEI JINGSHENG

Wei Jingsheng, China's most famous political dissident, rose to prominence in the 1978–1979 Democracy Wall Movement in Beijing. He was the founder and editor of a short-lived journal entitled Explorations, *in which he published his best-known political writings. He was sentenced to fifteen years in prison in 1979, but was briefly released in 1993 when China was trying to improve its image in an ultimately unsuccessful bid to host the 2000 Olympics. Wei was soon arrested and sentenced again to a long prison sentence. Under pressure from the United States to improve its human rights record, China released Wei from prison in 1997 and immediately put him on a plane to the United States, where he remains in exile. This article, which first appeared in* Explorations *in January 1979, remains one of the most eloquent statements in favor of democracy for China.*

What is true democracy? It means the right of the people to choose their own representatives to work according to their will and in their interests. Only this can be called democracy. Furthermore, the people must also have the power to replace their representatives anytime so that these representatives cannot go on deceiving others in the name of the people. This is the kind of democracy enjoyed by people in European and American countries. In accordance with their will, they could run such people as Nixon, de Gaulle, and Tanaka out of office. They can reinstate them if they want, and nobody can interfere with their democratic rights. In China, however, if a person even comments on the already dead Great Helmsman Mao Zedong or the Great Man without peers in history, jail will be ready for him with open door and various unpredictable calamities may befall him. What a vast difference will it be if we compare the socialist system of centralized democracy with the system of [the] capitalist "exploiting class"!

Will there be great disorder across the land and defiance of laws human and divine once people enjoy democracy? Do not recent periodicals show that just because of the absence of democracy, dictators big and small were defying laws human and divine? How to maintain democratic order is a domestic

615

problem requiring solution by the people themselves, and there is no need for the privileged overlords to worry about it. However, what they are worrying about is not the people's democracy but the difficulty of finding an excuse for destroying the people's democratic rights. Domestic problems cannot be solved all at once. Their solution takes time, during which mistakes and defects will be unavoidable. However, all these consequences, which concern us alone, should be far better than oppressions from the overlords which leave us no way to appeal for justice. Those who worry about the defiance of human and divine laws as a result of democracy are like those who had the same worry when the emperor was dethroned in the 1911 revolution. They are reconciled to this line of reasoning: Be at ease and submit to oppression. Without oppression, the roof of your house will fly sky high!

Let me respectfully remind these gentlemen: We want to be masters of our own destiny. We need no gods or emperors. We do not believe in the existence of any savior. We want to be masters of the world and not instruments used by autocrats to carry out their wild ambitions. We want a modern lifestyle and democracy for the people. Freedom and happiness are our sole objectives in accomplishing modernization. Without this fifth modernization all others are merely another promise.

Let me call on our comrades: Rally under the banner of democracy and do not trust the autocrats' talk about "stability and unity." Fascist totalitarianism can only bring us disaster. Have no more illusion. Democracy is our only hope. Abandon our democratic rights and we will be shackled once again. Let us believe in our own strength! Human history was created by us. Let all self-styled leaders and teachers go. They have for decades cheated the people of their most valuable possession. I firmly believe that production will be faster under the people's own management. Because the laborers will produce for their own benefit, their living conditions will be better. Society will thus be more rational, because under democracy all social authority is exercised by the people with a view to improving their livelihood.

I can never believe that the people can have anything from a savior without their own efforts. I also refuse to believe that China will abandon its goal because of difficulties. As long as people can clearly identify their goal and the obstacles on the way, they can surely trample on that mantis which bars the way. . . .

To accomplish modernization, Chinese people should first practice democracy and modernize China's social system. Democracy is by no means the *result* of social development as claimed by Lenin. Aside from being the inevitable outcome of the development of productive forces and the relations of production up to a certain stage, it is also the *condition* for the existence of productive forces and the relations of production, not only up to that certain stage but also at much higher stages of development. Without this condition, the society will become stagnant and economic growth will encounter insurmountable obstacles. Therefore, judging from past history, a democratic social system is the major premise or the prerequisite for all developments—or modernizations. Without this major premise or prerequisite, it would be impossible not only to continue further development but also to preserve the fruits of the present stage of development. The experiences of our great motherland over the past thirty years have provided the best evidence.

Why must human history take the road toward prosperity and modernization? The reason is that people need prosperity so that real goods are available, and so that there is a full opportunity to pursue their first goal of happiness, namely freedom. Democracy means the maximum attainable freedom so far known by human beings. It is quite obvious that democracy has become the goal in contemporary human struggles.

Why are all reactionaries in contemporary history united under a common banner against democracy? The answer is that democracy provides everything for their enemy—the masses of people—but nothing for them—the oppressors—to oppose the people with. The biggest reactionary is always the biggest opponent of democracy. As clearly shown in the history of Germany, the Soviet Union, and "New China" [that is, the PRC] the strongest opponent of democracy has been the biggest and most dangerous enemy of social peace and prosperity. From the history of these countries, we can also clearly see that the spearheads of all struggles by people for happiness and by societies for prosperity were directed against the enemies of democracy—the autocratic fascists. From the history of the same countries again, we can see that victory for democracy has always brought along with it the most favorable conditions and the greatest speed for social development. On this point, American history has supplied the most forceful evidence.

All struggles involving the people's pursuit of happiness and prosperity are based on the quest for democracy. Therefore, the result of any struggles involving the people's resistance to oppression and exploitation are determined by their success or failure in obtaining democracy. So let us dedicate all our strength to the struggle for democracy! People can get all they want only through democratic channels. They cannot get anything by undemocratic or illusory means, because all forms of autocracy and autocratic totalitarianism are the most open and dangerous enemies of the people.

Would the enemies be willing to let us practice democracy? Certainly not. They will stop at nothing to hinder the progress of democracy, deceive and hoodwink the people. The most effective method they, like all autocratic fascists, can count on is to tell the people that their present conditions are practically the best in the world. Has democracy really reached the stage it naturally should? Not at all! Any minor victory for democracy has been paid for at a high price, and democracy can be truly learned at the cost of bloodshed and other sacrifices. The enemies of democracy have always deceived the people by saying that democracy, even though achieved, will inevitably perish; so why should any energy be expended in striving for it?

However, let us look at the real history and not the history written by the hired scholars of the "socialist government." Every minute portion of democracy of real value was stained with the blood of martyrs and tyrants, and every step forward was met with strong attacks from the reactionary forces. Democracy has been able to surmount all these obstacles because it is highly valued and eagerly sought by the people. Therefore, this torrent is irresistible. Chinese people have never feared anything. As long as the people have a clear orientation, the forces of tyranny are no longer undefeatable. . . .

The struggle will certainly be victorious, though there will still be bloodshed and suffering. Liberation (about which there has been so much talk) will surely be attained. However much we may be covertly plotted against, the democratic banner cannot be obscured by the miasmal mists. Let us unite under this great and real banner and march toward modernization for the sake of the people's peace, happiness, rights, and freedom!

Suggestions for Further Reading

Deng Yong, and Fei-ling Wang, eds. *In the Eyes of the Dragon: China Views the World*. Lanham, MD: Rowman and Littlefield, 1999. An illuminating look at China's perspective on international affairs, told by leading Chinese scholars now teaching at U.S. universities.

Dickson, Bruce J. *Red Capitalists in China: The Party, Private Entrepreneurs, and the Prospects for Political Change*. New York: Cambridge University Press, 2002.

Economy, Elizabeth, and Michel Oksenberg, eds. *China Joins the World: Progress and Prospects*. New York: Council on Foreign Relations, 1999. An inclusive look at China's integration in the international community, including trade, the environment, human rights, and military and security affairs.

Hu Shaohua. *Explaining Chinese Democratization*. Westport, Conn.: Praeger, 2000. A brief overview of Chinese conceptions of democracy and the obstacles to its realization in China.

Johnston, Alastair Iain, and Robert Ross, eds. *Engaging China: The Management of an Emerging Power*. New York: Routledge, 1999. This book compares and contrasts how a variety of China's neighbors in East and Southeast Asia conduct their relations with China.

Li, Cheng. *China's Leaders: The New Generation*. Lanham, Md.: Rowman and Littlefield, 2001. An insightful analysis of the changing characteristics of China's leaders and their implications for China's future.

Zha, Jianying. *China Pop: How Soap Operas, Tabloids, and Bestsellers Are Transforming a Culture*. New York: The New Press, 1995. This is a refreshing account of how popular culture, including television, novels, films, and music, are both influencing and reflecting changes in Chinese society.

SOURCES[*]

GEOGRAPHY AND HISTORY

1. "China's Environmental History in World Perspective," by J. R. McNeill. In *Sediments of Time*, ed. Mark Elvin and Liu Ts'ui-jung, 31–41. Cambridge: Cambridge University Press, 1998. © 1998 by Cambridge University Press. Reprinted by permission.

2. "The Uniting of China." In *Ethnic Identity in China: The Making of a Muslim Minority Nationality*, by Dru Gladney, 11–20. © 1998. Reprinted with permission of Wadsworth, a division of Thomson Learning:www.thomsonrights.com.

3. "Confucius." In *Mountain of Fame*, by John E. Wills, Jr., 11, 14, 23–28, 30–32. Princeton, Princeton University Press, 1994. © 1994 by Princeton University Press. Reprinted by permission.

4. "History and China's Revolution," by John King Fairbank. From "Introduction: The Old Order," in *The Cambridge History of China*, ed. John King Fairbank, vol. 10, 1–6. London, Cambridge University Press, 1978. © 1978 by Cambridge University Press. Reprinted by permission.

5. "A Proclamation Against the Bandits of Guangdong and Guangxi, 1854." In *The Search for Modern China: A Documentary Collection*, ed. Pei-kai Cheng and Michael Lestz, eds., 146–49. New York: W. W. Norton & Company, 1999.

6. "The Boxer Uprising." In *History in Three Keys*, by Paul A. Cohen, 42–56. New York: Columbia University Press, 1997. © 1997 by Columbia University Press. Reprinted by permission.

7. "The Chinese Enlightenment." In *The Chinese Enlightenment*, by Vera Schwarcz, 4–8. Berkeley: University of California Press, 1986. © 1986 by the University of California Press. Reprinted by permission.

8. "Sun Yat-sen Opens the Whampoa Academy, 1924." In *The Search for Modern China: A Documentary Collection*, ed. Pei-kai Cheng and Michael Lestz, 253–55. New York: W.W. Norton & Company, 1999. © 1999 by W.W. Norton & Company, Inc. Used by permission of W.W. Norton & Company, Inc.

---

[*] Every effort has been made to locate the rights holders to all material used in this book. If you have pertinent information, please contact the publisher.

9. "Report on an Investigation of the Peasant Movement in Hunan," by Mao Zedong. In *Selected Works of Mao Zedong*, vol. 1, 23–29. Beijing: Foreign Languages Press, 1967. © 1967 by Foreign Languages Press. Reprinted by permission.

10. "Collapse of Public Morale." In *China On the Eve of Communist Takeover*, by A. Doak Barnett, 96–99. Encore Reprint Series. Boulder: Westview Press, 1986. © 1986 by A. Doak Barnett. Reprinted by permission.

11. "American Exclusion Act, May 6, 1882." In *The Search for Modern China: A Documentary Collection*, ed. Pei-kai Cheng and Michael Lestz, 164–66. New York: W.W. Norton & Company, 1999.

12. "Chinese Anti-Foreignism, 1892." In *The Search for Modern China: A Documentary Collection*, ed. Pei-kai Cheng and Michael Lestz, 166–67. New York: W.W. Norton & Company, 1999.

POLITICS

13. "Human Rights and American China Policy." In *China's Transition*, by Andrew Nathan, 246–62. New York: Columbia University Press, 1997. © 1997 by Columbia University Press. Reprinted by permission.

14. "Chinese Intellectuals' Quest for National Greatness and Nationalistic Writing in the 1990s," by Suisheng Zhao. *China Quarterly*, no. 152 (Dec. 1997): 725–45. © 1997 by Cambridge University Press. Reprinted by permission.

15. "A Quiet Roar: China's Leadership Feels Threatened by a Sect Seeking Peace," by Erik Eckholm. *New York Times*, 4 Nov. 1999. © 1999 by The New York Times. Reprinted by permission.

16. "China's Emerging Business Class: Democracy's Harbinger?" by Margaret Pearson. *Current History*, 97, 1 (Sept. 1998): 268–72. © 1998 by Current History. Reprinted with permission from *Current History* magazine.

17. "Village Elections: Democracy from the Bottom Up?" by Tyrene White. *Current History*, 97, 1 (Sept. 1998): 263–67. © 1998 by Current History. Reprinted with permission from *Current History* magazine.

18. "The Virus of Corruption." In *The Legacy of Tiananmen: China in Disarray*, by James Miles, 147–67. Ann Arbor: University of Michigan Press, 1996. © 1996 by The University of Michigan Press. Reprinted by permission.

19. The Political Sociology of the Beijing Upheaval of 1989," by Andrew Walder. *Problems of Communism*, 38, 5 (Sept.-Oct. 1989): 30–40.

20. "China since Tiananmen." In *The World and I, April 1996*, by Stanley Rosen, 36–43. © 1996 by The Washington Times. Reprinted by permission.

SOCIETY

21. "Family and Household." In *The Return of the God of Wealth*, by Charlotte Ikels, chapter 3. Stanford: Stanford University Press, 1996. © 1996 by the Board of Trustees of the Leland Stanford Junior University. Reprinted with the permission of the publishers, Stanford University Press.

22. "Home-Cured Tobacco—A Tale of Three Generations in a Chinese Village," by Daniel Wright. *Institute of Current World Affairs Letters*, DBW-11 East Asia, August 1998. © 1998 by the Institute of Current World Affairs Letters. Reprinted by permission.

23. "How Come You Aren't Divorced Yet?" by Zhang Xinxin. In *Unofficial China*, ed. P. Link, R. Madsen, and P. Pickowicz, 58–71. Boulder: Westview Press, 1989. © 1989 by Westview Press. Reprinted by permission.

24. "Human Rights Trends and Coercive Family Planning in the PRC," by Martin King Whyte. *Issues and Studies*, 1998, 34: 1–29. © 1998 by Issues & Studies. Reprinted by permission.

25. "McDonald's in Beijing: The Localization of Americana," by Yunxiang Yan. In *Golden Arches East*, ed. James Watson, 39–72. Stanford: Stanford University Press, 1997. © 1997 by the Board of Trustees of the Leland Stanford Junior University. Reprinted by permission.

26. "The *Fengshui* Resurgence in China," by Ole Bruun. *China Journal*, 1996, 36: 47–65. © 1996 by The China Journal. Reprinted by permission.

27. "Chinese Catholics." In *China's Catholics*, by Richard Madsen, 1–10 (excerpts). Berkeley: University of California Press, 1998. © 1998 by the University of California Press. Reprinted by permission.

28. "Urban Spaces and Experiments in *Qigong*," by Nancy N. Chen. In *Urban Spaces in Contemporary China*, ed. D. Davis, R. Kraus, B. Naughton, and E. Perry, 347–61 (excerpts). Cambridge: Cambridge University Press, 1995. © 1995 by Cambridge University Press. Reprinted by permission.

29. "Chinese Women in the 1990s: Images and Roles in Contention," by Stanley Rosen. In *China Review 1994*, ed. M. Brosseau and Lo Chi Kin, 17.6–12, 17.22–23. Hong Kong; The Chinese University Press, 1994. © 1994 by The Chinese University Press. Reprinted by permission.

30. "Hey Coolie!—Local Migrant Labor," by Daniel Wright. *Institute of Current World Affairs Letters*, DBW-15 East Asia, August 1999: 1–7. © 1999 by the Institute of Current World Affairs Letters. Reprinted by permission.

31. "Second Class Citizen," by Ge Fei and "Homosexuals in Beijing," by Jin Ren. In *Streetlife China*, by Michael Dutton, 65–74. Cambridge: Cambridge University Press, 1999.

32. "Elementary Education." In *The Return of the God of Wealth*, by Charlotte Ikels. Stanford: Stanford University Press, 1996. © 1996 by the Board of Trustees of the Leland Stanford Junior University. Reprinted by permission.

ECONOMY

33. "Understanding the Present," in *China 2020*, 1–9; Figs. 1.2, 1.4. Washington, D.C.: The World Bank 1997. © 1997 by The World Bank. Reprinted by permission.

34. "Is a Rich Man Happier than a Free Man?" In *Rediscovering China: Dynamics and Dilemmas of Reform*, by Cheng Li, 244–46, 250–53, 256–58 (excerpts). Lanham, Md.: Rowman & Littlefield, 1997. © 1997 by Rowan & Littlefield. Reprinted by permission.

35. "How to Reform a Planned Economy: Lessons From China," by J. McMillan and B. Naughton. *Oxford Review of Economic Policy*, 8, 1 (1991): 132–41 (excerpts). © 1991 Oxford University Press. Reprinted by permission.

36. "Rural-Urban Migration of Labour." In *Rural-Urban Divide: Economic Disparities and Interactions in China*, by John Knight and Lina Song, 277–78, 294–96, 308, 313–15 (excerpts). Oxford: Oxford University Press, 1999. © 1999 by Oxford University Press. Reprinted by permission.

37. "Development in Chinese Corporate Finance and its Implication for Ownership Reform," by Zhang Weiying. In *Asia Pacific Financial Deregulation*, ed. G. deBrouwer and W. Pupphavesa, 183–93, 196–99, 201–2 (excerpts). London: Routledge, 1999. © 1999 by Routledge. Reprinted by permission.

CULTURE

38. "Medicine," by Lu Xun. In *Lu Xun Selected Works*. 4 vols. Beijing: Foreign Languages Press, 1980, vol. 1, 58-67. © 1980 by Foreign Languages Press. Reprinted by permission.

39. "Autumn Night," by Lu Xun. In *Lu Xun Selected Works*. 4 vols. Beijing: Foreign Languages Press, 1980, vol. 1, 317-19. © 1980 by Foreign Languages Press. Reprinted by permission.

40. Excerpts from "Yan'an Talks," by Mao Zedong. Trans. Bonnie MacDougall. In *Mao Zedong's 'Talks at the Yan'an Conference on Literature and Art,'* by Bonnie MacDougall, 55–72. Ann Arbor: Center for Chinese Studies, The University of Michigan, 1980.

41. "Sealed Off," by Zhang Ailing. Trans. Karen Kingsbury. In *The Columbia Anthology of Modern Chinese Literature*, ed. Joseph S. M. Lau and Howard

Goldblatt, 188–97. New York: Columbia University Press, 1990. © 1990 by Columbia University Press. Reprinted by permission.

42. "The Unglovable Hands," by Zhao Shuli. Trans. Nathan K. Mao and Winston L. Y. Yang. In *Literature of the People's Republic of China*, ed. Hsu Kai-yü, 494–502. Bloomington: Indiana University Press, 1980. © 1980 by Indiana University Press. Reprinted by permission.

43. "On the Other Side of the Stream," by Kong Jiesheng. Trans. Charles W. Hayford. In *Roses and Thorns: The Second Blooming of the Hundred Flowers in Chinese Fiction, 1978–80*, ed. Perry Link, 168–94. Berkeley: University of California Press, 1984. © 1997 by Perry Link. Reprinted by permission.

44. "Responsibility." In *Evening Chats in Beijing*, by Perry Link, 249–55. New York: Norton, 1992. © 1992 by Perry Link. Used by permission of W. W. Norton & Company, Inc.

45. "On the Road at 18," by Yu Hua. Trans. Andrew F. Jones. In *The Past and the Punishments*, by Andrew F. Jones, 3–11. Honolulu: University of Hawaii Press, 1996. © 1996 by The University of Hawaii Press. Reprinted with permission.

46. Excerpts from *Deathsong of the River: A Reader's Guide to the Chinese TV Series Heshang*, by Su Xiaokang and Wang Luxiang. Trans. Richard W. Bodman and Pin P. Wan. Ithaca: Cornell East Asia Series, 1991. © 1991 by Richard Bodman and Pin P. Wan. Reprinted by permission of Bodman, Wan, and the Cornell University East Asia Program.

47. "I Have Nothing," by Cui Jian. Trans. Andrew F. Jones. In *Like a Knife: Ideology and Genre in Contemporary Chinese Popular Music*, by Andrew F. Jones, 134–35. Ithaca: East Asia Series, Cornell University, 1992. © 1992 by Andrew F. Jones. Reprinted by permission of Andrew Jones and the Cornell University East Asia Program.

48. Excerpt from *Playing for Thrills: A Mystery*, by Wang Shuo. Trans. Howard Goldblatt. New York: Penguin Books, 1997, 39–49. © 1997 by Wang Shuo. Reprinted by permission of HarperCollins Publishers.

49. "The Revolution of Resistance," by Geremie R. Barmé. In *Chinese Society: Change, Conflict and Resistance*, ed. Elizabeth J. Perry and Mark Selden, 202–8, 216–17. London and New York: Routledge, 2000. © 2000 by Taylor & Francis, Limited. Reprinted by permission.

50. "Fin de Siècle Splendor," by Zhu Tianwen. Trans. Eva Hung. In *The Columbia Anthology of Modern Chinese Literature* ed. Joseph S. M. Lau and Howard Goldblatt, 444–59. New York: Columbia University Press, 1990. © 1990 Columbia University Press. Reprinted by permission.

51. "Four Stanzas on Homesickness," by Yu Guangzhong. Trans. Michelle Yeh. In *Anthology of Modern Chinese Poetry*, ed. Michelle Yeh, 102. New Haven: Yale University Press, 1992. © 1992 by Yale University Press. Reprinted by permission.

FUTURE TRENDS

52. "The New Guard: Five Younger Officials Make Their Way to the Top," by Susan V. Lawrence. *Far Eastern Economic Review*, Sept. 24, 1998. © 1998 by Far Eastern Economic Review. Reprinted by permission.

53. "Chinese Web Opens Portals to New Way of Life," by John Pomfret. *Washington Post*, Feb. 13, 2000. © 2000 by The Washington Post. Reprinted by permission.

54. "The Chinese Future," by Michel Oksenberg, Michael D. Swaine, and Daniel Lynch. Pacific Council on International Policy, RAND Center for Asia-Pacific Policy, 1998. © 1998 by Pacific Council on International Policy. Reprinted by permission.

55. "Prospects for Democratization in China," by Martin King Whyte. *Problems of Communism*, 41, 3 (May–June 1992): 58–70. © 1992 by M. E. Sharpe, Inc., Armonk, New York, 10504. Reprinted by permission.

56. "The Fifth Modernization," by Wei Jingsheng. In James Seymour, ed., *The Fifth Modernization: China's Human Rights Movement, 1978–79.* Stanford-ville, N.Y.: Human Rights Publishing Group, 1980.

FIGURES

Cover: "Family Portraits" © by Chen Shun Chu. Used by permission of the artist.

Late Qing lithograph (1870s). From *Vignettes from the Chinese: Lithographs from Shanghai in the Late Nineteenth Century*. Hong Kong: Research Centre for Translation, The Chinese University of Hong Kong, 1987. © The Chinese University of Hong Kong. Reprinted by permission.

Sun Sun Company Advertisement (1926). From *Liangyou huabao* (Companion illustrated), no. 2 (March 25, 1926).

Republican Fashion (1926). From *Liangyou huabao* (Companion illustrated), no. 3 (April 15, 1926).

"Waiting" (1933), by Chen Tiegeng. "China, Roar!" (1936), by Li Hua. From *Zhongguo xinxing banhua wushi nian xuanji* (Selections from fifty years of new Chinese woodblock prints), (vol. 1 of 2), 1931–1949. Ed. Zhongguo xinxing banhua wushi nian xuanji weiyuanhui. Shanghai: Shanghai renmin meishu, 1981.

"In Following the Revolutionary Road, Strive for Even Greater Victory." "Destroy the Old World; Establish a New World." Shanghai Publishing System Revolutionary Publishing Group. From the University of Westminster Chinese Poster Collection. Reprinted with permission.

White Haired Girl (closeup); White Haired Girl liberated.

"Book from the Sky" (1978–1991). © by Xu Bing. Reprinted with permission of the artist.

"Great Castigation Series: Coca-Cola" (1993). © by Wang Guangyi. Reprinted with permission of the artist.

Rocker Cui Jian (still). From "The Soul of the Master," part three of *China: Unleashing the Dragon.* © First Run/Icarus Films, 1995. Reprinted by permission.

"House—Family Parade series" (1995–1996). © by Chen Shun Chu. Reprinted with permission of the artist.

Illustrations of the Lu Xun story "Medicine," by Feng Zikai. From Feng's *Huihua Lu Xun xiaoshuo* (Illustrated stories of Lu Xun). Hong Kong: Xianggang wanyue, 1954.

THE EDITORS

Thomas Buoye is associate professor of history at the University of Tulsa where he teaches courses on Chinese and Japanese history. Before moving to Tulsa in 1992, he was director of the China Statistics Archives and taught history at the University of Illinois at Chicago. His research focuses on the social, economic, legal history of the Qing dynasty (1644–1911). He is the author of *Manslaughter, Markets, and Moral Economy: Violent Disputes over Property Rights in Eighteenth-century China* (Cambridge: Cambridge University Press, 2000) and articles in *Peasant Studies*, and *Late Imperial China*.

Kirk Denton is an associate professor of East Asian languages and literature at Ohio State University. His research and teaching interests include modern Chinese literature and culture, literature in translation, and popular culture. He is currently studying the cultural complex of self, gender, nation, tradition, and modernity surrounding images of *guxiang* (hometown) in a range of cultural forms in early modern China (1915–1930). He is the author of *The Problematic of Self in Modern Chinese Literature: Hu Feng and Lu Ling* (Stanford: Stanford University Press, 1998) and the editor of *Modern Chinese Literary Thought: Writings on Literature, 1893–1945* (Stanford: Stanford University Press, 1996). He has also published articles in *The Columbia Companion to Modern East Asian Literature, Modern Chinese Literature and Culture*, and the *Journal of Chinese Philosophy* and has translated several works of Chinese literature and scholarly articles.

Bruce Dickson is associate professor of political science and international affairs at George Washington University. His research and teaching focus on the domestic politics of China and Taiwan, particularly the role of political parties in promoting and adapting to political, economic, and social change. He is the author of *Democratization in China and Taiwan: The Adaptability of Leninist Parties* (New York: Oxford University Press, 1997) and articles in *Asian Survey, China Quarterly, Comparative Political Studies, Comparative Politics, National Interest, Political Science Quarterly*, and several edited volumes. He is also associate editor of the journal *Problems of Post-Communism*.

Barry Naughton is an economist who specializes in China's transitional economy, concentrating on issues relating to industry, foreign trade, and macroeconomics. He was named the first So Kuanlok Professor of Chinese and International Affairs at the Graduate School of International Relations and Pacific Studies of the University of California at San Diego in 1998. His study of Chinese economic reform, *Growing Out of the Plan: Chinese Economic Reform, 1978–1993* (New York: Cambridge University Press, 1995) won the Masayoshi Ohira Memorial Prize. He is currently researching provincial economic growth and interprovincial trade in the People's Republic of China, as well as science and technology policy in China, and the political economy of socialist transition.

Martin K. Whyte is professor of sociology at Harvard University. Before moving to Harvard in 2000, he taught at the University of Michigan and at George Washington University. He studied physics at Cornell University as an undergraduate and then did graduate work in Russian Area Studies and sociology at Harvard, where he received his Ph.D. in 1971. Over the course of his career he has conducted research on many different aspects of social life in contemporary China, first through intensive interviewing with Chinese émigrés in Hong Kong, and more recently primarily through sample survey research conducted in the People's Republic of China. His books on China include *Small Groups and Political Rituals in China, Village and Family in Contemporary China* (Berkeley: University of California Press, 1974) and *Urban Life in Contemporary China* (Chicago: University of Chicago Press, 1984), the latter co-authored with William Parish. An edited volume, *China's Revolutions and Intergenerational Relations*, is forthcoming from the University of Michigan, Center for Chinese Studies. He also teaches and does research in family sociology and the sociology of development, an effort that resulted recently in the publication of an edited volume, *Marriage in America: A Communitarian Perspective* (Lanham, Md.: Rowan & Littlefield, 2000).

INDEX

Religion, 149, 156, 171, 261, 551–52, 601
  underground church, 272
Republic of China. *See* Taiwan
Republican period, 16–17
  fashion, *415*
  literary trends, 400
  social order, 210–12
Resident committees, 213, 233
Responsibility (Link), 406, 487–91
Revenue, state, 375–76, 385–86
Revolution of Resistance, The (Barmé),
  514–22
Revolutionary dramas, 404
Revolutionary literature, 402, 436–38
Rice, 7, 330
Rightists, 106, 111
  See also Anti-rightist campaign
River Elegy (documentary), 140, 407
Ronglu, 71
Rule of law, 114, 149, 153–54, 562, 586,
  601
Rural industry, 375
  See also agricultural economy
Russian Revolution, 79–80

Sage kings, 47
Sakharov Prize, 154
Sang Ye, 518
Savings rates, household, 356–57, 375
  Huaxi village, 362
  rural *vs.* urban households, 384–87
Scholar-officials, 4–5, 44–45, 54, 396–98
Schools. *See* education
Science, 75, 77, 395
Scramble for Concessions, 54
Sealed Off (Zhang Ailing), 403, 440–51
Secessionist policy, 35–37
"Self-strengthening" period, 13–15
Seven black categories, 465
Severe strike campaign, 303
Sexual activity
  AIDS, 308–9, 530
  homosexuality, 221, 305–8
  premarital, 225–28, 242–43
Seymour, Edward, 67
SEZs (Special Economic Zones), 339–42
Shang dynasty, 4
Shanghai, 12, 18, 129

literary center, 401, 403
  newspapers, 413
Shanghai protests (1986), 129
Shen Congwen, 403
Shen Taifu, 195–98
Shenzhen lottery incident, 192–95
Shi, 42, 46
Shun, 43, 47
Silk Road, 6
Sincerity (*cheng*), 49
Sino-Japanese War, 14, 54
Sino-Soviet split, 603–4
Sino-Soviet Treaty of Friendship, Alliance,
  and Mutual Aid, 21
Sino-Tibetan languages, 32
Social order
  imperial period, 207–10
  Mao-period, 103, 212–15, 602
  migration restriction and household
    registration, 299
  post-Mao period, 215–21
  Republican period, 210–11
Social trends, 585–86
SOEs (state-owned enterprises), 338, 340,
  341, 382–89, 553, 584, 590
  debt-asset ratios, 382, 384
  distinguished from capitalist firms,
    387
  nonperforming loans to, 348, 384,
    388–89, 590–91
  performance, 371–74, 375
  rate of growth, 553–55
Son of Heaven, 53
Song dynasty, 6–7, 330
South Korea, 140, 156
Soviet Union, 130, 218, 611
  1989 Conference of the Communist
    Party, 129
  effects of dissolution, 129, 144, 162,
    165
  ethnic composition, 606–7
  four commons, 35
  literary influences, 404
  model of collectivism, 212
  Sino-Soviet split, 603–4
  support of Nationalist Party, 17–18,
    79–80
  trade relations with China, 334

#1   408.24   4 PELICAN
394.24
394.24